History of Dodge and Washington Counties, Nebraska, and Their People Volume 2

History of

Dodge and Washington Counties, Nebraska

And Their People

Editors

REV. WILLIAM H. BUSS, Fremont
THOMAS T. OSTERMAN, Blair

VOLUME II

THE AMERICAN HISTORICAL SOCIETY
CHICAGO
1921

Vol II—1

Geo. L. Loomis

History of Dodge and Washington Counties

JUDGE GEORGE L. LOOMIS has been a prominent and representative member of the Nebraska bar since 1876, ranking as the pioneer attorney in this judicial district of six counties, and is the head of the law firm of Loomis, Laird & Loomis of Fremont, in which city he centralized his large and important law practice until his appointment to his present office, that of collector of internal revenue for the District of Nebraska, his appointment to this position having been made early in the first administration of President Wilson In his official capacity Mr Loomis maintains his headquarters in the City of Omaha, but he still resides at Fremont, where he began the practice of his profession forty-four years ago.

Mr Loomis was born in Chautauqua County, New York, on the 28th of November, 1849, and he was reared and educated in the old Empire State, where, in 1875, he received the degree of Bachelor of Law, upon his graduation from Union University, Department of Law, Albany, New York In 1876 he established his residence at Fremont, county seat of Dodge County, Nebraska, where success has attended his professional activities. He has long been recognized as one of the specially able members of the Nebraska bar, the while his law practice came to be one of broad scope and important order. As an effective advocate of the principles and policies for which the democratic party stands sponsor, Mr. Loomis has been influential in political affairs in the state He served two terms as city attorney of Fremont, was for two terms county attorney of Dodge County, has represented this county as a member of the State Legislature two terms, and was for eleven years a member of the Board of Education of his home city His civic loyalty has been intense, and no citizen has been more appreciative of the advantages and attractions of the State of Nebraska, in whose prosperity and progress he has taken the deepest interest Mr. Loomis was one of the founders of the Commercial Law League of America in 1895, has served with characteristic efficiency as a member of the Board of Directors of Doane College at Crete, Nebraska, for twenty-three years In his home city he has been a director of the Commercial National Bank and the Home Savings Bank since their organization nearly thirty years ago, and for more than twenty years of the Equitable Building and Loan Association He represented Nebraska as a delegate at large to the democratic national convention in Baltimore where Woodrow Wilson was first nominated for the presidency, and he has wielded much influence in the councils and campaign activities of the party in his home state. He has been long and actively affiliated with the Independent Order of Odd Fellows and was grand master in 1889-90, grand representative to the Sovereign Grand Lodge eight years, grand instructor fifteen years Has been a member of the Board of Home Trustees nearly twenty years and was president of the board at the time of erecting and equipping the Odd Fellows Home at York, this state He and his family hold membership in the Congregational Church Is past state regent of Sons of the American Revolution

On the 21st of July, 1880, was solemnized the marriage of Mr Loomis to Miss Alice Hadley, who was born in the picturesque little City of Hillsdale, Michigan, November 1, 1856, her parents having been pioneer citizens of that state, where they continued to reside until their death Mr. and Mrs. Loomis have six children Bayard is engaged in the moving-picture business in the City of Omaha; Floyd is a successful newspaper man in the City of Portland, Oregon; Leo is the wife of Fred C. Laird, of whom individual mention is made on other pages of this volume; Zela H. is vice president of the Telegram Company, publishers of the leading newspaper at Columbus, Nebraska; Howard W is the youngest member of the Fremont law firm of Loomis, Laird & Loomis, and concerning him further mention is made in appending paragraphs of this review, and Wayne is a student in the University of Nebraska as a member of the class of 1922

Howard W Loomis was born at Fremont, and after here completing the curriculum of the public schools he entered Fremont College, in which institution he was graduated as a member of the class of 1912 In preparation for the profession of his choice he then entered the law department of the University of Nebraska, in which he was graduated as a member of the class of 1915, his reception of the degree of Bachelor of Laws being practically coincident with his admission to the bar of his native state. He forthwith became associated with his father in active general practice at Fremont and is now the youngest member of the law firm of Loomis, Laird & Loomis, his father being the senior member and the third member being Fred C Laird, whose wife is a daughter of the senior member of the firm, as noted in the preceding paragraph In his professional work Howard W Loomis is well upholding the prestige of the family name and is one of the leading lawyers of the younger generation in his native county The firm of which he is a member controls a large and important law business, and incidental to the same he has proved himself a resourceful lawyer and well fortified counselor When the nation became involved in the World war he promptly subordinated his professional ambition to the call of patriotism He entered service in November, 1917, received his preliminary training at Camp Johnson, and finally became a member of the American Expeditionary Forces in France, where he was in active service fifteen months, his honorable discharge having been received in September, 1919, after the close of the war and his return to his native land He is an appreciative and popular member of the local post of the American Legion in his home city

Mr Loomis is found aligned as a stanch supporter of the principles of the democratic party, and is affiliated with the Independent Order of Odd Fellows, the Benevolent and Protective Order of Elks, the Alpha Tau Omega college fraternity and the Phi Delta Phi fraternity of the law school He holds membership in the Congregational Church at Fremont, where he remains at the parental home, as his name is still found listed on the roll of eligible young bachelors in his native county.

Ross L. Hammond In writing of the men that have been prominent and influential in developing and promoting the highest and best interests of Dodge County, special mention should be made of Ross L Hammond, widely known as one of the most enterprising and popular newspaper men of the state, who was editor of the Fremont Tribune for forty years, and in addition to his duties in that capacity helped to build up an extensive and remunerative business by the Hammond Printing Company of which he was president In October, 1919, he disposed of his principal interests in Fremont, and is now, in 1920, located at Riverside, California, engaged in investments and banking. A son of George and Jane (Leech) Hammond, he was born May 13, 1861, in Le Grand, Marshall County, Iowa, coming on both sides of the house of English colonial stock and of honored Quaker ancestry.

Born in Jefferson County, Ohio, George Hammond migrated to Iowa in early life, and as a pioneer settler of Marshall County bought land and began the improvement of a homestead He met with good success as a farmer and stock raiser, and also engaged in mercantile pursuits, building up a prosperous business as a dealer in lumber and grain A man of strong individuality, he was influential in advancing the prosperity of Le Grand, his home town, and was identified with the establishment therein of two colleges, and was a generous contributor toward their support

Scholarly in his tastes and ambitions, Ross L Hammond received his preliminary education in Le Grand, Iowa, attending the public schools and Friends' Academy, and subsequently continuing his studies at Penn College, in Oskaloosa, Iowa Yielding, no doubt, to a natural tendency, he began his connection with printing and journalism soon after leaving college, and in September, 1879, came to Fremont to assume a position on the Fremont Tribune, which was then owned by his father and his brother Frank under the firm name of Hammond & Son Becoming of age in 1882, Mr. Hammond was admitted to partnership in the firm, and the name was changed to Hammond Brothers The publishing business grew with surprising rapidity and in 1901 was incorporated, with a paid-up capital of $100,000, the Hammond Printing Company, Mr Hammond being made president of the concern He also became officially connected as vice president with the Hammond & Stephens Company, an entirely separate concern, which has a capital of $50,000 and is devoted to educational publications and supplies

He was for twenty-five years a director of the Nebraska Building and Loan Association, the largest financial institution of Fremont For several years before leaving the city he was its vice president He was for twenty years a member of the City Library Board and for several of the latter years its president. He was a director of the First National Bank and interested in several other banks of the state, and a farm owner in Nebraska and Minnesota

Under the wise control of Mr. Hammond the Tribune greatly prospered and grew in influence, and with the development of the paper, the job printing industry grew in a corresponding manner, its business having become extensive and lucrative, it being at the present time one of the most important industrial concerns in the city.

Mr. Hammond obtained his rudimentary knowledge of printing and journalism on the home farm, he and his brothers having set up a small press in their mother's pantry Working evenings, rainy days and holidays these enterprising boys became familiar with the art of printing, and subsequently began the publication of the "Amateur Star," a miniature weekly paper which they published two or three years, supplying copies to about 150 regular subscribers

An active and influential member of the republican party, Mr Hammond served as a delegate to every state convention within the past quarter of a century, and often assisted in the framing of the party platforms, and as a pleasing and effective speaker has been prominent in campaign work He was a candidate for Congress from the Third District in 1896, when the republican party was defeated by the fusion element In 1897 he was appointed postmaster at Fremont by President McKinley and having afterwards been reappointed by President Roosevelt, served in that capacity five years, when he resigned the position, his business requiring his entire attention In March, 1908, Mr. Hammond became collector of internal revenue for the State of Nebraska, holding the position for six years, when he resigned

An active and influential member of the Nebraska Press Association, Mr Hammond served as a delegate to many meetings of the National Editorial Association He was long prominent in the State Association, which he has served as secretary and as president, and was first president of the Fremont Men's Club, which was organized by sixty of the leading men of the city for the purpose of considering questions of interest to the general public In 1918 he was candidate for the United States Senate, and while he polled a big vote was narrowly defeated A highly esteemed citizen, popular with all classes of people, Mr Hammond and his family were entertained in Fremont many times at dinners given in their honor after their decision to go to California The climax of this series of functions doing them honor was a public banquet given at the Hotel Pathfinder Two hundred prominent men and women of the city gathered to pay testimony of the high esteem in which they were held A loving cup, suitably engraved was presented as an enduring proof of this regard As a means of giving his friends throughout the state a similar opportunity to attest their esteem a banquet was given at Lincoln to him and his family under the auspices of the Nebraska Press Association This was a brilliant and unusual affair, attended by men and women of prominence in and out of the editorial profession A gridiron performance followed the dinner in which Mr. Hammond was given a mock trial on the charge of desertion The indictment was preferred by the governor, the chief justice of the supreme court presided, the attorney-general and two or three former attorneys-general took part in the prosecution and defense While the unique affair was filled with mirth it afforded a vehicle for giving expression of the universal regret that Mr Hammond was leaving Nebraska

Mr. Hammond married in Fremont in 1885, Louise F. Reynolds and into their home four children have made their advent, namely: Louise, Le Ross, Howard and Constance Fraternally Mr Hammond is a member of the Independent Order of Odd Fellows of the Modern Woodmen of America and of the Ancient Order of United Workmen. Religiously he was reared in the Quaker faith, being a birthright Quaker, but for many years he has been a member of the Congregational Church, being for a long time before leaving Fremont chairman of its board of trustees

Joseph G Widhelm is one of the representative business men of the younger generation in Dodge County, where he has built up a most prosperous enterprise as executive head, as well as founder, of the Widhelm Remedy and Manufacturing Company, through which he has produced a valuable line of livestock remedies and a complete line of sanitary feeders' supplies, which he has protected with patents granted him by this and other governments This industry which he has established in Fremont is one of the fastest growing enterprises in the city

Mr Widhelm was born in Platte County, Nebraska, February 28, 1880, and is the son of Joseph and Theresa (Weimer) Widhelm, natives of Austria, who established their home in Platte County, Nebraska, prior to the admission of this state into the Union and here the father developed one of the finest farm estates in that county Joseph G was the fifth son of this worthy couple At the early age of sixteen he started out to make his own way in the world and to achieve his heart's greatest desire, a more advanced education By putting in a portion of each year at hard labor, he was enabled to spend the remainder of the year at the Fremont College until he completed a course of study which entitled him to a state certificate After spending a few years in the schoolroom as instructor he finally retired from the work and engaged in the remedy and manufacturing business in the year of 1908 He began his business career with only a few hundred dollars, but by making every dollar do full duty, preparing his remedies by night and selling them by day, he quickly forged ahead The worth of his goods soon became evident and their wide and ever-increasing sale attracted the attention of a number of Dodge County's most substantial citizens who came forward and offered to assist him in incorporating the business under the name of the Widhelm Remedy and Manufacturing Company In the year of 1918, he received his permit from the state and the business was incorporated for $100,000 Joseph G Widhelm became its first president and general manager. The products of this plant are now being shipped to all parts of the United States

Mr Widhelm is a liberal and progressive citizen even as he is a business man. He is an active member of the Rotary Club, Commercial Club and Knights of Columbus, in which last-named he has held some of the highest offices He also holds membership in the Modern Woodmen and the Eagles

October 23, 1907, recorded the marriage of Mr Widhelm to Miss Margaret V O'Donnell, who was born and raised in Saunders County, Nebraska, a daughter of Thomas and Margaret O'Donnell, both natives of Ireland Mr O'Donnell was for many years in the employ of the Union Pacific Railroad Company and was one of those who took part in the ceremony of the driving of the golden spike incidental to the joining of the Union Pacific with the Southern Pacific at Promontory Point, Utah, which completed the great transcontinental line linking the east with the west for the first time in the history of America

Mr. and Mrs Widhelm have two children, Virginia and Eugene.

THE MARSHALL FAMILY The firm of Marshalls Nurseries, composed of George A, Chester C and Harvey W Marshall, nurserymen, is one of the solid institutions of Arlington, and the history of their family is interesting enough to merit special attention in a work of this high class. They are the sons of Benjamin Clark and Catherine (Nonnamaker) Marshall, he born in Trumbull County, Ohio, and she in Hancock County, the same state Both families were old established ones of Ohio, where Benjamin C. Marshall continued to reside until 1881, at that time he with his family coming west to Nebraska and locating 3½ miles northeast of Arlington There he bought land and lived on it until 1910, and then retired, moving at that time to Arlington, where he lived until his death which occurred on February 15, 1919 After the death of his wife in 1904, he did not maintain a home of his own, but lived with his daughters He and his wife had nine children, eight of whom are living, namely: Eli W, who is a stockholder of the company of Marshalls Nurseries, and is its representative at Lincoln, Nebraska, and he married Josie Dalley, their children being Clark, May, Shirley, Eula, Tina and Dorothy; Ami, who represents Marshalls Nurseries at Bayard, Nebraska, married Minnie Marquard, and their children are: Maude, Cora, Lula, Irma and Chet, Chester C, who is vice president of Marshalls Nurseries, married Mary Fellers and their children are Gail, Leta and Eva; George A, who is president of Marshalls Nurseries, married Dora Goltry and their children are Vernon, Catherine, Ruth, Ralph and Maurice, Harvey W, who is treasurer of Marshalls Nurseries, married Allie Snodgrass and they have one child, Esther, now attending National Park Seminary, Forest Glen, Maryland, Dora, who is the widow of G M Whitford, who died in August, 1917, leaving her and two children, Murray and Bernice, the three now living at Arlington: Lucy E, who is the wife of William A Whitford, a retired resident of Arlington, and they have one child, Gladys, Austin C., who is engaged in farming in Washington County, married Nettie McMillan and they have six children: Leslie, Hazel Clayton, Julia, Howard and Georgia Benjamin C Marshall was a democrat in politics His wife was a consistent member of the Evangelical Church. Starting out in life with a very small capital, through persistent effort and strict economy, Mr Marshall accumulated a comfortable property and died a man of means

The elder of the Marshall children were educated in Ohio Austin was graduated from the Fremont, Nebraska, Normal School, Harvey graduated in the commercial course at the Shenandoah, Iowa, College, and those younger than he received their education in the schools of Washington County, Nebraska They were all reared on the farm, and in 1887 the sons started in the nursery business in a small way, grafting 40,000 apple trees and a smaller number of cherry and plum trees, and carrying a general line of small fruits, shrubbery and ornamental trees The firm was originally composed of C C Marshall, George A Marshall and Harvey W Marshall In June, 1916, they incorporated with a paid-up capital of $60,000, all owned by the family, and of this company George A Marshall is president, Chester C Marshall is vice president and Harvey W Marshall is treasurer, while C G Marshall is secretary

The company ships all over the United States, but the principal trade comes from Nebraska, Iowa and South Dakota The annual amount of business runs from 10,000 to 20,000 orders In 1915 they built a modern plant at Arlington, and in 1917 they enlarged same in order to handle the increase of business. At present their main frost-proof storage building, which is one and a half to two stories high, covers a space of 140 by 160 feet At one time they had a forty-acre apple orchard, which during the last seven years that it was productive, bore from 10,000 to 15,000 bushels annually, and they shipped a large proportion of these apples to Europe. This orchard, which was planted in 1893, is now, of course, practically extinct The company have two diplomas received from the Paris Exposition for apples there displayed, and also a gold medal awarded them for apples in the fruit display at the Omaha Exposition They have Government diplomas for fruit displays at both the Columbian and St Louis expositions, and won nine sweepstakes during nine years, seven years in succession and one year between, from the Nebraska state fairs The plant is perfect in every respect and the brothers own from 1,200 to 1,500 acres of land near Arlington, and this present immense business is the outgrowth of the small nursery established with $1,000 each, given the original partners by their father Employment is given to as many as 100 persons, according to the season, and including salesmen and laborers The somewhat remarkable success attained by the Marshall family would not have been possible if the individual members had not been men of sterling character, whose efforts have always been directed along constructive lines and with a definite end in view. Reared by careful and high-minded parents, they have grown into very desirable citizens and Arlington is fortunate in having them as residents and holders of valuable property interests here

JOHN P EATON A Dodge County pioneer, one of its oldest and best-known citizens, an honored survivor of the Civil war, and a man whose work and influence have always been on the better side of the changes and developments in this section of the West

A New Englander, he was born in New Hampshire August 18, 1843, son of Peter and Elizazbeth (Libby) Eaton His father was a machinist by trade and died in New Hampshire prior to the Civil war In the family were the following children Mary, James, Sarah, George, Abigail, John, Martha and Carrie Of these John is the only survivor Others of the family who also came to Nebraska were George, Martha and Carrie.

John P. Eaton had a common school education and was enrolled as a student in Pittsfield Academy for about a year when the war broke out and he finished his college course in the army. He was a fighting Union soldier four years He enlisted August 16, 1862, in Company B of the Twelfth New Hampshire Regiment and fought in the battle of Gettysburg On April 24, 1864, he was commissioned first lieutenant of Company G of the First United States Volunteer Infantry He was put in command of that company and served in that regiment on the western frontier until after the close of the war. He was honorably discharged May 21, 1866, at Fort Leavenworth, Kansas

He had not been out of the army long when he determined to establish a home in the new country west of the Missouri River and reached Nebraska soil in 1867, traveling by train as far as the river He homesteaded eighty acres in what is now section 14, township 18, range 6, in Cotterell Township, and that land has been his home and the scene of his activities for over half a century His first house was a five-room board dwelling, which subsequently gave way to the modern residence in which he still lives

Mr Eaton owns 485 acres of Nebraska farm lands For thirty-five years he was county correspondent for the Department of Agriculture and has always shown a willingness to exert himself for community benefit He organized the first school in his section of Dodge County and for three years filled the office of county commissioner He also laid out the star postal route from Fremont to Glencoe. Politically he is a republican of the same faith today as when he was fighting under the Union flag during the administration of President Lincoln. He is a member of the Grand Army of the Republic of North Bend, Nebraska, is a Mason and he and his family have long been identified with the First Congregational Church at Fremont, Rev W. H. Buss having been their pastor and intimate friend for a quarter of a century

After making his preliminary improvements on his Nebraska homestead Mr Eaton returned to New Hampshire and on September 10, 1868, married Miss Francena J Sawyer They lived happily together for more than half a century Mrs Eaton was born November 4, 1845, in the Town of Lee, New Hampshire, daughter of Jefferson and Elizabeth Sawyer Her parents were of Puritan ancestry and lifelong members of the Free Will Baptist Church Francena Sawyer inherited strength of New England character and met all the tests of true womanhood during her early life in New England and later among the pioneer circumstances of Nebraska She attended the public schools, the Walnut Grove School of her native town and the Framingham, Massachusetts, Normal, where she graduated, and for several years she was a teacher at Walnut Grove in her native state and at Westboro and Charlestown in Massachusetts

Mrs Eaton as a bride was introduced to the pioneer environment of Eastern Nebraska, and her first years in the state were marked by much solitude and unavoidable privation But she never lost the inbred refinement and culture acquired during early womanhood, and she made her home and her life a source of radiating influence over an entire community She was unceasing in devotion to duty, a helpful friend and neighbor and a conspicuous exemplar of Christian faith and fortitude Hers was a life of service, but it was also generously rewarded and enriched with the essentials of human happiness Her last years were spent in a beautiful home which she and Mr Eaton and their daughter planned and which was complete with every comfort and appointment When she first came to Nebraska she united with the Centerville Congregational Church, and later with her family became active in the First Congregational Church at Fremont After a life of seventy-four years five months and two days she died April 6, 1920, and she was buried from the First Congregational Church at Fremont Mr and Mrs Eaton had one child, Gertrude Francena, who received most of her early advantages at home and from her mother, and subsequently graduated from the South High School of Minneapolis and from Wellesley College.

WILLIAM REALPH. A skillful and progressive farmer of Dodge County, William Realph has had an extended practical experience in everything relating to agriculture, and is considered an authority on the various branches of this highly important industry He was born October 19, 1870, in Dodge County, Nebraska, the son of John Realph, one of the sturdy pioneers of this section of the country

Born and bred in Ireland, John Realph left the Emerald Isle in early life, making his way to the United States, which was known across the ocean as the land of plenty, and for a time was variously employed, working industriously to support his wife and children In 1870 he came by train as far west as Omaha, Nebraska, and from there, looking for a tract of good land, he walked into Dodge County, and having homesteaded eighty acres of land installed his family in a dugout and began the improvement of his newly acquired property The country roundabout was in its primitive condition, and the wily red man was everywhere evident, while wild beasts roamed at will Although somewhat hampered by the lack of cash, he labored with indomitable perseverance and not only improved a valuable homestead, but contributed his full share in advancing the growth and prosperity of the community in which he lived His wife, Mrs Bridget Realph, died on the old homestead at the ripe old age of fourscore years He is still living, making his home with a daughter in Custer County, this state

The fourth child in order of birth in a family of eight children, William Realph was brought up in pioneer days, and well remembers when Indians were numerous, and generally peaceful Beginning life for himself at the age of twenty years, he selected the occupation with which he was the most familiar as his life work, and has since been

MR. AND MRS. HENRY PANNING

actively engaged in general farming and stock raising and feeding, finding both pleasure and profit in his labors His land, advantageously situated on section 30, Logan Township, is under an excellent state of culture, the buildings are in good repair, the farm well stocked, and everything about the place bespeaks the ability, industry and wise supervision of the owner He also owns a half section of land in Colorado, near Julesburg Mr Realph is a good democrat in politics and religiously is not connected with any church organization

Mr Realph married in 1895 Christina Larson, and into their pleasant home eight children have made their advent, namely Mrs. Julia Bullock of Julesburg, Colorado; Harvey, Bryant, Edward, John, Mabel, Floyd and Norman, all of whom are at home with the exception of Mrs Bullock Harvey Realph, the eldest son, was drafted during the World war, going into the Three Hundred and Fifty-Fifth Infantry, Company A, Eighty-Ninth Division, and during the year he spent overseas took part in various battles of note, including the engagements at St Mihiel, on the Meuse, and in the Argonne Forest Returning home after the signing of the armistice, he was discharged at Camp Funston in 1919

HENRY PANNING of Winslow, now retired, belongs to the real pioneer element of Dodge County, coming here when he was twenty years of age, and for half a century contributing an important share in the labors by which this wilderness region was reconstructed and made into a wonderful landscape of valuable farms and homes

He was born April 15, 1844, in Hanover, Germany, and was eight years of age when in October, 1852, with his parents he reached the United States His parents, Henry and Margaret (Wolf) Panning, located at Watertown, Wisconsin, but left there in 1864 and with wagons and ox teams crossed the country beyond the Missouri to Nebraska Henry Panning, Sr, paid $1,200 for 360 acres of land partly improved, including a small house At that time any amount of land was still open for homestead settlement, but he preferred this and was willing to pay a larger price for just what he wanted On that farm he and his wife lived out the rest of their years, she dying at the age of fifty-eight and he at sixty-seven Henry Panning early took his sons, Henry and Frederick, into partnership with him, and their holdings increased to about 1,000 acres, were kept intact until after the death of Henry Panning Sr, when the land was divided

Henry Panning, Jr, acquired most of his education after coming to this country and in the State of Wisconsin He was just twenty when he came to Nebraska and many of his youthful years were devoted to the clearing up and improvement of the land in the community where the family settled He was very successful as a general farmer and stock raiser, and continued his work in the rural district until 1916 when he turned the management of his farm over to his sons and then built his present home in Winslow and retired He is one of the men of property in Dodge County, is a stockholder in both the Winslow State Bank and the Hooper Telephone Company, and has always assumed his share of duties and obligations in the community welfare He is a stanch democrat and both he and his wife are valued members of the Lutheran Church at Winslow

Mr Panning married Miss Meta Meyer, who was born in Oldenburg, Germany Eleven children were born to their union, six dying young Those to grow up were Mary, wife of J G Berght, a farmer in Wayne County, Nebraska, Louise, wife of Henry Kuss, manager of the Nebraska & Iowa Grain Elevator at Winslow, whose individual career is sketched elsewhere, Anna, wife of Paul Schmidt, manager of an elevator at Thayer, Nebraska, Frederick G and Gustave C., each of whom receives individual mention in this publication

FREDERICK G PANNING Thoroughly acquainted with the art and science of agriculture carried on by the present-day methods, Frederick G Panning, owner of a valuable farm in Hooper Township, occupies a noteworthy position among the active and thriving farmers of Dodge County, his diligent toil and good management having won him an assured success He is a son of Henry Panning of Winslow, and an account of this pioneer family of Dodge County is presented more in detail elsewhere in this publication

Mr Panning was born in Dodge County February 14, 1874, acquired his education in the local public schools, and the Fremont Normal School, and worked for his father until reaching his majority. Not liking farm life well enough to continue it, he entered merchandising, and operated a general store at Altona, Nebraska, for sixteen years Afterwards he was cashier of the Farmers State Bank of Altona four years On account of ill health disposing of his interests in that locality Mr Panning in 1912 returned to Dodge County, and has since resumed his early occupation and is prosperously engaged in agricultural pursuits, including general farming and stock raising He possesses marked business and financial ability, and is now serving as vice president of the Farmers State Bank of Winslow, in which he is a stockholder, also stockholder in the Hooper Mill, and is secretary and a director of the Farmers Mutual Insurance Company

Mr. Panning married in 1909 Miss Emma Pflueger, a native of Wayne County, Nebraska The seven children born to their marriage are Victor, Leona, Theodore, Arthur, Esther, Ruth and Ervin In politics Mr. Panning is a straightforward republican and religiously he and his wife are valued members of the Lutheran Church.

RAY HINDMARSH Actively engaged in the prosecution of one of the most independent and important industries to which a man may devote his time and energies, the wealth of the nation depending largely upon the success of the farmer, Ray Hindmarsh is successfully employed in his chosen calling on section 19, Elkhorn Township A native of Dodge County, he was born in Dodge, May 12, 1896, of English ancestry

His father, Adam Hindmarsh, was born, bred and educated in Newcastle, England Desirous in early manhood of trying the hazard of new fortunes, he immigrated to the United States, and for awhile resided in Illinois Coming from there to Nebraska, he took up a homestead claim in Dodge County, and with true pioneer courage and industry began the labor of improving his land, and placing it under culture Succeeding well in his efforts, he carried on general farming for many years residing in the county until his death, at the age of seventy-two years A man of far more than average intelligence and ability, he was active in public affairs, and served for many terms as county assessor. He was an active member of the Methodist Episcopl Church, and belonged to the Independent Order of Odd Fellows His wife, whose maiden name was Sarah Harkins, preceded him to the better world, passing away at the comparatively early age of forty-six years. She was a most estimable woman, and helpmeet in every sense of the term

Brought up on the homestead which he had helped to clear and improve, Ray Hindmarsh early woke up to the fact that there was both profit and pleasure in agricultural pursuits, and having decided to take up farming as his chief occupation started in life for himself in 1916, ere becoming of age Endowed with native ability and intelligence, his labors have been so eminently successful that he now has a valuable farm of 360 acres, lying a mile and a half south of Arlington, a most advantageous location In addition to carrying on general farming, Mr Hindmarsh raises thoroughbred stock, including Holstein cattle and Poland China hogs, a branch of agriculture on which he is considered an authority, and on which he has written papers of value and interest He likewise feeds stock on a somewhat extensive scale, being one of the largest feeders in Elkhorn Township

Mr. Hindmarsh married in Council Bluffs, Iowa, in 1916, Julia Larson, whose father, Nels Larson, is now a carpenter in Fremont, Nebraska. Mr Hindmarsh invariably supports the men and measures he deems best, voting independent of party lines or distinctions

CHARLES H BALDUFF Among the strong and influential citizens of Dodge County the record of whose lives have become an essential part of the history of this section, the gentleman whose name appears above has exerted a beneficial influence throughout the community where he resides His chief characteristics are keenness of perception, a tireless energy, honesty of purpose and motive and every-day common sense, which have enabled him not only to advance his own interests, but also to largely contribute to the moral and material advancement of the community

Charles H Balduff is a native son of Dodge County, having been born here on July 21, 1870, and is the son of Charles and Christina (Basler) Balduff These parents were both born in Germany, being brought to the United States in their infancy Here they were reared and educated and in 1868, after their marriage they came to Dodge County, where Mr Balduff homesteaded a tract of land He was a baker by trade and after living on his land for a time he moved into Fremont and started a bakery, his being one of the first bakeries and restaurants in this city He prospered in this enterprise and afterwards also engaged in the meat business, which also proved a good investment, so that some time before his death he was enabled to retire from active business pursuits He had also been interested in the ice business, and as a result of his energetic efforts in these various lines he accumulated a valuable lot of real estate, being numbered among the substantial citizens of the community. He and his wife were at first members of the Lutheran Church, but Mrs Balduff changed her membership to the Congregational Church In politics Mr Balduff was an earnest supporter of the democratic party, and took an active interest in local public affairs, having served several terms as a member of the city council and as supervisor To him and his wife were born seven children, six of whom are living, namely Charles H, Carrie, who is unmarried and lives at home, Fred, who is associated with Charles H. in the meat business, Louis M is an engineer and lives in Fremont, William S, who is assistant cashier for Nye, Schneider & Company of Fremont, Amelia, who is employed in the Commercial National Bank.

Charles H. Balduff attended the public schools, graduating from the high school and then attended the Fremont Normal School After completing his education he formed a partnership with his brother Fred and they engaged in the meat business in Fremont They have been prospered in their enterprise, which they have continued to the present time, and are numbered among the enterprising and successful merchants of their city Their success has been gained by close attention to business and the wants of their customers, and they enjoy the largest volume of business in their line in the city Charles H Balduff has been wisely economical and judicious in his investments and is the owner of considerable valuable real estate in Fremont

In 1900 Mr Balduff was married to Emma Day, a native of the State of Illinois, and the daughter of W B Day, now deceased, who came to Fremont in an early day and here successfully carried on a contracting business To Mr and Mrs Balduff have been born two children, George and Richardson

Mr. Balduff is independent in his political action, voting at all times according to the dictates of his own judgment Fraternally he is a member of the Masonic order, in which he has attained to the degree of a Royal Arch Mason, and he is also a member of the Royal Highlanders and the Independent Order of Odd Fellows, in which last named order he has passed all the chairs in both branches He is essentially a man of affairs, sound of judgment and farseeing in what he undertakes, and he has won and retains the confidence and esteem of all classes

J FRANK SCHWAB, one of the substantial agriculturists of Dodge County, identified with the agricultural interests of Hooper Township for many years, belongs to a family whose persistence and energy have been of inestimable benefit to that part of Nebraska whose strides in growth and material progress of the best type have been a source of credit to the community and of just pride in the commonwealth itself

Mr. Schwab was born in Dodge County, Nebraska, in 1882, a son of Henry Schwab and a grandson of Henry and Katherine (Veight) Schwab The grandparents, natives of Germany, were married in that country, where their son Henry was born in 1852, and in 1855 came to the United States, locating first in Dodge County, Wisconsin, and subsequently, in 1861, coming to Dodge County, Nebraska Here the grandfather homesteaded 160 acres of land on which he proved up, and continued to be engaged in farming and the raising of livestock until the time of his retirement, when he took up his residence at Hooper His death occurred at that point in 1902, when he had reached the remarkable age of ninety-three years, his wife having passed away at the age of seventy-two years, in 1888 Mr. Schwab was a democrat, and he and his worthy helpmate were devout members of the Lutheran Church and the parents of four children Katherine, the widow of Theo Uehling; Jacob, deceased: Adam, engaged in ranching in Colorado; and Henry Henry Schwab, the younger, was three years of age when he accompanied his parents to the United States and nine years old when the family located in Dodge County, Nebraska He remained with his parents on the home place, being associated with his father in his agricultural operations, until 1874 when he bought land of his own and followed an agricultural life until his retirement in 1910, when he moved to Hooper, his present home. Mr Schwab, during the active period of his career, was a successful farmer and stock raiser and at all times has been a man whose integrity has been impregnable In 1874 he married Louise Weigle, daughter of George and Christina (Cramer) Weigle, natives of Germany, who were among the first settlers of Dodge County, coming here from Cuming County, where they had spent one year. Mr Weigle died in 1895, at the age of seventy-three and his wife in 1904 at the age of seventy-five They passed through a number of exciting experiences on the frontier, including the Pawnee Indian raids, in one of which the red men stole an ox from the Weigle farm There were nine children in the family: Pauline, the widow of Jacob Schwab; Godfred, who is still engaged in farming in Dodge County; Rachael, the wife of Adam Schwab, a farmer of Colorado, John, engaged in farming in Dodge County; George, who is deceased, Mary, also deceased; Louise, who is now Mrs Henry Schwab; and Gustaf, who is operating his father's old homestead Seven children have been born to Mr and Mrs. Schwab Mannie, the wife of Henry Wagner of Hooper; Harry, farming the old homestead, J. Frank, Edward H, engaged in the hardware business at Hooper; Louise, the wife of P J Ewald of the Hooper Garage, Robert L, cashier of the Dodge County Bank of Hooper; and Elmer A, associated with his brother-in-law, Mr. Ewald, in the garage business at Hooper Henry Schwab is a democrat, and in past days was one of the influential members of his party in this locality, being a member of the Legislature in 1887 For a period of twenty years he contributed to the maintaining of high educational standards through his service as a director of School District No 15 He is past master and the oldest member of Hooper Blue Lodge of the Masonic fraternity He and his worthy and faithful wife are consistent members of Grace Lutheran Church J Frank Schwab was educated in the public schools and the normal school at Fremont and was reared to agricultural pursuits on the home farm In 1910 he began operations on his own account, at the time of his father's retirement, and at the present time has a well-cultivated farm, on which there are numerous improvements and the most up-to-date machinery and equipment of every kind In a capable and well-directed manner he carries on his activities as a farmer and a raiser of good livestock and his business affairs are conducted in a straightforward manner that has given him an excellent reputation and standing among those with whom he associates

In 1917 Mr Schwab married Anna Sommers, who was born in Dodge County, a daughter of John Sommers Mr and Mrs Schwab have two children, Myrtle and Louis, and are members of Grace Lutheran Church Mr Schwab is a Mason and an independent voter

William C Condit is the avowed apostle of good behavior in Dodge County, where he is giving a vigorous and effective administration in the office of county sheriff, a position of which he has been the efficient incumbent since 1901 and his retention of which indicates the popular estimate placed upon his services

Mr Condit was born on a farm in Jones County, Iowa, May 12, 1874, and is a son of William G and Emily (Crane) Condit, the former of whom was born near Sunbury, Union County, Ohio, and the latter in the State of New York, not far from the shores of Lake Ontario The marriage of the parents was solemnized in Iowa, to which state the father made his way by driving overland with team and wagon, from Ohio, in 1856, he having been accompanied by his father and an older brother, and the family having thus gained pioneer distinction in the Hawkeye State William G Condit was a skillful mechanic and was injured while working at his trade in Peoria, Illinois, the result being that he went to Iowa and turned his attention to farm enterprise He developed one of the valuable farm properties of Jones County, that state, and after the death of his wife he came to Nebraska in 1907. Later he removed to Lebanon, Missouri, and there he died at a venerable age. He was a republican in politics, was affiliated with the Masonic fraternity, and both he and his wife were members of the Congregational Church. Of the five children the sheriff of Dodge County is the eldest of the four surviving, Ernest is a prosperous farmer in South Dakota; Bessie M is the wife of Orrin Reed, who is engaged in the restaurant business at Oelwein, Iowa, and Orrin B resides in the southern part of the Canadian Northwest From this section Orrin B enlisted in the Canadian army in the early stages of the World war, he having accompanied his command to France, where he continued in active service two years and four months and in his arduous and perilous trench service he contracted rheumatism, and he was in bad physical condition when he returned home Orrin Condit has not failed to gain from the Canadian government recognition of his gallant service, for after remaining for a time in his native land after his return from France, he went to Canada and took up pre-emption and homestead claims of 160 acres each and has instituted the development of the property, the Canadian government loaning to its former soldiers $8,000 to develop and improve properties thus secured and to supply livestock

William C. Condit acquired his early education in the public schools of Iowa, including the high school at Anamosa, and there also he initiated his independent career as a farmer In 1898 he came to Fremont, Nebraska, where for one year he was employed at the marble and monument works of Hodges & Baldwin, the following year having found him employed in connection with the operations of the Frank Davis dray line, for which service he received $20 a month At the expiration of one year Mr Condit purchased this draying business, which he successfully conducted for the ensuing six years He then sold out, and for the next two years he was employed as freight foreman and baggageman at the local station of the Chicago, Burlington & Quincy Railroad For the next eighteen months he was traveling for the firm of Hodges & Baldwin, previously mentioned, and at the expiration of this period he was appointed deputy sheriff of Dodge County. Seventeen days later, taking his first insane patient to the asylum while waiting for his train, the patient threw himself in front of the train with the intention of committing suicide and Sheriff Condit, at the risk of his life, threw the patient to safety and lost his own leg by the engine running over it while making the rescue. After serving three years as deputy sheriff he was, in 1901, elected sheriff, and by successive re-elections he has since continued the incumbent of this office. His political allegiance is given to the republican party, and during the period of the nation's participation in the World war he served as chairman of the draft board of Dodge County He is affiliated with the Knights of Pythias, the Royal Highlanders and the Modern Woodmen of America His wife holds membership in the Congregational Church

February 8, 1898, recorded the marriage of Mr Condit to Miss Sylvia J. Walker, who likewise was born and reared near Anamosa, Iowa, and the one child of this union, Wolcott B, is attending the public schools of Fremont

BERNARD MONNICH No other class of men contributed so directly to the upbuilding, development and subsequent prosperity of any community as do those who are devoting their talents and energies to the handling of real estate. This is a line of business which requires grit, determination and enthusiasm in order that the one engaged in it rise above the ordinary operator and these are just the qualities needed for the making of the aggressive and dependable citizen who can promul-

L S Dykeman
Mrs J. S Dykeman

gate and carry out plans which ultimately will result in the betterment of the majority One of the men thus directly responsible for the attracting to Dodge County and its adjoining territory much of the attention it is now enjoying, is Bernard Monnich of Hooper.

Bernard Monnich is a native son of Dodge County, where he was born in 1869, and of which his father, Gerd Monnich, was a pioneer An extended notice of the Monnich family in connection with the development of Dodge County in the early days will be found elsewhere in this work.

Brought up in Dodge County to a life of industry, Bernard Monnich attended its schools and began at an early age to make himself useful, and in 1891 was able to establish his own business at Hooper, first being a dealer in hardware After two years in this line he branched out and handled agricultural implements for two years In 1897 he began handling real estate, and found in it a congenial occupation, although in the interval between then and now he was also in a garage business for seven years in partnership with his nephew, John, they erecting the garage at Hooper, and doing a general repair business, but in 1917 he disposed of his interest in it so as to give all of his attention to his real-estate operations, and is one of the leaders in this line in Dodge County

In 1891 Mr Monnich was united in marriage with Barbara Achling, born in Nebraska, and they became the parents of the following children: Charlotte, who is employed in the Dodge County Bank, Dora, who is the wife of Ward Thompson of Los Angeles, California, Bernard, who is associated in business with his father, and Carl, who is attending the Hooper schools Mr Monnich is a Blue Lodge Mason He belongs to Grace Lutheran Church of Hooper and is active in church work An independent in politics, at one time he was postmaster of Hooper, Nebraska, but aside from that has not entered public life Both he and Mrs Monnich are held in the highest esteem by their associates, and their friends are to be found all over this region

John G. Dykeman. If one desires to gain a vivid realization of the rapid advance in the civilization which the last few decades have brought, he can listen to the stories that men who are still living among us can tell of their early experiences when the country was new and conditions in the part of the country were in their formative period Conspicuous among the silver-haired veterans of a period long past is the venerable and highly-respected citizen, now living a life of honorable retirement, to a brief review of whose career the following lines are devoted.

John G Dykeman was born in New Jersey on January 31, 1842, and is the son of Gilbert and Mary (Johnson) Dykeman, who died in New Jersey. But three years of age at the time of his mother's death John G Dykeman was thereafter reared by strangers In young manhood he went to Illinois, where he applied himself to agricultural pursuits In 1872 Mr Dykeman came to Dodge County and bought 160 acres of land, to the improvement and cultivation of which he applied himself with energy and ambition Conditions here in those days were comparatively primitive and farming operations were not conducted with the ease of later years But his persistent efforts were rewarded with abundant success and in 1910 he relinquished the active labors of the farm and moved to Fremont, where he has since resided In 1913 he sold that farm and bought 800 acres of land near Potter, which he now rents.

In Illinois, on December 7, 1872, Mr Dykeman was married to Anna M Bull, who was born March 23, 1854, in New York state, the daughter of Harry and Elvira (Otis) Bull, both of whom were natives of New York state and both of whom are now deceased Mrs Dykeman was reared by strangers and knows practically nothing of her parents She is one of three children born to them To Mr. and Mrs Dykeman have been born twelve children, of which number nine are living, namely: Mary, the wife of N J Gidley, who is employed in a garage in Fremont; Allen G, a farmer near Potter, Nebraska, Lula, the wife of Cornelius Davis, a farmer near Potter; Elva, the wife of John Moody, a farmer of Saunders County, Bertha, the wife of Chris Ogard, a farmer near Potter, Lillian, the wife of Charles Christensen, a farmer near Foster, Nebraska; Verna, the wife of Fred Lowdon, of Wahoo, Nebraska, Wilma married Chas. Jennings, of Fort Wayne, Indiana, and Clair is in the employ of the Standard Oil Company at Potter

Mr. Dykeman and his family are identified with the Methodist Episcopal Church, and in politics he is an earnest supporter of the democratic party Mr Dykeman has played well his part at all times in the work of upbuilding his community and has always been fully abreast of the times, doing such good as he could in all the relations of life, consequently he is respected and admired by all who know him, for he is a man of sterling character and public spirit

HERBERT T RING A number of the flourishing journals of the country, especially those issued in the smaller communities, are owned, edited and published by men who know the practical end of the business and have reached these higher positions from the case Understanding every detail of the work, they know its possibilities and can meet the problems in an efficient and satisfactory manner, and while making a good living also render their community a service by giving it a wide awake organ Belonging distinctively to this class is Herbert T Ring of Hooper, who owns, edits and publishes the Hooper Sentinel, a weekly journal, and also carries on a general printing business

Herbert T. Ring was born in Minnesota in 1882, a son of John and Anna L (Goode) Ring, both of whom were born in Sweden, and came to the United States in the late '60s, locating first in Minnesota, but later coming west to Hooper, Nebraska, where John Ring became one of the prominent men, and served as postmaster for many years

A child when his parents came to Hooper, Herbert T. Ring was reared here and was graduated from the Hooper High School in 1898 Following his graduation he began learning the printer's trade with J I Broody on the Sentinel, later going with E W. Renkin for two years Mr Ring then worked for Shipley & Thompson, and then became an employe of the Hooper post office under his father, who was then postmaster, and held his position for nine years. In 1913 he returned to the Sentinel under Glenn Howard, and later formed a partnership with C. W Sedgwick which continued a year, when Mr Ring bought out Mr Sedgwick's interest While he is a republican, Mr. Ring conducts his paper along independent lines, and has an excellent circulation, and the patronage of his job printing establishment is large and steady for he turns out fine work

In 1915 Mr Ring was married to Elizabeth Schumacher, born in Nebraska, and they have one son, Theodore Herbert, who is a bright little fellow Mr Ring belongs to the Ancient Order of United Workmen, the Knights of Pythias, Ancient Free and Accepted Masons, and the Tribe of Ben Hur Both he and his wife are charter members of the Grace Lutheran Church of Hooper, and active in its good work.

A sound, dependable and public-spirited young man, Mr Ring is correctly numbered among the representative men of Dodge County

A. M TILLMAN A man of versatile talents and forceful individuality, A M Tillman, of Hooper, has long been identified with the interests of Dodge County, contributing toward the advancement of its manufacturing, agricultural and financial prosperity, and is eminently worthy of the high position he has attained in business and social circles A son of the late Frank M Tillman, he was born, August 1, 1870, in Dodge County, Nebraska, of German and Swiss ancestry

Born, bred and educated in Germany, Frank M Tillman remained in the fatherland until twenty-nine years old Coming then to this country, he located in Detroit, Michigan, where he subsequently married Anna Enderley, a native of Switzerland Settling with his bride in Holton, Michigan, he ran a hotel there for thirteen years. In 1868 he came with his family to Dodge County, Nebraska, and began life as a farmer in Ridgeley Township. Moving to Hooper in 1881, he managed the Tillman Hotel successfully for several years, being a very genial and popular host Retiring from active pursuits in 1888, he continued a resident of Hooper until his death, in 1915, at the venerable age of ninety-one years His wife preceded him to the better world, dying in 1908, aged eighty-two years He was a democrat in politics, and served as county commissioner from 1873 until 1879, and also served one or more terms as supervisor To him and his wife seven children were born, as follows: Joseph, deceased, Mary, deceased, wife of Peter Parkert, of Hooper, Margaret, wife of Charles S Basler, of Hooper, Lizzie, wife of W F Basler, also of Hooper, Frank A, of Hooper, a dealer in soft drinks, A M, and Catherine, wife of Edward Wiekhorst, of Santa Ana, California, the inventor of a fruit branding machine

Brought up and educated in Dodge County, A M Tillman has been associated with various enterprises, his first business venture having been in connection with the making and selling of soft drinks Continuing in Hooper, he was next engaged in the hotel business, later working as a plumber, and then being employed in the bottling business In 1904 Mr Tillman was made president of the First National Bank, of Hooper and in that capacity had charge of its affairs until he removed to Omaha in order that his children might have better educational advantages

At the end of six years, Mr Tillman settled in Knox County, this state, and was there successfully engaged in agricultural pursuits until 1917, when he returned to Hooper, and resumed his banking business, again becoming officially connected with the First National Bank He is likewise vice president of the Logan Valley Bank of Uehling, of which he was one of the organizers, and is secretary of the Dodge County Stock Association

Mr Tillman has been twice married His first wife whose maiden name was Tillie von Essen, died in early womanhood, leaving two children, namely Luella, of San Francisco, California, and Cornelius H, who enlisted in the World war in 1917, and served in the Oberlin, Ohio, Ambulance Unit until his death, January 24, 1918 Mr Tillman married again in 1908, Mrs Edna (Hartung) Uehling, and they have one child, M Auralea Tillman Mr. and Mrs Tillman are worthy and consistent attenders of the English Lutheran Church Politically Mr Tillman supports the principles of the democratic party by voice and vote Fraternally he is a member of the Knights of Pythias, and of the Fraternal Order of Eagles

WARREN MERSELIS was not yet five years old at the time when his parents established their home in Dodge County, where he was reared to manhood, where he gained his early education in the schools at North Bend and where the passing years have afforded him the opportunities which he has so embraced as to have gained a place among the representative exponents of farm industry in Cotterell Township His well improved farm of eighty acres is situated in section 28 of the township mentioned, and the pleasant home receives service on one of the rural mail routes centering at North Bend

Mr Merselis was born in New York in 1887, and is a son of William and Cora (Collins) Merselis, both likewise natives of the old Empire State, where the father learned and followed the miller's trade In 1891 William Merselis came with his family to North Bend, Dodge County, where for some time he operated the flour mill Later he here turned his attention to farm enterprise, and he now owns an appreciable tract of farm land in the State of Texas, where he maintains his residence, his wife having died in 1908, Warren Merselis being their only surviving child The father is a republican in political adherency and is an active member of the Methodist Episcopal Church, as was also his wife

Warren Merselis gained his initial experience in the basic industry of agriculture through his association with the activities of his father's farm, and since 1910 he has been engaged in farming in an independent way He owns eighty acres of the fine soil of Dodge County, and from the same gains the maximum returns, as he is essentially vigorous and progressive in the management of both the agricultural and live-stock departments of his farm enterprise He has had no desire for political activity, is independent of partisan lines as a voter and he and his wife hold membership in the Methodist Episcopal Church at North Bend

The year 1910 recorded the marriage of Mr Merselis to Miss Bertha Wagoner, who was born in Saunders County, this state, a daughter of Lewis Wagoner, now a resident of Fremont, Dodge County Mr and Mrs Merselis have one son, Harold

CHARLES H BRUNNER In all that constitutes true manhood and good citizenship Charles H Brunner, one of the best known business men in Fremont, is a notable example and none stands higher than he in the esteem and confidence of the community honored by his citizenship His career has been characterized by thrift and wisely directed efforts and he has acquired a fair share of this world's goods, besides earning a reputation as a man of sterling character and public spirit

Charles H Brunner was born in Ottumwa, Iowa, in 1853, and is the son of Henry and Ernestine (Denkman) Brunner, both of whom were born in Germany They came to the United States in their youth and were married here Henry Brunner had studied medicine in Wurzburg and Heidelburg University, Germany, and entered upon the practice of his profession in Davenport, Iowa, where he remained until 1868, when he came to Fremont, Nebraska, and practiced medicine here successfully up to the time of his death, which occurred in 1881 He was a democrat in his political affiliations and his wife was a member of the Congregational Church For a short time while he was located at Prairie du Chien, Wisconsin, he served as city physician and also as county coroner Of the four children born to him and his wife, the following are living: Charles H, John M, who was engaged in the banking business at Mildred and Elkhorn, Nebraska, for a number of years, but is now living in Long Beach, California; William R, who was in the printing business in Fremont for a number of years, is now retired and is living in Long Beach, California

Charles H Brunner was educated in the public schools of Wisconsin, where his father was engaged in the practice of his profession, and he then entered the University of Michigan, where he was graduated He then located in McGregor, Iowa, where he engaged in the drug business for two years, and in 1870 he came to Fremont and engaged in the same business in partnership with Mr Mageneau In 1893 Mr Brunner bought his partner's interest in the business and conducted it alone until 1900, when, on account of ill health, he sold out and from that time until 1918, he spent his time mainly in recovering his health In this he was successful and in the fall of 1918 he returned to Fremont and purchased the drug store owned by Mrs Laura L. Pohl He now has a partner, I H Langjahr, but the business is conducted under the name of Brunner Drug Company They carry a full stock of drugs and also carry a large line of sundries and accessories such as are usually to be found in a well-appointed drug store, and because of the high quality of their goods, their right prices and the courteous treatment accorded every customer who enters their store, they enjoy a large and representative patronage Mr Brunner is also a stockholder and director of the Fremont National Bank, is a member of the Fremont Commercial Club and the Retail Merchants' Association

In 1888 Mr Brunner was married to Lizzie Knoell, who was born, reared and educated in Dodge County, the daughter of J. Knoell, one of the early settlers and land owners of this county Mr Brunner is independent in his political thought and action, voting according to the dictates of his own judgment Fraternally, he is a member of the Ancient Free and Accepted Masons and the Independent Order of Odd Fellows. While he has never taken an active part in political affairs, he maintains a healthy interest in the public welfare and has rendered appreciated service as a school director By a straightforward and commendable course he has maintained an enviable position in the business and social circles of his adopted city, earning a reputation as an enterprising, progressive man of affairs and a high place in the confidence and esteem of all who know him

THEODORE UEHLING Sixty years ago when Dodge County was still part of the original Washington, one of the important accessions to the citizenship of the district was the late Theodore Uehling, who during a long life became prominent as a Nebraska pioneer and a man fitted by character, industry and integrity to adorn the annals of early settlement

Born in Saxe Meiningen, Germany, January 11, 1836, son of Casper and Gottliebetta (Deusing) Uehling, German farmers, who died when Theodore was young, he had a limited attendance at the common schools of his native land until 1847, when at the age of eleven years he came to America with his older brother, Frederick, who located in Wisconsin Theodore grew to manhood in Wisconsin and achieved American citizenship there In May, 1860, shortly after his marriage he left Wisconsin with an ox team, and after many days' journey reached Omaha on the second of July From Omaha they came up into what was then Washington County, and settled in section 18, township 19, range 9. When Dodge County was set off from old Washington County, his location fell in the former division After the passage of the Homestead

Act he homesteaded his property and gave his labors to its development for eighteen years Though he came to Nebraska with only a wagon, two yoke of oxen and $150 in money, he was able to see his affairs prosper and everything he touched respond to the benefit of himself or his community He proved a true friend of education, serving as school director for a number of years, and in 1891 was elected supervisor of Logan Township.

January 2, 1860, Theodore Uehling married Miss Kathrina Schwab, a native of Germany, who came to the United States in 1855 The children born to their union were Otto, Henry, Edward, Ludwig, Theodore, deceased, Martin A, Frederick J, Leonora L, Frank Theo and Louise F Most of the living sons have special sketches in this publication

Theodore Uehling after acquiring American citizenship allied himself with the democratic party and cast his vote true to that allegiance until 1897, after which he was equally stanch in his support of the republican ticket He was a Mason and a member of the Lutheran Church

When in 1905 the Sioux City and Western Railroad built through his farm he accepted the opportunity and laid out a town, which bears the name of this honored pioneer He had seen the little community grow to considerable proportions before his death, which occurred February 13, 1912, at the age of seventy-six years, one month, two days

EDWARD UEHLING, one of the sons of the late pioneer, Theodore Uehling, is a native son of Dodge County, has always retained more or less interest in the land and its resources, but primarily has been a business man His connections for a number of years past have been centered at the town of Uehling and his individual enterprise has done much to prosper and develop that commercial center

He was born at his father's home in what was then Washington but is now Dodge County, March 13, 1863 He attended the common schools of his home district until he was about thirteen On leaving school he went to work in a hardware store at Hooper, and the six years spent there gave him a fundamental training in business For about a year after leaving Hooper he was with a general mercantile establishment at Oakland, Nebraska, and then returned to the general merchandise business at Hooper, where he remained five years He next entered the Dodge County Bank, of Hooper, and in 1905 he helped organize the Farmers State Bank at Uehling and in connection with the bank of which he was cashier handled a stock of hardware Mr Uehling has been cashier of the bank from its inception and has had much to do with the financial service the institution has renderd in that community Its capital has always been $15,000 and while the deposits in 1906 were only $14,000, those for 1920 showed an aggregate of $247 000

Mr Uehling married in July, 1890, Miss Charlotte Herre, who was born in New Jersey They were married at Fremont, where her father, C F Herre, was for many years a tailor and where he died Mr and Mrs Uehling became the parents of four children: Mrs Vera L. Hout, the oldest, lives at Uehling, Harold T, who spent two years in the Ordnance Department of the army and saw service of eighteen months in France, is now connected with his father's bank, having received his honorable discharge in May, 1919, Elletha, the third child, is a student in the State University of Nebraska, and Clifton, the youngest, is at home

M A Uehling

Mr. Uehling has always been a factor in the school affairs of his community, serving for a number of years on the school board of Hooper and also at Uehling For six years he has been treasurer of the Town Board of Uehling He is a member of the Masonic Lodge and his family belong to the Congregational Church

MARTIN A UEHLING The kind of farming that gets results and contributes to the general upbuilding and prosperity of an entire community is in evidence on the place of Mr Uehling in section 8 of Hooper Township, Dodge County Mr Uehling is a veteran farmer and stock man, and belongs to the pioneer class of Dodge County citizenship

He was born in Dodge County August 20, 1869 More extended reference to the Uehling family is made on other pages of this publication, in sketch of his father Theodore Uehling. Mr Uehling spent his boyhood in a day when life was still primitive in Nebraska He attended the common schools and also spent one term in the Fremont Normal School In 1893 at the age of twenty-four he began farming for himself and for over a quarter of a century has looked after his crops and fields every season His farm comprises a 160 acres, all with high class improvements He keeps thoroughbred and high grade stock, both cattle and hogs, and the Sunny Slope Stock Farm has long enjoyed a high reputation in agricultural circles

Mr Uehling has also given time to public affairs and at present is county supervisor, entering the duties of his office in 1919, his term expiring in 1923 He is a member of the Grace Lutheran Church at Hooper, has held all the prominent chairs in the Masonic Lodge, and he and his wife are members of the Eastern Star Mr Uehling was for five or six years Worthy Patron and Mrs Uehling was Worthy Matron of the Eastern Star

March 31, 1893, the year he started farming on his own account he also established a home of his own by his marriage to Dora Keller, also a native of Dodge County Her father, William Keller, is living retired at Hooper Mr and Mrs Uehling have two children, Eva and Vyrle

FRED KNOELL has been a witness of many developments and changes in Dodge County, and for over twenty years has been a factor in promoting some of these developments, particularly in his home locality of Platte Township He is owner of one of the good farms in section 12, and has earned a substantial place in a community which has long esteemed this family name.

Mr Knoell was born in Dodge County February 18, 1878, son of Mr. and Mrs Thomas Knoell His father, a native of Germany, came to Dodge County at the age of seventeen, spent an earnest and effective life as a farmer and good citizen and died at the age of sixty-four

Fred Knoell grew up on the old homestead, attended the district schools and made himself helpful to his parents at the same time serving a practical apprenticeship in farming, so that when he started for himself in 1900 he was no stranger to the business of agriculture Mr Knoell has a well improved eighty acres, and along with the crop has made a specialty of Shorthorn cattle. His farm is six miles from Fremont, and is one of the most attractive places in Platte Township

Mr Knoell, like many of the younger generation, is an independent in politics His church affiliation is Lutheran He married Miss Alice Fairchild of Fremont, and they have one child now one year old

CHRISTIAN SASS In Christian Sass, Dodge County has a practical and zealous farmer, and one who, for a long period, has promoted the best interests of the community. For nearly thirty years he has been engaged in the cultivation of the soil in Cuming Township, and has not only developed a property that places him among the substantial agriculturists of his community, but at the same time has conducted his affairs in such an honorable manner as to gain him public confidence and esteem

Mr Sass was born March 19, 1868, on a farm in Dodge County, a son of John and Sophie (Kroeger) Sass His parents, natives of Germany, immigrated to the United States in 1868 and made their way to Omaha, from which point they came overland by team to Dodge County and homesteaded on township 43, the same land as that which now forms the farm of their son John Sass was a man of marked industry who worked faithfully in the development of a farm and the establishment of a home He had few interests aside from his farm and his family and did not thrust himself forward for public preferment Yet at his death, which occurred in 1900, when he was sixty-two years of age, his community lost a good and reliable citizen and his many acquaintances a kind and considerate friend His widow, who still survives him, has attained the phenomenal age of ninety-seven years. In their family there were four children, the first two being twins: Mary, who is the widow of George Mundlow, of Beemer, Nebraska; Sophia, who is the wife of John Ross of that community, August, who is engaged in agricultural pursuits near the town of West Point, and Christian. Mr Sass voted the republican ticket, and belonged to the Lutheran Church, to the faith of which his worthy widow still adheres

To the country schools of Dodge County Christian Sass is indebted for his educational training He was reared in an agricultural atmosphere and it was but natural that he should adopt farming as his life calling when he came to man's estate He was twenty-three years of age when he embarked upon activities of his own, and from that time to the present has applied himself assiduously to the work of farming and raising stock He has a good grade of cattle and raises all the standard crops and is generally accounted an able and thoroughly informed farmer and a good judge of live stock His property, lying in section 34, Cuming Township, has all the ear-marks of being under good management, and his reputation in business circles is that of an honorable and fair-dealing man

Mr Sass was married in 1891 to Miss Anna Meyer, who was born in Germany, and to this union there have born eight children Alma, who is unmarried and resides with her parents, Adelia, the wife of Herman Horst, a Dodge County farmer, John, who is engaged in farming in Dodge County, and Harold, Norman, Wenna, Christian and Roland, at home The family belongs to the Lutheran Church. Mr Sass is an independent voter and has never sought office

C JULIAN KOEHNE is the efficient and popular business manager at Ames, Dodge County, for the Farmers' Union Co-operative Association, and his executive functions include the directing of a substantial business in the handling of grain, lumber and farm implements and machinery

Mr Koehne was born at Wentworth, South Dakota, and is a son of Frederick E and Eunice (West) Koehne, both of whom were born and reared in the state of Wisconsin The father became a farmer in South Dakota, where he remained until 1886, when he came with his family to Dodge County, Nebraska, where he purchased a farm and continued his successful activities as an agriculturist and stock-grower He and his wife still reside in this county, where he is now living practically retired

C Julian Koehne accompanied his parents on their removal to Dodge County, where he gained his initial experience in connection with business affairs, his early education having been acquired in the public schools For six years he was in the employ of the Nye-Snyder-Fowler Grain & Lumber Company, and at the expiration of this period he became associated with a leading lumber company in the state of Washington In 1918 he established his residence at Ames, Nebraska, and entered vigorously upon the executive duties of the responsible position of which he is now the incumbent, and he has shown marked progressiveness and efficiency in the handling of the business of the Farmers' Union Co-operative Association at this point in Dodge County It should be noted that after the removal of the family to Dodge County, Mr Koehne availed himself of the advantages of the high school at Fremont, and that later he pursued a higher course of study in the University of Nebraska. He is a democrat in his political affiliation, and his wife is a communicant of the Protestant Episcopal Church

The year 1911 recorded the marriage of Mr Koehne to Miss Delia Tompkins, who was born and reared in the State of Washington, and they have two children—Frederick D and Charles Arthur

WILLIAM M STONE Practically all his life William M Stone has been a resident of Nebraska, being a representative of one of its early families His life has been one of signal usefulness and honor and his memory links the later pioneer epoch inseparably with the present era of prosperity and achievement As a representative citizen and enterprising business man, he has won the favorable opinion of all who know him and it is eminently consonant that a review of his life history be incorporated in a work of the character of the one in hand

William M Stone was born in Chatsworth, Illinois, on January 26, 1869, and he is the son of Addison and Catherine (Joyce) Stone They were natives respectively of Olean, New York, and of the State of Maine Leaving their respective states, they settled in Illinois soon after the close of the Civil war and there they met and were married They remained in Illinois until 1872, when they came to Nebraska and made permanent settlement at Central City, where Addison Stone followed mercantile pursuits during the rest of his active business life He was successful in his affairs and was held in high repute among his fellows His death occurred in 1903 and he is survived by his widow, who still lives in Central City They were members of the Roman Catholic Church and in his political views Mr Stone was a democrat To these parents were born four children, namely: William M, John, who lives with his mother at Central City, is a carpenter, C A, a physician, who has been very successful both professionally and in his financial affairs, lives in Hastings, Nebraska, and is the owner of several farms in Nebraska, James G is also a successful physician and is located at Sutton, Nebraska

William M Stone attended the public schools of Central City, supplementing this training by attendance at St Mary's College, at St Mary's, Kansas, and in the Fremont Normal School He then engaged in teaching school, following that profession for a number of years in Merrick County, Nebraska, and serving for one term as County Superintendent of Schools He also gave some attention to farming pursuits and engaged in mercantile pursuits at Central City and Greenwood, Nebraska In May, 1912, Mr Stone came to Fremont and engaged in the insurance business, to which later he added the real estate business He has been eminently successful in both of these lines and has handled a vast amount of farm and city property He possesses an accurate knowledge of land values and his opinions are held in high esteem by his contemporaries In January, 1920, Mr Stone was chiefly instrumental in organizing the Nebraska Land & Emigration Company, of which he is the office manager This company has taken over a large amount of irrigated land in the Arkansas River Valley, and it is their intention to sell this land in tracts of forty acres and upwards

In 1895, Mr Stone was married to Elizabeth C Owens, who was born in Canton, Ohio, and to them have been born six children, namely: Clarence L, who is employed by the Nye-Schneider-Fowler Company, Bernard R, who is a student in the Creighton Law School, at Omaha, Nebraska, Mabel, a teacher in the public schools at Ames, Nebraska, Zeta, Mary and Catherine are at home and attend the public schools.

The Stone family are members of the Catholic Church and in politics Mr Stone gives his support to the democratic party He is a member of the Knights of Columbus, the Royal Higlanders (in which he has passed through the chairs) and the Insurance Union of America A man of high moral character, persistent industry and excellent business ability, he stands "four square to every wind that blows," and occupies an enviable position among his fellow citizens of Dodge County.

H H Boyd The record of Nebraska's business men demonstrates that none of them who have risen to enviable positions have been thus successful unless they possessed more than average ability, and applied to their work a conscientious thoroughness which in the end justified the trouble and time expended Competition is greater today than it was in the antebellum period when such a thing as a world's shortage of foodstuffs was unbelieveable, so that greater efforts have to be made to establish and build up desirable connections, and to maintain the excellence of a product which has gained favor with the public One of the men of Dodge County who has for some years proven himself worthy of the trust reposed in him and measured up to the requirements of his undertaking is H H Boyd, miller and manager for the Hooper Milling Company, Incorporated, of Hooper

H H Boyd was born in Randolph County, Illinois, in 1876, a son of Fillmore and Elizabeth (Warnock) Boyd, both of whom were natives of Illinois Fillmore Boyd was a carpenter by trade, who died in Illinois during 1900, aged fifty-eight years In his religious faith he worshipped in accordance with the creed of the United Presbyterians A man of upright life and sober habits, he recognized the evils of intemperance and gave a strong support to the cause of prohibition

Mr Boyd came to Onawa, Iowa, from Illinois and there he learned the milling business, but when he reached Nebraska in 1904, he was first engaged in farming. After a brief period, however, he engaged with Teeter & Emerson of North Bend, Nebraska, and remained with that firm for eight years, leaving it for the mills at Fremont There he was in the employ of the Brown Milling Company, Incorporated, for two years, and then came to Hooper as miller and manager for the mills at this point C H Moeller is president of the company; H J

Krueger is vice president, and Peter Parker is secretary and treasurer A general grain and flour business is carried on and the specialties of the company are the Gold Drop and White Rose flours

In 1911 Mr Boyd was united in marriage with Margaret Tedy, born in Nebraska, and they have two children, namely. Wendell, who is attending school, and Marion, who is at home Mr and Mrs Boyd belong to the Methodist Episcopal Church Like his father, Mr Boyd is an ardent supporter of the principles actuating the prohibition party, and no one is more gratified than he over the passage and ratifying of the Eighteenth Amendment for in it he sees a fruition of years of earnest and sincere effort on behalf of his associates and himself, and those who were pioneers in the movement at a time when any idea of a concerted national movement toward doing away with the liquor traffic was scouted at even by those who would have been glad to see such action taken It is certain that the saloons would never have been abolished had it not been for the years of work by these self-same enthusiasts who, upheld by their conviction of right, labored on in the face of almost overwhelming opposition and discouragement, and their reward today is not a light one, nor can anyone criticise their satisfaction in the course of events.

ANDREW P NELSON In section 21, Maple Township, is situated a fine homestead farm whose general appearance clearly denotes the enterprise and progressiveness of its owner, Andrew P Nelson, who is one of the representative agriculturists and stock-growers of Dodge County He was born in Denmark in the year 1856, and is a son of James C C and Magdalena Nelson, who immigrated to America in 1863 and established the family home in Wisconsin, where the father found employment at farm work and began to make advancement toward the goal of independence and prosperity About the year 1863 he came with his family to Dodge County, Nebraska, and took up a homestead in Maple Township, where he reclaimed and improved a good farm, upon which he continued to reside until 1883, when he retired and removed to Fremont, the county seat, where he passed the remainder of his life, his widow passing away in 1909 at a venerable age He was a republican in politics, was a communicant of the Lutheran Church and his wife was a member of the Methodist Episcopal Church Of their twelve children, eight attained to years of maturity Morris is now serving as township supervisor and is one of the substantial farmers of Dodge County, Andrew P, of this review, is the next younger, Charles G is a farmer near Fremont, this county, James C is a retired stockman, living at Grand Junction, Colorado, as is also Frederick, Martin resides in the home of his brother, Morris, Anna is the wife of Charles C Johnson, of Fremont, and Otto died in 1919

Andrew P Nelson was about eight years of age at the time of the family emigration from Denmark to the United States and his early education was acquired principally in the public schools of Nebraska He was eight years old at the time of removal of the family to Nebraska and has since continued to be actively identified with the farming industry, in connection with which he has achieved substantial success His homestead farm comprises 120 acres, the place is well improved and though he is living practically retired, he still remains on his farm and gives to the same his general and effective supervision He is a stanch supporter of the principles of the republican party, has served as a member of the county board of supervisors, is affiliated with the Modern

Woodmen of America and his wife is an active communicant of the Lutheran Church

In 1887 Mr Nelson wedded Miss Mary Hold, who was born in Germany and who is survived by two children—Alfred C, who has active charge of his father's farm and Margaret E, who is the wife of Matthew Apple, a farmer in Everett Township, Dodge County After the death of his first wife, Mr Nelson married Miss Jennie Hold, who was born in Germany and no children have been born of this union

DUNCAN LIVINGSTON, who lived at Fremont over twenty years, was undoubtedly one of the best known citizens of Dodge County He was a railroad man, a merchant, and was honored with some of the important responsibilities of public affairs

He was born in Toronto, Canada, March 19, 1862, of old Scotch lineage, his parents being natives of Canada When he was a boy thirteen years old, his parents removed to South Carolina, where he was reared and educated After reaching manhood he went to Western Canada, to the new province of Manitoba, and for several years followed farming at Binscarth Coming to Nebraska in 1894, Duncan Livingston established his home at Fremont, and entered the service of the Chicago & Northwestern Railroad He was in that service for sixteen years before he resigned, and for several years had held the position of night yardmaster He became well known among the railroad men making their headquarters at Fremont In 1910 he established himself in the grocery business, and assisted in building up the store of which his son, J Stewart Livingston, is now proprietor

A democrat in politics he never shirked the responsibilities of public office, and was serving his second term as county supervisor at the time of his death on November 29, 1915 He was first elected to this office to represent District No 7 in Dodge County in 1912, and in 1914 was re-elected for a four-year term He had more than three years to serve at the time of his death His associates on the Board of Supervisors entertained the greatest respect for his judgment and gave full recognition of his views in matters affecting the public interest

He also stood high among Fremont business men, being a director in the Fremont Dealers' Association, and a member of the Commercial Club He was a Presbyterian and for a number of years served as trustee of the church at Fremont Fraternally he was affiliated with the Masonic Order, the Independent Order of Odd Fellows, the Ancient Order of United Workmen, and Knights of Pythias. He was a citizen of kindly purpose, a friend to the poor and needy, and his life was such that the city and community felt a deep sense of loss at his taking off He was survived by four sisters, one of whom is Mrs William A Carroll, of Fremont, by a brother, John Livingston, also of Fremont, and by his aged mother, who was with him at Fremont when he died

In 1886 Duncan Livingston married Miss Annie Peddie of Binscarth, Manitoba She was born in Canada and continued to make her home at Fremont Five children were born to Mr and Mrs Livingston Their son Robert lost his life while a brakeman on the Northwestern Railroad Two other children died young, a son being burned to death. The two surviving children are J Stewart Livingston, mentioned elsewhere as a Fremont business man, and Catherine, still in school

J STEWART LIVINGSTON One of the energetic and progressive citizens of Fremont, J Stewart Livingston is a prosperous and reliable business man of Dodge County, and as a merchant has an extensively

S Livingston

J. Stewart Livingston

patronized grocery carrying all the staple and fancy groceries found in the best establishments of that kind anywhere

Mr Livingston, a son of the late Duncan Livingston, was born August 26, 1888, in Binscarth, Manitoba, and was six years of age when his parents located at Fremont. He grew up, acquired his education in the local schools, graduating from the Fremont High School in 1908 He soon afterward began his business career as clerk in a grocery store, and for two years gave full measure to his routine of work and acquired much valuable knowledge and experience at the same time In 1910 with his father he opened a store at the corner of Main and Second streets, and since the death of his honored father has had entire control of the large and constantly increasing business

Mr Livingston is a democrat in politics but has never been active in political circles, his time and attention being devoted to his business affairs Fraternally he is a Scottish Rite Mason and a member of the Mystic Shrine, and is affiliated with Fremont Lodge No. 514 of the Elks He also belongs to the Country Club, is a member of the Retail Grocers' Association and the Nebraska State Retail Grocers' Association Mr Livingston was married in 1920

C A. KEENE Business interests of great importance are connected with the name of Keene in Dodge County, these including land, banking, real estate and insurance, C A Keene, manager of his father's large and valuable property, situated five miles from Fremont, on the Lincoln Highway, having built up a very substantial business reputation

C A Keene was born at Fremont, Nebraska, in 1884, a son of Lewis McClain and Jennie (Marr) Keene, the latter of whom was born at Simcoe, Ontario, Canada, in 1850, and died in Nebraska in 1897 Lewis McClain Keene has long been prominent in the affairs of Dodge County. He was born in 1844, at Appleton, Maine, and was twenty-three years old when he came to Nebraska in 1867, with a determination to succeed in his undertakings, and with a cash capital of $50 During his first winter in Dodge County he operated a sorghum mill, and afterward for some years, taught school during the winters and worked on farms during the summers, sometimes accepting much more laborious employment He has been heard to say when some case of willful idleness or lack of ambition in a young man has been brought to his attention, that if he had followed such a method in his youth, he would never have gained the confidence and respect of his solid, hardworking neighbors nor have reached his state of financial independence

After homesteading, Mr Keene lived alone on his claim until the land was his, and with this as a nucleus, acquired tract after tract until he became one of the heaviest landowners in Dodge County He still owns 1,705 acres in addition to a large amount of fine residence property in Fremont His extensive and highly cultivated farm lying five miles from Fremont, on the magnificent Lincoln Highway, has seven sets of farm buildings He entered into partnership with L D Richards, first as Richards & Keene, later as Richards, Keene & Company, as a real estate, insurance and investment firm, which continues and is one of the stable business concerns of old Fremont Mr Keene became prominent also in other ways For twenty-eight years he was president of the Fremont National Bank and is still chairman of its board of directors In politics a zealous republican, he has been personally acquainted with many of the party leaders with whom he has often been called in council, and in earlier days served for a number of years as county clerk

Mr Keene was married at Fremont to Miss Jennie Marr and two children were born to them, Lewis Marr and C A, both of Fremont Their mother was a devoted member of the Episcopal Church Lewis M Keene has reached high distinction in Masonry, is past grand commander of the Knights Templar of Nebraska and has attained the thirty-third degree He is a life member of Fremont Lodge No 514 Benevolent and Protective Order of Elks

C A Keene was reared at Fremont and was graduated from the Fremont High School in 1901, and afterward spent three years in Oberlin College, Oberlin, Ohio Upon his return to Nebraska, well equipped for almost any line of endeavor but more closely interested in farming than any other vocation, he found plenty of responsibility awaiting him in the management of his father's large and valuable farm, which commands $500 an acre.

In June, 1909, Mr Keene was united in marriage to Miss Hazel Rice who was born at Ainsworth, Nebraska, and is a daughter of Frank S Rice. Her grandfather was Brigadier-General Samuel Rice of Des Moines, Iowa, who was killed at the battle of Jenkins Ferry, during the Civil war Mrs Keene had one younger sister, who died in childhood In 1910 Mr Keene built a beautiful bungalow residence at 550 East Fourth Street Fremont, that he and his wife have occupied since February 11, 1911, one of the most attractive of this class of cozy homes in the city Mr Keene also owns a farm of 160 acres in Dodge County

Like his honored father Mr Keene has long been identified with the Masonic fraternity He has attained the thirty-second degree and at present is eminent commander of Mount Tabor Commandery No 9, and belongs also to the Mystic Shrine He belongs additionally to Fremont Lodge No 514 Benevolent and Protective Order of Elks In political life he has always been a sturdy republican but public office has never appealed to him and just at present he finds his time fully engaged in the stupendous work of managing a large modern farm, looking after his father's other business matters, and paying attention to his own

Capt Miner H Hinman This gentleman was born April 5, 1836, in Wysox Bradford County, Pennsylvania, and died at Fremont, Nebraska, January 3, 1917 He was the son of a Presbyterian minister—Abner Curtis Hinman and wife By occupation Miner H Hinman was a carpenter During the Civil war he enlisted in the Ninety-Day Men of the Pennsylvania State Militia, and was at Antietam and Gettysburg engagements He then returned home and raised a company for the One Hundred and Seventy-First Pennsylvania Volunteers and was made its Captain After the war ended he crossed the western plains with a caravan of ox teams, carrying supplies and engines, and landed at Cheyenne, Wyoming, where he took a contract for grading parts of the Union Pacific Railroad from Cheyenne to Ogden, Utah

He returned to Pennsylvania in 1869, and on April 8th, that year, married Emma A Ackley, came to Fremont, Nebraska, engaged in various occupations, was a county commissioner and purchased for the county the present poor farm He retired in 1892 from active life Mr Hinman was a member of the Ancient Free and Accepted Masons, Royal Arch Masons and Knights Templar of the Masonic Order, also an honored member of the Grand Army of the Republic

GUY M. HINMAN

MINER H. HINMAN

BEACH HINMAN

GUY M HINMAN. The fact that Mr Hinman is serving as mayor of his native city bears its own significance, in attesting not only to his ability and civic loyalty but also to the secure vantage-place that is his in popular confidence and esteem He is a scion of one of the honored and influential pioneer families of Dodge County, as may be better understood by reference to the memoir dedicated to his father, the late Capt Miner H Hinman, also in this publication, in which connection are given adequate genealogical data also

The present progressive and popular mayor of the City of Fremont was here born on the 11th day of April, 1873, and after having duly availed himself of the advantages of the excellent schools of his native city he pursued a higher academic course in Doane College at Crete, this state. He there made not only an excellent student record but was also a prominent figure in college athletics, especially in his effective work as halfback on the football team After leaving college Mr Hinman became bookkeeper in the Fremont National Bank, and with this institution he continued his connection fifteen years Thereafter he was associated with other banking institutions and finally he released himself from business exactions by indulging in a six months' hunting and fishing trip in Wyoming Upon his return to Fremont he became associated with the Fremont Saddlery Company, a wholesale concern, and he not only served as secretary and treasurer of this corporation but also as its credit man As an expert accountant he has been called upon to do much auditing work for the leading business concerns, a service to which he is still frequently called, but aside from his official duties as chief executive of the municipal government of Fremont he now gives the major part of his time to the management of his own financial and property interests

Mayor Hinman is unswerving in his allegiance to the republican party and while he has never been affiliated with office-seeking proclivities, he was made candidate for the office of mayor of his native city and was elected April 1, 1919, for the prescribed term of two years Since assuming his official duties he has instituted a careful and progressive administration that is clearly justifying his election That the popular mayor is "heart whole and fancy free" must be inferred from the fact that his name is still enrolled on the list of eligible bachelors in Dodge County. He has never abated his interest in outdoor sports and as a hunter he has a goodly assemblage of fine trophies, including bears and deer He is emphatically a "booster" for his home city, county and state, and his loyalty is marked by deep appreciation of the manifold attractions and advantages of Nebraska He is affiliated with both York and Scottish Rite bodies of the Masonic fraternity, including the Fremont Commandery of Knights Templar, and he has served continuously as treasurer of Fremont Lodge No 514, Benevolent and Protective Order of Elks, from the time of its organization

BEACH HINMAN, attorney-at-law, practicing at the City of Fremont, is a son of Minor H Hinman, whose biographical sketch appears on preceding pages

He attended the University of Michigan, receiving the degree of Bachelor of Laws in 1895

Politically Mr Hinman is a supporter of the republican party and is a member of the Masonic order

SYLVESTER A PRESTON, M D, now one of the representative physicians and surgeons engaged in practice in the City of Fremont, had achieved marked success in the pedagogic profession prior to preparing himself for that of which he is now an able and successful exponent. Doctor Preston was born in the City of Toronto, Canada, and is a scion of influential pioneer families of that immediate section of the beautiful Province of Ontario The date of his nativity was January 15, 1867, and he is a son of Robert S. and Isabelle (Atkinson) Preston, both of whom were likewise natives of Toronto, where the former was born February 28, 1837, and the latter on May 5, 1843 The parents were reared and educated in Toronto, where their marriage was solemnized and where they continued to reside until about 1870, when they removed to Greensboro, North Carolina, in which state they maintained their residence for a term of years They finally removed to the Province of Manitoba, Canada, where the father secured land and developed a productive farm, though prior to that time he had followed contracting and building and been actively identified with lumbering operations, as the owner and operator of sawmills Robert S Preston continued his residence in Manitoba until his death, July 3, 1917, and his devoted wife did not long survive him, as she passed to the life eternal on the 15th of May of the following year Of the four children three are living Dr Sylvester A of this review; Eugene, engaged in the jewelry business in the City of Vancouver, Canada, and Edgar S, residing upon and having active management of his father's old homestead farm near Winnipeg, Manitoba The parents were earnest members of the Baptist Church, with which the family has been affiliated for several generations —even prior to the coming of its first representatives to America Thomas Preston, grandfather of the doctor was born and reared in England and came to Ontario, Canada, about 1820 He had been a cattle dealer in his native land and upon coming to Canada he took up land near Toronto and developed a productive farm He there passed the remainder of his life, and in addition to operating his farm he was associated with Robert F Atkinson (maternal great-grandfather of Doctor Preston of this sketch) in the establishing and operating of the first sawmill in the vicinity of Toronto, this substantial old mill being still in operation at the present time Mr Atkinson likewise was a native of England, but was a lad of six years when his parents came to America and established their home in Ontario, Canada There he grew to manhood and there he became prominently concerned with lumbering operations, in connection with which he was concerned in the establishing of the historic old mill mentioned above

Doctor Preston was about four years of age at the time of the family removal to Greensboro, North Carolina, and he there attended the public schools until he was eligible for admission to Guilford College, this state where he continued his studies for some time He accompanied his parents on their removal to Northwestern Canada, and in 1895 he was graduated in the provincial normal school in the City of Winnipeg Previously to his graduation he taught school and he continued his efficient service as a teacher for ten years thereafter, his pedagogic service having been initiated in 1884 He came to Nebraska in the year 1896 and in pursuance of a cherished ambition he entered the medical department of the University of Nebraska, in which he was graduated as a member of the class of 1900 After thus receiving his coveted degree of Doctor of Medicine he engaged in practice at Howell, Colfax County, and later he was for a time retained as physician and surgeon in the service of the United States Steel Company in the mining district of the Upper Peninsula of Michigan He finally returned to Nebraska, and in September, 1908, he established his permanent residence at Fremont, where he has since continued in the general practice of his profession and where his success and popularity are attested by the large and representative practice which is now his The doctor served as local surgeon for the Chicago & Northwestern Railroad from 1903 to 1908, since which latter year his private practice has demanded his undivided attention, though he is medical examiner for the various fraternal insurance orders with which he is affiliated, and was at one time city physician of Fremont. Doctor Preston has served as president of the Dodge County Medical Society and the Elkhorn Valley Medical Society, and in addition to his active association with the affairs of these two professional organizations he is a member also of the Nebraska State Medical Society and the American Medical Association Unswerving in his allegiance to the work of his profession, Doctor Preston has had neither time nor inclination to enter the arena of practical politics, though he is a loyal supporter of the cause of the republican party. He and his wife are members of the Methodist Episcopal Church, and he maintains affiliation with the Masonic fraternity, the Knights of Pythias, the Modern Woodmen of America, the Woodmen of the World, the Royal Neighbors, the Degree of Honor and the Royal Highlanders

In 1901 was solemnized the marriage of Doctor Preston to Miss Ella Bonine, who was born at Perry, Iowa, a daughter of Calvin L Bonine, now a resident of the City of Omaha Dr and Mrs Preston have two children, Robert Louis and Isabelle, both of whom are attending the public schools of Fremont, Robert L. being a member of the class of 1922 in the high school

Luther C Larson The man who possesses the initiative to enter a new line of business generally succeeds, particularly if he is wise enough to select something which meets with popular approval Luther C Larson possessed just this quality and also grit, determination and the ability to overcome obstacles, when he commenced handling automobiles at Fremont, and now is doing one of the largest businesses in Dodge County and represents a number of standard companies

Luther C Larson was born in Omaha, Nebraska, in 1885, a son of L P and Althea (Granath) Larson, both natives of Sweden They were married in Kewanee, Illinois, where he had come when only twelve years of age In 1876 they came to Nebraska, and he was associated with Mr. Cummings in a wholesale grocery business at Omaha, Nebraska Later he moved to Fremont and carried on a wholesale liquor business until Nebraska went dry Not only was he a successful business man, but was also a leader in democratic politics and represented Dodge County in the State Assembly in the '70s The doctrines of the Christian Science movement so impressed him that he adopted them as his own Early in life he connected himself with the Knights of Pythias and the Elks He and his wife became the parents of the following children Lida, who married John C Hein, a confectioner, Laura, who is the widow of Otto Pohl, formerly a druggist of Fremont, Louis P, who is a manufacturer of chewing gum, lives at Chicago, Illinois, Lillie, who married C J Marr of Fremont, and Luther C, who was the youngest

Luther C Larson attended the Fremont schools until old enough to go into his father's business as bookkeeper Later he was made secretary and treasurer of the firm of L P Larson & Company, but left it in 1910 to engage in the automobile business, first representing the Stoddard Dayton car At present he represents the Hudson, Essex and Overland cars and the Republic trucks, and is the oldest automobile dealer in Fremont

On January 15, 1910, Mr Larson was married to Edna May Welch, born at Fremont, a daughter of J J Welch, a railroad man, now of Pierre, South Dakota Mr Larson is a Christian Scientist and his wife Episcopalian Fraternally Mr. Larson belongs to the Elks, Masons and Knights of Pythias, and in politics he is a democrat One of the live young business men of the city, he sets an example others would do well to follow, and is held in high esteem by all with whom he is associated

FRED VOLPP Thrift, honesty and industry have been the steppingstones by which many men of present day prominence have acquired fortune and public regard and this fact can scarcely be too often commented on when considering the means by which some men succeed and others fail in their life efforts When Fred Volpp, the leading banker of Scribner, came to Nebraska thirty-two years ago, he was practically empty-handed, while today he is not only at the head of one of the state's solid, substantial banking institutions, but has many other financial interests, and additionally he has been signally honored in the highest governing body in the commonwealth His whole life has been one of cheerful industry and the rewards that have accrued have been natural results

Fred Volpp was born April 18 1868, in Germany, where his father, Henry Volpp, was a farmer He died in 1884 and the mother in 1889 Of their eight children, Fred is the fourth in order of birth He has two brothers living at Bloomfield, Nebraska, and one brother, Carl, who is a truck farmer living in Pennsylvania He also has two sisters and two brothers living in Nebraska It was in his native land that Mr Volpp received his schooling and other training, and was twenty years old when he came to Nebraska He had learned the butcher's trade and opened a shop at Wayne which he conducted for sixteen years, retiring then from its personal supervision, although retaining part ownership, when he was elected county treasurer in 1900 With the greatest efficiency he served four years in this office, after which, for nine months he was cashier of the First National Bank of Bloomfield, Nebraska In 1905 he came to Scribner and became cashier of the Scribner State Bank, in which office he continued until 1909, when he was elected president of the bank He commands public confidence and under his clear-sighted policy the institution has grown in importance and stands as one of the bulwarks of safety and security in the state He has additional business interests and is officially connected with the Lion Bonding Company of Omaha, of which he is vice president

Not only has Mr Volpp been successful in business but his foresight, prudence and good judgment were early recognized in public affairs, and the democratic party first proved its appreciation by electing him county treasurer, as mentioned above, and in 1909 further honored him by electing him to the State Senate in which body he proved the possession of statesman-like qualities that reflected honor both on himself and on his constituency Senator Volpp served four years at Lincoln and retired from public office with an enviable record

In 1889 Fred Volpp was united in marriage to Miss Sophie Lerner He is a thirty-second degree Mason and a Shriner, also is an Odd Fellow and is treasurer of the Sons of Hermann for the State of Nebraska.

ARTHUR G CHRISTENSEN Possessing unquestioned business ability, integrity and judgment, Arthur G Christensen of Fremont, vice president of the First National Bank, holds a noteworthy position in financial circles, and is considered an authority on all questions concerned with banks and banking He was born August 6, 1880, in Fremont, which has always been his home, being a son of Christian and Maria (Paulsen) Christensen, both of whom were born in Denmark, came to this country in early life, and were married in Nebraska, and are now living in Fremont.

Arthur G Christensen was educated in Fremont, and soon after his graduation from the high school, with the class of 1898, became a clerk in the Commercial National Bank Proving himself eminently capable and trustworthy, he won promotions, and on leaving the institution on June 1, 1914, was serving as cashier On July 1, 1914, Mr Christensen was made vice president of the First National Bank of Fremont, and is still serving in that capacity, being also one of its directors, positions for which his knowledge, experience and business judgment and sagacity amply qualify him, and is a director in the Fidelity Trust Company

Mr Christensen married in 1906 Mary Roberta Hammond, a daugh-of Frank Hammond, a prominent newspaper man of Fremont, of whom mention is found elsewhere in this volume, and into their pleasant home three children have made their advent, namely Roberta, nine years old; William, seven years of age, and Mary Elizabeth, five years of age. Both Mr and Mrs Christensen are active and valued members of the Methodist Episcopal Church Fraternally Mr Chistensen is a prominent member of the Ancient Free and Accepted Masons, belonging to Lodge Chapter, Council, Commandery and the Shrine, and he is a member and past exalted ruler of Fremont Lodge No 514, Benevolent and Protective Order of Elks, of which he was secretary a number of years

ARTHUR G. SCHOENECK One of the representative citizens of Scribner, Nebraska, is Arthur G Schoeneck, postmaster, who is a member of one of the oldest settled families in Dodge County Its history includes much pertaining to pioneer hardships, for when the Schoenecks first came here the country was but sparsely settled, transportation facilities were absent and for years afterward the cultivation of the land was carried on under difficulties

Arthur G Schoeneck was born in 1874, in Dodge County, the second in his parents' family of five children His father, Carl F, and his mother, Emily (Radtke) Schoeneck were both born in Germany and were young when they came to the United States and to Dodge County, Nebraska Carl F Schoeneck homesteaded within one mile of Scribner, where he developed a fine farm and prospered as a stockman, in later years retiring and moving into Scribner, where his death occurred in 1917, at the age of seventy-four years Aside from Arthur G, his other children were as follows William, who conducts a garage at Snyder, Nebraska, Alma, who is deceased; Hilda, who is the wife of Carl Bleyhl, a farmer, and Ella, who is the wife of Sidney Spurling, a merchant at Scribner The mother of the above family still resides in Scribner She is a member of the Congregational Church

Arthur G. Schoeneck attended the common schools in boyhood but later went to Omaha and took a commercial course in a business college He remained on the home farm until he was twenty-one years of age, after which for some years he worked as a farmer through the home neighborhood Later he came to Scribner and became interested in the hardware business, subsequently entering into a business partnership in this line, and for some years the hardware firm of Marquardt & Schoeneck did a large business In 1914 Mr Schoeneck was appointed postmaster and has been continued in the office ever since He is a careful and efficient public official

On August 12, 1904, Mr Schoeneck was united in marriage to Miss Alice Clement, who was born and educated in Nebraska, and they have four children, namely Merton, Arthur, Marvin and William, all of whom attend school Mrs Schoeneck is a member of the Roman Catholic Church

Postmaster Schoeneck may be said to have been reared in the democratic party for his father had always been a staunch supporter of its principles and candidates Prior to his appointment as postmaster, Mr Schoeneck had served most acceptably in other public positions, for some years having been assessor and constable He belongs to the order of Royal Highlanders and also to the Sons of Hermann

William A Schoeneck It has been the privilege of William A. Schoeneck to realize many of his worthy ambitions, and through the exercise of good judgment and business sagacity to wrest from his opportunities financial and general success During his career he has been identified with diversified enterprises, and at the present time his name is associated with the operation of a successful soft drink establishment at Snyder, where he is also conducting a well-patronized garage

Mr Schoeneck was born on a farm in Dodge County, Nebraska, in 1871, a son of Carl F Schoeneck, a review of this family being found elsewhere in this work in the sketch of A G Schoeneck He received his educational training in the school at Scribner, in which locality his boyhood and youth were passed, and when he entered upon his independent career it was as a farmer on the property of his grandfather, located near Scribner For eleven years Mr Schoeneck continued to follow the pursuits of agriculture, after which he disposed of his farming and stock-raising interests in the country and came to Snyder, where, in 1904, he established himself in the liquor business. With this enterprise he continued to be identified for twelve years, when the Eighteenth Amendment, following the war-time prohibition act, abolished the saloon business, and Mr Schoeneck converted his establishment into a soft drink parlor, which he continues to conduct with much success, having built up a large and representative patronage in this connection At the same time, in partnership with John Seebeck, he opened a garage, but later disposed of his interest in this enterprise, and, with his son, opened another garage, under the business style of Schoeneck & Sons This is now enjoying a profitable trade as a garage, in addition to which the firm acts as sales agents for Nash and Chevrolet automobiles and carries a full and up-to-date line of standard accessories A general repair department is maintained, with skilled mechanics in attendance, the establishment furnishing an excellent service station for the convenience of local or out-of-town motorists.

In 1893 Mr Schoeneck was united in marriage with Miss Sophia Siems, who was born in Germany, and brought to the United States in childhood by her parents, who became farming people in Nebraska To this union there have been born four children: Hilbert and Arlan, who are associated with their father in the conduct of the garage at Snyder; and Norma and Eldon, who are attending school Hilbert Schoeneck joined the United States Air Service during the great World war, as a mechanic, and was in training in Texas at the time of the signing of the armistice The family's religious connection is with the Lutheran Church, the movements of which they have supported liberally. Mr Schoeneck is a broad-minded and progressive man, well-posted on current events, and entertaining sensible opinions on questions of public opinion In political affairs he maintains an independent stand

CHARLES ARNOT Two interests, those of education and finance, have entered the career of Charles Arnot, who since 1915 has been directing the affairs of the First National Bank of Scribner. His experience as an educator in Nebraska began many years ago, and he still maintains a helpful and constructive interest in school work that has done much to advance the cause of education in Dodge County

Mr Arnot was born at Greenville, Virginia, and received his education in public and private schools in his native state He was still a young man when he migrated to Nebraska in 1887, and during the next several years taught rural schools in Johnson and Richardson counties, subsequently becoming an instructor in Howell's public school. In 1896 he came to Scribner as superintendent of the school here, a position which he retained until 1901, when he resigned to take up his duties as superintendent of schools of Dodge County, to which he had been elected He served in that capacity for two terms, to the great satisfaction of the people, and in 1906 turned his attention, at least partly, to financial matters, being the organizer in that year of the Logan Valley Bank of Uehling He was president of that institution for five years, and in the meantime, in 1907, accepted the superintendency of the schools of Schuyler City, acting in that capacity until 1915 Mr Arnot then became acting manager of the First National Bank of Scribner, a position which he has since retained He is widely and favorably known in both financial and educational circles, and is a valued and popular member of the Nebraska Schoolmasters' Club He is also affiliated with the Masons, the Knights of Pythias, the Modern Woodmen of America and the Woodmen of the World Politically he is a democrat

In 1910 Mr Arnot was married at Schuyler to Miss Mabel E Johnson, a daughter of Gus and Sarah L Johnson, the former deceased, and to this union there have been born two children Ruth E and Charles P

JOSEPH F REZNICEK A wide-awake, progressive business man of Dodge, well educated and talented, Joseph F Reznicek is a worthy representative of the men of foreign birth who have brought to their adopted country the habits of industry, frugality and honesty that have won them success in various fields of endeavor He was born October 12, 1874, in Bohemia, and there spent his childhood days

His parents, Vaclav and Magdaline Reznicek, immigrated to the United States in 1886, coming directly to Nebraska Purchasing land in Saunders County, they labored unceasingly in their efforts to improve a homestead, and on their farm reared their family of five children, all of whom are now living

An ambitious student, noted for his good scholarship, Joseph F Reznicek was given good educational advantages after coming to this country, having attended the Joseph Medill High School in Chicago, two years, later taking a course in the Chicago Business College, and on his return to Nebraska studying two summers in the Fremont Normal School. Equipped for a professional career, he taught school in Saunders County four years, being quite successful as a teacher Embarking then in mercantile pursuits, Mr Reznicek conducted a general store at Morse Bluff, Saunders County, for twelve years Selling out there in 1914, he established his present store in Dodge, putting in a well-selected stock of general merchandise, and in its management has met with unquestioned success, his trade being far-reaching and remunerative.

Mr Reznicek married February 6, 1899, Anna Pavel, who was born in Butler County, Nebraska, near Abie, and to them nine children have been born, namely · Louis, employed in the First National Bank of Dodge; Joseph, a clerk in his father's store, William, attending school near Chicago, Helen, Rosie, Albin, Lucy, Marie and Tillie A stanch republican in politics, Mr. Reznicek has always taken a prominent part in the administration of public affairs, while living at Morse Bluff having served as village trustee, village clerk, village treasurer and as a school director He is ex-mayor of Dodge and he performed the duties devolving upon him in that capacity with ability and fidelity He is also ex-president of the Dodge Community Club, organized for the purpose of advancing the best and higher interests of the city Religiously he is a Catholic, and socially he is supreme president of the Catholic Workmen and one of the board of directors of Z C K J, a Bohemian Fraternal society

George F Wolz One of the most important developments of nation-wide importance is that which has brought about a recognition of the necessity for good roads, and the consequent building of magnificent highways in every state in the Union Much remains to be done, but the initial stage is past, and there are few who do not acknowledge the value of what has been accomplished and plan for an extension of the movement One of the men who has played a very important part in this progressive work in the State of Nebraska, is George F Wolz of Fremont, now serving as president of the Good Roads Association of the State of Nebraska For many years Mr Wolz has been connected with the business life of Fremont, was its mayor for several terms, and his name is one which carries weight, so that his present connection is one of great value to the people who have the welfare of the state at heart.

George F Wolz was born in the City of Philadelphia, Pennsylvania, on December 30, 1861, a son of George and Christianna (Basler) Wolz, of German descent George Wolz, Sr, died during the war of the '60s from disabilities incurred during his period of service in the Union army, and at that time his son, George F. Wolz, was but three years old The widow was later married to C Balduff, both deceased.

When he was only six years old his mother brought George F. Wolz to Fremont, and here he has spent practically all his life since that time Here he acquired his educational training, as well as that of business life, beginning the latter as a clerk in a store, of which later he became the proprietor, buying the business on time before he had reached his majority He had no one to back him, but the man from whom he bought knew him and his reliability, and was willing to take his notes, and this man, like everyone else with whom Mr Wolz has had any transactions, never had cause to regret his action in trusting to the young man's honesty and unusual ability.

It was in 1882 that Mr Wolz became the owner of his own business, which was a bakery and confectionery establishment, and he remained in one building for a period of thirty-four years, or until 1916, when he sold so as to devote more of his time to affairs of public moment This business was located at 530 Main Street, and was established in 1872

by C. Balduff During the first three years Mr Wolz had a partner, W S Balduff, now of Omaha, Nebraska, but bought the interest of his associate As time went on Mr Wolz gradually expanded his business and did a very large wholesale trade Still later he branched out as a caterer and for years was the only man in this business at Fremont He did an immense business in ice cream, fruits and bakery goods During the life of the Commercial Club, he was among its active members and for the past ten years has been its secretary and later president and now commissioner

Among the first to realize the necessity for improving the roads of Dodge and surrounding counties, Mr Wolz brought to bear upon the matter the same steadiness of purpose and efficiency of method and today has the pleasure of realizing that his efforts have borne such fruit, that the requisite laws have been enacted, principally through his instrumentality, and that the preliminary work has all been carried out At present he is president of the Good Roads Association of Nebraska, his success in local matters having brought him to the attention of the enthusiasts on this subject in the state, and many of his ideas have been adopted by similar organizations in other states For six successive years he was mayor of Fremont, and after a lapse of several years was again elected and served for two years more, so that much of the work of taking the municipality out of the village class and putting it where it belongs, among the thriving cities of the state, was done during his administration All of the work was not done, of course, while he was in the office, but he laid the foundation, made the plans and assisted his successors to bring about the ends all of the good citizens held so dear, and his name will always be associated with constructive work in Fremont He also served one term as senator from Dodge and Washington counties in the 1913 Legislature.

On February 15, 1883, Mr Wolz was united in marriage to Maggie L Pfeiffer, born at Philadelphia, Pennsylvania, and they have two daughters, namely Ida, who was born on April 4, 1885, married Glenn O Pope, train dispatcher at Chadron, Nebraska, and Laura, who was born on January 14, 1891, married Ray V Stock, assistant cashier of the Farmers and Merchants Bank of Fremont.

Mr. Wolz has been very successful in everything he has undertaken, and owns considerable real estate, is a director of the Farmers and Merchants Bank of Fremont, but devotes the greater portion of his time at present to carrying out the plans of his association, traveling all over the state in the interests of the good roads movement

He is well known in fraternal orders, being a member of the Scottish Rite, Mount Tabor Commandery, Tangier Temple, Ancient Arabic Order Nobles of the Mystic Shrine of the Masonic fraternity, past officer of different branches of the Independent Order of Odd Fellows and Knights of Pythias, is a member of the Elks, Lodge No 514, Rotary Club, Travelers' Protective Association and United Commercial Travelers, past commander of Nebraska Division and member L D Richards Camp No. 5, Sons of Veterans, and many other benevolent organizations

From the beginning of his career Mr Wolz has maintained a high standard of helpfulness and integrity. He has always been a hard-working, clear-headed man of affairs, but, while for years he was deeply immersed in intensely practical matters, he always found the time to devote to his civic duties and his ability to solve problems of large moment has brought him conspicuously before the public

ARTHUR BLEYHL, manager of the Farmers Union Milling and Grain Company, at Snyder, is a worthy representative of the younger business element of Dodge and Washington counties. To a very considerable extent it is this element in any community, especially outside of the large cities, which infuses spirit and zest into the activities of the place. It is this element whose entrance upon the arena of active life dates not farther back than a decade of years, which monopolizes much of the vigor, zeal and pushing energy which keep the nerves of the commercial world ramifying through all the lesser towns of the country strung to the full tension of strenuous endeavor. A pronounced type of the type of tireless workers thus described, Mr. Bleyhl has done much to advance the business interests of his company and of the community of his adoption.

Arthur Bleyhl was born on a farm in Dodge County, Nebraska, in 1893, and is a son of Albert and Katherine Bleyhl, natives of Germany. He was reared in an agricultural atmosphere, spending his boyhood in the country and obtaining his elementary education in the public schools of his native county. At first it was his ambition to follow the vocation of an educator, and with this end in view he pursued a teacher's course at the Fremont Normal School. After graduating from that institution, he commenced his work as an instructor, and for one year taught in the rural schools of Boone County, then going to Dodge County, where he instructed the mind of youth for two terms. At the end of this time, Mr. Bleyhl's experience had convinced him that a teaching career would not prove congenial, no matter how successful, and he therefore turned his attention in another direction, deciding to enter business matters. Accordingly, he sought and obtained employment in the hardware establishment of William J. Wolsleger at Snyder as a clerk and bookkeeper, positions which he retained during the year that he remained in Mr. Wolsleger's service. When he resigned these posts it was to accept the position of bookkeeper with the Farmers Union Milling and Grain Company at Snyder in 1917. He displayed energy, foresight, industry and fidelity and in 1918 the officials advanced him to the post of manager, which he has since retained. Mr. Bleyhl is an exceptionally energetic and enterprising young man and thoroughly competent in business transactions. The honesty of his dealings is fully recognized by his fellow-townsmen, and although his advent at Snyder is of comparatively recent date, the general confidence which he has acquired presages a successful future. Under his management the business, in which he is a stockholder, has enjoyed a healthy and consistent growth, its products meeting with a steady demand, and at this time six men are given employment. Mr. Bleyhl has a number of civic, social and business connections, and is a popular member of the local lodge of the Hoo Hoos, the well-known lumbermen's fraternal organization.

HENRY SIEVERS. Among the representative citizens of Scribner, Nebraska, none are better known or held in higher esteem than Henry Sievers, who is vice president of the Scribner State Bank and officially connected with other organizations, in all of which his business sagacity is highly valued and his sterling character recognized as a distinct asset. He has been a resident of the United States since he was fifteen years old, and of the State of Nebraska for more than fifty years.

Henry Sievers was born in Germany, December 16, 1843. His parents were Christian and Christina Sievers, who came with their children to the United States in 1858. Three of the children, David, William and John, are deceased. Of the other three, Henry resides at Scribner; Charles is a farmer in South Dakota; and Christian is a retired resident of Scribner The parents located at Moline, Illinois, where the father followed his trade of brickmaker for several years, moving then on a farm in Rock Island County He spent his last years with his children, surviving to the age of eighty-seven years, the mother passing away at the age of seventy-seven They were faithful members of the Lutheran Church

Henry Sievers had attended school in his native land His first occupation after reaching Illinois was farm work in Rock Island County, and he continued farming in that state until 1869, when he decided to become a resident of Nebraska At the present time a journey from Illinois to Nebraska is but a pleasant and comfortable railway trip of a few hours, but fifty years ago it was a much more serious matter Mr. Sievers was at that time a man of family and property, and it took much preparation before the start for the new home was made The family traveled into Dodge County in a pioneer covered wagon having more or less adventure on the way but finally reaching the land that Mr. Sievers had homesteaded It was entirely unimproved but the wagon sufficed for a home until a sod house could be made comfortable, and this humble dwelling remained the home of the Sievers family for some years

In Illinois, in 1867, Henry Sievers was married to Ida Kleeman, also a native of Germany, and to this marriage the following children were born Henry J, who is a farmer in South Dakota, Charles, who also lives on his farm in South Dakota, Frank, who lives retired at Huron, South Dakota Ferdinand, who conducts a meat market at Scribner; Augusta, who is the wife of George Cartens, a retired farmer in South Dakota, Anna, who is the wife of Henry Dringuis, a retired farmer of Scribner, Emil, who is a farmer in Dodge County; Ida, who is the wife of Dwight Martin, who is in the Government mail service at Scribner, Walter, who lives retired at Scribner Clara, who is the wife of Walter Aders, in the banking business at Dix, Nebraska; and Alexander, Edward and Arthur, all of whom are deceased

Although Mr Sievers and his family did not entirely escape pioneer hardships, they were patient, resourceful and industrious, and the homestead was rapidly developed and through careful cultivation became one of the most valuable farms in Dodge County Mr Sievers continued to farm and raise good stock for many years, resigning his heavy duties to younger hands at length and on retirement moved into Scribner Here he has continued an active business man up to the present As mentioned above, he is vice president of the Scribner State Bank, a solid, prosperous financial institution of Dodge County He is also treasurer of the German Mutual Insurance Company of Dodge County For many years he has belonged to the fraternal organization of Sons of Hermann and takes part enjoyably in its social features In political life he has always been an independent voter, and every public measure designed to permanently benefit Nebraska has his support During his long residence here he has seen so many changes and has known intimately so many people of consequence, that his reminiscences are more than usually interesting

Robert C Byers, M D A member of the medical profession whose position is a highly creditable one and whose reputation is well extended over Dodge County, Doctor Byers has practiced in this section of Nebraska for seventeen years, and most of the time in the Nickerson community

Doctor Byers, who comes of a family of physicians, was born in Ontario, Canada, in 1877, a son of Dr John N and Jeannette (Hadwen) Byers His mother was a native of England His father who was born in Canada in 1842, completed his medical education in Victoria College of Ontario, graduating in 1868, and was engaged in an extensive country practice in his native province until 1900 In that year he moved to Fontanelle, Nebraska and continued the general practice of medicine He was a member of the Episcopal Church and an independent in politics The children of Dr John N Byers were five in number; S J, a physician in Rimbey Alberta Canada, George A, who is also in the family profession, practicing at Snyder, Bernard, a farmer in Alberta, Canada, Eleanor, wife of Dr O C Hopper of Stanton, Nebraska, died April 20, 1920, and Robert C

Robert C Byers was liberally educated and graduated in 1903 from Western University of London, Ontario He then came to the home of his father at Fontanelle and was engaged in practice in that community for four years, since which date he has looked after his professional interests at Nickerson, and gives all his time to the busy demands of his profession

In 1907 he married Miss Laura Sexton, daughter of Dr and Mrs. T C Sexton of Fremont, a well-known family of Dodge County. Dr and Mrs Byers have four children Margaret, born in 1909; Eleanor, born in 1911; Patricia, born in 1917, and Robert C, born in 1919

Doctor Byers is a member of the Elkhorn Valley, Dodge County and State Medical Association He is a Knight Templar Mason a member of the Episcopal Church in which he was reared, while Mrs Byers belongs to the Baptist Church of Fremont

WILSON B REYNOLDS has gained precedence as one of the most successful exponents of the insurance business in his native state, and is one of the progressive men of affairs, of the younger generation, in his native City of Fremont, where he was born January 19, 1888 Here he is president of the corporation entitled Reynolds, Morrison & Rathburn Company, which is incorporated with a capital stock of $50,000, and which, in addition to maintaining the leading local insurance agency at Fremont, controls a large and constantly expanding general insurance business, with sub-agents not only in Nebraska but also in Kansas and South Dakota This company is conceded to be the most important and successful concern of its kind in Nebraska, and conservative yet progressive policies govern all features of its widely extended service in the domain of insurance indemnity Mr Reynolds is also secretary of the Farm Home Realty Company which is developing a splendid enterprise in the buying and selling of western farm lands, with its general headquarters at Fremont

Mr Reynolds is a son of B W and Mary (Davies) Reynolds, the former of whom was born at Fremont, where his parents were numbered among the earliest pioneer settlers, and his wife is a native of Wales He has been a specially successful business man and influential citizen of Fremont for many years, and he is now president of the Farm Home Realty Company, of which his son is secretary and which does an extensive business in the handling of western land, as noted above. He and his wife are numbered among the honored citizens of Fremont, and with them their son, Wilson B, continues to maintain his home

He whose name initiates this review continued his studies in the public schools of Fremont until his graduation in the high school as a member of the class of 1905 From the initiation of his independent career he has been continuously identified with the insurance business. He became secretary of the Colson-Reynolds Company, and later purchased the interest of Mr Colson and effected a reorganization of the business, under the present corporate title of the Reynolds, Morrison & Rathburn Company He has proved vital in his initiative and administrative ability and has furthered policies that have inured greatly to the success of the two important business enterprises with which he is identified He is an active and enthusiastic member of the Fremont Commercial Club, of which he served two years as vice president, and he was made president of the Fremont Advertising Club at the time of its organization. He is a republican in political adherency and is affiliated with Fremont Lodge No 514, Benevolent and Protective Order of Elks

WILLIAM J WOLSLEGER With the coming of Herman Wolsleger to Dodge County during the early '70s an element of strength and purpose was added to the upbuilding forces of a promising and prosperous community That the ideals of work and citizenship cherished by this frontiersman have been transmitted to those succeeding him in the race is not questioned by those familiar with the history of the family Mr Wolsleger purchased a couple of years after it was founded at Snyder the town's first hardware establishment, and this is still being conducted by a member of the family, the son, William J Wolsleger, who has also taken an important part in the various activities which have served to develop the community

William J Wolsleger was born in 1875 in Dodge County, Nebraska, a son of Herman and Clementina Wolsleger, the latter a native of Switzerland Herman Wolsleger was born in Germany and was little more than a lad when he came to the United States, his first home here being in Illinois, where he located in 1860 During the war between the North and South he fought as a Union soldier for one and one-half years, being a member of the Ninth Illinois Cavalry. During the early '70s he made his way overland to Nebraska, where he was shortly afterward married, and here homesteaded eighty acres in Dodge County and a like acreage in Saunders County During the early days he hauled ties for the Union Pacific Railway, but his chief interest was in his farming and stock-raising operations, in which he continued to be engaged after he had opened a hardware store at Snyder He was a good citizen and was recognized as such by his fellow-citizens, who elected him to various offices, including those of member of the Board of County Commissioners and road overseer. His political support was given to the principles and candidates of the democratic party He and his worthy wife were the parents of ten children, as follows. Henrietta, the wife of Gus Becker, a farmer carrying on operations in Dodge County; Katie, who is deceased, William J, of this review; Julius and Emma, who are deceased, Lizzie, the wife of John Meyer, a farmer of Dodge County, Carrie, the wife of Albert Orlley, a South Dakota ranchman, Ida, the wife of James Lynch of Omaha, Edward, who is in the garage business at Snyder, and Arthur, deceased

William J Wolsleger acquired his education in the public schools of the rural districts of Dodge County, and as a youth became acquainted with business methods in his father's hardware store After conducting this establishment for the elder man for about eight years, he bought the business and for a time handled harness and implements in connection with hardware Later, however, he disposed of these lines, and at the present time carries a general and complete line of shelf and heavy hardware and paints, and is doing a thriving business, necessitating the employment of three men. During the twenty years that he has conducted his present establishment, Mr Wolsleger has built up and maintained a splendid reputation for honorable dealing and high business principles

In 1902 Mr Wolsleger was united in marriage with Miss Emma Schneider, daughter of Conrad Schneider, a pioneer business man of Snyder, and to this union there have been born six children Magdalena, who is attending Hardin College, at Mexico, Missouri· Herman, who is deceased; two children who died in infancy, and William and Conrad, with their parents Mr and Mrs Wolsleger are consistent members and generous contributors of the Lutheran Church As a fraternalist, Mr Wolsleger holds membership in the Independent Order of Odd Fellows, the Ancient Order of United Workmen, of which he is financier, and the Modern Woodmen of America, in which he is a member of the venerable council While he is democratic in principle, he is an independent voter At the present time he is serving efficiently as township clerk, and in the past has been justice of the peace two years and a member of the city council of Snyder He is a stanch friend of education and was for five years treasurer of his school district He is an enterprising and capable man, thoroughly posted on current events and in close sympathy with everything which tends to the development and growth of his native county

H P Weitkamp A man of distinctive and forceful individuality, active and progressive, H P Weitkamp occupies a position of note among the leading business men of Winslow, where he is prosperously engaged in mercantile pursuits, owning and conducting the only hardware and furniture store in the place A son of the late Herman Weitkamp, he was born September 15, 1867, in St Louis, Missouri, of German ancestry

Born and bred in Westphalia, Germany, Herman Weitkamp came with his wife, Mary Weitkamp, to the United States in 1867, and spent the ensuing four years in St Louis Coming to Nebraska in 1871, he bought land in Washington County, near Fontanelle, and was there successfully engaged in tilling the soil until his death, December 23, 1917, at the advanced age of seventy-nine years His wife preceded him to the better world, dying in 1906 Four children were born into their household, as follows· H P, Mrs Louis Frank, living on a farm in Washington County, Mrs Frank Krohn, whose husband is also farming in Washington County, and W H, living on the parental homestead, near Fontanelle

Receiving his early education in the rural schools, H P Weitkamp became familiar with the various branches of agriculture when young, and choosing the free and independent occupation of a farmer began life on his own account in 1891 Renting from his father a tract of land not far from Etna, he continued there engaged in agricultural pursuits for sixteen years, meeting with good success in his work Looking for broader fields of action at the end of that period Mr Weitkamp located in Washington County, and having organized the Winslow State Bank was actively assocated with its management four years In 1909, still retaining his connection with that bank, he embarked in the hardware business, which he has managed successfully, gradually enlarging his

Henry Edelmaier

operations, and now is proprietor of the only hardware and furniture establishment in Winslow. In 1919, Mr. Weitkamp, with characteristic enterprise, established the Farmers State Bank of Winslow, of which he is president, and is managing its affairs most ably and satisfactorily

In February, 1891, Mr Weitkamp was united in marriage with Minnie Richter, who was born in Washington County, Nebraska, a daughter of the late Herman Richter, and they have one daughter, Esther, born in 1904. Mr Weitkamp is independent in politics, voting according to the dictates of his conscience, without regard to party affiliations Ever interested in local affairs, and never shirking the responsibilities of office, he has served as township clerk, village clerk, assessor, road overseer, and for twenty-five years was a member of the school board Both he and his wife are active members of the Lutheran Church

HENRY EDELMAIER. In naming the representative men of Scribner, Nebraska, Henry Edelmaier immediately comes to mind as one who has engaged public attention for a number of years because of business enterprise and achievement Mr Edelmaier is vice president of the Farmers State Bank at Scribner and in other ways also is a foremost citizen.

Henry Edelmaier was born April 6, 1870, in Belmont, Ohio, and is a son of David Edelmaier, extended mention of whom will be found in this work His education was obtained in the public schools, supplemented by a commercial course in the Gem City Business College at Quincy, Illinois He came to Washington County, Nebraska in 1887 and worked on farms by the month two years and in a brick yard and earned money to pay for his commercial course—1890-91

In 1893 Mr Edelmaier came to Scribner as office man in the Marquardt & Groetche elevator, and continued in that capacity with that firm for four years, after that going to Hadar, Nebraska, as manager for the Nye, Snyder, Fowler Company, operating a grain elevator and in the lumber business He later was stationed at Leigh, Nebraska, for the same firm and continued for some years From there he went to Hooper, Nebraska, as manager of the Farmers Grain and Stock Company, from Hooper coming to Scribner, where he operated a brick yard for one year In 1909 he entered the First National Bank of this city as assistant cashier, in which position he continued until inducements were offered that led to his going back to Hooper to take charge of the Farmers Elevator Company, where he remained for the following four years

In 1918 Mr Edelmaier returned to Scribner, when he was elected vice president of the Farmers State Bank, and he has been identified with all that pertains to the welfare of this prosperous little city ever since The Farmers State Bank of Scribner, Nebraska, commenced business February 4, 1918, and the report of its condition at the close of business November 15, 1919, shows that the institution has made safe and steady growth, with profits beyond expectation and with equally prosperous prospects for the future The officers of the Farmers State Bank are as follows: Arthur H Shultz, president, Henry Edelmaier, vice president, and Herman F Meyer, cashier All are men of independent fortune and of the highest possible personal character

In 1894 Mr Edelmaier was united in marriage to Miss Ida S Stoetzel, who was born in Nebraska and is a daughter of John Stoetzel, who came early from Germany and was a pioneer farmer in this section of Nebraska Mr and Mrs Edelmaier have three children, one son and two daughters, namely: Raymond, who is a business man at Hooper, Nebraska; Gladys, who is the wife of John H Bader, who is a successful farmer well known in Dodge County, and Helen, who resides with her parents All the children have been well educated and given many advantages Mr Edelmaier is a Scottish Rite Mason In politics he has always been an outspoken republican although never willing to accept any political office He is looked upon as one of the sound, reliable business men of Dodge County

GEORGE F BASLER The life of George F Basler, a well-known and public-spirited citizen of Fremont, has been such as to elicit just praise from those who know him best, owing to the fact that he has always been true to the trusts reposed in him and has been upright in his dealings with his fellow men, at the same time lending his support to the advancement of any cause looking to the welfare of the community at large Mr Basler was born in Philadelphia, Pennsylvania, in 1859, and is the son of Jacob Basler The latter was a native of Germany who came to the United States in young manhood and located in Philadelphia He has learned the trade of a stone mason, and also that of a shoe fitter, and to the latter vocation he turned his attention during the Civil war period With keen foresight he had purchased a large stock of leather and, owing to the big advance in the value of that material, he was enabled to make considerable money This he invested in Philadelphia real estate, which also enhanced in value to his financial advantage. In 1868 he moved with his family to Nebraska and bought a large farm near Nickerson, Dodge County, on which he lived for ten or fifteen years He then moved to Fremont and bought property, through which he still further profited, so that he was considered a man of substantial means To him and his wife were born five children, of which number George F is the only survivor

George F Basler received his educational training in the public schools of Fremont and then he engaged in the grocery business, in which he continued for twenty-two years He also served as constable for a number of years and was appointed city clerk of Fremont, serving a short time For a number of years he has been employed in the plant of the Rogers Tent and Awning Company, owned by his nephew, Henry W Rogers, who is represented elsewhere in this work Mr Basler's career has been characterized by persistent industry and faithfulness to duty and he enjoys the confidence of those with whom he is associated

In 1900 Mr. Basler was married to Mayme Milland He is a democrat in politics and takes an intelligent interest in the public affairs of his community. Fraternally, he is a member of the Ancient Free and Accepted Masons, the Independent Order of Odd Fellows and the Royal Neighbors of America and, with his wife, belongs to the Order of the Eastern Star, the Daughters of Rebekah and the Pythian Sisters Though a man of unpretentious demeanor, he possesses those qualities which win friends, and he is deservedly popular among those with whom he associates and enjoys the respect of the entire community

GEORGE N PARKERT The Parkert name has been one of honored consideration in Dodge County for a long period of years, and while some of the records of the family are given attention on other pages, the following is devoted primarily to the career of George N Parkert, who has achieved a distinctive success as a stock farmer and whose well equipped farm and attractive home are in section 13 of Everett Township

Mr Parkert, who both on the farm and in association with progressive organizations illustrates the modern type of American farmer, was born in Dodge County March 15, 1884, a son of Peter Parkert, Sr As a boy he attended the public schools of Hooper and acquired part of his education at Fremont At the age of twenty-four in 1908 he began farming for himself, and in twelve years has done a great deal to demonstrate his abilities For several years he specialized in Shorthorn cattle, but more recently has made his farm notable for its Poland China hogs He conducts annual sales, frequented by numerous stockmen looking for high-class hogs He also feeds for the market

Mr Parkert is a stockholder in the First National Bank of Hooper, a stockholder in the Farmers' Co-operative association, in the Dodge County Agricultural Association of Hooper, and Hooper Milling Company

In 1910 he married Miss Josephine Bradbury, a daughter of James Bradbury of Hooper The Bradburys are one of the old and solid names in the citizenship of Dodge County Mr and Mrs Parkert have one daughter, Mary Georgean Mrs Parkert is a member of the Grace Lutheran Church at Hooper, while Mr Parkert is affiliated with the Catholics of that community He is a member of the Knights of Columbus at Fremont, the Modern Woodmen of America and in politics is a democrat

JOSEPH SNYDER, one of the historic pioneers of Dodge County, has lived here for over half a century, and has been a contributor as well as a witness of the progress of development.

Mr Snyder, who is now enjoying the comforts won by early years of self denial and industry with home at Fremont, was born in Germany December 28, 1842 He was eight years of age when in 1850 he came to the United States, and lived in Illinois for the next ten years In 1860 he went to Wisconsin, and in the meantime had served an apprenticeship at the shoemaker's trade In 1861 he enlisted as a Union soldier in the Ninth Wisconsin Infantry and was in a number of battles and campaigns until he received his honorable discharge in the fall of 1864 Having performed his duty as a good soldier he resumed his trade, lived in Iowa one year, and in the spring of 1866 came to Fremont, Nebraska That was before any railroads were built and he had some difficulty in getting his tools and equipment out to this frontier locality In the absence of tools he had to work at anything that offered As the pioneer shoemaker he was in business at Fremont for five years, and among the customers of that period he recalls that he made a pair of boots for Mr L D Richards, when that pioneer business man and citizen first came to Dodge County. On leaving the cobbler's bench Mr Snyder went out to his homestead three miles east of Fremont, and during many successive years gave his undivided time and attention to the improvement and cultivation of his land He went through all the years of adversity that afflicted Nebraska farmers, involving loss from grasshoppers and high water, and many times he worked in the fields husking corn, furnishing his own team and wagon at wages of 60 cents a day He proved up his homestead of eighty acres and subsequently bought other land at $2 50 and $7 00 an acre until at one time he owned a complete farm of 320 acres Some years ago he sold his land and has since lived retired in Fremont

In 1868 at Fremont Mr Snyder married Miss Mary Nuel She was born in Bavaria, Germany, and was brought to the United States when young They were companions on life's highway for forty years until the death of Mrs Snyder in 1910 Nine children blessed their home Josephine of Fremont, Louis, a farmer of Dodge County; Alice, who lives in Montana, Sylvester of South Dakota, Carrie, who died in 1918; Viola, who lives in Alaska, Eva of Dodge County, Albert, a resident of Montana; and Mollie of Omaha.

Mr Snyder is an honored member of the Grand Army Post of Fremont While living in the country he served as a director of his home school board, was a member of the Township Board, and also justice of the peace of his precinct. For a man who has lived actively nearly fourscore years he is exceedingly well preserved

Louis Snyder is a native of Dodge County, and during his mature career of nearly thirty years has been a member of the farming community of Elkhorn Township He owns a well improved farm in section 16, and while he has worked out his material prosperity on the land, he has not been unmindful of those responsibilities which come to every good citizen and has readily co-operated with community enterprises

He was born at Fremont September 30, 1873 His father, Joseph Snyder, was a native of Germany but was brought to the United States at the age of eight years He grew up at Galena, Illinois, where General Grant was then an obscure merchant He learned the cobbler's trade and from Galena entered the ranks of the Union army After the war he came to Nebraska and homesteaded in Dodge County

Louis Snyder grew up on his father's farm, acquired a common school education and at the age of twenty-one began making his own way in the world He worked as a farm hand and for five years operated a hay baler, and by thrift and industry accumulated the modest capital for the purchase of land, and for a number of years has owned a farm of 160 acres, well improved, adapted for all the crops of this section, and he feeds all the land produces to stock on the place His specialty in stock is blooded red hogs Mr. Snyder is an independent voter, and for one year filled the office of road overseer in his district

February 8, 1905, he married Melia Loges at Arlington, Nebraska They, have a family of six children, all still at home, most of them attending school, named Joseph, Ted Nie, Margaret, Esther and Jessie

Peter Loges, father of Mrs Snyder, was born in Germany and came to the United States as a youth. He served as a Union soldier, thus proving his sterling American citizenship Except for his army experience he was a farmer all his life He married Marie Tews in Omaha She is now deceased, and of their seven children Mrs Snyder is the fourth All are still living except one son

John W Stevenson is sole owner and active manager of the North Bend Nursery, and his initiative and administrative ability has been significantly demonstrated in the development of this now important and far-reaching business enterprise, which has contributed much to the prestige of Dodge County and the vital little City of North Bend, where Mr Stevenson maintains his home and business headquarters He was a boy at the time of the family removal to Iowa, where he grew to manhood and became deeply imbued with the progressive western spirit

Mr. Stevenson claims the old Buckeye State as the state of his nativity, his birth having occurred in Muskingum County, Ohio, on February 14, 1843 He is a son of James and Eliza (Wallace) Stevenson, the former of whom was born in Ireland, of Scotch ancestry, and

Harlow. Carpenter Ellen. G Carpenter

the latter was born and reared in Ohio, where their marriage was solemnized. James Stevenson was a young man when he came to the United States and established his residence in Ohio, where he acquired land and turned his attention to farm enterprise In 1857 he removed with his family to Iowa and became a pioneer settler in Delaware County He developed one of the excellent farms of that county and there continued to maintain his home until his death in 1879, at the age of seventy-two years, his wife having passed away in 1876, at the age of seventy years, John W. of this review being the only survivor of their ten children James Stevenson was an ardent abolitionist in the climacteric period leading up to the Civil war and his home in Ohio had been a station on the historic "underground railroad" by means of which many slaves were assisted to freedom He was independent in politics and both he and his wife were earnest members of the Reformed Presbyterian Church

John W Stevenson gained his rudimentary education in his native state and was a lad of twelve years at the time of the family removal to Iowa, where he attended the pioneer schools and also assisted in the reclamation and general work of the farm home When about 23 years of age he went to Nashville, Tennessee, where during 1866-7 he was employed in the wholesale millinery establishment of Beard Brothers He then returned to Delaware County, Iowa, where for the ensuing three years he was engaged in the grain and lumber business For several years thereafter he was associated with a general merchandise business at Hopkinton, that state, and in 1879 he came to Dodge County, Nebraska, where he purchased a tract of land and instituted its improvement In 1882 he founded the North Bend Nursery, and in this connection he has developed a large and far-extended business, which is conducted exclusively through the medium of mail orders and which is of general order, though Mr Stevenson gives special and primary attention to the propagation and sale of fine strawberry plants His nursery utilizes twenty acres of ground, in the immediate vicinity of North Bend, and is conducted according to scientific methods, as well as with the most approved of modern facilities

As may well be expected of a man of such progressive business policies, Mr Stevenson is loyal and public-spirited in his civic attitude He has been a stanch advocate and supporter of the prohibition movement but is independent in politics, rather than being dominated by strict partisanship Both he and his wife are zealous members of the United Presbyterian Church of North Bend, in which he is serving as an elder and also as secretary of the Sunday school He has given effective service as a member of the city council of North Bend and has otherwise done all in his power to further the civic and material advancement and the prosperity of his home community

In 1882 was solemnized the marriage of Mr. Stevenson to Miss Elizabeth Marshall, at Hopkinton, Iowa, Mrs Stevenson having been born in the State of Pennsylvania They became the parents of three children: the first child, a daughter, died in infancy, Elsie P is the wife of Floyd S Haverfield and they reside with her parents, their one child being a daughter, Elaine, and Edna May died at the age of five years

Harlow J Carpenter was one of the very first men to become acquainted with the section of Dodge and Washington counties and afterwards make his permanent home here He was not only an early settler but a man of distinction in business and civic affairs after Dodge and Washington counties had become well settled

He was born in New York State in 1830 He acquired only a fair knowledge of the fundamentals of learning, and was educated largely by contact with the world He was a worker, always ready to accept duties away from the comforts of civilization For two years of his youth he worked on railroad construction in Canada

It was in 1855 when the great Kansas-Nebraska question was the principal object of controversy in the halls of Congress that Harlow Carpenter came to Nebraska Territory and pre-empted some land near Fontanelle. He made the journey up the river by boat as far as Omaha This country was then far out on the frontier and he found it difficult to make a living entirely from the land To supplement his efforts as a farmer Harlow Carpenter engaged in freighting, making several trips to Fort Kearney and also going as far as Denver Those who followed him to this new country recognized his qualities of manhood and his reliability, and at their hands he was honored with the office of county clerk when Fremont was the county seat of Washington County In addition to farming he was associated with Julius Brainard as a hardware merchant at Fremont for about two years Besides the county office just named he served several terms as county commissioner and for many years was a justice of the peace He voted as a republican and was an active member of the Grange Harlow Carpenter was seventy-three years of age when he died in 1903 and his character is still safe in the memory of most of the older citizens of the two counties Harlow Carpenter married Helen Griffin, a native of Illinois They were married in Fontanelle, Nebraska, and she died in 1914 at the age of seventy-seven. She was a very earnest member of the Baptist Church

Nine children were born to Harlow Carpenter and wife Florence and Charles F , both deceased Lucelia, wife of James Daffer, a farmer in Red Willow County, Nebraska, Emma, deceased, Eva, wife of Ned Carpenter, a clothing merchant at Denver, Elmer, connected with a flour milling company at Omaha; Ernest H , a well-known farmer citizen at Fontanelle, Jessie, deceased, and Winifred deceased wife of Henry Brand of Fontanelle

ERNEST H CARPENTER represents a thoroughly progressive element in the agricultural district around Fontanelle He knows the country by lifelong experience, is a practical farmer, an expert in the stock industry, particularly as a grower and breeder of Duroc swine, and a very live and capable business man and citizen

He was born at Fontanelle August 28, 1871 and is a son of the late Harlow J Carpenter, whose career as one of the earliest pioneers of Washington County is recited on the preceding page Ernest H Carpenter acquired a common school education in Washington County and for three years taught in a country district Leaving the schoolroom he became associated with I E Cahoon in the creamery industry, and he was a factor in the creamery business for fifteen years, having charge of cream routes Since then he has devoted his time and energies to his individual farming interests Since 1908 he has specialized in the breeding of Duroc Jersey hogs, and for several years past has held annual sales that have attracted buyers from all over this section of the Missouri River Valley Mr Carpenter is a member of the Duroc Jersey Association and of the Washington County Breeders' Association. He is a Blue Lodge Mason and a member of the Modern Woodmen of America and the Royal Neighbors, and in politics follows the fortunes of the republican party.

Mr Carpenter has an interesting family and three of his sons were with the colors during the World war In 1894 he married Lena Meier, who was born in Washington County. Her father, Henry Meier, came from Germany and pioneered in Washington County as early as 1868, taking up a homestead and spending the rest of his years as a farmer To Mr and Mrs Carpenter were born five children Ray W, who is now connected with the State Agricultural Extension Department at Lincoln, was in the naval aviation branch of the military, being trained in the Great Lakes Naval Training Station and at Seattle, and was discharged at Seattle fourteen months after he enlisted Ivan H, a farmer in Dodge County, was a supply sergeant in the ammunition train of the heavy artillery corps and was trained at Camp Taylor, Kentucky, and Camp Kearney, California, being eight months in service and being discharged at Camp Kearney Gilbert, the third son, now at home, spent four months in the Students' Army Training Corps at the Peru Normal The two younger children are Howard and Helena, both high school students at Fremont.

IRA E CAHOON A resident of Washington County forty years, Ira E Cahoon has made the best interests of the community his own, and has made his initiative and business enterprise count for development of these counties. For a quarter of a century most of his time and energies have been devoted to the prosperous creamery plant at Fontanelle, an industry which he founded and which he has promoted

Mr. Cahoon was born in Massachusetts January 4, 1858, a son of Ezarias and Fannie (Holland) Cahoon. His parents called Massachusetts their home all their days, though his father was a seafarer and was captain of an ocean-going vessel until he retired at the age of fifty

Ira E Cahoon acquired his education in the common schools of his native state, and learned the trade of bricklayer there It was as a mason that he was first known in Nebraska, settling at Arlington in March, 1880. Altogether he followed the mason's trade for twenty-two years

In 1895 Mr. Cahoon built the plant known as the Fontanelle Creamery, and has made that one of the leading establishments of its kind in eastern Nebraska The plant has a capacity of 5,000 pounds of butter per day Besides the creamery industry he is also a buyer and shipper of eggs Mr Cahoon owns the controlling interest in the Fontanelle Mercantile Company, is a stockholder in the Beatrice Creamery Company of Deadwood, South Dakota, a stockholder in the Baker-White Pine Lumber Company of Oregon, and in the Goose Lake Elevator Company in Canada. He owns a 400-acre farm in Holt County, near O'Neill, and an orange grove in Florida All these property interests bespeak the energy with which he has prosecuted his affairs since coming to Nebraska, a comparatively poor man

In 1883 he married Manda A Jones, a native of Illinois. Her father, W. R. Hamilton, was one of the early settlers of Washington County Mr and Mrs Cahoon are the parents of seven children Robert, a merchant at Hooper, Rossie, wife of Edward Uehling of Hooper; Percy, who is in the motorcycle business in California, Irving, proprietor of a confectionery store at West Point, Nebraska, Parke, interested in the creamery at Fontanelle, George Dewey, a student in Coe College at Cedar Rapids, Iowa; Lourene, at home The family attend the Union Church Mr Cahoon is a member of the Masonic Lodge, the Royal Highlanders, the Modern Woodmen of America and politically has always cast his vote in the interests of the republican party.

GOTTLIEB HARTUNG Representing one of those substantial families that comprised an important colony of Washington County settlers who came from Quincy, Illinois, Gottlieb Hartung has lived most of his life in Washington County and a large farm with splendid improvements demonstrate the success he has achieved here His home is in section 21, a mile south of the Town of Fontanelle

Mr Hartung was born at Quincy, Illinois, February 21, 1869, son of Fred and Sophia (Kruger) Hartung His parents were natives of Germany. His father, a carpenter by trade, went to Quincy, Illinois, in early life and both farmed and followed his trade for several years Subsequently he came west by prairie schooner and located among old friends and neighbors in the Fontanelle colony, where he bought land and continued farming and stock raising He also built many of the homes of the earlier settlers He had a long and useful life and died honored and respected at the age of sixty-nine in 1903 His widowed mother is still living, aged eighty-five Both were active members of St. Paul's Lutheran Church and his father was a democrat To their marriage were born eight children: August, William and Julius, all farmers in Washington County; Mary, wife of Henry Pluggy, a farmer in Washington County, Lizzie, deceased, Catherine, wife of Fred Huewman, living on a Washington County farm; Emma, wife of Fred Brackett, a farmer in Washington County and Gottlieb

Gottlieb Hartung attended his first school in Washington County and completed his education before he settled down to the serious responsibilities of life He assisted his father on the farm for a number of years, and at the age of thirty-one established a home of his own His has been a record of straightforward progress and today he owns 355 acres, with fine improvements, and operated as a stock farm Mr Hartung is also a member of the progressive organizations in his section, being a stockholder of the Farmers' Union and the Fontanelle Mercantile Company

In 1898 he married Miss Emma Jacobs, a native of Washington County and a daughter of Henry Jacobs To their union were born ten children Agnes, Obert, Mata, Freda, Violet, Verna, Ervin and Merle, all at home, while the youngest were twin daughters, Lorraine and Lorretta, the latter being deceased The family are members of St Paul's Lutheran Church Mr Hartung casts his vote according to the dictates of his independent judgment The father of a large family, he is naturally interested in their education, and for fifteen years has served as a member of the School Board in District No 5

GEORGE FRANKE, who was brought to Washington County when a child more than forty years ago, has securely established himself in a community of prosperous farmers and farm owners around Fontanelle He owns a valuable farm a mile east of the town in section 10, and while absorbed in the duties of his farm he has found time to participate and help influence for the good various community projects.

The Frankes, like so many of the substantial families of Fontanelle, came from Quincy, Illinois George Franke was born at Quincy in 1873, son of William and Anna (Stiegel) Franke. His parents were natives of Germany and the father was a cooper by trade and was employed in that line in a factory at Quincy, Illinois, until he came out to Washington

County in 1879 In Nebraska he applied himself successfully to general farming and stock raising and died in 1890 at the age of fifty, his widow surviving him until 1915, being eighty-four at the time of her death Of eight children six are still living· Adam, a farmer in Washington County; Louis, a Washington County farmer, Anna, widow of Henry Neiderhofer who lives near Arlington; Lizzie, wife of August Hartung, Martha, wife of Reinhart Sick of Hooper, Nebraska and George The father of these children was at one time a trustee of the Lutheran Church at Fontanelle. In politics he was independent

George Franke acquired his education in the schools of Fontanelle and after the age of twenty-five became a farmer on his own account He has always combined cattle feeding with the raising of crops, and for several years has specialized in Shorthorn cattle Like his father he is an independent voter and he and his family are members of the Lutheran Church at Fontanelle.

In 1897 Mr Franke married Wilmena Kampf, who was born in Germany, a daughter of William Kampf Their home life has been blessed with four children, all at home, named Wilmena, George, Chester and Helen.

William O Anderson, whose home is in section 22 of Hooper Township, has always looked upon Nebraska as a state of opportunities However, the opportunities were not the kind that a man would seek desiring an easy life and income He has realized his rewards at the expense of a great deal of labor many sacrifices, and a persistent going ahead and doing the duties that came nearest to him, no matter how circumstances might frown and forbid

Mr Anderson was born on an Illinois farm in 1875 and a year later his father, David Anderson, took his family to Iowa W O Anderson grew up in a home of simple comforts, acquired a common school education, and at the age of nineteen, with a sister and a brother aged seventeen, came to Nebraska His first location was in Colfax County and having no money with which to buy land he made out as a renter for thirteen years, gradually accumulating some capital He remained near North Bend as a renter until 1907 when he bought a farm in Boone County, Nebraska, where he remained four years, when he sold and moved to North Bend for five years, then in 1916 he came to his present place near Winslow and purchased 615 acres. On this land his enterprise has greatly expanded, and he is one of the leading farmers and stock men of the locality In livestock he specializes in the raising of sheep

Mr Anderson is a stanch republican in politics, and fraternally is affiliated with the Masons and Modern Woodmen of America He and his family are Methodists

Mr. Anderson married in June, 1897, Miss Anna Banghart They have four children, capable young people who have grown up to appreciate the value of education as well as industry These children are Frank D, Edward L, Harvey D and Mabel L Frank D enlisted August 13, 1918, when nineteen years old at Fort Logan in the engineers, Camp Humphrey, Virginia, was made bayonet instructor and was on board train to go overseas when the armistice was signed He obtained a release and came home Discharged December 13, 1918

Mrs Anderson is a daughter of Vangilder Banghart, a pioneer of Dodge County, who in 1868 homesteaded eighty acres in Ridgeley Township His first home was a dugout, but gradually he gave his family all the substantial comforts of life and made a farm that is still rated as one of the best in that section of the country. He was one of the early fruit growers, setting out a large orchard, and placed many shade trees around his home When he first came to the county his nearest market was the little Village of Fremont, containing only a few buildings

Vangilder Banghart was born in Ohio in December, 1835, son of Henry and Mary A Banghart, natives of New Jersey Their four children were Vangilder, Isaac, Mary J and Henry Vangilder Banghart lived in the Buckeye State until he was thirty years of age, and when he reached Nebraska he was $5 00 in debt, having borrowed that sum at Omaha At that time he was a veteran of the Civil war, having enlisted in 1861 in Company I of the Twelfth Ohio Infantry He was in a company commanded by Captain Cable, and during his first three months' enlistment served in the West Virginia campaign After being discharged he again enlisted in Company G of the Second Ohio Infantry and served with the Fourteenth Army Corps in the army of the Cumberland Altogether he gave three years and five months to the cause of winning the Union Among other battles he was at Iron Mountain, West Liberty, Perryville, Stone River, Chickamauga and Missionary Ridge, and went through the heat of the conflict without a wound. He was mustered out at Columbus, Ohio, and in March, 1865, he married Catharine A Roat, daughter of Jacob and Nancy Roat, the former a native of Pennsylvania and the latter of New Jersey Mr and Mrs Banghart became the parents of ten children · Thomas, Ida, William T, Lillie, Mrs Anna Anderson, Jesse and Frank, both deceased, John L, Nellie and Roy G The Bangharts are members of the Methodist Church.

GEORGE G HINDMARSH was one of the capable, honest, public-spirited citizens who gave the greater part of his life to the development of a Dodge County farm, making a home, providing for those dependent upon him, and associating himself with every worthy cause in his community

He was born in Illinois and died in Dodge County January 21, 1915, at the age of fifty-three, having come to Nebraska as a youth On January 1, 1888, he married Miss Emma Pollock, then sixteen years of age She was born in Douglas County, Nebraska, daughter of Joseph and Elizabeth Pollock Her father, a native of Scotland, came to the United States at the age of eighteen, lived for a time in Illinois, from which state he went into the Union army during the Civil war, and after the war went west to California, but eventually settled in Douglas County, Nebraska, where he homesteaded and where he spent the rest of his life improving a farm Of the eight children of Joseph Pollock and wife Mrs Hindmarsh is the oldest The others were Irvin, Bert, Olive, Nellie of Minneapolis, Leander, deceased, Allen of Minneapolis, while the youngest died in childhood

George Hindmarsh was a practical young farmer when he married and during the rest of his life he looked after his landed interests, farmed on a rather extensive scale, and converted a tract of prairie into a farm improved with good buildings and now an attractive feature of the landscape A republican voter, he was always progressive in matters of citizenship and for the last four years of his life held the office of township assessor.

After her husband's death Mrs Hindmarsh made her home in Arlington, but finally moved back to the farm to assist her son in operating the 160 acres. The family enjoy the comforts of one of the good rural homes of Dodge County Mrs Hindmarsh has shown much capability

Ed. A. Niebaum. Anna S. Niebaum

as a business woman and practical farmer She is the mother of nine children: Pearl, John, Irvin, Wesley, Clarence, Stuart, Marvin, Donald and Genevieve Mrs Hindmarsh has been a member of the Methodist Church since the age of fourteen years

OTTO LANGHORST, SR, has the distinction of having made his home continuously on one tract of land in Washington County forty-three years That farm indicates the quality of enterprise, industry and good management that have always prevailed there. The Langhorst homestead is in section 22 of Fontanelle Township, the home being a mile and a half south and a mile east of Fontanelle Village

Mr. Langhorst was born in Germany October 12, 1843, son of Henry Langhorst, a German farmer who spent all his life in the fatherland Otto Langhorst was reared and educated in his native land and soon after his marriage started for America, reaching Washington County May 4, 1869. To begin life in America he had come practically to the very western frontier After reaching Omaha he traveled to his destination by wagon For a time, having limited capital, he rented land, and then engaged in farming on his own property In 1877 he bought his present place, and through all the years has handled good livestock in connection with his crops

In 1869, in Germany, he married Mary Brunkost Eight children were born to their marriage Anna, at home, Henry, a Washington County farmer; Otto, A, Jr, of Fontanelle; Edward, who lives on a farm in Dodge County, William, Albert and Louis, all at home, and Mary, who died in infancy The mother of these children died September 11, 1912, at the age of sixty-six, forty-three years after her marriage, and after she had seen her sons and daughters grow up to useful manhood and womanhood Mr Langhorst is actively identified with the Lutheran Church at Fontanelle and politically casts his vote with the republican party

EDWARD NIEBAUM, whose farm home is in section 9, a mile northeast of the Town of Fontanelle, grew up in this community and has lived here for more than half a century He has prospered in his farm activities, and has also acquired many interests to identify him with the substantial citizenship of Washington County

Mr Niebaum was born at Quincy, Illinois, March 15, 1865, and was brought to Washington County in 1868 as part of the Quincy colony that began settlement here in pioneer times His parents, Herman and Recia (Monke) Niebaum, were born in Germany, lived on a farm near Quincy, Illinois, for several years and in 1868 established their home in Nebraska among many of their former friends and neighbors from Illinois They made the journey from Quincy by wagon and team Herman Niebaum for many years was an industrious farmer around Fontanelle and died in 1892, while his widow survived him until 1912 at the age of eighty-three. He served a number of years as a trustee of the Lutheran Church at Fontanelle and was a republican in politics

Edward Niebaum was educated in the common schools of Washington County, finished his education in Midland College in Kansas, and for thirty years has been practically identified with farming He owns one of the well-improved places of the township, and from the farm his interest has gone out to other enterprises He is a stockholder in the First Bank of Nickerson, in the Great Western Tire and Body Company of Omaha, the Lyon Bonding Company of Omaha, Blackstone Hotel,

Omaha, in the Baker White Pine Lumber Company of Oregon and in the Farmers' Union at Nickerson In 1891 Mr Niebaum married Miss Anna Sprick, daughter of Henry Sprick, Sr, one of the most prominent of the old Quincy colony at Fontanelle, of whom a complete sketch is found on other pages of this volume They have four children: Leah and Dorothy, both graduates of the Fremont High School, and Clarence and Willis, who are still getting their education in the local schools The family are Lutherans and Mr Niebaum is a republican

William J. McVicker, who is now living practically retired in the thriving little City of North Bend, Dodge County, was a lad of thirteen years when, in 1864, he accompanied his parents on their immigration to Nebraska Territory, the family home being established in Dodge County, where he was reared to manhood under the conditions that marked the pioneer days Few men in Nebraska have had as wide and varied an experience as has Mr McVicker, for, as a skilled millwright and practical mining engineer, he has held important executive positions in South Africa, Australia and Mexico

Mr McVicker was born in New York City on November 24, 1850, and is a son of Robert and Margaret (McKee) McVicker, both natives of Ireland, where the former was born January 3, 1824 Robert McVicker was reared and educated in his native land, whence, in 1850, he came with his young wife to America and established his residence in the City of New York Later he was engaged in farm enterprise in New Jersey, and finally he removed to Ohio, where he followed the same vocation until 1864, when he came with his family to Nebraska and settled in Dodge County, where he reclaimed and improved a pioneer farm and became one of the successful exponents of agricultural and livestock industry in that county. In order to afford his children requisite educational advantages he finally removed from his farm to Peru, Nemaha County, and there he lived virtually retired until his death, at a venerable age, his wife having passed away in April, 1875, at the age of forty-eight years, both having been active members of the United Presbyterian Church and his political allegiance having been given to the republican party. Of the seven children William J is the eldest; Anna is the wife of Alonzo Tate and they reside in the State of Oklahoma, Joseph is a resident of Long Beach, California, James is living retired, at Schuyler, Nebraska, Mary is the wife of William J Gregg, a farmer near Kress, Texas; Margaret is the wife of Edward Lippitt, a talented teacher of music, and they reside at Liberty, Indiana· and Hugh is night editor of the Nebraska State Journal, in the City of Lincoln

William J McVicker gained the major part of his early education in the public schools of Ohio, and supplemented this by attending the pioneer schools of Nebraska He early gained a full quota of experience in connection with the activities of his father's pioneer farm, and his initial enterprise of independent order was made when he engaged in farming in Cuming County He became influential in public affairs in Cuming County and represented that county in the Nebraska Legislature in 1877 In the following year he went to the Black Hills, where, as a millwright, he continued to be actively identified with mining operations for nine years He passed the following year in Dodge County, Nebraska, and in the meanwhile served as deputy sheriff of the county In 1888 Mr McVicker went to Johannesburg, South Africa, under commission to assume charge of mills there operated by an important English mining syndicate. He remained three and one-half years. He then went to

Mexico, to make an examination of mining property, and his next experience was in connection with the equipping and developing of mining properties in Australia Incidental to this service he was enabled to make the trip around the world From Australia Mr McVicker returned to Dodge County, Nebraska, and soon afterward he here recruited and was captain of a company for service in the Spanish-American war. He took his command to Cuba and continued in active service one year He then passed three years in the handling of important construction work, as a construction engineer, on the west coast of Africa, and in this connection he was absent from his home for four years Since his return he has continued his residence in Dodge County and has not responded again to wanderlust save in one instance He represented this county in the State Legislature for two terms His peaceful quietude has been broken by three years' association with mining enterprise in Nevada and his broad experience makes him an authority in the technical details of mining industry Mr McVicker is a man of broad views and well poised intellectual powers, is a stanch democrat in politics, is affiliated with the Modern Woodmen of America and the Ancient Order of United Workmen, and he and his wife hold membership in the United Presbyterian Church, in the faith of which he was reared.

In April, 1872, was solemnized the marriage of Mr. McVicker to Miss Jennie H Miller, daughter of Robert and Jane (Bennett) Miller, who were numbered among the very early settlers in Dodge County, where they established their home in 1856, more than ten years before the admission of Nebraska to statehood, the journey from Illinois was made with wagon and ox team, and the family arrived in Dodge County July 4th of the year mentioned, Mr Miller having here secured land and developed one of the first productive farms of the county, he having passed away in 1911, and his wife having died the preceding year Their names merit enduring place on the roll of the honored pioneers of Nebraska In conclusion is given brief record concerning the children of Mr and Mrs. McVicker. Margaret is the wife of Charles K Watson, who is engaged in the lumber business at North Bend, Ella is the wife of Albert Wood of Lead City, South Dakota; Irma is the wife of James P Gillis of Boise, Idaho, Robert, now residing at Ranger, Texas, was one of the gallant young men who served with the American Expeditionary Force in France during the nation's participation in the World war, and thirteen days after his arrival in France he was taking part in the great Argonne campaign, with which he continued forty-one days, he having held the rank of first sergeant at the time of his discharge, Jessie is the wife of John Emerson, manager of the North Bend flour mills; and Frederick is manager of a lumber yard in the City of Omaha

LEANDER B SMITH, M. D—After many years of earnest, faithful and efficient service in the practice of his exacting profession, Doctor Smith has well earned the retirement which he now enjoys, as the shadows of his life lengthen from the West, where the sunset gates are open wide. The doctor built up an excellent general practice in Dodge County and has maintained his home at Fremont, the county seat, since 1867, the year that marked the admission of Nebraska to the Federal Union of commonwealths Commanding a high place in the confidence and loyal friendship of the people of Dodge County, and honored as one of the sterling pioneers of this section of the state, Doctor Smith is entitled to special recognition in this history of Dodge and Washington counties

Doctor Smith was born in Wyoming County, Pennsylvania, January 27, 1846, and is a son of Isaac O and Sarah (Bunnell) Smith, who passed their entire lives in the old Keystone state, where the father was a prosperous farmer in Wyoming County for many years prior to his death, the old homestead place being still in the possession of the family Isaac O Smith supported the cause of the republican party from the time of its organization until the close of his long and useful life, and both he and his wife were earnest members of the Methodist Episcopal Church Of their five children three are living, Doctor Smith, of this review, being the eldest of this number, Malissa M. has never married and still maintains her home in Wyoming County, Pennsylvania; and Hernando C still resides in that county, where until recent years he continued to have the active management of the old home farm on which he was born

Reared to the sturdy discipline of the farm, Doctor Smith acquired his early education in the schools of his native county, and he continued his residence in Pennsylvania until 1867, when he came to the new state of Nebraska and established his residence at Fremont Here he gave his attention principally to the drug business during the earlier period of his pioneer experience, but finally, in consonance with his ambitious purpose and previously formulated plans, he entered the College of Physicians and Surgeons in the city of Keokuk, Iowa, in which institution he was graduated as a member of the class of 1878 and with the well won degree of Doctor of Medicine. He forthwith established himself in practice at Fremont, and this city continued as the central stage of his long and successful service in his humane profession, to the work of which he gave his close attention until 1915, when he retired However, many of the families to whom he long ministered as physician and friend, have continued to ask for his presence in times of illness—a call which he has never refused to meet unless circumstances made his visitation impossible Doctor Smith is one of the veteran and honored members of the Dodge County Medical Society, and is at the present time one of its oldest members He is affiliated also with the Elkhorn Valley Medical Society, the Nebraska State Medical Society and the American Medical Association He served several years as city physician of Fremont, and two terms as county coroner He was reared in the faith of the republican party and has never deviated therefrom The doctor has been affiliated with the Masonic fraternity for fully half a century, has served as senior warden of the local lodge of Free and Accepted Masons, is a member of Mount Tabor Commandery, Knights Templar, in his home city and has received the thirty-second degree of the Ancient Accepted Scottish Rite, besides being affiliated with the Mystic Shrine and holding membership in the Independent Order of Odd Fellows He has for many years been an earnest member of the Methodist Episcopal Church, of which his wife likewise was a devoted adherent until her death.

The year 1878 recorded the marriage of Doctor Smith to Miss Cora M Albertson, who was born in Colfax County, this state, a daughter of Alexander Albertson, who came to Nebraska Territory in 1856 and became one of the earliest settlers of Colfax County, where he took up land and instituted the development of a farm, his death having there occurred in 1866 Doctor and Mrs Smith became the parents of two sons who survive the loved wife and mother, who passed to the life eternal in December, 1906, and whose memory is revered by all who came within the compass of her gracious influence Victor B, the elder son, resides in the City of Omaha, where he is associated with the Omaha Bee, one of the leading newspapers of the state, Floyd A is in the automobile business in Fremont.

GUY H TEETER is identified with a line of industrial enterprise with which his father has been prominently concerned for many years and he is now secretary of the North Bend Milling Company, which owns and operates a thoroughly modern merchant mill at North Bend, Dodge County, his father being president of the company and John A Emerson, the treasurer, the latter being individually mentioned in the paragraphs that immediately follow this sketch

Guy H Teeter was born at Hampton, Iowa, on the 5th day of April, 1885, and is a son of John and Elizabeth (Watson) Teeter, the former a native of Pennsylvania and the latter of Sheffield, England The father was actively associated with milling operations for more than sixty years, and though he is now living virtually retired at North Bend, he is still president of the North Bend Milling Company He was secretary and treasurer of the company until the death of his honored coadjutor, the late William Emerson, and upon the death of the latter, in 1913, he succeeded to the presidency of the company. It is gratifying to record that the active management of the substantial business is now vested in the sons of the original partners. John Teeter had broad and varied experience in connection with milling operations, he having served an apprenticeship in the old Star & Crescent Mills in the City of Chicago, having worked in the dressing down of the buhr stones in mills operated under the old-time system, at Minneapolis, Minnesota, prior to the adoption of the roller process in that great center of the flour manufacturing industry, and as a skilled workman at his trade he held responsible positions in turn at Waterloo and Cedar Falls, Iowa Later he was for fourteen years manager of the operation of the Wahoo Mills, at Wahoo, Nebraska, and in 1902 he became allied with the late William Emerson in the ownership and operation of the mills at North Bend, under the present corporate title of the North Bend Milling Company These mills have a capacity for the daily output of 250 barrels of flour, steam power is used and the products are of the highest grade, with the result that a substantial and prosperous merchant-milling business is controlled by the company

Guy H. Teeter gained his youthful education principally in the public schools of Nebraska, and after having availed himself of the advantages of the high school at Beatrice, judicial center of Gage County, he attended the University of Nebraska for two years He has been actively associated with the North Bend Milling Company since 1909, and prior to that year had been for four years employed by the firm of Nye, Snyder, Fowler Grain Company, which operates the largest terminal grain elevator in the City of Omaha He has been secretary of the North Bend Milling Company since 1913. He is a member of the directorate of the Nebraska Millers' Association, is a republican in politics, and his Masonic affiliation includes membership in that jocund order, the Mystic Shrine.

JOHN A EMERSON, whose technical and executive powers have proved of marked value in connection with the operations of the North Bend Milling Company, at North Bend, Dodge County, is now serving as treasurer of this representative industrial corporation and is one of the progressive business men of the younger generation in this part of the state

Mr Emerson was born at LaPorte City, Iowa, on the 23d of August, 1881, and is a son of William and Alfretta (Smith) Emerson, the former of whom was born in England and the latter in the State of Pennsylvania At Waterloo, Iowa, as a young man, William Emerson learned the milling trade, and later he traveled somewhat extensively as an expert miller in the service of the Barnard & Leas Manufacturing Company, of Moline, Illinois Finally he became associated with J. H. Patterson in establishing the milling business at North Bend, Nebraska, under the title of the North Bend Milling Company, and he continued as president of this corporation until his death, in 1913 He was a man of marked ability in the practical work of his chosen vocation, as well as in connection with the directing of commercial policies, his having been a secure vantage place as one of the prominent business men and honored and influential citizens of North Bend, where his widow still resides He was a republican in politics and held membership in the Methodist Episcopal Church, as does also his widow Of their children John A, of this review, is the eldest, Howard is employed by the North Bend Milling Company, Harry E. is vice president of the company, Ruth is the wife of George Snyder, a prosperous farmer in Colorado, and Joseph and Paul are stockholders in the North Bend Milling Company

John A Emerson is found aligned as a supporter of the cause of the republican party holds membership in the Presbyterian Church, is affiliated with the Masonic Lodge and is recognized by the milling fraternity as one of the leading hard wheat millers of his state

H O BERGQUIST A prominent and prosperous member of the farming community of Dodge County, H O Bergquist, of Logan Township, is in very truth a native, and to the manner born, his birth having occurred May 22, 1876, on the farm which he now occupies, and which he is managing with such marked ability and success

Oscar A Bergquist, his father, was born and educated in Sweden, and early in life came with his parents, two brothers and two sisters to the United States, and for a short time thereafter lived in Illinois In 1867 the father, who was a farmer by occupation, came with his family to Dodge County, Nebraska, making the long, tedious trip with wagons Taking up a homestead claim in Logan Township, on section 24, he lived for a few seasons in a dugout, as did nearly all of the pioneers at first, and began the improvement of a farm His earnest labors were well rewarded, and on the farm which he redeemed he spent the remainder of his life, passing away at the age of sixty-six years His wife, whose name before marriage was Nellie Nelson, survived him, and is now a resident of Hooper, this county.

Brought up on the parental homestead, where his entire life has been spent, H O Bergquist began as soon as old enough to assist in the manual labor of the home farm, and since assuming its management has met with assured success, his improvements being of an excellent character, while everything about the premises bears evidence of the thrift and good judgment of the proprietor Mr Bergquist is a general farmer and stock raiser, making a specialty of breeding Polled Shorthorn cattle Mr Bergquist has also acquired considerable other property, being a stockholder in the Lion Bonding Company, of Omaha, and in the Logan Valley Bank, of Uehling Mr Bergquist is a Lutheran in religion, and acquired his business education in the Lutheran College after attending the Fremont Normal School

Mr Bergquist married, in 1906, Edith Tunberg, the oldest daughter of Frederick and Matilda Tunberg, Knox County farmers, who reared a family of eleven children Mr and Mrs Bergquist have two children, Harold and Hazel, both attending school.

C J SCHOW has been a resident of Dodge County since he was a boy of five years, has imbibed deeply of the progressiveness for which Nebraska stands forth most distinctly and in his career as a farmer and stock-grower he has achieved the success that marks him as one of the representative exponents of these basic industries in the county He continued to be actively associated with his father in farm operations until the latter's death, and since that time has independently carried forward the activities of the fine farm of 292 acres, which they together accumulated and improved and which is attractively situated in section 25, Maple Township The buildings and other improvements on this farm estate offer little suggestion of conditions that existed when the father here established his home in a rude dugout of the type common to the pioneer days, and the remarkable changes that have occurred, but offer evidence of the splendid rewards which Nebraska pays to those who earnestly and industriously call forth returns from the willing soil of this fine commonwealth

C J Schow was born in Denmark, April 28, 1871, and is a son of John and Catherine Schow, who continued their residence in their native land until 1876, when they immigrated to America and established their home in Dodge County, Nebraska, where they passed the remainder of their lives, the father having died at the age of sixty-nine years and the mother having passed away when sixty-eight years of age. Both were devout communicants of the Lutheran Church. As previously noted C J Schow was a lad of five years when his parents came to Dodge County, and here he was reared on the pioneer farm, his father having at first rented eighty acres of land and then having purchased the property, to which he and his son continued to add until they developed the present fine farm of 292 acres now owned by the latter Hans J Schow, a brother two years older than C J, lived at the parental home until his death at the age of twenty The first team which John J. Schow owned and used in connection with the work of the farm was a yoke of oxen, but these slow-moving animals soon gave place to horses, while today Mr Schow uses the best of modern facilities in the varied operations of his farm C J Schow gained his early education in the schools of Dodge County, and that in later years he has taken loyal interest in the public schools of the county is shown by his having served six years as a member of the school board of his district He is a democrat in his political adherency and he served two years as treasurer of Maple Township, a preferment indicative of the unqualified confidence and esteem in which he is held in his home community Mr Schow has been a member of the board of directors of the Farmers' Union Co-operative Association of Nickerson, Nebraska, since it began business in 1913 and he is now president of the organization He is also president of the Peoples Co-operative Store of Fremont, one of the leading business houses of the city at present doing a mercantile trade of $200,000 annually

At Fremont, this county, in 1895, was solemnized the marriage of Mr Schow to Miss Christine Eidam, who was born and reared in Dodge County, where her father, Casper Eidam, was an early settler Mr and Mrs Schow have three children Lydia is the wife of Harry

Christensen, who is engaged in farming in Dodge County; and Harry and Marie remain at the parental home Both C J Schow and his wife are earnest communicants of the Lutheran Church

OTTO A LANGHORST The Langhorst family became identified with Fontanelle a few years after the establishment of the colony here and the Langhorst farm near Fontanelle is one of the oldest places under continuous ownership in that community Representing the second generation of the family in Washington County, Otto A Langhorst has spent all his life here and for a number of years was a leading merchant at Fontanelle, but has latterly found an interesting and profitable vocation as a grower of fancy poultry

He was born at Fontanelle November 20, 1874, son of Otto and Mary (Brunkhorst) Langhorst His parents were natives of Germany The family established themselves at Fontanelle in 1865, when Otto Langhorst bought the land comprising the old homestead Many years ago he set out a good orchard, and also carried on an extensive enterprise as a farmer and stock raiser He has lived retired since the age of seventy-six His good wife, who was born in 1845, died in 1913 Both were supporting members of the Lutheran Church Special mention made of them on other pages of this volume

Otto A Langhorst attended the common schools of Washington County and took a one-year commercial course in the Midland College. After some years of general farming experience he became a clerk in the mercantile house of Sprick & Burkheimer at Fontanelle, later bought out the firm, and altogether continued in business for fourteen years He finally sold to Block & Flaton, who had previously been associated with him About the time he left the store, Mr Langhorst started the development of his noted flock of rose comb Rhode Island Red chickens, and has been steadily at that business for eleven years, his farm being a highly specialized industry

In 1902 he married Miss Emma Sprick, a member of the prominent Sprick family of the Fontanelle community, her father, Henry Sprick, having been one of the founders of Fontanelle of whom special mention is given on other pages of this volume Mr and Mrs Langhorst have four children. Marion, attending high school at Fremont; Mildred, Margaret and Gerald, all at home The family are active members of the Lutheran Church Mr Langhorst is venerable consul of the Modern Woodmen of America and in politics is a republican

GUY B BAIRD, D D S, was formerly one of the reputable dental surgeons of Dodge County, where he enjoyed a well-earned practice of large proportions He is a carefully trained and skillful operator and one who gives conscientious service to his patients. Doctor Baird was born on a farm in Floyd County, Indiana, in 1873, a son of William H. H and Nancy C (Smith) Baird William H H Baird was born in Kentucky, and his wife was born in Illinois, and they were married in Indiana Two brothers of William H H Baird, Wesley and Thomas Baird, were Confederate soldiers, but he was a Union man, this division in the family being but one of the innumerable instances during that unhappy conflict when brother was opposed to brother, and each one was actuated by the highest of principles

In 1889 William H H Baird brought his family to Nebraska, homesteading in Box Butte County, and remaining on his claim for two years He then moved to a farm near Central City, Nebraska, where

MR. AND MRS. OTTO A. LANGHORST

both he and his wife later passed away, having been successful farmers In religious faith he was a Methodist, and she a Presbyterian. Made a Mason in Illinois in 1884, William H H Baird rose in his lodge and held a number of offices during a long period of years In politics he was a republican The children born to Mr and Mrs Baird were as follows: Mrs J. F. Wallace, a widow of Central City, Nebraska, G B Baird, who was second in order of birth, and Frank, who is a farmer in the vicinity of Central City

Doctor Baird attended the public schools of Horace, Illinois, and Chapman, Nebraska, and then spent four years on a Nebraska farm He matriculated at the Omaha Dental College of Omaha, Nebraska, in 1897, and then in the fall of 1900 entered the dental department of the Northwestern University, at Chicago, Illinois, and was graduated therefrom in 1901 On May 1 of that year he established himself in practice at Fremont, and remained there recognized as one of the leaders of his profession in Dodge County until his removal to Los Angeles

On October 25, 1911, Doctor Baird was united in marriage with Bertha A Rine, born on a farm north of Fremont, a daughter of Philip S Rine, a prominent banker of Fremont They have no children Doctor and Mrs Baird are Christian Scientists

In 1894 Doctor Baird was made a Mason and has risen until he is now a Knight Templar and Shriner Mason He had held all of the offices in the Blue Lodge, and was eminent commander of Fremont Commandery in 1906, and he also belongs to the Benevolent and Protective Order of Elks

For a number of years he has been connected with the various societies of his profession, and has held all of the offices in the Nebraska State Dental Association, including that of president in 1918 and 1919, and he also belongs to the National Dental Association For a number of years he has been a member of the Woodbury Study Club A close student, Doctor Baird has taken up much post graduate work under Dr E D Campbell, of Kansas City, Missouri, and a course under Dr. Rupert E Hall, of Chicago, Illinois, completing the last in 1919. During the late war Doctor Baird did considerable missionary work in dentistry in the various states from New York to California, and he is extremely well known all over Nebraska His specialty is gold fillings and Prosthodontia, although he does a large amount of oral surgery A man interested in civic betterment, he was active in the Commercial Club, while he found congenial social diversion and companionship in the Country Club

At present Doctor Baird is located in Los Angeles, California, specializing in Prosthodontia

P J Ewald. The almost universal use of automobiles by the general public has brought into being a new line of business within recent years, that of providing an efficient service in the way of repair work, the handling of accessories and the selling of standard makes of these cars Hooper, like every other community in the country, has its representatives in this business, and one of them who has been more than ordinarily successful because of his capability and probity, is P. J Ewald, senior member of the firm of Ewald & Schaub

P J. Ewald was born at McCloud, Minnesota, a son of Martin and Anna (Kulbflesh) Ewald, natives of Denmark and Illinois, respectively Mrs Ewald died in 1911 aged sixty-two years, but Mr Ewald is still living, making his home in Minnesota. When he came to the United States in young manhood, he located in Minnesota and there was engaged in general farming and dairying until he retired He and his wife had twelve children, all of whom are living In her religious belief Mrs Ewald was a member of the German Methodist Church. Mr Ewald is a thirty-second degree Mason He never definitely connected himself with any political party, but voted independently

P J Ewald attended the public schools and was graduated from the high school course After leaving school Mr Ewald spent five years with a dredging company, and then for a time engaged in contracting In 1911 he came to Hooper and was employed by Tunberg & Ruty as floorman and repairer of automobiles After a year Mr Ewald bought a half interest in the business, and eighteen months later became the sole proprietor Subsequently Mr Daw bought an interest and remained in the business for over a year, when he sold to Mr Schaub, and the present firm of Ewald & Schaub was organized The firm represent the Ford and Republic cars, carry a complete line of accessories and do a general repairing business, and have a fine and constantly growing trade among people who appreciate good service

In 1913 Mr Ewald was united in marriage with Louisa Schaub A sketch of her family is to be found elsewhere in this work Mr Ewald is a Mason and his wife belongs to the Eastern Star, and she is also a member of Grace Lutheran Church, of Hooper Like his father, Mr Ewald is an independent voter He is a man widely and favorably known and has always taken an intelligent interest in civic matters, although never willing to go into politics as an office seeker

HERMAN H F WATERMAN The manufacturing interests of a section of country are exceedingly important and their healthy growth an indication of public prosperity Directly connected with the growth are the men whose knowledge, judgment, foresight and energy are necessary in the organization and maintenance of these enterprises Capital with no wise directing hand would be useless and the results of unregulated effort would be unsubstantial Especially important are those industries which are in any way connected with building activities for the problems of providing proper housing facilities are increased when the normal output of building material is disturbed. Herman H F Waterman, of Hooper, brick manufacturer, is one of the men of Dodge County who has won his way step by step to his present position in his community, through industry, natural aptitude and persevering effort

Herman H F Waterman was born at Fontanelle, Nebraska, in 1886, a son of Herman and Caroline (Nolte) Waterman, natives of Germany Herman Waterman was a brick maker, beginning his apprenticeship to the trade when only fourteen years old, in Germany He came to the United States with his father, and they located in Washington County, Nebraska, where he established a brick plant and operated it at Fontanelle for five years Moving to Scribner, Nebraska, he bought the plant owned by Mr. Romburg and conducted it for five years, and then he came to Hooper, and in 1893 bought the brick yard at this point, then owned by John Heimrick, who had established it At that time there were four kilns, but the plant has been enlarged so that there are now ten, all of which are in operation, and the capacity of the plant is 50,000 brick per day. Associated with Mr Waterman in this business are his son and John Edelmeier The plant including the land covers

157 acres, and shipments are made to Wyoming, South Dakota, Iowa and different parts of Nebraska.

Herman H. F. Waterman was married in 1909 to Emma Bayer, born in Dodge County, Nebraska, a daughter of Henry Bayer, now a resident of Omaha, Nebraska Mr and Mrs Waterman have one child, namely, Melba, who is attending school. Mr. Waterman is an independent voter Fraternally he belongs to the Ancient Order of United Workmen and the Knights of Pythias Both he and his wife belong to Grace Lutheran Church, of Hooper

Herman H F Waterman is a Dodge County man, and received his educational training in Hooper High School, Fremont Business College and Boyles College of Omaha, where he completed his commercial course The brick yards are conducted as an incorporated concern with Herman Waterman as president, John Edelmeier as general manager, and Herman H. F Waterman as secretary and treasurer

JOHN J. HANSEN To a stranger in Nebraska perhaps the finely cultivated farms and sleek stock might not convey the lesson taught one who was conversant with the history of agricultural development in these western states, or the proof this advancement affords of the fine quality of the character of the citizens who have brought this about While it is now many years since Dodge and Washington counties were included in the class of pioneer communities, yet that day is not so far distant that men still in the very prime of life were participants in the most strenuous period of this constructive development Perhaps because of the vivid contrast afforded between those days and the present ones, these same men are able to appreciate what they and their contemporaries have accomplished, and to look forward into the future and see that the time is not so far distant when a much greater advance will be shown along all lines

One of the constructive agriculturists of Dodge County, whose finely cultivated rural property is the homestead of his family for two generations, is John J Hansen of section 27, Maple Township

John J. Hansen was born on this farm on August 3, 1878, a son of Hans and Ellen Hansen, natives of Sweden, who came to the United States in 1852 For a period after reaching this country Hans Hansen worked at different jobs as he found them, but finally came West to Nebraska and bought forty acres of land, later increasing his holdings until he owned 160 acres at the time of his demise. His widow survives him and makes her home at Fremont

John J Hansen was reared on his present farm and learned under his father's careful supervision to be a practical farmer, and in his agricultural ventures he has been eminently successful. For the past ten years he has been conducting the homestead and doing general farming and stockraising, averaging forty head of cattle of a good grade but no thoroughbred strains.

In 1912 Mr. Hansen was united in marriage with Miss Minnie Harnes, who was born in Dodge County. Mr and Mrs Hansen have three children, namely: Mabel, Victor and Merl In his political sentiments Mr. Hansen is an independent republican, but he has never sought to come before the public for consideration for public honors, his time being too much occupied with his agricultural work For some years he has maintained membership with the Modern Woodmen of America, and finds congenial companionship among his lodge brothers. A man of solid and dependable characteristics, Mr Hansen is an admirable type of citizen and is a credit to his state, and his parents, and is rearing his children along the same lines followed in his upbringing so that they, too, will be worth-while representatives of the great state they claim as their place of birth

MRS MAE GILMORE is one of the honored residents of Fremont and a lady who possesses many of the desirable attributes of her sex She has reared a family of fine children, has been very active in church work, and proven herself a kind neighbor and good friend to those in adversity

Mrs Gilmore was born at Fontanelle, Iowa, a daughter of Hiram and Marie (Dearinger) Miller Hiram Miller was born on a farm near Pella, Marion County, Iowa, and his wife also was born in Iowa They were married in that state and made it their home for some time, before coming to Nebraska For many years Mr Miller was a stockman, buying and selling horses upon quite an extensive scale, and he made a success of his undertakings His death occurred at Omaha, Nebraska, in 1917, but his widow survives him and still makes her home at Omaha. In politics Mr Miller was a democrat Both he and his wife early joined the Christian Church, and she still maintains her membership in it They had the following children Harry, who lives at Omaha, Dollie, who married Peter Hanson, a stationary engineer of Omaha, Mrs Gilmore, who was third in order of birth; Pearl, who is unmarried, lives at Billings, Montana, Maude, who married William Fisher of Scottsbluff, Nebraska, who runs an engine at the sugar factory of that city, and Loren, who is a resident of Omaha

Mrs. Gilmore attended the public schools of Iowa and Omaha, Nebraska, and was brought up carefully by her parents In 1895 she was married to Oliver Gilmore, and they became the parents of seven children, namely. Olive, who married Walter Schrader, a druggist of Elkhorn, Nebraska, Lela, who is unmarried, is a stenographer and lives at home, William, who is a brakeman, also lives at home, Dora, who works at the canning factory at Fremont, and Murel, Norma and Bessie, all of whom are attending school Mrs Gilmore was reared in the faith of the Christian Church, and when she reached a suitable age, joined the church Her children belong to the Baptist Church Her older children are doing well, and the ones in school give promise of being equally successful, all of which is largely due to her careful training of them and her inculcation into their plastic minds of lessons which cannot but result in character building and good citizenship

W HOWARD HEINE, M. D Among the dependable and skilled physicians of Dodge County none stands higher in public confidence and esteem than Dr W Howard Heine, of Hooper He was born at Reading, Pennsylvania, in 1877, a son of Fred F and Lydia (Babb) Heine, both natives of Pennsylvania, who came to Dodge County, Nebraska, in 1883. Fred F Heine established himself in the plumbing business and conducted it at Hooper until he retired, when he moved to Omaha, Nebraska, where he and his wife are now living She is a consistent Lutheran Mr. Heine became a charter member of Hooper Lodge, Ancient Free and Accepted Masons In politics he is a republican

Fred F Heine and his wife became the parents of the following children: Dr W. Howard, who is the eldest, Fred, who is a locomotive engineer at Philadelphia, Pennsylvania, Harry, who is a farmer, operat-

ing near Creston, Nebraska, John, who is deceased, was killed in a gasoline accident, Dr Clinton, who was born in Dodge County, secured his degree in Pharmacy at Creighton University in 1906, his scientific degree at the Nebraska State University, and that of Doctor of Medicine at Rush Medical College, Chicago, Illinois, and served six months interneship at St Joseph Hospital, Chicago, and two years interneship at St Luke's Hospital, Chicago, is now in partnership with his brother, Dr W Howard, at Hooper, and during the World war served one and one-half years overseas with Base Hospital No 53 with the rank of captain; Olivia, who is the wife of Herbert Bush, a cattle and sheep raiser of Sheridan, Wyoming, Lydia, who is a stenographer of Omaha, Nebraska, Edith, who is a teacher in the graded schools of Omaha, Nebraska, and Minerva, who is a stenographer of Omaha, Nebraska

Dr W Howard Heine was graduated from the Hooper High School in 1894, and then for three years served his apprenticeship with E L Geisert, a druggist, passing by examination the State Board of Pharmacy as a registered pharmacist and then for three years was manager of Doctor Zellers' pharmacy He then entered the medical department of the University of Nebraska and was graduated therefrom in 1905, with the degree of Doctor of Medicine For the subsequent eighteen months he served as interne in the Douglas County Hospital Returning to Hooper, Doctor Heine was associated in a general practice with Doctor Zellers for three years, and then in 1910 opened an office for himself. Still later his brother, Dr Clinton Heine, came into partnership with him, and the association is regarded as one of the strongest medical firms in this part of the state They have a general medical and surgical practice Dr. W Howard Heine was in the United States service during the World war and was stationed at Base Hospital No 75, Oglethorpe, Georgia, with the rank of captain, and received his honorable discharge on January 1, 1919, after which he returned to Hooper and resumed his practice.

In 1908 Doctor Heine was united in marriage with Edgard Lyman, born at Hooper, Nebraska, a daughter of the late Thomas Lyman, one of the oldest pioneers of the town Doctor and Mrs Heine have two children, namely: Lyman Howard, who is attending the Hooper public schools, and Mary, who is also attending school Doctor Heine is a Shriner Mason. He belongs to Grace Lutheran Church, and his wife is an Episcopalian In politics he is a strong republican Doctor Heine is a man of personal charm, culture and wide intellectual interests and possesses high ideals with reference to professional obligations, living up to them to the best of his capabilities, and rendering to his community a whole-souled service which is meeting with appreciation to judge from the regard in which he is held by all classes.

CHARLES H PEASE As one of the leading dairymen of Dodge County, Charles H. Pease, now living retired from active business cares in Fremont, was for many years conspicuously identified with one of the more important and useful industries of which our country can boast, more especially while delivering the products of his dairy in Fremont, for on the supply of pure and wholesome milk the life and health of this, and future generations largely depends Coming from honored New England ancestry, he was born, January 31, 1856, in Appleton, Maine

His father, Harrison C Pease, spent the major part of his life in Maine, his native state. He was very prominent in his community, and was successfully engaged in business as a shoe merchant and manufacturer, having a large factory and a well-patronized shoe store He was a straightforward republican in politics, and a member of the Independent Order of Odd Fellows He married Mary E Keene, a native of Maine, and of their six children five are living, as follows: Charles H, with whom this sketch is principally concerned; Mrs S G. McAlmon, of Maine; Edwin R, a bookkeeper in Los Angeles, California; Carrie E, residing in Rahway, New Jersey, and Harry C, of Maine, who was formerly there engaged in mercantile pursuits, but is now a bookkeeper

Having acquired a practical education in the public schools of Appleton, Maine, C H Pease began work at an early age, and for three years was in the employ of the American Express Company, remaining a member of the parental household In 1881, following the tide of emigration westward, he located in Fremont, Nebraska, in December of that year, and very soon after embarked in the dairy business He bought land near Fremont, and rented adjoining tracts, and having purchased a goodly number of cows delivered milk in Fremont for fourteen years Increasing his operations, Mr. Pease sold the milk from his fifty cows to the local creamery, and continued in his extensive and profitable industry until 1915, when he disposed of his dairy interests, and moved to his present home in Fremont He is a republican in politics, but not an office seeker, and is a member of the Royal Highlanders

Mr Pease married, in October, 1884, Edith M Sherman, who was born in Maine, a daughter of Judson A Sherman, a prominent business man, having a shoe factory in both Maine and Massachusetts. Mrs Pease passed to the life beyond February 21, 1915, leaving two children, namely. Mary H, working for the Plumfield Nursery Company, of Fremont, and Hazel A, bookkeeper for Eddy Brothers Both daughters are members of the Congregational Church

George Foster When an ever-busy man, from the feverish turmoil of politics and the harassing cares of business, is retired to a peaceful, quiet and happy life, such an individual naturally excites the friendly envy of his less-fortunate fellowmen Without ostentation or apparent conscious superiority, he mingles in the society of his neighbors, and enjoys with them the affairs of the present and a pleasant retrospect of a life well spent In this connection mention is due George Foster, now living retired in Scribner, who was for a number of years agent for the Chicago & Northwestern Railroad and who filled that office with success and capability.

Mr. Foster was born in England, March 23, 1852, son of George Foster, a tallow chandler, who never left his native land Fred Foster, a brother of George of this review, came to the United States and located at Scribner, where for a time he was identified with railroad work, but subsequently went back to England George Foster was educated in the public schools of England and in 1873 immigrated to the United States For a time he worked on a farm near Cedar Bluffs, and subsequently was employed first by Jack Statts and later by H. B. Nicodemus, on farms, later going to Arlington, where he secured employment on a railroad While in this employment he came to Scribner for the first time, but later moved on to Onawa, Iowa, and, while working around the railroad depots, learned telegraphy Thus he was able to secure an appointment as agent of a railroad at Mondamin, Iowa, and remained there two years In 1889 Mr Foster again came to Scribner, this time as depot agent for the Chicago & Northwestern Railroad, and during the five years that he remained formed numerous friendships that have continued to the present time At the end of the period mentioned, he was transferred by his road to the station at Blair, and there, likewise, he served two years Mr Foster then resigned his post with the railroad and purchased 160 acres of land in Pierce County, Nebraska After he had farmed this property for a short time, he conceived the idea of laying out a town thereon, which was subsequently named Foster in his honor Mr Foster was able to clear quite a handsome sum on this transaction, and while residing at Foster served efficiently in the capacities of postmaster and assessor. When he left Foster it was to go to Lindsay, and there he was appointed station agent and telegrapher, a position which he held one year, being then reappointed agent at Scribner, where he continued to discharge the duties of that position until 1917, at that time retiring to his comfortable home, where he is surrounded by every modern convenience He has a number of important business connections and is a stockholder and director in the Scribner State Bank. Mr. Foster is a Blue Lodge Mason, and in politics is an independent voter.

In 1879 Mr. Foster was united in marriage with Miss Caroline Driggs, a native of Iowa, and to this union there have been born three children: LeRoy, who is superintendent of the Cuban Railway in Cuba, Fred, agent for the Chicago, Milwaukee & St Paul Railroad at Elwell, Iowa; and Byrne, telegraph operator at Scribner station, who resides with his parents

Grover C Spangler It is a well-authenticated fact that success comes as a result of legitimate and well applied energy, unflagging determination and perseverance in a course of action when once decided upon She is never known to bestow her largesses upon the indolent and ambitionless, and only those who seek her untiringly are recipients of her blessings In tracing the history of the influential business man and representative citizen whose name introduces this sketch, it is plainly seen that the prosperity which he enjoys has been won by commendable qualities and it is also his personal worth that has gained for him the high esteem of those who know him

Grover C Spangler, who owns one of the best-appointed jewelry stores in Eastern Nebraska and who for a number of years has been a potent factor in the commercial affairs of Fremont, was born near that city on May 19, 1888, and is the son of L C and Alveretta (Bordner) Spangler Both of these parents were born in Pennsylvania and came to Dodge County in an early day, their marriage occurring after their arrival here L C Spangler and a brother bought a tract of farming land north of Fremont, but he later sold his interest at $25 an acre, and moved to Colfax County, this state. He was a well educated man, having graduated from college; and after his location in Colfax County he was elected superintendent of schools Sometime later they moved across the river to a town called Edholm, where he engaged in the mercantile business, establishing a large store, which he operated for about ten years, when he was burned out In 1900 he came to Fremont and entered the employ of Nye, Schneider & Company, with whom he still remains He and his wife are members of the Methodist Episcopal Church, while in politics he has been active in support of the democratic party He has been a prominent member of the Knights of Pythias, having served for many years as master of finance of his lodge.

To him and his wife were born five children, namely: Ray, who is station agent for the Northern Pacific Railroad at Manhattan, Montana, Nettie, who assists her brother in the jewelry store, Grover C, of this sketch, Lottie is the wife of Walter Wohenburg, a professor in Yale College, at New Haven, Connecticut Mason, who is engaged in the jewelry business at Scotts Bluff, Nebraska

Grover C Spangler received his elementary education in the public schools of Fremont, graduating from the high school, after which he attended technical trade schools in Chicago and Milwaukee Then for a short time he was employed in the jewelry trade, but soon started into the business on his own account During the days when he served as an employee he worked in Fremont, Nebraska Butte, Montana, Livingston, Montana, and Milwaukee, Wisconsin In May, 1912, Mr Spangler engaged in the jewelry business on his own account in Fremont and his record since then has been one of steady and continuous progress Starting modestly, and with a small stock of goods and a working bench as his main assets, he has advanced both in volume of business and in popular esteem, increasing his stock and enlarging and improving his salesroom until today he possesses one of the handsomest stores and most complete stocks of jewelry in the State of Nebraska He devotes his attention closely to his business and has reached a very comfortable station in life In addition to his jewelry business, Mr Spangler also does a good deal of speculating in farm lands, in which he has met with splendid success

In 1914 Mr Spangler was married to Bessie Christensen, the daughter of C Christensen, and they are the parents of two children, Stephen and Joan Fraternally, Mr Spangler is a member of the Ancient Free and Accepted Order of Masons and the Benevolent and Protective Order of Elks Personally, Mr Spangler is affable and popular with all classes and stands ready at all times to encourage and aid all laudable measures and enterprises for the general good Because of his consistent life and his fine personal qualities, he has won the esteem and good will of all who know him

John Gumb With the passage and enforcement of the Eighteenth Amendment, the men who had formerly been engaged in the manufacture of beverages stronger than those now permitted, wisely turned their attention to the production of other lines of goods and already many of them are meeting with an astounding success The skill and knowledge which in the past enabled them to furnish an excellent grade of fermented goods, are just the qualities required in the manufacture of non-alcoholic beverages and similar products One of these energetic business men and manufacturers of Fremont, is John Gumb, secretary of the Fremont Beverage Company

John Gumb was born in Hesse Darmstadt, Germany, on June 29, 1860, a son of Philip and Barbara (Kobberger) Gumb, who came to the United States in 1870, locating at Chicago, Illinois, where he received his naturalization papers. He was a brick contractor and was engaged in that line of business until he died, both he and his wife passing away at Chicago Their three children were as follows John, whose name heads this review, George, who died at Fremont in 1916, was in the retail liquor trade; and P W, who was also in the retail liquor business, is a resident of Chicago, Illinois The parents were devout members of the Roman Catholic Church, and the father was a democrat in politics

Growing up in Chicago, John Gumb attended its schools, but early learned to be self-supporting and worked at mechanical engineering, for ten years being connected with the erection of engines of various kinds Later he was connected with a concern manufacturing mining machinery, and for two years traveled through the West in its interest, and in this way became impressed with the possibilities of this region, so, in 1891, he came to Fremont as supervising architect of the brewery then in process of erection, and although he had to leave to carry out a contract for the erection of a brewery at St Louis, Missouri, he made arrangements to return, doing so in 1892 For the subsequent two years he carried on a cigar business in partnership with Mr Bridenfeldt. Going back to Chicago, he spent four years in that city erecting breweries and elevators April, 1899, brought him to Fremont again, and this time he took charge of a brewery, and has been with it ever since, forming a company and served as its secretary The company is now placing on the market a beverage that is meeting with popular favor, and also a malt syrup that has been found to be admirable for sweetening purposes in the households of the country to take the place of the high-priced sugar.

In March, 1887, Mr Gumb was united in marriage with Elizabeth Nuernberger, born at Peru, Illinois, and they became the parents of five children, namely Philip, who is in the employ of the Union Pacific Railroad at Grand Island, Nebraska, Fritz, who is a musician of Fremont, John, who is studying law at Chicago, Illinois, Harold G, who is attending the Shattuck School, Faribault, Minnesota; and George Arthur, who is attending the public schools of Fremont. The family all belong to the Episcopal Church In his fraternal relations Mr Gumb maintains membership with Elks, Eagles and Woodmen of the World A strong democrat, Mr Gumb served on the board of public works for twelve years, and has always taken a prime interest in the improvement of the city. He owns considerable property, including 120 acres of land in Douglas County and city realty, and he is vice president of the Arctic Creamery Company, of Fremont While he has these other interests, Mr Gumb is devoting all of his time to the beverage company, and has built up a trade which extends all over the state and as far east as Sioux City, Iowa, and expects to have it expand until he covers at least all of the Western states, for he feels that his products possess sufficient merit to popularize them wherever he introduces them

BENJAMIN W REYNOLDS Enterprising, energetic and progressive, Benjamin W Reynolds is a fine representative of those native-born citizens of Fremont, Dodge County, who have spent their lives within its boundaries, and have been actively identified with the development and promotion of its best interests, whether relating to its agricultural, industrial or financial affairs A son of Wilson Reynolds, his birth occurred in Fremont, November 11, 1860 His paternal grandfather, Benjamin Reynolds, a native of Whitehall, New York, spent the earlier part of his life in the Empire State, migrating to Racine County, Wisconsin, in 1836, although his death occurred in Fremont, Nebraska, where he came when well advanced in years

Born December 25, 1825, at Virgil Corners, New York, Wilson Reynolds migrated to Wisconsin in early manhood, and lived there until after his marriage In 1857 he settled in Fremont, Nebraska, pre-empted a claim in Dodge County, a portion of which is now the site of the Fremont Country Club, and he subsequently built up an extensive business as a dealer in real estate and live stock Industrious, enterprising, and far-seeing, he accumulated a competency, and afterward lived retired from business pursuits in Fremont until his death, in May, 1910 He married Sarah Morilla Harmon, who was born in Warren County, Ohio, July 3, 1834, a daughter of Hiram Harmon, who moved with his family from Ohio to Racine County, Wisconsin Two children were born to their union, as follows: Cassius S, of Fremont, who acquired much wealth as an extensive dealer in land and live stock, and is now retired from active business cares, and Benjamin W, of this brief personal record.

Having completed the course of study in the public schools of Fremont, Benjamin W. Reynolds attended the University of Nebraska in Lincoln, for two years, and at the age of nineteen years began his career as a stockman, for a number of years driving stock across the plains In addition to his large dealings in live stock, Mr Reynolds has for many years bought and sold real estate on an extensive scale, at the present time being the owner of several valuable farms

On December 29, 1880, Mr Reynolds was united in marriage with Mary A Davies, and into their household three children have been born, namely: Mary M, formerly teacher in the public schools of Baker, Oregon, now the wife of Albert Rodamor of that city; Wilson B, and Cassius James both engaged in the insurance business. A straightforward republican in politics, Mr Reynolds served as chairman of the republican committee for many years, and represented his district in the State Senate one term, during the session of 1902 and 1903 He served, under President Taft, as postmaster at Fremont four years, and during the World war was food administrator Fraternally Mr Reynolds is a member of the Ancient Free and Accepted Order of Masons, belonging to Lodge and Chapter · and of Fremont Lodge No 513, Benevolent and Protective Order of Elks He attends the Episcopal Church, while Mrs Reynolds worships at the Baptist Church In 1904, at 901 North I Street, he erected his attractive home, which is a center of social activity

PAUL L KELLER As long as such safe, careful, conservative financial institutions as the Scribner State Bank, of Scribner, Nebraska, easily bear the strain of readjustment after a great war, the general interests of the community may be considered in a prosperous condition This bank has large capital back of it making its resources, for business purposes, practically illimitable, has no concealed liabilities, and is officered and directed by men who possess the confidence and high esteem of their fellow citizens

The officers of the Scribner State Bank are as follows: Fred Volpp, president; Henry Sievers, vice president; P L Keller, cashier; P. L Bauer and W. E. Fahnestock, assistant cashiers Deposits in this bank are protected by Guaranty Fund of the State of Nebraska

Paul L Keller was born in Germany, March 6, 1891, and was brought to the United States by his widowed mother in 1892 She is now a resident of Bloomfield, Nebraska, and a member of the Lutheran Church. His parents were John and Caroline (Volpp) Keller, both of whom were born in Germany, and the father died there when aged thirty-three years He was a stone cutter by trade and followed the same almost all his life His death left two little sons fatherless, namely· Fred and Paul L Both are in the banking business, the

P. L. Keller

former being cashier of the Cheyenne County State Bank at Cheyenne Wells, Colorado

Paul L Keller was as stated an infant when his mother brought him to America She located at first at Wayne, Nebraska, but later removed to Bloomfield, in Knox County Paul L attended the public schools at Bloomfield, then took a commercial course at Fremont College In 1912 he came to Scribner and entered the Scribner State Bank as assistant cashier, seven years later, in 1919, becoming cashier, a position for which, both by talent and temperament, he is admirably fitted

On August 20, 1919, Mr Keller was united in marriage to Miss Magdalene Wupper, who was born in South Dakota They have a daughter, Annette Irene Their pleasant home at Scribner is one of great hospitality Mr Keller is a thirty-second degree Mason, and belongs to the Mystic Shrine and to other fraternal organizations He has never united with any political party but is not indifferent as a citizen, on the other hand being faithful to what he believes the best interests of Nebraska and the country at large Mr and Mrs Keller are members of the Lutheran Church, and Mrs Keller is interested in many benevolent enterprises connected with the church and outside that organization.

SAMUEL A ZAPP, secretary and general manager of the Zapp Garage, is one of the successful men of Fremont who has made his own way in life and not only has the satisfaction of knowing that he has gained a material prosperity, but that he has at the same time won appreciation from his associates for his sterling traits of character The birth of Samuel A Zapp took place at Chicago, Illinois, in December, 1877 He is a son of Charles and Dilomer (Greenwood) Zapp, natives of Holstein, Germany, and Canada, respectively They were married at Chicago, and came to Nebraska about 1880, and following his arrival in this state Charles Zapp was engaged in a contracting business although in early life he was a sailor His death occurred in 1905, but his widow survives him and makes her home with her son, Samuel A She and her husband had three children, two of whom survive, namely: Samuel A, who was the eldest, and George W, who is a farmer of Winnebago, Nebraska In religious faith Charles Zapp was a member of the German Lutheran Church, and his wife belonged to the Methodist Episcopal Church His political views were such as to place him in accord with the principles of the democratic party, and he always voted its ticket While he did not acquire any great amount of wealth, he was fairly successful, and was always highly respected

The educational training of Samuel A Zapp was obtained at the Emerson High School and Highland Park College of Des Moines, Iowa, and following his completion of his courses he taught school for a year He then worked at the carpenter trade at Emerson, and did some contracting, and in 1910 came to Fremont, and opened up his present automobile business, operated as the Zapp Auto Company In 1916 he incorporated the business under the name of the Zapp Garage, with a capital stock of $25,000, of which he has been secretary and general manager since the incorporation papers were taken out. The company sells the Dodge and Chevrolet cars

In October, 1915, Mr. Zapp was united in marriage with Zena Johnsen, who was born in Norway They have a little daughter, Ruth Irene, who received first prize in the baby contest at Fremont, and is considered as one of the most perfect babies in the country Mrs Zapp belongs to the Lutheran Church, while Mr. Zapp affiliates with the Methodist Episcopal Church Fraternally he belongs to the Odd Fellows, in which he has passed all the chairs, the Knights of Pythias and Elks In politics he prefers to cast his vote independently of party ties. A very hard-working man he devotes himself to his business and does not care for outside diversions, either political or social, aside from those amusements in which his family can share.

IRA F RICHARDSON The science of osteopathy is not understood by many and is misunderstood by some so that in considering the life and work of Dr Ira F Richardson of Fremont, an osteopathic practitioner, it may not be out of place to state briefly the principles upon which he works The motto used as the working creed of the modern osteopath is "God has made man's body perfect, as long as the body is normal, health will reign" Osteopaths hold that the human body contains all the remedial agents necessary for the maintenance of health, and that these curative fluids are distributed when and where needed, except when such distribution is interfered with by structural disorder The province of the osteopath is, therefore, to restore structural harmony, so that the inherent healing power of nature may gain control, making the administration of drugs unnecessary. From its name it might be inferred that osteopathy deals only with the adjustment of the bones This idea is erroneous Muscles, ligaments, and the various organs of the body are included in the term structure, and in seeking to restore function, the practitioner endeavors to secure the proper adjustment of any or all of these parts to each other in regard to position, relation and size Many kinds of mechanical treatments have been known and practiced for centuries, but the osteopathic theory, both as to the cause and the treatment of disease, differs widely from that of the older thinkers and practitioners Instead of working blindly for results, the osteopath seeks to find an intelligent reason for the disorder, and much of his treatment is based upon well-known principles of mechanics

Ira F Richardson was born in Sanders County, Nebraska, in 1872, a son of George and Lizzie (Husnetter) Richardson, natives of Michigan and Iowa, respectively They came to Nebraska, homesteaded in Sanders County and lived there for a number of years Later they moved to Linwood, Nebraska, where the father conducted a general store, but they are now residing at Fremont Having been such early settlers of the state, they recall many interesting events of pioneer days Both belong to the Congregational Church In politics Mr Richardson is a republican and he served as postmaster while living at Linwood.

Doctor Richardson, who is the only child of his parents, attended the schools of Linwood, Franklin Academy, and Weeping Water Academy He then went into his father's store for a time but having decided upon a professional career, he entered the National School of Osteopathy at Kansas City, Missouri, and was graduated therefrom in 1900, and from the S S Still College of Osteopathy, Des Moines, Iowa, and after a brief period, he took a course at Hahnemann Medical College, Kansas City, Missouri and was graduated therefrom in 1903 Doctor Richardson then located at Fremont and since that time has been actively engaged in practice as an osteopath meeting with a very gratifying success

In 1912 he was married to Nina Phillips, who was born on a farm in Dodge County, a daughter of Ezra Phillips Mr Phillips was one of the early homesteaders of Dodge County, but he and his wife are now living retired at Fremont Mrs Richardson is a member of the Christian Church, but Doctor Richardson is not connected with any religious organization, although he contributes liberally to the one to which his wife belongs He is a Knight Templar Mason, and also belongs to the Elks, of which he was exalted ruler in 1911 and 1912, and represented the Fremont Lodge at the Grand Lodge at Portland, Oregon, in 1912 Doctor Richardson has also filled a number of offices in the Commandery, and both he and his wife belong to the Order of Eastern Star, and she is past matron of the Fremont Chapter of that order In politics Doctor Richardson is a republican, but he has never entered public life, all of his interest being centered in the practice of his profession Not only as a practitioner does Doctor Richardson stand well in his community, but also as a man and citizen his earnestness and dependability being recognized and admired, and he is justly numbered among the worth-while persons of Dodge County

ANTHONY F PLAMBECK is junior member of the firm of Springer & Plambeck, which conducts one of the leading general insurance agencies in the City of Fremont, and he has not only achieved prominence as one of the successful insurance men of his native city but is also a representative of an honored pioneer family of Dodge County

Mr Plambeck was born at Fremont on the 12th of September, 1870, and is a son of Claus H. and Anna C (Kuehl) Plambeck, who were born and reared in Holstein, Germany, where their marriage was solemnized Utterly opposed to the rigorous military regime in his native land, Claus H Plambeck decided to come to America, where he was assured of freedom of thought and action, as well as opportunity for the achieving of independence through personal effort He arrived at Fremont, Nebraska, July 5, 1869, and he and his young wife were entirely without financial resources, though rich in good health, ambition and earnest purpose

Mr Plambeck became actively identified with farm enterprise, as one of the pioneers of Dodge County, and later he was engaged in the mercantile business at Fremont, where also he conducted a hotel for a number of years A man of utmost integrity and superior mentality, he gained and retained the confidence and esteem of the people of Dodge County, and became influential in community affairs He served five years as county judge, but prior to this had engaged in the insurance business at Fremont, a line of enterprise to which he continued to give his attention after his retirement from the bench of the county court and until the time of his death, in 1910, at the age of sixty-seven years He served also as a member of the city council, was a staunch supporter of the cause of the democratic party, was affiliated with the Knights of Pythias and the Ancient Order of United Workmen, and was a zealous communicant of the Lutheran Church, as is also his widow, who still resides at Fremont and who celebrated in 1919 the seventy-seventh anniversary of her birth Of their fine family of fifteen children nine are living Of these five live in Fremont of whom Anthony F is the eldest, Frederick is associated with the Ideal Laundry, of Fremont, Jeanette is the widow of Charles J Johnson and resides at Fremont; Otto is a carpenter and contractor in this city, and Ernest is connected with a leading automobile garage here.

In the public schools of Fremont Anthony F Blambeck continued his studies until his graduation in the high school, as a member of the class of 1888 Office work has engaged his attention throughout his entire active career, and he early gained in his father's office a thorough experience in connection with the details of the insurance business, his continuous association with which has given him authoritative knowledge In 1907 he formed a partnership alliance with D J Springer and engaged in the general insurance business, under the present firm name of Springer & Plambeck, their agency now controlling a substantial and representative business. That Mr Plambeck has the fullest measure of popular confidence and good will in his native city is shown by the fact that he has served continuously since 1914 as city treasurer of Fremont. His political allegiance is given to the democratic party, he is affiliated with the Knights of Pythias, and he and his wife hold membership in the Congregational Church

In 1901 Mr Plambeck was united in marriage to Mrs. Jean (Hughes) Boyd, she being a native of Carroll County, Illinois Mr. and Mrs Plambeck have no children, but Mrs Plambeck has by her former marriage one daughter, Jeanne Boyd, who is now a successful and popular teacher of music in the City of Chicago

William M Sanders, who has been for nearly a quarter of a century in continuous service as the efficient and popular county engineer of Dodge County, and who is known as one of the representative civil engineers of this section of the state, claims the old Keystone state as the place of his nativity, and is, on the paternal side of English lineage, while on the maternal side he is of Holland Dutch ancestry, both families having early been founded in America Mr Sanders was born in Lancaster County, Pennsylvania, in April, 1857, and is a son of Emanuel and Barbara (Kapp) Sanders, both likewise natives of Pennsylvania, where the former was born in 1819 and the latter in 1825 The father passed his entire life in the Keystone state, where he died in 1878 His entire active career was marked by close association with agricultural industry and he was one of the early and influential members of the Grange or the Patrons of Husbandry in his native state He was a stalwart republican and served in various township offices as one of the influential men of his community He was a strong abolitionist during the climacteric period culminating in the Civil war, and he employed two substitutes to serve as soldiers in that great conflict. Both he and his wife were zealous and devout members of the United Brethren Church Mrs Sanders survived her husband by nearly forty years, she having come to Dodge County, Nebraska, in the early '80s and having established her home at Hooper, where she continued to reside until her death, in 1917, at the venerable age of ninety-two years. Of the eight children William M of this review is the eldest of the three now living, Jacob B is a merchant at Hooper, Dodge County, and John is the manager of the grain elevator in that village.

William M Sanders is indebted to the public schools of his native state for his early educational discipline, which included that of the high school, and he was an ambitious youth of twenty-two years when, in 1879, he came to Dodge County, Nebraska, where for a time he worked on a farm near Hooper Prior to coming to Nebraska he had given close study to and gained practical experience in surveying, and in 1880, the year after his arrival in Nebraska, he went to the Territory of New Mexico, where he became a Deputy U S Surveyor in connection with government surveying service He thus continued in government employ five years, and his work was not only in New Mexico, but also in Arizona At the expiration of the period noted, Mr Sanders returned to Dodge County, where for a time he was engaged in the contracting business at Hooper In 1897 he was elected county engineer, and of this office he has continued the incumbent during the long intervening period, the while it has been within his province to do a large amount of important surveying and other professional service for the county, his long retention of office affording the best evidence of the high estimate placed upon his ability and service He has held also various township offices, including that of assessor, and he was for six years a member of the school board at Hooper, where he maintained his home until his removal to Fremont, the county seat He is unwavering in his allegiance to the republican party and is well fortified in his political convictions In addition to being county engineer at the present time he is also filling the office of highway commissioner Mr Sanders is actively affiliated with the Masonic fraternity, in which he has received the fourteenth degree of the Ancient Accepted Scottish Rite, and both he and his wife are affiliated with the adjunct organization, the Order of the Eastern Star Mrs Sanders and her three younger daughters are members of the Presbyterian Church, and the eldest daughter holds membership in the Methodist Episcopal Church

In 1882 Mr Sanders was united in marriage to Miss Elizabeth McBroom, who has the distinction of having been the first white girl born in Dodge County, where she has continuously maintained her home and remains as a popular representative of one of the old and honored pioneer families of the county Her father, the late Hugh McBroom, here established his home in 1857, ten years before Nebraska was admitted to the Union, and he took up a tract of wild prairie land, on Clark Creek, where he developed one of the early farms of the county, both he and his wife having continued to reside in Dodge County until their death In conclusion is given brief record concerning the children of Mr and Mrs Sanders: Lyman is assistant cashier in a bank at Roswell, New Mexico, Boyd is manager of the Pecos Valley Light and Power Company, at Carlsbad, that state, Miss Esther remains at the parental home and is employed as a skilled stenographer and bookkeeper, Ruth likewise is at home and holds a position as stenographer in an office at Fremont, Grace is attending the public schools of Fremont; and Frances likewise is attending school in her home city.

William J. Davies, M D, has been a resident of Nebraska since he was a lad of nine years, but can claim Wales as the place of his nativity and long ancestral record, his birth having there occurred on December 31, 1862; five years later, in 1867, marked the immigration of his parents to the United States. He is a son of James and Mary (Williams) Davies, and upon coming to this country the family residence was first established in Wisconsin At Columbus, that state, the father continued to be engaged in the drug business until 1871, when he came with his family to Nebraska and engaged in the same line of enterprise at Fremont, where he continued to conduct a well-appointed drug store until his death, in 1879, at the age of forty-two years His widow survived him by thirty years and was one of the venerable and loved pioneer women of Fremont at the time of her death, in 1909 Of the six children, the eldest is Mary, who is the wife of B W. Reynolds, a prominent citizen of Fremont, Dr William J, of this review, was the next in order of birth, Emily died at the age of thirty-five years; Catherine is the wife of Charles Marshall, who is engaged in the jewelry business at Fremont, Rupert A resides at Arlington, Washington

County, Miss Glendora holds a clerical position in the Fremont post-office The father was independent in politics and within the comparatively short period of his residence in Fremont he served for a time as village clerk, long before the county seat of Dodge County had been incorporated as a city Both he and his wife were earnest members of the Baptist Church

Doctor Davies profited fully by the advantages afforded in the public schools of Fremont, where he was reared to adult age, and where he gained practical business experience in his father's drug store, he having been seventeen years of age at the time of his father's death In 1883 he entered the celebrated Rush Medical College, in the City of Chicago, and in this institution he was graduated as a member of the class of 1887, with the degree of Doctor of Medicine Thereafter he was engaged in the drug business in connection with his practice until 1893, when he began the active practice of his profession in the City of Fremont, where he has since continued his humane mission and won marked prestige in his able service in the alleviation of human suffering and distress Such has been his faithful stewardship that he has responded to calls with utmost self-abnegation, has endured the winter's cold, has traversed the worst roads, both night and day, and has not permitted any adverse condition to baffle him in his work No man has completed the curriculum ot Rush Medical College without coming forth admirably fortified for the work of his profession, but Mr Davies has not been content to remain in statu quo but has been a close student and otherwise availed himself of every possible means of keeping abreast ot the advances made in medical and surgical science. He has long controlled a large and remunerative practice, is one of the leading physicians of Dodge County and in his home City of Fremont is known for his civic loyalty and progressiveness He has served as health officer of Fremont and is actively identified with the Dodge County Medical Society, of which he has served as president, besides which he is affiliated with the Nebraska State Medical Society, the Elkhorn Valley Medical Society and the American Medical Association He is a democrat in political allegiance and he attends and supports the Congregational Church of Fremont, of which his wife is a zealous member

In 1890 Doctor Davies wedded Miss Jessie Hinman, daughter of Miner H Hinman, of whom specific mention is made on other pages of this volume Dr and Mrs Davies have three children Allen holds a position in a banking institution at Silver Creek, Merrick County, Martha, a graduate of Nebraska State Normal School at Fremont and of the Thomas Training School in the City of Detroit, Michigan, is now a popular teacher in the schools of Republican City, Harlan County, Nebraska, and Ruth, now Mrs J A Maxwell, likewise a graduate of the State Normal School at Fremont, was an efficient teacher in the public schools at Silver Creek, Merrick County

Charles C, Johnson Although born on foreign soil, Charles C Johnson was brought up and educated in this country, and in his youth imbibed the respect for American institutions, and the knowledge and patriotic spirit that has made him a loyal and valued citizen of the United States, and one of the honored and respected men of Fremont, his home city He was born, January 19, 1869, in Denmark, which was also the birthplace of his parents, G. P and Annie (Christensen) Johnson

Some years after his marriage G P Johnson immigrated with his family to the United States, locating in Casey, Iowa, in April, 1869 He

Chas C Johnson

was there employed in railroad work for two years, when, in 1871, he came to Saunders County, Nebraska, traveling with his family in a prairie schooner. Taking up a homestead claim, he cleared and improved a farm, laboring diligently in his agricultural work until ready to retire from active pursuits, when he moved to Fremont, where he spent the closing years of his life. He was a stanch republican in politics, and a member of the Lutheran Church, to which his wife also belonged Seven children were born of their marriage, three of whom are living, as follows Nels, a farmer, living near Fargo, North Dakota, John, owning and occupying the parental homestead; and Charles C of this sketch

After leaving the rural schools of the community in which he was reared, Charles C Johnson continued his studies in the Fremont Normal School Leaving the home farm at the age of sixteen years, he entered the employ of the Northwestern Railroad Company with which he remained for fifteen years, at first being a freight handler, and later being promoted through different departments to that of freight agent, a position that he resigned in 1905 Locating in Fremont, Mr. Johnson became bookkeeper for the Fremont Milling Company, of which he is now an active member This company was incorporated with a capital of $35,000, and its plant has a capacity of 600 barrels a day, and makes and sells up to that limit, its productions being in demand throughout Nebraska and the East During the World war some of its productions were bought by the Government, and sent over to France for the army boys Mr Johnson is both secretary and treasurer of the company, and is kept busily employed

Mr Johnson married, in April, 1894, Annie Nelson, who was born in Fremont, Nebraska, where her father, James Nelson, located on coming to this country from Denmark, his native land, and where he continued his occupation of a farmer Mr and Mrs Johnson have three children, namely · Evelyn, wife of A K Lane of Fremont, Stanley, who enlisted in the navy in May, 1918, and returned to Fremont in March, 1919, and is now with the Ford Company at Des Moines, Iowa; and Howard, attending the Fremont High School Mrs Lane was graduated from the high school, and before her marriage taught school, and Mr. Lane, who served in the navy a year is now with Reynolds, Morrison, Rathburn Company Fraternally Mr Johnson is a member of the Independent Order of Odd Fellows, and has filled all of the offices of the Lodge, Canton and Encampment. He and his family are members of the Methodist Episcopal Church He is a republican in politics but has never sought public office, his time and energies having been wisely devoted to his business interests, more especially since the Fremont Milling Company took over the Brown Mill, merging the two companies into one Mr Johnson is prominent in religious circles, being an active worker in the church, and at different times has filled the pulpit very acceptably.

EDWARD W HOOKER Ability to overcome obstacles and a determination to get ahead have been characteristics which have worked to the advantage of Edward W Hooker so that he is today one of the men of means in Dodge County and is living at Hooper retired from the exactions of business He was born at West Hampton, Hampshire County, Massachusetts, on November 26, 1840, a son of Festus and Mary B (Strong) Hooker, farming people of Massachusetts, and a descendant of Rev Thomas Hooker, first minister of Hartford, Connecticut The great-grandfather of Edward W. Hooker was a physician and a man of great activity, who, when over eighty years of age, pulled some of the teeth of his great-grandson, Edward Both parents of Edward W Hooker died in Massachusetts. Their children were as follows Allen F, who died at the age of twenty years; Henry C., who is also deceased; Edward W, whose name heads this review, Lucy A, who is the widow of George E Knight, resides at West Hampton, Massachusetts, Worthington, who is deceased, was a farmer in Massachusetts; and Charles H, who is deceased, was a farmer Both parents were Congregationalists. After the organization of the republican party, the father espoused its principles, and upheld them the remainder of his life At one time he was a member of the town board and was a man of considerable prominence in his community

Growing up on the home farm, Edward W Hooker, like so many of the young men of his generation, was aroused by the outbreak of war, and enlisted on July 17, 1862, in Company D, Thirty-Seventh Massachusetts Volunteer Infantry, being mustered into the service at Pittsfield, Massachusetts, and at once was sent to Arlington Heights, Virginia He participated in the battles of Fredericksburg, Marye's Heights, Salem Church and Gettysburg In 1863 his regiment was sent to New York City to enforce the draft, and then returned to the front, and Mr Hooker was in the engagements on the Rappahannock, at Mile Run, the campaign in the Wilderness, the battles of Spottsylvania, Cold Harbor, Petersburg and Fort Stephens, in the latter engagement the regiment being equipped with Spencer rifles For eighteen months Mr. Hooker was color bearer, and was promoted to the rank of second lieutenant. He brought colors from his last engagement in which he was wounded in both hands, the enemy shot at him from the side, and the flagstaff splintered in his hands, injuring both of them, but aside from this he escaped in spite of the exposed position he occupied as color bearer.

Following his return from the war Mr Hooker worked at his trade of millwright for six years, and then in 1872 came west to Nebraska He had a soldier's claim and homesteaded and on it carried on general farming and stock raising The only work he has done at his trade since coming to the state was the erection of his own house on his homestead. Hardly had he managed to get things in working order than the plague of grasshoppers descended upon him and utterly destroyed his crops for several seasons so that in order to tide over he engaged in teaching school This he was able to do very efficiently for he had been well educated in the common schools of his native place, Westfield Academy and Willison Seminary, but as soon as he was able he resumed his farming and continued it until 1907 when he retired and located permanently at Hooper

In July, 1862, Mr. Hooker was united in marriage with Jennie E Clark, born at Elbridge, New York, January 15, 1841, a daughter of Zenas S and Eliza Clark, natives of Massachusetts Mr and Mrs Hooker became the parents of the following children Henry C has been postmaster of the Leigh postoffice for eight years, Edward F was a farmer and died at the age of thirty-one, Anna W died at the age of three years, Nellie is the wife of Chester Bridgman, a farmer and stockman of Fairmount, Nebraska, Charles S died in childhood, and May married J R. Phillips, a farmer of Maple Township Both Mr Hooker and his wife are devout members of the Methodist Episcopal Church He is a republican, and he was a member of the county board of Dodge County for six years For many years he has been a member of Upton Post,

Grand Army of the Republic, and enjoys meeting his old comrades He is a stockholder in the Dodge County State Bank of Hooper, and is otherwise interested in sound investments in this region When his country had need of his services as a soldier, he did not shirk his duty, nor has he failed to render a good account of himself ever since and it would be difficult to find a man more representative of the best and most substantial element of the county than he

ADOLPH HAGENBAUMER Out of nearly eighty years of his long and useful life Adolph Hagenbaumer has spent more than fifty in Dodge County, and the greater part of this time as a resident on one farm in Hooper Township, in section 24 As a farmer he has achieved much success, represented in extensive land holdings, and in every way has been substantially identified with the welfare and progress of the community.

His career has been a typical American achievement, though he is foreign born He was born in Germany September 3, 1841, and had only a common school education in his native land Seeking the better and broader opportunities of America he came to the United States in 1869, and came direct to Fontanelle, Nebraska. All the others of his immediate family remained in the fatherland He had been brought up on a farm, and turned to agriculture as the vocation he knew most about For about two years he was a renter, and then with limited means he bought 160 acres of prairie land The first house in which he lived was a small shack of lumber He was a hard worker, practiced thrift, was always a good manager, until he totaled his possessions as nearly 1,000 acres of good Nebraska soil Most of this has since been divided among his family, and he is now able to take life at leisure, turning over the heavy responsibilities of the farm to his boys

Mr Hagenbaumer's first wife was Hannah Sigmann, whose two children, Henry and Fred, now live in Washington County. For his second marriage he took Charlotte Bickmier. To this union were born eight children Annie, John, Edwin, Augusta, William, Adolph, Louise and Charles The sons, William, Adolph and Charles, are still on the home place Mr Hagenbaumer looks out upon many broad acres which his diligence improved, and besides his comfortable home has a complete equipment of other fine buildings, making this one of the progressive farmsteads of Dodge County Though he had a limited education himself he has done much to foster the cause of good schools and for four years was a member of the School Board of Washington County. He and his wife are Lutherans and he is a republican voter.

HERMAN WATERMAN Having learned the trade of a brickmaker in his native land, and not finding there the opportunities he sought in order to develop a paying business, Herman Waterman came to the United States, accompanied by his father, and since that time has become one of the substantial men of Dodge County The opening given him upon his arrival was not especially encouraging, but he is one of those men who sticks to anything once he has begun, and he is now reaping a well merited reward for his years of endeavor

Herman Waterman was born in Germany April 14, 1856, a son of Herman and Marie Waterman The former was a laborer. They had three children, namely Fred, who is living retired at Fontanelle, Nebraska; Sophia, who is deceased, and Herman, whose name heads this review.

After coming to the United States Herman Waterman worked in a brickyard, and then established one of his own at Fontanelle, and conducted it for five years, and was then connected with a similar enterprise at Scribner for another five years In 1893 he came to Hooper and bought the brickyard which had been built by John Heimrick At the time Mr Waterman bought the yard from Mr Heimrick there were four kilns, but he has so enlarged it that there are now ten kilns and the daily capacity of the plant is 50,000 brick, which are shipped to Wyoming, South Dakota, Iowa and Nebraska This plant covers, with the land, 157 acres and the equipment is modern in every respect The business has been incorporated, with Mr Waterman as president, his son, Herman H F, as secretary and treasurer, and John Edelmeier as general manager

Mr and Mrs Herman Waterman became the parents of the following children Carrie, who is the wife of Frank Wagner, a farmer, who lives near Leigh, Nebraska, Herman H F, whose sketch appears elsewhere in this work, John, who is employed in his father's brickyard; Lydia, who is the wife of R. Krebell, a farmer of Dodge County, Elbert, who is also employed in his father's brickyard, Dora, who is attending school, the next one died in infancy, and so did the youngest; and Rose, who was eighth in order of birth, died at the age of eighteen years Both Mr and Mrs Waterman are held in high esteem in their neighborhood, and their children are a credit to them and to their bringing up, for they show that they have had careful and watchful parents who have tried to teach them to become useful men and women

James Balding For upwards of forty years a resident of Dodge County, the late James Balding of Fremont witnessed in that time many wonderful transformations in the county, the dugouts and sod houses of the early pioneers being replaced by substantial frame houses, while the hamlets of those days developed into thriving villages and populous towns He was born July 1, 1838, in London, England, and died in Fremont, Nebraska, May 23, 1906

His parents, Mr. and Mrs Thomas Balding, immigrated to the United States in 1850 and settled on a farm in the vicinity of Milwaukee, Wisconsin They subsequently removed to Minnesota, and on the farm which they improved spent their remaining years. They reared three children, as follows Harriet, a resident of Minnesota, Thomas, a venerable man of fourscore and four years, was for many years a stock broker in Milwaukee, Wisconsin, where he is now living retired from active pursuits, and James

Twelve years of age when he came with the family to this country, James Balding completed his early education in Wisconsin, and under his father's instructions became familiar with the various branches of agriculture. Locating in Fremont, Dodge County, Nebraska, in May, 1865, Mr Balding established a meat market, which he operated successfully for a time, giving it up later to devote his attention to the buying and selling of stock, an industry in which he found both pleasure and profit Possessing good business ability and judgment, he accumulated a good property, including among other pieces of real estate 300 acres of valuable land lying one mile west of Fremont He was a stanch republican in politics, and served one term as councilman

About a year after coming to Fremont, on January 1 1867, Mr Balding married Fannie Bullock, a native of the Empire State, born December 21, 1848. Her father, Daniel Bullock, was born in New York State and his wife whose maiden name was Lettie Ross, was a native of Canada In the fall of 1865 they came with their family to Dodge County, locating in Fremont, where for many years he was employed in carrying the mail from the postoffice to the railway station and vice versa Of the twelve children that were born of their union three are surviving, as follows Melissa, living in Fremont, is the widow of Edward Fuller, who was here engaged in the furniture business for many years; Fannie, Mrs Balding, and Mrs Rebecca Carter, a widow, residing in Lincoln, Nebraska

Four children blessed the union of Mr and Mrs Balding three of whom have passed to the life beyond Jessie, the only child living, married Frank Fowler, president-manager of the Nye, Schneider & Fowler Company, and they have one son, James Fowler, a student in the Fremont Normal School Mrs. Balding is a faithful member of the Methodist Episcopal Church, of which Mr Balding was a regular attendant, and a generous contributor towards its support Mrs Balding, who lives alone, has a fine home at 432 West Military Avenue, where she enjoys all the comforts of life, receiving from her husband's large estate a handsome annual income.

Dr Samuel G Glover, now deceased for many years, was one of the distinguished members of the medical profession at Arlington, where his memory is still cherished for his sympathy his knowledge of his calling and his real humanity He was born in Oberlin County, Ohio, on June 24, 1834, and died on November 14, 1907 He was educated in Ohio, and enlisted in the Union army from Indiana, serving for three years in a cavalry regiment and rose to be a company official

After the close of the war he returned to Indiana and from there moved to Altoona, Iowa, and there he conducted a drug store and practiced medicine. In 1871 he came to Arlington, Nebraska, where he found the conditions for which he was looking and here built up a large practice and also was interested in a drug store Still later he identified himself with the banking business, and finally retired, living in leisure the last years of his life. He was a skilled physician and experienced druggist and acquired his medical training under Doctor Ross, one of the old-time medical practitioners of Indiana

In March, 1874, Doctor Glover was united in marriage with Jennie Mansfield, born in Pennsylvania in 1857, a daughter of Albert and Lydia A (Rosa) Mansfield, both of whom were natives of Pennsylvania, who came to Arlington in 1870 and built the first store of this city, in which Mr Mansfield carried on merchandising for a few years, and then retired Both he and his wife died at Arlington Of their five children, two survive, namely Mrs Glover and Fred The latter is engaged in a draying business at Arlington, Nebraska Dr and Mrs Glover became the parents of two sons, namely Guy L Glover, who is in the confectionery and ice cream business at Arlington, married Anna Bluckett of Omaha, Nebraska and they have one daughter, Dorothea Glover, and Albert L, who is in the investment and loan business at Omaha, Nebraska, married Maude Miller and they have one son, Roland Glover. Mrs Jennie Glover is a member of the Methodist Episcopal Church. Doctor Glover was a well-known democrat and was receiver of the land office at Valentine under President Cleveland for four years He was a Knight Templar Mason and belonged to the Order of Eastern Star, and Mrs Glover still holds membership in the latter order Beginning their married life as poor young people with their way to make, Dr and Mrs Glover became people of ample means while still young enough to enjoy their prosperity, and in 1884 built the comfortable home Mrs Glover now occupies at Arlington

Doctor Glover came of English and Irish stock, his father, Joseph Glover, being a native of the former country and his mother, Eliza Glover, of the latter They came to Nebraska during the formative period of the commonwealth, and both died at Aurora, Nebraska

CHARLES E. ABBOTT was graduated as member of the class of 1897 in the law department of the University of Nebraska, and on the 1st of January of the following year he established his residence at Fremont, judicial center of Dodge County Within the intervening period of nearly a quarter of a century he has here clearly demonstrated his ability as a lawyer and counselor, and he has long controlled a substantial and representative law business, as one of the leading members of the Dodge County bar He gave about twelve years of effective service as city attorney of Fremont and is now president of the Fremont Commercial Club, an organization of state-wide reputation for business ideals and progressive policies Mr. Abbott is deeply appreciative of the advantages and attractions of his home city and county, and aside from the activities of his profession he has become closely assocated with agricultural industry of the county, as the owner of 600 acres of valuable and well-improved farm land He is a stanch advocate of the principles and policies for which the republican party stands sponsor and is affiliated with the Masonic fraternity, the Independent Order of Odd Fellows and the Benevolent and Protective Order of Elks

Mr Abbott was born at Taylorville, Illinois, on December 1, 1871, and is a son of Miles J and Jennie (Scribner) Abbott Miles J Abbott had been a newspaper publisher in Illinois and in 1879 he came with his family to Nebraska and settled near Hastings, Adams County. In 1885 he moved to western Nebraska and was prominently concerned with the organization of Hayes County, and published a weekly newspaper at Hayes Center, the county seat, for twenty years He engaged also in the practice of law and was for many years one of the most prominent and influential citizens of Hayes County, where his protracted incumbency of public office included service as county attorney and county judge

November 28, 1900, at Fremont, was recorded the marriage of Charles E Abbott to Miss Gertrude Sexton, daughter of Dr Thomas C. and Emma (Peters) Sexton, her father having been a pioneer physician in Washington County, where he established his home in 1865, about two years prior to the admission of Nebraska to statehood Dr and Mrs Sexton are now venerable and revered pioneer citizens of Fremont, and it is practically assured that Mrs Sexton is now the oldest native-born citizen still residing in Dodge County Mr and Mrs Abbott have two children—Katherine and Charles Wade

WILLIAM FRIED A man of superior business ability and tact, talented and cultured, the late William Fried was for many years actively associated with the higher interests of Fremont, whether relating to the advancement of its mercantile, industrial, financial or political prosperity, and his death was a cause of general regret, being a loss not only to his home city, but to the county and state A native of Sweden he was born May 20, 1841, a son of Samuel Fried, and died in Fremont, Nebraska, July 21, 1914 Samuel Fried was a well-to-do merchant in Sweden, where both he and his wife, whose name before marriage was Carrie Sanden were lifelong residents They were the parents of five children none of whom are now living

Wm. Fried

William Fried received excellent educational advantages in his native land, acquiring his elementary education in Wexio, and afterward attending school in Stockholm Coming when young to the United States, he continued his studies in this country, thus preparing himself for any work in which he might wish to engage He first located in Henry County, Illinois, where three of his brothers were living, Samuel, John and Carl A In 1863 he and his brother, Carl A Fried, enlisted in Company I, Illinois Engineering Corps, and served two years, taking part in several engagements of the Civil war Being discharged from the army at the close of the conflict, Mr Fried took a commercial course of study in Albion, Michigan, and for two years thereafter served as a clerk on the Steamer Benton, plying between St Joseph, Michigan, and Grand Haven

In 1867 Mr Fried and his brother, Carl A Fried, located in Fremont, Nebraska, and there the brother, who became a prominent and successful business man, passed the remainder of his life, dying at the comparatively early age of forty-four years. William Fried settled in Fremont soon after coming to Nebraska, and having secured a position with Nye, Colson & Company, continued with the firm as an employee until 1871, when he was admitted to partnership Proving himself eminently capable and trustworthy, he was later made vice president of the firm, and when that firm was merged into the Nye, Schneider & Fowler Company, Mr Fried was continued as vice president of the new organization, and retained the position until his death A man of fine business qualifications, he accumulated a large estate, leaving his family with abundant means

Mr Fried was a loyal republican in politics and influential in local and county and state affairs In 1891 he was elected mayor of Fremont and served acceptably for eight years, and when, in that year, the city insisted on his retaining the position still longer, both he and his wife rebelled and he refused another re-election He filled many positions of trust and responsibility beside that of mayor, and in 1880 served as a representative to the State Legislature He belonged to the Grand Army of the Republic and was a member of Fremont Lodge Ancient Free and Accepted Masons; Signet Chapter No 8, Royal Arch Masons; Tabor Commandery No 9, Knights Templar, a Scottish Rite and also a thirty-third degree Mason Mr Fried owned valuable city property and had title to considerable land in Dodge County He was a stockholder in the Fremont National Bank and in the Stockyard and Land Company, and had served as president of the Fremont Board of Trade

Mr Fried married, May 20, 1875, in Des Moines, Iowa, Carrie C Lobeck, who was born in Illinois November 29, 1857, a daughter of Otto Lobeck A native of Germany, Otto Lobeck immigrated to the United States at the age of twenty years, and located first in Henry County, Illinois, where he subsequently embarked in mercantile pursuits Coming from there to Nebraska, he opened a real estate office in Omaha, and was there successfully engaged in business until his death His wife, whose maiden name was Anna Erickson, was born in Sweden, and they became the parents of ten children, one of whom, Charles O Lobeck, who served in the United States Congress for eight years, recently died in Omaha, where the larger part of his life was spent Of the four children born of the union of Mr. and Mrs Fried, two are living, namely William, born in 1880, is engaged in the lumber and grain business at Beemer, Nebraska, where he has an elevator; and Thyra, wife of Walter C Jones of Fremont, a bookkeeper Mrs Fried is a member of the Methodist Episcopal Church, in which she is an active worker She belongs to the Order of the Eastern Star, and is first vice president of the Eastern Star Home at Fremont She resides at 1505 North Nye Avenue, occupying a modernly constructed brick house, her home being very pleasant and attractive

COMMODORE PERRY MASTERS One of the important elements in any community is that composed of men who after years of strenuous endeavor as agriculturists have reached the time of life when they feel justified in retiring from former activities and, being thus relieved from the responsibilities formerly their portion, are able to give thought and attention to civic problems with resultant good to their community Such a man is Commodore Perry Masters of Arlington

Commodore Perry Masters was born in Indiana on June 5, 1856, a son of Azariah and Sarah (Kepler) Masters Azariah Masters was born in Greene County, Pennsylvania, on October 8, 1831, and he is now making his home at Arlington, Nebraska His wife was born in DeKalb County, Indiana, on October 1, 1837 and died on May 5, 1909. They were married in Indiana on April 1, 1855.

While a resident of Indiana Azariah Masters was engaged in farming, but seeking better opportunities came west to Nebraska in 1857, and pre-empted land to which he later added more land by purchase, living on his land until about 1900, when he moved to Arlington, and since then has lived retired For a time after his retirement he retained his farm, but later gave it to his sons Six children were born to him and his wife, as follows: Commodore Perry, who was the first born; Alfred M, who is on his father's farm; Mrs J. E Brice, whose husband is a farmer and cattleman, Bryan F, who is on the homestead; Clara V, who married J M. Marshall, a farmer of Arlington, and one who is deceased. Both as an Odd Fellow and democrat Azariah Masters was a well-known man

Commodore Perry Masters was reared on a farm and attended the rural schools, and when he attained to manhood estate he naturally adopted farming as his life work and he followed an agricultural life until his retirement in 1910, at which time he moved to Arlington and here he has since lived retired In 1914 Mr Masters built a beautiful home at Arlington, which is one of the best in Washington County In his religious faith he is a Methodist, and in political convictions a democrat. Although he has always taken an intelligent interest in everything pertaining to civic affairs he has not sought office, preferring to exert his influence from the standpoint of a private citizen

On December 25, 1884, Mr Masters was married to Dora Wages, born in Wisconsin, a daughter of Gustav and Dorothea (Lubens) Wages, natives of France and Hanover, Germany, respectively They came to the United States when young people. Her death occurred in Wisconsin, and he passed away in Iowa in 1909 They had three children, namely Lillie Pomroy, who lives north of Arlington, Ernest, who is a retired farmer of Arlington, and Mrs Masters Mr. and Mrs. Masters have one daughter, Gertrude, who married F I Pfieffer, cashier of the First National Bank of Arlington It would be difficult to find a man more highly esteemed than Mr Masters He has not sought to bring himself before the public in any undue manner, but has tried to do his duty to his fellow man and his country, and to hurt no one by word or deed, thus taking into his every-day life the religion he professes, and earning and holding that approval which means so much to the right-minded person

HERMAN G MEYER It means something to be a successful self-made man in the true sense It means character, independence, poise, self-respect and moral strength The self-made man has behind him developing experiences that have bestowed gifts of compassion and liberal-mindedness that cannot be misunderstood or appreciated by one who has never made an unaided struggle upward A very prominent citizen of Arlington, Nebraska, who well understands this situation is Herman G Meyer, vice president of the Arlington State Bank

Herman G Meyer was born March 25, 1871, in the Province of Oldenberg Germany, the youngest in a family of five children born to Herman and Katherine (Hillen) Meyer The father was a farmer and both parents spent their entire lives in Germany Mr Meyer has three brothers Henry, William and John, all of whom are farmers in Germany, and one sister, Hermine, who is the wife of Henry Hillen, also a German farmer

When Herman G Meyer was seventeen years old, he had had the usual school privileges of his class He was a youth filled with ambition and believing that better opportunity to advance in life could be found in the United States, he found a way to come to America and landed on American soil in 1888 By the time he reached a German settlement in Wisconsin his slender means were exhausted, but he easily secured farm work, to which he applied himself no more faithfully than he did to the task of learning the English language He spent the summer in Wisconsin then went westward and landed in Dodge County, Nebraska, in 1889, again without means During the next three years while working on farms in Dodge County, he learned American customs and language, while carefully saving his money The use he put his capital to was to attend the normal school at Fremont and afterward the State University at Lincoln, where he made such rapid and substantial progress that he secured a certificate to teach school and for years afterward taught in country and town schools in several counties to the entire satisfaction of all concerned He spent nine years teaching in Nebraska, being principal five years of this time

In the meanwhile Mr Meyer had progressed in citizenship as well as materially and became influential in republicans politics but not as a seeker for office for himself It was in 1904 that he entered the banking field, serving first as assistant cashier of the Snyder State Bank at Snyder, Nebraska, for two years, then as cashier for six years, going then to Hooper, Nebraska, where he served four years as cashier of the First National Bank In 1916 he came to Arlington and became financially interested in the Arlington State Bank, of which he is vice president His time has been devoted mainly to the affairs of the bank for the past four years, but he still owns a fine farm property in Dodge County

In 1904 Mr Meyer was united in marriage to Miss Emily McClean, who was born in Saunders County, Nebraska, and is a daughter of Robert McClean, a prominent farmer of Saunders County, of Scotch ancestry Mr and Mrs Meyer have two children, Gretchen and Allen, aged respectively twelve and ten years, both of whom are doing well at school The family attends the Congregational Church Mr Meyer is a thirty-second degree Mason, and he belongs also to the Odd Fellows and the Modern Woodmen of America.

G I PFEIFFER, cashier of the First National Bank of Arlington, is one of the most representative men of Washington County, and one intimately associated with its growth and development, and also with the expansion of the banking interests of this region He was born near Stuttgart, Germany, on January 31, 1874, a son of Solomon and Katherine (Wagner) Pfeiffer, both natives of Germany, where he was born on October 12, 1833, and she on September 21 of the same year He died on October 15, 1916, but she survives and makes her home at Arlington They were married in Germany and came to the United States in 1881, locating first at Fontanelle, Nebraska, but in 1893 moving to the vicinity of Arlington, where they bought and later developed a farm They had eight children, namely: Solomon, who is a retired farmer of Arlington, Fred C, who is a farmer of Fontanelle, G John, who moved to Oklahoma, is still engaged in farming in that state; William G, who is a blacksmith and mechanic of Arlington Henry, who is on the old homestead· G I, whose name heads this review; Charles, who is a salesman of Norfolk, Nebraska; and Martha, who married E H Woerner, a florist of Arlington The parents were Lutherans in their religious faith, and in politics the father was a democrat. When he came to this country he was penniless, and yet when he died he was a well-to-do man, and had made everything himself His farm comprised 160 acres and was well improved and in a high state of cultivation

G I Pfeiffer attended the public schools and then gained a working knowledge of business fundamentals by taking a correspondence course, and in 1902 became bookkeeper for the First National Bank of Arlington, rising in two years to be assistant cashier In 1906 he became cashier and is still holding that very responsible position The capital stock of the bank is $25,000, the surplus is $10,000, and the deposits are $200,000, and this bank is recognized as one of the sound financial institutions of Washington County

On May 29, 1906, Mr Pfeiffer was united in marriage with Elsie Roberts, born in Arlington, a daughter of R E Roberts, who was a pioneer freighter of this region, who came here in the '50s, walking from St Joseph, Missouri, to Omaha, Nebraska Although a poor man when he came into the state he became wealthy and at the time of his death owned 2,000 acres of land and three elevators Mr and Mrs Pfeiffer have one son, Robert who is now attending the State University at Lincoln, Nebraska During the World war he served for two years, enlisting in the Sixth Nebraska Infantry, from which he was transferred to the One Hundred and Ninth Military Police, Thirty-Fourth Division He was sent to France and was there from October, 1918, until July, 1919. During the last three months he was in France he attended the University at Toulouse, and received credit for his work there when he entered the University of Nebraska

The Pfeiffer family attend the Congregational Church Mr Pfeiffer belongs to the Masonic order, and has served as master of his lodge for two years While he is a democrat he is inclined to be independent. For twenty-four years he has been an Odd Fellow, passed all of the chairs in the lower lodge and was district deputy grand master of the state Mr Pfeiffer was township clerk for two years and treasurer of the village, and has been on the School Board for the past nine years, but of recent years he has devoted the greater part of his time to his bank In addition to other honors conferred upon him, Mr Pfeiffer is president of the Men's Club of the Congregational Church Since Mr Pfeiffer assumed charge of the duties of cashier there has been a very material increase in the amount of business done by the bank, as at that time the deposits did not exceed $50,000, and the greater part of this expansion is the direct result of his own efforts He has always been greatly interested in Arlington and Washington counties, and his excellent common sense and sound financial judgment are so generally recognized and appreciated that his advice is generally asked before any movement of any importance is promulgated His standing is such that his approval of a measure is just about all that is needed to carry it through, but he will not sanction any lavish expenditure of the people's money, for he is conservative when it comes to finances Such men as Mr Pfeiffer exert a very constructive influence in their community and are a valuable addition to any locality

CHARLES E MAJERS Possibly there is no other vocation in which men are so certainly but quietly influential as journalism The printed thought that comes under the eye has a chance to make an appeal that circumstance and the spoken word might render ineffective, and the newspaper may have an audience of thousands where the speaker may not have hundreds Hence a grave responsibility rests with those who interpret the happenings of the world to others, be they of nation-wide interest or of affairs close at home This responsibility is felt and acknowledged by such able and experienced newspaper men as Charles E Majers, a well-known journalist, owner and editor of the Scribner Rustler, at Scribner, Nebraska

Charles E Majers was born in 1889, in Taylor County, Iowa, and is a son of Abner and Rosanna (Spencer) Majers He was reared on his father's farm and attended the neighborhood schools until fourteen years of age, when he entered the office of the Free Press, at Bedford, Iowa, to learn the newspaper business from the ground up. He remained with the Free Press for seven years, in various capacities, then went to Topeka, Kansas, where he remained with the Trapp Printing Company for the next eight years Mr Majers then bought the Monitor, at Harveyville, Kansas, conducted it one year and then went back to Iowa, and for the next seven and a half years was editor of the Moorhead Times, at Moorhead, in Monona County, Iowa, making that newspaper one of the most reliable mediums in the state. In December, 1919, Mr Majers came to Nebraska and purchased the office, good will and entire plant of the Scribner Rustler, which journal he has ably conducted ever since It is a large newspaper, non-political in policy, and is issued weekly. Mr Majers devotes his columns mainly to matters in which his large list of subscribers are most particularly interested, but nevertheless readers of the Rustler are kept well informed on all questions of world-wide importance In connection with his newspaper, Mr Majers has a well-equipped job office that turns out work that would be creditable to any printing establishment

During his residence at Topeka, Kansas, Mr Majers was united in marriage to Miss Jennie Ferrell, and they have one daughter, Helen L Mr. Majers has never had any political ambitions but as a watchful private citizen, with a sense of public responsibility, he works for what he believes the welfare of the country, state and city Personally he is genial and hospitable and those who make his acquaintance on coming to Scribner, are given a very favorable impression

NORMAN E SHAFFER Prominent in both business and public affairs at Hooper, Nebraska, is Norman E Shaffer, cashier of the First National Bank of Hooper, and a former member of the State Legislature He is a representative of one of the substantial old families of Dodge County that was founded here forty-four years ago Its members have been identified creditably with many of the developing agencies of this section, and few families are better or more favorably known

Norman E Shaffer was born in Dodge County, Nebraska, in 1884, and is a son of Jacob G and Eliza (Winey) Shaffer. Jacob G Shaffer was born in Pennsylvania October 18, 1848, a son of William T and Barbara Shaffer, natives of Germany They had four children John, Alice, Jacob G and Elizabeth, the only survivor being Jacob G, who lived in his native state until 1876 When a boy he earned his first money by picking stones from land that could not have been otherwise cultivated, then worked as a day laborer until 1868, when he was engaged to drive mules on the towpath along the canal, from that getting into regular canal-boat work, keeping on until he was first made boatswain and then captain At that time in his neighborhood in Pennsylvania, canal traffic was heavy and transportation by water was of more importance than now, when much of it is diverted to the railroads

Mr Shaffer left the canal in 1875 and in that year was married to Eliza Winey, who was also born in Pennsylvania On March 18, 1876, they came to Dodge County, Nebraska, renting a farm near Hooper, on which they lived until 1884, when Mr Shaffer bought 240 acres, where he carried on general farming and stock raising very profitably for many years He also owned a threshing outfit and did the most of the corn shelling in his neighborhood for a long time In 1913 he retired from the farm and moved to Hooper, where he is one of the men of ample fortune, interested in numerous sound business enterprises He is a stockholder in the Farmers Co-operative Company of Dodge County, and a stockholder in both the First National Bank and the Dodge County Bank at Hooper

To Jacob G Shaffer and his wife the following children were born: Dorsey, deceased, William V living in Lincoln, Nebraska, Harvey W., who farms the old homestead; John A, who served in a United States infantry regiment in the Great war and now with the Farmers Co-operative Company of North Bend, Norman E, cashier of the First National Bank of Hooper; Mary, who is connected with a business house at Hooper, May, a trained nurse in the Methodist Episcopal Hospital at Omaha, Stanley, in the Government employ, is a druggist by profession; Rose, a school teacher at Gordon, Nebraska, Clark, office man for the Avery Harvester Company of Omaha, and Jay, who is connected with a business house at York, Nebraska

Norman E Shaffer attended the local schools and assisted his father on the home farm until twenty-one years old, then, after a commercial and shorthand course at the Fremont Normal School, he became bookkeeper for the Farmers Co-operative store at Hooper, where he remained through 1907 and 1908, when he turned his attention again to agricultural pursuits and from 1909 until 1918 raised grain and fine livestock In the meanwhile he became prominent in democratic politics and in 1917 was elected to the State Legislature He proved able and capable as a statesman but political honors did not succeed in luring him from the business field, for which he is particularly well qualified, and in 1918 he came to the First National Bank, of which he is a director, and continues as cashier of this stable institution, of which his careful, conservative policy is a recognized asset

In 1909 Mr Shaffer was united in marriage with Miss Anna Antoinette Monnich, who was born in Dodge County, and they have three children, namely Donald, Charlotte and Cornelius Mr and Mrs Shaffer are members of Grace Lutheran Church Mr Shaffer is a

Scottish Rite Mason In all that concerns Nebraska and Dodge counties in particular he takes deep concern and although one of the younger men in the county's public affairs, has made a favorable impression as a fearless, upstanding citizen not afraid to defend his convictions on any subject, when convinced they are right and for the general welfare

JOHN N MONNICH, proprietor of the Monnich Garage, is one of the aggressive young business men of Fremont, and one who is held in high esteem by his competitors and the public generally on account of his fair treatment and good judgment He was born at Hooper, Nebraska, on January 26, 1885, a son of Herman and Margaret (Parkert) Monnich, natives of Iowa and Michigan, respectively, who were married in Dodge County, to which they had come about 1869 They are now living on their farm north of Hooper, their residence being one of the nicest country homes in the county Ever since coming to Nebraska Herman Monnich has been a farmer and stockman In politics he is a republican Mrs Monnich is a Catholic and Mr Monnich is a member of the Lutheran Church They became the parents of the following children George, who is on the home farm; John N, whose name heads this review, Bernard, who is also on the farm; Antoinette, who married Norman Shaffer, cashier of the First National Bank of Hooper, Edward, who lives at Oakland, California, was in the service during the late war for six or seven months, Ardelia, who is a trained nurse, lives at Akron, Ohio, and Clarence, who was in the service for nine months during the late war, was sent overseas, participating in four big drives and at present is living with his parents The paternal grandfather was Gerard Monnich, born in Germany

John N Monnich attended the rural schools of Dodge County and Highland Park, where he took a course in electrical engineering, afterward finishing in the Fremont Normal School Until he was nineteen years of age he was engaged in farming, but then with the money he had saved up, took his courses in electrical engineering Completing them he went into the automobile business at Hooper, holding an agency for the Ford cars As a partner in this business he had his paternal uncle, Bernard Monnich In 1912 he came to Fremont and established the Ford agency and built a large brick garage with a floor space of 28,000 square feet on its two floors in 1916 At present he owns this garage and one each at North Bend and Valley, Nebraska, being the second oldest Ford agent in Nebraska in point of service

In March, 1911, Mr Monnich was united in marriage with Bertha Olson of Fremont, a daughter of N. P Olson They have a daughter, Priscilla, who was born on April 13, 1912, and a son, John Charles, born November 10, 1920 Mr and Mrs Monnich belong to the First Congregational Church of Fremont Mr Monnich is a Knight Templar and thirty-second degree Mason and a member of the Mystic Shrine He also belongs to Fremont Lodge No 513, Benevolent and Protective Order of Elks, and other fraternal organizations A strong republican he is now serving as a member of the board of public works of Fremont

Beginning in a small way Mr Monnich has expanded his business until he owns several well-equipped garages in different communities and gives employment to thirty-five persons. His present prosperity has not come to him without effort, but it is all the more appreciated because it is the result of his energy, foresight and excellent judgment, and he is proud of it and the place he has gained in public esteem.

WILLIAM J CRANE There must be an immense amount of satisfaction to a man to be able to look back over a long and well-spent life and realize that he has attained not only to a material success, but that at the same time he has won and held the confidence and respect of business associates and social intimates William J Crane of Arlington, now enjoying the contentment of honorable retirement, has achieved more than ordinary success in his business ventures, and no man of Washington County stands any higher in public confidence

Mr Crane is a New Yorker, as he was born in Owego, Tioga County, New York, November 30, 1840, a son of John G and Sarah (Day) Crane, both of whom were born in New York State John G Crane was born in that state on February 9, 1809, a son of Henry Crane, a native of New Jersey, who moved to New York State at an early day and died at Wellsville, that commonwealth, having been a shoemaker by trade During the second war with England he served as a soldier, and his father was a soldier of the American Revolution Mrs Sarah Day Crane was born at Gilderland, Albany, New York, in 1799 Her father was a physician and a very wealthy man, owning a tract of land ten miles square and including much of the present City of Albany John H Crane and his wife were married in New York State on May 27, 1830 During his younger life he was a worker in the woolen mills of his native state, but later became a minister of the Methodist Episcopal Church and as such was stationed at different points, one being Blossburg, Pennsylvania, but for the most part he was in his native state, and he continued in the ministry for a long period, only leaving it when he had reached his seventy-fifth birthday. He and his wife had seven children, of whom three are now living, namely: Henry P, a retired business man, who has traveled considerably and is now living at Rochester, New York, Sarah, who married Joel Davis, a banker of fifty years' standing, lives at Blossburg, Pennsylvania; and William J, whose name heads this review When the slavery question was the living issue of his day John G Crane was a strong abolitionist, but later espoused the principles of the republican party For over sixty years he was an active member of the Independent Order of Odd Fellows

Growing up in his native state, William J Crane secured his educational training in the public schools, and was engaged in mercantile pursuits when he felt the urge of patriotism which prompted his enlistment in the Union army in August, 1861, as a member of Company H, Eighty-Fifth New York Volunteer Infantry, and served with his command until the battle of Fair Oaks, at which time he was wounded, the bullet passing through his left lung, and he has never recovered fully from its effects.

In 1858 Mr Crane went to Kansas for a period of two years, and then returned to New York, but during that time he acquired a love for the west, and so, in 1871, returned to it, but selected Arlington, Nebraska, as the location of his new home The first season he was there he raised a crop of corn but found that his health was not equal to the strain put upon it by agricultural pursuits, and so secured the position of station agent in the Arlington depot in 1872, and held it for three and one-half years In 1878 Mr Crane embarked in a banking business, and conducted it until 1886, when he went to Wyoming, although continuing to maintain his residence at Arlington He was interested in the oil fields of that state and was the first to take machinery into them Later he became interested in mining, this industry absorbing the major portion of his time and attention until his retirement The various ventures in which Mr Crane has been interested have proven very successful, and Mr. Crane has reaped abundantly from his business acumen and able handling of his large and varied affairs Always, from the organization of the Grand Army of the Republic, he has been a forceful factor in it, and since 1890 has been on the committee on the finances connected with the operation of the Old Soldiers' Homes

In 1865 Mr Crane was united in marriage with Miss Mary Harding, born in Tioga County, Pennsylvania, and they became the parents of one son, William H Crane, who was born on December 15, 1872 He was educated at Arlington and in Doane College, and following the completion of his education he returned to Arlington and established himself in a real estate business Still later he went to Colorado in order to homestead During the Spanish-American war he served as a soldier, but the war terminated before he was sent further south than Chickamauga Park Mrs Crane died in 1906, a consistent member of the Congregational Church, and Mr. Crane maintains his connection with that body This church organization was started in the Crane home, and Mr Crane is the only living charter member of it For over fifty years Mr. Crane has been an Odd Fellow, and organized the lodge of that order at Arlington in 1873 While he has always been very active in the republican party he has never aspired to office His residence at Arlington is one of the best in the city, and here he is living in comfort

Although handicapped almost at that most important period of a man's career, the beginning by his disability incurred during his military service Mr Crane has not allowed it to hamper him unnecessarily, but has gone straight ahead, rendering an efficient service, and bringing to bear on each undertaking, no matter how small, the full force of an unusually intelligent mind, with the result that in his declining years he occupies the place in his locality to which his abilities and accomplishments entitle him and there are few men who have as many warm, personal friends as he Generous in his contributions to civic undertakings Mr Crane has always advocated those improvements which his experience taught him were practical and not unduly extravagant, and his advice is generally sought before a movement is launched, for his fellow citizens rely on his judgment and desire his advocacy of a plan before it is placed before the public for decisive action Mr Crane is an inspiring example to the veterans of the late war of what can be accomplished by one who came out of his country's service in a much worse condition that when he went into it, and the young heroes of this generation, learning from him need not be discouraged but go ahead as did he, and rest assured that they, too, can attain to ample means and prestige among their fellows, provided of course that they are willing to put up a good fight against the obstacles that will of course rise in their path

W R Adams Among the self-made, substantial business men of Fremont is W R Adams, of the W R Adams Company, Incorporated, who came to the community some years ago Mr Adams was born in 1865 at Laurel, Indiana He is a son of W D and Nellie (Blue) Adams The father was born at Everton Indiana, while the mother came from Hamilton, Ohio They were married in Indiana and always lived there Mr. Adams was a farmer and also had a sawmill

There were six children in the family of W D Adams Only three are living today They are Lillian wife of B F Christy, a farmer near Oklahoma City, W R Adams; and Anna, wife of J. F. Kehoe of Clay City, Indiana, president of the Kehoe Preserving Company, which raises and preserve pimentos The parents have gone the way of the world W D Adams was a soldier in the Civil war and was in Morgan's raid through Kentucky He voted the republican ticket, and was a successful farmer and lumberman, as stated, owning a mill and getting out much building material in the days of the rural sawmills

The son, W. R Adams, was educated in the public school at Laurel and in the Terre Haute Normal School, and his first business opportunity was in the sawmill with his father Later he engaged in the butcher business in Indiana After coming to Nebraska in 1890 he worked on a farm for three or four years by the month until he saved enough to engage in the butcher business in Hastings in 1894 In 1896 he started traveling on the road buying hides and in 1898 bought a half interest in the firm he was traveling for and devoted his time to management of same This firm was the Hastings Hide and Tallow Company In 1900 Mr Adams purchased the other members' interests and conducted the business successfully until 1907 when he sold out and came to Fremont He then bought out J H Hoebner, who had the hide, fur and woolen business in Fremont

Mr Adams at once enlarged the business and the buildings by adding fifty feet and a second story. He buys and sells hides, furs and wool, shipping in carload lots to the Eastern markets He supplies tanneries with the hides and furs The W R Adams Company is incorporated as a $100,000 concern, and Mr Adams is its president and general manager He is a director in the Commercial Bank of Fremont and devotes all of his time to his business interests As a means of recreation he is an enthusiastic golf player, realizing that the efficient business man must have recreation

On June 1, 1899, Mr Adams married Gertrude Stilson She is a daughter of S T. Stilson and was born at Earlville Illinois Her people located in Cherry County, where they had a stock ranch Now, however, they live at Keisling, Washington, where they have a fruit ranch Mr and Mrs Adams are members of the Episcopal Church, while he belongs to the Benevolent and Protective Order of Elks, Knights of Pythias and is a Rotarian

WILLIAM E HILLIKER One of the successful business men of Fremont who has built up his present prosperity entirely through his own efforts, and at the same time secured for himself the place in his community to which he is entitled, is William E Hilliker. He was born at La Crosse, Wisconsin, on May 28, 1861, a son of William E and Cornelia (Stout) Hilliker, natives of Pennsylvania and Wisconsin, respectively They were married in Wisconsin, and it was from that state that William E Hilliker, the elder, enlisted in the Union army as a member of the Wisconsin Twenty-Second Volunteer Infantry, and was in the army for eighteen months, when he was honorably discharged

Following the close of the war he returned to Wisconsin and having previously learned the machinist trade in the shops of the Chicago Milwaukee & St Paul Railroad, worked at it in Milwaukee, Wisconsin Later he moved to Reno County, Kansas, and for a time continued to work at his trade, and then homesteaded near Hutchinson, Kansas Still later he moved to Red Oak, Iowa, where he died, his wife having passed away at La Crosse, Wisconsin They had four children, as follows: Maggie, who married a Mr Schwerin of Omaha, Nebraska, William E, whose name heads this review, Mark, who lives in California, and one who is deceased He was a member of the Methodist Episcopal Church, and his wife was a Catholic In politics he was a democrat, but he never took any active part in public affairs, being too much occupied with his own concerns

William E Hilliker, the younger, attended the public schools of Kansas and Iowa, and when still not much more than a lad began handling horses, and has continued in this line ever since In June, 1904 he located permanently at Fremont, erecting a large barn, with a comfortable residence nearby, and began to deal in horses and mules upon a very large scale Within recent years he opened up a commission business at Omaha, Nebraska, which makes the third time he has embarked in this line at Omaha, incorporating as the South Omaha Horse and Mule Company in 1912, and when he had the business well under way, sold at a profit in 1914 In 1917 he again sold a business he had built up, and in 1920 he incorporated as Hilliker & Simpson Mr Hilliker divides his time between Fremont and Omaha The firm sold to the United States, Italian and French governments over 73,000 head of horses and mules They handle about 2,500 per month at both places and sell locally

In March, 1884, Mr Hilliker was married to Catherine Talty, born in Cass County, Iowa, and they became the parents of the following children William, who is associated with his father in business, Blanche, who married A C Denney of Fremont; Laura and Nellie, both of whom are unmarried, and four who died in infancy Mrs Hilliker was a Catholic and died firm in the faith of her church on August 26, 1916, mourned by a wide circle of warm personal friends, as well as by her family Mr Hilliker belongs to Fremont Lodge No. 514, Benevolent and Protective Order of Elks In politics he is a republican

Frank Martin Haun An impressive instance of the power of innate energy, self-reliance, indomitable resolution and incessant perseverance in moulding an unaided career is manifest in the life of Frank Martin Haun, now a retired resident of Fremont, who during his active career was one of the most influential and extensive farmers of Dodge County, as well as one of its most prominent and useful citizens

Mr Haun was born in Houghton County, Michigan, December 11, 1867, and was still a lad when he accompanied his parents to Nebraska, a history of the family being found elsewhere in this work in the sketch of his father, John Haun Frank M. acquired a public school education and grew up in an agricultural atmosphere, and at the time that he attained his majority entered upon a career of his own, renting from his father a farm of eighty-seven acres After four year of renting he purchased 120 acres of farm land, and this proved the nucleus for his subsequent extensive operations which brought him steadily to the forefront as one of the large and successful agriculturists of his day and locality His good management and business foresight, his constant industry and his wise investments enabled him to accumulate a large and valuable property, and at this time he is the owner of 657 acres, of which 240 acres are in Maple Township, 340 acres in Cotterell Township and seventy-seven acres in Elkhorn Township Seventy acres are in pasture land, the rest being improved

While engaged in general farming, Mr Haun was also quite a feeder of cattle, maintaining a large herd of high-grade stock He likewise raised chickens to a considerable extent In all of his agricultural work he displayed a progressive spirit that manifested itself in his willingness to give a trial to new methods and inventions and to adopt them if they proved practicable While Mr Haun's success was remarkable, it was gained in a strictly legitimate manner, and his associates have always known him as a man of the highest integrity In 1919 he decided that he had done his share of hard work and accordingly turned over active labors to younger hands and shoulders and moved to Fremont, where he had purchased a pleasant modern home at 1255 North Brand Street Here he has shown an intelligent and helpful interest in civic affairs and has demonstrated himself as ready to give his support to all worthy movements

Mr Haun was married February 10, 1890, to Miss Anna Edam, and to this union there have been born three children Mrs. Ottilene Waywood of Dodge County, Mrs Olga Emanual, residing near Webster, in Pleasant Valley Township, and Anna, who died in infancy. Mrs Haun is a member of the Christian Church, while Mr Haun is a Catholic In political views Mr and Mrs. Haun are democrats During his residence in the county Mr Haun served on the School Board and as treasurer thereof for twelve years He also took an important part in the Liberty Loan drives in his county during the war period His only fraternal connection with the Knights of Columbus

EDWARD F. LANGHORST In the Township of Nickerson in Dodge County one of the capable, upright and progressive farmers is Edward F Langhorst, whose home is in section 13, and whose affairs as a farmer and citizen deserves consideration in this publication

Mr Langhorst was born in Washington County, Nebraska, in 1877 His father, Otto Langhorst, was a native of Germany and was one of the earliest settlers in this section of Nebraska. He prospered as a homesteader and land owner, and of whom complete mention is made on other pages of this volume Edward F Langhorst grew up in a home of more than average comfort, acquired a substantial education, and started life for himself at the age of twenty-eight He bought some land from his father and at the present time owns 160 acres thoroughly improved and operated as a general crop and stock farm

February 14, 1907, Mr Langhorst married Miss Lizzie Lallman, who was born and reared in Washington County, where her people were early settlers Mr and Mrs Langhorst have two children, Florence and Mabel, both at home.

In addition to looking after his farm Mr Langhorst has taken much interest in church and public affairs, serving as township clerk for a long period of years He is a republican voter and he and his wife are members of the Lutheran Church

FRANK THEODORE UEHLING The career of the honored Dodge County pioneer, the late Theodore Uehling, in whose honor the Town of Uehling was named, is the subject of a separate article in this work. A son of Theodore, and his wife Catherine (Schwab) Uehling, is Frank Theodore Uehling, who now owns the old family homestead He has lived there all his life, and was born at the home place October 26, 1877.

During his boyhood he attended the local public schools and in preparation for a serious vocation as an agriculturist and stock man attended two sessions of the State Agricultural College For five years he managed the home place for his parents, and subsequently bought out the interests of the other heirs and has given the old farm distinction as one of the centers of pure bred livestock in Northern Dodge County He has bought an additional 160 acres, making 320 acres This is

C. L. Dudley. Ina B. Dudley

known as the Oak Hill Stock Farm and is one of the model farms pointed out to visitors in Dodge County

September 12, 1908, Mr Uehling married Miss Bertha Pauline Von Seggern She was born in Dodge County where her parents, Henry and Sophia (Brockhus) Von Seggern were pioneer settlers, they having come from Germany Mr and Mrs. Uehling have five children: Thelma A., Raymond F., Lucile H., Wilma L., and Frank Theodore, Jr Mr Uehling is a stanch republican in politics. He has served as township treasurer, is secretary of the Farmers' Co-operative and Mercantile Association of Uehling, a member of the school board, and is a member of Oakland Lodge No. 91, Ancient Free and Accepted Masons

CHARLES L DUDLEY With attractive appointments and large and select stock, the Dudley Music Store figures as one of the popular and prosperous retail establishments in the City of Fremont Here is found a general line of musical instruments, sheet music in required variety and scope, and the various supplemental stock that marks a high grade musical emporium of modern facilities

Mr Dudley began selling musical merchandise soon after leaving college He was very fortunate in his marriage, Mrs Dudley being an accomplished musician as well as a thorough-going housewife and mother, and since they came to Fremont she has been closely associated with every phase of the developing business

Mr Dudley was born in Seward, County, Nebraska, October 14, 1882, son of Rolland and Senith (Ogden) Dudley, the former a native of Kendallville, Indiana, and the latter of the State of Ohio They were married at Weeping Water, Cass County, Nebraska, Rolland Dudley having come to Nebraska in 1868, about a year after the admission of the state to the Union He took up and improved a homestead in Seward County where eventually he became the owner of a large and valuable landed estate and was long one of the representative farmers of the county He is now living virtually retired, he and his wife having a pleasant home in University Place, a suburb of the City of Lincoln Of the six children all are living except one, and of the number the oldest is Raymond, an accountant in the employ of Amour & Company at Sioux City, Iowa, Charles L comes next in order of birth; Lulu at home, Eugene and Clarence engaged in the automobile business at Hastings, Adams County The parents are members of the Methodist Episcopal Church, while the father is a republican in politics and is affiliated with the Modern Woodmen of America. He and his wife are numbered among the honored pioneer citizens of Nebraska

Charles L Dudley acquired his early education in the public schools, including the high school at Ulysses, Butler County In 1900 he graduated from Nebraska Wesleyan University at University Place For the eleven subsequent years he was in the employ of the Matthews Piano Company of Lincoln After severing his association he was for a short time engaged in the general merchandise business at Glenwood, Iowa In 1915 he established himself in the music business at Fremont, where he has built up a substantial and prosperous enterprise and is numbered among the city's representative business men of the younger generation

Both Mr and Mrs Dudley are stanch republicans and take loyal interest in the furtherance of its cause Mrs Dudley cast her first vote for Mr Harding The only official position he has held was as a member of the Municipal Council while a resident of Glenwood, Iowa. Mr and Mrs. Dudley are active members of the Methodist Episcopal Church Fraternally he is a Knight Templar Mason, affiliated with the Modern Woodmen of America and the Brotherhood of American Yeomen

March 15, 1905, was marked by the marriage of Mr. Dudley to Miss Ina Finch She was born in Troy, Wisconsin, June 20, 1881, daughter of Charles L. and Clara L (Brigham) Finch, both natives of Wisconsin, who removed to Lincoln, Nebraska, in 1888 Her father was an engineer on the Burlington Railway for about twenty-three years and subsequently in the real estate business and also operated a hotel at Wahoo and York, Nebraska, until his death which occurred in 1917 at the age of sixty-seven Mrs Finch who is a member of the Reformed Church makes her home at Fremont Mrs Dudley was about seven years old when brought to Nebraska, was educated in the grammar and high schools of Lincoln, spent three years in the Nebraska School of Music and the old L Street Conservatory of Lincoln, and had private instruction as well She took a business course and was a stenographer in the music department of the Matthews Piano Company at Lincoln when she became acquainted with Mr Dudley She taught music for about three years in Glenwood Iowa When they opened their store in Fremont in 1915, Mrs. Dudley took an active share in the work and fully shares in the credit with her husband for building up the business Mrs Dudley possesses much real business ability, is a thorough musician, and individually and through the store has contributed much to the raising of sound musical standards They now have the leading general music store in Fremont, and their business is widely extended, since four traveling salesmen represent the establishment over a large Nebraska territory Mr. and Mrs Dudley have two children, Lavone and Charles

Ray Nye Throughout the great Middle West, more especially mayhap in Nebraska and Iowa, the name of Nye is synonymous with enterprise, influence and prosperity, in the grain marts and lumber districts standing pre-eminent, one Theron Nye having been the founder and promoter of the very extensive and substantial grain and lumber business with which his son, Ray Nye, is now actively identified

Theron Nye was born July 26, 1828, in Brookfield, Madison County, New York, where his parents, Thomas and Anna (Goldsmith) Nye, located on migrating from New England to the Empire State The father, a soldier in the War of 1812, was a manufacturer of potash, but never accumulated great wealth Brought up in his native county, Theron Nye acquired a practical education in the public schools, and as a young man learned the druggist's trade He afterwards embarked in mercantile pursuits in Hubbardsville, New York, where he remained four years Early in 1857, responding to the lure of the then distant West, he bade farewell to his family, and on May 1, 1857, landed in Omaha, Nebraska, having come to that city from St Louis, Missouri, by boat He was variously employed for a very short time, but finding nothing that suited him in the line of employment, he came to Fremont on May 27, of that year, with a limited capital of $25 at his command.

Pre-empting 160 acres of land, Theron Nye embarked in agricultural pursuits, and also engaged in freighting across the plains to Denver Hard working and thrifty, he accumulated some means, and in 1866 formed a partnership with S B Colson, J T. Smith and J G Smith, and embarked in the lumber and grain business as head of the firm of Nye, Colson & Company, to which William Fried was subsequently admitted and from which the Smith brothers withdrew. In 1884 Mr Nye sold his interests in the business to his son Ray, and in 1887 this firm together with two others was consolidated and the Nye, Wilson, Morehouse Company was incorporated, later becoming the Nye, Schneider, Fowler Company, which operates grain elevators in seventy Nebraska, Iowa and South Dakota towns, along the lines of the principal railways of those states

Active and prominent in advancing the interests of Fremont, his home city, Theron Nye was one of the organizers of the First National Bank of Fremont, and served as its president during the first fourteen years of its existence A republican in politics, he served as mayor of Fremont two terms, and was county treasurer of Dodge County an equal length of time After his retirement from the firm of Nye, Colson & Company, he lived a comparatively quiet life in Fremont until his death, which occurred on March 6, 1901

The marriage of Theron Nye and Caroline M Colson was solemnized in New York State on May 22, 1853. Two sons blessed their union, as follows: Fred, who has passed to the life beyond, was a prominent journalist, having served on the staff of the New York World several years, and prior to that having edited the Omaha Republican, and Ray, of this sketch The mother survived her husband a number of years, living in Fremont until her death

Born in Fremont, Nebraska, October 7, 1861, Ray Nye was educated in the Fremont schools, and when a boy of fifteen years entered the office of Nye, Colson & Company as bookkeeper, a position that he ably filled for six years, gaining in the time valuable business knowledge and experience In 1882 he was admitted to partnership in the concern, and in 1884 bought his father's interests in the business Three years later that firm consolidated with the firms of W R. Wilson & Company and B F Morehouse & Company, and was incorporated as the Nye, Wilson, Morehouse Company In 1890 Messrs Nye and R. B Schneider purchased the interests of Messrs Wilson and Morehouse, and Mr Nye was made president of the new firm of the Nye & Schneider Company, later the Nye, Schneider, Fowler Company which operates 200 or more elevators in Nebraska, Iowa, Kansas, South Dakota, and annually handles millions upon millions of bushels of grain, and operates extensive lumber yards in different cities of Nebraska and nearby states.

Mr Nye has other interests of importance and value, and for a number of years has been a large stockholder, and the president of the Omaha Printing Company, one of the most extensive printing and stationery manufacturing concerns in the West. He has been an important factor in promoting the highest interests of Fremont, the city in which his entire life has been spent, and although he is a prominent member of the republican party, he has never held any public office, his entire time and attention having been devoted to his business affairs Fraternally he is a member of the Ancient Free and Accepted Order of Masons, belonging to Lodge, Chapter, Commandery, and Shrine

On November 22, 1883, Mr Nye was united in marriage with Miss Annie End, of Sheboygan, Wisconsin. Their only child, George Theron, born August 30, 1884, died June 20, 1886

EDWARD R STEWART, M D Distinguished not only as the longest established physician and surgeon of Blair, but for his professional success, and his high standing as a man and a citizen, Edward R

Stewart, M D, is a fine representative of the medical fraternity of Washington County, and eminently worthy of the respect and esteem so generally accorded him A son of the late John G Stewart, he was born in Center County, Pennsylvania, April 8, 1862

Born and reared at Spruce Creek, Pennsylvania, John G Stewart acquired a good education when young, and being an intelligent reader kept in touch with the topics of the day throughout his life In 1867 he moved with his family from Tyrone, Pennsylvania, to Moweaqua, Illinois, where he bought land, and was engaged in tilling the soil many years Going, in 1883, to Union Star, Missouri, he improved a farm, and there both he and his wife spent their remaining days He was a republican in politics, and a member of the Presbyterian Church, to which his wife likewise belonged Of the nine children born of their union, eight grew to years of maturity, and four are living, as follows Maggie B., wife of S H Shomers, a general merchant of Linwood, this state; John, of Urbana, Illinois, a retired farmer, Abraham E, a retired farmer, lives at Nickerson, Nebraska; and Edward R, of this sketch One of their sons, Samuel Stewart, served in the Civil war from 1863 until the surrender at Appomattox

Edward R Stewart received his preliminary education in Illinois, and after attending the State Normal School about a year then taught in the public schools for a time, and entered the Missouri Medical College, at St Louis, Missouri, which at that time was a department of the Missouri State University, and was there graduated in 1887 with the degree of Doctor of Medicine

Coming directly to Nebraska, Doctor Stewart located at Linwood, Butler County, where he remained for four years, his practice being extensive Coming from there to Blair in 1891, the doctor soon won a position among the leading physicians and surgeons of Washington County, and through his professional skill and ability which are recognized and appreciated, has maintained it until the present writing While living in Linwood, he managed a drug store, and in Blair he is owner of the Stewart Pharmacy, which is now managed by his son, John H

In January, 1889, Doctor Stewart was united in marriage with Estelle Diefendorf, who was born in New York State, where her parents spent the major part of their lives, her birth having occurred in Canajoharie Five children have blessed their union, namely Ethel, who completed her early studies in Rockford, Illinois, is now teaching in Riverton, Wyoming, being engaged in primary and second grade work, John Harold, in charge of the Stewart Pharmacy, is a graduate of the Blair High School, Donald D, of Milwaukee, Wisconsin, enlisted in the World war October 1, 1917, trained at Camp Cody, went across in July, 1918, joined the Thirty-second Division as replacement man, was in action on three fronts, Chateau Thierry, Soissons, and the Argonne Forest, and after receiving his discharge in June, 1919, returned home, and Keith Edward and Kenneth Arthur, twins, both pupils in the Blair High School.

The doctor is a member of the State Medical Society, and of the Washington County Medical Society, which he has served as president He is independent in politics, casting his vote for the best men and measures regardless of party restrictions, and has served for a term as member of the Blair City Council Fraternally he is a member of the Ancient Free and Accepted Order of Masons, of the Knights of Pythias, and of other fraternal and social organizations Mrs Stewart and her children are members of the Congregational Church

JOHN H. WITT deserves a long and worthy memory in Dodge County for the part he played as a pioneer, developing and improving land that never before had borne the crops of civilization. He was a good citizen in every respect apart from his industry and success as a business man He favored those institutions and improvements that raised the standard of living in the community

His life record began in Holstein, Germany, in 1836, and after getting a common school education he served an apprenticeship as a carpenter and as a journeyman he traveled about and saw much of many European communities before he came to the United States in 1865 His first location was at Freeport, Illinois, but in 1868 he crossed the Missouri River and homesteaded eighty acres in Dodge County He married about that time, but for a year kept his residence in Omaha where he worked at his trade He moved out to his land in 1869, and he and his bride endured a rather lonely existence, since their little frame house had only one other residence between it and Fremont twenty-five miles away. He worked hard, proved thrifty and saw his affairs prosper, and at the time of his death in June, 1911, he was owner of 600 acres, constituting a highly valuable estate He was also active in association with his fellow farmers and for twenty-five years served as treasurer of the Farmers Club. Politically he acted with the democratic party and as a member of the Lutheran Church

His first wife, whom he married in 1868, was Sophie Meeves She died the mother of four children Mrs Amelia Peters, of Scribner; Henry, of Scribner; John Witt Miller, of Leigh, Nebraska, and one that died in infancy For his second wife John H' Witt married Anna Paulsen, and to their union were born fourteen children, six of whom died in infancy, the others being Mrs Emma Diedrichsen, of Scribner, Dr. Bernhard, a veterinary surgeon at Scribner, Rudolph, who served as a soldier in the World war; Mrs B Diedrichsen, of Scribner; Arnold Reinhold in Ohio, Mrs Erna Kellner, Scribner, and Ewald at home

JOE S COOK One of the first names to appear in the pioneer annals of the Blair community in Washington County is that of Cook Several of the family have lived here as honored residents and one of them is Joe S Cook, now retired, who was a gallant Union soldier in the Civil war, came to Washington County, Nebraska, a few years later, and has lived here more than half a century Mr Cook has always sustained the character of a substantial and successful business man and the honors and responsibilities accorded him as a citizen comprise nearly all the offices in the gift of his home township and county

Mr Cook was born in Pennsylvania September 8, 1841, and is now in the shadow of his eightieth birthday His parents, John and Eliza (Shoup) Cook were also native Pennsylvanians and in 1868 came out to Nebraska and homesteaded in Washington County, where they lived out their years. The father was a republican and both parents were identified with the Presbyterian Church Of their large family of eleven children, eight are still living Mrs T F Martin, whose late husband was a deputy county clerk of Washington County, Jane of Pender, Nebraska, Rebecca, widow of James Hayes and now living in one of the western states; Sue, widow of Doctor Love, a resident of Carroll, Nebraska, Amelia, a widow living at Indiana, Pennsylvania, Joe S; James, a painter and paper hanger at Pender, Nebraska, and Harriet, also of Pender.

Joe S. Cook during his youthful days in Pennsylvania had only limited opportunities to acquire a public school education He found tasks to busy himself on the farm and in a country district, and was not twenty years of age when the war broke out He enlisted in April, 1861, at the very beginning of the struggle, joining Company F of the Eighth Pennsylvania Reserves He fought for the flag of the Union three years, until honorably discharged May 30, 1864 Mr. Cook was in some of the greatest battles of the war in Virginia, including Second Bull Run, South Mountain, Antietam, Fredericksburg the wilderness where he was on duty for twelve successive days, and also participated in the seven days fighting around Richmond He was captured there, and for three or four months was confined in a Southern prison

His patriotic duty discharged, Mr Cook returned to Pennsylvania and in 1868 came West to Washington County, Nebraska, where he improved a homestead, shared with other pioneers in the hardships and vicissitudes of the early years, and in all his varied relationships has shown a prompt readiness to discharge his duties to the best of his ability.

Mr Cook has been a resident of Blair since 1879, and is now one of the oldest residents of that community In November, 1865, when he had been out of the army about a year he married Miss Harriet C Gates, also a native of Pennsylvania, where her parents, Peter and Nancy (Benner) Gates spent all their lives Mrs Cook is a member of the Methodist Episcopal Church while Mr Cook still gives his preference to the church in which he was reared, the Presbyterian He is affiliated with the Independent Order of Odd Fellows and has long been prominent in the Grand Army of the Republic and is Past Commander of the local post In politics he has been stanchly aligned with the republican party since casting his first vote during the Civil war Besides all the local offices of his community, Mr Cook was for two terms a member of the board of county commissioners, was also county treasurer, county clerk two terms, and for a number of years served as clerk of the district court He has been deeply interested in the welfare of local schools and for twenty-two consecutive years served as a member of the home school board

Mr. and Mrs Cook had four children, three of whom are still living The oldest is Mrs T. F Martin, now deputy county clerk The second, Miss Mary, has for over twenty years been cashier of the banking house of E Castetter, at Blair The only son, William P Cook, is cashier of a bank at Calhoun, Nebraska

Aaron W Murphy A man of versatile talents, Aaron W. Murphy, of Fremont, has been variously employed since locating in Dodge County, and has contributed his full share in advancing its agricultural, industrial and material interests Beginning life for himself poor in pocket, but rich in energy, he has met with well deserved success in his undertakings, and obtained a noteworthy position among the useful and esteemed citizens of his community A son of Isaac Murphy, he was born May 23, 1864, in Grant County, West Virginia

A native of West Virginia, Isaac Murphy succeeded to the occupation of his ancestors, and carried on general farming for a number of years During the latter part of the Civil war, he enlisted in the Union Army, and was killed very soon after his enlistment He married Jemima C Crites, who was born in West Virginia, and they became the parents of one child, Aaron W Murphy, with whom this sketch is

Henry Rebbe

chiefly concerned The mother subsequently married for her second husband T Reel, and of that union had three children, all of whom live in West Virginia, where her death occurred in 1913. The father was a republican in politics, and both he and his wife belonged to the Lutheran Church

Educated in the rural schools of his native state, Aaron W Murphy remained on the farm until attaining his majority Anxious to try the hazard of new fortunes, he started westward, and on February 7, 1885, made his first appearance in Fremont, Nebraska He first found employment in a dairy, and later followed the carpenter's trade a while, after which he worked in a foundry for three months Trying to better his fortunes, Mr. Murphy subsequently teamed for a time, and then took contracts for putting up hay, keeping busily employed at something all of the time Resuming the occupation to which he was reared, he rented a tract of land, and when he had accumulated a sufficient sum to warrant him in so doing, he bought land, and though he has always lived in Fremont, engaged in farming More recently, in association with his son, Mr Murphy has been extensively and prosperously engaged in the sand business, which has proved a paying proposition, while as a farmer and stock raiser he is meeting with equally good success

Mr Murphy married, in 1884, Carrie E Parks, a native of West Virginia, and of their union three children, triplets, were born, one of whom, a boy, died at the age of two years, and two are living, namely Leander Smith Murphy, formerly in the Government employ at Fort Logan, is now in the sand business with his father, and Leona, in the employ of Cain & Johnson, lawyers

Politically Mr Murphy is identified with the republican party, and for five years served ably in the City Council, resigning therefrom to accept his present position as county supervisor, an office which he has filled satisfactorily for the past fourteen years, a record of service bespeaking his ability and fidelity Religiously he is a member of the Christian Church, to which Mrs Murphy likewise belongs, and fraternally he belongs to the Modern Woodmen of America

HENRY REBBE While Henry Rebbe came to Dodge County in the early '70s and became one of the largest land and property owners, his life had a wide range of interest and activity outside the county He had the spirit of a pioneer, willing to undergo labor and risk and hardship, and was a splendid example of the stalwart Americanism that subdued the western half of the continent.

He was born in Hanover, Germany, May 12, 1841 His parents were poor and small farmers in the old country While Henry had the regular common school education of Germany, his life from early youth was one of regular toil He was nineteen years old when in 1860 he crossed the ocean to New York and for about two years he was a fireman on steamships making several voyages from New York to European ports Following that for about a year he clerked in a store in New York City

At that time the Great West was a country largely unexplored and unknown and presented every variety of fascination for the youth of energy Henry Rebbe responded to the call of the wild in 1863 and went to Montana, where gold had been recently discovered, and where a territorial organization was perfected by the first pioneers in that year He staked out a gold mining claim in Stinking Creek District at what is now Virginia City He remained there about six years, and when he sold his interests in 1869 he left with a modest fortune to his credit Having spent nearly ten years engaged in strenuous work he took a well earned vacation, returned to Germany, and there met and on September 12, 1871, married Miss Wilmina Siever She was born in Germany January 12, 1853

In March, 1872, the bride and groom set sail for the United States and this time Mr. Rebbe came direct to Dodge County, Nebraska He bought 320 acres of prairie land in Maple Township. Financially he was in a better situation than many of the early settlers, and his first home was a comfortable frame house and much above the average of the type found in Dodge County fifty years ago In handling the resources of the soil he was as successful as he had been as a miner, and from year to year he saw his possessions broaden and expand, until at the time of his death he was said to be the heaviest tax payer in the county. He owned 2,440 acres of good land, most of it in Dodge County, and also financially interested in banks and had other properties He was one of the hard working citizens of Dodge County for over thirty years. With the approach of his seventieth birthday, he began arranging his affairs so as to turn the active management of his lands over to his sons, and he bought a pleasant home in the village of Hooper. He was denied the privilege of occupying it and enjoying a few years of leisure He was stricken and after three days died on March 22, 1908 He was a faithful member of the Lutheran Church, and altogether one of the very constructive citizens of Dodge County

The children born to Mr. and Mrs Rebbe were. Henry C., the oldest, now makes his home with his mother and sister at Hooper and assists in looking after the large estate, Louis J, a prominent Dodge County farmer, concerning whom an article appears on other pages, Oscar and Emma, both deceased; August, a Dodge County farmer, also mentioned elsewhere, and Katherine at home with her mother Mrs Rebbe, who was the faithful companion of her husband for thirty-seven years, since his death has lived in the pleasant home at Hooper, has shown much skill and good judgment in the management of her business affairs and she and her son and daughter are active in local societies and other events of the village community

John O Milligan, Sr A prominent family of Dodge County, Nebraska, bears the name of Milligan, and it has belonged to this state for over a half century During this period of great development, it has been continuously identified with leading interests in Dodge and other counties. A well known member of this important family is John O Milligan, Jr, who is one of the foremost business men of Scribner He was born here in 1878, and is a son of John O and Kate L. (Neff) Milligan.

John O Milligan, Sr, was born in Stark County, Ohio, in 1840 His parents were Joseph and Rebecca S (Winner) Milligan, the former of whom was born in Ohio and the latter in Delaware Joseph Milligan was a farmer in Ohio until 1850, when he moved to Illinois John O. Milligan, Sr, was reared on the home farm but was afforded educational advantages that included a course in Union College, Ohio In 1862 he enlisted for service in the Civil war, entering Company C Ninety-third Illinois Volunteer Infantry, was wounded in action near Memphis, Tennessee, and was honorably discharged in 1865 He returned to Illinois but in 1868 came to Nebraska and homesteaded in

Dodge County, proved up, and mainly devoted his attention to raising stock until 1877. In that year he came to Scribner and opened a general mercantile store, in which he continued to be interested until 1890 He had many additional interests, being a man of unusual business enterprise He became interested in the grain business and in lumber, starting a lumber yard at Wayne, in Wayne County, and in 1884 built a flour mill at Wakefield He was president of the Farmers & Merchants Bank, of Scribner, for a number of years, and was a director of the Farmers & Merchants Bank of Fremont for thirty-eight years For years he was prominent in republican politics in Dodge County and was a member of the State Legislature from 1905 until 1907. Failing eyesight caused his practical retirement from business but he remains one of the most highly esteemed residents of Scribner

John O Milligan was married in 1865 to Kate L Neff, who was born in Muskingum County, Ohio, and the following children were born to them· J L, who is a railroad man in Oklahoma, Glenn J, who lives retired at Redlands, California· John O, who is a merchant at Scribner, Granville W, who died in Mexico, was treasurer of the Pan-American Railroad there, Emmett, who operates the old Milligan ranch in Dodge County, Rena, who resides at Scribner; Dora M, who is the wife of August Jaiser, who is an insurance and real estate broker at Kansas City, Gertrude B, who is teaching school in Wyoming; and Emma, who is the wife of Emil Horseman, with the Rocky Mountain Fuel Company, at Denver, Colorado The mother of the above family is a member of the Methodist Episcopal Church The father belongs to the Grand Army of the Republic post at Scribner

John O Milligan, Jr, was mainly educated in the public schools at Wakefield, and the normal school at Fremont From 1890 until 1905 he was associated with his father in the milling, grain and livestock business at Wakefield In 1910 he bought the Milligan mercantile interests at Scribner, since which time he has devoted himself mainly to the management of this enterprise, which has grown to large proportions through his progressive methods He employs nine people in his store and implement department

In 1910 Mr Milligan was united in marriage to Miss Maggie Steiper, who was born in Dodge County and is a daughter of John Steiper, a prominent resident of Scribner, and they have four children, namely, John O, Harlan, Arline and Burdette Mrs Milligan is a member of the Congregational Church In politics, Mr Milligan has always been identified with the republican party At times he has served in local offices and at present is a member of the town board In addition to other business interests, Mr Milligan is a stockholder in the First National Bank of Scribner, and also in the Farmers & Merchants Bank of Fremont An honorable, upright business man and connected only with enterprises of worth, he stands as a representative citizen of his native county and state

CHRISTOPHER CUSACK was a pioneer of Dodge County, coming to this section of Nebraska half a century ago, and during his lifetime achieving all the success and honor of business and good citizenship For a great many years he was closely identified with the financial affairs of the county

He was born May 10, 1848, at Moffat, Ontario, Canada, and practically all his mature life was spent in Nebraska When he came West in 1869 he performed among other duties those of section foreman on the line of the Union Pacific Railroad in Wyoming From that modest station in life he rose through his own ability and efforts until he became one of the substantial capitalists and influential citizens of Dodge County In the earlier period of his residence at North Bend he developed a prosperous business in the buying and shipping of hogs, and later became a dealer in lumber and agricultural implements

In July, 1886, Christopher Cusack was elected cashier of the First National Bank of North Bend, after having served for some time previously as a member of its board of directors He continued his efficient service as cashier until 1905, when he became president of the institution Of that position he continued the incumbent until November, 1912, when he resigned owing to his seriously impaired health, and his death occurred in the following month The entire community united in an expression of its sense of loss in the passing of a citizen who had merited the fullest measure of confidence and esteem and who had contributed much to the civic and material advancement of his home town and county His political allegiance was given to the republican party, and in a fraternal way he was affiliated with the Masonic Order and the Ancient Order of United Workmen

Christopher Cusack married Eliza J Scott, who was born in the City of Philadelphia, Pennsylvania, August 28, 1858, and still maintains her home at North Bend, where she is an earnest member of the United Presbyterian Church of the city. Mrs Cusack's parents were pioneers of Dodge County, and some other facts regarding their early residence and activities are detailed on other pages of this publication

Of the four children of Christopher Cusack the oldest is John S, identified with a leading commission firm at Denver, Colorado, Roy J, his father's successor as a banker and his career is sketched elsewhere, Harry C is assistant cashier of the First National Bank of North Bend and Marie I is the wife of Russell R Goody, cashier of the Montrose National Bank of Montrose, Colorado

Roy J Cusack, who is cashier of the First National Bank of North Bend, Dodge County, succeeded his honored father as executive head of this substantial financial institution, of which he had previously been cashier, and his own life has contributed to the civic and business prestige of a family name long one of prominence and influence in Dodge County The part played by his father, the late Christopher Cusack, in Dodge County, is found on the preceding page

Roy J Cusack was born at North Bend May 24, 1882, and in the public schools of his native town continued his studies until he had profited by the advantages of the high school He also attended the United Presbyterian College at Tarkio, Missouri, and after completing his education began a business career as assistant cashier of the First National Bank of North Bend Subsequently he was promoted to cashier and that office he filled until the retirement of his father in 1912, when he was elected president This representative bank of Dodge County has a capital of $50,000, with surplus and profits aggregating $30,000, and its deposits are now in excess of $400,000

Mr Cusack takes a lively interest in all things touching the welfare of his home village and county and is a liberal and progressive citizen and enterprising young business man His political faith is that of the republican party. He is affiliated with the Masonic Order and the Mystic Shrine also with the Independent Order of Odd Fellows and the Modern Woodmen of America He was reared in the faith of the

United Presbyterian Church and his wife is an earnest communicant of the Protestant Episcopal Church

September 18, 1919, he married Miss Adys Huberle, who was born at Nebraska City She has become a popular factor in the representative social activities of North Bend They have one son, David

JAMES R SMITH Washington County offers many instances of remarkable business expansion, but in every case upon investigation it is found that the men who have achieved such prosperity have been those who have been willing to work hard for it, and have not sought to get something for nothing James R Smith, senior member of the dependable firm of Smith Brothers, implement dealers of Blair, is one of the men of Nebraska who belongs to the above-mentioned class, and his success is not confined to commercial circles for he has been honored by election to public office at the hands of his appreciative fellow citizens

James R Smith was born in County Fermanagh, Ireland October 10, 1852, a son of Richard and Florence A (Fife) Smith, both of whom were born in the same county as their son They left Ireland in 1882, and coming to the United States located at Burlington, Iowa, where they spent the remainder of their lives In his native land Richard Smith was a gun and lockmaker, but lived practically retired after reaching this country He and his wife had nine children, of whom the following four survive James R, whose name heads this review, Edward Robert, born January 4, 1858, came to the United States with his parents, having been educated in Ireland and taught the gunmaking trade, located at Blair in 1883, at first working for his brother, but is now a partner in the firm of Smith Brothers, and is unmarried, Emily, who married Dan Ryder, is now a widow residing at Burlington, Iowa, and Florence, who married Bert Hood, a mechanic of Burlington, Iowa The family all belonged to the Wesleyan Methodist Church. In politics Richard Smith was a conservative before leaving Ireland, but while he took an intelligent interest in public affairs in the United States, did not affiliate with any party here He and his family came to this country under much better conditions than many of their fellow countrymen, for he was a man of ample means, as he has been very successful as a business man, and so had been able to give his children excellent opportunities.

James R Smith attended the schools of his own country before the family's immigration, but learned the blacksmithing trade after his arrival in the United States Going to Greensburg, Ohio, he spent seven years in a blacksmith shop there, and in 1878 came to Blair, and followed blacksmithing for ten years, then, in 1888, he established himself in an implement business, and now he and his brother, in point of service, are the oldest implement dealers at Blair They carry a full and varied line of goods, and have built up a very wide connection, their trade showing a steady and healthy increase

In 1882 Mr Smith was married to Nellie H Stewart, who was born in Guelph, Canada, a daughter of Peter Stewart, who came to Washington County, Nebraska, at an early day, and here homesteaded His death, however, occurred in California, but his widow survives him and makes her home at Blair. Mr. and Mrs Smith have two children, namely Florence Maude, who is at home, and Grover Irwin, now a traveling salesman, is a veteran of the great war He came to Nebraska from Pennsylvania in order to volunteer from his native state, and enlisted in the Sixth Infantry, but was transferred to the quartermaster's department After two years of service he was honorably discharged with the rank of second lieutenant Mrs Smith is a member of the Congregational Church Well-known in Masonry, Mr Smith was entered as an apprentice August 15, 1885, became a fellowcraftsman, October 7, 1885, and was given the third degree November 10, 1885 He is now a Knight Templar, and has served his Commandery as eminent commander Mr Smith also belongs to the Woodmen of the World. In politics a democrat, he is one of the local leaders of his party, and was elected on its ticket commissioner of Washington County, and served for one term Keen, self-reliant and experienced Mr Smith knows his trade and how to supply its demands Having lived at Blair during its formative period, he takes a pride in the fact that he participated in its constructive work, and is anxious to further its growth in the future

C R MEAD, D D S The record of Dr C R Mead proves the value of persistent endeavor and the fact that no intelligent effort is lost He has so developed his natural faculties that today he is justly numbered among the leading practitioners of his learned profession and is recognized as one of the public-spirited men of Blair, where for some time he has been intimately identified with the development of this section of the state.

Doctor Mead was born at Marengo, Iowa, on June 16, 1869, a son of J. H and Ellen E (Kepner) Mead, natives of New York and Pennsylvania, respectively They were married at Marengo Iowa, and lived there during their early married life but then, in 1882 came to Blair, Nebraska, and before his death, which occurred some years later, he developed into a farmer and stockman of more than local prominence and a man of large means His widow survives him and makes her home at Blair They became the parents of four children, namely Guy K, who is manager of the Blair Garage Company of Blair, Gertrude, who is at home, Doctor C R, who was third in order of birth, and Ethel, who is at home The family are all devoted members of the Methodist Church The father belonged to the Masonic Order, the Grand Army of the Republic, and was a republican During the war between the North and the South, he served in the Twenty-fourth Iowa Volunteer Infantry until he was transferred to the Sixty-second United States Colored Infantry of which he was a lieutenant

Doctor Mead attended the public schools of Blair and Central City, Nebraska, and he studied dentistry in the Chicago College of Dentistry, from which he was graduated in 1898, and returning to Blair, entered at once on the practice of his calling Since then he has built up a large and valuable connection and is recognized as one of the leading dentists in this part of the state

In 1900 Doctor Mead was married to Eda Jones, born at Fontanelle, Nebraska The children born of this marriage are as follows: James, who is now in the preparatory school of the United States Navy at Newport, Rhode Island; and Robert, Elizabeth, and Paul, all of whom are attending school They are all members of the Methodist Episcopal Church Doctor Mead has been superintendent of the Methodist Episcopal Sunday School for twenty years He is a Royal Arch Mason, and belongs to the Knights of Pythias, serving as master of the former for one term and as chancellor of the latter for three terms, and represented the Blair Knights of Pythias at the grand lodge A very strong republican, Doctor Mead was the successful candidate of his party for mayor of Blair in 1908, the year that the city went dry He served fifteen years on the school board He has lived up to the highest standards of American citizenship, and deserves the consideration accorded him by those associated with him.

WILLIAM E BARZ In a comparative sense Nebraska is to be designated as one of the younger commonwealths of the Union, even though she has maintained the dignity of statehood for more than half a century, and it is gratifying to record that within her borders are now found many native sons whose loyalty and eligibility are shown in their incumbency of various offices of public trust In Dodge County Mr. Barz has maintained his home from the time of his birth, and here he has been called upon to serve in various official positions, including that of county clerk, of which he is the present efficient and popular incumbent

Mr Barz was born on a farm near Scribner, Dodge County, December 15, 1884, and is a son of Carl and Anna (Ollermann) Barz, both natives of Germany and both pioneers of Dodge County, where their marriage was solemnized Carl Barz was active in the development of farm industry in this county and after having been engaged in agricultural pursuits a number of years he operated a brick yard at Snyder, this county, for another term of years He finally purchased a farm in the State of Louisiana, and there he and his wife have resided since 1916, his attention being given mainly to the improvement and cultivation of his farm Of the two children William E of this review is the elder, and Ottilie is the wife of Walter Gustin, their home being now in the States of Louisiana

He whose name introduces this sketch acquired his preliminary education in the district schools of his native county, and thereafter he continued his studies in the Fremont Normal School and Business College After a due experience in connection with farm work he attended the public schools at Snyder, and in the meanwhile clerked in a local drug store Thereafter he served a few years as deputy postmaster at Snyder, and his later activities in that village were in the operation of a brick yard, besides which he gave considerable attention to the feeding of cattle for the market

After removing to Fremont, the county seat, he was appointed deputy county assessor and served in 1908-1909 His next occupation was in connection with a lumber yard and grain elevator at Snyder, and he has served as clerk in a number of the retail mercantile establishments of Snyder In 1912 he was appointed deputy county clerk and served until 1917 Mr. Barz was elected county clerk, and the best voucher for the ability he displayed in this office was that given in his re-election in 1918 He has given a very efficient administration of the multifarious affairs of this important county office and his service has met with unequivocal popular approval

Mr Barz has been unwavering in his support of the cause of the democratic party, and he is prominently affiliated with both the lodge and encampment bodies of the Independent Order of Odd Fellows, in which he has passed the various official chairs in both, and he is identified also with the Fraternal Order of Eagles

In 1908 Mr. Barz was united in marriage to Miss Mary Pateidl, who likewise is a native of Dodge County, and they have one child, Carl, who is a student in the Fremont schools

OTTO H. SCHURMAN, president of the Commercial National Bank of Fremont, one of the leading financial institutions of Dodge County, was a lad of ten years at the time of the family removal to Fremont, where he was reared to adult age and where his entire business career has been marked by close association with the bank of which he is now the executive head and of which his honored father was the founder and first president

Mr. Schurman was born at Pekin, Tazewell County, Illinois, August 12, 1870, and is a son of Ernest and Onnoline (Looschen) Schurman, who were born and reared in Germany and whose marriage was solemnized in the State of New York, whence they removed to Illinois in 1865, where the father was enabled to exchange his modest supply of gold coin and buy "greenbacks" with a material profit At Ottawa, that state, he made the application and filed the papers which resulted in his becoming a naturalized citizen of the land of his adoption, and it may well be said that no man proved more loyal and appreciative than did he, for in this country he found the opportunities that enabled him to achieve large and worthy success At Pekin, Illinois, this future banker found employment in a wagon and hardware establishment, at a salary of $75 a month, and he continued his residence in that state until 1880 In the meantime his earnest and well ordered activities in connection with business had resulted in the advancement of his financial prosperity, and when, in the year noted, he came to Fremont, Nebraska, he here established himself in the wholesale grocery business In addition to developing one of the leading wholesale industries of the vigorous little city he soon made his influence still more pronounced, by effecting the organization of the German-American Bank in 1889 The new institution received the fortifying power of his exceptional energy and business acumen and soon took rank with the foremost institutions of its kind in Dodge County. Eventually it was reorganized as the Commercial National Bank, and Mr Schurman continued as president of the institution until his death, at the age of fifty-five years, his wife having passed away at the same age and both having been earnest communicants of the Lutheran Church Mr Schurman had a capital of about $20,000 at the time of establishing his home at Fremont, and through his progressive business enterprise in Nebraska he accumulated a fortune that marked him as one of the wealthiest men of Fremont at the time of his death, even as he was one of the most loyal and respected citizens His political allegiance was given to the republican party, he was prominently affiliated with the Masonic fraternity and he held membership also in the Independent Order of Odd Fellows Of the three children, Otto H, of this review, is the eldest, Ernest A is engaged in the banking business at Elkhorn, Douglas County; and Rudolph B conducts a prosperous automobile business at Fremont

In the public schools of Fremont Otto H Schurman continued his studies until he had profited by the advantages of the high school, and thereafter he completed a course in a business college in this city He then became a bookkeeper in the bank established by his father, and his advancement came as a matter of efficient and faithful service rather than through paternal influence He passed on through the various stages of official promotion and finally, after the death of his father, he was made president of the institution The Commercial National Bank bases its operations on a capital stock of $100,000, has a surplus fund of equal amount, its undivided profits are fully $50,000, and its average deposits are in excess of $1,250,000 These figures bear their own significance as indicating the solidity and popularity of this old and well ordered banking institution, whose history has been one of conservative management and cumulative success

Henry Sprick

Sophie Sprick.

Though unwavering in his allegiance to the republican party and essentially progressive and public-spirited in his civic attitude, Mr Schurman has had no ambition for official preferment and has given close attention to his business affairs, rather than entering the arena of practical politics A deep student of the history and teachings of the time-honored fraternity, Mr Schurman has taken great satisfaction in his affiliation with the various bodies of both the York and Scottish Rites, in the latter of which he has the distinction of having received the thirty-third, or maximum, degree, the Red Cross of Constance, and Royal Order of Scotland He was raised to the sublime degree of Master Mason May 19, 1909, received the capitular degree on the 16th of the following October, was made a Knight Templar on the 20th of December of the same year, and received the thirty-second degree of the Ancient Accepted Scottish Rite on the 17th of March, 1910, while the final honor of the thirty-third degree was conferred November 26, 1917. Mr. Schurman was for many years actively identified with the Nebraska National Guard, from which he received his discharge November 5, 1892 He was treasurer of Fremont Lodge No. 15, Ancient Free and Accepted Masons, from 1912 to 1920, was high priest of the local chapter of Royal Arch Masons in 1914-15; was captain-general of Mount Tabor Commandry, No 9, Knights Templar, in 1915-16, having previously held the office of generalissimo of this commandary, and having served as its eminent commander in 1915-16 He was reared in the faith of the Lutheran Church, but is now a member of the Congregational Church, as is also his wife

In April, 1895, was solemnized the marriage of Mr Schurman to Miss Myra L Lee, daughter of Henry Lee, a prominent and influential citizen of Fremont Mr. and Mrs Schurman have three daughters: Lee Ottila is a student in Sweetbriar College, in the State of Virginia, as is also Phyllis, and Hortense Ruth is a student in the Fremont high school The family is prominently identified with the Congregational Church of Fremont, of which Mr Schurman is a trustee and also treasurer

Henry Sprick The early history of Fontanelle is intimately associated with the colony which in the spring of 1855 emigrated West from Quincy, Illinois, and made the first settlements on the prairie around what is now that thriving town One of the prominent men in the colony was the late Henry Sprick, whose early residence in Nebraska Territory and subsequent achievements as a business man and citizen, and all around wholesome character, entitle him to a special place in the history of his county.

Henry Sprick was born March 1, 1826, in Westphalia, Germany, and in 1853 settled at Quincy, Illinois, at that time a favorite colony of Germans He worked on the farm for a time, but in 1855 joined the party of about fifty people who set out from Quincy in prairie schooners drawn by oxen going to Washington County, Nebraska He was perhaps the only native German in the entire colony Nebraska was then a territory, and settlement was being attracted within the borders largely as a result of the tremendous and vital discussion going on in Congress over the Kansas-Nebraska bill Henry Sprick made several trips back and forth between the Nebraska colony and Quincy, and in 1858 he returned to Quincy to marry Sophie Wilkening She was born in Germany May 30, 1837, and came with her parents, Henry Wilkening and wife to Quincy in 1856 After their marriage Henry Sprick and bride made their wedding journey out to Fontanelle, Nebraska, a distance of nearly four hundred and fifty miles, in a wagon drawn by a yoke of oxen Henry Sprick in the course of time became prominent in the new community In 1873 he was elected to the lower house of the Nebraska Legislature, and served three successive terms In 1878 he was chosen a member of the State Senate, and in 1884 was a presidential elector on the republican ticket.

After having been active in the development of his community for fifty years, successful in business and exemplifying a philanthropic spirit, he passed away honored and esteemed July 21, 1906 While his first home in Fontanelle was a log cabin, he later enjoyed the comforts of a fine brick residence His wife survived him about ten years, passing away in September, 1916, at the age of eighty Of this honored pioneer couple portraits appear in this work

They were the parents of ten children. Mary, wife of Christian Sick of Sterling, Nebraska Henry C, who though born and reared in Fontanelle, went back to Quincy, Illinois, some thirty years ago and has achieved great prominence as a banker, business man and citizen of Quincy; Sophie, wife of Carl Krueger, a minister living in New York State, Anna, wife of Ed Niebaum, a Washington County farmer whose sketch appears elsewhere, Albert W, whose interests in the Fontanelle community are also described, Emma, wife of Otto A Langhorst of Fontanelle, a record of whom appears elsewhere, Clara, widow of George D Roth of Quincy, Illinois; Louise, George, who died in infancy; and Alfred, who died in 1901 at the age of twenty-three

Albert W Sprick, a son of the prominent Fontanelle pioneer, the late Henry Sprick, has been a life long resident of this section of Nebraska, is a former merchant of Fontanelle, and one of the leading farmers and stockmen of Washington County

He was born at Fontanelle March 18, 1871, and has well exemplified the high minded and progressive spirit of his family He was educated in the common schools of Washington County, spent one year in Iowa College at Grinnell, and completed his education with a four year course in Midland College in Kansas On leaving college he applied his efforts to general farming and stock raising, but from 1898 until 1902 was a member of the well known mercantile firm of Sprick & Berkheimer After selling his mercantile business he resumed with renewed energy the stock raising and farming industry and this is the field in which his enterprise has brought him substantial material rewards

In 1911 Mr Sprick married Miss Bertha Westhold of Quincy, Illinois They are active members of the Lutheran Church and Mr. Sprick, like his father, is a republican Respected for his sound judgment in business and public affairs and though quiet and unassuming he has a host of loyal friends and has rendered valuable service in a public way He was a member in 1919 and 1920 of the Nebraska Constitutional Convention and in 1920 was elected a member of the House of Representatives in the State Legislature Mr Sprick occupies his father's fine old home place at Fontanelle

Mrs Elizabeth A Maxwell of Fremont is the widow of the late Judge Samuel Maxwell, for many years one of the most prominent jurists of the state

Mrs Maxwell was born in Andrew County, Missouri, September 5, 1845 Her father, Jacob Adams, was a native of North Carolina but

Albert W. Sprick   Bertha W. Sprick

spent his early life in Henry County, Indiana He was a carpenter by trade but for many years a farmer. As a pioneer Nebraskan he took up a claim and then returned to Iowa During his absence the claim was jumped and when he returned he bought out the occupant in later years He made the journey from Iowa by wagon and passed through Plattsmouth when it contained only two houses Jacob Adams died at the age of fifty-nine He married Rachel Wyles, who became the mother of six children, Mrs Maxwell being the oldest

In 1866 at Plattsmouth, Nebraska, Miss Elizabeth Adams was married to Samuel Maxwell, who was born May 20, 1825, in Lodi, New York, his parents having come from Scotland At the time of his marriage Mr. Maxwell was a farmer but had studied law under his brother and in 1866 he opened a law office in Plattsmouth and in Fremont in 1873, when he had been appointed district judge of the North Platte district, which office he filled several terms, when he was made supreme judge of the state. He then moved to Dodge County and in this county achieved his greatest eminence as a lawyer and judge He was a Presbyterian, a Mason and Odd Fellow, and died February 11, 1901, at the age of seventy-six

Mrs Maxwell was the mother of nine children: Mrs Maggie Ferguson of Brookland, Henry E of Omaha, Jacob, Elizabeth L, at home, Andrew C of Sioux City, Iowa, Marilla, at home Mrs Anna Jefford of Jamaica, New York, Samuel of Fremont, and Sarah, at home

Herman F Meyer Among the stable business men of Scribner, no one is held in more confidence or higher esteem than Herman F Meyer, who is cashier of the Farmers State Bank of this city This institution is one of large importance in Dodge County and its growth has been steady and satisfactory since its organization Its officers are all men of ample means and banking experience, and are recognized as able, upright business men

Herman F Meyer was born in 1876, in Dodge County, the second in a family of twelve children born to J G and Marie (Stoever) Meyer Both parents were born in Germany and both came when young people to Dodge County, Nebraska, the father in 1867 and the mother in 1869 They were married in Dodge County, where the father secured a homestead, proved up and for many years afterward occupied his land, in the course of time becoming a substantial farmer and stock raiser Since retirement they have lived at Uehling, Nebraska

The brothers and sisters of Mr Meyer were as follows Anna, who is the wife of Charles Heneman, a banker at Spring View, Nebraska, Sophia, who is the wife of Joseph Marsh, a farmer near Spring View, Mary, who is the wife of William Heneman, a ranchman near Millboro, South Dakota, Bernard, who is a farmer in Dodge County. Matilda, who is the wife of Lars Jorgenson of Uehling, Nebraska; Bertha, who is the wife of Hans Jorgenson, a farmer in South Dakota, Kate is a student in a business college at Grand Island, Nebraska; Freda, who is principal of the public schools at Spring View, Nebraska, Margaret, who resides at home, and Deidrich, who is deceased The parents are faithful members of the Lutheran Church

Herman F Meyer remained at home and assisted his father on the farm until he was twenty-eight years old He attended the public schools in Dodge County and afterward spent one year in the Fremont Normal College, where he completed a commercial course After leaving the farm he went to Uehling, and there embarked in the insurance business, but later sold out in order to become assistant cashier of the Farmers State Bank of Uehling, where he continued until 1918, when he came to Scribner to accept the position of cashier in the Farmers State Bank of this city Mr Meyer devotes himself closely to the affairs of this institution Officially and otherwise he has made many friends since coming to Scribner, his courteous accommodation in business being appreciated, and his interest in all matters pertaining to the welfare of the community being welcomed

Mr Meyer was married on June 26, 1907, to Miss Lena M Young, who was born at Omaha, Nebraska, and they have two children, namely: Donald and Delma, both of whom are in school Mr and Mrs Meyer belong to the Congregational Church Mr Meyer belongs to Scribner Lodge, Ancient Free and Accepted Masons, and to the Woodmen of the World

CARL F KOLTERMAN In mercantile circles of Blair a name that is becoming increasingly prominent with the passing of the years is that of Carl F Kolterman. During the past nine years Mr Kolterman has been the proprietor of a variety store at Blair, and his energetic spirit, progressive views and excellent management have served to introduce him to the people of this community in a favorable light, while his ideas of public-spirited citizenship have caused him to be a contributing factor in the success of various movements of civic moment

Mr. Kolterman was born at Millard, Nebraska, September 24, 1882, a son of John Carl F and Anna G (Kanenbley) Kolterman, the former a native of Pomerania, Germany, and the latter of Jersey City, New Jersey The father learned his trade in his native land and on coming to the United States settled at Omaha, where he was married and where he conducted a mill at West Point Later he came to Blair, where he also followed milling, and at the time of his death was one of the highly respected citizens of his community He was a republican in his political views, and he and Mrs Kolterman were members of the Lutheran Church Mrs Kolterman, who survives her husband, resides at Red Oak, Iowa, with her son The seven children, five of whom are living, are Carl F., Fred, the proprietor of Kolterman's Racket Store, at Seward, Nebraska, Ewald W, who is a grading contractor at Lamoni, Iowa, Herman, who met an accidental death by electrical shock while working for his brother Carl being then aged twenty years, John, who conducts a general store at Red Oak, Iowa Frank, who is employed by his brother Carl, and Ernest, who was a twin of Frank and died at the age of nine years

Carl F Kolterman acquired good educational advantages in his youth, first attending the public schools of Millard and Blair and later Dana College at Blair for two terms When he left school he began working with his father, with whom he was associated until reaching the age of twenty-one years, at which time he secured a position with a coal, lumber and grain company at Scribner Mr Kolterman continued to be thus occupied until 1911, when he decided he was ready to embark upon an enterprise of his own, and accordingly established his present store at Blair, where he has worked out a substantial success Mr Kolterman has what is known as a variety store, handling a large stock of useful articles, modern in design and moderate in price He has acquired the confidence of his fellow-townsmen, a quality necessary for the conduct of any successful commercial enterprise and his success may be largely traced to his honorable methods, ready enterprise and unfailing courtesy The growth and development of his business have made necessary his close application thereto, but he is not indifferent to the responsibilities of citizenship, and worthy measures meet with his approval and support He is a republican in his political views, and he and Mrs Kolterman are members of the Lutheran Church

In January, 1906, Mr Kolterman was united in marriage to Miss Christina Von Lauken, who was born at Arthur, Illinois, daughter of George Von Lauken, a native of Germany To this union there have been born three children: Carl F, Jr, born in 1907, Frederick, born in 1910, who are attending school, and Herbert, born in 1918

OLE HANSEN A real pioneer of Dodge County, Ole Hanson, who is now retired in a comfortable home at Fremont, has known this section of Nebraska for more than half a century and has been a participant in its farm, rural and civic development

He was born in Denmark February 23, 1849, and his father also came to America Ole, who acquired his early education in Denmark, came to the United States in 1866 and at once located in Dodge County, Nebraska. His brother Rasmus had preceded him five years to this state. Ole was too young to enter a homestead, but pre-empted some land He had the misfortune to have his claim "jumped" and thus failing in his first efforts to establish himself in the country he left Nebraska and spent a year as a sailor on the Great Lakes He then returned and formally entered a homestead of eighty acres ten miles northwest of Fremont His first home in which he lived for three years was a dugout Later he acquired better living facilities, improved his land, put up substantial buildings, and to the homestead of eighty acres added until he had 210 acres He went through the various hardships to which the early settlers of this section of Nebraska were subjected, though the country afforded a plentiful supply of wild game and there was always enough to eat

November 7, 1874, Mr Hansen married Miss Hansena Anderson, a native of Denmark She was born in 1847 and died in 1906 During their married life of over thirty years six children were born into their home: Celia Olsen, who is married and lives in Colorado, John, a farmer in Dodge County, Edward, who lives on the homestead, Andrew, of Dodge County, Walter, who lives near Ames, and Anna Ketrina of Dodge County Mr. Hansen married for his second wife Christina Wilson, who was born in Schleswig, Germany, but recently reunited as a Province of Denmark She was born in 1865 In June, 1919, Mr and Mrs Hansen left their home farm and moved into Fremont, where they enjoy the comforts of a good home Mr Hansen is an independent voter, a member of the Lutheran Church, and during his life in the country gave much of his time to the welfare of schools and served fifteen years as school director and for twenty years occupied the office of assessor.

C EDWARD HANSEN Son of an old homesteader in Dodge County, C Edward Hansen has chosen to remain identified with the community in which he was born and reared and has made himself a prominent factor in the agricultural and stock raising activities of Maple Township He has a well ordered and systematized farm in section 26, and besides the daily routine of duties on the farm he has interested himself in church, schools and other local interests

Mr Hansen was born in Dodge County November 19, 1878 The facts of the family history are detailed in the preceding sketch

Mr Hansen grew up on his father's homestead, made the best possible use of his advantages in the schools, and for about twenty-five years has been working steadily towards independence as a farm owner and citizen He gives much attention to fine stock, particularly thoroughbred hogs of the Duroc and Poland China strains

October 18, 1911, he married Mary M Harms. They have two children, Raymond and Ruth Mr Hansen is a democrat in his political affiliations and has served both on the School Board and two years as township clerk He and his family are members of the Danish Lutheran Church

R J MURDOCH, M D A prominent citizen of Blair, and one of the foremost physicians and surgeons of Washington County, R J Murdoch, M D, is actively engaged in the practice of one of the most exacting professions to which a man may devote his time and talents, and is meeting with unquestioned success A native of Canada, he was born January 8, 1870, in Lanark County, of honored Scotch ancestry, his Grandfather Murdoch, a man of culture and a native of Scotland, having been sent by the British government to Canada at an early day to superintend the Canadian schools.

James Murdoch, the doctor's father, spent his entire life in Canada, during his active career having been a tiller of the soil To him and his wife, whose name before marriage was Elizabeth Moffatt, were born three children, as follows Edith, wife of C A Wilson of Kelowna, Canada, R J, of this personal review, and Maude, wife of John Black, a farmer residing in Kelowna, Canada Both parents were devout members of the Presbyterian Church

Acquiring his preliminary education in the Winnipeg Collegiate Institute, R J Murdoch subsequently entered the medical department of the University of Nebraska, from which he was graduated in 1898, with the degree of Doctor of Medicine Locating immediately in Petersburg Boone County, this state, Doctor Murdoch established a good practice and remained there seven years, gaining experience, confidence and skill In 1905, desirous of broadening his field of endeavor, he came to Blair, where he has built up a very large and lucrative patronage and gained an enviable reputation, not only as a physician but for his judgment and skill as a surgeon

The doctor is actively identified with various professional organizations, belonging to the American Medical Association, the Nebraska State Medical Society, the Elkhorn Valley Medical Society and the Washington County Medical Association, which he has served as president He is also a member of the County Insanity Board, is local surgeon for the Chicago & Northwestern Railway Company, a member of the Blair Board of Health, and during the World war served on the Board of Draft Examiners Fraternally the doctor is a member of the Ancient Free and Accepted Masons, belonging to Lodge and Chapter; of the Knights of Pythias, of the Woodmen of the World, and the Highlanders, and both he and his wife are active members of the Order of Eastern Star

Doctor Murdoch has been twice married He married first, in 1898, Lela Bonine, who was born in Iowa, and died in 1916 at her home in Blair Of the three children born of their union two are living, namely. Evelyn M attending Doane College in Crete, Nebraska, and Louis, a

Clark O'Hanlon

pupil in the Blair High School The doctor married in 1917, Ruth Palmer, who was born in Blair, a daughter of Dr W H Palmer, a pioneer physician of this place, and they have one child, Margaret Religiously Mrs Murdoch is a member of the Presbyterian Church, while the doctor belongs to the Congregational Church

CLARK O'HANLON Well equipped for his chosen profession, Clark O'Hanlon of Blair occupies a noteworthy position among the active and successful attorneys of Washington County, his broad knowledge of law, and his keen and lucid powers of exposition having won him an assured place in the legal world He was born February 24, 1869, in Washington County, Nebraska, on the parental homestead, which was situated just north of the present site of Blair

His father, Richard O'Hanlon, was born, reared and married in Washington County, Ohio Seeking a favorable location for conducting his chosen vocation, he came to Nebraska with his wife and their growing family in 1865, and for a few months was engaged in railroad work In 1868 he took up a homestead claim in Washington County, and by dint of persistent toil improved a good farm He subsequently bought a ranch not far from Herman and managed it successfully until 1893 His health becoming impaired, he went South, hoping to recover his former physical vigor, and died at Gueda Springs, Kansas, in 1897. He was a self-made man, having begun life even with the world, and in addition to bringing up and educating a large family of children accumulated considerable property, acquiring title to 280 acres of valuable land He was a democrat in politics and a member of the Independent Order of Odd Fellows

The maiden name of the wife of Richard O'Hanlon was Sarah Joy She was also born in Washington County, Ohio, and she died in 1904 in Hartford, Kansas To her and her husband fourteen children were born, ten of whom are living, Clark, the fifth child in succession of birth, being the only one residing in Washington County, Nebraska She was a consistent member of the Methodist Episcopal Church, but her husband was not affiliated with any religious denomination

Spending several years of his earlier life in Iowa, Clark O'Hanlon attended the public schools of Herman, Nebraska, and the State Normal School at Shenandoah, Iowa, subsequently studying law under Col. L W Osburn, he was admitted to the bar in 1891 and began the practice of his profession with his former tutor Leaving the colonel's office in 1897, Mr. O'Hanlon established himself in Blair, and has continued in active practice ever since, having built up an extensive and highly remunerative clientele In order to give proper attention to his numerous patrons Mr O'Hanlon has secured a partner to assist him in his work, and now his son is to be admitted to the firm, the firm being O'Hanlon, Maher & O'Hanlon In 1910 Mr O'Hanlon helped organize the Commonwealth Life Insurance Company of Omaha, of which he has since been a director, and the general legal counsellor, positions that demand considerable of his time and attention.

Mr O'Hanlon married, in 1893, Bertie Reed, a native of Monmouth, Illinois and into the household thus established four children have made their advent, namely. Reed, Philip, attending the Blair High School, Luther, and Francis. Reed O'Hanlon, the eldest child, entered the army as a member of the National Guard in 1916, and as lieutenant of his company spent seven months on the border He was afterward transferred to the One Hundred and Twenty-Seventh Field Artillery, in which he served as adjutant and as captain, being first stationed at Camp Cody, and later at the School of Fire in Fort Sill, Oklahoma Going overseas in September, 1918, he was commissioned major in the Seventh Division Regulars, while in France, and after the signing of the armistice he had charge of over 700 of the soldiers employed in reconstruction work, near Metz In 1919, soon after his return home, he, having previously studied law in the University of Nebraska, was admitted to the bar, and is now associated in practice with his father

An influential member of the democratic party, Clark O'Hanlon served as county attorney from 1895 until 1899, was mayor of Blair in 1903 and 1904, and having been elected county judge in 1908, served in that capacity until 1911, when he resigned from the bench to resume his practice, which required his whole attention Fraternally Mr O'Hanlon is a prominent member of the Ancient Free and Accepted Masons, belonging to Lodge, Council, Commandery and is also a member of the Ancient Arabic Order Nobles of the Mystic Shrine, and is likewise a member of the Independent Order of Odd Fellows, of which he is past grand master Both he and his wife are members of the Congregational Church

CHRISTIAN G FRITZ Having proven himself a reliable business man and worthy of favors from the Government of his adopted country, Christian G Fritz was appointed postmaster of Hooper by President Wilson in 1913 and has held this important office ever since. He is a man well and favorably known all over Dodge and Washington counties and deserves the confidence he inspires

Christian G Fritz was born in Germany May 13, 1869, a son of Frederick and Dorothy (Maier) Fritz, both natives of Germany, the former of whom was a tailor by trade They had the following children born to them Carl, who is a tailor of Fremont, Nebraska; Albert, who is a barber of Hooper, Ernest, who was also a barber, was killed accidentally, Jacob, who is a resident of Omaha, Nebraska, and Christian G, whose name heads this review.

In 1884 Mr Fritz came to the United States and located in Dodge County, Nebraska, and for two years was engaged in farm labor From 1886 until 1888 he was in the employ of the Plambeck grocery and crockery establishment at Fremont, and then went to Oklahoma, where he homesteaded, but relinquished same back to the Government and returned to Dodge County and conducted a barber shop at Hooper until 1905. He and a brother then turned their attention in another direction, opening a bakery and restaurant that they conducted very profitably under the name of Fritz Brothers Mr Fritz has also been quite extensively identified with the real estate operations of this neighborhood, and has handled some large transfers In 1913 he was appointed postmaster of Hooper, and has since been in charge of the postoffice here, under his systematic conduct its affairs being in excellent condition

In 1897 Mr Fritz was united in marriage with Martha Nehling, born in Dodge County, a daughter of Oswald Nehling, one of the pioneers of this region Prominent in the ranks of the democratic party, Mr Fritz has held a number of local offices, including those of village trustee for a number of years and justice of the peace Zion Lutheran Church of Hooper holds his membership He belongs to the Knights of Pythias and the Ancient Order of United Workmen

Mr Fritz is a man who has succeeded because he has never shirked hard work, or failed to give honest value in return for what was accorded him Both as a business man and private citizen he measures up as an honest, dependable and capable man, and it would be difficult to find one who is more deserving of popular regard than he, for he has earned this confidence, as well as his prosperity, through his own unaided efforts

JOHN SANDERS With a firm and abiding faith in the ultimate reward of the homely virues of honest, diligence and unselfish loyalty to the task at hand, John Sanders has developed more than average ability and justifies in every transaction the confidence placed in him He is of a superior type of the self-reliant, clear-brained business man, and is one of the most valued buyers and salesmen of the Nye-Schneider-Fowler Company of Hooper

John Sanders was born in Pennsylvania February 2, 1865, a son of Emanuel and Barbara (Capp) Sanders, natives of Pennsylvania Emanuel Sanders was a millwright by trade, and was also engaged in farming, and he spent his entire life in Pennsylvania, where he died at the age of sixty-eight years He and his wife had eleven children, three of them living, namely: William, who is county surveyor of Dodge County, lives at Fremont Jacob B owns and operates a grocery at Hooper, and John, who was the youngest born In politics Emanuel Sanders was a republican He and his wife belonged to the United Brethren Society.

John Sanders attended the public schools of Pennsylvania and Dodge County, Nebraska, coming to the latter in 1882, and was employed in farm work for a time He then engaged with May Brothers, wholesale grocers of Fremont, for a short time, but returned to the farm, and continued to be an agriculturist for fifteen years During that experience he gained a thorough knowledge of grain and in 1894 decided to put this to some practical use, so became manager for Henry Roberts of Hooper, handling his grain and lumber business very acceptably for five years Leaving Mr Roberts, he formed connections with Nye-Schneider-Fowler and has been with this concern for nine years, devoting his attention to buying grain, livestock and similar commodities, and selling lumber and coal

In 1892 Mr Sanders was united in marriage with Miss Emma Ruysert, born in Nebraska a daughter of William K Ruysert, one of the homesteaders of Dodge County Mr Sanders is a republican, but has never sought public office, his time being too much occupied with his own affairs He belongs to the Knights of the Maccabees and the Knights of Pythias. Possessed of admirable and effective qualities and not easily deceived in men or misled in their motives, he has been able to render his concern a valuable service and is held by it in high esteem

WILLIAM D HOLBROOK The long and honorable career of William D Holbrook, who has been a resident of Dodge County for forty-two years, has been characterized by successful achievements in the vocation of agriculture as well as by business success and splendid public service in offices of marked responsibility and trust. Belonging to that class of men who have watched the wonderful development of their section since they themselves initiated the forward movement by breaking the sod of the prairies, he has combined his activities for personal advancement with conscientious and able labor in behalf of his adopted county and state and has served in both bodies of the Nebraska Legislature, in addition to having been a justice of the peace for thirty-two years

Mr Holbrook was born April 17, 1850, on a farm in Sullivan County, Missouri, a son of William N and Mary (Osborn) Holbrook, natives of Virginia. His father was educated for the law in his native state, whence he went to Indiana and subsequently to Missouri He became a practitioner of some reputation and at one time was district judge of Sullivan County, in addition to which he served as county superintendent at Milan, Sullivan County, in which community he was the owner of valuable land He was a Mason, fraternally, and he and his worthy wife held membership in the Methodist Episcopal Church They were the parents of ten children, of whom two are living Nancy, the wife of Charles Kingsolver, a retired citizen of York, Nebraska, and William D

William D Holbrook was educated in the public schools of Missouri and was still a youth when, in 1863, he went to Illinois and became a farm hand His opportunities for advancement were few, and it was not until he came to Dodge County, in 1878, that he really entered upon his career In March of that year he rented a property in section 6, Maple Township, and broke the virgin sod of the prairie Later he purchased the land, and at this time is the owner of a finely-improved farm of 160 acres, which boasts of the most modern equipment and improvements He has been a general farmer who has kept thoroughly abreast of the times and modern methods have always been a feature of his work Although primarily an agriculturist, Mr. Holbrook has not allowed opportunities of a business character to pass unnoticed He assisted in the drafting of the constitution and by-laws of the Farmers Mutual Insurance Company of Dodge County, in which he held policy No 1, and at this time is a stockholder in the Farmers Union Elevator of Hooper and Ames, and in the Farmers Telephone Company of Hooper

From early manhood Mr Holbrook has been interestedly active in politics and has been a stanch and unwavering republican After filling several minor offices, in 1895 his fellow-citizens sent him to a seat in the State Senate, and in 1897 he was elected a member of the House of Representatives He was returned to the former body in 1899, and was again elected in 1907 His service in the Legislature was constructive and valuable, and in addition to being the father of some very useful legislation he was always found supporting movements making for the betterment of his county and state and tending to advance the interests of his constituents in an honorable way He has likewise served as a member of constitutional conventions of 1919 and 1920, and for thirty-two consecutive years has been a justice of the peace His religious connection is with the United Brethren Church

Mr. Holbrook was married in 1875 to Miss Adda R Mahan, a native of Ohio, the ceremony being performed in Illinois They have been the parents of five children Myrtle, the wife of W A Hough, an agriculturist of Dodge County, Mabel, deceased, was the wife of Arthur Bowring, a ranchman of Cherry County, this state, Edith, the wife of D F Head, a Dodge County farmer, Frank, a chiropractor of Sheridan, Wyoming, and Ethel, the wife of C O Hull, connected with the Hooper Milling Company

H. O L OLLERMANN A resident of Blair since September, 1881, and consecutively identified for nearly forty years with the jewelry business in the county seat of Washington County, Mr Ollermann represents a pioneer family in Dodge and Washington counties Apart from their substantial enterprise as homesteaders, business men and citizens, the Ollermanns, particularly with the older settlers, are widely known all over this section of Nebraska on account of their musical gifts and abilities The Blair merchant was for many years prominent in all musical events in his home city

Mr Ollermann was born in the Province of Pomerania, Prussia, Germany, January 5, 1855, son of Franz and Othelia (Krahn) Ollermann. His father was a thoroughly educated musician and gave his son the benefit of musical instruction in Germany The father at one time was a traveling musician with a concert band and spent one season with a circus band By trade he was a tailor

The Ollermann family came to America and settled in Dodge County, Nebraska, in 1869 They took up their residence on a homestead two and a half miles from Snyder in section 32, township 20, range 6 The mother lived on the homestead until her death, while Franz Ollermann died at Scribner They were devout Lutherans, and the father followed the fortunes of the democratic party in politics There were six children, two daughters and four sons The three now living are Gustav, a farmer near St Charles, South Dakota, H O L, and Anna, wife of Carl Barz, owner of extensive plantation interests and a banker at Morganza, Louisiana

H O L Ollermann learned to play the violin when a child and at the age of nine played for a wedding in his native country He was twelve when he came to America and settled on the homestead in Nebraska He and his three brothers and their father comprised a family orchestra that forty years or more ago was in constant demand to play at all the dances in Fremont and adjacent towns They were musicians of sound taste as well as skill in the use of their respective instruments

After his removal to Blair H O L Ollermann organized a band and for a number of years played both in the band and orchestra On locating at Blair in September, 1881, he took charge of the jewelry department of the local drug store He had learned the jeweler's trade in Fremont, and he was actively identified with the jewelry business at Blair until September, 1911, when he opened a jewelry store of his own He now conducts the leading establishment of its kind in the county seat, carries a large and well selected stock of jewelry of all kinds, and also does repair work He keeps two people employed in the business

In 1880 at David City, Nebraska, Mr Ollermann married Hattie S Woodruff, a native of Hartford, Connecticut Four children were born to their marriage Parker, who served in the United States navy for five years and is now at home assisting his father in business, Agnes, a teacher in the schools of Weeping Water, Nebraska, Hermine, at home; and Frederick, still attending school at Lincoln, taking the agricultural course and in his senior year.

Mr Ollermann attends the Lutheran Church while his wife is a Universalist He is affiliated with the Independent Order of Odd Fellows, casts his vote independently, and is a citizen who has given close attention to business but incidentally has exercised a good influence on the community and achieved the thorough respect and esteem of his fellow citizens

ULYSSES S CAIN A man of good business ability, possessing in a large measure the energy, intelligence and tact necessary for the successful conduct of his chosen work, Ulysses S Cain of Fremont has built up a large and profitable business as agent for the Central Life Insurance Company of Des Moines, Iowa A native of Iowa, he was born August 28, 1868, in Brooklyn, Poweshiek County

Milligan J Cain, his father, was born and educated in Ohio, from whence he migrated in early manhood to Iowa, where he first found employment in a tailoring shop He married soon after going there, and at the outbreak of the Civil war enlisted in Company K, Thirty-Ninth Iowa Volunteer Infantry, of which he was commissioned first lieutenant Returning to Brooklyn, Iowa, at the end of the conflict, he opened a general store and meat market, but later moved to a farm lying east of Brooklyn, and was there engaged in agricultural pursuits for twenty years. He lived to a good old age, dying in Brooklyn, Iowa, in 1913 He was a republican in politics, and soon after the formation of the Union Labor party ran on that ticket for governor of Iowa, but, naturally, the party being new, was defeated at the polls He was a member of the Grand Army of the Republic, and for forty years belonged to the Independent Order of Odd Fellows

Milligan J Cain married, in Iowa, Nancy Morey, who was born February 16, 1840, and on February 16, 1920, celebrated, in Brooklyn, Iowa, the eightieth anniversary of her birth Of the eleven children born of their union eight are living, two of them being residents of Nebraska, as follows: Edward L, of Omaha, was for twenty years overseer of the parcel post terminal for the Chicago, Burlington & Quincy Railroad Company, and is now associated with the Jones Construction Company, and Ulysses S, with whom this sketch is principally concerned Both parents were worthy members of the Methodist Episcopal Church

After leaving the Brooklyn, Iowa, High School, Ulysses S. Cain made good use of every offered opportunity for advancing his knowledge, reading and studying as time allowed, and in the fall of 1888 entered upon a professional career, teaching in Iowa two years, and then in the rural schools of Washington County, Nebraska, for an equal length of time Abandoning the desk, Mr Cain was engaged in mercantile pursuits in Blair, Nebraska, for three and a half years Moving then to Omaha, he worked first for Browning & King Clothing Company and for the past ten years was connected with Central Life Insurance Company of Des Moines, Iowa Coming to Fremont in 1915 Mr. Cain accepted a general agency with the company and having made good from the start is now district manager, having control, not only of Dodge County, but of several adjacent counties, the territory in which he is so successfully working

Mr. Cain married, September 24, 1896, Harriet T Tracy, who was born at Mount Pleasant, Iowa, a daughter of Jonathan L Tracy, who moved from Ohio to Iowa, and thence to Blair, Nebraska, where he engaged in farming and dairy business Mr and Mrs Cain have two children, namely. Stanley and Ruth Stanley Cain was born in Blair, Nebraska, June 6, 1897, and as a boy and youth received good educational advantages, having attended the Central High School at Omaha, and later the high schools of Morris, Minnesota, and of Fremont, Nebraska He subsequently studied pharmacy at Highland Park, Des Moines, Iowa, and there afterward worked for a few years in a drug store At the present time he is profitably engaged with his father in the life insurance business He is a member of the Ancient Free and Accepted Masons and of the Order of the Eastern Star. Ruth L Cain, the only daughter of the parental household, is attending Wesleyan University, in Mount Pleasant, Iowa

Politically Mr Cain is a stanch republican Fraternally he belongs to the Ancient Free and Accepted Masons, and to the Independent Order of Odd Fellows, and both he and his wife are members of the Order of the Eastern Star Mrs Cain is vice president of the Rebekah Assembly of Nebraska Mr and Mrs Cain are prominent members of the Methodist Episcopal Church, and take an active part in church and Sunday school work

JOHN C CHERNY was a lad of about ten years when he accompanied his parents on their emigration from their native Bohemia to the United States in 1870 and the same year recorded the arrival of the family in Saunders County, Nebraska, where the father took up a homestead and vigorously turned his attention to the development of a productive farm. With the passing years he became one of the successful exponents of agricultural and livestock industry in that county, where both he and his good wife passed the remainder of their lives on their old homestead They were fine representatives of that sturdy element of Bohemian citizenship that has played large part in the civic and industrial progress and prosperity of Nebraska Their names, Venzelslaus and Anna (Shavlich) Cherny, merit enduring place on the roll of the sterling pioneers of Saunders County, both having been devout communicants of the Catholic Church and the father having supported the cause of the republican party after he had become a naturalized citizen of the land of his adoption Of the six children, John C of this review is the eldest, Albert remains on the old home farm, James is a successful farmer in Dodge County, Anna is deceased, Kate is the wife of F A Hines, a farmer near Morse Bluff, Saunders County and Joseph is engaged in the insurance and real estate business at Walthill, Thurston County

John C Cherny gained his rudimentary education in his native land and attended school when opportunity offered after the family home had been established in Nebraska He early began to assist in the work of the home farm and there remained with his parents until 1880, when, at the age of twenty years, he came to North Bend, Dodge County, where he found employment in the lumber yard of Christopher Cusack After having been thus engaged two years he became a partner in the firm of which the other members were Mr Cusack, his former employer, and J Y. Smith and J R Acom After having thus been actively engaged in the lumber and livestock business two years he sold his interest in the business to C L Coleman of La Crosse, Wisconsin He then became associated with F C Cavan in purchasing the well-established implement and lumber business of J B Foote The new firm continued to control a substantial and profitable business until the partnership alliance was severed by the death of Mr Cavan, in 1899, and within a short time thereafter Mr Cherny admitted C K Watson to partnership, under the firm name of Cherny & Watson This progressive firm has a large and substantial business in the handling of lumber, coal and heavy and light farm machinery and implements. In addition to the headquarters enterprise at North Bend the firm maintains branch yards at Rogers, Colfax County, Morse Bluff, Saunders County, Walthill, Thurston County, as well as at Winnebago, that county, and at Mineola, Iowa This mere statement of conditions marks the firm as conducting a business of broad scope and importance and testified to the distinctive success that has attended the independent activities of the Bohemian boy who was born in 1860 and was but ten years old when he came with his parents to the state which has been the stage of his progressive movement in the field of normal and useful business enterprise.

Mr. Cherny is one of the specially loyal and liberal citizens and business men of North Bend, and has been influential in public affairs in Dodge County. His political allegiance is given to the republican party, he served nine years as a member of the municipal council of North Bend, as well as one year in the office of mayor, and he was for ten years a member of the Board of Education, while he also gave two years of effective service as township assessor. In his activities as a dealer in agricultural machinery Mr. Cherny introduced the first twine-binding reaping machine that was placed in operation not alone in Dodge County but also the first in this section of the state. In a fraternal way he is affiliated with the Independent Order of Odd Fellows.

In 1885 Mr. Cherny was united in marriage to Miss Victoria Sedlacek, who likewise is a native of Bohemia, and of this union have been born five children: Mildred is a popular teacher in the public schools of North Bend; James is bookkeeper in the office of his father's business at North Bend; Leland J. is manager of the firm's business at Rogers; Alice is at the parental home, and Helen is, in 1920, a student in the University of Nebraska.

HERMAN HOLSTEN. A prominent, prosperous and highly esteemed citizen of Dodge, Herman Holsten has for upwards of thirty years been conspicuously identified with the promotion of the financial prosperity of his home city, and as president of the Farmers State Bank is wisely managing one of the more prosperous and substantial institutions of the kind in Dodge County. Of German parentage, he was born, February 24, 1867, in Benton County, Missouri.

His father, D. Holsten, was born in Germany, and as a lad of seventeen years came to the United States in search of more favorable opportunities for earning a living. He located in Missouri, and during the Civil war enlisted in Company C, Missouri Cavalry, in which he bravely served four years. Resuming his agricultural labors on leaving the army, he remained in Missouri until 1874, when he came with his family to Dodge County, Nebraska. Buying a tract of wild land situated near Scribner, he improved a valuable ranch, on which he lived and labored many years. Subsequently giving up the management of his large farm, which he afterward sold, he lived retired, first in Scribner, and then Redlands, California, where his death occurred on June 12, 1917.

D. Holsten married, in Warsaw, Benton County, Missouri, Marguerite Behrens, and they became the parents of three children, as follows: Herman, of this sketch; Emma Diels, of Redlands, California; and a child that died in infancy. The father was a republican in politics, and both he and his wife were members of the German Lutheran Church.

Completing his early education in the country schools, Herman Holsten took a business course of six months in the Fremont Normal School. Although he had been well trained in the agricultural arts on the home farm, he early decided to seek some other occupation than farming, and as a young man started out for himself. On March 1, 1889, soon after attaining his majority, Mr. Holsten organized the Farmers State Bank at Dodge, of which he is president, and has managed it most successfully, and to the entire satisfaction of all connected with it. The original capital of this bank was $10,000, which has been increased to $30,000, while its individual deposits, which amounted to less than $50,000 the first year, are now $750,000, an increase indicative of the institution's prosperity and popularity. Mr. Holsten has made wise investments and has valuable farming interests as well as city property.

Herman Holsten

In 1891 Mr. Holsten married Ella Dierker, who was born near Westpoint, Cuming County, Nebraska, being one of the ten children of Henry and Mary Dierker, who are now living retired in Orange, California. Mr. and Mrs. Holsten have four children, namely: Harry, cashier in the Farmers State Bank; Marguerite Johnson, San Bernardino, California; Leona Stecher; and Viola, engaged in teaching. A republican in politics, Mr. Holsten has served the Town Board for twenty years, and has been secretary of the School Board an equal length of time. He and his wife are members of the German Lutheran Church, but the children belong to the Congregational Church.

WILLIAM A. G. COBB. Distinguished not only for his service in the regular army, more especially during the Civil war, but as a man of sterling worth and integrity, the late William A. G. Cobb, for nearly half a century a resident of Fremont, was eminently deserving of the high position he attained among the esteemed and valued citizens of his community. He was born February 8, 1841, in Wurtemburg, Germany, a son of Simon and Wilhelmina Cobb, and died at his home in Fremont, Nebraska, April 1, 1918.

Immigrating to the United States in 1857, he first found employment as a farm hand in Michigan, where he remained two or three years. Going from there to Illinois he enlisted July 5, 1860, as a private in the United States army, becoming a member of Company E, Eighth Regiment, United States Infantry, which was under the command of John T. Sprague. He then went with his comrades to Fort Leavenworth, Kansas, from there marching across the plains to Hatcher's Run, and a week later continuing his journey to Fort Fillmore, New Mexico. Leaving there in March, 1861, with his command, he marched 700 miles across the country to San Antonio, Texas, where the entire company of 315 men was taken by Van Dorn's Confederate brigade, and he and his comrades were being held as prisoners when the outbreak of the Civil war was announced.

Rejoining his regiment when paroled, Mr. Cobb took part in several important engagements of the war, including the first battle of Bull Run, the engagement at Fredericksburg, and the battle of Gettysburg. Soon after the latter battle, he and his company were ordered to New York City to suppress the draft riots. Going then to Warrenton, West Virginia, with his command, which became the provost guard of the Ninth Corps, he took an active part in all the movements of that organization. His term of enlistment having expired, Mr. Cobb was honorably discharged from the service, at Indianapolis, Indiana, on July 12, 1864, and subsequently re-enlisted in the same company for another term of three years.

For meritorious and efficient service, he was promoted to the rank of first sergeant, and on January 1, 1867, was made regimental commissary sergeant. Just after his re-enlistment Mr. Cobb joined his old company at Baltimore, Maryland, and was detailed as clerk at the headquarters of General Hancock, a position that he filled ably and most satisfactorily. On July 12, 1867, his term of enlistment having expired, he was honorably discharged from the army, at Raleigh, North Carolina, and returned north to resume his duties as a private citizen.

Coming to Dodge County, Nebraska, in the spring of 1869, Mr. Cobb located in Fremont, and first clerked in a grocery, and later in a hardware store, entering the employ of a Mr. Carter. Taking up a claim a short time later, he lived on his homestead three years, there beginning the improvement of a farm. The work not proving to his liking,

Mr Cobb returned to Fremont, and ran an elevator for several years He subsequently bought an elevator and a lumber yard in Hooper, Nebraska, and managed it ably for several years Again returning to Fremont, he established a lumber yard and built an elevator, and operated both for some time He then engaged in the horse business, but the venture was a losing one, and he then lived retired from active business cares until his death He was a self-made man in every sense implied by the term, and by his own efforts accumulated a fair share of this world's goods, at his death leaving considerable property He built, in 1889, the large and conveniently arranged home at 1612 East Military Avenue, the valuable lot on which it is located containing eighteen acres of land, and Mrs Cobb still occupies it

Mr Cobb married October 9, 1870 Eliza A Mefferd, who was born in Logan County, Ohio, a daughter of Andrew and Nancy (Wellingsford) Mefferd, who came from Ohio to Dodge County, Nebraska, in the fall of 1869 Her father first rented land and later took a homestead claim in Colfax County, where both he and his wife spent their remaining years Mr and Mrs Cobb reared one child, Gustav L Cobb, who was born February 10, 1872, and after his graduation from the Fremont High School attended a business college for a year This son who was general passenger agent for the Chicago, Milwaukee & St Paul Railroad at Chicago while the Government operated the railway, but is now in New York City, was recently given a medal by King Albert, who greatly appreciated the courteous attention tendered him when he traveled over that railway while visiting this country William Cobb was a republican in politics, and a loyal member of the Grand Army of the Republic He was reared in the Lutheran Church and his wife was a member of the Methodist Episcopal Church

MYRON G SNYDER For many years actively engaged in agricultural pursuits in Dodge County, Myron G Snyder used excellent judgment and good business methods in the care and management of his farm lands, and met with such signal success that he acquired much wealth, and is now living retired from active labor in Fremont, enjoying all the comforts of life He was born April 3 1856, in New York State, which was likewise the birthplace of his father, George Snyder

George Snyder, who was of English ancestry, was a lifelong resident of the Empire State, where he carried on general farming throughout his active career He was a steadfast republican in politics, and served as sheriff of Herkimer County, New York His wife, whose maiden name was Lydia Case was born in Massachusetts, and died on the home farm in New York State They became the parents of several children, as follows: William, a soldier in the Civil war, was wounded in the battle of Antietam and died eighteen days later, in October 1862, Charles, a resident of Herkimer, New York, visited his brother Myron in Fremont, Nebraska, in December, 1919, and died very soon after his return home, his death occurring January 1, 1920, Horace N, foreman of a factory in Utica New York· Myron G of this sketch and Albert E foreman of the Remington Gun Works at Ilion, New York

Educated in the public schools of his native state, Myron G. Snyder was there first engaged in tilling the soil, and later taught school there for two years Coming to Nebraska in the spring of 1878 he taught school in Saunders and Dodge counties several seasons, and subsequently worked in a store, and clerked in a bank In 1882 he invested a part of his savings in Fremont real estate, and later bought seventeen acres of land in the vicinity of Fremont Mr Snyder met with success in his undertakings, and having accumulated some money invested it in a farm of 400 acres, situated two miles west of Fremont In addition to carrying on general farming, he made a specialty of dairying, which he continued until moving into Fremont, in March, 1910 He has sold all his land.

Mr Snyder married, in 1883, Nettie N Burt, who was born in New York State, where her parents, Henry and Caroline Burt, were lifelong farmers Five children are living and two deceased of those which have blessed the union of Mr and Mrs Snyder, namely Frank B, of Fremont, is shipping clerk for the Hammond & Stevens Company, in which he is a stockholder, George, engaged in farming in Colorado, Winifred, living at home, Ray H, of Fremont is in the employ of the Nye, Schneider & Fowler Company, Lydia, at home, Ethel, who married James E Nerray and died at the age of thirty-nine years, leaving one son Eldon, and Berne C, died when nineteen years old

Politically Mr Snyder invariably casts his vote in favor of the republican party. He is liberal on local affairs

George S Brown Prominent among the representatives of the farming and stock growing industry of Dodge County, one of this county's native sons who has worked his own way to position and independence is George S Brown Mr Brown, who is the owner of a valuable property in section 12, Maple Township, was for some years an operator in Nance County, but the call of his native soil brought him back thereto, and in the Fremont community he is making the most of his opportunities and is steadily acquiring a higher position and richer emoluments

George S Brown was born on his father's farm, about nine miles northwest of Fremont, in Dodge County, in 1879, a son of David and Catherine (Raycraft) Brown His father was born in Ontario, Canada, in 1839, a son of John and Ellen Brown, the former being a native of Erin's Isle who settled in young manhood in Canada and there passed the rest of his life as a farmer, dying at the age of seventy-two years David Brown acquired a public school education in Ontario and for nine years followed the vocation of educator When he came to the United States, in 1866, he first settled in Benton County, Iowa, and was engaged in farming for one year, but following that moved around considerably until 1871 In that year, after spending a short time at Fremont, he rented a farm nine miles northwest of that city, which he later acquired by purchase He developed into one of the substantial agriculturists of his community, but for several years has been in retirement, having reached the advanced age of eighty-one years He is a prohibitionist and a man of integrity and probity, and is a faithful member of the Presbyterian Church. He married, in Ontario, Catherine Raycraft, who died in 1917, at the age of seventy-two years, and to them there were born six sons and three daughters: Alfred D, William J, Emma V, Agnes S, Helen M, George S, Earl R, Owen D and Ernest H Of these Agnes S is deceased

George S. Brown attended the public schools of his native community and was given the further advantages of attendance at the normal school at Fremont. He made his home under the parental roof until he reached his majority, and at that time went to Nance County, where he began operations on his own account For sixteen years he continued in that community, carrying on general farming and also meeting with success in the raising of Shorthorn cattle and Poland China hogs, but eventually disposed of his Nance County holdings and returned to Dodge County in 1917 Here he has duplicated and even bettered, the record for agricultural achievement which he had made in the other community, and today he is numbered among the most progressive and prosperous of the agriculturists of his part of the county. His farm is modern in every respect, and includes in its appointments all the latest machinery and equipment, while the buildings are commodious and substantial and the farm bears a general air of prosperity that evidences the managerial ability of its owner

Mr Brown was married in 1901 to Miss Theo D Taylor, who was born in Illinois, daughter of Alfred J Taylor, one of the early settlers of Dodge County, and to this union there have been born four children: Clara, Alta F, Ruth G and Margaret Mr and Mrs Brown are faithful members of the Presbyterian Church, which they attend at Fremont, and are liberal contributors to its movements Mr Brown is a stalwart prohibitionist and a man of sound integrity and probity of character His only fraternal affiliation is with the local lodge of the Royal Highlanders

G G Hines Besides its importance as a county seat and commercial center of Washington County, Blair is the home of some business institutions and business men whose relations are broadly extended beyond the limits of Washington County One of these is G G Hines, a contractor and builder whose material achievements are represented in the prominent architecture of both Washington and Dodge counties and in many other sections of the state He has been a resident of Blair for many years, his father was a successful contractor in the west for a long period, and the present firm of Struve & Hines enjoys the highest rating all over the west

G G Hines was born at Avoca in Shelby County, Iowa, December 10, 1876, son of T J. and Elizabeth (Carmen) Hines His paternal grandfather, Thomas J. Hines, was a native of Pennsylvania and in the early '60s came west with his family traveling in a wagon drawn by ox team to Iowa He homesteaded in Iowa and spent the rest of his life there The maternal grandfather of G G Hines was Doctor Carmen a physician who practiced in Iowa for many years Elizabeth Carmen was born in Quincy, Illinois, and T J Hines was born in Warren County, Pennsylvania They were married at Avoca, Iowa T J Hines took up railroad contracting at a pioneer period in the construction of western railroads He did a large amount of contracting for the Union Pacific, and built the stone arch over Green River in Wyoming, and also the depots in Ogden and Logan, Utah, these being the more conspicuous among the many important contracts he handled He also built the school building at one of the large Indian agencies in the State of Wyoming, and in this contract used a million and a half bricks, having established the kilns and supervised the manufacture of the brick He was in the business on a large scale until he lost his life in a cyclone at Herman, Nebraska, in 1900 T J Hines was a Methodist, was affiliated with the Ancient Order of United Workmen, the Woodmen of the World and the Knights of Pythias, was a republican, and took considerable interest in politics and served two terms as sheriff of Shelby County, Iowa He and his wife had nine children, seven daughters and two sons G G Hines was the third in age and is the only one now living in Nebraska His brother, Driscoll, is a successful contractor at Denver

G. G. Hines finished his early education in the Omaha High School, and subsequently took technical correspondence courses to aid him in his profession He learned the building trades with his father, and for over twenty years has been engaged in contracting Many of the principal buildings of Blair are monuments to his enterprise, including the Public Library, the State Bank Building, and he also erected the first bank at Kennard, a large garage in Fremont, and the firm of Struve & Hines now has a contract for building a large bank building at Neeley, Nebraska

In 1901 Mr Hines married Alma Gochenour. She was born in Iowa, daughter of Adam and Mary J. (Burgess) Gochenour, who came to Blair in 1888 and the family name has been a prominent one in that city ever since Her father was in the butcher business in Blair for a number of years Both her parents died there Mrs Hines was one of twins, the youngest of six children Mr. Hines is a member of the Congregational Church, is affiliated with the Independent Order of Odd Fellows and with his wife is a member of the Rebekahs, and in politics is a republican

FRED E KOEHNE Endowed with the habits of industry and thrift, and the keenness of intellect that win success in any line of industry, Fred E. Koehne has made diligent use of his time and opportunities, and having acquired sufficient wealth to assure him a comfortable income is now living retired from active business cares in Fremont, his home being at 435 West Ninth Street A son of the late Charles Koehne, he was born July 11, 1858, in Wisconsin, coming on the paternal side of German lineage

Born and bred in Germany, Charles Koehne immigrated to the United States when young, locating in Milwaukee County, Wisconsin, where he subsequently followed the blacksmith's trade for thirty-seven or more years, doing all kinds of pioneer work, even making nails for the farmers' use Coming to Dodge County, Nebraska in 1871, he purchased 560 acres of land, paying $6 25 an acre for the larger part of it, but never lived upon it He afterward moved to South Dakota, and there he and his wife spent their declining years, dying on the homestead which he had improved. He was a republican in politics, and while a resident of Wisconsin served many years as postmaster at Paynesville His wife, whose maiden name was Mary N Meyer, was born in Rochester, New York Six children were born to them, as follows: Charles, a veterinary surgeon, lives on the old homestead in Milwaukee, Wisconsin, Fred E, of whom we write; Albert, engaged in the implement business at Oldham, South Dakota, Caroline, a widow, resides in Milwaukee, Wisconsin, John, who owns and operates an elevator at Oldham, South Dakota, and Mary Ann, who lives with her widowed sister in Milwaukee

Brought up in Milwaukee County, Wisconsin, Fred E Koehne was educated in the district schools, and afterwards served an apprenticeship at the wagon and carriage maker's trade, which he followed three or four years Migrating to South Dakota, he took up a homestead claim on which he lived and labored seven years before selling it Coming to Dodge County, Nebraska in 1887, Mr Koehne purchased the large tract of land belonging to his father, and occupied it from 1888 until 1899, in the meantime adding each year to its improvements. Mr Koehne then sold the farm, receiving $300 an acre for the same tract that his father bought for $6 25 an acre Removing then to

Fremont, he has since lived a life of leisure, enjoying the fruits of his earlier years of toil He is independent in politics, and has never been an aspirant for official honors

Mr Koehne married, February 25, 1880, Eunice A V. West, who was born in Milwaukee County, Wisconsin, August 25, 1858, where her father, Quincy P West, was a prosperous farmer Five children blessed the marriage of Mr and Mrs Koehne, four of whom are living, namely Charles Julian, manager of the Farmers Co-operative Union at Ames, Nebraska, Sadie, wife of Fred Wislicen, of Fremont, manager of the New York Bakery, Carrie, single, is employed in the Anderson Jewelry Store, and lives with her parents, and Freida, living at home Mr Koehne and his family attend the Congregational Church, and contribute towards its support For upwards of a quarter of a century Mr Koehne has been a member of the Independent Order of Odd Fellows, in which he has passed all the chairs, and he, and all of his family, with the exception of the youngest son, are members of the Daughters of Rebekah, two of his daughters, Sadie and Carrie, are past noble grands

EDWARD C JACKSON There is nothing in the world more beautiful than the spectacle of a life that has reached its autumn with a harvest of good and useful deeds It is like the forest in October days when the leaves have borrowed the richest colors of the light and glow in the mellowed sheen of the Indian summer, reflecting all the radiance of their existence The man who has lived a clean and useful life cannot fail to enjoy a serenity of soul, and when such a life is preserved in its strength and integrity so that even in age its influence continues unabated, it challenges the added admiration of those whose good fortune it is to be brought into contact with it Such a life has been that of Edward Charles Jackson, for fifty years one of the substantial and enterprising citizens of Washington County Such a life merits a record of its deeds, but his record is too familiar to the people of the locality of which this history deals to require any fulsome encomium here, his life work speaking for itself in stronger terms than the biographer could possibly employ

Edward Charles Jackson, clerk of the district court at Blair, was born in Columbus, Georgia on December 10, 1844, and is the son of George H and Harriett M (Allen) Jackson Both of these parents were natives of New York State, the father having been born at Peru, and the mother at Troy They were married at Troy and in 1842 they went to Columbus, Georgia, where George Jackson had a contract for the erection of a cotton mill In his work as a contractor he necessarily was located in different places from time to time, but he finally returned to Troy, New York, and engaged in the manufacture of wagons and buggies. Subsequently they moved to Ashton, Maryland, where they spent their remaining years and died They were members of the Baptist Church and he also held membership in the Independent Order of Odd Fellows He gave his political support to the republican party and was active in public affairs, having served a number of years as a member of the county board at Troy To him and his wife were born eight children, namely William H, of Detroit, Michigan, where he is engaged as a landscape photographer, owning a large establishment and enjoying a wide reputation for the excellence of his work, Edward C, Mary Elizabeth, the widow of George Brown, Frederick D, who is now retired and living in Ashton, Maryland, Frank H, now deceased, who

Edward C. Jackson

was an architect in the employ of the Federal Government, Emma K, an artist and colorist in Detroit, Jennie, deceased, Allen, who was an actor for many years, but is now retired and living at East Hadam, Connecticut

Edward C Jackson received his educational training in the public schools of Troy, New York His first occupation was as a wagon-maker, which trade he learned Later he was employed as a bookkeeper, and also was employed as a copyist in an attorney's office In August, 1862, Mr Jackson enlisted as a private in Company K, Twelfth Regiment Vermont Volunteer Infantry, at Rutland, Vermont, with which he served his enlistment period of nine months He then returned to Troy and in February, 1864, enlisted as a private in Company A, One Hundred and Twenty-fifth Regiment New York Volunteer Infantry, with which he served until June 14, 1865, when he was honorably discharged Mr Jackson's army record was one of which he is deservedly proud and in evidence of which were his promotions, on May 27, 1864, to sergeant on December 5, 1864, as first lieutenant, and the captaincy of Company B on March 28, 1865 His regiment was a part of the Army of the Potomac, with which he took part in many of the most important engagements of that great army up to Lee's surrender

In December, 1867, Mr Jackson came to Nebraska, locating first at Omaha, where he was associated with his brother in the photographic business for three years In 1870 he came to Washington County and for five years was engaged in farming In 1875 he was elected county clerk and clerk of courts, serving as such from 1876 to 1879 and then during 1880-81 he served as clerk of courts From 1881 to 1887 Mr Jackson served as deputy county treasurer, and then from 1888 to 1891 as county treasurer Mr Jackson was admitted to the bar in 1879 and so favorable an impression had he made on the voters of the county that in 1893 he was elected county judge, occupying the bench from 1894 to 1901 After his retirement from the bench, he was engaged in the practice of law until 1911, when he again became clerk of the district court, which office he is still filling He has devoted himself indefatigably to the discharge of the duties of the office and because of his faithfulness and painstaking care of details he has not only made himself well-nigh invaluable to the court, but has also gained the confidence and good will of all who have come into contact with him

On November 28, 1867, Mr Jackson was married to Elizabeth Smith, who was born in New York City, and to them have been born three children, namely George H, died in infancy, Ada, died November 22, 1912, aged thirty-seven years and Joseph, a lumber broker in Minneapolis

Edward C Jackson is a member of the Episcopalian Church and of the Ancient Free and Accepted Masons In the latter order he has attained to the degrees of Knight Templar and he has received preferment in all the subordinate bodies in which he has passed the chairs He was grand junior deacon in the grand lodge of Masons and is now grand commander of Knights Templar of the State of Nebraska He is a stanch supporter of the republican party and while in the army he voted for Abraham Lincoln before he was twenty-one years old He keeps alive his old army associations through his membership in John A Dix Post No. 52, Grand Army of the Republic, which he has served as commander In the life history of Mr. Jackson are found evidences of characteristics that always make for achievement—persistency coupled with fortitude and lofty traits—and as the result of such a life he has long been one of the best known, most influential and highly esteemed citizens of his county

NATHAN SAMPTER For many years actively identified with the mercantile interests of Dodge County, the late Nathan Sampter displayed marked ability and sound judgment in the management of his business, and as one of the leading clothiers of Fremont acquired considerable property He was born November 20, 1853, in Germany, where the days of his early boyhood were spent At the age of thirteen years, unaccompanied by relatives or friends, he bravely crossed the ocean to seek a living in a land where there were fewer restrictions

Locating in New York State, Nathan Sampter continued his studies there for a brief time, and later attended school in Peoria, Illinois. There, in the employ of an uncle, he became familiar with the work associated with a clothing store, and was subsequently engaged in the clothing business at Independence, Iowa, for five years Coming to Fremont, Nebraska in 1883, Mr. Sampter opened a clothing store, and managed it with signal success until 1909, when he sold out his interests in the establishment He thereafter lived retired from active business until his death, which occurred November 15, 1910, at his pleasant home on North Nye Street Industrious, thrifty, and a wise manager, Mr Sampter accumulated a fair share of this world's goods, his business having been extensive and lucrative

Mr Sampter married, March 26, 1888, in Fremont, Nebraska, Carrie Myers, a native of Independence, Iowa Her father, August Myers, emigrated from Germany to the United States as a young man, settling in Independence, Iowa, as a clothing merchant Subsequently moving to Nebraska, he spent the last thirty-two years of his life in Omaha. He was a Democrat in politics, and a member of the Jewish Church Mr Myers married Babette Baum, who was also born in Germany, and of the seven children born to their union, Mrs Sampter was the sixth child in succession of birth, and one of the five now living

Mr and Mrs Sampter became the parents of three children, namely Mrs John Sonin, whose husband is a well known merchant of Fremont, Mrs Hyman Fishgall, of Sioux City, Iowa, and Gerald, member of the firm with Mr Sonin Politically Mr Sampter was a sound republican; fraternally he was a Mason, and religiously he and family belonged to the Jewish Church

ALEXANDER THOM came to Nebraska in January, 1882, and after having long been actively and successfully identified with agricultural and livestock industry in Dodge County he retired from the farm and established his home at North Bend, where he has since continued to enjoy the merited prosperity gained through former years of earnest endeavor. He has passed the psalmist's span of threescore years and ten and is a sterling citizen to whom is accorded the fullest measure of popular esteem

Mr Thom was born in Aberdeenshire, Scotland, September 25, 1847, and is a son of William and Christina (Chalmers) Thom, who there passed their entire lives, the father having been fifty-three years of age at the time of his death and the mother having passed to eternal rest at the age of sixty-eight years William Thom was a farmer by vocation and both he and his wife were zealous members of the Free Church of Scotland in which he served as an elder for a number of years prior to his death. Of the six children three came to the United States William, who became a resident of Nebraska and whose death occurred in a hospital at Omaha, December 13, 1919, Isabelle, who became the wife of James Tham, of Illinois, and who was in the home of her brother, Alexander, of this review, at the time of her death, and Alexander, whose name initiates this sketch. Of the other three children, James and George died in Scotland, and there Andrew has been for half a century pastor of a church in Stirlingshire, as a representative clergyman of the Free Church of Scotland in that section of the land of hills and heather

Alexander Thom was afforded the advantages of the schools of his native land and there continued his association with farm enterprise until 1877, when he came to the United States and became foreman of the large farm estate of Henry B Sherman in Dodge County, Wisconsin. He retained this position five years, and in January, 1882, he came to Nebraska and became associated with the firm of Smith & Mallon, at North Bend, an important concern engaged in the importing of horses. In the interests of this firm Mr Thom purchased high grade horses in Scotland and shipped the stock to the United States, his operations in this field of enterprise having continued about four years He then purchased land in Dodge County and turned his attention, with characteristic vigor and judgment, to general farming and stock-raising, in which connection he made a specialty of raising blooded Clydesdale horses and Chester White swine On his farm, comprising 320 acres, he made the best of improvements, including the erection of a barn that is still considered the finest in the county, and he continued his active work on the farm until 1892, since which time he has lived virtually retired, at North Bend, his farm property still remaining in his possession

Mr. Thom was one of the organizers and incorporators of the First State Bank of North Bend, of which he has continuously served as president from the inception of the enterprise and to the success of which his mature business judgment and conservative policies have contributed in large degree He is an elder and member of the board of trustees of the United Presbyterian Church at North Bend, and as a citizen of his adopted state he is most loyal and appreciative

In 1887 Mr Thom wedded Miss Margaret Agen, a native of the state of Illinois, and she passed to the life eternal in 1892 Of the three children of this union two died in infancy, and the one surviving is Mabel, wife of Dr Andrew Harvey, a representative physician at Fremont, judicial center of Dodge County, of whom mention is made on other pages of this work For his second wife Mr Thom married Anna Collins, and she passed away a few years later, the only child of this marriage likewise being deceased April 15, 1913, recorded the marriage of Mr Thom to Laura Miller, who was born and reared in Dodge County and who is the popular chatelaine of their pleasant home.

Mr. Thom is a radical prohibitionist in his political allegiance and has been active and zealous in furtherance of national prohibition, the success of the great movement being a source of marked gratification to him He has a high place in the confidence and esteem of his home community and the year 1920 finds him serving his third consecutive term as mayor of North Bend

ROBERT FRAHM It is a matter of grave import to the people of a community to know that their banking institutions are sound, that their entire business methods are carefully and well advised, that their assets are entirely adequate, and that the officers and directors are men of stable character and of thorough banking experience From the prosperity attending the Snyder State Bank at Snyder, Nebraska, it may be inferred that all these requirements are being held satisfactory, and since 1919, when Robert Frahm became president, a still larger measure of public confidence has been shown Although Mr Frahm is yet a young man, he has had a large amount of banking experience

Robert Frahm, president of the Snyder State Bank, is a native of Nebraska, born in 1886, in Saunders County His parents were Hans H and Margaretha K Frahm, the latter of whom was born in Germany, and the former, also of German ancestry, was a native of Illinois From Illinois the father came to Nebraska in 1869, locating first in Douglas County, but one year later moving into Saunders County, where he made his home for forty-four years His death occurred in 1914 He carried on farming and stockraising and prospered through industry and frugality The mother of Robert Frahm still survives, being a highly esteemed resident of Snyder He has two brothers and one sister, namely: Elliot H, who is cashier of the Snyder State Bank Fielda, who is assistant cashier of the Snyder State Bank, and Alvin, who served as assistant cashier for years of Snyder State Bank and one year as cashier of Bank of Morganza, Louisiana, and is now head bookkeeper of Scotland Lumber Company Ravenswood, Louisiana

Robert Frahm attended the public schools at Prague, Nebraska, had further school privileges at Fremont, and took a commercial course in Mosher-Lampman Business College, Omaha His first business experience was as a clerk in a general store at Memphis and later, in the same capacity was at Cedar Bluffs, Nebraska, following which he entered the Corn Exchange Bank at Spencer, in Boyd County, where he continued one year as bookkeeper After that he served four months as bookkeeper in the Nebraska National Bank at Norfolk Nebraska, going from there to the First National at Pilger, in Stanton County He was thus well posted in Nebraska banking law before going to South Dakota, where he was associated for two months with the Bank of Winner, and for nine months with the First National Bank of Fairfax in Gregory County In 1911 he returned to Nebraska to become cashier of the Snyder State Bank, of which he became president in March, 1919 While the affairs of the bank engage the greater part of his time, he gives some attention to his farm interests, mainly specializing in hogs and poultry, growing nothing but Poland China and Chester White hogs, and pure-blood Leghorn and Wyandotte chickens. He finds much pleasure and needed recreation in looking after the above interests

In 1910 Mr Frahm was united in marriage to Miss Martha Klug who was born in Madison County, Nebraska, though she was reared and educated in Boyd County, Nebraska They have a pleasant home and a wide social acquaintance at Snyder, and both are active members of the Lutheran Church, in which they were reared by careful parents In political life Mr Frahm has followed in the footsteps of a father whose good judgment he had never occasion to doubt, and has been quite prominent in local republican circles and is serving at present as village clerk and on the school board as moderator

NATHAN H BROWN, M D Well equipped for the duties demanded of the members of the medical profession, not only by natural gifts and temperament, but by mental training and untiring industry, the late Nathan H Brown, M D, of Fremont was for many years actively and successfully engaged in the practice of his chosen profession, having gained the confidence and good will of the community, and his death, which occurred while he was yet in manhood's prime, was a cause of deep regret A native of New York, he was born November, 30, 1851, near Saratoga, and died at his home in Fremont, Nebraska, November 29, 1903.

But two and a half years of age when his parents moved to Warrenville, Illinois, Nathan H Brown acquired his rudimentary education in the public schools of Dupage County, that state Turning his attention to the study of medicine, he was graduated from the Chicago Medical School, after which he took two or more post-graduate courses in New York City Locating in Racine County, Wisconsin, soon after his graduation, Doctor Brown remained there for eight years, in the meantime building up a large country practice, at first riding on horseback, with medicines in his saddle bags, but later making his rounds with a horse and buggy Then, after spending a brief time in Western Connecticut, he located in Fremont, Nebraska, in June, 1882, where he built up an extensive and very satisfactory practice, his professional skill and ability having won him an extensive patronage, and a position of note among the more successful physicians and surgeons of his day In 1894 the doctor, accompanied by his son, crossed the ocean, and had a most enjoyable time visiting points of interest in many parts of Europe, taking especial interest, however, in medical and surgical methods and institutions

Doctor Brown married, December 22, 1875, Gratia C Hamilton, who was born January 24, 1841, in Western New York, but at the age of three months was taken by her parents to Wisconsin, where she was educated Her father, William Hughes Hamilton, became well versed in legal lore, and was for several years engaged in the practice of law in Racine, Wisconsin Removing from there to Nebraska, he spent the closing years of his life in Fremont His wife, whose maiden name was Adelaide Palmer, died in Wisconsin Six children were born of their marriage, as follows. Gratia C, now Mrs. Brown, Alvah, a soldier in the Civil war, was killed in battle, Harriet A, wife of James M Brearley, a retired railroad man of Minneapolis, Minnesota, Martha C, died at the age of twenty-nine years, Stephen H, an attorney in Washington, Kansas, and James H, engaged in the grain business at Peoria, Illinois Mr. Hamilton was a republican in politics, and he and his family were Episcopalians

Two children blessed the union of Doctor and Mrs Brown, namely Francis H and Adeline Eliza Francis H Brown, M D, was educated for a physician, and for two and a half years was engaged in practice with his father in Fremont He became interested in the grain business, with which his father was also associated, and after the death of his father gave up the practice of medicine, and has since devoted his time and attention to the buying and selling of grain, being located in Omaha He married Daisy Goff, a daughter of J. W Goff, of Fremont, and they have one child, Francis Hilliard Brown Adeline Eliza Brown married F. H Richards, of Fremont, who is in business with his father, L D Richards, and they have one child, Fred H Richards, Jr, a bright and capable youth of eighteen years, who was graduated from the Shattuck School, in Faribault, Minnesota, with the highest honors of his class, and is now a student in the University of Nebraska, at Lincoln.

Mrs Brown is a woman of talent and culture, and is held in high esteem throughout the city, her beautiful home at 114 East Military Avenue being ever open to her many friends She was educated primarily in Manitowoc, Wisconsin, and subsequently studied for a while in the University of Wisconsin, at Madison She is a devout member of the Episcopal Church, of which the doctor was an attendant. He was a stanch democrat in politics, and a thirty-second degree Mason

WILLIAM SAEGER An active and thriving business man of Fremont, William Saeger is identified with the mercantile and manufacturing interests of Dodge County, being a member of the firm of Saeger & Sons, one of the most extensive and best known cigar making concerns in this section of the state He was born in Germany, a son of Henry Saeger, and there spent a part of his early life

Born, bred and married in Euger, Westphalia, Germany, Henry Saeger emigrated from the fatherland to the United States in 1887, coming directly to Fremont, Nebraska After working in the cigar factory of George Godfrey for a brief time, he started in business on his own account, becoming junior member of the firm of Stork & Saeger, continuing under that name until 1890, a period of two years On June 5, 1890, the present firm of Saeger & Sons was formed, and has been actively engaged in manufacturing cigars ever since, the members of the company comprising Henry Saeger, Sr, William Saeger, August Saeger, Peter Saeger, and Henry Saeger, Jr

This enterprising firm began business at the corner of Fourth Street and Nye Avenue, and subsequently occupied the Loomis Building on Main Street, five or six years Its constantly increasing business demanding more commodious quarters, Saeger & Sons erected, on the corner of Main and Fourth streets, a large two-story factory, the largest cigar manufactory in the state, it having a frontage of 44 feet, and being 120 feet deep The entire upper floor is used for manufacturing purposes by the firm, which also devotes the first floor of the north part of the building to its own uses, selling the products of its factory at retail, while the first floor of the south portion of the building is rented to other parties The firm carries on a very large business, both in making and selling cigars, employing about fifty people.

Henry Saeger, Sr, married, in Germany, Johanna Schroeder, who died in Fremont, Nebraska in 1916 Seven children were born of their marriage, as follows. William, of this sketch, August, born in Germany, is married and has four children, Alfred, Victor, Roland, and Elsie, Peter, born in Germany, married and has three children, Gretchen, Hulda, and George; Henry, Jr, is married, and has one child, Warren; Lizzie, wife of Arthur Fox, who is engaged in the laundry business at Great Falls, Montana. Gusta, wife of Fred Moller, a mail carrier in Fremont, and Minnie, wife of Francis Eagle, of Fremont, a traveling salesman Both parents united with the Lutheran Church when young The father, now a venerable man of eighty-five years, became quite homesick after spending seven years in Fremont, and went back to Germany to stay permanently, but after a short stay in his native land decided that life in the United States was far preferable, and returned to Fremont, where he has since lived, contented and happy

William Saeger, married in 1891, Dora Kaufman, and into their pleasant household nine children have made their advent, namely· Will; Paul, Edward, Fred, Rudolph; Homer, who secured the first prize in the baby contest on July 4, 1918, Kate, Elizabeth, and Minnie.

Mr. Saeger, who came to Fremont in 1886, a year before his father and family came, devotes his entire time and attention to his cigar business, which is extensive and lucrative.

WALTER C. BLISS A live, wide-awake young agriculturist of Dodge County, Walter C Bliss occupies a position of prominence among the enterprising and progressive farmers of Elkhorn Township, and is held in high esteem as a citizen of worth and ability A son of F C Bliss, he was born in 1891, at Howell, Colfax, County, Nebraska, coming from honored New England stock

Born and bred in Vermont, F C Bliss grew to manhood in New England, and received his education in the public schools Coming to Colfax County, Nebraska in 1886, he took up land near Howell, and for several years was engaged in farming Subsequently removing to Omaha, he embarked in the commission business as head of the live stock firm of Bliss & Wellman, one of the best known organizations of the kind in the city, and in the management of its affairs is meeting with excellent success. To him and his wife, whose name before marriage was Ada Pattee, three children have been born, as follows Huishel, deceased, H P, of Omaha, in business with his father, and Walter C

Well trained in agricultural pursuits as a boy and youth, Walter C Bliss began life for himself with fair prospects for a prosperous future, and his energetic labors, ability and good business tact have already placed him among the prominent and successful agriculturalists of Dodge County He has 360 acres of rich and fertile land in Elkhorn Township, on which he has made many wise improvements, his farm in regard to its appointments and equipments being one of the best in the community In addition to carrying on mixed husbandry after the most approved modern methods, Mr. Bliss makes a specialty of raising stock, breeding about three hundred and fifty Hampshire hogs every year, and feeding a hundred head of cattle

Mr Bliss married, June 24, 1914, Vivian Wright, who was born in Richford, Vermont, and acquired her early education in the public schools of her native state Her father, Mathew Wright, never came to Nebraska, but since his death her mother has made her home with Mr and Mrs Bliss, who have one child, Ethlada Bliss Ever interested in local progress, Mr Bliss, although not an office seeker, has served as school director a number of terms He is a member of the Congregational Church, and Mrs Bliss, true to the faith in which she was reared, belongs to the Baptist Church

MRS MAY (SMITH) MOREHOUSE A daughter of the late Joseph Towner Smith, Sr, Mrs Morehouse was born in Fremont of honored pioneer ancestry Her father, a native of Pennsylvania, came to Nebraska with two of his brothers long before it was admitted to statehood Locating in 1856 in what is now Dodge County, he helped lay out the Town of Fremont, and was thereafter conspicuously identified with its development and growth

A man of distinctive and forceful individuality, Mr Smith was conspicuously identified with the upbuilding of Fremont, being a leading spirit in the establishment of beneficial enterprises, and in addition to having been the pioneer merchant of the place served as its first fire chief, and his brother and partner, James G, was the first postmaster. Full of energy and vim, he extended his business operations from time to time, and through wise management and good investments accumulated a large estate, to a part of which Mrs Morehouse is heir

Mr. Smith married first Charlotte Adelia Miller, who died in early life He subsequently married, November 25, 1882, Augusta Wilhelmine Knopp, and into the household thus established three children were born, as follows May, now Mrs Morehouse, Franklin Perry, who was born in 1888, and died March 10, 1919; and Joseph T, who has charge of his father's estate A more complete sketch and a steel portrait of Joseph Towner Smith will be found on other pages of this work

Mrs Morehouse received her rudimentary education in Fremont, and after leaving the high school attended St Mary's Boarding School in Knoxville, Illinois, for two years, and then studied a year in Liberty, Missouri On June 28, 1905, she was united in marriage with Carlos Morehouse, who was born in Hooper, Nebraska, and acquired his first knowledge of books in the rural schools of his native county, completing his early studies at the Culver Military Academy, in Culver, Indiana For two years thereafter, Mr Morehouse was engaged in the grain business, having an elevator at Gresham, York County, coming from there to Fremont, he was employed in the bottling works for a time, after which he became a member of the firm of Wiley Morehouse & Company, wholesale dealers in fruit, with which he was connected until recently

Mr and Mrs Morehouse have three children, namely Gene, born September 30, 1907, Joseph Franklin, born in 1909, and Richard Carlos, born in 1911 Religiously, Mrs Morehouse is an active member of the Congregational Church Mrs. Morehouse is a member of the Order of the Eastern Star, and belongs to the Fremont Woman's Club, and to the Charity Club

ALLEN JOHNSON is one of the representative younger members of the bar of Dodge County and is engaged in successful general practice in the city of Fremont, as junior member of the firm of Cain & Johnson, his partner being William M Cain, of whom individual mention is made on other pages

Mr Johnson was born in Dodge County, August 3, 1880, and is a representative of a pioneer family of the county, where his father established residence in the year that marked the admission of Nebraska to statehood. Mr Johnson is a son of Andrew J and Martha (Sampson) Johnson, who were born and reared in Sweden and whose marriage was solemnized in Dodge County, where the father established his home in 1867, the mother having come to this country in the early '70s Andrew Johnson came to this county with very limited financial resources, and he took up and instituted the development of a homestead, in the meanwhile adding to his revenues by working at intervals on the Union Pacific Railroad for a period of about three years After his marriage he and his wife remained on his homestead farm a few years, and finally they removed to Burt County, where Mr Johnson purchased a goodly acreage of land and developed a valuable farm property. There he continued to reside until his death, November 10, 1916, at the age of sixty-seven years, his devoted wife having passed away on the 13th of the preceding April, aged sixty-seven years The eldest of the four children is Charles W, a retired farmer residing at Oakland, Burt County, Sarah is the wife of Charles E Lunberry, of Craig, that county, Miss Anna C resides at Oakland, Burt County, and Allen, of this review, is the youngest of the number Through his own ability and efforts Andrew J Johnson gained substantial success in connection with farm industry in Nebraska, and he was one of its loyal and progressive citizens His political allegiance was given to the republican party and he and his wife were zealous communicants of the Lutheran Church Though Andrew J Johnson was of Swedish birth, his paternal grandfather was an Englishman named Allen, who left his native land on account of religious intolerance manifested toward him and made his way to Sweden, where he became successful in his temporal affairs and where he passed the remainder of his life The change of the name of his descendants to Johnson was in consonance with the common practice in the Scandinavian countries, where the son took as his surname the personal, or Christian name of the father, with the additional terminal of "son" Two sisters of Andrew J Johnson married brothers by the name of Pollock and the two Pollock families were the earliest settlers of Dodge County, Nebraska.

Allen Johnson was a child at the time of the family removal to Burt County, where he was reared on the home farm and profited by the advantages afforded in the public schools This discipline was supplemented by a course in the Fremont Normal School at Fremont, and in preparation for his chosen profession he entered the law department of the University of Nebraska, in which he was graduated as a member of the class of 1908, with the degree of Bachelor of Laws. He was forthwith admitted to the bar of his native state, and he has been admitted also to practice before the Federal Courts in the state All of these privileges were granted him on the day of his graduation, and the next day he opened an office at Fremont and girded himself for his professional novitiate He proved himself well fortified as a trial lawyer and counselor, and his law business has continuously expanded in scope and importance. Since 1917 he has been associated in practice with William M Cain, under the title of Cain & Johnson, and this is recognized as one of the strong and successful law firms of Dodge County The firm has a representative clientage and is retained as local legal representative of the Chicago & Northwestern Railroad Company. Mr Johnson is the owner of valuable real estate in Fremont, including his attractive home He is a republican in his political allegiance and he and his wife hold membership in the Methodist Episcopal Church of their home city

August 2, 1908, marked the solemnization of the marriage of Mr Johnson to Miss Lottie Morter, who was born in Hand County, South Dakota, a daughter of Henry and Fedora (Barr) Morter, who are now residents of Burt County, Nebraska, where the father is a prosperous retired farmer Mr and Mrs Johnson have one child, Forrest Allen Johnson, who was born May 13, 1917

William H Belknap has been a resident and active business man of Blair for a quarter of a century and is manager of the Haller Proprietary Remedy Company Mr. Belknap first came to Washington County, Nebraska, soon after the close of the Civil war, but through the stress of circumstances abandoned his intention of developing a homestead and returned east to take up a business career

He was born at Yonkers, New York, July 30, 1845, son of Charles F. and Abigail Jane (O'Dell) Belknap His parents were lifelong residents of New York State and his father was a contractor and builder and followed the business until his death There were three children Ethelbert, a retired hat manufacturer at Yonkers; W H., second in age; and Mrs Ida Morrell, who still lives in New York State Charles F Belknap was the first member initiated into the Lodge of Odd Fellows at Yonkers and was faithful and loyal to that order all the rest of his life and was honored with all the chairs and offices He began voting as a whig and subsequently became a republican

William H Belknap acquired his early education at Yonkers, attending the Star Commercial Collegiate Institute of that city At the age of sixteen he began work as clerk in the grocery store of Walter Paddock at Yonkers, but soon gave up his place behind the counter to enlist as a soldier in Company A of the Thirteenth Regiment of New York Militia He was in the Hundred Day service and did picket duty and acted as a guard on the pike road and railroads around Richmond He and his regiment went by boat from Fortress Monroe to New York City for the purpose of being discharged The boat was wrecked during the voyage and seven lost their lives while being transferred to life boats Following his military experience Mr Belknap was for two years entry clerk with a hatter's supply house of New York

In 1867 he came as a pioneer to Washington County, Nebraska. He entered a homestead and earnestly devoted his time to its development and improvement for a year and a half There were many trials and discouragements, and the last straw was a severe hail which completely destroyed all his crop prospects for that year. Leaving his place in charge of a neighbor, he returned east to better his finances He had paid eight hundred dollars for lumber for building purposes and has practically nothing to show for nearly two years of hard work He was offered five hundred dollars for his homestead and decided to sell it, though something interfered with carrying out the transaction and he continued to own the land for a long period of years, until 1910, when he finally sold the property at a hundred dollars an acre

Mr Belknap, after his Nebraska homesteading experience, remained in New York State for twenty-five years and became very successful in business, as president of the Yonkers Hat Manufacturing Company. Then in 1896 he returned to Nebraska and located at Blair, and has since been manager for the Haller Proprietary Company, a company incorporated for fifty thousand dollars capital This company manufactures a large line of home remedies and the product is sold and widely distributed over the country

December 22, 1867, at Woodbine, Iowa, Mr Belknap married Miss Emma A Royster. She became the mother of four children, two of whom are still living The son Rolland is chief auditor for the Sperry & Hutchinson Company at Yonkers, and the other son Stanley is in the repair department of the Remington Typewriter Company in Omaha In 1901 at Blair Mr. Belknap married Marie F. Peterson, who was born on a Nebraska farm They have two children, William H Jr, a schoolboy, and Adeline Priscilla Mr Belknap and his family are all members of the Baptist Church He has been a loyal member of the Masonic Order since 1866 and is also affiliated with the Grand Army of the Republic and is a republican voter

OTTO HOEGERMEYER Located in a rich agricultural region, Otto Hoegermeyer stands high among the enterprising and self-reliant men who are so ably conducting the farming interests in Everett Township, the greater part of his land being in a yielding condition, and the improvements on his place being of a good, practical, and substantial character Although native born, his birth having occurred November 18, 1887, in Dodge County, he is of foreign ancestry, his parents, Henry F and Mary Hoegermeyer, having been born on German soil

Brought up in Germany, Henry F Hoegermeyer was educated in the public schools, and, in common with his youthful companions, served the required time in the German army He subsequently learned the blacksmith's trade, which he followed for a while In 1872 he came to the United States, and having settled in Dodge County, Nebraska, secured work on a farm Having accumulated some money, he wisely invested it in land, and having made good improvements on it continued life as a farmer and stock raiser, branches of industry that proved profitable On his well cultivated estate he resided until his death, in 1914 He was not affiliated with any political party, being an independent voter Religiously he was a member of St John's Lutheran Church, to which his widow, who is now a resident of Dodge County, belongs. Nine children were born to their union, as follows Anna, wife of Mr. Heermann, a farmer in Stanton County, Louise, wife of William Moeller, who is engaged in farming in Dodge County; Minnie, wife of Otto Langewisch, a Dodge County agriculturalist, Mary, Augusta; Henry, a farmer in Cuming County, Fred, engaged in farming in South Dakota, Herman, farming in Washington County, and Otto, subject of this sketch.

Completing his early education in the rural schools, Otto Hoegermeyer worked with his father several seasons in the parental homestead Starting in life for himself in 1914, Mr Hoegermeyer has since carried on general farming with good results, making a specialty to some extent of raising a good grade of stock. He is a stockholder in the Hooper Mill and Grain Company, which is doing an extensive business In politics he is independent, as a voter being bound to no party Religiously, true to the faith in which he was reared, he is a Lutheran, being a trustworthy member of St John's Church

Mr. Hoegermeyer married, in 1916, Lydia Whitman, who was born in Indiana, and they have two children, Walter and Hugo

James M Shaffer has been actively identified with the agricultural interests of Maple Township, Dodge County, for more than a quarter of a century and ranks among the extensive successful farmers of the locality. His success has been self-attained, and in its gaining he has used strictly legitimate methods, which have served to substantially place him high in the confidence and esteem of his associates and acquaintances

Mr Shaffer was born in Pennsylvania in 1863, a son of Abel and Mary Ann (Hellwick) Shaffer, natives of the Keystone State His father learned the shoemaker's trade in his youth and followed that vocation in Pennsylvania until 1878, when he came to Nebraska and rented a farm in Dodge County He was an industrious man and eventually accumulated sufficient means with which to buy his land, the rest of his life being passed in agricultural operations He was a capable farmer and a good judge of live stock, while his citizenship and integrity were never questioned In politics he was a republican, and he and his worthy and estimable wife were members of the Lutheran Church They were the parents of six children· James M., William, who is engaged in farming in Dodge County, Emma, the widow of Joe Barner, of Kearney, Nebraska; Lucinda, the wife of Henry Stever, an agriculturist of Dodge County; Jacob, a resident of Kearney, and Abel, deceased

James M Shaffer was educated in the public schools of Pennsylvania, and was fifteen years of age when he accompanied his parents on their overland trip to Nebraska He was reared to agricultural pursuits and remained on the home place with his father until he reached the age of twenty-nine years, at that time buying 160 acres of land From that time to the present Mr. Shaffer has been extending his operations annually, and at this time is accounted one of the successfully substantial farmers and stockraisers of Maple Township He has a good grade of live stock and his improvements and equipment indicate that he is progressive in principle and that he takes a pride in his surroundings While farming has been his chief work, he has not let opportunity pass him by when business prestige has been at stake, and is a stockholder in the Union Elevator of Hooper, and the Lion Bonding Company, of Omaha. In politics he is a republican

Mr. Shaffer was married in 1895 to Miss Elizabeth Brugger, who was born in Pennsylvania, and to this union there have been born two children LeRoy and Iva, both at home.

CHARLES M MILLER Ten miles distant from North Bend. Dodge County, is to be found the attractive rural home of Charles M Miller, who here has a well improved farm of 120 acres, in sections 2 and 11, Cotterell Township As an agriculturist and stock-grower he has well upheld the high standards that have long been a marked feature of industrial enterprise in Dodge County, and his success has been substantial. His tangible rewards are especially pleasing to note in view of the fact that he came from Iowa to this county when a young man of twenty-one years, driving through with a team and covered wagon and reinforced with a capital of only ten dollars at the time when he crossed over the Missouri River and made his appearance in Nebraska

Mr Miller was born in Mahaska County, Iowa, on the 7th of August, 1861, and is a son of John T and Elizabeth Miller, who were numbered among the sterling pioneers of Iowa, where the mother still maintains her home, at a venerable age, the father having been a native of Terre Haute, Indiana, and having been seventy-two years of age at the time of his death He reclaimed and improved a pioneer farm in Iowa and was still a resident of Mahaska County, that state, at the time of his death

In the public schools of the Hawkeye State Charles M Miller acquired his early education, and in the meanwhile he had gained a plethora of experience in connection with the work of the home farm He continued to be there associated with agricultural enterprise until he had attained to his legal majority, when, in 1882, he set forth with his team and covered wagon to establish a home in Nebraska and to work his way toward the goal of independence and enduring prosperity. Soon after his arrival in Dodge County he purchased eight acres of wild land, in section 2, Cotterell Township, and for this property he paid at the rate of thirty dollars an acre With definite plans for providing a home, the young bachelor erected a modest dwelling and other necessary buildings on his new farm, and valiantly began the work of bringing the land under cultivation His original tract is an integral part of his present well improved farm of 120 acres, and the modern house and other excellent buildings give evidence of the prosperity that has attended the earnest enterprise of Mr Miller as an agriculturist and stock-grower In past years he gave special attention to the feeding of cattle and hogs for the market, but he now limits this feature of his farm enterprise, in order to develop to the fullest extent the agricultural resources of the land He is a democrat in politics and is known as a loyal and progressive citizen of his adopted county

Not long did Mr Miller feel content to maintain a bachelor home on his farm, as is shown in the fact that the year 1884 recorded his marriage to Miss Elizabeth Haberer, who likewise is a native of Iowa, and who has proved a devoted companion and helpmeet The while the passing years have brought a fine family of eleven children into the pleasant home, namely Iva, Josephine, Alfred, Elsie, Zora, Goldie, Lyda, Sylvia, Onnie, Walter and Carl

DON C VAN DEUSEN, editor and proprietor of the Pilot, the oldest newspaper of Washington County, is one of the representative men of Blair, whose influence is far-reaching and effective He was born in Beverly, Ohio, on October 12, 1871, a son of Barrett S and Hannah (Green) Van Deusen, born February 21, 1843, natives of Canajoharie, New York, and Ohio, respectively They were married in Ohio and came to Blair, Nebraska, in 1873 and bought railroad land five miles west of Blair Mr Van Deusen has retired and now lives at Blair, but continues to own 320 acres of land, a portion of which he bought for $10 per acre This land was all improved by him and is now very valuable He and his wife became the parents of nine children, five of whom are still living, namely: C C, who is on the old homestead, served in the Nebraska State Legislature for two sessions, Don C, whose name heads this review, H G, who is living retired at Kennard; Lena, who is now Mrs Henry Kasbaum and lives near Dunbar, Neb, was for a number of years a trained nurse and lived in Omaha, and Mrs Don J Gammel, who lives at Tekamah, Nebraska, where her husband is manager of the Farmers Elevator Company The mother is a member of the Methodist Episcopal Church, but the father does not belong to any religious organization During the war between the states he served as steward on the battleships Sachem and Uncas under his brother, Maj-Gen George H Van Deusen, and was fortunate enough to be stationed at Newport News at the time of the battle between the historic Merrimac and Monitor which ended the hope of the Confederacy for naval supremacy, and was an eye-witness to what was at that time the greatest naval engagement of the age

After attending the country schools of his neighborhood, Don C. Van Deusen went to high school for one year at Omaha, completing his high school work at Blair, where he was graduated in 1889 For the subsequent four years he was a student at Doane College, and while there managed the Doane Owl, the college paper, for two years In 1895 Mr Van Deusen bought the Courier at Blair and edited it until 1907, when he sold it to T T Osterman, and then bought his present journal, The Pilot, the leading republican organ in this part of the State. Within recent years he bought the building he occupies, modernized it and now has an up-to-date newspaper and job printing plant, fully equipped to issue his newspaper and carry on his large job printing business His paper has a paidup circulation of 2,000 and is recognized to be one of the best papers in Dodge and Washington counties

In 1899 Mr Van Deusen was united in marriage with Miss Minnie Wiseman, born at Salem, Indiana, but brought to Fort Calhoun, Nebraska, many years ago by her parents She was assistant cashier of the banking house of A Castetter for eight years There are no children Both Mr and Mrs Van Deusen belong to the Congregational Church. He is a Mason and also connected with the Modern Woodmen and both belong to the Order of Eastern Star One of the leading republicans of this locality, he was elected an alternate to the national convention of his party held at Chicago, Illinois in 1912

Mr. Van Deusen followed in the footsteps of his father when he became a member of Company E, Third Nebraska Infantry, serving under Col Wm J Bryan, and as such went to Cuba during the Spanish-American war, remaining in the service for one year While his time is taken up with his paper, during the late war he served as chairman of the Four Minute Men and also as chairman of the fuel committee of his county. He was a member of the executive committee of the local Red Cross Chapter on the Board of Instruction for the new soldiers and was tenor for the "Liberty Quartet," which sang all over the county in the interest of various war activities At present he is serving as a member of the executive committee of the Nebraska Press Association, and has been on the republican state central committee at different times A forceful man, fearless and energetic, he has always been a leader and as he knows how to handle men his work for any cause is very effective, and when the people of this region have in mind the promotion of any public enterprise they try to get his endorsement and co-operation, for they realize the value of such a service

FRED G PIERCE is handling with marked circumspection and efficiency the multifarious records and other details pertaining to the office of city clerk of Fremont and is one of the popular executives of the judicial center and metropolis of Dodge County He was born at Plymouth, Pennsylvania, May 11, 1863, and is a son of James B and Leonora (Remmell) Pierce, the former a native of Connecticut and the latter of Pennsylvania, where their marriage occurred and where they passed the remainder of their lives, the father having first been engaged in farming in the old Buckeye State, and later having become a successful contractor and builder He learned the carpenter's trade in his youth and thus was well fortified when he initiated independent operations as a contractor and builder He served two years as a member of a Pennsylvania regiment in the Civil war, was a republican in politics, was affiliated with the Masonic fraternity, and both he and his wife held membership in the Presbyterian Church He became the owner of a considerable amount of coal land, and the exploitation of the coal deposit added materially to his financial prosperity Of the six children only two are now living, Fred G being the elder, and his brother Harry being a resident of Wilkesbarre, Pennsylvania, where he owns and operates a greenhouse and is successful in floriculture.

The present city clerk of Fremont acquired his youthful education in the schools of the old Keystone State, including a course in Wyoming Seminary, at Kingston, besides which he attended Wilkesbarre Academy two years, and then entered LaFayette College, one of the well ordered institutions of Pennsylvania, where he continued his studies four years and in the civil engineering department, of which he was graduated as a member of the class of 1885 Thereafter he was employed for a short interval in the coal fields of West Virginia, but before the close of the year 1885 he had accepted a position as a railroad conductor in that State He continued his residence in West Virginia until 1891, when he came to Fremont, Nebraska, and entered service as a conductor on the Chicago & Northwestern Railroad He continued his efficient service in this capacity until 1913, and in the meanwhile had continuously maintained his home at Fremont. In the year mentioned he purchased the popular Brunswick Restaurant in this city and he successfully conducted the same four years, when he sold the business For eighteen months thereafter he was employed in the local offices of the Chicago & Northwestern Railroad and for three months in the office of the state land commissioner in the city of Lincoln He was then elected city clerk of Fremont, of which position he has since continued the incumbent He was for two years a member of the City Council and in the election of 1919 he was the republican candidate for the office of county clerk, his defeat having been encompassed by only 137 votes. Mr. Pierce has long been deeply interested in the history and teachings of the Masonic fraternity, in which he is affiliated with both York and Scottish Rite bodies, in the former of which he is a member of the Fremont Commandery of Knights Templar He still holds membership also in Brotherhood of Railway Conductors, and he figures as one of the veteran and retired railroad men of Nebraska, his service having been principally on passenger trains He and his wife are active members of the Presbyterian Church in their home city, and their circle of friends is limited only by that of their acquaintances

In January, 1888, was solemnized the marriage of Mr Pierce to Miss Bertha Kurtz, who likewise was born and reared in Pennsylvania, and concerning their children brief record is given in conclusion of this review Russell K, who is now associated with the business of Bader Brothers, of Fremont, was in service during eighteen months of the World war and for one year of this period was mess sergeant at Base Hospital No 49 in France Lenora is the wife of Joseph T Smith of Fremont Rebecca is the wife of Earl J Lee, who is engaged in the practice of law in this city Lawrence, now a traveling salesman for the Hoover Sweeper Company, was in service two years during the World war, and was mess sergeant in the military base hospital at Houston, Texas Beth Evelyn is attending the public schools of Fremont

JUDGE CONRAD HOLLENBECK, a resident of Dodge County almost two score years, was during a large part of that time judge of the Sixth Judicial District, and the distinctions achieved by him as an able lawyer, a profound jurist and a man of affairs made him one of the State's best known citizens Since his death Mrs Hollenbeck has continued to reside at Fremont, where for many years she has exercised a prominent influence in the social and civic affairs of the community and State

The late Judge Hollenbeck was born at East Hebron, Potter County, Pennsylvania, November 19, 1847 His first American ancestor, his great-grandfather, came from Holland when a young man and settled at Coxsackie, Greene County, New York, where he married His son, Conrad Hollenbeck, lived to the unusual age of 106 years and is buried at Sweden Valley in Potter County, Pennsylvania This Conrad Hollenbeck was married in Cortland County, New York, to Rebecca Edwards Their son, John Hollenbeck, became a prosperous farmer in Hebron, Pennsylvania, whither he removed after his marriage with Emily Parker, a native of Virgil, Cortland County, New York

A son of John and Emily (Parker) Hollenbeck, Conrad Hollenbeck, grew up in a home equally removed from poverty and from luxury, and his training was such as to bring out the sturdy and self-reliant qualities of his character He attended a district school, and at the age of nine years earned his first money building fires for the school teacher He worked on his father's farm, and in the spring of 1864 before he was seventeen years of age he enlisted as a private at Williamsport, Pennsylvania, in the 207th Pennsylvania Infantry. He was in the great Battle of the Wilderness and with the army of the Potomac until Lee's surrender After the war he resumed his education and in June, 1869, graduated from the college at Mansfield, Pennsylvania He took up the study of law in the office of Isaac Benson at Coudersport, Pennsylvania, was admitted to the bar in 1871 and remained there in active practice for six years While in Pennsylvania he gained his first recognition as a public leader, being elected to the Legislature in 1874 and again in 1876

May 9, 1877, he married Janet Knox at Coudersport Their wedding journey brought them out to Nebraska and they arrived in Fremont on the 15th of May Judge Hollenbeck came to Dodge County with a proved record as a lawyer and was not long in securing a position of advantage and influence in the bar of this State After some years of private practice he was elected county attorney in 1890, and held that office until 1895 In 1896 he sat as a delegate in the Chicago National Convention, where Bryan was first nominated Two years later in 1898 he was elevated to the bench as judge of the Sixth Judicial District and discharged the duties of that position with eminent abilities for eighteen years He was elected chief justice of Nebraska in 1914 and served until his death on January 21, 1915, in Lincoln, Nebraska, holding court only five days before he died

Mrs Hollenbeck was born at Lisle in Broome County, New York, April 21, 1856, and represents several family lines of great distinction in America Her parents were Franklin William and Catherine (Johnson) Knox Her father was a prominent Pennsylvania lawyer and a railroad president, practiced at Coudersport, Pennsylvania, for forty-seven years, and died at his winter home at Charlottesville, Virginia, in 1891 Catherine Johnson, mother of Mrs Hollenbeck, was born at Lisle, New York graduated from the Homer Academy at Cortland and died in 1869 Her grandfather, John Johnson, was born in Connecticut and was a soldier in the Revolutionary war for seven years, holding the rank of lieutenant and captain He was at Valley Forge with Washington, and after the war drew a pension for his service Captain John Johnson married Clarissa Rock Cyrus Johnson, grandfather of Mrs Hollenbeck, was a captain in the War of 1812, served as a member of the New York State Legislature and was a successful merchant of Lisle, New York He married Abigail Wheeler granddaughter of a French physician named Quigley, who came with General Lafayette to America at the time of the Revolution. An uncle of Mrs Hollenbeck was a captain of the Civil war, so that there were three generations of her family that gave captains to the military service of this country

Through the paternal line she is a member of the distinguished Knox family of America Her great-grandfather, William Knox, married Margaret Colton. He moved from Connecticut to Pennsylvania and built a block house on the site of what is now Knoxville, Tioga County, Pennsylvania His son, James Knox was the first white child born in that county James Knox married Anna Faulkner, who was born in Otsego County, New York in 1798 In this block house was born Franklin W Knox, father of Mrs Hollenbeck, and he lived there until one year of age The land on which the block house was built is still owned by members of the Knox family Seven generations of the Knox family have been born in America since the first ancestor came from Scotland

Mrs Hollenbeck was educated in a private school, in the Pennsylvania Female College at Philadelphia, and the interests and activities of her life have been those of a cultured and patriotic woman She served as a member of the Woman's Board of Management of the Trans-

Mississippi and International Exposition at Omaha in 1898, representing the Third Congressional District of Nebraska She is a member of the Charity Club, has been president of the Woman's Club, and has long been prominent officially in the Daughters of the American Revolution, having organized the Lewis and Clark Chapter at Fremont

Judge and Mrs Hollenbeck had two children Franklin Knox, born June 18, 1878; and Oscar Lowry, born September 13, 1884, and died in 1885.

The only son now living graduated from the Fremont High School and the University of Nebraska in the Law Department, and was married November 15, 1905, to Mae B Alexander, daughter of a prominent Montana rancher and business man of Forsyth, Montana, where Franklin K Hollenbeck now lives They have five children Thomas Alexander, Janet K. Gretchen L, Prudence J and John Conrad At the time of his marriage Franklin K Hollenbeck was city treasurer of Fremont He also conducted a bank at Harrisburg and is now postmaster of Forsyth, Montana

JOSEPH VINCENT HINCHMAN, M D A well known physician of Blair, Joseph Vincent Hinchman, M D, is devoted to his practice, which is a large and lucrative one, and well deserves the reputation which he enjoys of being one of the most able and faithful physicians of the city A son of John Hinchman, he was born January 14, 1846, in Rush County, Indiana, coming, on both sides of the house, of pioneer stock

John Hinchman was born and bred in Virginia, and as a youth came with his parents as far west as Rush County, Indiana, where his father, Joseph Hinchman, redeemed a homestead from the wilderness He assisted in the pioneer task, and subsequently bought land, and continued in agricultural pursuits throughout his active life. He married Charlotte Blacklidge, a native of Rush County, she having been a daughter of John Blacklidge, who migrated from Kentucky to Indiana when the vast forest was the happy hunting ground of the Indians, and who, by true pioneer labor, hewed from the dense woods the farm on which he and his faithful wife spent their remaining years Of the five children born of their union, four are living, as follows Joseph Vincent, Mrs Nan Adams, a widow, resides in Greenfield, Indiana, J M, also of Greenfield, is a farmer and implement dealer; and Mrs R A Goldsmith, a widow, living in Kinsley, Kansas. The father, a republican in politics, served as county commissioner, and was a member of the Independent Order of Odd Fellows He was not identified with any religious organization, but his wife was a member of the Methodist Episcopal Church

Brought up and educated in his native state, Joseph Vincent Hinchman offered his services to his country during the Civil war, enlisting in Company B, Ninth Indiana Cavalry, and serving for eighteen months and eighteen days. Captured by General Forrest, at Sulphur Trussell, Alabama, he was confined as a prisoner at Cahaba, Alabama, until the close of the conflict. Taking up the study of medicine a few years later, he was graduated from the Indiana Medical College with the class of 1885, and during the next year was engaged in the practice of his profession at Mound City Missouri Coming to Nebraska in the autumn of 1886, Doctor Hinchman continued his practice at Fall City for six years Locating in Hebron, Thayer County, in 1892, he remained there eleven years, after which he established himself in Blair, where he has since built up a very satisfactory practice, and gained to an eminent degree the confidence and respect of his fellow-men

Doctor Hinchman has been three times married He married first, in 1867, Irene Crane, who was born in Greenfield, Indiana, and died at Falls City, Nebraska, leaving one daughter, Mrs Alice Headley, of Edinburg, Texas He married for his second wife Candace Firkins, who bore him one child, Mrs Helen Anderson, of McCook, Nebraska. The doctor subsequently married Hannah Moynihan, a woman of culture and refinement

Doctor Hinchman is an active member of the Nebraska State Medical Society and of the Washington County Medical Society, of which he was president two years He was physician for seven months for the Soldier's Home at Burkett, Nebraska, and is a valued member of the Grand Army of the Republic, being past commander of the posts at Hebron and at Blair For full thirty-three years the Doctor has been a member of the Independent Order of Odd Fellows, in which he has passed all the chairs

William H J Meyer While it is truly claimed that by using present opportunities a man may be sure that he can and will use greater opportunities, and that in the development of his skill, judgment, initiative and determination, he is taking advantage of the openings offered by his everyday life, but if he does not possess sterling characteristics, this is not possible Therefore, if man is not honest, capable and mentally alert, there is but little use to expect him to develop into a citizen of probity, ample means and intellectual attainments From the above it is certain that no man is found in high position, especially in those connected with the banking business, unless he has these qualities and has made proper use of both small and great opportunities Such a man without doubt is William H J Meyer, vice president of the Dodge County State Bank of Hooper, and secretary of the Fremont Joint Stock Land Bank

The birth of William H J Meyer occurred in Germany in 1878, and he is a son of Claus and Anna (Kruse) Meyer, who came to the United States from Germany in 1881, and located in Dodge County, where they bought land and were engaged in carrying on general farming and stockraising until they retired and moved to Fort Collins, Colorado, and there they are still living in comfort after their years of toil In politics the father is a democrat, and both he and his wife are members of the Lutheran Church in their religious affiliations Their children are as follows Mary, who was the eldest born, William H. J, whose name heads this review; Lena, who is with her parents; Emma, who married E R Brown, a Dodge County farmer Herman, who is living in retirement at Fort Collins, Colorado, Maggie, who is a trained nurse, lives at Denver, Colorado, Edith, who is in the employ of a bank at Fort Collins, Colorado, Edward, who is now at Fort Collins, Colorado, was in the United States service during the World war, Louise, who is a stenographer at the Agricultural College at Fort Collins, Colorado, Alvina, who is with her parents, and Bertha, who is a public school teacher lives with her parents

Until he was twenty-three years old William H J Meyer lived with the family on the farm, and attended the Fremont College for two years, following which he took a commercial course, and after he had completed it, he became bookkeeper for the Farmers Grain and Stock Company of Hooper and held the position for three years, when he entered upon what was to be his life work as bookkeeper of the Dodge County Bank at Hooper in 1905, rising to be assistant cashier, and in 1910 to the position of cashier. In 1918 he was elected vice-president of the bank, and is now devoting all of his time to the banking business, serving the Fremont Joint Stock Land Bank as secretary, as well as discharging the duties pertaining to the vice presidency of the Dodge County Bank The latter is in very sound financial condition, having a capital of $25,000, a surplus of $40,000, and deposits of $646,000

In 1902 Mr Meyer was united in marriage with Miss Luruqua Bradbury, a native of Pennsylvania, daughter of James and Mary (Sweinhart) Bradbury, of whom mention is found on other pages of this volume Mr and Mrs. Meyer have one child, Darelle L, who is attending the Hooper High School Fraternally Mr. Meyer belongs to the Elks of Fremont and the Modern Woodmen of America of Hooper. In his politics he is a democrat, but aside from exercising his right of suffrage he has not taken an active part in public life Both he and Mrs Meyer are consistent members of Grace Lutheran Church of Hooper A sound, dependable man, Mr Meyer gives solidity to the banks with which he is connected His efforts have always been directed toward constructive citizenship, and he has contributed liberally of his means and time to bring about developments which he has felt would be advisable and practical, and his ideas upon public matters are generally sought and followed for his good judgment and knowledge of human nature are recognized and admired.

CHARLES H HOOPER An old and substantial family of Dodge County bears the name of Hooper, the prosperous Village of Hooper perpetuating the memory of the father of Charles H Hooper, of Fremont, Richard Hooper, for whom it was named He came to Dodge County in 1859 and did much to aid in the material development of this section

Charles H Hooper was born in Racine County, Wisconsin, February 7, 1859, and was an infant and the oldest of ten children, when his parents, Richard and Elizabeth (Goodman) Hooper settled in Dodge County The father was born in County Cornwall, England, and the mother in Derbyshire, and both came to America and settled in Wisconsin when young and married there Richard Hooper worked for J I Case as a carpenter in early days, but later became a farmer, in which latter business he took so much interest that it determined him to migrate to Nebraska where a poor man could secure land on reasonable terms. The family, father, mother and infant son, set out in a covered wagon, taking with them as many household goods as possible, and in June, 1859, reached Fremont The mother of Charles H Hooper cooked her first family meal in Nebraska where the Congregational Church now stands

Richard Hooper homesteaded south of Scribner and after proving up on his tract, bought a farm north of Fremont, where he engaged in farming and hog and cattle raising During those early days he also did freighting to Denver He acquired property through his industry, reared a large family comfortably, took an interest in public matters, was a republican because of his hatred of slavery, and was one of the liberal supporters of the Congregational Church to which both he and his wife belonged They had five sons and five daughters, as follows Charles H, Elizabeth, who is the wife of L H Hole, railroad man at Lincoln, Mrs Mary Zorn, who died in the summer of 1919, William, who is a lawyer at Leavenworth, Kansas, Henry, who is a farmer near Cedar Rapids, Boone County, Nebraska, Mrs Belle Sandusky, who lives at Denver, John, who is a farmer northwest of Fremont, Lennie, who is the wife of James Kervin, Lula, who is the wife of Ora Thompson, a farmer near Ames, Nebraska; and Richard, who is a farmer near Cedar Rapids

Charles H Hooper attended school at Fremont, Nebraska, remaining with his father on the farm until he reached his majority, when he went into the ice business with E N Morse He continued to deal in ice for some time, then became associated with H. Furhman in the wholesale dry goods line, remaining about seven years Mr Hooper is now practically retired from business but owns some very valuable Dodge County land, and for that northwest of Fremont has been offered $300 an acre. He has been quite active in democratic politics and served as deputy sheriff for five years

On February 20, 1888, Mr Hooper was united in marriage to Miss Mary Savage, who was born in Nebraska, a daughter of Anton Savage and his wife, natives of Germany They came to Butler County, Nebraska, in 1867, where the mother of Mrs Hooper died, when the father came to his daughter's home in Fremont and later died here Mr and Mrs Hooper have four children, namely: Thomas H, who is in the automobile business at Fremont, Emma, who is the wife of Earl Ropp, a mail clerk at Fremont, Irene, who is the wife of E C Olson, and Charles H who is a farmer in South Dakota The family belongs to the Congregational Church Mr Hooper belongs to the Odd Fellows and the Eagles and has held offices in the former organization. In 1898 with a party of eleven others, Mr Hooper took charge of fifty-two cars of cattle across the Atlantic Ocean to Liverpool, and after the delivery was made the visitors enjoyed a trip of sixty-four days during which they visited Ireland, England and Germany For four years Mr Hooper conducted the first Business Men's Club at Fremont

HENRY J. LEE, of Fremont, is one of the few survivors of those Dodge County pioneers who arrived here about the time the American Civil war was coming to a close Most of those who came then or somewhat later have gone Many of them achieved only a moderate degree of success, and never reached the full benefits of early settlement Henry J Lee's career has been conspicuous not only for his residence of more than half a century in Dodge County but for the wonderful ability with which he has handled his business affairs He is still one of the leading men of Fremont and deserves all that can be said of a man of sterling integrity and pronounced business acumen

A son of James and Jane (Dougherty) Lee, he was born August 25, 1837, in Bradford County, Pennsylvania, and was reared there on a farm His father, a native of Ireland, came to the United States when a young man and until after his marriage remained in New York City. Subsequently buying land in Bradford County, Pennsylvania, he improved a farm and was prosperously engaged in tilling the soil until his death while yet in manhood's prime He became active in republican politics, holding many local offices, and both he and his wife were active members of the Baptist Church In New York City he married Jane Dougherty, also a native of the Emerald Isle. Of their six children three are now living, Margaret Jane, a widow living at Camptown, Pennsylvania Henry J, and Joseph P, of Wyalusing, Pennsylvania, who although past eighty years of age runs a foundry and sells machines, having established an extensive and substantial business

H. Y. Lee

After leaving the common schools of Bradford County, Henry J. Lee completed his early studies at the Laceyville Seminary A young man when his father died he and his brother bought the parental homestead and managed it successfully a number of years, teaching school in the meantime during the long winter terms, and working on the farm during seed time and harvest He subsequently engaged in the hardware business in his native state for a year

In 1865 imbued with the restless spirit characteristic of the Americans, Mr Lee came to Fremont, Nebraska, and during his first year in the state freighted across the plains and during the following four years sold goods on the road In January, 1870, he entered the hardware business, buying a $4,000 stock of hardware. To this he added by degrees and soon began a jobbing business on a small scale, increasing as trade demanded The first four or five years he did most of the traveling himself, and after that put traveling representatives on the road In 1878 he erected a large three-story and basement store building, 125 by 33 feet, which then and for some years was one of the most complete hardware stores in that section of the state He continued this local business at Fremont until 1917 when he sold out In the meantime, in 1880, with C A Fried, a wholesale hardware company was organized in Omaha under the name of H J Lee & Company, but soon changed to Lee, Fried & Company From 1880 the Lee-Fried Hardware Company, wholesale, was operated at Omaha and continued its growth and prosperity under that name until Mr Fried's death a few years later The business then acquired the title of Lee, Glass, Andreesen Company, and in 1917 was changed to Lee, Coyt, Andreesen Hardware Company, and is still operated under that name Mr Lee owns the building, though he sold his interest in the business in 1918 This is one of the leading wholesale establishments of Omaha, with a trade territory extending over Iowa, Nebraska, the Dakotas, Colorado, Wyoming and Utah

Mr Lee is a stanch republican and served with credit as a member of the school board and city council and for three years on the board of county commissioners March 16, 1869, he married Sophronia S Ellsworth, who was born in Bradford County, Pennsylvania, April 1, 1849, daughter of Charles and Ruth Ellsworth, who were both genuine Yankees Mr and Mrs Lee had two children, Eva L and Myra F Eva, widow of T W Miller, living with her parents, assists her father in looking after his extensive business interests and is herself a very competent business woman She has three daughters, Eva Irene, Florence and Alice Miller The daughter, Myra F, is the wife of Otto Schurman, a Dodge County citizen whose career is sketched elsewhere

Though Mr Lee is now eighty-three years of age he is still hale and hearty, and attends to all his private business, representing responsibilities of much magnitude He was for many years past president of the First National Bank, of which he was one of the founders, until January, 1920, when he resigned He is also a director and stockholder in the Commercial National Bank Mr Lee has one of the beautiful homes of Fremont It was built in 1891 and 1892 on the corner of Sixth and C streets

JACOB J KELSER, who is now living retired at North Bend, is one of the venerable and honored pioneer citizens of Dodge County and during his active career he did well his part in connection with the civic, industrial and business development and advancement of this county He was born in Holmes County Ohio, March 13, 1842, and is a son of Lewis and Margaret (Spreng) Kelser, the former a native of Alsace and the latter of the adjoining section, Lorraine, France. They were reared and educated in their native land, their home district having passed to Germany at the time of the Franco-Prussian war and later having become the stage of gigantic military operation in connection with the late World war Lewis Kelser became a sailor in his youth and continued to follow a seafaring life until he came to the United States in 1824, his marriage having been solemnized in New York City, where his wife had established her residence a short time previously. From the Empire State the young couple removed to Ohio, and there the father continued his active association with agricultural industry until his death in 1852, his widow having remained on their old home farm for a number of years thereafter and having been a resident of Wayne County, Ohio, at the time of her death in 1887, her religious faith having been that of the Evangelical Church and her husband having become an adherent of the democratic party after he gained citizenship in the land of his adoption Of their fine family of thirteen children six are still living Lena is deceased, the second child died in infancy, Lewis, Jr, now deceased, served as a member of an Ohio regiment in the Civil war, Catherine is deceased, Frederick is a resident of the State of California; John is deceased, Philip, a retired clergyman of the Methodist Episcopal Church, resides in Medina, Ohio, Jacob J, of this sketch, was the next in order of birth · Christian, now a resident of Hermosa, California, was a member of the same regiment as was the late President William McKinley in the Civil war, Sarah, the widow of John Shearer, resides in Ohio, Henry is a merchant at Fulton, Michigan, and Barbara and William are deceased

Jacob J Kelser was reared to manhood in the old Buckeye State, where he duly availed himself of the advantages of the common schools and where he continued his association with farm industry until there came the call of higher duty, when the Civil war was precipitated on a divided nation He forthwith showed his patriotism by enlisting as a member of Company H, Twenty-third Ohio Volunteer Infantry, with which command he continued in service three years and four months He lived up to the full tension of the conflict between the states of the North and the South and took part in numerous important engagements, including the historic battles of Antietam and South Mountain While participating in the battle of Cloyd Mountain, West Virginia he was wounded, but he was not long incapacitated, and his service as a gallant young soldier of the Union continued during the major part of the great war He received his honorable discharge in the City of Columbus, Ohio, and thereafter supplemented his interrupted education by attending Greensburg Seminary, in Ohio, two years Impaired health then led him to abandon his studies and he took charge of his mother's old home farm, in Wayne County, Ohio In 1867, however, he assumed the operation of a grain elevator at Lakeville, that state, and within the same year his marriage occurred Thereafter he continued his residence at Lakeville until 1871, when he came with his family to Dodge County, Nebraska, and took up a homestead of eighty acres, in Union Township He reclaimed and improved this property and there continued his activities as a farmer and stock-grower for seven years, the farm having been finally sold at satisfactory profit For fifteen years thereafter Mr Kelser conducted a general store at North Bend, and the following ten years here found him successfully engaged in the real estate business, with which he continued his association until his retirement He served several years as justice of the peace, has been unwavering in his allegiance to the republican party, is an appreciative and honored member of the North Bend Post of the Grand Army of the Republic and his wife is an active member of the Presbyterian Church Mr Kelser found his loyalty again raised to a high pitch when the nation became involved in the late World war, and he was earnest and liberal in support of the various governmental agencies advanced in furtherance of war preparation and exploitation

November 28, 1867, recorded the marriage of Mr Kelser to Miss Marian E Newkirk, who was born and reared in Wayne County Ohio, and of this union have been born six children Grant and Emma are deceased, Bessie is the wife of William W Roberts, engaged in the drug business at Fremont, judicial center of Dodge County John N is conducting a meat market in that city, and Chauncey and Marian E are deceased, the latter having passed away in 1914

William G J Dau A purpose in life is as the helm of a ship for it shapes direction to the goal; it stirs ambition, arouses determination and is the mainspring of success It is necessary for a man to have some definite aim in life for without it he stagnates A number of men whose earlier years were spent in farming, discover this when they retire from an agricultural life and seek to find contentment in a life of leisure, for they find that they cannot adapt themselves to their new environment Having always had something to work toward, some purpose in view with each day, the hours hang heavy on their hands, and those who are sensible, when once they realize this, do not wait, but embark in some other line, and usually succeed in it too, for back of them is that purpose which enables them to endure difficulties and hardships, take blows and rebuffs of fortune, and tolerate disappointments One of the representative and energetic men of Hooper, who, after he had terminated his experience as a farmer, opened up a garage and is now operating it, acting as agent for several well-known cars and tractors and handling accessories, and doing a fine business in all lines, is William G J Dau, mayor of the city

The birth of Mr Dau took place in Germany in 1868, and he is a son of Peter and Marguerite (Schomacher) Dau, natives of Germany, both of whom are deceased, he passing away in 1897, aged fifty-eight years, and she in 1916, aged seventy-five years They came to the United States in 1878, and located at Fremont, Nebraska, where he obtained employment as a brick mason for seven years, and then bought a farm near Hooper, on which he carried on general farming and stockraising until his death. Of the thirteen children born to him and his wife, five survive, namely: John, who is a resident of Scribner, Nebraska, drives a car; William G J, who is second in order of birth, George, who is a Dodge County farmer, Ernest, who is manager of the elevator at Scribner, Nebraska, and Edward, who is living retired at Hooper Peter Dau was a democrat after coming to this country He and his wife belonged to the Lutheran Church and were active in it

William G. J Dau accompanied his parents to Dodge County, Nebraska, and assisted his father with the farm until the latter's death, after which he bought out the other heirs and continued to conduct it until 1917 when he retired to Hooper After coming here he opened a garage which he conducts under the name of the Farmers Garage, and he is sales agent for the Nash automobiles and Nash and Reo trucks, and he carries a full line of automobile accessories.

In 1894 Mr Dau was united in marriage with Anna Studt, born in Iowa, a daughter of John Studt, one of the early settlers of Dodge County Mr and Mrs Dau have two children, namely Peter J, who is with his father in the garage, and Lillian, who is at home Like his father, Mr Dau is a democrat, and he was twice elected to the State Assembly of Nebraska, in 1915 and 1917, and served two terms Later he was honored by being placed on his party ticket for the office of mayor of Hooper, and elected by a gratifying majority, and is the present incumbent of the chair of chief executive of his municipality A constructive citizen, Mr Dau has sought since he has been in office to further practical improvements, and in spite of the restrictions of the times, has been able to make considerable progress and has plans for further advancement in the near future He is a thirty-second degree Mason, and belongs to the Modern Woodmen of America Mrs Dau is a member of Grace Lutheran Church of Hooper While Mr Dau's educational training was confined to the public schools of Dodge County, he is a very well informed man, and his advice is sought and taken by a number of his fellow citizens who recognize his sound business sense and good judgment

FRANCIS M CASTETTER The Castetter family is one of the oldest and most prominent in the history of Washington County, where they have lived since almost the first dates of pioneer settlement Many of the important interests of the family are associated with the banking house of A Castetter at Blair, an institution that has enjoyed the highest financial standing in the county for years and in the management of which the heirs of the bank's founder are still active

The founder of the family in Nebraska was the late Abraham Castetter, who came to Washington County about 1856 He was one of the first county clerks of the county, and for a number of years lived at De Soto He owned and operated one of the first flour mills in that section of the state and in 1869 founded the Castetter banking house, an institution which has now rounded out a full half century of service as a factor in the business and financial community This bank was originally conducted at De Soto, and subsequently at Blair

A son of Abraham Castetter was the late Francis M Castetter, who was born in De Soto, Nebraska, in 1858 and died at Blair in 1912 He was reared and educated in Washington County, and as a young man became actively associated with his father in the banking business, and served as president of the bank at Blair for a number of years prior to his death He was prosperous and a highly regarded business man, showing a keen interest in everything that concerned the welfare of his community He was a republican in politics and a member of the Woodmen of the World

August 5, 1884, Francis M Castetter married Anna Catharine Noble, who during the life of her husband and since has been leader in the social affairs of her community She is also a director of the Castetter banking house Mrs Castetter was born in Sharon, Canada, daughter of Hiram and Jane Ann (Thompson) Noble, also natives of Canada. Her father was a physician and surgeon, having been educated for his profession in McGill University He practiced for several years in Canada and in 1870 moved to Onawa, Iowa, where he practiced for a decade, and about 1881 established his home at Blair, Nebraska, and devoted his professional service to that community the rest of his life. He died at eighty-two and his wife at eighty-seven, they having celebrated their sixtieth wedding anniversary Doctor Noble was a Universalist and his wife a Congregationalist. Mrs Castetter, who is an active member of the Episcopal Church at Blair, is the mother of three daughters. May Noble is at home Shirley is the wife of George W Donaldson, a business man of Omaha Frances Marion was graduated from Brownell Hall in Omaha in 1919 and also from Lincoln School at Providence, Rhode Island

JOHN CUSACK is one of the venerable and honored pioneer citizens of Dodge County, where he is now living retired, at North Bend, and where he formerly served as postmaster He was born in the Province of Ontario, Canada, near the Town of Moffatt, and the date of his nativity was May 10, 1844 His parents, William and Anna (Semple) Cusack, were born in Ireland and both were residents of Ontario, Canada, at the time of their death, the father having passed away in 1879, at the age of seventy-five years, and the mother having been seventy years of age when she was summoned to the life eternal The father was a young man when he immigrated to Canada, where he purchased land and became a successful exponent of farm industry He was a man of pronounced views and was somewhat of a reformer in his political attitude He was a communicant of the Catholic Church, but his wife held the faith of the Church of England, a faith represented in the United States by the Protestant Episcopal Church William and Anna Cusack became the parents of nine children Mary and Catherine are deceased, James is a farmer in Ontario, Canada, William remains on the old homestead farm of his father in Ontario, Alexander is identified with mining enterprise in British Columbia, John, of this sketch was the next in order of birth; Christopher is deceased, of whom mention is found elsewhere in this work; Anna is the wife of Jerry Dion of North Bend, Nebraska; and Sarah is the wife of George Gallop, their home being in Ontario, Canada

John Cusack was reared on the old home farm and is indebted to the schools of his native province for his early educational discipline He remained with his parents until 1869 when he came to Nebraska and took up a pre-emption claim in Dodge County He began the reclaiming and improving of this property, in Webster Township, but he availed himself of other means of adding to his financial resources, as shown by the fact that for nine years he served as a railroad section foreman in Dawson County He finally sold his farm, and in 1881 he engaged in the lumber and agricultural implement business at North Bend He continued in control of a successful business in this line about twenty years After selling this business he devoted his attention for some time to the feeding of live stock for the market, and in 1906 he was appointed postmaster at North Bend, a position of which he continued the incumbent eight years, since which time he has lived virtually retired He has long been a stalwart supporter of the cause of the republican party and has been influential in its affairs in Dodge County, though he has never sought office He has, however, given effective service as a member of the Board of Education of North Bend He and his wife are earnest members of the United Presbyterian Church, he is affiliated with the Masonic fraternity and both he and his wife hold membership in the North Bend Chapter of the Order of the Eastern Star.

April 22, 1872, recorded the marriage of Mr. Cusack to Miss Mary Ann Richie, who was born in Fifeshire, Scotland, December 18, 1849 a daughter of James and Anna (Burns) Richie, who came from Scotland to America in 1870 and forthwith established their home in Fremont, Dodge County, Nebraska, where the father purchased land and instituted the development of a farm, besides which he continued in zealous and faithful service as a layman clergyman of the Presbyterian Church and temperance worker The parents were residents of North Bend at the time of their death Mr and Mrs Cusack had five children Anna is the wife of T J Castle, a banker at North Bend, Mabel C holds a position in a bank at Cozad Dawson County, Alice M is the efficient and popular supervisor of the primary work in the public schools of the City of Lincoln, Susie J is the wife of C P Hord, who is engaged in the banking business at Cozad, and William James died at the age of four years

JOHN H GIBSON A man of versatile talents, far-sighted and eminently capable, John H Gibson of Blair, president of the Farmers State Bank, has been identified with the agricultural, industrial and financial interests of Washington County for many years, and is widely known in business circles throughout city and county Of substantial Danish ancestry, he was born September 19, 1877, in Paxton, Illinois, where he lived until four years old.

His father, Hans Gibson, was born and reared in Jutland, Denmark Immigrating to the United States when young, he secured work on a farm, and for many years was engaged in agricultural pursuits in Illinois, near Paxton Accumulating money, he wisely decided to invest it in a newer country, where land was cheaper Coming, therefore, to Nebraska in 1881, he bought a ranch near Hampton, Hamilton County, and in its management met with characteristic success, remaining upon it until 1915 In that year, still retaining the ownership of his valuable farm, he settled at Long Beach, California, where he is living retired from active business cares, enjoying to the utmost the fruits of his earlier years of toil He is a fine example of the men who have come to this country from across the sea, and who, by diligent labor and thrift have arisen from a state of comparative poverty to one of affluence, he being worth now upwards of $100,000

Hans Gibson married, in Paxton, Illinois, Karen Rasmussen, a native of Fyen, Denmark, and they are the parents of four children, as follows Mary, wife of Harold B Larson, a wealthy citizen and philanthropist of Hollywood, California, who was for many years associated with a fuel company in Racine, Wisconsin, and is now making good use of the money he there acquired, giving liberally to churches and charitable organizations; John H, of this brief sketch, Jabe B, of Norfolk, employed in the Nebraska State Bank, and Peter H, managing the home farm. An independent democrat in politics, the father served as road overseer eighteen years, and as a member of the local school board a number of terms He is a member of the Woodmen, and both he and his wife are faithful members of the Danish Lutheran Church

Obtaining his preliminary education in the rural schools, John H Gibson took a business course in Fremont, this state, and subsequently became familiar with the rudiments of agriculture on the parental homestead Laboring faithfully, he acquired fame, especially as a corn husker, having husked on an average over 100 bushels of corn a day Leaving the farm on attaining his majority, Mr Gibson was engaged in the hardware business with his uncle, C Newaman, at Hampton, this state, for seven years, and the ensuing six years again worked on the farm Making a change of occupation and residence, he was then for four years assistant cashier of the Rock County State Bank at Newport, Rock County Then, after spending a brief time in York, Nebraska, Mr Gibson bought an interest in the Citizens State Bank at Blair, and for five years served as assistant cashier of that institution On November 1, 1919, he organized, in Blair, the Farmers State Bank, which has a paid up capital of $35,000, and in which he has a controlling interest, and has since served acceptably as its president, an office for which he is eminently qualified This bank, although comparatively new, its charter number being 1 542, is in a highly prosperous condition, its report at the close of business on February 14, 1920, being highly satisfactory to all interested, including its officers and patrons

Mr Gibson married, in 1904, Miss Grace Miller, a native of Bradshaw, Nebraska, and they are the parents of two children, Forrest, born in 1906, and Leta, four years younger than her brother Mr Gibson is an independent democrat in politics, but takes no active part in political affairs, his business demanding his time and attention True to the religious faith in which he was reared, he belongs to the Danish Lutheran Church, while Mrs Gibson is a member of the Christian Church

JAMES A MURRELL, retired groceryman and capitalist of Fremont, was born November 30, 1849, at Clarksville, Clinton County, Ohio He is a son of Alexander and Amanda L (Penquite) Murrell The father was born in Virginia and the mother in Ohio, where they married and always lived Mr Murrell was a farmer in Clinton County They had five children and those living today are Mrs E J Mooney of Duncansville, Illinois, Mrs M E Mail of Fremont, and James A Murrell. A brother, G. A Murrell, who was born January 3 1852, and died February 18, 1920, came to Fremont April 1, 1880 He was mayor of Fremont and a deputy in the office of the county clerk two terms and was then elected county clerk for two terms He was route agent for a creamery company about Fremont for several years James A Murrell's parents were members of the Baptist Church and the father was a whig before he became a republican

James A Murrell secured a common school education in Ohio, and his first work was farming, although he clerked in a store before the Civil war In 1871 he went to Mingo, Jasper County, Iowa, and bought a farm where he lived for thirteen years In February, 1884, he came to Fremont and for almost eight years he clerked in the W H Turner grocery store He went into business for himself in 1892 and continued it until 1916, when he sold and is now living in retirement

Mr Murrell is a member of the Board of Directors of the Fremont State Bank, and he owns stock in other banks and in the Fidelity Trust Company When Mr Murrell was only two years old his father died and he was thus early thrown upon his own resources, and when eleven years old he was taking care of himself. On February 17, 1876, Mr. Murrell married Sarah V Rumbaugh She was born at Lima, Ohio Her father, G W Rumbaugh, once owned the county hospital farm in Allen County, Ohio

Mr and Mrs Murrell have three children Amanda Leta is the wife of Dr J R Bell, an Omaha dentist, Delbert L has a sheep ranch at Red Elm, South Dakota, and George W owns one-half section of land at Faith, South Dakota The latter enlisted in the World war, June 26, 1918, and after short training at Camp Funston and Camp Dodge he sailed on August 17 for France He was in the Eighty-Eighth Division and was on the firing line the day of the signing of the armistice He was almost one year in the service and was wounded by shrapnel while carrying a message on a motorcycle

In Fremont the Murrells belong to the Methodist Episcopal Church, and the father is a Knight Templar, thirty-second degree Mason and a Shriner He was king and high priest in the Royal Arch Masons and illustrious master in the Council, and has held all chairs as a Knight Templar He also belongs to the Independent Order of Odd Fellows Mr Murrell owns a modern home in Fremont and other desirable rental property He has been a successful business man

RUDOLPH B SCHNEIDER The late Rudolph B Schneider, one of the founders and secretary and treasurer of the Nye, Schneider Company of Fremont, was one of the biggest men this region ever produced, and his wide-reaching operations affected all this part of the state, and always along constructive lines. During his many years' residence at Fremont he not only became a towering figure in its business interests, particularly in the grain trade, but also attained the full measure of the popular heart and confidence of its people, and was recognized to possess in rare degree tact, courtesy, intelligence and good judgment

Rudolph B Schneider was born at Beardstown Illinois, on February 25, 1853, youngest son of B W and Elizabeth (Crow) Schneider, natives of Germany and Illinois, respectively When he was twenty-five years of age B W Schneider came to the United States, arriving here in 1830 His death occurred in 1853 when he was forty-eight years old, he having been born in 1805 Although still in middle age when he died, he left a considerable fortune which he had accumulated through his own efforts after reaching this country, in mercantile and real estate lines His widow died at Fremont, Nebraska, on December 12, 1884 Their children were as follows. Mrs Anna McPherson, who lives at Fremont, Charles W, who is a resident of Milwaukee, Wisconsin, L A, who is a druggist of Arlington Nebraska, and Rudolph B, whose name heads this review

Until he was fifteen years old Rudolph B Schneider attended the public schools of Beardstown, but at that time began working, and two years later came West to Fremont, Nebraska His first employment in this city was with W R Wilson, a grocer, but after a couple of years he returned to Illinois, and for the subsequent five years was engaged in farming, taking charge at that time, although only eighteen, of the family affairs, both his mother and sister being widows

About 1877 Mr Schneider returned to Fremont, once more resuming his connections with Mr Wilson, and during the six years that followed he made himself so useful that he was taken into partnership, the new firm becoming W. R Wilson & Company, with headquarters at Nickerson, Nebraska In January, 1887 the firm of Nye, Wilson, Morehouse Company was launched and Mr Schneider was one of the stockholders and directors of the concern, which he had assisted in organizing Upon the retirement of Mr Wilson and Mr Morehouse, the Nye, Schneider Company came into existence of which Mr. Schneider remained secretary and treasurer until his death.

Mr Schneider had other interests including large investments in the Fremont Stock Yards and Land Company, the Fremont Foundry and Machine Company and he was one of the stockholders of the First National Bank and the Fremont National Bank, the Fremont Street Railway and other prosperous enterprises of Fremont and Dodge County A man of great public spirit he possessed that sense of larger responsi

bilities and broad vision which made him labor for the good of his community and he was one of the promoters and the first president of the Christian Park and Assembly Association of Fremont

A strong republican he was very active in his party and served for several years as chairman of the county central committee In 1889 he was chairman of the Board of Supervisors, and was on that board for a number of years It was while he was chairman of that board that the new courthouse was erected, and as such rendered a capable service in securing the best of work and materials for the building Mr Schneider belonged to Centennial Lodge No 59, Independent Order of Odd Fellows, and also the Encampment and Canton of this order He owned realty at Fremont and also at Salt Lake City, Utah

On June 29, 1882, Mr Schneider was united in marriage at Nickerson, Nebraska, to Miss Isabelle D Spangler, born in Pennsylvania, a daughter of Adam Spangler, who with their three daughters survive him Both Mr and Mrs Schneider early connected themselves with the Methodist Episcopal Church, to which Mrs Schneider still belongs On July 26, 1913 Mr. Schneider passed away from the scene of his numerous activities, and left behind him a record for great mental resourcefulness and surprising and big achievements He was a man who was thoroughly prepared to take advantage of the opportune moment, and was not readily deceived in men or misled as to their motives Early in life his economic necessities were sufficiently urgent as to compel him to increase his fortune very materially, and he never lost this vigor, but was just as eager to make a success of his undertakings at the close of his career as he was in young manhood While advancing himself, he carried others with him and not only added to their prosperity but also so firmly impressed upon them his deep and abiding faith in the ultimate reward of the homely virtues of honesty, direct diligence and unselfish loyalty to the task at stake, that they never forgot the lessons taught by his own actions

Mr. and Mrs Schneider became the parents of three daughters, namely Etta Schneider Turner, widow, who resides with her mother, was in the government service during the late war and was sent overseas to France. Clara and Marguerite who are also with their mother, went to France during the war as members of the Red Cross Canteen Department Mrs Schneider has a beautiful residence on Tenth Street, and she owns stock in several concerns as well as considerable realty at Fremont, and is one of the most charitable ladies in the county, her benefactions having been especially heavy while this country was at war

WILLIAM NICHOL. It was given to the late William Nichol to render valuable service in connection with bridge construction enterprise in Nebraska and also to do his part in the furtherance of agricultural industry in this state A man of marked ability and sterling character, he made his life count for good in its every relation and he was one of the honored and influential citizens of North Bend, Dodge County, at the time of his death, July 11, 1913, when nearly seventy-three years of age He served three terms as mayor of the thriving little City of North Bend, where also he gave eleven years of effective service as a member of the Board of Education His political allegiance was accorded to the republican party and he was well fortified in his opinions concerning governmental and economic policies. He was a zealous member of the Methodist Episcopal Church at North Bend, as is also his widow, and he was a member of its Board of Trustees at the time of his death

A scion of the stanchest of Scottish ancestry, Mr Nichol was born at Westminster, Province of Ontario, Canada, on November 20, 1840, and in the schools of his native province he acquired his early education, his alert mentality later enabling him to profit greatly from the lessons gained in connection with the activities of a signally busy and useful career He was a son of Jonathan and Sadilano Nichol, both of whom were born in Scotland and the Province of Ontario, Canada, having become their place of abode upon their immigration to America In that province Mrs Nichol passed the remainder of her life and there Jonathan Nichol continued his activities as a farmer until he came to Nebraska and became a pioneer settler in Saunders County, where he secured land and developed a productive farm and where he continued to reside until his death, when venerable in years

William Nichol accompanied his father on the removal to Nebraska and here he purchased railroad land, in Saunders County A skilled carpenter and bridge builder, he traveled extensively through Nebraska for a number of years and gave his attention to the construction of high-grade bridges, as a representative of the American Bridge Company He also developed and improved his farm property and upon his retirement from active business, in 1890, he established his home at North Bend, where he passed the remainder of his life and where his widow still resides, sustained and comforted by the companionship of friends who are tried and true

Mr Nichol married December 8, 1877, Miss Sarah Wilcox, who was born at Durnham, Ontario, March 10, 1848, where she was reared and educated She was a daughter of Hiram Wilcox, also a native of Canada, and he came to Saunders County, Nebraska, where he homesteaded near Morris Bluff and where he died at about seventy years of age Mrs Nichol came to Saunders County in 1877 to her brother's and was married that same year Mr and Mrs Nichol had no children, but have reared a girl who still makes her home with Mrs Nichol Mrs Nichol is a member of the Methodist Church

Joseph C Newsom, editor and publisher of the North Bend Eagle, in the vital and progressive little City of North Bend, Dodge County, was a child of three years at the time the family home was established in this county, and thus he gained in his childhood and youth a due share of the inspiring western spirit, which he has effectively shown in his business career Personally and through the medium of his attractive and well conducted newspaper he stands as a true apostle of progress in his field of enterprise, and has made the North Bend Eagle one of the representative newspapers of Dodge County He is a son of Judge Joseph E Newsom, the present postmaster of North Bend, and on other pages is given a brief record of the career and family history of his father, so that a repetition of the data is not demanded here

Joseph C. Newsom was born at Worthington, Indiana, November 28, 1875, but he was not long permitted to breath the air of the Hoosier State, as his parents came to Nebraska in 1878 and established their home in Dodge County, where they still reside Joseph C Newsom received his education in the public schools of North Bend, while soon afterward he entered upon the practical apprenticeship to the printers' trade, a discipline that has consistently been pronounced if carried to proper limits, the equivalent of a liberal education His first experience in the "art preservative of all arts" was acquired in a printing office at North Bend under the direction of Elmer Davis and later he was employed two years in the office of the Fremont Herald, at the judicial center of his home county Soon after his return to North Bend he purchased the plant and business of the North Bend Republican, and in 1897 consolidated with the North Bend Argus, with incidental elimination of both original names and the adoption of the present title of the North Bend Eagle Mr Newsom has a well equipped office for the execution of both newspaper and job work, and the pages of the Eagle show the best of modern linotype composition, the pages being a six-column quarto edition, published on Thursday of each week and constituting a most attractive and effective exponent of community interests He has served as city clerk of North Bend and also as a member of the Board of Education Within the period of the nation's participation in the World war he showed his patriotism and loyalty by leaving his family and his business and doing effective service with the Young Men's Christian Association in France. He is affiliated with the Masonic fraternity, the Modern Woodmen of America and the Ancient Order of United Workmen, and he and his wife hold membership in the Christian Church

November 26, 1908, recorded the marriage of Mr. Newsom to Miss Adda M Guttery, who was born at Brookfield, Missouri, and who was a child at the time of her parents' removal to Nebraska, the family home being established in Dodge County Mr. and Mrs Newsom have two children—Philip and Betty Jane.

JOHN H C MOELLER. An active, enterprising and practical farmer, John H. C. Moeller of Cuming Township, is an able assistant in maintaining the reputation of Dodge County as a superior agricultural and stock-raising region, his success as a husbandman being unquestioned A son of Casper Moeller, he was born, September 22, 1885, in Dodge County, where he has always resided

Born, bred and educated in Germany, Casper Moeller left his native land in 1859, crossing the ocean in a slow-sailing vessel, and came directly to Dodge County, Nebraska, in search of a favorable location Homesteading a tract of land, he improved a fine farm, and was not only very successful as a farmer and stock-raiser, but attained a place of prominence and influence in the community where he lived, having served at one time as president of the Dodge County Bank, and having also been president of the Farmers Mutual Insurance Company Giving up active pursuits in 1908, he has since lived retired at his pleasant home in Hooper He married Joanna Langermeyer, a native of Germany, and of their union five children were born, as follows Henry, engaged in farming in Dodge County, Louise, wife of Rev J H Hartenberger of Red Bud, Illinois, Caroline, wife of Amiel Neiborn, a farmer, Fredericka, wife of Emil Rink, a Dodge County farmer, and John H C, of whom we write. The father is an independent voter, and both he and his wife belong to St John's Lutheran Church

Completing the course of study in th common schools of Dodge County, John H C Moeller attended the Fremont Normal School, thus materially advancing his education Working with his father, he early acquired a thorough knowledge of the modern methods of farming, and in 1908 embarked in agricultural pursuits on his own account He has since carried on general farming extensively and prosperously, as a stock raiser, making a specialty of Poland China hogs, in the raising of which he has been very fortunate He is also interested to some extent in other affairs, being one of the stockholders of the Hooper mill

Mr Moeller married February 24, 1908, Frieda Rink, who was born in Dodge County, where her father, Jacob Rink, was a pioneer settler Five children have been born of the marriage of Mr and Mrs Moeller, namely Lois, Agnes, Eugene, Elhardt and Etta May Independent in his political affiliations, Mr Moeller votes according to the dictates of his conscience Religiously he and his wife are members of St John's Lutheran Church

CASPER HOEGEMEYER is one of the old and honored settlers of Dodge and Washington counties, and for nearly fifty years has applied his industry as a farmer and stock raiser in Dodge County His home is in section 36 of Cuming Township

Mr Hoegemeyer was born in Germany March 22 1849, son of Casper H and Louise (Hilker) Hoegemeyer, both of whom spent all their lives as German farmers One other son Henry also came to Nebraska and settled in Dodge County Casper Hoegemeyer was twenty years of age when he came to the United States in 1869, and he journeyed east by railroad as far as Council Bluffs, Iowa and came by boat to Washington County For a year or so he was employed as a farm hand, and in that time learned the American language and rapidly adapted himself to American ways

Mr Hoegemeyer in 1871 took up a homestead in Dodge County, and by much industry and thrift improved it He has a small frame house at the beginning, and for nearly half a century has used his lands for general farming and stock raising He has also become a stockholder and director in the Dodge County Bank of Hooper During his long residence in Dodge County Mr Hoegemeyer has fed and fattened many carloads of livestock for the markets

In 1873 he married Miss Anna Mary Stork, member of a well-known family of Washington County. To their marriage were born seven children. William, a Dodge County farmer, Christ, also a farmer in that county, August, who has a farm in Burt County, Nebraska; Casper H, a farmer of Cuming County, George, at home, Emma wife of H Heitshusen of Burt County, and Louise, wife of Emil Miller of Cuming County The mother of these children died September 6, 1914, more than forty years after their marriage and after she had seen her sons and daughters well placed in life Mr Hoegemeyer and family are members of the St John's Church. In politics he casts his ballot independently. He has been interested in the affairs of his community, particularly good schools, and for a number of years was a director of District No 16

MRS MARY C. DEBEL It is a compliment worthily bestowed to say that Washington County is honored by the citizenship of her whose name forms the caption to this sketch for she has achieved definite success through her own efforts and is discharging the duties of the office which she fills to the entire satisfaction of the voters of the county Mary C Debel was born at Lincoln, Nebraska, and is the daughter of C M and Mary (Knudsen) Christensen, both of whom were born in Denmark After coming to the United States, their respective families came to Lincoln, where their marriage occurred Mr. Christensen was engaged in the meat business at Lincoln for some time, but later engaged in farming, to which he devoted his efforts for seventeen years He also became interested in livestock, as a buyer and shipper, buying his animals in Blair and shipping to the Omaha market He was suc-

Seymour D. Sidner

cessful in his business affairs and in March, 1909, became a resident of Blair, where he and his wife now reside They are earnest members of the Lutheran Church Mr Christensen is a democrat in politics and fraternally is a member of the Woodmen of the World To him and his wife were born three children, namely: Anton, who is employed as a chauffeur in New York City; Holger, who is manager of a Thompson restaurant in Chicago, and Mary C., of this sketch

Mary C Christensen Debel received her elementary education in the public schools, and then she attended Dana College at Blair For a number of years after leaving school she was engaged in clerical work in Blair, and in 1918 she was elected to the office of county clerk, of which she is the present incumbent Thoroughly competent by natural ability and training for the performance of her official duties, Mrs Debel has won the hearty commendation of all who have dealings with her office, for the promptness, courtesy and thoroughness with which the duties of the office are discharged

On October 12, 1918, Mary C Christensen was united in marriage with Anders C Debel, who was born in Denmark and who is now a successful and well-known attorney at Blair and county judge of Washington County, to which office he was elected in 1920 He was in the military service during the World war, though the major portion of his time was spent in training camps in California

Mrs Debel is a member of the Lutheran Church Mr Debel is a democrat in his political views and he sustains fraternal relations with the Ancient Free and Accepted Masons Because of her charming personality, her genuine worth and her business ability, Mrs Debel has won and retains the sincere respect and good will of all who know her

SEYMOUR S SIDNER The profession of law is peculiarly a field for men of strong personality No other profession demands so much of personal ability and address A lawyer cannot buy his business and cannot receive it by inheritance Clients demand personal capability, so that underlying all must be the fundamental element of good judgment and sound principles, just as it must in all callings, and these attributes dominate Seymour S Sidner, one of the shrewd and successful young attorneys of Fremont

Seymour S Sidner was born at Stillwater, New Jersey, on January 12, 1875, a son of John and Martha (Van Horn) Sidner, both of whom were born in New Jersey, farming people who came to Dodge County, Nebraska, in 1888 They are now living in retirement at Fremont Their children are as follows Ida, who lives with her brother, S S, Sadie, who married Albert Lucas, lives in Oregon; Kathryn Amelia, who married W A. Yoder, a high school teacher; Seymour S, whose name heads this review, Martha, who is a teacher in the Omaha, Nebraska, public schools, Harry J, who is a Dodge County farmer, and Clarence, who is cashier of the First National Bank at North Bend, Nebraska The parents belong to the Methodist Episcopal Church, and the father is a democrat in his political sentiments

Seymour S. Sidner attended the Fremont public schools and the Fremont Normal School, and then for a year he was engaged in teaching school, and then studied law in the office of Judge Cartright until he was able to pass the examinations which enabled him to be admitted to the bar in June, 1899 Following this he formed a partnership with W J Cartright, and later the firm became Cartright, Sidner, Lee & Jones, which association is still maintained, and it is one of the strongest in this region, and has been connected with some very important jurisprudence in this part of the state

Mr. Sidner was married on October 31, 1899, to Myrtle Cramer, born at Harrisburg, Pennsylvania, and they became the parents of four children, namely Arthur C, John E, Seymour S, Jr, and Robert D, the latter dying May 20, 1920, and the first two being in a college at Cedar Rapids, Iowa Well known in Masonry, Mr Sidner belongs to the Commandery, and is past master of Fremont Lodge, Ancient Free and Accepted Masons. In politics a democrat, he was elected on his party ticket county attorney for two years, and was delegate to the democratic convention in San Francisco in 1920 The Rotary Club has the benefit of his membership and he is an enthusiastic booster for Fremont and Dodge County Both he and his wife belong to the Presbyterian Church. Some idea of the regard in which he is held by his fellow citizens is shown in his selection by them in November, 1919, as a member of the constitutional convention, for they realized that in him they would have an able representative and one who would know how to prepare the new constitution so that there would be no future disputes regarding the legality of its provisions On June 1, 1920, he was elected president of the First National Bank

WILLIAM H TURNER With the death of William H Turner on February 23, 1920, Dodge County chronicled the passing of its oldest pioneer citizen, one who had come into the wilderness of eastern Nebraska more than sixty years ago and had been a sharer in every phase of development from about the time Nebraska attracted the attention of eastern settlers He was a man who kept in close touch with passing events He came here when Nebraska was largely a country of Indians, buffalo and other wild game. The rivers and the overland trails were the only avenues of transportation He helped build some of the pioneer railroads of the state He saw the various advances and improvements in agriculture, the change from the nomadic life of the open range to settled agriculture, witnessed the introduction of manufactures and industry, was here when the Civil war was being fought, and saw the close of the World war, and by his individual experience could measure and appreciate the wonderful changes recorded between these wars

William H Turner was born in Massachusetts January 27, 1843, and died when he was a little past seventy-seven years of age His father, John Turner, and his mother, Margaret Slee Turner, were both natives of England, and from that country they came to the United States in the early '30s The father brought with him an outfit with which he established the first knitting factory at Needham, Massachusetts, and subsequently developed a large and important factory for the manufacture of stockings and underwear. Here he continued to live and operate his factory until his death Of sixteen children born to him and his wife the last two were William H and Mrs Carrie Rice, widow of John Rice and a resident of Omaha

Growing up in his native state William H Turner attended the public schools, and lived there until 1856, when he went out to Dubuque, Iowa, and a year later, in 1857, arrived on the Nebraska frontier at Fremont A youth willing to participate in all the arduous and hazardous undertakings of that time, he spent some five years engaged in freighting between Fremont and Denver. He also opened and conducted the old Valley House, a historic place of entertainment known to the travelers of the region for years In conjunction he conducted a stage station

All of this was in the pre-railroad era With the construction of the Union Pacific Railroad he took contracts for grading and supplying ties With the development that ensued following the building of the first railroad, Mr Turner engaged in the grocery business at Fremont in partnership with Andy Brugh and E N Morse, and continued active in that line for nearly a quarter of a century For the last fifteen years of his life Mr Turner had lived retired. He was a man highly esteemed for his business ability and integrity, and not less for the public spirit that made him a working factor in all community movements and kept him in the ranks of progressive citizenship to the close of his life He was deeply interested in the cause of public education and served for many years on the school board He was a member of the Masonic fraternity and in politics a democrat

October 12, 1869, Mr Turner married Miss Lucinda Gilley A few months before his death they had quietly observed their golden wedding anniversary Mrs Turner, whose parents were Elisha and Hannah (Stanley) Gilley, resides at 405 East Fifth Street in Fremont She is the mother of two daughters, and with them belongs to the Episcopal Church The daughter Maud is the wife of Thad Quinn, a Fremont merchant, while Nona is unmarried and lives at home

John Hendricksen. The little Kingdom of Denmark, small in size and in population, but great in history, has sent to the New World some of its best citizens, men of sturdy purpose and high aims, ot resolute principles and sound integrity, who have invaded the newer sections and have contributed in marked degree to the work of development that has changed the face of Nature and brought forth prosperity where only waste was known before. Denmark was the birthplace of John Hendricksen, one of the substantial farmers of Maple Township, Dodge County

Mr. Hendricksen was born April 6, 1858, a son of Henry and Gertrude Johnson, and one of seven children He grew up in an agricultural atmosphere, his father being a small land owner, and was educated in the public schools, also seeing nine months of military training in the Danish infantry Mr Hendrickson was twenty-seven years of age when he immigrated to the United States and when he arrived in Dodge County, Nebraska, in 1885, was without means He secured employment as a farm hand from Lars Olsen and continued to be thus engaged for several years, but for a time thereafter turned his attention to railroading, and in this connection worked in the states of Idaho and Washington Returning to Dodge County with his small savings, he invested them in a tract of 160 acres of land, and for the next few years worked unceasingly until he had fulfilled his obligations Since that time he has acquired, through purchase, eighty additional acres, in Maple Township, so that he is now the owner of 240 acres of valuable and productive land, on which he carries on successful operations as a general farmer and a raiser of a good grade of live stock Mr Hendricksen has splendid improvements on his land, including a modern, commodious home, erected in 1918 He is accounted one of the progressive agriculturists of his community and his reputation is one that has been built substantially through long years of honorable dealing and fair transactions. Mr Hendricksen is a democrat, but has shown no inclination to participate actively in political affairs, although as a good citizen he manifests an intelligent interest in the movements which affect the welfare of his community and state

In 1907 Mr. Hendricksen was united in marriage with Miss Florence Peterson, who was born in Henry County, Iowa, and they are the parents of one child, Glen Peterson, who is attending school in Dodge County. Mrs. Hendricksen is a member of the Fleihlars Fraternal National Union.

EDWIN L. HUSTEAD, M. D. Speaking in the language of the day, how poorly equipped would any modern community seem without its complement of able professional men, all of whom have their place, with particular stress perhaps laid on its medical men. Notwithstanding the perpetuation of feuds and the continuation of wars, the preservation of human life is still acknowledged the most important earthly factor of existence, and it is to the trained medical scientist that the world turns in its times of deep physical distress. To the growing City of Scribner, Nebraska, have come young men of professional ability who have found here recognition of their talent, and one of these is Dr. Edwin L. Hustead, a skilled physician and surgeon.

Doctor Hustead was born in 1885, at Omaha, Nebraska, where his mother still resides. He is the eldest of three children born to Charles M. and Caroline (Zimmerman) Hustead, of German ancestry but natives of Fort Madison, Iowa. For many years the father was a grocery merchant in Omaha, in which city he died in 1917. As a business man he was held in high regard, and as a republican was frequently tendered political honors which he would not accept. Doctor Hustead has one sister, Elvera, and one brother, Charles M., Jr., both of whom reside at home.

After completing his public school training in the Central High School at Omaha Edwin L. Hustead went into the offices of the Cudahy Packing Company, where he remained for five years, during all this time cherishing the intention of becoming a medical practitioner, and in a quiet way did considerable medical reading before he entered Creighton Medical College in 1912. After completing his studies there he was associated with Dr. L. T. Petersen of Omaha and in 1914 came to Scribner, where he has built up a large and satisfying practice. He has handled many cases with rare skill and has made an excellent impression wherever his services have been requested. He belongs to the Dodge County, the Nebraska State and the American Medical societies.

In 1914 Doctor Hustead was united in marriage to Miss Ida S. Procter, who was born, reared and educated in Nebraska. They have one daughter, Dorothy L., and one son, Arthur Procter, who contribute greatly to the sunshine prevailing in the home. Doctor Hustead belongs to the Masonic fraternity and to the Royal Highlanders. He has never found time, even if he had the inclination, to be active in a political way, not, however, being a negligent citizen, but preferably casting an independent vote. As a citizen of Scribner he takes keen interest in her schools and moral agencies, in outdoor sports from a physician's standpoint, and in public improvements along sanitary lines.

N. M. BOGGESS. A gifted and accomplished musician, Prof. N. M. Boggess, of Fremont, formerly an instructor in the Fremont College, was endowed by nature with musical talent of a high order, and as a teacher won an enviable reputation. Since resigning his professional position in the college he has been actively and prosperously engaged in business as proprietor of a finely equipped music store. A son of Henry Boggess, he was born, December 29, 1878, in Carrollton, Illinois, and in the Prairie State was reared and educated

Born, reared and educated in Illinois, Henry Boggess served for four years as a soldier during the Civil war, being a member of Company I, Ninety-First Illinois Infantry. He took an active part in several important engagements, being wounded at Elizabethtown, Kentucky, and was there captured by Morgan's raiders, and taken to prison, but was soon exchanged. Returning to Illinois, he settled as a farmer in White Hall where he is now living retired from active pursuits, although he has been connected to some extent with the postoffice the past few years. He is a republican in politics, and a member of the Grand Army of the Republic. He married Ellen Ragan, a native of St. Louis, Missouri, and of their five sons, three are living, as follows: John, a well known horse and stock man of White Hall, Illinois; N. M., of this sketch, and Ernest, engaged in farming near White Hall, Illinois. Both parents are consistent members of the Christian Church.

Educated in the public schools of his native county, and at Shurtleff College, in Alton, Illinois, N. M. Boggess studied music in Chicago, under the instruction of W. S. B. Matthews, a teacher of note. Coming to Fremont, Nebraska, in 1906, he entered Fremont College in a professional capacity, and taught music there for seven years, being dean of his department. In 1912, a year before leaving the college, Mr. Boggess established his music store, to the management of which he has devoted his entire attention since 1913, the business being carried on under the name of the Boggess Music Company. He has built up a large and constantly increasing business, handling sheet music and musical instruments of all kinds, his stock being very complete. Until recently he had branch stores in both Scribner and North Bend, this state, but has closed them. He sells music and musical instruments in all parts of Nebraska and Illinois, having especially large sales in Greene County, Illinois, where his parents live.

Mr. Boggess married, in 1907, Kathryn Holland, who was born in Pennsylvania, and as a child came to Nebraska with her parents. Her father died in this state, and her mother resides in Fremont. Mr. and Mrs. Boggess have one child, Harold, a schoolboy. Mr. Boggess is a republican in politics, and while a resident of White Hall, Illinois, served as a member of the City Council, and as city clerk. Both Mr. and Mrs. Boggess are active members of the Christian Church.

August L. Rebbe. The younger generation of the intelligent and progressive agricultural element in Dodge County is capably and worthily represented by August L. Rebbe, who is carrying on successful operations in farming and stock raising in section 1, Maple Township, where he is the owner of 360 acres of valuable and highly productive land. Mr. Rebbe has acquired his success in his home community, for he is a native son of Dodge County, born February 28, 1880, in Maple Township, his father being Henry Rebbe, Sr., a sketch of whose career will be found elsewhere in this work in the review of Henry Rebbe, Jr.

Mr. Rebbe is indebted to the district schools of Maple Township for his educational training, and to his father's instruction for his training along agricultural lines. He was reared to habits of industry, integrity and probity, and remained under the guidance of his parents until the time of his marriage. Following that event, he embarked upon a career of his own, in the same county and township, where he has since been successful in his operations as a general farmer and a breeder of purebred Herefords. His farm consists of 360 acres, upon which there are improvements and equipment of the latest kind. Aside from his agricultural interests, Mr Rebbe is a stockholder in the Dodge County Bank of Hooper and the First National Bank, also of that place. He is a Mason and belongs to the Mystic Shrine and the Knights of Pythias In politics he votes independently

January 29, 1897, Mr. Rebbe was united in marriage with Miss Ida Carstens, who was born November 2, 1884, in Dodge County, Nebraska, daughter of Henry Carstens, an early settler of Dodge County, and to this union there have been born three children—Emma, Lloyd and Carson—all of whom reside with their parents and are attending school.

JOHN B CARTER At present a retired citizen of Blair, John B Carter has been one of the industrious men of Washington County, linking his name with all that is admirable in farming and wise and progressive in individual life While general farming occupied his chief interest during the active years of his career, he was also widely known as a breeder of cattle, and in the field of fruit raising gained a reputation that extended far beyond the boundaries of his own state

Mr Carter was born in Adams County Ohio, May 20, 1856, a son of Jacob and Frances L (Harris) Carter, who were married in Ohio, the former being a native of Ohio and the latter of Virginia Coming to Nebraska in 1856, with their three children, Charles, Mary and John B, they secured a pre-emption claim in Washington County, on which they proved up, and obtained land at $1.25 per acre Here they spent the rest of their lives in farming, gaining well-merited success and the esteem and respect of their neighbors, and reaching advanced years, the father dying when seventy-five years of age and the mother when she had attained the remarkable age of ninety-two years They were faithful members of the Baptist Church Mr. Carter, a democrat in politics, was one of the early supervisors of Washington County, and in his public life as in his private affairs gave evidence of the possession of the sturdy traits of character inherited from his English ancestry There were ten children in the family, of whom five are living · Charles, who is engaged in farming in Washington County, Mary, the wife of Z T Brunton, of Blair, John B, Dora, who is unmarried and resides at Blair, and Julia, the wife of William J Lippincott a farmer of Webster County, Nebraska

John B. Carter was an infant when brought by his parents to Washington County and here his education was acquired in the public schools As a youth he took up farming and was his father's assistant until he was thirty-six years of age, at which time he began independent activities on his own account During the long period that he followed active farming, Mr Carter made many improvements on his property, which is still known as one of the most modern as to equipment to be found in the county It includes a windmill, running water in the residence and other modern advantages, and during his occupancy its general air of prosperity attracted much favorable comment While he sold his farm stuff in 1914 and located in a pleasant home at Blair, Mr Carter retains the ownership of 440 acres of valuable land For a number of years Mr Carter raised Polled Angus cattle, having a large herd of these registered animals and being considered an authority upon the subject of their breeding He also had two acres of orchards on his farm, where he raised all kinds of fruit, and was a frequent exhibitor thereof at state fairs, etc Of such a high grade was his product that during one year it took seven first prizes at the Nebraska State Fair, while in another year his apples took three first and four second prizes at the Iowa State Fair

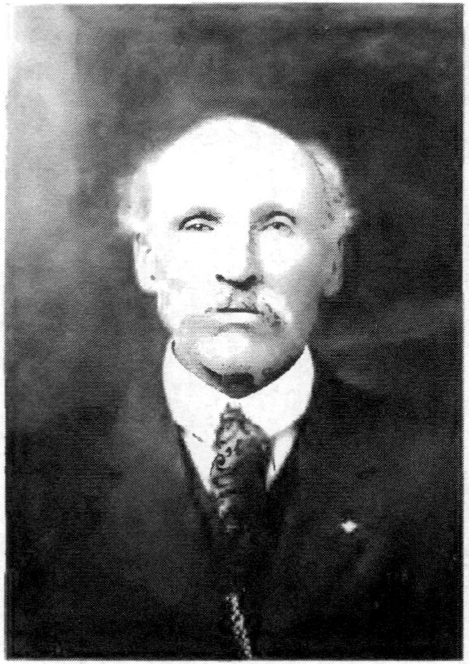

J B Carter

Mrs J. B. Carter

Mr Carter was married November 24, 1892, to Miss Margaret Nettie Stilts, who was born in Washington County, Nebraska, daughter of Ela and Margaret (McClelland) Stilts, natives of Ohio, who came to Washington County in 1856 and settled on a pre-emption claim near Fort Calhoun and later near Blair, upon which both died, he at the age of sixty-four and his wife at seventy years They had eleven children, of whom five are living Ernest, a farmer of the community of Elbert, Colorado, Philip, a fruit farmer of Corning, California, Mrs John B Carter; Eliza, who is single and a resident of Corning, California and Harry, a fruit farmer and stock raiser of that locality

Mr and Mrs Carter are members of the Baptist Church They belong to the Order of the Eastern Star, in which Mrs Carter has held all the chairs and is past matron, and Mr Carter is likewise a Knight Templar Mason and a Shriner. In politics he is a democrat in national affairs, although inclined to independent views In 1920 they built a modern home at the corner of West Front and Second Streets, the first tile-brick house in Blair, and it stands on the land that Mr Carter's father pre-empted from the Government in 1857.

T. A F Nusz Recognizing the fact that in the field of journalism there exists plenty of room for men of brains and vim, T. A. F Nusz early chose for his calling the newspaper profession, with what degree of success is shown in his present well-equipped establishment at Snyder, where he publishes the Banner and carries on a prosperous business in job printing He was born at Frederick City, Maryland, in 1851, a son of George M and Susan M Nusz

George M Nusz was a brick and stone mason by trade, and brought his family to the West in 1856, locating at Cedar Rapids, Iowa, where he met an accidental death, his widow surviving him for some years They were the parents of ten children Mary, the widow of H F Fitch, of Cedar Rapids, Iowa, F T, a harnessmaker of Bay City, Michigan; George D, deceased; Henry, who died in infancy, T. A F., Lucretia, the wife of C C Bushnell, a carriagemaker of Marion, Iowa, Ida, who is deceased, Myra and Harry, who died in infancy, and Ida, the wife of George Elkle a merchant tailor of Cedar Rapids The parents were members of the English Lutheran Church, and in politics Mr Nusz, the elder, was a republican In his youth he received his education in the schools of Baltimore, Maryland, and received a congressional appointment to West Point, but never took advantage of this opportunity

T. A F Nusz was five years of age when he accompanied his parents to Cedar Rapids, Iowa, and his education was acquired in the public schools of that city When he was eighteen years of age, in 1869, he entered the job printing office of the Weekly Times, at Cedar Rapids, and during the next fifteen years followed printing as a trade, visiting various points in Montreal, Canada, Vermont and New York Returning to Cedar Rapids, he accepted the foremanship of the Daily Republican, with which he remained for some years, after which he went to Des Moines to become superintendent of the state printing office, a position which he retained eight years In 1900 he came to Fremont, Nebraska, as superintendent of the Hammond Printing Company, remaining eleven years, after which he came to Snyder, and in 1913 leased the office of the Snyder Banner Here he has since been engaged in publishing a reliable and interesting weekly newspaper, the circulation of which has increased steadily and the value of which as an advertising medium is generally conceded A well-equipped job printing office is operated where all kinds of high-class work is done, and Mr Nusz has found his journalistic and business duties sufficient to demand his entire attention to the exclusion of outside interests.

In 1886 Mr. Nusz married Miss Alice Goodell, who was born in Illinois, and who bore her husband two children George, who died in infancy, and Stoddard, now a resident of Fremont, who spent twenty-three months in the medical corps of the United States Army and saw service on the Mexican border Mr Nusz was again married, at Des Moines, Iowa, to Jessie Davis, a native of Iowa Mr. and Mrs Nusz are members of the Christian Church, the movements of which they have supported liberally, while he maintains an independent stand as to political matters

J H C MEYER A thorough-going, enterprising farmer of Dodge County, J H C Meyer is proprietor of a well-kept and well-appointed farm in Cuming Township, where he has been profitably engaged in his independent calling for a number of years He was born December 27, 1879, in Germany, a son of J H G Meyer

Born, reared and educated in Germany, J H G Meyer immigrated to this country in 1879, bringing with him his wife and family, which then consisted of five children Coming directly to Dodge County, this state, he bought land that was still in its primitive wildness, and having cleared and improved a good farm was actively and successfully engaged in tilling the soil until 1910, when he moved to Scribner, Dodge County, where he has since lived retired from active labor He has never been active in local affairs, but is independent in his political relations, and is a worthy member of the Lutheran Church, to which his good wife, who died in 1917, aged three score and ten years, also belonged He married Anna Lewis, and they became the parents of six children, as follows Anna, wife of Chris Sass, who is engaged in farming in Dodge County, Mary wife of Frank Hartung, a Colorado farmer, Sophia, wife of John Hargens, Gesina, wife of Fred Kitzrow, proprietor of a bakery at Beemer, J H. C, of this sketch, and George, a prosperous farmer of Dodge County

Educated in the district schools of Dodge County, J. H C Meyer was well drilled in the various branches of agriculture when young, and finding the occupation not only pleasant, but profitable, began life for himself as a farmer at the age of twenty-six years, and having met with desired results in his operations as a farmer and stock raiser, realizes that he made no mistake in selecting his future occupation

Mr Meyer married, in 1910, Amelia Klusendorf, who was born in Wisconsin and came to Nebraska when an infant and was educated in the Lutheran schools They have two children, Florence and Mildred, both attending the Lutheran schools Mr Meyer invariably cast his vote for the best men and measures, regardless of party prejudices Both Mr and Mrs Meyer are Lutherans in religion, belonging to St John's Church

ERIC G ERICKSON A well-known and highly esteemed farmer of Dodge County Eric G Erickson of Logan Township, materially assists in maintaining the reputation of this section of Nebraska as a good agricultural region, and thoroughly identifies himself with whatever will promote the highest interests of his community A son of the late Ambrose Erickson, he was born, in 1864, in Buffalo, New York

Born in Sweden, Ambrose Erickson grew to manhood in his native country, residing there until after his marriage with Carrie Chapman

Coming to America in 1863, he stopped a short time in Montreal, Canada, after which he lived in Buffalo, New York, for a while Having some means of his own, he decided to take advantage of the opportunity for buying cheaper lands in the West, and moved to Omaha, Nebraska, from whence he freighted out to Dodge County, Nebraska Homesteading 160 acres of land in Logan Township he began the pioneer labor of redeeming a farm from its primitive wildness, and in addition to carrying on general farming worked for a few years in the Union Pacific car shops at Omaha He was exceedingly prosperous as an agriculturist, continuing as such until his death, when but three score years of age He first lived in a dugout, and that was replaced by a substantial log structure, which in time gave way to a good frame house, each advancing step taken in improving the estate betokening the owner's prosperity

Brought up on the parental homestead, Eric G Erickson gleaned his early knowledge of books in the rural schools, and as a youth clerked for a short time in a mercantile establishment Turning his attention to agriculture, Mr Erickson took up a homestead claim in Box Butte County, Nebraska, where he tilled the soil for a few seasons Returning to Dodge County, he was employed as clerk in a general store at Hooper for seven years Subsequently, responding to the lure of the land, he took charge of his present farm in Logan Township, and in its care has shown marked ability and excellent judgment

Mr Erickson married in 1883, Christina Dahl, a daughter of Peter and Justina Dahl, neither of whom are now living Mr and Mrs. Erickson are worthy and active members of the Congregational Church. Mr Erickson is a decided democrat in his political views, and socially he is a member of the Farmers' Union, at Hooper Mr and Mrs Erickson have no children

O B Wegner Not only is there an immense demand for a high grade of ice cream by the retail dealers, restaurants and hotels, but from careful housewives who are recognizing the fact that this delicious article is not only the best, but also, everything considered, the most economic dessert they can furnish their families The latter however, are even more particular than other consumers in their requirements for a product that may be safely used as a part of the daily menu, and the manufacturers of the commodity who are achieving the best results are those who are putting on the market a pure article Such a concern is the one operated under the caption of The Arctic Cream Company of Fremont, of which one of the energetic officials is O B Wegner, a veteran of the Great war, and one of the live, young business men of Fremont

O B Wegner was born at Fremont on February 17, 1891, a son of Rev Herman and Mary (Fry) Wegner, natives of Germany and Illinois, respectively Rev Mr Wegner was only a lad of eight or nine years of age when he was brought to the United States, and his parents became early settlers of Nebraska He became a minister of the German Lutheran Church and has had pastorates in Saunders County and Washington County, Nebraska, where he remained for five years, and at Fremont, where he was located for some time, and he is now in charge of a church of his denomination at Loveland, Colorado Of his seven children, six are living, but O B. Wegner is the only one of them who is a resident of Fremont Rev Mr. Wegner is a strong republican

O B Wegner received his educational training in the grade and high schools of Omaha, Nebraska, and after completing his schooldays, engaged with the Toledo Scale Company at Omaha, and remained with this concern in that city, and also at Kansas City, Missouri, Minneapolis, Minnesota, and Duluth, Minnesota Mr Wegner is one of the young men of the country who entered the United States service as a member of the Seventy-Ninth Field Artillery, Seventh Division, attached to the medical department, and was in France for six months, but in the service for two years Mr Wegner received his discharge on February 22, 1919

Prior to going into the army, Mr. Wegner had been interested in what was then known as the Fremont Ice Cream Company. In 1918, while he was away, the company bought another plant at Sioux City, Iowa, and re-organized under the present name of The Arctic Cream Company, with a capital of $100,000 This company manufactures ice cream exclusively, and ships the product to different parts of Nebraska, South Dakota and Iowa, in addition to doing an immense trade locally Mr Wegner resumed his connections with this company upon his return from the war, and is devoting all of his time to his duties with relation to it

In September, 1918, Mr Wegner was married to Allie Phillips, born near Fremont, a daughter of Ezra and Louise Phillips

In former years Mr. Phillips was extensively engaged in farming in Dodge County, but is now retired and living at Fremont Mrs Wegner is a member of the Christian Church Fremont Lodge No 514, Benevolent and Protective Order of Elks, holds the membership of Mr Wegner as does the Fremont Rotary Club Like his excellent father Mr Wegner is a republican

J Howard Heine A man of keen judgment, clear-headed and far-sighted, J Howard Heine, of Fremont, has had a varied experience in business, and as vice president of the Farmers and Merchants National Bank of Fremont is actively identified with the management of one of the substantial financial institutions of Dodge County A son of the late John F Heine, he was born July 20, 1873, in Philadelphia, Pennsylvania, of German and Scotch ancestry

Born in Germany, June 2, 1843, John F Heine came to America with his parents when about four years of age, settling in Pennsylvania, near Reading, where he followed his trade of an iron moulder Coming to Nebraska, he located at Hooper, Dodge County, on July 10, 1882, and subsequently was engaged in the hardware and implement business with his brother, George F Heine, until his death, which occurred May 24, 1919 A sound republican in politics, he held some of the local offices During the last year of the Civil war he served in Company D, One Hundred and Ninety-Eighth Pennsylvania Volunteer Infantry, taking an active part in several engagements, one of the most important having been the battle at Five Forks, and was afterwards a prominent member of the Grand Army of the Republic, and a delegate to several national conventions of the organization His wife, whose maiden name was Sarah J Bush, was a life-long resident of Pennsylvania, her birth occurring there September 12, 1850, and her death on September 16, 1881 She was a daughter of Mathew and Julia A Bush, also natives of Pennsylvania Of the six children born to Mr. and Mrs Heine, five are living, as follows George W, in the hardware business at Hooper, Laura G wife of J A Hunker, lives on a ranch near Howell, South Dakota, J Howard, Ada I, of Hooper; and Julia F, also of Hooper, Nebraska. The mother was a member of the Lutheran Church, and the father was a Catholic in religion

At the age of seventeen years, having completed his studies in the public schools of Philadelphia and Hooper, Nebraska, J. Howard Heine began his business life as a clerk in his father's hardware store He subsequently accepted a position as cashier of the First National Bank of Hooper, and retained it until January, 1912. Going then to Twin Falls, Idaho, he was engaged in the orchard business a short time, and later served in the Twin Falls Courthouse as deputy county auditor, and then as deputy treasurer. In 1914, continuing in that city, Mr Heine was elected county treasurer, and served in that capacity a year Resigning the position, he returned to Hooper, and resumed his connection with the First National Bank and held its cashiership two years. Mr Heine gave up that position to become cashier of the Farmers and Merchants Bank of Fremont, and on January 1, 1919, was elected vice president of the same institution, and has since, as vice president and cashier, had charge of the bank and its extensive financial affairs. That the bank's business has nearly doubled in quantity and value since Mr Heine assumed its charge is proof of his ability, fidelity and wise judgment

Mr Heine married, September 6, 1897, Julia Farrell, a native of Schuylkill County, Pennsylvania, and they are the parents of three children, namely Zita, head bookkeeper in the Farmers and Merchants National Bank of Fremont, Comer, a senior in the Fremont High School, and Phyllis, a sophomore in the same school A republican in politics, Mr. Heine served for two years on the Republican State Central Committee, and while living in Hooper held all of the offices within the gift of his follow townsmen While there he organized the Hooper Stock Show Company, the Hooper Telephone Company, and the Hooper Ice Company Fraternally Mr Heine is a member of Fremont Lodge No 514, Benovelent and Protective Order of Elks, and of the Knights of Columbus, which he has served as district deputy Religiously he belongs to the Catholic Church

HENRY A HAUN has been a resident of Dodge County from the time of his birth, which here occurred in the year 1882, and here he has become not only a successful agriculturist but has also achieved no little prominence as a breeder and grower of fine Belgian draft horses and the highest type of shorthorn cattle His farm comprises 400 acres, is improved with good buildings of modern type, is supplied with the best of equipment and accessories for the furtherance of the general activities of the place, and is one of the attractive rural estates in section 2, Cotterell Township Mr. Haun is indebted to the public schools of Dodge County and the State Normal School at Fremont for his youthful education and has been independently engaged in farm enterprise since he attained to his legal majority. He is one of the substantial and popular citizens of Cotterell Township, where he has served as a member of the school board of district No 30, his political allegiance being given to the democratic party in national affairs but in local matters his vote being cast in support of men and measures meeting the approval of his judgment, irrespective of strict partisan lines He and his wife are communicants of the Catholic Church at Ridgeley, in which village Mrs Haun taught school prior to her marriage Mr Haun is affiliated with the Knights of Columbus

In 1903 was solemnized the marriage of Mr Haun to Miss Nellie O'Connor, who likewise was born and reared in Dodge County, and who is a daughter of Matthew O'Connor. Mr and Mrs Haun have seven children · Helen, Floyd, Kermit J. Charlotte, Marion, Katherine and Regina All except the two youngest of the children are attending school

John Haun, father of him whose name initiates this sketch, was one of the pioneer homesteaders in Dodge County, of whom a complete sketch and portrait are found on other pages of this work He and his sons are now engaged in breeding full-blood spotted Poland-China hogs.

GRACE BALLARD A wide-awake, brainy woman, full of vim and energy, Grace Ballard, of Blair, a successful lawyer, now serving as county attorney of Washington County, gained an almost nation-wide reputation as one of the most enthusiastic and valuable workers in the cause of equal suffrage, of which she is an ardent champion A native of Blair, she was born August 12, 1877, a daughter of the late Martin Ballard

Born in Kentucky, Martin Ballard received excellent educational advantages, and as a young man was admitted to the bar Coming to Nebraska in 1869, practiced law in Blair until 1885, being quite successful His health failing, he went to Chadron, Nebraska, hoping to recuperate, and there continued his legal work until his death, in 1889 While living in Blair, he served as county judge, and at the time of his death was county attorney of Dawes County A lawyer of much prominence, he was financially successful, and for a number of years was in partnership with W C. Walton, a well-known and popular attorney. In his political relations, he was a republican, and much interested in public affairs

Martin Ballard married in Millersburg, Iowa, Sarah D Strong, who was born in Ohio four score years ago, and is now a resident of Blair, having a pleasant little home on the edge of the city She is a woman of culture, and a worthy member of the Methodist Episcopal Church. Of the four children born into her home, three are living, namely A N., engaged in farming at Coleman, South Dakota, Harriet N, profitably engaged in the millinery business at Wichita, Kansas, and Grace, of whom we write

After her graduation from the Blair High School, Miss Grace Ballard continued her studies at the Nebraska State University, in Lincoln, and at the age of eighteen years began to read law, her great ambition having been to enter the legal profession In September, 1911 Miss Ballard entered the law department of the University of Nebraska, and at the same time secured a position with the Lincoln Safety Deposit Company, earning a salary with which she paid her college expenses A brilliant student, she made an excellent record in her class work, and in 1914 was admitted to the bar.

An active supporter of equal suffrage, Miss Ballard went to Pennsylvania in the spring of 1915, and there championed the cause with good effect In the spring of 1914 she spent four months similarly engaged in Iowa, and in January, February and March of the following year worked in Nebraska, having been one of the prominent and popular supporters of the cause in the state

In May, 1918, Miss Ballard opened a law office in Blair, and in August, of that year, filed a petition for county attorney, and was subsequently elected by a majority of 200, an exceedingly large majority for the county She has met with almost unprecedented success, both as a lawyer, and in her official capacity as county attorney In 1913 she had the honor of being elected president of her class in the law school, being the first woman ever elected to that position, and she also has the distinction of being one of the very few women in the United States to serve as county attorney

Grace Ballard

HENRY W ROGERS Clearly defined purpose and consecutive effort in the affairs of life will inevitably result in the attaining of a due measure of success, but in following out the career of one who has attained success by his own efforts there comes into view the intrinsic individuality which made such accomplishment possible, and thus there is kindled a feeling of respect and admiration The qualities which have made Mr. Rogers one of the prominent and successful men of Fremont have also brought him the esteem of his fellow townsmen, for his career has been one of well-directed energy, strong determination and honorable methods

Henry W. Rogers is a native of the community now honored by his citizenship, for he was born in Fremont on May 10, 1872 He is the son of Henry W. and Catherine D. (Basler) Rogers Henry W Rogers, Sr., was born in Philadelphia, Pennsylvania, in 1840, and his death occurred on November 30, 1916 He learned the vocation of a steam engineer and for a number of years ran an engine on the Philadelphia & Reading Railroad Later he joined the Philadelphia fire department and he ran the first fire steamer in that department In 1868 he came to Dodge County, Nebraska, and settled on Maple Creek, where he homesteaded a farm, on which he lived for about five years He then moved to Fremont and was here employed for a time in setting up machinery for a harvester company, and was afterwards employed by May Brothers, wholesale grocers, for a number of years His last employment was with the Fremont Water Company, with whom he remained until the infirmities of advancing years compelled his retirement from active affairs Catherine D Basler was born on a steamer on the Atlantic Ocean while her parents were emigrating from Germany to the United States in 1846, and her death occurred at Fremont in December, 1904 Her marriage to Henry W Rogers occurred in Philadelphia Her father, Jacob Basler, was but a young man when he came from Germany with his young wife and they settled in Pennsylvania. To Henry W. and Catherine D Rogers were born six children, namely Jacob, who is employed as engineer by May Brothers, at Fremont; Emma is the wife of Arthur Gwynn, a wealthy ranchman living near Lucerne, Wyoming; Henry W., Katie is the wife of Charles Green, who runs the Green House at Fremont, Lucy is the wife of Fred Lanz, of Columbus, Nebraska, an engineer on the Union Pacific Railroad, and a veteran of the United States army, having served in the Philippines and was captain of a supply company in the army during the World war Etta is the wife of Henry Yenney, a car repairer on the Chicago & Northwestern Railroad at Fremont. The parents of these children were earnest members of the Lutheran Church and in politics the father was a democrat

Henry W. Rogers, Jr, received his educational training in the Fremont public schools and the Fremont Normal School His first employment was as a newspaper carrier, by which means he was able to pay his way through the normal school He then went to work for the Omaha Tent and Awning Company, with whom he remained for twelve years, during which time, by faithful and conscientious work, he rose from a modest position to that of manager of the Lincoln office, where he was stationed for three years He then traveled in the interests of this company for eight years, and then for two months he served as assistant superintendent of the George B Carpenter Company of Chicago, the largest awning company in the world In 1904 Mr Rogers came to Fremont and organized the Rogers Tent and Awning Company, for the manufacture of tents, awnings and canvas covers of every description.

He has been successful in this enterprise even beyond his expectations and now his company is the second largest of its kind in the State of Nebraska, their products being shipped throughout Nebraska, Kansas, Wyoming and the Dakotas Mr Rogers has gained a wide reputation because of the high quality of his products and during the past nine years he has supplied and handled the tents for the National Power Tractor Shows, which are exhibited in nine different states

Fraternally Mr Rogers is a member of the Ancient Free and Accepted Masons, in which he has attained to the thirty-second degree of the Scottish Rite, and to the Ancient Arabic Order Nobles of the Mystic Shrine and the Independent Order of Odd Fellows, being a past noble grand in the latter order In his political faith he is a democrat He takes a keen interest in every movement for the advancement of the community, along material, civic or moral lines, and, because of his generous public spirit and his excellent personal qualities of character, he is held in deservedly high repute among his fellow citizens

BYRON B HAUSER, M. D Medical science has never been stationary, but from the earliest days, advances have been made, some of which revolutionize existing theories. Specializing observation on disease have worked marvelous changes in treatment; tireless theoretic experiments have proven the truth of contentions, and only after results have been demonstrated beyond reasonable doubt, are discoveries given to the public In the work of the past quarter of a century are to be noticed such practical advances as the development of bacteriology, the particularly successful efforts to wipe out tuberculosis, bubonic plague, cholera, diphtheria, typhoid, spinal meningitis and similar maladies, while great control has been gained over cancer and miracles performed in connection with the restoration of lost or diseased tissue during the late war This marvelous progress has not come naturally, but is the outcome of the tireless, aggressive and self-sacrificing work of the men who have devoted themselves to the profession of medicine One of these men whose names will always be connected with this most honored of all callings, especially in Dodge County, is Dr Byron B Hauser, of Hooper

Doctor Hauser was born December 29, 1871, at Yadkinville, North Carolina, a son of Theophilus C and Martha L (Martin) Hauser, the former of whom was a farmer, merchant and operator of flour mills at Yadkinville His death occurred in 1887 when he was seventy-seven years old, and his wife passed away in 1904 when she was sixty-seven Of their children, Sidney L died at the age of thirty-seven, five survive Walter C is a farmer of Yadkinville, William A is a farmer of Fullerton, North Dakota; Charles M, who is a banker of High Point, North Carolina; Sallie is the wife of Robert Dalton, of Winston-Salem, North Carolina, a hardware merchant; and Doctor Byron B, whose name heads this review Doctor Hauser's father had by a previous marriage the following children: John H, who is a farmer of Yadkinville, Martha who is the widow of Virgil Wilson, of Pfafftown, North Carolina, and Amelia, who is the widow of Dr. Henry Wilson, of Fremont, Nebraska A man of considerable prominence, T C. Hauser was elected to the State Assembly of North Carolina for one term on the democratic ticket The mother of Doctor Hauser was a Baptist, but his father did not belong to any religious organization.

Doctor Hauser attended the public schools of Yadkinville and Guilford College, and then secured his medical education at the College of Physicians and Surgeons at Baltimore, Maryland, from which he was graduated in 1898 For the subsequent year Doctor Hauser was engaged in a general practice at Booneville, North Carolina, and then spent a year at Yadkinville, North Carolina, but in 1900 came west to Nebraska and located permanently at Hooper, where he has since been engaged in practice, and has built up a large and profitable connection

In 1896 Doctor Hauser was married to Rose E Vestal, born in North Carolina, and they became the parents of three children, namely Byron Terrell, who is now attending Columbia University, was in the United States service during the late war, being trained at base hospital No 49, Nebraska, and was sent overseas with that contingent and served until after the armistice was signed; Herbert S, who was also in the service, in the naval training department of the University of Nebraska, is now operating a ranch at Grant, Nebraska, and George, who is with his brother on the ranch at Grant.

Doctor Hauser has long been an enthusiastic member of the Dodge County Medical Association, and is now serving as its president He also belongs to the state and national medical associations, and the Elkhorn Medical Association Both he and Mrs Hauser are members of the Society of Friends In politics he is a democrat Fraternally he belongs to the Knights of Pythias, Odd Fellows, Maccabees, Woodmen of the World and Modern Woodmen of America From the beginning of his professional career Doctor Hauser has lived up to the highest ethics of his calling, and has won and retains the confidence of the public in his skill, dependability and good judgment, and these qualities are deeply appreciated as is shown by his increasing practice and the place accorded him in his community

Henry Witt One of the good country homes of Dodge County is in section 36 of Pebble Township, and its owner is also one of the high class progressive farmers of the locality, Henry Witt His home is in a rather historic locality, at the site of what is still known by the old timers as the Town of Pebble, which was platted even before the Town of Scribner

Henry Witt is a son of that sterling pioneer, the late John H Witt, whose life story has been told on other pages Henry Witt was born in Dodge County on the old homestead in 1871, and came to manhood with a good education in the local schools, and with a practical training as a farmer He lived at home until he was twenty-five, and then began farming on his own account Three years later he joined his brother John in the operation of the Pebble Roller Mills They were associated in that milling enterprise for ten years and then dissolved partnership, he returning to the farm while his brother is now a miller at Lee, Nebraska. Henry Witt is proprietor of 120 acres where he lives and still handles the greater share of the work himself. He keeps good live stock and feeds practically all his crops on the place He is a director in the Farmers Telephone Exchange and has affiliated himself with the various progressive organizations of the county. He served six years on the local school board, is an independent voter in politics and is affiliated with the Knights of the Maccabees

In 1905 he married Miss Emma Ruff, who was born and reared in Dodge County where her father, Charles Ruff, a native of Illinois, was an early settler Mr and Mrs Witt have five children: Sophie, John Henry, Elsie, Willis and Louise

ARTHUR K DAME It is well within the province of this publication to accord specific recognition to those who stand as representative figures in the various lines of professional activity in Dodge and Washington counties, and in even a cursory survey it becomes evident that Arthur K Dame is in secure vantage place as one of the leading members of the bar of Dodge County, with residence and professional headquarters at Fremont, the judicial center of the county

A scion of a family that was founded in New England in the Colonial period of our national history, Mr Dame was born at Orford, New Hampshire, October 8, 1860 He is a son of Henry A. and Harriet F (Moulton) Dame, the former of whom likewise was born at Orford, and the latter of whom was born at Lyman, that state, though their marriage was solemnized at Newbury, Vermont, their residence in the old Green Mountain state having been of comparatively brief duration In his native town in New Hampshire Henry A. Dame died in 1879 at the age of fifty-one years, and his venerable widow now resides in the home of her son, Arthur K of this review, she having celebrated in 1919 the eighty-first anniversary of her birth and being revered by all who have come within the compass of her gentle and gracious influence Arthur K is the elder of two children and William M who is in the railway mail service, resides in the City of Lincoln, this state Henry A Dame was a democrat in his political proclivities and was actively engaged in agricultural and live stock industry during virtually his entire active career He served in various township offices and his religious faith was that of the Congregational Church He was a son of Theodore and Lucy (Stebbins) Dame, the former of whom was born on virtually the same spot in which the son, Henry A, and the grandson, Arthur K, were born—in fact that shows that the ancestral homestead in Orford, New Hampshire, early came into the possession of the family The fine old residence, erected in 1817 and of the beautiful Colonial type, is a spacious dwelling, with nine fireplaces, and is still in excellent preservation Theodore Dame passed his entire life in New Hampshire, and he served either as sheriff or deputy sheriff of his county for more than forty years His father, Theodore Dame Sr, was born near Portsmouth New Hampshire, in 1750, and his death occurred in 1799 He was one of those who took part in General Montgomery's historic expedition against Quebec in the Revolutionary period, and he took part also in the battles of Bennington and Saratoga

Rinaldo and Harriet (Kent) Moulton, maternal grandparents of Arthur K Dame of this review, likewise were natives of New Hampshire, where the former died in 1895, his widow having long survived him and having been a resident of Michigan at the time of her demise, in 1895 The lineage of the Dame family is traced back to staunch English origin, and the first American representatives, headed by Deacon John Dame, settled at Dover, New Hampshire in 1627 The Moulton family also is of English origin, and Noah Moulton, Jr, great-great-grandfather of Arthur K Dame, served as a patriot soldier in the War of the Revolution, in which he took part in the expedition against Quebec, his father, Noah, Sr, having been killed while serving in this expedition in the attack on Quebec Col Jacob Kent, Capt Timothy Barron, Ensign Richard Peabody and John Tillotson were other Revolutionary patriots with whom Arthur K Dame can claim family kinship

Mr Dame gained his early education in the schools of his native state, and in 1882 he was graduated in historic old Dartmouth College, with the degree of Bachelor of Arts Thereafter he studied law in the office of the firm of Keating & Dickerman, of Muskegon, Michigan, and in 1885 he was admitted to the bar of that state For two years thereafter he was engaged in practice at Menominee, Michigan, and he then, in November, 1887, came to Fremont, Nebraska, where he has since continued in the active practice of his profession and where he is now one of the veteran members of the Dodge County bar He is a democrat in politics, and he is now serving his second term as municipal police judge of Fremont Prior to his assuming this judicial office he had served twenty-three consecutive years as justice of the peace In his law practice he now gives his attention almost exclusively to probate business, and he has been called upon to act as attorney for a number of large and important estates in this section of Nebraska With a broad and accurate knowledge of the science of jurisprudence, Judge Dame has contributed three valuable works to the literature of his profession He is author of a work entitled "Probate and Administration," which was published in 1902, to which he added a supplement in 1909, the work meeting with such demand that in 1915 he issued a second edition, which has had still larger sale and which is considered a standard in the province of law which it exploits with all of authority and conciseness In 1918 Judge Dame published another valuable work, entitled "Nebraska Inferior Court Practice," and this, too, is meeting with most favorable reception on the part of members of the bar of the state

For fully a quarter of a century Judge Dame has maintained active affiliation with the Nebraska state organization of the Society of the Sons of the American Revolution, for membership in which no citizens of the state can claim greater eligibility He is affiliated also with the Independent Order of Odd Fellows, including the Encampment, and the Ancient Order of United Workmen and the Improved Order of Red Men Though a man of engaging social qualities, he has remained a bachelor, a fact that does not in the least militate against his popularity in the county that has long represented his home

FRANK DOLEZAL has been, save for an interval of six months passed in the State of Utah, continuously engaged in the practice of law at Fremont, judicial center of Dodge County, since the year 1881, and his high reputation in his chosen profession has so far transcended local limitation as to give him secure vantage-ground as one of the essentially representative members of the bar of the state His success and prestige are the more pleasing to note by reason of the fact that he has been a resident of the vital West since his boyhood days and is a member of a sterling pioneer family of the State of Iowa He controls a large and important law practice and has appeared in much notable litigation in the various courts of Nebraska, including the supreme court of the state and extending also into the federal courts

Mr Dolezal was born in Bohemia, January 16, 1858, and is the only child of John and Dorotha (Kubik) Dolezal, the latter of whom died in his childhood In 1867 John Dolezal, accompanied by his son, Frank, then a lad of about nine years, immigrated to America and became a pioneer settler in Jones County, Iowa, whence he later removed to Tama County, that state, where he won substantial prosperity through his resourceful activities as a farmer and where he continued to reside until his death, at an advanced age He contracted a second marriage after coming to the United States, and his second wife lives in Tama County, Iowa He is survived by three children Fannie is the wife of Joseph Hansus, a farmer in Tama County, Iowa Bertha resides in the City of

Cedar Rapids, that state, and Lester remains on the old homestead farm in Tama County The parents were Catholic people and the father was a stanch and well fortified advocate of the principles of the republican party, with which he continued active affiliation until his death

Frank Dolezal is indebted to the public schools of Iowa for his early educational discipline, and in 1879 he completed his higher course of study in the Southern Iowa Normal Institute, at Bloomfield On January 1st of the following year he began reading law in the office and under the effective preceptorship of the firm of Stivers & Bradshaw at Toledo, Iowa, and his ambition was marked by the resolute purpose that enabled him to make rapid progress in his absorption and assimilation of the science of jurisprudence, with the result that he secured admission to the Iowa bar in December, 1880 In the following January he engaged in the practice of his profession at Fremont, Nebraska, where he became associated with Judge Joseph E Frick, who had been a fellow student of law at Toledo, Iowa, but who had completed his course of technical study one year earlier than Mr Dolezal The firm of Frick & Dolezal built up a fine law business in Dodge County, and the professional alliance continued fifteen years The two partners then removed to Salt Lake City, Utah, where the partnership was dissolved about six months later. Judge Frick remaining in that state and later becoming a member of its supreme court Mr Dolezal returned forthwith to Fremont, in 1897, and here he has continued in successful independent practice during the intervening years He has been local attorney for the Union Pacific Railroad for thirty-five years, and his general clientage has long been of important and representative character He is a stanch republican and though he has taken lively interest in party affairs he has sought no political office, virtually the only public office which he has consented to fill having been that of city attorney of Fremont He is unswerving in his devotion to the work of his profession, and to this fact has been in large measure due the high reputation he has achieved therein He is affiliated with the Masonic fraternity, and is past chancellor of the Fremont Lodge of Knights of Pythias

The year 1885 recorded the marriage of Mr Dolezal to Miss Catherine Feidler, who likewise is a native of Bohemia, and immigrated directly to Nebraska They have three children Frank is a locomotive fireman on the Chicago & Northwestern Railroad and resides at Fremont, Bessie is the wife of Henry Ptacek, who is engaged in the cigar business in the City of Denver, Colorado, and Miss Elsie remains at the parental home The women members of the family are communicants of the Catholic Church

Louis J Rebbe Reared in an agricultural community and atmosphere, and having all his early training along the lines of farming, Louis J Rebbe adopted the tilling of the soil as his vocation when he entered upon his independent career However, the development of his abilities and the opening up before him of opportunities for success along other lines of endeavor, have caused him to branch out into business ventures, in which he has met with the same measure of prosperity that has attended his activities in farming and stock raising

Mr Rebbe is one of the native sons of Dodge County, having been born here December 20, 1873, a son of Henry Rebbe, Sr., a review of whose career will be found elsewhere in this work in the sketch of Henry Rebbe, Jr Louis J Rebbe acquired a public school education and became his father's associate in his farming operations, remaining

MR. AND MRS. LOUIS J. REBBE

with his parents until the father passed away At his death he succeeded to a share of the home property, upon which he has made extensive and modern improvements, making it one of the valuable properties of the locality devoted to the industries of general farming and the raising of a good grade of live stock As before noted, Mr Rebbe has not confined his activities to the work of the husbandman, for business affairs know him as a shrewd, far-sighted man of affairs, capable of holding his own with others in competition, yet unquestionably honorable in all his dealings He is a stockholder and vice president in the Farmers State Bank of Ames, and his interests also include the holding of stock in the Farmers Co-operative Store at Fremont, the Lion Bonding Company of Omaha, and the Superior Cement Company of Superior, Nebraska.

In 1909 Mr Rebbe married Miss Augusta Knoell, who was born in Dodge County, Nebraska, and to this union there have been born five children. Daisy, Velma, Katherine, Louise, who died in infancy, and Henry Mr and Mrs Rebbe are consistent members of the Lutheran Church, which they attend at Fremont Fraternally Mr Rebbe is identified with the Knights of Pythias, while in political matters he takes an independent position

FREDERIC W BUTTON, judge of the District Court of Dodge County, was a youth when he came with his parents to Nebraska, where he completed his higher academic education and where also he prepared himself for the legal profession, as a representative member of which he was engaged in active practice in the City of Fremont until his elevation to the bench of the District Court

Judge Button was born in Grundy County, Illinois, and is a son of Charles J and Elizabeth (Williams) Button, the former of whom was born in Lake County, Ohio, and the latter in the fine old seaport town of Swansea, Glamorganshire, Wales, she having been a girl of twelve years at the time when her parents established their home in Illinois, and her husband likewise having been a member of a pioneer family of that state Charles J Button continued his residence in Illinois until 1888, when he came with his family to Nebraska and established his home at Hastings, the judicial center of Adams County He purchased a farm in that county, but continued to maintain his residence at Hastings until the time of his death, he having retired from active business even prior to coming to Nebraska and having achieved substantial prosperity through well directed industrial and business enterprise He was a republican in politics and was influential in community affairs in Adams County, where he served a number of years as a member of the Board of County Commissioners His religious faith was that of the Protestant Episcopal Church and his wife held membership in the Methodist Episcopal Church. Of the two children Judge Button, of this review, is the elder; William F, the younger son, received the advantages of Hastings College, became a successful member of the bar of Adams County, where he served nine years as judge of the County Court, and he was one of the honored and influential citizens of Hastings at the time of his death, in 1917

Judge Frederic W Button acquired his early education in the public schools of his native state and after the removal of the family to Nebraska he attended Hastings College and also Fremont College, in which latter he completed both classical and scientific course and in which he was graduated as a member of the class of 1896 Thereafter, in consonance with his ambition and well formulated plans, he began reading law in the office of a representative member of the Hastings bar, and later he continued his studies in the law department of the State University of Colorado He was admitted to the bar of Nebraska in 1893, and in 1898 he established himself in practice at Fremont, where he has since maintained his home and where he built up a substantial and representative law business Prior to engaging in the practice of law he had served two years as superintendent of the public schools of Hartington, Cedar County, and after his retirement from this position he was associated with Judge Hollenbeck in the practice of law for two years He then, upon the election of Judge Hollenbeck to chief justice of the Supreme Court of the state, succeeded the latter upon the bench of the District Court at Fremont his appointment to this office having been made by Governor Morehead in January, 1915, and the following year recorded his election to the office with no opposing candidate Well fortified in the science of jurisprudence and by a judicial cast of mind, Judge Button has given a signally effective administration on the bench, and few of his decisions have met with reversal by courts of higher jurisdiction He had been elected to a second term in the office of county attorney, but resigned this office to accept appointment to the bench on which he is now serving His judicial district comprises the counties of Dodge, Colfax, Platte, Merrick, Nance and Boone, in each of which he holds court He is a stanch advocate of the basic principles of the democratic party, and his advancement and success have been won entirely through his own efforts, the while he has so directed his course as to merit and receive the unqualified confidence and respect of his fellow men The judge is now the only representative of the immediate family in Nebraska, and in fact, he has no close kinsfolk He has become the owner of a considerable amount of real estate in Fremont, including his modern and attractive residence

The year 1895 recorded the marriage of Judge Button to Miss Lillie Ruegg, who was born in the City of Milwaukee and who was a popular piano instructor in the musical department of Fremont College at the time her future husband was a student in that institution She is still active and is a decided success as a pianist and soloist Mrs Button has made a close study of ornithology and has become specially adept in discerning and interpreting the various bird songs and calls She has achieved no little reputation in this connection and is actively identified with the Nebraska Ornithological Society, the Audubon Society in the City of Omaha and the Wilson Ornithological Society, a national institution Judge and Mrs Button have no children Their home is known for its gracious hospitality and is a center of much representative social activity, with Mrs Button as its gracious and popular chatelaine

Rutherford H Haverfield owns and conducts one of the leading general merchandise stores in the vital little City of North Bend, Dodge County, and has been a resident of this county from the time of his birth His parents here established their home within the decade following the admission of the state to the Union, and thus he can claim a due measure of inherited pioneer distinction

On his father's old homestead farm near North Bend, this county, Rutherford H. Haverfield was born on May 23, 1878, a son of Wilson and Hannah (Griffith) Haverfield, the former of whom was born in Harrison County, Ohio, April 2, 1842, and the latter of whom was born in the State of Indiana in the same year, she having passed the closing years of her life at North Bend, where she died March 18, 1903, at the age of sixty-one years Prior to coming to Nebraska Wilson Haverfield had been engaged in farm enterprise in Mercer County, Illinois, whence he came to Dodge County, Nebraska, in 1876 He purchased land not far distant from North Bend, and there became a prosperous agriculturist and stock grower He erected on his farm a large house, with accommodations far superior to the average house of the locality and period, and in this hospitable home semi-hotel entertainment was given to many travelers who passed through the county Wilson Haverfield remained on his farm until March, 1881, when he removed to North Bend Here he conducted a restaurant for a time and later a hotel, which he made a popular place of entertainment of the traveling public As a civil engineer of much practical ability he served twenty-nine years as city engineer of North Bend, where he still maintains his home, as one of the sterling pioneer citizens of Dodge County He is a republican in politics and his wife was a devoted member of the Christian Church Of their seven children the eldest is Charles Elliott, a resident of North Bend, Kitty Louise remains with her father, James Edward, a painter by vocation, now resides in the City of New Orleans; Lena is the wife of Frederick Herfurth, a contractor engaged in business at Fremont, judicial center of Dodge County, Rutherford H, of this sketch, was the next in order of birth, Effie May is the wife of Ernest Hahn, county treasurer of Dodge County, at Fremont, and Floyd S died October 13, 1912, at North Bend

Rutherford H Haverfield acquired his youthful education in the public schools of North Bend, where also he gained his initial experience in practical merchandising In 1900 he opened a general store at Webster, Dodge County, where he continued the enterprise successfully until 1908, when he sold the stock and business and found a broader field of endeavor by opening his present well equipped general store at North Bend, where he has built up a substantial and profitable enterprise and is recognized as one of the progressive and representative business men of the town His political allegiance is given to the republican party and he is serving at the present time as a member of the Board of Education of North Bend He served as captain of the North Bend Home Guards, and is affiliated with the Woodmen of the World and the Modern Woodmen of America, in which latter he is banker of the local camp Both he and his wife hold membership in the Christian Church

The year 1901 recorded the marriage of Mr Haverfield to Miss Bertha M McClure, of Creston, Iowa, and they have six children—Lorraine, Bernice, Wilson, Donald, Stanley and Audrey All of the children are attending the public schools of North Bend, where Lorraine and Bernice are, in 1920, students in the high school

Chris L Poulson The little Kingdom of Denmark, small in size and population, but great in history, her people having a record second to none for courage, chivalry, prowess, the mastery of the professions and arts and the handling of business and financial affairs, has sent to Nebraska some of its best citizens, among whom may be mentioned Chris L Poulson, who for many years was engaged in agricultural pursuits but is now living in retirement at Blair

Mr Poulson was born in Denmark, January 13, 1859, a son of Nels and Christine Poulson, natives of the same country In Denmark Nels Poulson followed the trade of carpenter, but after coming to the United States and settling at Omaha in May, 1870, was employed for a time by a cooperage firm, and remained in that city for four years Of a frugal and saving nature, while he had arrived in this country without resources, during his residence at Omaha he was able to accumulate a property of sufficient value to trade for eighty acres of land in Washington County, and in the years that followed, while he was engaged in farming, he added from time to time to his holdings that when he died, in 1914, he was the owner of a large tract of land and accounted one of the substantial men of his community Following his death his widow moved to Blair, where she died in 1915, at the home of her son. She belonged to the Lutheran Church, as did her husband, who was a democrat in his political allegiance.

Chris L Poulson, the only child of his parents, received his early education in the schools of his native land and was eleven years of age when he accompanied his parents to the United States For three years following his arrival he familiarized himself with the English language through attendance at the Omaha public schools and when he laid aside his school books it was to begin work on his father's farm, on which he remained until he was twenty-two years of age During his career as an agriculturist, Mr Poulson remained on one farm for a period of forty-one years, during which he farmed on his own account for thirty-three years In the working out of his unquestioned success he made the use of every opportunity that presented itself, but refused at all times to take an unfair advantage As a result he gained a reputation for fair and honorable dealing that placed him high in the esteem of his fellow-citizens On May 3, 1915, Mr Poulson retired from active pursuits and moved to a comfortable modern home on Colfax Street, where he is surrounded by all the conveniences which are the award of a well-ordered, energetic life He is still the owner of 240 acres of highly improved farm land in Washington County, for which he has been offered $325 an acre How far his fortunes have advanced under the impetus of his good management and industry may be seen in the fact that he commenced his career by buying 160 acres of school land, the lease on which he later surrendered, then buying land under the old system Mr Poulson is a man well informed and well liked and belongs to Trap Boy Camp No 1295, Woodmen of the World, of Blair He is democratic in his political allegiance and he and the members of his family belong to the Lutheran Church

Mr Poulson was married May 20, 1881, to Katherine Nielsen a native of Denmark, whose parents came to Washington County in 1880 and purchased farming land, on which they resided for a few years Then they removed to Sioux County, Nebraska, where Mrs Nielsen died, Mr Nielsen then going to Nuckolls County this state, where he passed away. The six children of Mr and Mrs Poulson are Christina, who died in infancy, Nels N, who is engaged in farming in Washington County, Sorn J, who is engaged in farming with his brother; Nelse Martin, a farmer of Washington County, Christensen, unmarried and residing with his parents, and Carl Raymond, who enlisted in the United States Aviation Corps in November, 1918, and was in training at San Antonio, Texas, until August, 1919, since which time he has resided at Omaha

JOHN O'CONNOR claims Dodge County as the place of his nativity and that he is not like the scriptural prophet, who was "not without honor save in his own country," is significantly shown by the fact that he served as county assessor in which he fully justified the popular confidence reposed in him Mr O'Connor was born in Dodge County October 27,

1872, and is a son of Matthew and Ellen (Martley) O'Connor, the former of whom was born in Ireland, in 1831, and the latter in the Dominion of Canada, their marriage having been solemnized in Dodge County, Nebraska Matthew O'Connor came to Nebraska Territory about the year 1865, and he assisted in the construction of the line of the Union Pacific Railroad, while he continued in the employ of the railroad company a number of years after the great transcontinental line was in operation In 1870 he filed entry on a homestead claim in Dodge County, and this he developed into one of the productive and valuable farms of this section of the state He continued there his activities as one of the prosperous farmers and highly esteemed citizens of the county until his death in 1896 and his venerable widow died May 26, 1920 They became the parents of six sons and three daughters, all of whom are living. John, of this review, is the eldest of the number, Retta is the wife of James F Reddy, a prosperous farmer in Cheyenne County, Abram is one of the substantial farmers of Dodge County, Milton, also a Dodge County farmer, Ada is a popular teacher in the public schools at Lexington, Dawson County, Alvin holds a clerical position in a clothing store at Fremont, Irvin is a successful farmer in Dodge County, Nellie is the wife of Henry Haun, another of the prosperous farmers of Dodge County; and Harold, who was one of the gallant young men who represented Dodge County in the World war, he having entered service in 1917 and with his command saw eighteen months overseas, the most of this time having been passed in Germany, after the occupation of German territory by the entente allies, and his honorable discharge having been given him in September, 1919 The loved mother was a devout communicant of the Catholic Church, as was also the father, and the latter was a democrat in political allegiance

John O'Connor was reared to the sturdy discipline of the home farm and his early educational advantages were those afforded in the district schools He continued his active association with agricultural industry until he was twenty-nine years of age, and in the meanwhile had become the owner of a farm in his native county At the age noted he removed to Fremont, the county seat, and he was long retained in office in his home county Prior to leaving the farm he had held various township offices, and finally he was elected registrar of deeds of the county, an office in which he served two terms of four years each Thereafter he was for one year employed in the Commercial National Bank of Fremont and the following year found him succesfully engaged in the real estate business Then he was again summoned to public service, by being elected county clerk In this office, of which he continued the incumbent five years, he gave a characteristically efficient administration, and since 1916 served, with marked efficiency and acceptability as county assessor, his previous official service as county clerk having rendered him specially eligible for this post

Mr O'Connor has been one of the loyal and influential workers in the local ranks of the democratic party and has served as chairman of the Democratic County Committee of Dodge County In connection with his official duties he conducted a representative real estate business and maintained also the most authoritative abstract office in the county He has been essentially the artificer of his own success, which has been worthily achieved, and he is now the owner of 240 acres of good land in his native county, as well as valuable real estate, both improved and unimproved properties, in the City of Fremont He and his wife are communicants of the Catholic Church, and he is affiliated with the

Knights of Columbus, the Modern Woodmen of America, the Fraternal Aid Union and the Improved Order of Red Men

On June 3, 1903, was solemnized the marriage of Mr O'Connor to Miss Georgia Mowrer, who was born at Albia, Iowa, and who had been for nearly a quarter of a century an efficient and popular clerical employe in the Dodge County courthouse, her service having been in different offices. Mr and Mrs O'Connor have one child, Wilma, a member of the class of 1920 in the Fremont High School

William G Mercer Progress brings changes, and in nothing is this more clearly shown than in the advancement made in methods of locomotion The invention, improvement and final almost universal adoption of the motor-run vehicle in place of that drawn by horses, has resulted in the practical abolishment of establishments which formerly were connected with the sale, care and renting of horses, and the development of modern garages Fremont has a number of these business enterprises, and a number of them are run by men who had the vision and courage to make the change from one kind of commercial enterprise to the other One of these men is William G Mercer, a very successful business man of Fremont

William G Mercer was born at Ogdensburg, New York, on May 19, 1863, and he had the misfortune to lose both of his parents when he was a baby, but was reared by some of his uncles and aunts He attended the public schools of his native state and learned the horseshoers' trade at Ogdensburg After he came to Fremont, on July 7, 1883, he further increased his store of knowledge by attending night school He worked at his trade at Fremont from 1883 until 1917 when he opened the Mercer Auto Parts Company and has built up a very large business He buys all kinds of cars, breaks them up and assembles new cars from the undamaged parts thus secured Not only does he own his business property, but three other pieces of property at Fremont

In March, 1888, Mr Mercer was united in marriage with Anna Bohn, and they became the parents of two children, one of whom is living, Namely: George L, who is with his father in the Mercer Auto Parts Company Mrs Mercer is a member of the Evangelical Lutheran Church, but Mr Mercer is not connected with any religious organization He belongs to the Knights of Pythias, the Ancient Order of United Workmen and the Royal Highlanders In politics he is a democrat

Mr. Mercer reached Fremont with twenty-five cents in his pocket, and is now one of the substantial men of his community, but this prosperity has come to him through no favors, but is the result of his own unaided hard work, careful planning and initiative While he has been too much occupied with his business affairs to take any active part in politics, aside from voting, he is interested in the advancement of the city and county and can be counted upon to give his support to movements which he believes will obtain practical results and not waste the money of the taxpayers

George L Mercer is one of the enterprising young business men of Fremont who is proving his worth to his community, and doing credit to his parents He was born at Fremont on July 15, 1890, a son of William G and Anna (Bohn) Mercer, the former of whom is the originator and owner of the Mercer Auto Parts Company of Fremont, where he and Mrs Mercer are still living

L. D. Richards

After having attended the Fremont High School and Normal School, George L Mercer gained a knowledge of the fundamentals of business life as a hardware clerk, and remained in that line of endeavor for five years, after which he learned horseshoeing with his father, and then worked at his trade for seven years When his father organized the Mercer Auto Parts Company, George L Mercer assisted him in it for a year, and then established himself in the garage business as proprietor of the Fremont Garage, but April 8, 1920, he sold his garage and joined his father again in the management of the Mercer Auto Parts Company

On October 27, 1913, Mr Mercer was united in marriage with Anna L Godel, born at Fremont, a daughter of Henry Godel, one of the early settlers of Fremont, who is still a resident of the city, and a man highly respected by all who know him Mr and Mrs Mercer have one child, George L, Jr, who was born on January 27, 1916, a very bright little fellow Mr and Mrs Mercer belong to the German Salem Church of Fremont Fraternally Mr Mercer is connected with Fremont Lodge No 514, Benevolent and Protective Order of Elks, and the Odd Fellows, and is interested in the progress of both organizations A leader among the young republicans of his ward he is now chairman of the Fourth Ward Republican Committee, and is deeply interested in public matters, and well posted on current events

Lucius Dunbar Richards History is largely a record of men's deeds and experiences, and when an individual's activities reach out and influence the life of many communities the task of biography is exceedingly difficult. The following paragraphs while involving many matters of great historical import to Dodge and Washington counties, nevertheless fall short of adequately representing the career and character of the Fremont pioneer and distinguished citizen Lucius Dunbar Richards.

Mr Richards in his own career has been a living exemplification of Americanism, and in that respect has been true to the record of his ancestors who were among the early settlers of New England, and were participants in the French and Indian war, the War of Independence and the War of 1812 His own birth occurred on a farm at Charleston Orleans County, Vermont, November 26, 1847 The home being broken up when he was eleven years of age, he left the homestead and went to work fourteen to sixteen hours a day for neighboring farmers for board and clothes He also had the advantages of some limited terms of instruction in the Yankee district school

Before he was fifteen years of age on September 5, 1862, he enlisted in Company I of the Fifteenth Vermont Infantry He succeeded in getting to Brattleboro the rendezvous of the regiment, and by the intercession of the colonel with the United States mustering officer was accepted in spite of his youth His regiment was commanded by Redfield Proctor, who was not only an able soldier but afterwards governor, secretary of war and senator from Vermont Young Richards served out his nine months' term and was mustered out in August, 1863. Before going to the front he was detailed as orderly to Colonel Proctor and this relationship was cemented by a lifelong friendship between the commander and the boy soldier Mr Richards has a memento of Colonel Proctor's handwriting on the discharge which reads "No longer a soldier under my command May the stronger relations of friendship continue through life is the wish of your colonel and friend"

Not satisfied with his first term of enlistment, in the summer of 1864 he re-enlisted in Company K of the Seventeenth Vermont Infantry and carried a musket until the close of the war He was with his regiment in the front line before Petersburg when that stronghold fell on April 2, 1865, and when Lee surrendered he was detailed as a guard, and the regiment leaving soon afterward he was never relieved on his post, until he took it upon himself to discharge himself from that duty, the only instance of his military career when he was not faithful to orders

After the war he joined his mother in Michigan, worked on a farm, and in the fall of 1865 entered Eastman's Business College at Poughkeepsie, New York In March, 1866, he went west to Hannibal, Missouri, and was employed by his uncle, F R Lockling, then city engineer of Hannibal, and assisted in laying out additions to the towns along the Hannibal & St Joseph Railroad He also was on the railway survey between Hannibal and Moberly This gave him a knowledge of engineering Starting for Colorado in July, 1867, he ran out of money and stopped at Missouri Valley, Iowa, then the headquarters of construction of the Sioux City & Pacific Railway While he tried to qualify as an engineer, his first work was on a pile driver, but later he accepted an engineering job at smaller wages In April, 1868, he was promoted to transit man on the survey of the Sioux City & Pacific Railway from California Junction to Fremont Thus a little more than half a century ago Mr Richards in line of duty became identified with the city of his present residence After this work was completed he was a member of an engineering party that made the survey for what is now the Illinois Central from Sioux City to Fort Dodge, and he then returned to the Sioux City & Pacific road

One morning at breakfast the superintendent of construction, Burnett, laid an order upon his plate directing him "to take charge of all railway work between the Missouri River and Fremont," giving him due authority and instructions to harmonize and bring efficiency between the track laying, pile driving and bridge forces This responsibility was thrust upon the young man not yet twenty-one years of age

Track laying was completed to Fremont in February, 1869 Going thence to Cherokee on the Sioux City and Fort Dodge Line Mr Richards had charge of construction of a division crossing the Little Sioux River until November, 1869, after which returning to Fremont he built in about six weeks the first ten miles of the Fremont, Elkhorn & Missouri Valley Railway. Under his charge this road was completed during 1870 to West Point and early in 1871 to Wisner During this period Mr Richards also surveyed and platted the towns of Scribner, Hooper and Nickerson Railway construction having for the time ceased he became roadmaster and superintendent of bridges and buildings on the line from Sioux City to Wisner, so continuing until August, 1872 During this time he exercised his right under the land laws and homesteaded and proved up eighty acres near Scribner. This constituted his first real estate possession

The young railroad builder returning from out of the West to his native state of Vermont was married January 9, 1871, to Miss Carro E Hills, of Burlington His bride returned with him to Fremont, subsequently lived at Missouri Valley until the fall of 1872 when Mr Richards took his wife and child back to Burlington and accepted an advantageous offer from the Henry Meggs' railroad interests in Costa Rica, Central America, and for nearly two years was engaged in engineering and superintending construction and operation of railroads in Costa Rica

In April, 1875, he returned with his family to Fremont Railroad construction had absolutely ceased following the financial panic of 1873 and he was confronted with the necessity of finding some other line of work At that time he entered the real estate and insurance business with W C Ghost as a partner for about a year, later was associated with Mr Reynolds, and still later the firm and corporation of Richards, Keene & Company

Having reviewed briefly the experiences which preceded his permanent residence and interests at Fremont and in Nebraska, an effort should be made to describe in broad outlines the larger service and influence rendered by Mr. Richards His dominating characteristic has always been a constructive spirit. With other empire builders he has been best satisfied in giving concrete reality to broad plans that affect for good the welfare of large regions and numerous population This characteristic was reinforced by his early experiences as a railroad builder, when responsibilities far in advance of his years were laid upon him The group of railroad builders with which he was mainly associated included that great pioneer, John I Blair, and was the group which built and owned what afterwards became a part of the Great Northwestern system in northern and eastern Nebraska, known for many years as the Sioux City & Pacific and the Fremont, Elkhorn & Missouri Valley His co-operation and council were long valued by those roads. In compliance with the Nebraska law his office for a considerable time was the corporate Nebraska office of the Fremont, Elkhorn & Missouri Valley road He was the general agent for their state land grant lands and townsites He supervised the preliminary investigations and surveys in the middle '80s of a proposed railroad northwestward from Fremont midway between the Union Pacific and the main line of the Northwestern, which afterwards materialized as the Scribner-Albion line of the Northwestern He was in close touch with the construction management when in 1886-87 the Northwestern lines were built out from Fremont to Lincoln, Hastings, Superior and Omaha

His constructive genius was combined with the vision of a financier and that led him to make strong financial and business connections in New York and New England, through which he was able to take a still larger participation in the development of the eastern Nebraska country and his home town in particular

From the first he conceived that strong confidence in Fremont and the surrounding country which their great intrinsic merit warranted At a time when he owned but little real estate his high public spirit led him to work for the realization of everything calculated to develop the town and country One of the first fundamental resources of Fremont which he interested himself to develop was in 1880, the dairy industry Taking into consideration the wide surrounding valley of hay and corn lands, he foresaw scarcely any limit to the future of the industry Largely through his initiative and financial co-operation a modern brick creamery was built in 1880, a building of a size considered large even now He has lived to see the Fremont creamery industry and interests and closely related lines developed into eight prosperous companies and plants with an annual volume of business of more than $3,000,000

Closely related to the dairy industry and farming generally and vital to the best interests of Fremont was the extensive drainage of the extremely wet valley lands adjacent to the city Here Mr Richards' skill and experience as an engineer came into play and peculiarly fitted him to solve and direct the complicated work carried on through a period of thirty years His service in this connection has undoubtedly been one of the greatest credited to his personal energies Tributary to Fremont were 200,000 acres of Platte and Elkhorn River valley lands, presenting during the greater part of the year a morass unproductive of little more than wild hay and incapable of good roads While the engineering problems involved were serious and expensive, the human elements were equally difficult to line up, since any project however well conceived inevitably aroused antagonism and resulted in litigation and obstruction Under Mr Richards' leadership in 1886-88 the first adequate ditch was initiated and constructed, crossing the wide flat valley diagonally from the northwest to the southeast into the Platte a number of miles west of Fremont and known as "the Fremont cut-off ditch" It was followed by two other similar main cut-offs further west in the county, and more recently by a comprehensive highly detailed ditching system for the eastern end of Dodge and the western end of Douglas County This latter system involved reducing the length of the Elkhorn River by eighteen miles and the dredging of many waterways into that river

The culmination of his persevering efforts came in 1907 with the organization of a special district at Fremont of levees, dykes and diversion work on the Platte River to prevent the periodical river overflows which had always distressed the southern portion of Fremont and that general locality This organization was made possible solely through Mr Richards' financial and legal support and through the large real estate holdings he represented in that locality The plan was effectively accomplished by an expenditure of $100,000 and a dozen years of careful, painstaking engineering work

While so much is to be credited to his personal initiative and enterprise, in all the years of his residence in Fremont Mr Richards has retained and advanced his influence through his faculty of leadership and co-operation with his fellow citizens He has always realized the power of united effort and concentration of energies involving all the progressive elements of the community In 1880 while mayor of the city he brought about the organization of the Fremont Board of Trade, which under the later name of Commercial Club has been an efficient body for forty years While even in larger cities such clubs have had alternating periods of stagnation and feverish energy, largely through the unremitting efforts of Mr. Richards the Fremont organization has been kept going and working, and now in its fortieth year is one of the strongest and most efficient organizations of its kind in the state

Mr Richards for many years has been regarded as one of the foremost business men of Nebraska In 1885 he organized and incorporated the first trust company in Fremont and to this corporation he turned over the great trust and investment business he had personally built up For several years previously he had been doing business in twenty counties of eastern Nebraska and western Iowa, where he was the exclusive confidential representative of large eastern land and farm loan investors He organized and conducted the first savings bank, and in 1886 organized the Fremont Stock Yards and Land Company with a paid-up capital of $200,000, owning 1,400 acres of land adjacent to Frement for the feeding in transit of western sheep, cattle and general stock This company has extensive yards, covered sheds, grain elevators, three miles of industrial railroad of its own and many other facilities Mr Richards has always been the president and leading stockholder of the company. He was largely instrumental in the organization of the Fremont National Bank, in which were combined the private banking interests of Richards & Keene and Hopkins & Millard

After Mr Richards returned to Fremont to make the city his permanent home he resurveyed the town. He was a member of the Board of Public Works for twenty-five years, served as surveyor of Dodge County three years, as city engineer of Fremont, and for two terms held the office of mayor.

His political career has some interesting incidents though as a whole it has been subordinate to the larger affairs with which he has been busied In 1888 he was unanimously chosen chairman of the Republican State Central Committee and was re-elected the following year He was one of the delegates at large in the national convention in 1892 when President Harrison was renominated, and a delegate at large and chairman of the Nebraska delegation to the Chicago convention in 1920 which nominated Harding and Coolidge In 1890 he was chosen the republican candidate for governor That year three tickets were in the field, the populists then showing great strength Moreover the republican candidate showed no disposition to win at the expense of some deeply cherished convictions of his own, and that independence and loyalty to principles, one of his chief characteristics, was a contributing factor in the final results of the election True to his New England instincts he has never neglected his duties as an American citizen He has interested himself in politics altogether to promote the cause of good government and to oppose what his judgment and experience have shown him to be unsound and essentially un-American

During his railroading experience in Costa Rica he was made a Mason and has had many honors of the craft He has attained the thirty-third honorary degree in the Scottish Rite, is past grand high priest of Grand Royal Arch Chapter of Nebraska, past commander of Mount Tabor Commandery No 9, Knights Templar. He is also a past president of the Nebraska Sons of the American Revolution, and is a past department commander of Nebraska Grand Army of the Republic For many years he was a trustee of Brownell Hall, the Episcopal School for Girls at Omaha and was also deeply interested financially and otherwise in Clemons Fremont College, Midland College and the Young Men's Christian Association at Fremont

The marriage companionship of nearly forty-five years was terminated by the death of Mrs Richards in December, 1915 She was the mother of four children Josephine R Sears; Fred H, a partner with his father, Katharine R, wife of B W May, a wholesale grocer at Fremont, and Redfield Proctor Richards, also associated with his father in business

Joshua S Devries, M D, has been established in the general practice of his profession at Fremont for more than thirty years and is one of the able and honored representatives of his profession in Dodge County The large scope of his practice attests most fully his technical ability, his personal popularity and his fine sense of professional stewardship. He commands the high regard of his professional confreres and has long been one of the influential members of the Dodge County Medical Society, besides which he is affiliated with the Nebraska State Medical Society, the Elkhorn Valley Medical Society, and the Missouri Valley Medical Society Doctor Devries has been a resident of Nebraska since his boyhood, here he received his academic and professional education, and here has found opportunity for the achieving success and prestige in his chosen vocation

The lineage of the Devries family is traced back to French origin, and representatives of the name came to America in the Colonial period of our national history Doctor Devries was born in Carroll County, Maryland, September 23, 1864, and is a son of Elias Perry Devries and Elizabeth E (Shipley) Devries, who were born and reared in Maryland and the latter of whom there passed her entire life, her death having occurred in 1869 In 1878 Elias P Devries came with his children to Nebraska and established a home in the City of Omaha He was a resident of Fontanelle, Washington County, this state, at the time of his death He was a democrat in politics and prior to the Civil war had been a slave owner in Maryland His religious faith was that of the Christian Church and he was long affiliated with the Masonic fraternity. Of the five children, Doctor Devries, of this review, is the younger of the two now living, his sister, Mary J, being the wife of A P Manning, cashier of the First National Bank of South Pasadena, California

Doctor Devries gained his rudimentary education in his native state, and after the family removal to Nebraska he continued his studies in the public schools of Omaha In preparation for his chosen profession he there entered the medical college that is now the medical department of the University of Nebraska, and in this institution he was graduated as a member of the class of 1888, with the degree of Doctor of Medicine While a student he gained a valuable clinical experience as an interne in the Douglas County Hospital, at Omaha, his entire service in this capacity having covered a period of twenty-two months Within a short time after his graduation, and before the close of the year 1888, he came to Fremont, where he formed a professional partnership with Dr. L J. Abbott, with whom he was thus associated two years Since that time he has conducted an independent practice of general order, has kept in touch with the advances made in medical and surgical science and has long controlled a large and representative practice It has already been noted that he is actively identified with the Dodge County Medical Society, and it may further be stated that he has served as president of the same His political allegiance is given to the democratic party, and at one time he held the office of coroner of Dodge County He and his wife are communicants of the Protestant Episcopal Church, and he is prominently affiliated with the Masonic fraternity, in which his maximum York Rite association is with Mount Tabor Commandery of Knights Templars, besides which he has received the thirty-second degree of the Ancient Accepted Scottish Rite, holds membership in the Mystic Shrine and is identified also with the Independent Order of Odd Fellows

On the 27th of August, 1889, was solemnized the marriage of Doctor Devries to Miss Miriam Woodman, who was born in the City of Chicago The marriage service occurred in Trinity Cathedral of the Episcopal diocese, in the City of Omaha To Doctor and Mrs Devries have been born five children James Arthur, who is now living at Fort Worth, Texas, was in the government service during the nation's participation in the World war and was for two years an instructor in the aviation service, Perry O is engaged in the drug business at Fremont, Miriam G is the wife of Carl Byorth, assistant postmaster at Fremont, Herbert J is studying law in the University of Colorado, at Boulder, and was for some time employed in the office of the district attorney at Sante Fe, New Mexico, and Donald E is a student in the Fremont High School

WILLIAM M ZELLERS. Hooper is so located as to afford excellent transportation facilities, and attract to it men of brains who are handling grain and other farm products, offering a market for the agriculturalists of the surrounding country, and shipping a substantial amount to the trade centers for further distribution One of these men is William M Zellers, manager of the Farmers Union Elevator Company, and a sound citizen of Dodge County

William M. Zellers was born in Pennsylvania in 1880, a son of Dr M T Zellers, one of the best known men and eminent physicians and surgeons of Dodge County, an extended sketch of whom appears elsewhere in this work Brought to Dodge County by his parents, William M Zellers attended the Hooper High School, Midland College at Atchison, Kansas, and the Creighton College of Pharmacy at Omaha, Nebraska. During his early years at Hooper, Doctor Zellers was interested in conducting a drug store, and it was in it that the son gained his practical experience in the drug business, remaining with it for twelve or thirteen years He then went into the grain trade, and for three years was associated with the Farmers Grain & Stock Company, leaving it to form connection with the Farmers Union Co-operative Association, and in behalf of this concern went to Uehling, Nebraska, but returned in 1917 to become manager of the Farmers Union Elevator of Hooper He devotes all of his time and attention to handling grain, lumber, coal and livestock and feed John Havepost is president of the company, and George Meier is secretary, and it is admitted to be one of the sound institutions of the county.

In 1903 Mr Zellers was united in marriage with Nora A Bayer, born in Dodge County, a daughter of Henry Bayer, an early settler of the county Mr. and Mrs Zellers have two children, namely: Erdine, who is attending school, and Clinton, who is at home Fraternally Mr Zellers is a member of the Knights of Pythias and the Masonic Order Mrs Zellers belongs to Grace Lutheran Church of Hooper, but Mr. Zellers is not a member of any religious organization, although he gives his support to the one his wife attends A man of strong convictions Mr Zellers prefers to select his own candidate so votes independently Mr Zellers is noted for the vigorous and efficient manner in which he carries on his business and the resourcefulness he displays in solving the various problems presented to him, and he has fairly earned the confidence felt in him and his abilities by the people of his county, and this portion of the state generally.

JOSEPH E NEWSOM has been a resident of Dodge County for more than forty years and is thus entitled to a due measure of pioneer distinction, besides which he has had marked influence in connection with the civic and industrial development and progress of the county He was appointed postmaster at North Bend on the 26th of April, 1914, and has continued the efficient and honored incumbent of this position to the present time Previously to assuming this position he had served as township assessor, as judge of the police court of North Bend, as city marshal and as justice of the peace—preferments which denote his strong hold upon popular confidence and good will in the county that has long represented his home and in which he was originally engaged in farm enterprise. Judge Newsom is a loyal and vigorous advocate of the principles of the democratic party, and is affiliated with the local organizations of the Masonic fraternity, the Independent

Order of Odd Fellows, and the Modern Woodmen of America, while both he and his wife hold membership in the Christian Church at North Bend

Judge Newsom was born at Worthington, Indiana, May 17, 1844, and is a representative of a sterling pioneer family of the Hoosier State He is a son of Jacob and Delitha (Miller) Newsom, both of whom were born in North Carolina. Jacob Newsom was a lad of eight years at the time when his parents removed to Indiana, where the father became a pioneer farmer and where both parents passed the remainder of their lives Jacob Newsom became one of the substantial farmers of Greene County, Indiana, and for many years he also owned and operated a grist mill He died in 1868, at the age of forty-six years, and his widow passed away in 1882, at the age of sixty years He was independent in politics and was long affiliated with the Masonic fraternity. Of the ten children Joseph E is the eldest of the four now living, Henry J is a prosperous farmer in Indiana, Celia A, the widow of Joseph Wingler, still resides in Greene County, Indiana, and Nancy Jane, widow of John H Thompson, resides at Hooper, Dodge County, Nebraska

The present postmaster of North Bend, Nebraska, was reared and educated in his native state and there continued his active association with agricultural industry until 1878, when he became a pioneer settler in the State of Kansas There he raised one crop and then sold and came to North Bend, Dodge County, Nebraska, in July, 1878, with his family where he acquired a tract of land and engaged in general farming, in which due success attended his energetic labors He remained on the farm until 1886, when he removed to the City of North Bend, where he has since maintained his residence and where, as previously noted, he has held various positions of public trust As postmaster he has given a signally efficient administration, and he takes much interest in all things pertaining to the prosperity and progress of his home community and county

In 1869 was solemnized the marriage of Mr. Newsom to Miss Sarah J Sargent, who likewise was born and reared in Indiana, and of this union have been born ten children Olive B holds a position in the postoffice at Wahoo, Saunders County; Jacob A died when about thirty-two years of age, Joseph C, publisher of the North Bend Eagle, is individually mentioned on other pages of this volume, James A died at ten years of age; Jessie A is the wife of Arthur B Skinner, of Fremont, Bessie P died at the age of eighteen years and Ethel L at the age of thirty-one years, Minnie H is a clerical assistant in the North Bend postoffice Marie is the wife of Ernest O Sweeney, of Alma, Nebraska; and Henry J is assistant postmaster at North Bend

John McKay In the list of business citizens of Blair who have started as poor boys and through individual effort have advanced themselves to positions of commercial independence, is John McKay, the proprietor of a flourishing feed business. Mr McKay has been a resident of this city for a quarter of a century, during which time he has made use of his opportunities to impress himself upon his community as a sound and reliable business man and a public-spirited and constructive citizen

Born September 16, 1869, on Prince Edward Island, Canada, he is a son of James and Sarah (McQuarrie) McKay, natives of the same place The family is of Scotch descent and is identified with the Scotch Presbyterian Church The parents of Mr McKay passed their entire lives on Prince Edward Island and in their community were known as honest, industrious and God-fearing people They were the parents of four children, John, Rebecca, who is the wife of Robert Miltigan, of Prince Edward Island; Alexander, a farmer there; and Dolland, of Sussex, New Brunswick.

The public schools of his native community furnished John McKay with his educational training, and when he was nineteen years of age he came to Blair and secured a position with his uncle, John McQuarrie, by whom he was employed for a period of eight years He then embarked in the feed and milling business on his own account, and from a modest start has built up a thriving enterprise of important proportions, one which has its recognized place in the business life of Blair. He is energetic, thoroughly reliable and markedly progressive and has the full confidence of his associates While his business interests have claimed his chief attention, he has also taken a helpful part in civic affairs and has served as a member of the city council In politics he is a republican, while as a fraternalist he holds membership in the Masons and Odd Fellows, in the latter of which he has passed through the chairs

In 1895 Mr McKay was united in marriage with Miss Luttie Irmi Newell, and to this union there have been born two children John Willard, a farmer in the Blair community, and Madeline, who is a student at Ames (Iowa) College

John Willard Newell, the father of Mrs John McKay, was born July 5, 1837, at Pelham, Massachusetts, a son of S A and Rebecca (Hall) Newell, the former a native of Massachusetts and the latter of Connecticut The parents were married in Massachusetts, and in 1865 came to Nebraska and settled on a homestead, on which they lived until reaching their declining years The mother died in Kansas at the home of a daughter, while the father, after his retirement, moved to Blair and died at the home of his son Of their ten children, six are living J A, who is engaged in farming in Washington County, Nebraska, John Willard Mrs Selden, a widow of Blair, Elizabeth, the wife of J. L. Skinner, of Coffeyville, Kansas, who formerly had a large draying outfit but is now living retired, Martha, the widow of Mr Davis, of Omaha; and Myron D, proprietor of a meat market at Arlington, Nebraska. The parents were members of the Methodist Episcopal Church and in politics the father was a republican

John Willard Newell received his education in the public schools of Massachusetts, and on completing his training began to assist his father, who was in modest financial circumstances Times were hard in Massachusetts at that time, however, and the youth, finding that he was making no progress, decided to try his fortunes in the West To do this he had to rely upon his own resources, for his capital was decidedly small, but he possessed the optimism of his years and his self-reliance was great After getting as far as Quincy, Illinois, he took a boat for St Louis, and with but $30 in his pocket embarked for Leavenworth The times were troublous, as passions were inflamed due to the controversy arising from the unsettled conditions that were to eventuate in the Civil war When he arrived at Leavenworth he found the town crowded, and his first night's bed was the floor of a bar room His money now being spent he went to a Kansas farm where he worked for two weeks and secured $10, then returning to Leavenworth he took a boat up the river Omaha was the destination of Mr Newell and a young companion, but after sleeping on the floor of a heavily-overladen and unsafe vessel, the partners agreed that traveling by land was more desirable, and accordingly, after giving the porter 50 cents to unload their trunks at Omaha, they left the vessel at Brownsville and made their way by foot from that point to Omaha, where they arrived weary and footsore three days later Mr Newell, upon his arrival at that city, was possessed of just ten cents, but soon found employment digging a ditch, and after two days' work received $2 For two or three days thereafter he worked in a brick yard, but while thus engaged was unfortunate enough to contract mumps and measles and had to give up his position Next he hired out on a farm, on which he worked during the summer and followed the trade of shoemaker in the winter In 1858 he and his partner rented a farm and raised a crop of corn that brought them $400 in gold, and in 1859, during the gold excitement, went to Pike's Peak Colorado, making the journey by wagon Camping at Clear Creek, the youthful associates traded with the people that were going and coming from the gold diggings and remained there until 1861, when they sold out and returned to Omaha There they divided, Mr. Newell settling at Omaha and his former partner going to Kansas They had the distinction of being the first settlers in Polk County, Colorado.

After his return to Omaha, Mr Newell built a barn, but sold out and purchased a bakery, in connection with which he had the first cracker machine in Omaha During 1862 he ran this establishment both night and day in order to supply the demand, but in 1863 disposed of his interests Mr Newell had some experience in freighting to Denver, Colorado, and Nebraska City, Nebraska, and during this period had many adventures, both exciting and interesting, the Indians being numerous, and on occasions, very troublesome Leaving Omaha May 10, 1863, with a party of fourteen or fifteen, in ox-teams, he arrived at Bannock City, Montana, in September, and then went to Virginia City and engaged in getting out drift timber and in freighting from Virginia City to Salt Lake City, Utah, making three trips in one year While on this journey to Montana, his party was attacked by a large band of hostile Indians, who were driven off only after they had killed three of Mr. Newell's freighting companions

Mr Newell returned to Omaha in 1864, and in 1865 made a trip to Denver with a load of whiskey His last freighting trip was made to California in 1866 In February, 1868, he came to Washington County and for two years had a store at Cummings City, following which he resided on a farm near Herman for nine years He then moved to a farm in the vicinity of Blair, on which he made his home and centered his activities for fifteen years, after which he engaged in the flour and feed business at Blair and was the proprietor of this establishment until he sold out to his son-in-law, since which time he has lived in comfortable retirement

Mr Newell was married in the fall of 1865 to Miss Mary E Wait, who was born in Rhode Island, and to this union there were born two children Mrs John McKay, and John Willard, Jr, proprietor of an electrical supplies store at Blair Mr Newell has the distinction of being the only charter member of Omaha Lodge of the Odd Fellows fraternity now living and is one of the few living charter members of Blair Lodge of that order, having been an Odd Fellow for fifty-eight years, in 1920 In the year mentioned he was given a piece of jewelry by his lodge emblematic of long service and containing twenty-three jewels In politics a republican, Mr Newell has taken an interest in local affairs and for three or four years occupied the position of township treasurer. During his long, honorable and successful career, he has attached to himself many friends, and his life is one in which the value of the homely virtues of honesty, perseverance and fidelity has again been demonstrated

JOE STECHER is one of Nebraska's famous sons, and as a farm boy near Dodge he developed that prodigious strength and skill which enabled him still to retain the championship of the world as a wrestler.

He was born a few miles from Dodge in Cuming County, Nebraska, April 5, 1893 His parents, Frank and Anna Stecher, are still living, being retired residents of Dodge Frank Stecher was born in Bohemia and came to the United States in 1876 at the age of twelve years He developed a farm from the prairie of Cuming County a mile and a half north of Dodge, and followed agriculture until he retired

Joe Stecher is the youngest of three sons, and received his education in the common schools near his father's farm. He has done a great deal of practical farm work, not only while he lived at home with his father, but even now is the owner of a well improved farm in Cuming County As a youth he easily surpassed all the neighbor boys in the wrestling game, and for two years did a great deal of training before he became a professional wrestler He has been a contender for championship honors since 1914, and has participated in about three hundred wrestling matches He first achieved championship honors June 4, 1915, and by a well merited victory in New York over Ed Strangler Lewis April 16, 1920, retained his honors Mr Stecher's business manager is his brother, Antone Stecher

December 6, 1916, Joe Stecher married Frances Ehlers, a daughter of Claus Ehlers, a well known stock buyer and farmer at Scribner Mr Stecher built his fine bungalow home in Dodge in 1917 He is an independent voter, was reared a Catholic and is a member of the order of Elks, while his wife belongs to the Congregational Church

R P TURNER The record of R P Turner is that of a man who by his own unaided efforts has worked his way from a modest beginning to a position of comfort and influence in his community His life has been one of unceasing industry and perseverance and the systematic and honorable methods he has followed have won for him the unbounded confidence of his fellow citizens of Dodge County whose interests he has at heart and which he seeks to promote in every practical way

R P Turner was born in Waukesha County, Wisconsin, on June 2, 1874, and is the son of R. C and Isabelle A (Foster) Turner Both of these parents were natives of New York State, but were taken to Wisconsin in an early day by their respective parents, and in the latter state their marriage occurred They are both now deceased They were members of the Presbyterian Church and in his political views the father was a republican Of the nine children born to them, eight are living, namely W R, a farmer at Holton, Kansas. Edith, the wife of Alex Will, a farmer at Dennison, Kansas, L H, a farmer at Glenwood, Minnesota, L B, a farmer at Sovereign, Canada, Mrs John Knowles, whose husband is engaged in the shoe business at Fremont; Mary D, the wife of E D Smart, an automobile dealer at Eagle, Wisconsin; R P, of this sketch, Etta M, the wife of Rev T H Melville, of Pawnee City, Nebraska

R P Turner received his elementary education in the district schools of his native community, supplementing this by attendance at Carroll College, at Waukesha, Wisconsin His first employment was as a clerk in a shoe store at Grand Island, Nebraska, but his vocation was interrupted by the outbreak of the Spanish-American war He enlisted in Company L, Firty-first Regiment Iowa Volunteer Infantry, and was sent to the Philippines After about a year's service, Mr Turner received an honorable discharge and again returned to the pursuits of civil life, going on the road as a traveling salesman for a shoe house After following this line for eight years, he came to Fremont in 1893 and bought a shoe store, which he has owned and managed continuously since He has always carried a large and well selected stock of shoes of all lines and has enjoyed a large and representative patronage, being numbered among the leading merchants in his line in this locality During the World war, Mr Turner rendered effective service with the Young Men's Christian Association, being in France about a year with the American Expeditionary Forces

In 1904 Mr Turner was married to Bessie W Doyle, a native of Kentucky, and they are the parents of two children, George M and Kathleen, both of whom are in school Mr and Mrs Turner are members of the Presbyterian Church Politically, Mr Truner is a republican and he is a member of the Spanish-American War Veterans Earnest effort, unabating perseverance, a laudable ambition and good management are the elements which have contributed to the splendid success which is now his, and because of these qualities he has won and retains to a marked degree the confidence and good will of his fellow citizens

GEORGE J HASLAM, M D, B Sc, F A C S, M R C S, London Unfaltering in his devotion to the work and service of his exacting profession and keeping in close touch with the advances made in medical and surgical science, Doctor Haslam has been engaged in practice in the City of Fremont, Dodge County, since 1889, the while he has gained specially high repute in the surgical department of his professional service. It may consistently be said that few physicians in Nebraska have been fortified by as fine preliminary training and education of technical order as has Doctor Haslam, for his professional education was obtained under most authoritative auspices in England, Ireland and the continent of Europe, and reinforced by effective clinical experience in leading hospitals

Doctor Haslam was born near Manchester, England, on the 18th of May, 1858 He acquired his preliminary education in the Manchester Grammar School and completed a higher academic course in the Owens College After graduating from the University in Ireland and from the College of Surgeons of London, he served a period of nine years in various internships both in England and on the continent of Europe

In 1889 Doctor Haslam came to the United States, and within the same year he established his residence at Fremont, Nebraska, which has since continued the central stage of his very successful professional activities He had come to America primarily to accept a position as a member of the faculty of Shattuck Military Academy, at Faribault, Minnesota, but upon his arrival he found that this post had been filled Under these conditions he returned to New York City, where he found his available capital reduced to the lowest point, but he proved efficient in devising ways and means and soon made his way to Nebraska, his exchequer having shown a balance of only $53 when he arrived in

Geo. Haslam

Fremont His ability and personality forthwith gained him recognition, and his professional success has been cumulative from that time, the result being that he has accumulated a competency, as well as high reputation as a physician and surgeon Prior to coming to America he had written and published an authoritative work on the Anatomy of the Frog, his student work having involved a specializing in physiology He had lectured on physiology in Owens College at Manchester, England, and later was scientific investigator in the University at Zurich, Switzerland, and he had done an appreciable amount of fine surgical work prior to coming to the United States At the present time he specializes in surgery, and his services in this field of practice are by no means confined to Dodge County He is identified with the Nebraska State Medical Society, the American Medical Association, is a Fellow of the American College of Surgeons, and a member of other representative professional organizations, and his active affiliation with these associations is made to subserve his keeping fully in advance of modern medical and surgical methods and service

Doctor Haslam has completed the circle of York Rite Masonry, in which his maximum affiliation is with the Fremont Commandery of Knights Templars, and in the Scottish Rite he has received the thirty-second degree, besides being affiliated also with Mystic Shrine, the Knights of Pythias, the Independent Order of Odd Fellows and the Royal Highlanders As a citizen he is liberal and progressive and in politics he maintains an independent attitude

In 1893 was solemnized the marriage of Doctor Haslam to Miss Mary Dern, who was born and reared at Fremont and who is a daughter of John Dern Mr Dern was an early settler of Fremont and served at one time as County Treasurer of Dodge County He is now one of the most prominent and influential citizens of Salt Lake City, Utah Doctor and Mrs Haslam have three children Gretchen is now teaching in the University of Nebraska, George Alfred Haslam is at the present time, 1920, a student in the medical department of the University of Nebraska, and Gertrude is attending the public schools of Fremont

ARCHIBALD H WATERHOUSE To be given the opportunity of educating the youth of the land is the aim and the compensation of the true teacher To him it is a worth-while achievement to lead into fields of knowledge, to develop talents that might otherwise remain dormant, and by inspiring to onward and higher effort, bring deeper meaning and value to life Aside from all choice of congenial vocation and its many pleasant aspects, the man or woman who devotes a lifetime to this responsible work, has this idea of beneficence as a basic motive The world today needs true education more than ever before There are some sections of the country that have seemingly recognized this fact and have called to their help teachers tried and true, and have benefited accordingly. In this connection mention may be made of the able superintendent of the city schools of Fremont, Nebraska, Archibald H. Waterhouse, a veteran in the educational field

Mr Waterhouse was born May 2, 1858, on a farm in Berrien County, Michigan, the third in a family of four children born to John H and Minerva (Hanna) Waterhouse His father was born in Vermont, and his mother in Ohio They both went to Indiana, met there, married and lived there subsequently, the father being a farmer and mill man Later they lived in other states and the father died in Michigan and the mother in Iowa He was a man of some prominence in his community and was a democrat in his political views The mother was a devoted member of the Congregational Church and impressed her children with the beauty of a Christian life

Archibald H Waterhouse attended the country schools near his father's Inana farm, in boyhood, later the Rolling Prairie High School in Laporte County, from there entering the Northern Indiana College at Valparaiso While doing some preliminary reading of law, as he had made up his mind to follow the law as a vocation, he taught a few terms of school and then took a course in law at Ann Arbor, Michigan, finding, however, by the time he was qualified for practice, that his deeper interest rested in educational work Afterward Mr Waterhouse taught school in great states of the Union, Indiana, Iowa and Nebraska, coming to the last named state in 1888

By this time Mr Waterhouse had a creditable teaching record to refer to He took charge of a school at Weeping Water, in Cass County, remaining there for seven years and then accepted the principalship of the high school at Grand Island, and after two years was tendered the office of principal of the high school at Lincoln, two years later becoming principal at Omaha, where he remained nine years. From there he came to Fremont and for twelve years has been superintendent of the nine public schools of this city, having seventy teachers and 2,200 pupils under his direction

Mr Waterhouse has been married twice, first to Henrietta Lackey, of Washington, who died in 1892, and second to Clara E Parkins, of Weeping Water, Nebraska Two daughters were born to his first marriage Ula, the widow of Philip H Echols, is a resident of Fremont but connected with the public library at Omaha, and Ruth, who married Edward Fredrickson and resides in Fremont Two sons have been born to Mr Waterhouse's second marriage, Ronald A and Robert P, both of whom are attending school

In recognition of his scholarship, in 1908 the University of Nebraska, under Chancellor Andrews, granted Mr Waterhouse the honorary degree of Master of Arts

CHRISTIAN J CHRISTENSEN, the efficient and popular general manager of the business of the Farmers' Union Co-operative Association, at Fremont, was a child of three years when his parents came to Nebraska, soon after the admission of the state to the Union, and here he was reared to manhood under the condition that marked the pioneer days He was born in Denmark, March 9, 1866, and is a son of R. and Christina (Thompson) Christensen, who immigrated to America and became pioneer settlers in Saunders County, Nebraska, in 1869 The father there took up a homestead, and in the reclaiming and improving of the farm he did well his part in furthering the civic and industrial progress of that county, while he and his family had their full share of pioneer trials and hardships He developed one of the valuable farm properties of that county and there remained until his death, in December, 1919, his wife having passed away in 1903 Both were earnest members of the Baptist Church and in politics Mr Christensen was a democrat Of their children Christian J is the eldest, Christene is the wife of Martin Petersen, of Fremont; Sophie is the wife of Chris Nelsen, a farmer in Custer County, Arthur H. is a farmer and owns the old, home place in Saunders County, and Charles J is also a farmer in Saunders County

Christian J Christensen was reared to the sturdy discipline of the pioneer farm and acquired his early education in the rural schools of Saunders County. He continued his active association with farm industry until 1911, and in the meanwhile had become the owner of one of the excellent farms of Saunders County. In the year mentioned he removed to Kansas, where he continued in the employ of a hardware company until 1914, when he came to Fremont and assumed charge of the business of the Farmers' Union Co-operative Association's business, of which he has since been the efficient manager, the concern basing its operations on a capital of $50,000, and its functions including the handling of grain, flour, feed, farm implements, etc.

Mr Christensen is independent in politics and supports men and measures meeting the approval of his judgment. He is affiliated with the Woodmen of the World and he and his wife are members of the Methodist Episcopal Church.

In 1895 Mr Christensen was united in marriage to Miss Anna Barnett, who was born in the state of Illinois, and they have four children · Ethel is the wife of Forrest Booth, of Fremont, Elnora is the wife of Owen Pease, of this city, and Goldie and Lloyd remain at the parental home, the former having attended a business college and being a competent stenographer

HON WALDO WINTERSTEEN The dignity of the law is ably upheld by the jurists of Nebraska, who, both individually and as a body, exemplify the admirable results of long and careful training, wide and varied experience, contact with men and affairs, and the responsibility of grave duties It is not an exaggeration to say that the very life of this country rests upon the intelligence and incorruptibility of the bench Like many other sections of the state, Dodge County has been fortunate in its jurists, and one of them who is held in high esteem and is recognized as a man fully capable of sustaining this regard with dignified capability is Judge Waldo Winstersteen, county judge of Dodge County

Judge Wintersteen was born at Harrisonville, Meigs County, Ohio, on February 1, 1864, a son of James H and Mahala (Dunlap) Wintersteen, who, leaving Ohio in 1871, came West to Nebraska and homesteaded in Saunders County, but after about eleven years on this farm sold it and moved to Fremont, where the father followed his trade He and his wife had ten children, but only four of them survive, namely. Elizabeth, who is Mrs Wittman, a widow of Chicago, Illinois; Mary, who is Mrs. Lyon, a widow of Buffalo, New York, Judge Wintersteen, and Mrs J M Shively of Fremont, her husband being the traveling representative for the Union Pacific Railroad at that city The parents were active members of the Methodist Episcopal Church During the period antedating the war between the North and the South, the father was an abolition democrat and conducted one of the "stations" of the "Underground Railroads" For a number of years he served as postmaster at Harrisonville, and his integrity and fitness for office were so universally conceded that, although of a different political faith, President Lincoln continued him in office, and he was still its incumbent when he resigned in order to go West

Judge Wintersteen grew up in a household governed according to high principles, and while he was attending the district schools, he was at the same time learning to be a patriotic citizen and good man He later attended school at Wahoo, Fremont and Lincoln, in the intervals between school terms, working on Nebraska farms and breaking the prairie sod with a hand plow drawn by oxen Coming to Fremont in 1882, the future distinguished jurist acquired a speaking acquaintance with the general public as a clerk in a mercantile establishment owned by Ben Davidson, and, although his ambitions soared above his occupation, he gave satisfaction, for his is a nature which will not rest content with anything but the best of service During the winter of 1882 he was employed by the Hammond Printing Company, and later he engaged in house painting, and then in the spring of 1884 he entered upon a new phase of life, for he then became a range rider in northwestern Nebraska, and remained there as such for two years, returning to Fremont in 1886, and then, after a brief period, went to Wymore, Nebraska, and spent six months at that point closing out a stock of goods Once more he came back to Fremont, which he regarded as his home, and once more sold goods over the counter.

During all of this period he had been making friends and impressing people with his reliability, and in 1887 he was elected constable, thus beginning his connection with the enforcement of the law, and discharged the duties of that position for four years. He was also deputy sheriff under Sheriff J P Mallon From early youth he had cherished an ambition but it was years before he found the time and opportunity to indulge it, but finally he was able to begin the study of law, with N H Bell as his preceptor, and in 1895 was admitted to the bar However, in the meanwhile, in 1893, his fellow citizens elected him to the office of justice of the peace, and he held it until 1897, and that same year he was honored by election to the office of county judge of Dodge County and served for four years A vacancy occurring, Judge Wintersteen was appointed, in 1913, to fill the unexpired term, was again elected, and has been re-elected to succeed himself twice, without opposition, and is the present incumbent of this high office

On June 3, 1893, Judge Wintersteen was married to Grace Palmer, born at Spirit Lake, Iowa, and they have one daughter, Ruth, who is a graduate of the Fremont High School, and now one of the popular public school-teachers of her native city She prepared herself for her entry into the educational field by taking a special course at the National Kindergarten School at Chicago, Illinois, and is a very accomplished young lady Judge and Mrs Wintersteen and their daughter are all members of the Fremont Methodist Episcopal Church, and are recognized as valuable adjuncts to it Judge Wintersteen is a Mason, Modern Woodman, Highlander, and a member of the order of Ben Hur Always active in politics as a democrat, in 1912 he was one of the presidential electors to ballot in the electoral college, being the first elector of his political faith sent from Nebraska His election was owing to his personal popularity for he ran way ahead of his ticket Although he retains his interest in politics, he is now devoting all of his time to the duties of his office, which are very onerous owing to the fact that the business of it has doubled within the past five years

Judge Wintersteen comes of a long-lived family as his father lived to be ninety-two years of age, dying on May 16, 1913, his mother having passed away in June, 1903, when she was a venerable lady The fundamental gauge by means of which men are judged and their value to their community estimated at its true figure, is after all not a spectacular one, but rather is it formulated from the effects of a man's everyday life, and the methods he employs for enriching his generation, and the part he plays in the economic and intellectual development of his community Measured by such a gauge, Judge Wintersteen is easily one of the most important men of Dodge County, aside from the remarkable service which he has rendered in the several offices which he has held, and his name will always be connected with all that is progressive and sound during the period he has been placed in a position of authority

ROLAND G ALLEN This representative and honored citizen of Blair, Washington County, has been distinctively the architect of his own fortunes, has been true and loyal in all the relations of life and stands as a type of that sterling manhood which ever commands respect and honor He is a man who would have won his way in any locality where fate might have placed him, for he has sound judgment, coupled with great energy and business tact, together with upright principles, all of which make for success wherever and whenever they are rightly and persistently applied By reason of these principles he has won and retained a host of friends throughout the county of his residence

R. G Allen is a native son of Washington County and was born on December 20, 1880 He is the son of A T and Mary E (Lamb) Allen, the former a native of Ohio and the latter of Kentucky They both came to Washington in early life and their marriage occurred here A T Allen's residence here dates from 1868 and he followed farming here during all of his active years, being successful in his efforts, but in 1907 he sold his farm and moved to Blair, where he and his wife are now living They are members of the Methodist Episcopal Church and in political affairs he gives his support to the democratic party. They became the parents of four children, three sons and a daughter, as follows Charles R, who is connected with the firm of Cox, Jones and Van Alstine Company, at Omaha, Nebraska, Roland G, of this sketch, is next in order of birth, Leora died at the age of twenty-seven years; A Clyde is a rural mail carrier and lives at Blair

R G Allen received his educational training in the public schools and the Fremont Normal School He remained on his father's farm until he was twenty-one years old, when he became connected with the grain elevator business, serving for two years as manager of an elevator at Herman, Washington County Then for several years he was in the Plateau State Bank at Herman, and in 1913 he was appointed deputy county treasurer, serving in that position until he was elected county treasurer in 1916 He proved to be eminently qualified for that position and in 1918 he was again elected to the office and is its present incumbent In this responsible position Mr Allen has demonstrated business ability of the highest order and his official record has been universally commended by the voters of the county which he serves

On November 12, 1910, Mr Allen was married to Mabel Lowe, who was born in Tekamah, Burt County, and they are the parents of a daughter, Harriett, who is now a student in the public schools In their religious faith Mr and Mrs Allen are affiliated with the Baptist Church and in politics Mr Allen is a strong supporter of the republican party Fraternally, he is a member of the Ancient Free and Accepted Masons, in which he has attained to the degrees of the Royal Arch While living at Herman he was secretary of the Blue Lodge and also served as clerk of the village He and his wife are members of the Order of the Eastern Star Mr Allen is a man of likable personality, possessing to a marked degree the characteristics which beget esteem, confidence and friendship, and because of his success in both private and public business affairs he is entitled to specific mention in a work of the character of the one in hand

IRA M WILLIAMS Having accomplished a satisfactory work as an agriculturist, and acquired a competency to live on, Ira M Williams, of Fremont, is taking life easy at the pleasant home which he erected, in 1917, at 247 East Military Avenue, where he is enjoying to the utmost the well-merited reward of his long continued, unremitting, but remunerative toil A son of the late Milton Williams, he was born in Woodford County, Illinois, in 1862 His grandfather, Benjamin Williams, migrated from Ohio to Illinois in pioneer days, and having taken up government land, cleared and improved a homestead

Milton Williams was a life-long resident of Illinois, always claiming the Prairie State as his home Joining the gold seekers in 1849, he went to California, and as a miner in the gold fields made money and spent it When returning to Illinois, he walked across the Isthmus of Panama and subsequently made the trip home by way of Cape Horn Resuming his former employment, he was engaged in tilling the soil until his death, in 1873, at a comparatively early age He married Cordelia De Long, who was born in Illinois, and is now residing in Fremont, Nebraska He was a democrat in politics, and his wife belongs to the Methodist Episcopal Church Of the three children born of their marriage, Ira M is the only one now living

Acquiring his elementary education in the country schcools of Illinois, Ira M Williams, who was left fatherless at a tender age, came to Nebraska in 1876, and spent a few months in Dodge County before going back to Illinois. In 1880, responding to the lure of the West, he returned to Dodge County, and having bought a tract of wild land, began its improvement Successful in his operations, he bought, as he had means and opportunity, until now he has large and valuable landed interests in and around Dodge County, being one of the wealthy and prominent agriculturists of the county He rents his land, receiving a good annual income, and makes his home in Fremont.

Mr Williams married, in 1890, Phoebe Scholtz, who was born in Saunders County, Nebraska, where her father, John Scholtz, homesteaded, and on the farm, which he improved, resided until his death. Mr and Mrs Williams have one child, Andrew Williams, who assists his father in caring for his different farms He is married, and has one son, Howard Williams, who is a great favorite of his grandparents Mr Williams is a democrat in politics and a member of the Ancient Free and Accepted Order of Masons

JOHN HENRY MONKE was a pioneer in Washington County, possessing the stalwart enterprise and robust energy necessary to successful achievement in a section which half a century ago gave its rewards only after strenuous toil and exertion Those who enjoy the prosperity of the twentieth century are under a constant debt of gratitude to such men as John Henry Monke

He was born in Westphalia, Germany, March 21, 1830 and lived in the fatherland until well on towards middle age He married Fredericka Tappe in 1855 and their five children were born in the fatherland However earnest he was about his business, Mr Monke could see only meager prospects for himself and the children growing up about him, and therefore about the year 1869 he and his wife, accompanied by their children, started for America, landing in New Orleans A boat carried them up the Mississippi to St Louis, and after about a month's visit with relatives in that city they went on up the Missouri River to Omaha Leaving the river, they settled in the community of Fontanelle

MR. AND MRS. JOHN HENRY MONKE

MR. AND MRS. HENRY S. MONKE

in Washington County, and during the first year John Henry Monke rented land from Miss Mary Kimberlain He next strained his resources to purchase eighty acres of land at ten dollars an acre and that was the beginning and nucleus of the generous accumulations of land and other property which he built up during his lifetime He lived on the farm until 1902 and saw his acreage and his herds of livestock increase and prosper until at one time he owned 1400 acres When he left the farm he retired to Fontanelle and, honored and respected by all who knew him, he passed away December 12, 1916, at the venerable age of eighty-six His wife had died January 29, 1905, aged seventy-seven

Both were very devout Lutherans, attending church at Fontanelle After acquiring American citizenship, Mr Monke voted as a republican He lived in Washington County over forty-five years and well repaid his debt to America's opportunities by his constructive labors in developing farms from waste land, and by discharging his varied responsibilities to home and community He and his wife were the parents of five children Anna, who died in 1877, wife of Rev Henry Sohl, Christian, who died in infancy, Hannah, who died January 21, 1883, wife of John Sohl, now a California fruit farmer at Napa; Sadie is the widow of Carl Mengedoht of Washington County, and the youngest and only living son is Henry S Monke, a sketch of whose career follows

Henry S Monke Farming and stock raising, real estate and other interests have given Henry S. Monke a broad field of action and of service during his many years of residence in Washington and Dodge counties He was brought to the Fontanelle community as an infant and has witnessed practically all the changes in this community for half a century

Mr Monke was born in Westphalia, Germany, April 1, 1869, and was only six months old when he came to America with his parents, Mr. and Mrs. John Henry Monke The pioneer story of his honored father is told on preceding pages Henry S Monke acquired his education in the local district schools of Washington County and also took the commercial and normal course in Fremont College. He laid the foundation of his success as a farmer and stock raiser, an occupation continued until 1906, when he entered the real estate business at Fontanelle He has all the qualifications to make an expert judge of real estate values, and has made this knowledge of direct advantage to a large clientage Besides his beautiful modern home in Fontanelle he and Mrs Monke own about twelve hundred acres of valuable farm land in Washington and Dodge counties This land is operated by tenants and renters, and without deviation from strict commercial principles he has managed his property interests in a way to benefit the entire community

Mr. Monke is a very popular citizen, active in Masonry, having attained the thirty-second degree in Scottish Rite and is a member of the Council Degrees of York Rite Politically, he is a republican and is a member of the Central Committee at Fontanelle He and all the members of his family are active members of the Lutheran Church Mr Monke has had a very happy home life. March 10, 1896, he married Miss Lena Ruwe of Fremont They have two children Anna May, born May 8, 1900, now a student in Midland College at Fremont, and Luther, born December 1, 1902, also attending Midland College

CHRISTIAN CHRISTENSEN A prominent, honored and highly esteemed resident of Fremont, Christian Christensen, now retired from business pursuits, has had a varied experience in life and can tell many a thrilling tale of pioneer and frontier hardships, perils, and of labors crowned with success He was born, February 23, 1847, in Denmark, where his parents, Christen and Sophia Rasmessen, spent their entire lives

Prior to his marriage, Christen Rasmessen was a sailor, and in that capacity visited nearly every country on the globe After marrying, he was engaged in farming and gardening to a considerable extent, and likewise carried on a good business as a fisherman To him and his wife four children were born, as follows Rasmus, who immigrated to Nebraska in 1879, took up a homestead claim in Saunders County, and was there engaged in farming until his death, December 11, 1919, Julius, located in Saunders County, this state, in 1880, is there employed in tilling the soil; Christian, of this sketch, and a son that died in Denmark Both parents were members of the Lutheran Church

Acquiring his education in his native land, Christian Christensen was graduated from the church, or parochial, school, under the supervision of the minister At the age of eighteen years (1865), impressed by the stories regarding the vast wealth and magnificent resources of the United States, he immigrated to Brown County, Wisconsin, where he worked as a farm laborer for six months Going in the fall of that year to Chicago, he found employment at the carpenter's and cabinet maker's trade, and in that capacity not only laid one of the first planks in the Stockyards, but assisted in the construction of the water works

Coming to Nebraska in 1867, Mr Christensen continued at the carpenter's trade although he had learned that of a miller in his native country, and as an employe of the Union Pacific Railroad Company worked for some time on the bridges between Grand Island and North Platte Later working for the Government, he helped build the barracks at Omaha During the Indian massacre he was working on the railroad at Lexington, where all the trainmen were killed excepting the conductor and an Englishman, who was left on the field for dead but who recovered from his wounds Mr Christensen went to the railway terminus, Cheyenne, where he assisted in the building of a windmill, being all of the time harassed by the Indians, who were on the war-path

Locating in Fremont, Dodge County, in 1874, Mr Christensen followed his trade a short time, and in 1879 erected his beautiful home at 306 East Fifth Street The ensuing year, in 1880, he put up a large store building on Main Street, and having laid in a complete stock of choice groceries was there actively and prosperously engaged in mercantile pursuits for thirty-four consecutive years Retiring from active business in 1911 he has since kept busily employed in looking after his personal affairs, as he has large property interests in Fremont, and is a director and one of the organizers and the first vice president of the Commercial National Bank, which office he still holds, and also one of the organizers of the Home Savings Bank and a director in same

An active and influential member of the democratic party, intelligently interested in local matters, Mr Christensen has never shirked the responsibilities of public office, but has rendered able and appreciated service as a member of the City Council, as city treasurer, and as mayor, a position that he filled one term Fraternally, he is a member of the Independent Order of Odd Fellows, in which he has passed all of the chairs included in its different branches, and is a charter member of Fremont Lodge No 514, Benevolent and Protective Order of Elks He also belongs to the Country Club

On November 27, 1869, Mr Christensen was united in marriage with Marie Paulsen, who was born in Denmark and was there educated Her father, Nels P. Paulsen, came to the United States from Denmark in 1863, locating in Omaha, where he was employed as a gardener for a year and a half, although he had been a miller in his native country. Subsequently buying land in Washington County, Nebraska, he was there engaged in farming for eighteen years Retiring then from active pursuits, he moved with his family to Fremont, where both he and his wife spent their remaining days They had but three children in their family, as follows Mary, widow of John Hansen, lives in Blair, this state, Christina, wife of Christ Holstein, a farmer, living near Blair; and Mrs Christensen Eight children have been born of the marriage of Mr. and Mrs Christensen, namely Josephine Johnson, of Omaha; Nora, wife of Charles Kilpatrick, now assistant manager Lee Coyt Andreesen Hardware Company, Omaha, Emma, who married Edward Mills, died at the early age of thirty-one years, Walter, a banker at Norfolk, Nebraska; Arthur, vice president of the First National Bank of Fremont, Mabel, wife of John A Ryan, a successful attorney of Omaha; Bessie, wife of Grover Spangler, a jeweler in Fremont, and Eddie, who lived but four short years

FRANK HAMMOND, of Fremont, president of the Fremont Manufacturing Company, president of the Hammond Printing Company, and president of the Equitable Building and Loan Asssociation, is one of the most prominent and representative business men of Dodge County, and a responsible factor in the life of his city He was born in Marshall County, Iowa, a son of George and Jane (Leech) Hammond, both of whom were of Quaker stock, and migrated to Iowa from Ohio at an early day in the history of the former state

Until 1879 Frank Hammond remained in his native state and there acquired a knowledge of men and affairs which enabled him, when in that year he came to Fremont, Nebraska, to assume at once a commanding position in the newspaper field as publisher of the weekly Tribune in partnership with his brother, Ross Hammond Out of this partnership grew the present Hammond Printing Company, although before the present name was adopted the business had become George Hammond & Son, of which Frank Hammond was the junior member In addition to a large jobbing business the Hammond Printing Company publish the Fremont Tribune, issuing a daily, the circulation of which approximates 10,000 A force of 100 people are required to carry on the business, and this company is the largest individual concern in Fremont Frank Hammond was elected president of this company in January, 1920, his associates in this company being Ray W Hammond, vice president and general manager, Lucius R Hammond, secretary; and Walter B Reynolds, treasurer, and these gentlemen, together with Harvey C Kendall, constitute the board of directors The last named, Mr Kendall, is in charge of the advertising department, and he and Lucius R Hammond are new additions to the official force. Frank Hammond is also editor-in-chief of the Tribune and divides his time between this company and the other organizations with which he is connected

He assisted in developing the Hammond-Stephens Company, of which he was treasurer, but from which he has since retired, which was organized for the purpose of carrying school supplies for a large territory adjacent to Fremont, and this company is in a very flourishing condition under the present sole ownership of Dan V Stephens

Another of the leading concerns of Fremont which owes its existence to Mr. Hammond's organizing ability is the Fremont Manufacturing Company, formerly the Sure Hatch Incubator Company, of which Mr Hammond is now president. This concern was first located at Clay Center, but in 1906 was brought to Fremont and at that time the plant was greatly enlarged, a new building being erected with floor space of over 100,000 square feet, and a capacity of 50,000 incubators annually The company's products also include family refrigerators, ice cream cabinets, chocolate, vegetable and grocers' refrigerators The last named features are put out under the name of the Crystal Refrigerator Company Employment is given to 100 persons and the products are sold all over the world

Essentially a man of large affairs, Mr Hammond has extended his activities to include membership with the Fremont Commercial Club, which he served as president in 1913, during which year he was also secretary of the Board of Public Works, in the latter capacity having supervision of all of the public improvements made in Fremont for a period of fifteen years

The children born to Mr Hammond and his wife are as follows Ray, who is manager and vice president of the Hammond Printing Company, Mary Roberta, who married A G Christenson of the First National Bank of Fremont; Earl, who is treasurer of the Fremont Manufacturing Company, Lucius R, who is secretary of the Hammond Printing Company, and Everette, who is with the Fremont Manufacturing Company

Mr Hammond has possessed the strength of will and caliber of brain which have made it possible for him to forge ahead and accomplish results which would have been impossible to a man less generously endowed He is so many-sided in his abilities, so catholic in his sympathies, so deep in his understanding of human nature, that his friends are included in every rank of life From the time he located permanently at Fremont he has been called into counsel by the best elements, and is recognized as an authority on public questions

Herman Petersen is another of Dodge County's sterling citizens who can claim Denmark as the place of his nativity, and he has maintained his residence at Fremont since 1901 and who now controls a large and prosperous business as a merchant tailor and as a dealer in men's furnishing goods, with a trade of notably representative order

Mr Petersen was born in Denmark on the 10th of July, 1878, and is a son of Herman and Cina Petersen, the former of whom passed his entire life in his native land, where his widow still maintains her home, she being a devout communicant of the Lutheran Church as was he also The father was a merchant in Denmark for a long term of years and continued his association with this business until his death

The only child of his parents, Herman Petersen, Jr, was afforded the advantages of the excellent schools of his native land, where also he served a thorough apprenticeship to the tailor's trade, at which he became a skilled workman. He continued to work at his trade in Denmark until 1901, when, at the age of twenty-three years, he came to America, where he felt assured of better opportunities for winning independence and success in connection with business He first settled at Emmettsburg, Iowa, but before the close of the year 1901 he came to Fremont, Nebraska, where he found employment at his trade and soon established a reputation for technical ability therein In 1906 he expanded his field of activity by opening a small store and installing a stock of men's furnishing goods The success which attended the new venture has been cumulative, and in connection with his substantial merchant-tailoring business he now conducts a prosperous enterprise based on his large and select stock of furnishing goods for men Artistic draping and workmanship in the production of men's clothing and also high grade tailored suits for women have enabled him to gain a specially representative list of patrons in this department of his business, and he has secured place as one of the leading merchant tailors of Dodge County Mr Petersen is known as a reliable and progressive business man and as a loyal and appreciative citizen of the land of his adoption, while he has a wide circle of friends in his home city and county In the Masonic fraternity he has received the chivalric degrees as a member of the local commandery of Knights Templar, besides being affiliated with the Ancient Arabic Order Nobles of the Mystic Shrine and with Fremont Lodge, Benevolent and Protective Order of Elks His political allegiance is given to the republican party.

In 1907 was solemnized the marriage of Mr Petersen to Miss Ida Larsen, who was born and reared at Fremont, a daughter of Louis Larsen, a prosperous retired farmer of this city Mr and Mrs Petersen have three chilren, whose names and respective ages, in 1920, are here noted. Ralph, twelve years, Marjorie, eight years, and Louis, six years

Benjamin E Krajicek, D D S The dental profession is well represented at Scribner, Nebraska, and one of its leading members is Dr. Benjamin E Krajicek, who devotes his entire time to his practice which, on account of his professional knowledge and skill, has grown to large proportions in a comparatively short period

Doctor Krajicek was born in 1894, at Atkinson, Nebraska His parents were Frank and Mary Krajicek, natives of Bohemia, in Europe, from which section they came to the United States many years ago With others of their countrymen, they settled in Colfax County, Nebraska, where the father homesteaded, but, on account of unusual hardships and fears of Indian attacks, did not prove up He removed to Atchison, in Holt County, where he operated a flour mill for a time, later taking his family to Arlington, in Washington County, where he worked on the railroad as a section foreman He was an honest, hard-working man all his life and a faithful Catholic His death occurred at Arlington, in 1913

The brothers and sisters of Doctor Krajicek are as follows Stephen A, who is a civil engineer with a construction company at Grevbull, Wyoming; Amy, who is the wife of C. N Cook, a farmer near Arlington, Nebraska, Mary, who is the wife of Ross Marshall, a farmer near Arlington; Bessie, who teaches school near Fremont, Louis, who works for his brother-in-law, C N Cook, Joe, who is a mail carrier at Arlington; Frank, who operates a hotel at Reno, Nevada, and Julia, who is the wife of E J Christenson, an oil operator at Greybull, Wyoming The mother of the above family survives and resides at Arlington. The father was insured in the Bankers Reserve Life Insurance Company, showing that he was a prudent man, belonged to the Modern Woodmen of America, and voted with the republican party

In boyhood Doctor Krajicek attended the public schools, and in 1913 was graduated from the Arlington High school, shortly afterward entering the Lincoln Dental College, from which he was graduated in 1917. He immediately opened an office at Scribner and is very firmly established in the confidence of the people He belongs to the new school of dental practitioners, whose scientific work precedes that of the physician, in many cases making that of the latter entirely unnecessary He has a well located and thoroughly equipped office

Doctor Krajicek was married in 1918 to Miss Mable Hrabak, of Bohemian ancestry, but born and reared in Nebraska, her people having settled in Dodge County They are members of the Catholic Church Doctor Krajicek belongs to the Royal Highlanders, the Omaha Life insurance Company, the Business Men's Accident Association and retains membership in his old dental college fraternity, the Delta Sigma He is identified also with the Nebraska State Dental Society

WILLIAM EDWARD VLOCH Energetic and enterprising, full of vim and push, William Edward Vloch, of Dodge, is prosperously engaged in mercantile pursuits, as proprietor and manager of the Golden Rule Store, having built up a highly satisfactory trade, his patrons coming from far and wide. He was born, December 8, 1890, in Cuming County, being the fifth child in succession of birth of the ten children born to his parents, Vaclav and Mary Vloch, who came from Bohemia to Nebraska, and now, retired from agricultural pursuits, are living in Dodge

Acquiring his preliminary education in the district schools, William Edward Vloch completed his studies at the Fremont Normal School Although brought up on a farm, he didn't take kindly to agricultural work, and soon after leaving school entered the employ of his brother Joe, a general merchant, with whom he remained as a clerk for twelve years On June 26 1918, having obtained not only valuable experience, but a practical insight into the modern ways of business, Mr Vloch purchased his brother's interest in the Golden Rule Store, which he has since successfully managed, retaining its old customers and adding many new ones each season

Mr Vloch married, in November, 1913, Edna Yunek, and they have one child, Wilman In his political relations Mr Vloch is a steadfast republican

LUDWIG UEHLING A member of that old and substantial family of Uehlings who from pioneer days to the present have been decided factors in the agriculture, business and civic affairs of Dodge and Washington counties, Ludwig Uehling has applied his efforts almost entirely to farming, and in that vocation has achieved most substantial success, at the same time winning the confidence and trust of his home community His farm and home are in section 10 of Logan Township

Mr Uehling was born near Hooper in Washington County November 8, 1865, a son of Theodore Uehling, a prominent pioneer for whom the town of Uehling was named A sketch of Theodore Uehling and family is found on other pages Ludwig Uehling attended some of the pioneer schools of eastern Nebraska, but the best lessons were those he learned by practical contact with the land and with men He was strong, self-reliant and ambitious and soon after reaching manhood had acquired some lands for himself He married at the age of thirty, and since then has given a quarter of a century to the general farming and stockraising He has always favored good stock, and his efforts have served to advance the standards of livestock in his section His farm contains a herd of ten registered Holstein cattle He also keeps a good grade of horses His farm represents a growing business and a substantial degree of prosperity, all of which has been won from a very modest start

Ludwig Uehling Mrs Ludwig Uehling

In a public way he has served his township as treasurer two years and for many years as treasurer of the school board In politics he is a republican

In 1895 Mr Uehling married a daughter of Henry von Seggerson To their marriage have been born five children: Mrs Alma Osterlow, Edna, Orvel, Windsor and Kenneth

FRED A HERFURTH. One of the first-class examples of the self-reliant man who has made his own way in the world is Fred A Herfurth, a successful contractor and owner of a planing mill at Fremont He was born at Madison, Wisconsin, on June 14, 1868, a son of August and Ida (Dienald) Herfurth, both natives of Germany, who came to Wisconsin at an early day and were there married, and became the parents of five children, four of whom survive, namely. Millie, who married Earl Brink of Grand Island, Nebraska, Mrs Alma Leberman, who is a widow, of Fremont, Fred A, who was third in order of birth; and Max, who is a carriage trimmer, living at Fremont The parents were members of the Congregational Church In politics the father was a democrat. By trade he was a gunsmith and he worked at his trade at Madison, Wisconsin, and at Fremont, Nebraska, to which city he moved when Fred A Herfurth was a child, and here he died in 1884, but his widow survives him and lives at Grand Island.

Fred A. Herfurth attended the public schools of Fremont, and was graduated from its high school course in 1894 Beginning his apprenticeship in boyhood, Fred A Herfurth learned the carpenter trade and has always worked at it, developing into a contractor, and has done considerable building in and about Fremont In 1907 he established a planing mill that he sold to W R Reckmeyer, and in 1913 built another mill that he is still conducting in conjunction with his contract work In his mill Mr. Herfurth makes fixtures of all kinds used in woodwork, and his product is in great demand A skilled workman himself, he will not accept anything but first-class work and is noted for his faithfulness in living up to the specifications of his contracts

In March, 1913, Mr Herfurth was married to Lena Haverfield, born in Illinois They have no children Both Mr and Mrs Herfurth are members of the Congregational Church and active in all of its local organizations While he exercises his right of suffrage Mr Herfurth does not give much time to politics as his business cares are exacting, but he is interested in the progress of Fremont and willing to give his support to those measures which will result in practical results and not waste the people's money

GEORGE F STAATS A prominent and prosperous dealer in farm lands and city property, George F. Staats, of Fremont, is actively identified with a large and highly profitable industry, being one of the most extensive dealers in realty to be found in this section of Dodge County, he and his partner, Henry C Dahl, having won a large patronage. A son of the late Jeremiah F Staats, he was born, June 12, 1866, in Tazewell County, Illinois, where his childhood days were spent

Jeremiah F. Staats was born near Boundbrook, New Jersey, where his father, Peter Staats, was a life-long resident Learning the bricklayer and stone mason's trade, he followed it in his native state until 1858, when he migrated to Illinois, where he lived for fifteen years Coming from there to Nebraska in 1873, he bought, in Saunders County, railroad land, giving five dollars an acre for the tract, and on the farm that he improved resided until his death in 1898. Successful in his undertakings, he added by purchase to his original homestead, which is now owned by his son George, increasing its area to 400 acres. His wife, whose maiden name was Mary E. Hoagland, was born in Boundbrook, New Jersey, and died in Nebraska in 1903. Of the six children born to their union, four are living, as follows: Mrs. W. J. Harmon, of Fremont, whose husband is a retired farmer; Charles, of Omaha, accountant for the Woodmen of the World; Louis C., of Central City, Nebraska, a real estate agent; and George F. of whom we write. The father was a republican in politics, and a member of the Dutch Reformed Church. The mother, who inherited the religious faith of her father, Christian Hoagland, was a member of the Congregational Church.

After his graduation from the Fremont Normal School in 1888, George F. Staats turned his attention to agriculture, and for twenty years was prosperously engaged in general farming. Wisely investing a part of his annual profits in other tracts of land, Mr. Staats now has title to upwards of a thousand acres, a large part of which is under culture. On January 20, 1911, he took up his residence in Fremont, and has since dealt extensively in real estate, making a specialty handling farm lands and farm loans, branches of business with which he is familiar, and for which he is amply qualified both by knowledge and by experience.

Mr. Staats married, in March, 1891, in Fremont, Nellie Sanderson, who was born in Utica, New York, where her father, William Sanderson, was an early settler. Three children have blessed their union, namely: Roy, living in Fremont; Ruby, a teacher in the Fremont schools; and Mabel, attending school. A stanch republican in politics, Mr. Staats has held several township offices, and in 1917 was elected as a representative to the State Legislature. Fraternally, he is conspicuously identified with the Ancient Free and Accepted Order of Masons, belonging to Blue Lodge, Chapter, Council, Commandery, and to the Shrine, and is a member of the Knights of Pythias, in which he has passed all the chairs. Both Mr. and Mrs. Staats are faithful and valued members of the Presbyterian Church. During the World war Mr. Staats took an active part in the drive for bonds, and was active in Red Cross work, giving generously of his time and money.

James C. Robertson. A representative citizen of Dodge County who actively engaged in farm pursuits for many years, is James C. Robertson, capitalist, who is well known in business circles at Fremont, where he is interested in developing valuable property. Mr. Robertson has been a resident of Dodge County since he was fifteen years of age, found his business opportunity here, through thrift and industry built up an ample fortune and is held in high esteem by those who have known him for almost forty years.

James C. Robertson was born in Ayreshire, Scotland, June 22, 1866. His parents were Robert and Elizabeth (Wilson) Robertson, natives of Scotland, who came to Dodge County, Nebraska, in 1881, and both died here. They had the following children: Hugh, who was an early homesteader in Dodge County, died in 1916; Robert, who is a cabinetmaker by trade, still lives in Scotland; William, who is foreman in a copper mill at Butte, Montana; Jane, who is the wife of John Ferguson, who owns a cattle ranch in Blaine County, Nebraska; and James C., who resides at 350 East Tenth Street, Fremont.

James C Robertson was reared on a farm but had excellent educational advantages in Perth Academy, near Glasgow Although he was compelled to borrow his passage money to America, he insisted on accompanying his parents and after reaching Nebraska proved very helpful to his father Before very long he had cancelled his indebtedness and then set himself to the task of honestly acquiring land of his own Like other settlers of thirty or more years ago, Mr Robertson found many hardships to contend with, but he persevered and finally owned a large farm which he cultivated and improved, making it so valuable a property that when he decided to remove to Fremont in 1918, he was able to sell it for $50,000 He still owns about 600 acres in Nebraska and Colorado, together with valuable realty at Fremont.

On January 27, 1893, Mr Robertson was united in marriage to Miss Nellie Hastings, who was born in Illinois Her father, A J Hastings, now an octogenarian, resides in California Mr. and Mrs. Robertson have had the following children Anson, who was in military training at Camp Custer, during the World war, is connected with a mercantile establishment at Webster, Nebraska, Margaret, who fills a clerical position in a business house at Fremont, Bessie, who is a school teacher, Fred, who is a student in the Fremont High School, and Walter S, who died of influenza in November, 1918

After coming to Fremont, Mr Robertson bought property and is now having three lots near his home improved with buildings, occasionally doing a little carpenter work himself With his family he belongs to the Presbyterian Church In politics a republican, he has served as assessor of the First Ward, at Fremont, and while living on his farm was long a member of the school board at Webster

W F Hemphill, D. D S A well known and successful dentist of Blair, W F Hemphill, D D S, is actively identified with one of the most important branches of surgery, its application being required at some period of life by almost every member of the human family. Rapid strides in dentistry have been made in recent years, elevating it to a distinct science in which America has taken a foremost position, American methods being used not only in this country, but in countries across the sea A son of Theodore Monroe Hemphill, the doctor was born, August 7, 1892, in Litchfield, Illinois, his boyhood home

Born and bred in North Carolina, Theodore M Hemphill obtained an excellent education and, having adopted a teacher's profession, followed it successfully as a professor in some of the leading schools of Illinois and Kansas, his home at the present time being in Belleville, Kansas He is a man of sterling worth and ability, highly esteemed in his community, where he occupies a place of influence He is a republican in politics, a member of the Woodmen, and belongs to the Presbyterian Church He married, in Illinois, Clara Hamilton, who was born in Boston, Massachusetts, and died in Kansas in 1906 Eight children were born of their marriage, W. F, of this sketch, being the fourth child in succession of birth

Having laid a substantial foundation for his future education in the public schools, W F Hemphill entered the dental department of Creighton University, in Omaha, Nebraska, and was there graduated with the class of 1916 Locating in Blair soon after his graduation, Doctor Hemphill has established a large and rapidly increasing practice, and won for himself an assured position in the professional, business and social circles of the city.

In March, 1917, Doctor Hemphill was united in marriage with Lola Taylor, a native of Beatrice, Nebraska, and they have one child, Robert The doctor is independent in political matters, a member of the Ancient Free and Accepted Orders of Masons, and both he and his wife belong to the Methodist Episcopal Church

ANDREW FROST Actively and successfully engaged in the prosecution of a calling upon which the health, wealth and prosperity of our great nation is in a large measure dependent, Andrew Frost holds a noteworthy position among the foremost agriculturists of Dodge County, and is prominent in the public affairs not only of Uehling, his home town, but of his home district, which he now represents in the State Legislature. A son of Mats Frost, he was born, January 25, 1862, in Sweden, the abiding place of his ancestors for many generations

Born and educated in Sweden, Mats Frost lived in his native land several years after his marriage His prospects for earning enough to support his young and growing family not being very bright, he and his wife, Carrie, accompanied by their children, immigrated to the United States in 1865 Locating in Burt County, Nebraska, he homesteaded, and lived there eighteen months The results of his labors being unsatisfactory, he moved to Omaha, and for five years worked in the shops of the Union Pacific Railroad Company Resuming his former occupation, he bought land in Dodge County, just west of the present site of Uehling, and having improved a farm, both he and his wife spent the remainder or their days thereon, the wife passing away when seventy-six years old, while he attained the venerable age of ninety-four years Coming to this state while it was still in its primeval condition, Indians being numerous, though not unfriendly, he lived to see the country well settled and himself the owner of a good farm well and substantially improved To him and his wife five children were born, Andrew having been the third child in order of birth

Scarce three years of age when he came with his parents to this country, Andrew Frost was reared in Nebraska, and while young was initiated into the mysteries of agriculture, obtaining a practical knowledge of its various branches Becoming an agriculturist from choice, he has since, with the exception of two years spent in Canada, carried on general farming and stock raising in Nebraska, and in his undertaking have met with well deserved success A stanch republican in politics, Mr Frost has been active and influential in the public affairs of Uehling, having served on the town board, the school board, and as justice of the peace In January, 1919, he had the honor of being elected to the State Legislature, where he is performing the duties devolving upon him ably and faithfully, being ever mindful of the interests, not only of his constituents, but of town, county and state

Mr Frost married, March 17, 1888, Mary Anderson, born July 16, 1869, in Dodge County Nebraska, a daughter of P Anderson, a retired farmer, now living in Uehling, and to them five children have been born, namely. Hubert, an accountant in Duluth, Minnesota, served for eight months of the World war as a chemist; Irving, of Omaha, also an accountant, served as an electrician in the United States Army during the World war; Carroll, who enlisted in the Coast Artillery during that war, is now taking a course in art and science at the University of Nebraska: Emil, who enlisted in the Coast Artillery during the late war, is now at home; and Lewis, also at home

Mrs Frost's father, P Anderson, was born in Sweden March 16, 1843, and at the age of six years was left fatherless He was brought

Andrew Frost

up and educated in his native land. In 1868, accompanied by his sister and wife, whose maiden name was Carrie Erickson, he immigrated to the United States With but $100 to his name, he made his way directly to Nebraska, coming by rail to Omaha, where he located. He homesteaded, taking up eighty acres of land, and while improving a farm suffered all the privations and hardships of pioneer life Markets were few and far between, and he was forced to go to the Missouri River for wood, a long day's trip Succeeding in his labors, he subsequently added to the extent of his farm by purchasing 160 acres more land, and continued his agricultural labors until 1908 Retiring from active work in that year, Mr Anderson moved to Uehling, where he has a most pleasant and attractive home He is a republican and for several years has been a road overseer

Eight children have been born of the union of Mr and Mrs Anderson, namely: John Albert, John Frederic and Adolph, all deceased; Mary Victoria, wife of Andrew Frost, of this sketch; Maudie, wife of Matts Anderson, engaged in farming in Dodge County, Anna Josephine Westlin, a widow, Esther Margaretta, wife of August Westlin, and Lydia Caroline, wife of George Monnich.

JOHN B VAN PATTEN A prominent and prosperous farmer and stockman of Dodge County, John B Van Patten, of Fremont, has achieved marked success in his agricultural labors, and as a man of sound judgment and good business ability has acquired property of value, owning not only rich farming lands, but several pieces of city property, all of which are paying investments He was born, December 14, 1866, in Cayuga County, New York, which was also the birthplace of his parents, John A and Lucinda (Adams) Van Patten His grandfather, Peter Van Patten, a native of Albany County, New York, was one of the early settlers of Cayuga County

John A Van Patten was a life-long resident of his native county, where he was engaged in tilling the soil A man of integrity and worth, he won the respect of the community in which he resided He was a republican in politics and a member of the Methodist Episcopal Church. To him and his good wife four children were born, as follows Emma, wife of John Ingersoll, a retired farmer of Cayuga County, New York, John B ; George, engaged in farming in Cayuga County; and Nettie M, wife of Charles Wilda, of New York, an extensive land owner, and a successful produce dealer

Acquiring his early education in the rural schools of the Empire State, John B Van Patten spent his early life on the home farm, where he obtained an excellent knowledge of the rudiments of agriculture In 1886, ere attaining his majority, he decided to try life for himself in a newer country Making his way to Dodge County, Nebraska, he secured a position with W H. Turner and brother, noted stockmen, and for fourteen years was employed in driving cattle and sheep across the plains Forming then a partnership with Turner Brothers, Mr Van Patten assumed the entire charge of the extensive business and in its management displayed wisdom and ability When Mr Van Patten arrived in Dodge County he had but fifteen dollars to his credit, but he labored faithfully, was wise in his savings, and prudent in his expenditures, and soon found himself in comfortable circumstances, with plenty of work ahead of him, and no financial troubles Using sound judgment in his investments, Mr. Van Patten, in partnership with Ira Williams, owns a magnificent farm near Fremont, and is managing it most successfully. He also owns city property in Fremont, which he has always claimed as home, his residence at 450 North Bell Street being one of the most attractive in the community

Mr. Van Patten married, in 1893, Hannah M Carruthers, who was born at White Haven, England and came to the United States about thirty-five years ago with her parents Her father has passed to the life beyond, but her mother is living, being now a resident of California. Mr Van Patten is a steadfast republican in politics, and Mrs Van Patten is a member of the Episcopal Church, having never departed from the faith in which she was reared They have no children, but are always interested in advancing the welfare of the younger generation

CHARLES HRABAK Although born on foreign soil, Charles Hrabak, a well known merchant of Dodge, was brought up and educated in this country, and in the days of his youth imbibed the respect for American institutions, and the knowledge and patriotic spirit, that has made him an honored and valued citizen of the United States A native of Europe, he was born, December 28, 1858, in Bohemia, where he lived as a child

Crossing the ocean with his parents in 1867, Mr Hrabak settled with them in Zama County, Iowa, on August 23d, of that year, and during the ten years he lived there completed his early education, and also obtained a good knowledge of the various branches of agriculture Migrating to Kansas about 1879, he was there engaged in agricultural pursuits for five years, and the following three years was similarly employed in Scribner, Dodge County, Nebraska On August 23, 1886, Mr Hrabak established a store in Dodge, becoming the pioneer merchant of the town Having very limited means at his command, he labored industriously to get a start, among other labors having cut corn in the fields to get sufficient money to erect a building for his stock of merchandise He succeeded well in his efforts, winning a substantial patronage, but subsequently sold his business, and is now manager for the Ryan Company, who have an extensive trade in general merchandise

Mr Hrabak married, November 5, 1879, Josephine Hrutka, and of their union nine children have been born, namely Julia, Charles, William, Arthur, Edna, Edward, Carrie, Mabel, and Howard Arthur died when two years old, Edna when six months old, Edward at the age of one year, and Charles died at the age of thirty-six, leaving a wife and three children The other children are all married and successful. Mr Hrabak is a sound republican in politics, and has the distinction of having been a member of the first town board, and of the first school board of Dodge Fraternally he is a member of the Modern Woodmen of America, and of the Woodmen of the World In religion both Mr and Mrs Hrabak are of the Catholic faith.

G A SWEET An extensive and well-to-do agriculturist of Dodge County, G A. Sweet is actively and prosperously engaged in his independent occupation on one of the most attractive and desirable farms in Elkhorn Township Located on section 36, it comprises 360 acres of fertile land, and, with its comfortable set of buildings, invariably attracts attention, indicating to the observer the judicious manner in which the owner has employed his time and means A son of the late Perry Sweet, he was born, December 7, 1874, in St Joseph, Missouri, and there obtained his elementary education

Born in Illinois, Perry Sweet grew to man's estate in his native county, being variously employed. Subsequently migrating to Missouri, he lived for a time in St Joseph, from there coming with his wife and children, in 1889, to Nebraska Locating in Dodge County, near Fremont, he was there engaged in general farming until his death, when but fifty-four years of age His widow, Nellie Sweet, survived him, and now makes her home with one of her sons.

A lad of fifteen years when he came with his parents to Nebraska, in 1889, G A Sweet received an excellent training in the art and science of agriculture while yet a youth, and found the occupation very congenial to his tastes Beginning farming on his own account in 1908, Mr Sweet has made wise use of every opportunity to improve his methods, and advance his interests, as his means increased adding to his property from time to time He has 360 acres of well improved land in his home farm, and also owns 800 acres of land in Colorado. He is carrying on general farming with very satisfactory results, using the most approved up-to-date methods, and in addition to tilling his land is feeding cattle and hogs quite extensively, it being considered a profitable branch of agriculture in this state

Mr Sweet married, in 1910, at Council Bluffs, Iowa, Miss Phoebe Johnson, and they have one child, Gretchen Sweet A straightforward republican, Mr Sweet has served as a member of the local school board for eight years. Fraternally he is a member of the Ancient Free and Accepted Order of Masons, of the Independent Order of Odd Fellows, and of the Modern Woodmen of America

CHARLES McKENNAN Widely known as a prosperous agriculturist, Charles McKennan is numbered among the citizens of good standing and high repute of Dodge County, of which he is an honored pioneer, his farm being located in Elkhorn Township He was born, in 1858, in New York State, where his parents, John and Elizabeth McKennan, were life-long residents.

Born, bred and educated in the Empire State, Charles McKennan remained an inmate of the parental household until attaining his majority In 1879, following the advice of Horace Greeley, who said "Go West, young man," he came to Nebraska, locating in Dodge County in pioneer days, when the now flourishing City of Fremont was a mere hamlet, with no indication of its present prosperity The good roads hereabout were then but pathways, comparatively, Indians were numerous; and wild game of all kinds was abundant, furnishing an ample supply of food for the family larder Mr McKennan bought land at $5 an acre soon after his arrival, but deciding it was not worth the money relinquished it He afterwards bought land in section 26, Elkhorn Township, and by persevering industry and good management has a finely improved estate, well adapted for his occupation of a general farmer.

Mr McKennan married, in 1882, in Dodge County, Martha Close, a daughter of John A and Nancy Close, neither of whom are living. Mr. Close came from Wisconsin to Nebraska at a very early period of its settlement, driving the entire distance two ox teams and one cow team, being five weeks in making the long and wearisome journey He took up a tract of land from the Government, near the present site of Arlington, which had not then won a place on the map, on what was known as Bell Creek, and in a few years had improved a homestead of 160 acres He served as a soldier in the Civil war, and was quite active in public affairs, having served as school director, and as township assessor

He died on the homestead at the age of seventy-two years, and his wife lived to be seventy-four years old Both were faithful members of the Methodist Episcopal Church Mr and Mrs McKennan have six children, namely Bessie, living in Fremont, Frank M, of Reno, Nevada, Rollo, living in Wyoming, Edith Bricker, Gertrude, of Memphis, Nebraska, and John, living at home True to the faith in which they were reared, Mr and Mrs McKennan are members of the Methodist Episcopal Church

JOHN SAMPSON An honored representative of the early pioneers of Dodge County, John Sampson, of Swaburg, Logan Township, is a true type of the energetic and enterprising men who have actively assisted in the development of this fertile and productive region, and by his sagacity and keen foresight has at the same time been enabled to accumulate a comfortable share of this world's wealth A native of Sweden, he was born April 17, 1842, being one of a family of ten children born to his parents, Samuel and Sarah Sampson

The second child, and eldest son, of the parental household, John Sampson came to the United States in early life, and on June 5, 1868, located in Fremont, Dodge County, Nebraska, where he lived and labored for a year In 1869 he homesteaded a part of his present farm, and when he paid for his land had just 50 cents left to his credit At the end of six months, having assumed possession of the dugout, his first home in the township, he hired fifteen acres of his land cleared, paying $5 an acre for the work Finding ready money very scarce, Mr Sampson secured a job on the railroad, and making his headquarters in Fremont spent one night each month on his claim in order to hold it, walking the entire distance of twenty-five miles, and as there was no bridge across the Elkhorn, waded the river While improving his homestead, Mr. Sampson suffered all the hardships and privations incident to pioneer life, in fact meeting with more trouble than many had to endure as, in 1873, he had the misfortune to be completely burned out by a prairie fire, obliging him to start all over again Among the many cherished treasures brought with him from his old home in Sweden, which he lost in this fire, was his large Swedish Bible When he began farming for himself, Mr Sampson had but one horse, and few equipments the tractors and farm machinery of the present day having been not only unknown but undreamed of

Mr Sampson was a man of push and energy, not easily discouraged, and it is not at all surprising to learn that he became very successful in his career, and having purchased other land has now a well cultivated and highly improved farm of 200 acres, with fine and conveniently arranged buildings, a productive orchard, and broad, fertile and productive fields, his estate being a credit to him, and an ornament to the community Mr Sampson himself does but little active labor now, having given up all the responsibilities of farm ownership and management to his two sons He is a stanch republican in politics, and a valued member of the Lutheran Church at Swaburg, which he helped to organize and build, hauling material across the Missouri River on the ice in 1871 He is now one of the few remaining charter members of this church

Mr Sampson married, February 25, 1871, Marie Monson, who was born in Sweden in 1853, being the youngest daughter of John and Elna Monson, also natives of Sweden Mrs Sampson died August 9, 1895, leaving eight children out of the family of ten children that blessed their union The children are: Alice, now Mrs Fred Raber, of Winfred, South Dakota, Ingrid, Victor E., Anna, Emma, Hjalmer N., Esther and Luella

HENRY M KIDDER A survey of this publication will show that within its pages is to be found individual recognition of the greater number of the representative members of the bar of Dodge County, and a place of due relative precedence is consistently to be accorded to Mr. Kidder, who has been a resident of Nebraska since his boyhood and who has been engaged in the practice of his profession at Fremont, judicial center of Dodge County, since 1912, prior to which year he had gained secure vantage-place as one of the leading members of the bar of Custer County

Mr Kidder was born in Barry County, Michigan, February 11, 1859, and in that state he acquired his rudimentary education. He was eleven years of age when he accompanied his parents to Nebraska, in 1870, and his father secured a homestead near Norfolk, Madison County, where he developed a productive farm and became one of the substantial citizens of the county Henry M Kidder continued his studies in the public schools of that county, besides which he attended for three years a well ordered German school At Norfolk he initiated the study of law in the office of the firm of Wigton & Whitham, and under such able preceptorship he made substantial progress in his assimilation of the involved science of jurisprudence He was admitted to the bar June 7, 1886, upon examination before Judge Tiffany, who was then presiding on the bench of the District Court, and in the same year he became one of the early members of the bar of Mason City, Custer County, where he remained nine years and developed a prosperous law business At the expiration of this period he removed to Woodbine, Harrison County, Iowa, but he continued in practice in the Hawkeye State only one year He then returned to Mason City Custer County, but fifteen months later, on the 1st of June, 1897, he established his residence at Scribner, Dodge County, where he showed his versatility by entering the profession of journalism, as editor and publisher of the Scribner Rustler, which he conducted very successfully for twelve years, the paper having become under his management an effective exponent of community interests, as well as a leader in popular sentiment and action relative to political affairs and general public interests in the county In August, 1912, Mr Kidder removed to Fremont, the county seat, where he opened an office and continued the practice of law. His professional ability has never lacked for popular appreciation, and his success has been pronounced, the while his professional activities have involved his appearance in the courts of many Nebraska counties, including Custer, Sherman, Greeley, Hall, Buffalo, Dawson, Dawes, Sheridan, Antelope, Thurston, Pierce, Knox, Madison, Stanton, Cuming, Washington, Douglas, Dodge, Colfax, Platte, Boone, Howard, Lancaster, Clay, Red Willow, Chase and Cheyenne, as well as in Beadle, Gregory and Red Willow counties, South Dakota He has also presented a large number of cases before the Supreme Court of Nebraska He has appeared also before the Supreme Court of Kansas, and in the courts of Kansas City and St Joseph, Missouri, as well as the Superior Court of that state It is thus evident that his law business has been of broad scope and importance and that he has high standing at the bar In 1920 he was the republican candidate for judge of the District Court of the Sixth District of Nebraska, his opposing candidates being Judge F W Button, at that time presiding on the bench of this district, A M Post, and John C Martin He has been influential in republican councils and campaign work, and while a resident of Custer County he served for a time as city clerk of Mason City, his incumbency of this position having continued during the major part of his residence here While residing at Scribner, Dodge County, he assisted in the organization of the Farmers Grain & Stock Company, of which he was a director for some time, and for which he secured, from the railroad company, the site for the company's grain elevator He and his wife are members of the Baptist Church, and he has passed various official chairs in the Independent Order of Odd Fellows, including the Encampment, as well as in the Modern Woodmen of America, besides which he is affiliated also with the Sons of Hermann

January 5, 1887, recorded the marriage of Mr. Kidder to Miss Nora R Rumery, who was born in Jones County, Iowa, a daughter of Sewell C and Hannah (Cooper) Rumery, who came to Nebraska in 1894 and passed the closing years of their lives at Mason City, Custer County the father having devoted the greater part of his active career to agricultural enterprise Mr and Mrs Kidder have two children. Olive P became the wife of Peter C Conroy but she now resides at the parental home in Fremont, where she is employed by the Hammond-Stevens Company, Minnie M. is the wife of Soren C Hansen, of Fremont

Reverting to the parents of Mr. Kidder, it is to be stated that he is a son of Rev. James W and Mary Ann (Stevens) Kidder, the former a native of Enosburg, Vermont, and the latter of East Machias, Maine, in which latter state their marriage was solemnized From the Pine Tree State they removed to Ohio, where they remained one year. They then removed to Michigan, where for eleven years he was pastor of the Congregational Church at Middleville In 1870 he came with his family to Nebraska, and assumed a pastorate at Norfolk, as the pioneer English-speaking clergyman of that place There he continued his ministerial labors nine years, besides preaching at several other places in that section of the state He finally removed with his family to the farm which he had secured near Norfolk, but after his retirement he returned to that now thriving little city, where he and his wife passed the closing years of their lives, secure in the affectionate regard of all who knew them They became the parents of four children Hattie is the wife of Andrew U McGinnis, of Norfolk, Mary L is the widow of Peter C Stewart, who died in South Africa, and she now resides at Northfield, Minnesota, Miss Laura A resides at Norfolk Nebraska, but was for seventeen years an efficient and popular teacher in the public schools of Fremont, and Henry M, of this review, was the second in order of birth of the four children

MARTIN NELSON, the enterprising and efficient manager of the well equipped creamery of the Farmers Union Co-operative Company at Fremont, was born in Denmark, October 29, 1876, and is a son of Nels and Trine (Hendrickson) Nelson, the former of whom passed his entire life in his native land In 1881 the widowed mother came with her eight children to the United States and established her home in Dodge County Nebraska, where for some time she continued to give effective service as a practical nurse, in which capacity she won the affectionate esteem of the community Here she passed the remainder of her life and was a devout communicant of the Lutheran Church, as was also her husband,

Martin Nelson.

the latter having been a man of superior education and having been a successful school teacher in Denmark at the time of his death Of the eight children, seven are living Lars is a prosperous farmer near Potter, Cheyenne County, Dora is the widow of John Madison and resides in the City of Omaha, Mary is the wife of John Schon, a farmer near St Paul, Howard County, James is employed in the stockyards at Omaha, Lena is the wife of Peter J Lorenson, of Fremont; Nelsena is married and now resides in Denmark, and Martin is the subject of this review.

Martin Nelson was about five years old when he came with his mother to Nebraska, and his youthful education was obtained in the rural schools of Dodge County, where also he gained early experience in connection with farm work He continued to be actively identified with farm enterprise until he was nineteen years of age, when he went to California There he learned the technical work of the creamery business, and he continued to be employed five years in western creameries—in California and Idaho, in which latter state he organized and successfully operated a co-operative creamery He then returned to Dodge County, where he devoted the ensuing ten years to the operation of rented farm property He then purchased the Valentine Knoell farm, five miles northwest of Fremont, and here he has conducted successful activities as an agriculturist and stock grower since 1912 He still resides on this well improved farm, to which he continued to give a general and specially effective personal supervision, though he has had the active management of the co-operative creamery at Fremont since May 1, 1917 His thorough technical knowledge and progressive policies have contributed greatly to the success of this creamery, which bases its operations on a capital stock of $35,000 and of which he is general manager The greater part of the high-grade butter produced at this model creamery is shipped to the eastern markets, and the business for 1919 aggregated fully $540,000 Mr Nelson's farm comprises 160 acres, and for the property he has been offered $500 an acre Mr Nelson has been essentially the architect of his own fortunes, as his success has been entirely the result of his own ability and well directed efforts He is a republican in political allegiance and he and his wife are communicants of the Lutheran Church

The year 1909 recorded the marriage of Mr Nelson to Miss Marie Jeppeson, who was born and reared in Dodge County, a daughter of Jens Jeppeson, who still resides on his farm, northwest of Fremont Mr and Mrs Nelson have five children Lenta, Gladys, Leland, Marion, and Alvina

Morris Nielsen, M D, of Blair, occupies a noteworthy position among the foremost physicians and surgeons of this section of the state, and is well worthy of representation in a work of this character A son of Peter H Nielsen he was born, October 3, 1875, in Copenhagen, Denmark, where he lived for nine years

Born and brought up in Denmark, Peter H Nielsen received excellent educational advantages, having studied at the National School of Technology, in Copenhagen. Learning the carpenter's trade when young, he became a master builder, and as a journeyman traveled in France and Switzerland, following his trade in different places In 1884 he came with his family to the United States, locating in Omaha, Nebraska, where he is still a resident Poor in pocket when he located in that city, he followed his trade steadily and by means of industry and thrift accumulated some property, and is now living retired from active labor His wife, whose maiden name was Anna C Madsen, was born in Copenhagen, Denmark, and died, in November, 1915, in Omaha She was a member of the Lutheran Church, to which her husband also belonged He is a member of the Danish Brotherhood, an organization in which he takes great interest and much pleasure

The only survivor in a family of three children, Morris Nielsen acquired his rudimentary education in the public schools of Omaha, and in September, 1893, entered the Omaha Medical College Before completing his course, he was forced, on account of lack of funds, to leave school for a time He herded cattle, broke bronchos and freighted for a time, and later secured a position as commercial traveler for a firm from Scotland, and in that capacity visited many of the foreign countries Returning to Omaha in 1898, he resumed his studies in the Medical Department of the University of Nebraska, and was there graduated with the degree of Doctor of Medicine in 1900

Locating in Belden Nebraska, in that year, Doctor Nielsen remained there seven years, in the meantime building up a good practice Going to Boston, Massachusetts, in 1907, he took a post-graduate course at Harvard University, and during the succeeding two years was associated as an assistant with Doctor Rouse, at Sioux City, Iowa Wishing to still further fit himself for his professional work, the doctor went to Europe, and took post-graduate courses in two of the leading medical institutions of that continent, one in Berlin, and the other in Vienna Returning to the United States, he located in Blair in the fall of 1911, and has since continued here, his practice being extensive and highly remunerative Doctor Nielsen's work is so widely recognized that he has very little leisure, his professional duties demanding all of his time He is a member of the American Medical Association, of the Nebraska State Medical Association, of which he is now counselor, and of the Washington County Medical Society

Doctor Nielsen married, in 1903, Mary Nielsen, a native of Nebraska, and into their household four children have been born, namely Morris, Jr, born in 1904, Damon Jenner, born in 1908 Vance Aubrey, born in 1910, and Jules Peter, born in 1912 Politically the doctor is a republican Fraternally he is a member of the Ancient Free and Accepted Masons, of the Benevolent and Protective Order of Elks, and of the Independent Order of Odd Fellows, of which he is past grand Both he and his wife are devout members of the Episcopal Church

William Koyen Showing marked ability and skill in the management of his agricultural interests, William Koyen occupies an honored position among the industrious and progressive farmers of Dodge County, his well-kept farm in Elkhorn Township comparing favorably in regard to its appointments and improvements with any in the neighborhood A son of Frederick and Christina Koyen, he was born, in 1875, in Wisconsin, of Danish ancestry

Frederick Koyen, or, as the name was originally spelled Koyn, was born in Denmark, November 28, 1848, and at the age of twenty-one years immigrated to the United States Settling in Wisconsin, he was employed in the woods, or in tilling the soil, for eleven years Coming from there to Dodge County Nebraska, he bought 160 acres of raw land which he improved and on that farm he remained until ready to retire from active pursuits, when he removed to town He married in New York State, and to him and his wife, Christina Koyen, five children were born, of whom three are living, William, Albert, and Victor E. The wife died on the homestead aged sixty-nine years He was an independent voter, and a member of the Danish Lutheran Church

Coming with his parents to Dodge County in childhood, William Koyen obtained his early education in the rural schools, and in 1896 began life for himself as a farmer, renting land at first Energetic and industrious, he toiled early and late, and as his wealth accumulated invested it wisely, and now is owner of 120 acres of rich land, on which he is successfully engaged in general farming He has made noteworthy improvements on his place, having a modernly constructed home, and all the necessary barns and outbuildings required by a practical agriculturist In politics Mr Koyen is independent, voting without deference to party lines, and in addition to having served on the local school board has been township treasurer He was for two terms president of the Farmers' Co-operative Association, and was the first president to form a company.

Mr Koyen married, in Fremont, Nebraska, in 1897, Louisa Stiles, who was born in Iowa, a daughter of S F Stiles, who settled in Fremont, this state, in pioneer times, and took an active and influential part in its upbuilding, and there continued to reside until his death, at the age of sixty-nine years Mr Stiles was city clerk for several years, and also served as chief of police, and as deputy sheriff His widow still lives in Fremont. Mr and Mrs Koyen have four children, namely: Gertrude Hanson, of Fremont, Fred, Francis, and Ward Mr Koyen has never joined any fraternal organization Religiously he is a member of the Methodist Episcopal Church

G A Bushnell A skilled mechanic, thoroughly acquainted with all branches of the wood worker's trade, G A Bushnell, of Fremont, head of the Bushnell Repair Company has built up a thriving business in connection with the painting and repairing of automobiles, and won a position of prominence in the industrial circles of this part of Dodge County. A son of Robert Lay Bushnell, he was born, July 4, 1860, in Rock County, Wisconsin, coming from honored patriotic stock, Gen John Stark, of Revolutionary fame, having been his maternal great-grandfather

Robert Lay Bushnell was born, reared, and married in New York State Removing to Wisconsin, he bought land in Rock County, where he carried on general farming several years He afterwards continued his agricultural labors in Iowa, from there going to South Dakota, where he spent the closing years of his life He married Margaretta LeFevre who was born in New York State, and died in Mason City, Iowa Her father, Minard LeFevre, Mr. Bushnell's maternal grandfather, was a very prominent architect, and in addition to having furnished the plans for forty or more of the large and prominent buildings of New York City, drew the plans for several of its noted church edifices, including those for the Holy Trinity Church on Brooklyn Heights, the wealthiest Protestant Church in the world His designs were mainly of the Gothic style, and the Holy Trinity Church building designs were the last that he constructed Of the eight children born of the union of Mr and Mrs. Robert Lay Bushnell, five are living, as follows. Mrs Permelia Sherman, of Mason City, Iowa, Mrs Julia Read, of Carson, Iowa, G A, of this sketch, F E, of Fremont, working for his brother in the repair shop and Willie, an oil man in Los Angeles, California.

Obtaining the rudiments of his education in Wisconsin, G A Bushnell completed his early studies in Iowa, and subsequently learned the carriage maker and wood worker's trade in Mason City, Iowa, where he followed it for a while, from there going to Malvern, Iowa, where he continued as a carriage maker. Coming to Fremont, Nebraska, in 1890, Mr Bushnell began working for John Bunt, in the Fremont Carriage Company, and in 1913 bought the factory, which he has transformed into a repair shop From year to year he has enlarged his operations, and is now carrying on an extensive and substantial business as a painter and repairer of automobiles, repairing everything pertaining to automobiles with the exception of engine work Having begun life for himself with no other assets than strong arms and an unlimited amount of courage, he has met with excellent success in his undertakings

Mr Bushnell married, October 21, 1884, Minerva Edie, who was born May 17, 1863, in Emerson, Iowa She graduated from the public schools at the age of fifteen then entered Tabor College, of Iowa, and where she finished her education, she was one of Iowa's successful teachers until her marriage Her parents, A G and Sarah (Gustin) Edie, settled in Emerson on moving, in 1849, from Ohio, their native state, to Iowa Her father is still living on the old home place in Iowa, but her mother has passed to the life beyond Mr. and Mrs Bushnell have two children, namely Pearl, wife of Dalton Smith, manager of the Globe Milling Company, at Los Angeles, California, and Ralph, who is associated in business with his father Mr. Bushnell is a stanch republican in politics, and is an active and prominent member of Triumph Lodge No 32, Knights of Pythias, of Fremont, of which he is a very prominent and active member and past chancellor commander, and which he has several times represented at the Grand Lodge Mrs Bushnell is past grand chief of Calanthe Temple No. 3, Pythian Sisters, of Fremont, and past grand chief, Nebraska, and also past supreme representative of the Pythian Sisters She has been very active in the lodge work and has filled the highest offices in the local, state and supreme lodges

Morris Horstman Well trained in modern business ways and methods, Morris Hortman is actively identified with the advancement of the mercantile affairs of Fremont, where he has built up an extensive and remunerative trade as a dealer in shoes, his genial courtesy, prompt attention to the wants of his customers, and his honesty, having won him a highly satisfactory patronage, and given him a place of influence in the community He was born, July 9, 1874, in Germany, the birthplace, likewise, of his parents, Detlef and Catherine (Braker) Horstman

In 1885 Detlef Horstman immigrated with his family to the United States, the land of plenty, and sometime in the '90s made his way to Nebraska Buying a tract of land in Dodge County, near Scribner, he was there prosperously engaged in tilling the soil until his death, which occurred in 1917. A man of energy and enterprise he was very successful in his undertakings, acquiring a good property He was a republican in politics, and a member of the Lutheran Church, to which his widow, who still lives on the old homestead, belongs They were the parents of ten children, all of whom are living, Morris being the sixth child in succession of birth

Having completed his early education in the Avoca, Iowa, High School, Morris Horstman then engaged in farming and during the four years that he was thus employed gained an excellent knowledge of agriculture Migrating to Nebraska, he served as a clerk in a mercantile establishment at North Bend for seven years, and later was treasurer of Dodge County for five years, a position of responsibility and trust that he filled ably and faithfully. Locating in Fremont, Mr Horstman established his present shoe store in 1915, and has since built up a large and flourishing business, being now one of the foremost shoe merchants in this part of Dodge County

Mr. Horstman married, in 1901, Alvina Wickhorst, who was born in Dodge County, Nebraska, where her father, the late Jacob Wickhorst, was a pioneer agriculturist Two children have been born of the union of Mr and Mrs Horstman, namely Harold, born in 1906; and Blondell, born in 1909 Mr and Mrs Horstman are regular attendants of the Methodist Episcopal Church ' Politically Mr Horstman is an influential member of the republican party, and his popularity as a man and a citizen was clearly demonstrated when he was elected county treasurer by a large majority in a district that had been under the control of the democratic party for a full quarter of a century. Fraternally, he is a member of the Modern Woodmen of America, and of the Independent Order of Odd Fellows

SIRENO BURNELL COLSON A man of sterling and honest integrity and worth, possessing pronounced business acumen and ability, the late Sireno Burnell Colson was for full forty years identified with the leading interests of Fremont, and while advancing his own prosperity contributed in no small measure toward the progress of his home city A son of Thomas Paine Colson, he was born in Madison County, New York, February 3, 1828, being the lineal descendant of a member of the Swedish Colony that settled in New Jersey in 1700 He was also of Revolutionary stock, his grandfather, Abiah Colson, having fought in the Revolution while serving as a member of the Sixth Massachusetts Regiment, commanded by Colonel Millens

A shoemaker by trade, Thomas Paine Colson followed that occupation in New York State for many years, laboring industriously, but not making very much money In 1859, hoping to improve his financial condition, he came with his family to Nebraska, locating in Fremont, where he remained until his death. He married Mary Rice, the descendant of one of the earlier families of the Empire State, and a woman of many virtues

Brought up in Hamilton County, New York, Sireno B Colson was a delicate child, and though an ambitious student in his boyhood, was badly handicapped by ill health. After leaving the common schools of his neighborhood, he entered Hamilton College, but on account of his physical condition, and his father's financial condition, he was unable to complete the course of study therein Subsequently working with his father, he learned the shoemaker's trade, which he followed before coming to Nebraska, and for about six years after the family located in Fremont Although short of stature, and slight of frame, Mr Colson was an ambitious student, and having become proficient in the study of telegraphy, had the distinction of having been the first operator west of the Missouri River for the Atlantic and Pacific Telegraph Company, a position that he accepted in 1861

In 1866 Mr Colson was appointed local agent and telegraph operator at Fremont, being the first to be thus appointed by the Union Pacific Railroad Company outside of Omaha, and held the position until 1871 In 1867, with his brother-in-law, Theron Nye, as a member of the firm of Nye, Colson & Company, he began dealing in grain and lumber, and built up a large and lucrative business, which has continued in existence until the present time, and although the firm name has been several times changed, there has ever been a Nye at the head, Ray Nye, son of Theron Nye, the original founder of the firm, being now senior member of the present firm, known as the Nye, Schneider, Fowler Company. Mr. Colson retained his interest in the extensive lumber and grain business until his death, which occurred at his home in Fremont, September 28, 1896.

An earnest worker in the republican party, Mr. Colson was elected treasurer of Dodge County, Nebraska, in 1871, and re-elected to the same position in 1873, that having been the only public office that he ever held. He was one of the organizers of the First National Bank of Fremont, and was serving as its vice president at the time of his death. He never united with any religious organization, the only society to which he belonged being the Sons of the American Revolution. At Omaha, in the records of that society, may be found a review of the life of Mr. Colson, contained in a paper read before the society on February 22, 1897.

Mr. Colson married, January 21, 1868, Miss Frances I. Reynolds, who still survives him, residing in Fremont. She was born in Dansville, Livingston County, New York, in 1847. Later her family moved to Buffalo, and still later to Detroit, from whence they removed to Fremont in 1861, two brothers and a sister having preceded them. She participated in the hardships and trials that attended all the pioneers, and later attended school at Brownell Hall in Omaha. She then taught school in Papillion and Fremont and also for a short time at an Indian school in Kansas, where there was an Indian insurrection which threatened to be serious but fortunately was quelled with no loss of life. She was married when 20 years of age, and was the mother of four children, the eldest dying in infancy and three still living: Paul and Burnell Colson, living in Fremont, and May Colson Knowles, residing in New York City. Mrs. Colson was formerly a member of the Episcopal Church, later joining the Congregational Church, and has long been a faithful worker for the causes of prohibition and suffrage for women.

GERHARD MONNICH. Noteworthy for his good citizenship and many excellent traits of character, Gerhard Monnich, of Hooper, a retired agriculturist, is well known throughout this part of Dodge County as a man of honor and integrity, and as one who has contributed his full share toward advancing the material interests of his community. He was born, November 23, 1854, in Germany, which was the birthplace of his parents, Tonjes H. and Beta (Havelkamp) Monnich.

Immigrating to the United States with his family, T. H. Monnich located in Dodge County, Nebraska, in 1869, coming by train as far as Fremont. Taking up a homestead claim two miles north of Hooper, he labored with true pioneer grit and courage in his efforts to clear and improve a farm, and was thereafter engaged in mixed husbandry until his death, in 1897, at the advanced age of eighty-one years. He was a man of enterprise and energy, and one of the shareholders of the Farmers' Company of Hooper. He was a stanch democrat in politics, and both he and his wife were Lutherans in religion. They were the parents of four children, as follows: Gerhard, of this sketch; Gesine, widow of J. H. Kuhlman, of Dodge County; Catherine, deceased; and a child that died in infancy.

MR. AND MRS. GERHARD MONNICH

Acquiring an excellent knowledge of the common branches of study in the district schools, Gerhard Monnich received an extended education in the agricultural arts and sciences under his father's tutelage Choosing the occupation to which he was reared, he was prosperously employed in tilling the soil, and in raising and feeding stock, until 1903. Moving then to Hooper, Mr Monnich has since been looking after his large land interests, being one of the large land owners of the county, owning several farms in this county and also in Scott's Bluff County, Nebraska He is a man of good business ability, and one of the stockholders of the Farmers' Union He is a sound republican in politics, but has never been prominent in the management of public affairs

Mr. Monnich married, in 1903, Gesine Freese, who was born in Germany, August 25, 1867, and was an infant when she came to the United States with her parents, being a daughter of John D. Freese, who settled in Dodge County in 1869 in pioneer days Three children have blessed their union, namely Bertha, Henry and George, all attending school in Hooper Mr and Mrs Monnich are active and worthy members of the Lutheran Church.

August Westlin During a half century of residence the name Westlin has been constantly accumulating esteem and respect in Dodge County due to the energies, industry and thrifty character of those who bear that name in the agricultural community of Logan Township

The home and farm of August Westlin, one of the progressive men of Dodge County, is in section 4 of Logan Township. He was born in the same county in 1876 His father, the late N P Westlin, was born in Sweden in 1835 When he was thirty-two years of age he started for the United States and came on west as far as Council Bluffs, where his first employment was on the old asylum In 1868 he took up his homestead in Dodge County and in the fall of 1869 did the first breaking of prairie sod, using an ox team That homestead is near the present town of Uehling

When he departed for America Christina Nelson, whom he had learned to love and to whom he was betrothed, had remained behind, but on receiving word from Mr. Westlin that his affairs were prospering she came on to this country in 1870 and they were married in Omaha. Their first home was a sod house, and in 1876 they erected a more substantial frame structure, the home in which August Westlin spent his boyhood N P Westlin continued his career as a successful farmer in Dodge County until his death in 1890 and his wife passed away in 1889 They were the parents of five children Caroline Olsen, deceased, Albert, who was born in Dodge County and died in 1913, August, Olaf, associated with his brother August, and Mrs Ellen Larson, whose husband is a garage owner at Warsaw in Knox County

August Westlin acquired a common school education and grew up well trained for the vocation of farming and stock raising. For many years he has fed hogs and cattle for the market and is now the prosperous owner and manager of 260 acres devoted to general farming. In 1916 he built his present home, one of the finest and most modern in that section of the county. Mr Westlin and family are members of the Congregational Church and in politics he is an independent voter

In 1902 he married Miss Esther Anderson, who was born in Dodge County in 1877. Concerning her father, T. A. Anderson, of Uehling, more is said on other pages Mr and Mrs. Westlin have two children, Margaret and Sherman, both at home

HENRY SCHMIETENKNOP Widely known as a prosperous agriculturist of Everett Township, Henry Schmietenknop is numbered among the citizens of high repute in Dodge County, where he has lived for upwards of a quarter of a century He was born March 25, 1876, in Germany, the lifelong residence of his parents, Gerhard and Anna (Miners) Schmietenknop, who were industrious, hard-working farmers

Bred and educated in his native country, Henry Schmietenknop determined as a boy to find out, as soon as old enough, the truth regarding the wonderful stories of America's prosperity, and in 1893 left home and friends to come to the United States Making his way to Nebraska, he located in Dodge County, and for a time worked for John Heithausen Becoming familiar with agricultural pursuits, he engaged in farming on his own account, and met with such encouraging results that, in 1900, he rented the farm which he still farms, it being on section 12, Everett Township In 1911 he purchased a farm of 225 acres in Hooper and Everett townships which he rents out Laboring industriously and intelligently, Mr Schmietenknop has carried on general farming and stock raising most successfully, his land being well cultivated and well improved, while his farming implements and machinery are all that can be desired by the up-to-date agriculturist Interested in everything pertaining to the management of a farm, he is an active member of the Farmers' Union at Hooper August 4, 1898, Mr Schmietenknop was united in marriage with Anna Osterloh, who was born in Dodge .County, Nebraska, of German lineage Her father Gerhard Osterloh, was born in Germany, October 31, 1838, and there lived until after his marriage with Gesine Egbers Coming with his family to Dodge County, Nebraska, in 1868, he homesteaded, and was thereafter prosperously engaged in general farming and stock raising and feeding until his death, in 1894 He was independent in politics, and an active member of St Paul's Lutheran Church, to which his widow belongs

Three children have blessed the marriage of Mr and Mrs Schmietenknop, namely George, Clara and Fred An independent voter, Mr Schmietenknop casts his ballot in favor of the men and measures he deems best Both he and his wife are valued members of the St Paul's Lutheran Church, and are rearing their family in the Lutheran faith

JOHN H DIERKS An industrious and enterprising agriculturist, John H Dierks, late of Fremont, was one of the earlier settlers of Saunders County Nebraska, and with true pioneer courage cleared and improved a highly productive farm He was born November 22, 1845, in Germany, and died in Fremont, Nebraska, October 20, 1909

A small boy when he was brought by his parents to the United States, Mr. Dierks was educated in the public schools of Illinois, and having been of deeply religious nature, with strong personal convictions, he early determined to enter the ministry Circumstances changed his plans, however, and in 1878 he made his way to Nebraska, arriving in Saunders County with a capital of $1,500, a part of which he invested in land, buying 160 acres of virgin soil Laboring with unceasing toil, he cleared and improved a good ranch, and at the end of twenty years made his last payment on his farm, acquiring a clear title to it His health failing, he moved with his family to Fremont, Dodge County, in July, 1909, and the following October passed to the life beyond

Mr Dierks was an earnest and devout member of the Baptist Church, and after settling in Saunders County he and wife helped organize a church of that denomination there He was also influential in establishing a mission in Fremont, and having been made superintendent of its Sunday school drove a distance of seven miles every Sunday in order to assume charge of the school Mr Dierks paid $8 50 an acre for his farm in 1878 and in the spring of 1919 his widow sold it, receiving $250 an acre, a decided advance in price.

Mr Dierks married in 1870 Elise Folkers, who was born February 21, 1850, in Germany, and in 1857 was brought to this country by her parents, Ulrich and Catherine Folkers, who located permanently in Illinois Six children were born of their union, four of whom are living, namely: Edward, a barber, resides in San Diego, California; George, of Wahoo, Nebraska, is a chiropractor, Sophia, living in Fremont; and Emma, wife of Frederick Thielen, foreman of a harness and saddle factory in Lincoln, Nebraska Mrs Dierks is an active member of the Baptist Church, and takes great interest in the work of the Young Women's Christian Association She lives at 949 North Park Avenue, in the pleasant home which she purchased in 1913

J E LUTZ A man of strong personality, enterprising and keen sighted, J E Lutz, a well-known monument manufacturer and dealer of Blair, occupies a place of prominence and influence in the political and business circles of the city, and is a typical representative of the men of the day who have attained success through persevering industry and wise management of their affairs A son of Barnet Lutz, he was born in 1854, in Linn County, Iowa, of pioneer ancestry

Born in Fayette County, Pennsylvania, Barnet Lutz there married Ann Kramer, and two years after that important event migrated to Iowa with his bride, going the greater part of the way by boat, an eventful trip in that year of 1839, when but little was known of any part of the country lying west of the Alleghenies Buying a tract of Government land in Linn County, he cleared and improved a fine homestead in the vicinity of Kenwood Park, and there resided until his death The little town was laid out on his farm, and he had the honor of serving as its first mayor He was an influential member of the republican party, and he and his wife were active members of the Methodist Episcopal Church They were the parents of eleven children, three of whom are now living, as follows Mrs J J Wayt, of Springdale, Arkansas, where her husband is living retired from active business, Mrs J H Smith, a widow, living in Sigourney, Iowa; and J E, of whom we write In addition to their own large family of children, the parents, in the goodness of their hearts, brought up as their own two other children

The tenth child in order of birth of the parental household, J E Lutz, received superior educational privileges, after leaving the rural schools of his native town having attended the Cedar Rapids High School and Western College He subsequently made, and saved, his first $100 as a teacher in the country schools. In 1877 he embarked in the monument business at Kenwood Park, and continued in that little town until 1888 Coming to Blair, Nebraska, in that year, Mr Lutz here established himself in the same business, beginning in a modest way, and from year to year has gradually enlarged his operations, having now a very large and exceedingly prosperous business, and in addition to having been successful himself has helped several other men to start in the same line of industry

Active in local affairs, Mr Lutz, a strong republican in politics has served as a member of the City Council for fifteen years, and was a candidate for delegate at large for the National Republican Convention of 1920 He took up a homestead claim in 1905 in South Dakota and he bought land adjoining the homestead, and is now owner of 480 acres of choice land Fraternally Mr Lutz is a member of the Knights of Pythias, being past chancellor of his lodge and deputy chancellor of the state and is a member of the Independent Order of Odd Fellows Religiously he belongs to the Methodist Episcopal Church

Mr Lutz has been twice married He married first, in 1880, Georgia Miller, and of the three children born of their union, one is living, Daisy, wife of Layton Morris, a professor in Columbia University Mrs Georgia Lutz passed to the life beyond in 1890, while yet in early womanhood Mr Lutz married in February, 1892, Mary Augusta Campbell, a native of Pennsylvania, and they have two children living, namely Frank, now in business with his father; and Margaret Ann, wife of L Noies, who served in the World war, being sent from Camp Dodge to the border, and who is now in the employ of Mr Lutz

Frank Lutz, a member of the National Guard, was sent to the border in 1914, and was released in 1916 In 1917 he entered the World war, being sent, on March 26 of that year, to the Fort Snelling Training School, where, after receiving his commission as second lieutenant, he was transferred to Camp Miller, New York Sailing from Hoboken on October 14, 1917, he subsequently saw active service in France, going over the top, and in one engagement he was slightly wounded He belonged to the Rainbow Division until 1918, when he was transferred to the Thirty-Second Division Returning home, he received his discharge in May, 1919, and has since been associated in business with his father, as stated above Howard Lutz, the eldest child of Mr Lutz, served in the United States navy before the World war He subsequently assumed the management of his father's homestead property in South Dakota and was there killed in September, 1906, when but twnty-three years of age.

Charles Ross Inheriting in a large measure the habits of industry, economy and thrift characteristic of a long line of honored Scotch ancestry, Charles Ross of Blair has long been prominently identified with the development and advancement of the manufacturing interests of this part of Washington County, and as secretary and manager of the Blair Horse Collar Company is carrying on an extensive and lucrative business A son of the late Charles Ross, Sr, he was born May 2, 1867, in Scotland, where he spent the first three years of his earthly existence

Charles Ross, Sr, was born, bred, educated and married in Scotland Immigrating with his family to the United States in 1870, he located in Des Moines, Iowa, where he followed his trade of a stone setter, for ten years working on the state capitol Moving to Kansas, he became a homesteader and lived there five years Removing then to Omaha, Nebraska, he built the old courthouse, which was his last piece of work, and continued his residence in that city until his death, in 1901 He was first identified with the republican party, but subsequently supported the democratic ticket He was an active member of the Ancient Order of United Workmen, and a devout member of the Presbyterian Church Charles Ross, Sr, and his wife, Eliza Ross, became the parents of seven children, as follows: William, a merchant, lives in Colorado; James H, deceased, Charles, with whom this sketch is chiefly concerned, David, his twin brother, living in Los Angeles, California, is employed as a mechanic in the shipyards, George, deceased, Isabelle,

wife of Jack Durham of Salt Lake City, who is in the passenger service of the Oregon Short Line Railroad, and Robert, agent, in Columbus, Ohio, of the Booth Packing Company.

Acquiring his elementary education in Iowa, Charles Ross subsequently spent five years on the Kansas prairies, going there with the family at the age of twelve years. He afterward learned the trade of a horse collar manufacturer, which he has followed since attaining the age of nineteen years, first establishing a small factory in Omaha. Coming from there to Blair in 1906, Mr Ross continued at his trade, enlarging his operations each year, and in his large and well equipped plant now manufactures collars of all descriptions The business has been incorporated, with a capital of $50,000, and Mr Ross is secretary and manager of the firm In the management of the business Mr. Ross has two wide-awake men on the road, their territory covering the states of Nebraska, Iowa, Kansas and Colorado

Mr Ross married, in 1889, Lizzie Forgan, a native of Scotland, and into their pleasant home four children have been born, namely Ralph, with the Nebraska Power Company, in Omaha, Winfield, an attorney in Omaha, Grace, teaching school in Columbus, and Kenneth, in Omaha, with the Nebraska Power Company All of these children were graduated from the Blair High School, and Ralph was later graduated from the Armour School of Technology in Chicago, Winfield was graduated from the Creighton Law School in Omaha, and the other two children are graduates of the University of Nebraska in Lincoln Mr. Ross is a democrat in politics, and belongs to the Masonic fraternity and to the Woodmen.

LLOYD W PHILLIPS A young man of energy and enterprise, possessing excellent business and executive ability, Lloyd W Phillips is officially connected with one of the most essential of all of the public utilities, being general manager of the Fremont Gas, Electric Light and Power Company A son of the late Matthew Phillips, he was born October 25, 1890, at Table Rock, Pawnee County, Nebraska.

Matthew Phillips was born and reared in Ohio, but as a young man moved to Illinois, where he was variously employed for a number of seasons Moving to Table Rock, Nebraska, in 1875, he bought land and was there engaged in agricultural pursuits until his death. He was a straightforward republican in his political affiliations, a member of the Modern Woodmen of America and belonged to the Presbyterian Church He married, in Illinois, Jessie Weider, who was born in that state, and is now living in Minneapolis, Minnesota Three children blessed their union, as follows: Ross E, who attended the University of Nebraska for two years and was graduated from a business college, has served as secretary and treasurer of the Lincoln Gas and Electric Company for the past thirteen years, Nellie, wife of Charles Butler, who is connected with the White Motor Truck Company in Sioux City, Iowa, and Lloyd W, of this brief sketch

Acquiring his education in Nebraska, Lloyd W Phillips was graduated from the Lincoln High School with the class of 1911, and the following year became bookkeeper for the Lincoln Gas and Electric Light Company Continuing with the same company, he was subsequently transferred to Fremont, and promoted to cashier, a responsible position that he ably filled until April, 1916, when he was made secretary of the organization Three years later, in April, 1919, Mr Phillips was again advanced in position, and has since served ably and faithfully as manager, an office that he is filling with credit to himself, and to the entire satisfaction of all concerned

On May 13, 1916, Mr Phillips was united in marriage with Etta Hairhouse, who was born in Fremont, where her father, Julius T. Hairhouse, a jeweler, was an early settler. Mr and Mrs Phillips have one child, William Lloyd Phillips, born in the autumn of 1919 Mrs Phillips is a consistent member of the Congregational Church Politically Mr Phillips invariably casts his vote with the republican party Fraternally he is a member of the Ancient Free and Accepted Masons, belonging to Lodge and Chapter, and Mount Tabor Commandery No 9, and also to Fremont Lodge No 514, Benevolent and Protective Order of Elks

ANDREW E OLSON Noteworthy among the intelligent and self-reliant men who are ably conducting the agricultural interests of Dodge County is Andrew Olson, who owns and occupies a finely improved farm in Logan Township and in its management is meeting with marked success Coming on both sides of the house of thrifty Swedish ancestry, he was born, December 22, 1872, in Dodge County, where his entire life has been spent

Lars Olson, his father, was born, in 1843, in Sweden, and in 1868 immigrated to the United States, locating first in Omaha, Nebraska, arriving there with but $5 to his name Subsequently taking up a homestead claim in Logan Township, he brought a wagon load of goods across the country to the small shanty in which he was to live, and for many years thereafter was busily engaged in the pioneer task of clearing and improving a farm. Prospering far beyond his first expectations, he wisely invested his accumulations in more land, and at the time of his death, in 1916, had title to a valuable farm of 360 acres, a large part of which was under cultivation In 1871 he married, his wife being also born in Sweden She came to the United States in 1870 and was married in Omaha Mrs Carrie Olson is now sixty-eight years old and still lives on the home farm To Mr and Mrs Olson three children were born, as follows: Andrew E, of this sketch; Mrs Frances Erickson of Dodge County; and Mrs Mary Erickson, also of this county

Brought up on the parental homestead and educated in the rural schools, Andrew E. Olson chose for his life work the free and independent occupation with which he had become familiar while working with his father, and having inherited 120 acres of land in Logan Township immediately began general farming on his own account Industrious and enterprising, Mr Olson succeeded well in his undertakings, his land being now well cultivated and well improved, and amply supplied with farm buildings and farm machinery

Mr Olson married, in 1908, Carrie Hansen, who was born in Sweden, where her father still resides, and they have one child, Lillian Olson, a school girl. Politically Mr Olson is a steadfast supporter of the principles of the republican party, and in 1918 served as moderator of School District No 84 Fraternally he is a member of the Woodmen of the World and takes great interest in the order.

CLARENCE D BRIGGS One of the older residents of Dodge County, Clarence D Briggs devoted the best years of his life to farming, and while he has experienced practically all the vicissitudes that have beset the career of Nebraska agriculturists has persisted through bad years as well as good, and today has all the evidences of independence and the goodly esteem of his fellow men

Mr Briggs, whose complete and modern farmstead is in section 34 of Logan Township, was born in Mills County, Iowa, June 26, 1859 Five years later his father, George Briggs, drove with wagon and team across the country and homesteaded a claim in Dodge County near the Town of Fontanelle The brother of George Briggs, A C Briggs, at that time owned the old Logan mill on Logan Creek, one of the historic industries of pioneer times Though he came to Nebraska with no asset, George Briggs made himself prosperous before he died He passed away at the age of seventy-one, and his wife, Henrietta Briggs, died at the age of sixty-nine

C D. Briggs received his education in Dodge County and at an early age began acquiring property for himself, though he remained at home with his parents to the age of thirty-four At the age of twenty-one he bought eighty acres and he now has 500 acres, all constituting a modern farm with high-class improvements He has never concerned himself with fraternal organizations, but is an active member of the Methodist Church and a republican voter The Briggs family belongs to the pioneer era of Dodge County, since they came before the building of the first railroad and when the trains ran only to Council Bluffs.

September 29, 1897, Mr Briggs married Miss Mary Ruppert, who was born and reared in Dodge County. To their marriage have been born seven children, Hattie, Grace, Fern, Herbert, Earl, Lawrence and Violet.

Mrs Briggs is a daughter of Samuel Ruppert, who was born in Michigan October 3, 1853, and has lived in Dodge County since 1872 His father, Henry Ruppert, came to the county in 1871 but never homesteaded, though he followed farming as well as his trade as carpenter He died at the age of seventy-four and his wife Catherine at seventy-two Samuel Ruppert from the time he came to Nebraska farmed his father's place about four and a half miles northeast of Hooper In 1877 he married Sophie Gaster, who was born in Wisconsin and came to Dodge County when about ten years of age Mr and Mrs Ruppert were the parents of eight children, three of whom died young The others are Mrs Mary Briggs, Levi, Joseph, Mrs Rosie Mortison and Elmer Mr Ruppert has been a carpenter like his father and is still active in the management of his farm of forty acres a mile from Winslow He is a republican voter.

OVE T. ANDERSON, former county clerk of Washington County, has been a leader in politics and public affairs for a number of years, and in his home Town of Blair is now well established in a thriving abstract, real estate and insurance business Mr Anderson has spent the greater part of his life in Nebraska and in all his varied relations has shown those qualities that command respect and esteem

He was born at Cedar Falls, Iowa, February 5, 1873 His parents, James and Sophie (Peterson) Anderson, were both natives of Denmark His mother's family, after coming to America, adopted the name of Goldburg James Anderson came to the United States about 1859 or 1860, settling in Wisconsin In 1861 he volunteered to serve his adopted country in the Union army and was in the Fifteenth Wisconsin Infantry and was a brave and faithful soldier four years, participating in many of the historic battles of the war In 1886 he was married to Sophie Peterson He settled and lived in Iowa several years and about 1876 homesteaded in Webster County, Nebraska He was a resident of that county twenty-one years and while there took a prominent part in republican politics, holding township offices and justice of the peace In 1895 he removed to Washington County, settled on a farm near Blair, and after continuing his vocation as a farmer for eight years he retired and he and his wife now live in a comfortable home in Blair. They are active members of the Lutheran Church Of their eight children three are still living: Goldburg Anderson, a farmer in Washington County, Ove T., and Theodore, a farmer near Blair.

Ove T Anderson was a child when his parents moved to Nebraska and acquired his early education in the country schools of Webster County He also attended Dana College at Blair and the Fremont Normal School His liberal education has fitted him for his varied duties and responsibilities in public and business affairs For a number of years he confined his attention to farming and left the farm to become deputy county clerk of Washington County He filled that office five years and his experience thoroughly qualified him for his duties when he was elected county clerk Mr. Anderson was the capable and efficient county clerk of Washington County nine years, retiring from the courthouse in January, 1919 Since then he has devoted his time to the abstract business at Blair and has a complete record of abstracts enabling him to furnish prompt and reliable service in that line He does an extensive real estate business and also represents a number of the standard insurance companies Mr Anderson was secretary of the local exemption board during war times and gave much of his time to patriotic service

January 31, 1915, he was married to Margaret Nielsen, who came with her parents, Mr and Mrs Julius Nielsen, from Denmark to this country when she was only three months old They settled in Kimball County, Nebraska, where Margaret grew to womanhood Mr and Mrs Anderson have an adopted daughter, Margaret, now three years of age They are members of the Lutheran Church and politically Mr Anderson has always taken a working role in the republican party Besides his business interests at Blair he owns farming lands in Washington County, but these are cultivated by tenants and renters

REV C. A BEYERSDORFER All classes of citizens in the community of Blair have recognized a source of inspiration and substantial factor in improving the moral and civic standards of the locality in the person of Father Beyersdorfer, pastor of the Catholic Church of Blair Father Beyersdorfer is a highly educated young priest, is a constructive leader, and takes a willing interest in everything to promote the welfare of his home town and county

He was born at St Louis, Missouri, November 19, 1893, son of William and Anna (Connelly) Beyersdorfer His father was also born at St Louis and his mother at Bunker Hill, Illinois They were married at St Louis and lived there for many years William Beyersdorfer for a number of years conducted a shoe business and since then has been a traveling salesman for a shoe house He has been quite successful in business He votes independently, and he and his wife are devout Catholics They have two sons, Edward William and C A The former is employed in a St Louis bank

Father Beyersdorfer was educated in Holy Name Parochial School at St Louis, also attended a seminary in that city and the Kenrick Seminary at Webster Grove, Missouri, and on September 15, 1917, was ordained a priest in the Good Shepherd Convent at Omaha, Nebraska Following that he spent a year in post graduate study in the Catholic

University of America at Washington, and on July 6, 1918, was assigned to duty as assistant at St Patrick's Church at Omaha On Thanksgiving Day of the same year he was appointed priest of the Church of St. Francis Borgia at Blair, Nebraska, and has now rounded out two years of faithful and fruitful labors in this community. His parish comprises about fifty Catholic families He has done much to upbuild and strengthen the church and is earnestly working to establish a parochial school Father Beyersdorfer is a member of the Knights of Columbus.

ERNEST HAHN was a lad of fourteen years at the time the family home was established in Dodge County, and that in the passing years he has commended himself effectively to the confidence and good will of the people of the county is indicated in his incumbency of the office of registrar of deeds, as well as by his former tenure of the position of county treasurer Mr Hahn was born in Germany, where he received his preliminary school discipline, which was supplemented by his attending the public schools of Fremont after his parents here established their residence, the family immigration to America having occurred in 1881 and the same year having recorded their arrival in Dodge County Mr Hahn is a son of Ludwig and Martha (Looschen) Hahn, and the father died within a few years after coming to Fremont, where he became a clerk in one of the county offices and where he was serving as deputy county treasurer at the time of his death, in 1889, when fifty-five years of age He was a man of sterling character and superior mentality, was deeply appreciative of the land of his adoption, became aligned in the ranks of the republican party and took much interest in community affairs He was a consistent communicant of the Lutheran Church, as was also his wife, who survived him by nearly a score of years and who passed to the life eternal in December, 1918, her memory being revered by her children and by all others who came within the sphere of her gentle and kindly influence Of the nine children seven are living Carl is engaged in the banking business at Twin Falls, Idaho, Ernest, of this review, was the next in order of birth; Julia is the wife of Harry B Dodge, their home being at Fremont and Mr Dodge being an engineer on the Chicago & Northwestern Railroad; Fred is bookkeeper in the office of a leading business corporation at Fremont, Miss Lena remains at Fremont and is a popular clerk in a local mercantile establishment; Henrietta is the efficient housekeeper for her brother Fred and sister Lena, and Emil is secretary of the Nye, Schneider & Fowler Company, of Fremont

After leaving school Ernest Hahn became a clerk in the offices of the Nye, Schneider & Fowler Company Later he was appointed deputy county treasurer, and after retaining this position five years he was elected county treasurer, an office of which he retained the incumbency four years, with careful and effective administration of the fiscal affairs of the county In 1918 he was elected county register of deeds, and here his administrative ability again comes into play for the benefit of the people of the county. He is a stalwart in the camp of the republican party and has been influential in its councils and campaign activities in Dodge County, especially during his service as chairman of the County Central Committee of the party

The year 1913 recorded the marriage of Mr. Hahn to Miss Effie Haverfield, of North Bend, Dodge County, she being a daughter of Wilson and Hannah (Griffith) Haverfield, the former being a native of Ohio and the latter of Illinois, in which state their marriage was solemnized and whence they came to Dodge County, Nebraska, in the early '70s.

Mr Haverfield is a carpenter by trade and he became one of the leading contractors and builders at North Bend, where he still maintains his home and where occurred the death of his wife Mr and Mrs Hahn have no children

MARION E SHIPLEY Among the foremost men of Dodge County, no one has been more prominent for years past than Marion E Shipley, a former member of the Nebraska State Legislature, a capitalist, newspaper man and captain of industry He comes of English ancestry, the well-known Town of Shipley, England, having been named in honor of the family, the first American representative of which came very early to the Colonies His great-great-grandfather served under Washington in the Revolutionary war

Marion E Shipley was born July 16, 1868, in Knox County, Ohio, a son of Benedict F. and Mary C. (Anderson) Shipley His father was a lumberman and mill man, operating a water-power mill in Ohio and later a steam mill sawing hardwood lumber He disposed of his mill interests in 1879 and came to Nebraska, buying 140 acres of land near Fremont, in 1881 coming to Dodge County, trading his 140 acres for a tract of eighty acres near North Bend, where he engaged in farming Later he moved into North Bend in order to give his children better educational advantages than they could have in the country Still later he went to Wyoming and followed ranching there for some years and finally lived retired at McMinnville, Oregon, until his death August 22, 1920 The mother of Mr Shipley died October 4, 1902, at Green Forest, Arkansas, where both are buried. During President Cleveland's administration Mrs Shipley was appointed postmistress of Manville, Wyoming, but failing health caused her to resign and her husband served in her place Of the five children in the family Marion E is the eldest, the others being as follows· Price M , who is pastor of a Free Methodist Church at Oklahoma City; William B who lives at Lusk Wyoming, is county road engineer of Niobrara County; Lydia Ora, who is the wife of Monroe Dunlap, a farmer near Green Forest, Arkansas, and Guy R who is a farmer and telephone man at McMinnville, Oregon The parents reared their children in the Methodist faith The father was a democrat in politics and a Royal Arch Mason and member of the Sons of the American Revolution

Marion E Shipley accompanied his parents to North Bend, Nebraska, where he completed his school attendance, and then went to work in the printing and publishing office of the North Bend Flail, then conducted by C W Hyatt From there he went to the North Bend Eagle, under Charles Fowler In 1887, in partnership with his father, he bought the Brainard Journal, which he sold three years later and then returned to North Bend and remained until 1894, when he went to work as a printer on the Schuyler Herald, going from there to Cedar County, Iowa, where he bought the Stanwood Herald and conducted it for four years Mr. Shipley desired to return to Dodge County, however so he once more disposed of his newspaper interests and came back to Fremont, worked on the Tribune until 1899, when he came to the Hooper Sentinel, which he purchased in partnership with W G Thompson and conducted two years and then sold to Mr Thompson in order to take up an entirely different line of business

Mr Shipley was one of the organizers of the Hooper Telephone Company, in 1901, of which he has been general manager ever since and is a heavy stockholder This company was incorporated with a capital

M. E. Shipley.

of $50,000, and paid in capital of $37,000, the officers being the following capitalists: W G J. Dau, president, Herman Meyer, vice president, Norman E Shaffer, secretary, and Henry Windhusen, treasurer

Since 1901 Mr. Shipley has devoted the greater part of his time to telephone and electric light business For three and a half years he owned the Hooper Electric Light & Power system, which he sold in 1911, and built the telephone system at Lusk, Wyoming, which he owned and operated until 1914 He has large interests at Rushville, owning the electric light company there, known as the Sherida Electric Service Company, of which his son is in charge; owns the Opera House at Rushville and also a picture playhouse there, having a large amount of capital invested there and in other profitable enterprises, being a now heavy stockholder and a director in the Hooper Electric Light & Power Company of Hooper, Nebraska

On September 15, 1895, Mr. Shipley was united in marriage at North Bend, Nebraska, to Miss Lessie A Thompson, and they have one son, Trajan C, who manages his father's interests at Rushville. Mrs Shipley is a lady very highly esteemed at Hooper and is a member of the Christian Church. Mr. Shipley is a thirty-second degree Mason and is affiliated with the Knights of Pythias, Odd Fellows and the Knights of the Maccabees, Modern Woodmen of America, and by virtue of his long and honorable American ancestry is a member of the Sons of the American Revolution

From early manhood he has been interested in politics and in political affiliations followed in his father's footsteps In 1913 he was elected on the democratic ticket a member of the State Legislature from Dodge County, and throughout the Thirty-third Session proved himself a worthy and useful member of that body, punctual and attentive as to his duties and watchful over the best interests of his constituents

Naturally his position in the community made him a leader in local patriotic activities at the time of the World war He did not wait to be asked but pressed forward with all the influence at his command to build up the local organizations for raising funds and prosecuting other war matters He was commissioned chairman of the Four Minute Men, an organization at Hooper that made a splendid record He was also commissioned by the Governor Captain of the Home Guards and the Home Defense Guards, and employed his knowledge of military tactics to good advantage in drilling the company and maintaining its enthusiasm as long as the services were required

HERMAN MEYER. The Township of Logan, Dodge County, has no more thoroughgoing, systematic and diligent agriculturist than Herman Meyer, who has resided on his present farm, on Hooper Rural Route No 1, since 1889. Mr. Meyer was born in Germany, December 20, 1855, a son of John G and Meta Meyer

John G. Meyer was employed in his native land in work in caring for the government forest, at a wage of 25 cents per day, out of which he was expected to pay his own board. He had no prospects of bettering himself, and finally decided to come to the United States to seek his fortune In 1868, accordingly, he immigrated to this country with his father, John Herman Meyer, the little party arriving in Dodge County April 11th They homesteaded in section 26 Cuming Township, and the last of the little capital possessed by John G Meyer went for the purchase of a cow After many years of industrious labor, Mr Meyer accumulated a property approximating 1,188 acres, which went to his sons at the time of his death, when he was seventy-five years of age His widow survived him to the age of eighty-three years They were the parents of two sons Christoph and Herman.

Herman Meyer attended the public schools of Germany, and after coming to the United States gained some further education in the public schools of Dodge County He was brought up as a farmer's son, and has passed his entire career in agricultural pursuits, in which he has achieved an unqualified success. In 1889 he moved to his present property, in Logan Township, where he has the best of improvements and the most up-to-date equipment In addition to general farming, he is largely interested in hog raising and shipping, and this forms a large part of his work He has holdings in the Farmers State Bank of Uehling and the Farmers Co-operative Association of Uehling and Hooper As a citizen he has faithfully discharged all duties devolving upon him, and has served as township treasurer four years and as a member for many years of the school boards of districts Nos 16 and 18 He is a non-partisan voter, and he and Mrs Meyer belong to the Lutheran Church

Mr. Meyer was first married to Miss Elise Brockshus who was born and reared in Germany, and they became the parents of two children. George, who is engaged in farming near Wisner, Cuming County, and Mrs Martha Wobken whose husband is a farmer near Scribner, Dodge County Mr Meyer's first wife died, and in April, 1897 he was united in marriage with Miss Sophie Wobken and they are the parents of ten children Herbert, Christoph, Leona, Alma, Alice, Lawrence, Herman, Myra, Gerald and Laura The Meyer home is a pleasant and hospitable one and is always open to the many friends of Mr and Mrs Meyer

HENRY H LUENINGHOENER Until he recently retired Henry H Lueninghoener, a prosperous farmer of Dodge County, was actively engaged in the prosecution of his calling and has been very successful in his operations, having made improvements of practical value on his estate, which is one of the most attractive and productive of any in Hooper Township. A son of the late Peter Lueninghoener, he was born May 30, 1860, in Quincy, Illinois.

Born and brought up in Germany, Peter Lueninghoener, impressed by the wonderful stories he had heard of the glorious opportunities afforded the poor man in America, immigrated to the United States at the age of eighteen years, and soon secured work as a farm laborer. He lived in Illinois until 1868, when, with his wife and children, he came to Nebraska, bringing with him the $800 he had accumulated by hard work He came up the river as far as Omaha in a steamboat, and thence made his way to Dodge County where he bought a tract of wild land. As his means increased, he bought other tracts becoming owner of 800 acres of farming land ere his death, which occurred when about seventy-eight His wife, Anna Monke, was born in Germany, and as a lass of eighteen years came with her parents to this country Nine children were born to their marriage, three sons and six daughters a family of which they could well be proud.

Eight years old when he came with his parents to Washington County, Nebraska, Henry H Lueninghoener well remembers the desolate aspect of the country roundabout, and the arduous toil required of the courageous pioneer ranchmen Familiar with argicultural work from his youthful days, Mr Lueninghoener succeeded to the occupation in which he was reared, and at the age of twenty-three years bought the farm which he now owns and in its management met with unquestioned success, it now being one of the best in regard to its improvements and appointments of any in the neighborhood He recently turned over the management of the farm to his son, Irvin, and retired to Fremont to live.

Mr Lueninghoener married, in 1884, Helen Eisely, who was born in Omaha, where her father, Carl Eisely, was an early settler, while her mother was said to have been the first white woman to settle west of Fontanelle, Dodge County, Nebraska Three children blessed their union, namely Alma Marks, of Winslow, Irvin, operating the home farm, and Gilbert, living at home Mr and Mrs Lueninghoener are valued members of the Evangelical Church Politically an independent voter, Mr Lueninghoener has served as a member of the local school board for ten years

Fred Wolf. Occupying a position of note among the active and progressive farmers of Dodge County, Fred Wolf, of Hooper Township, shows decided ability and skill in the management of his agricultural interests, his farm being well improved, and furnished with good farm buildings, and plenty of machinery of the latest approved kinds, to successfully carry on his chosen work. A son of Frederick and Dora (Fullham) Wolf, he was born May 9 1865, in Dodge County, this state

Frederick Wolf, Sr, his father, was born, reared and educated in Germany Desirous of establishing a home in the land of bright promise, he immigrated to the United States, settling first in Wisconsin Hearing good reports regarding Nebraska, he started westward with his family, making the journey thither, according to the custom of that day, with ox teams, taking all of their household effects, and driving two cows Buying land at $11 an acre he improved a good farm, on which he and his wife resided the remainder of their lives, his death occuring at the age of seventy-two years, and hers at the age of seventy-three years Both, true to the religious faith in which they were reared, were devout members of the Emmanuel Lutheran Church

Brought up in Dodge County, Fred Wolf obtained a practical knowledge of books in the district schools, and on the home farm was well drilled in the various branches of agriculture Becoming a farmer from his inherited home farm where he was born, he bought land on section 7, Hooper Township, and immediately began its cultivation Laboring diligently and intelligently, Mr Wolf has been exceedingly prosperous in his undertakings, the rich and fertile soil, responding to his care, yielding abundant harvests each year, and well repaying him for his days of toil In addition to carrying on mixed husbandry successfully, he pays considerable attention to the raising of stock, which he finds quite profitable He has also other interests of value, being a stockholder in the Hooper Tile Company, and one of its organizers and directors since its organization also of the Winslow State Bank, and the Hooper Mill

In 1890 Mr Wolf was united in marriage to Emma Rabe, a native of Illinois, and into their home six children have been born, namely. Ida, wife of H. P Bartling, a Washington County farmer, Henry F, engaged in agricultural pursuits in Dodge County, Frederick H ; Louis E, George; and Elma Mr Wolf is independent in politics, being bound by no party restrictions, and though not at all active in public affairs served for twenty-seven years as school moderator in district No 14 He is a valued member of the Emmanuel Lutheran Church, of which he is a deacon, and to which Mrs Wolf also belongs.

HENRY G KENDRICK For many years engaged in the meat and live stock business in Fremont, the late Henry G Kendrick was a typical representative of those eminently able and intelligent men of Dodge County who brought to their respective callings good business methods and wise judgment, and whose labors were crowned with success He was born February 6, 1861, in Pecatonica, Illinois, of honored New England ancestry, his parents having lived for many years in Boston His paternal ancestors originated in England and Wales, while his mother's people emigrated from Ireland to the United States, settling in Boston

Educated in Illinois, Henry G Kendrick remained in his native state until after his marriage Adventurous and enterprising, he came with his young wife to Nebraska, and having decided that the opportunities for improving his financial condition were as good in Fremont as could anywhere be found, he established himself in the meat business, an industry that proved profitable, his specialty having been the buying and selling of live stock Successful in his operations, he bought land and raised and fed stock, which he shipped to Omaha and Chicago, building up a very extensive and lucrative trade He accumulated a fine property, and at his death, on June 2, 1919, left a valuable estate, including among other property a large farm in Saunders County He was independent in his political relations, and was never an aspirant for official honors, his time having been devoted to his business interests

Mr Kendrick married, in Illinois, Elizabeth Kenney, who was born in Stephenson County, that state, and is now living a quiet life in Fremont, where she has large property interests Three children were born of the union of Mr. and Mrs Kendrick, namely Verne, living with his mother travels for the Cluette Peabody Company; Pauline employed in an attorney's office in the courthouse, and William, engaged in the rendering business at Fremont. Mrs Kendrick is a member of the Catholic Church, to which her husband also belonged

CHARLES J MARR, president of the Marr-Hein Candy Company, a well-established and prosperous manufacturing concern of Fremont, is fully entitled to designation as one of the prominent and progressive business men of the younger generation in his native city and is a member of a representative family of Dodge County, as may be seen by reference to the sketch of the career of his father, Charles D Marr, on other pages of this volume

Charles J Marr was born at Fremont on September 15, 1883, and his early education was here acquired in the excellent public schools, besides which he pursued higher studies in the Nebraska State Normal School of this city After leaving school he was for three years bookkeeper in the office of the Fremont Foundry & Machine Company, of which his father is president, and he then purchased the bottling works of H. J. Archer, an enterprise which he still continues, under the title of the Fremont Bottling Works In 1919 he became one of the organizers and incorporators of the Marr-Hein Candy Company, the majority of the capital stock being held by Mr Hein and Mr Marr, and, with a well-equipped establishment with the best modern facilities, this company now manufactures high-grade candies, with an output of about four tons daily and with a trade that extends throughout Nebraska, as well as into Wyoming and South Dakota The business is constantly expanding in scope and constitutes one of the important industrial enterprises of Fremont In addition to being president of this company Mr. Marr is also president of the Fremont Bottling Works, which likewise controls a sub-

F. S. Pratt

stantial business He is a republican in politics, is affiliated with the local Blue Lodge, Chapter and Commandery of the Masonic Fraternity, and also with the Benevolent and Protective Order of Elks and the Fraternal Order of Eagles. Mrs Marr is an active member of the Christian Science Church

November 24, 1904, recorded the marriage of Mr Marr to Miss Lillie Larson, who likewise claims Fremont as the place of nativity, her father, L P Larson, being one of the venerable pioneer citizens of this city, where he is now living retired, after a specially successful career as a prominent business man of the city Mr and Mrs Marr have two children Helen Althea, and Peter.

FRED E PRATT There are few residents of Dodge County who have turned business opportunities to better account in a comparatively short time, than Fred E Pratt, president of the Golden Rod Creamery Company of Fremont, and one of the most extensive hog raisers in this section of the state He began with very small capital, and to close attention to business, excellent judgment and native thrift may be attributed the conspicuous success that has attended his various undertakings in Nebraska.

Fred E Pratt was born at Woodstock, in Windsor County, Vermont, June 20, 1863 His parents were Carlos A and Delphine (Rickard) Pratt, and his grandfathers were Laverne Pratt and Dr Benjamin Rickard, both of whom were lifelong residents of Vermont The father of Mr Pratt died on his Vermont farm in 1865, when but thirty-eight years old, but his mother survived to be sixty-eight years of age and passed away in 1897 Of the family of four children but two survive, Fred E and a daughter, Lilla D, who is the widow of F. H Vaughn, who died at Cheyenne, Wyoming, in the fall of 1919.

Mr Pratt obtained his education in the public schools of Windsor County and grew up on the home farm and continued interested in his native state in farming and dairying until 1897, when he came to Fremont After working in a creamery plant for a short time he determined to go into the business on his own account and matured plans that enabled him to start the Golden Rod Creamery Company, in 1901, in rather small quarters and with a small force of helpers The business prospered from the first as Mr Pratt was experienced in this line, and soon enlarged quarters had to be secured and so much expansion has taken place that Mr. Pratt now has seventy-eight men on his pay roll He carried it on as a private enterprise until 1919, when the business was incorporated with capital of $300,000, with $250,000 paid in In the meanwhile he has invested in land in Dodge County and gone into the business of raising hogs on a large scale, keeping exclusively to thoroughbred Red Durocs, and averaging 1,500 head annually He owns the large building on the corner of Broad and Military avenues, Fremont, which he erected in 1904, devoting it entirely to business purposes

In 1899 Mr Pratt was united in marriage to Miss Isetta D Doty, who was born at Mansfield, Massachusetts, and they have one daughter, Lura Madaline, who graduated from the Fremont High School in June, 1919, and expects to continue her education in the Northwestern University, Chicago. Mr Pratt and his family are members of the Congregational Church. Although never unduly active in the political field and never willing to accept a public office, Mr Pratt has continuously supported the candidates of the republican party He belongs to the Elks and the Highlanders The family spent a recent winter in California, making the journey in their high-powered, luxurious automobile

John Weigle has impressed himself upon the people of Hooper Township as a man of worth and stability, one whose experience, enterprise and enlightened views will add to the community's prestige and whose agricultural abilities will serve to assist materially in an elevation of standards Mr Weigle was born in Illinois March 7, 1857, a son of George Weigle, who was born in Germany George Weigle, upon his arrival in the United States in 1852 or 1853, spent two years in New York State and a like period in Illinois, and then came to Nebraska, where he took up a homestead He became a successful man and died, highly respected, at the age of seventy-two years His wife, Christine Kramer, is also deceased, having died when about seventy-eight years of age

John Weigle was educated in the public schools and began his independent career at the age of twenty-six years, when he began renting property from his father At the time of the elder man's death, he secured his first land, an inheritance of 160 acres, and so ably have his affairs been managed that at the present time he is the owner of 380 acres, all in a good state of cultivation, and devoted to general farming and the raising of live stock Mr Weigle came to Dodge County when about two years of age and has made a place for himself among the substantial and reliable men of Hooper Township, where his property is located on section 11 He has excellent improvements and substantial buildings and keeps fully abreast of all the progressive movements made in his vocation Mr Weigle is a popular member of the local lodge of the Sons of Hermann He is an independent voter, and he and Mrs Weigle are consistent members of the Lutheran Church

In 1883 Mr Weigle married Augusta Dickman, who was born in Germany November 4, 1866, and came to the United States when six months old with her parents Mr and Mrs Weigle are the parents of seven children Fredericka, Augusta, Amelia, Albert, Carrie, Minnie and Emma Another child, Ella, died in infancy

Jacob Sanders There are some very capable business men at Hooper, who are handling the local trade so successfully that outside custom is attracted to the city, with the result that this has come to be recognized as one of the centers of distribution for a wide territory One of these men is Jacob Sanders, one of the leading grocers of Dodge County

Jacob Sanders was born in Pennsylvania in 1859, a son of Emanuel and Barbara (Capp) Sanders, also born in Pennsylvania, where they passed their lives and died, he when sixty-eight years of age By trade he was a millwright, and he was at one time also engaged in farming The children born to him and his wife were as follows William, who is surveyor of Dodge County, lives at Fremont, Jacob, whose name heads this review, and John, who is connected with the grain and elevator business at Hooper

Growing up in his native state, Jacob Sanders there attended the public schools and attained a working knowledge of the fundamentals of an education In 1876 he came West to Nebraska, and for six years worked for P S Ryan on his farm near Fremont, and then, renting land, was engaged in farming for six years Having saved up some money by that time, he was able to purchase a farm of his own one-half mile south of Hooper, and for the succeeding twelve years was engaged in general farming and stock raising In 1900 he moved to Hooper and buying the stock of Hecker & Son, grocers, has since been engaged in the grocery business with very gratifying results

In 1882 Mr. Sanders was united in marriage with Linda Hartung, born at Watertown, Wisconsin, a daughter of William Hartung, an early settler of Dodge County Mr and Mrs Sanders have two children, namely William E, who is manager of the Hooper Theater and the Hooper Bottling Works, was in the service during the late war, being trained at the officers' training camp at Camp Taylor, and Cora, who is the wife of Fred Duty, a jeweler of Scribner, Nebraska Mr Sanders is a republican and was mayor of Hooper for fifteen years and was on the school board for six years Both he and Mrs Sanders belong to Grace Lutheran Church He maintains fraternal relations with the Knights of Pythias An enterprising business man, Mr Sanders deserves his present prosperity and the confidence he inspires has been earned by his probity and the interest he has always taken in civic matters, both as an official and private citizen

WILLIAM MIDDAUGH Owning and occupying a well-managed and highly productive farm in Platte Township William Middaugh is familiarly known throughout this section of Dodge County as a prosperous and progressive agriculturist whose labors have been crowned with success A son of the late J C Middaugh he was born July 11, 1872, in Mercer County, Illinois, but the major portion of his life has been spent in Dodge County

In 1873 J C Middaugh came with his family from Illinois to Nebraska, and settled on the broad prairies of Dodge County, being one of the earlier pioneers of the place The neighbors were few and far between, the range was free, there being nothing fenced; and land sold anywhere from $3 to $5 an acre Indians were numerous, and deer, which furnished much of the food of the early comers, and other wild beasts roamed at will through the country Buying a partly improved farm, he was engaged in agricultural pursuits until his death, at the age of seventy-six, in his undertakings being quite successful, though in the early stages crops were destroyed by grasshoppers for three years and by drought, etc Mr Middaugh, a prominent member of the Seventh Day Advent Church, took great interest in that organization His wife, whose maiden name was Nancy Braucht, survived him, and now lives with her only daughter

Growing to manhood on the parental homestead, William Middaugh assisted in the almost herculean labor of improving a good farm, and as a boy, youth, and young man, endured the hardships and privations incidental to life in a new country Laboring with unceasing toil, he has performed no inconsiderable part in helping to develop the resources of this section of the state, and since becoming a farmer on his own account has undergone many hardships Persevering and energetic, Mr Middaugh has courageously followed his chosen occupation, and now has a farm of 380 acres, on which he has placed improvements of value, rendering it one of the most desirable estates in the vicinity In addition to general farming, Mr Middaugh raises cattle, of no particular breed, however, and has built up an extensive and profitable business as a buyer and seller of stock, his dealings being quite remunerative

Mr. Middaugh married, in 1899, at Fremont, Nebraska, Louise Boyd, who was born and educated in Champaign County, Illinois, a daughter of William Boyd, who came from Scotland to Illinois with his parents when but five years of age, and early in life settled in Nebraska Mr and Mrs Middaugh have one child, David Middaugh Politically Mr. Middaugh is identified with the republican party in local affairs, but in county and state affairs is independent, casting his vote for the men and measures that he deems best True to the religion in which he was reared, he is a Seventh Day Adventist

J W DELANEY A worthy representative of the energetic, enterprising and progressive men who are so ably conducting the agricultural interests of Dodge County, J. W. Delaney, through his own efforts and wise management, improved one of the more valuable and attractive farming estates of Elkhorn Township He was born, January 26, 1865, in Davenport, Iowa, a son of John and Julia Delaney

John Delaney spent the first fourteen years of his life in Ireland Immigrating then to the United States, he lived in Pennsylvania about fifteen years, being employed in the steel works Moving from there to Davenport, Iowa, he bought land in that vicinity, and there engaged in farming eight years About fifty-three years ago, soon after the close of the Civil war, he came with his family to Nebraska, and having taken up a homestead claim of eighty acres in Elkhorn Township, Dodge County, redeemed a farm from its original wildness, and was subsequently engaged in mixed husbandry until his death, at the age of seventy-six years His wife, who was born in Ireland, and came to the United States as a girl of fifteen summers, died when but thirty-nine years old. They were married in Philadelphia, and became the parents of nine children, three boys and six girls, and of these four of the girls have passed to the life beyond

Brought up on the parental homestead, J W Delaney was educated in the rural schools of Dodge County, and in his tender years began to assist his father in the pioneer task of clearing and improving a homestead. He was an ambitious youth, full of push and vim, and having determined when young to pursue the independent occupation of a tiller of the soil, he began his agricultural operations on rented land At the end of six years, having been successful in his labors, Mr Delaney purchased 237 acres of land near Fremont, Nebraska, and managed it for a while He afterwards sold it at an advantage, and bought his present place of 160 acres, on which he has made all of the improvements, having erected his pleasant residence, and substantial barns and outbuildings, in addition having placed his land largely under tillage, rendering it exceedingly productive Although Mr Delaney had a hard time at first to make both ends meet, he labored steadily, conquering all difficulties that obstructed his pathway, and now stands in the front ranks of the prosperous and progressive agriculturists of his community

Mr Delaney married, at Fremont, Nebraska, in 1901, Jessie Charleston, who was born and educated in Illinois, and died on the home farm, April 4, 1919 Three children were born of their union, namely Marguerite, who lived but six years, a child that died at birth, and John Joseph An active and influential member of the democratic party, Mr Delaney has faithfully served in many important offices, having been a member of the town board six years a road overseer several terms; and justice of the peace six years Fraternally he belongs to Eagle Lodge He is not a member of any religious organization, but Mrs Delaney was a worthy member of the Christian Church

H GUS GUMPERT The true measure of individual success is determined by what one has accomplished, and, as taken in contradistinction to the old adage that a man is not without honor save in his own country, there is a particular interest attached to the career of H Gus Gumpert,

Dan V. Stephens

since he is a native son of Dodge County, where practically his entire life has been passed, and he has so directed his ability and efforts as to gain recognition as one of the representative citizens of the community, being a worthy scion of one of our worthy pioneer families.

H Gus Gumpert, one of the leading merchants of Fremont, was born in this city in 1872, and is a son of H F and Gretchen Gumpert, both of whom were natives of Germany Their marriage occurred in Fremont in 1871 and here Mr Gumpert established a barber shop, which he conducted during the greater part of his active business life, his shop being the first of the kind in Fremont Subsequently he engaged in the shoe business here for a number of years, but is now retired and living in Long Beach, California. He was a successful, self-made man and enjoyed the respect of all who knew him Of the three children born to him and his wife, H Gus is the only survivor They were members of the German Lutheran Church and in politics Mr Gumpert is a supporter of the democratic party.

H. Gus Gumpert received his educational training in the public schools, graduating from the Fremont High School His first employment was with Nye, Schneider & Company, with whom he remained for five years He then engaged in the mercantile business in partnership with his brother and father, some time later buying the interest of his brother in the business The father retained his interest in the shoe business until 1914, when he sold that to his son, who has since been sole owner of the business Thus H Gus Gumpert has been continuously engaged in the mercantile business here since 1898 and has been a witness of and a participant in the splendid growth which has characterized this section during the intervening years At one time he gave serious attention to the study of law under the direction of Judge Munger, and, though he did not follow that profession, his studies were of advantage to him in his future business career He now owns one of the largest and most complete department stores in this section of the state and enjoys a large and constantly growing trade In 1915 he built a large business block, three stories high and a half block in extent, at the corner of Main Street and Fifth Avenue, and here he has a well-stocked store, carrying a large line of goods in each department Courteous treatment, prompt service and right prices have been the elements which have entered into his success and he enjoys distinctive prestige among his fellow merchants

In 1898 Mr Gumpert was married to Dot Glenn, who was born in Glencoe, Nebraska, the daughter of James Glenn, a merchant and the postmaster at Glencoe, which town was named in his honor To Mr and Mrs Gumpert has been born a daughter, Zoe, who graduated from the Fremont High School in 1917 and remains at home Mrs Gumpert and daughter Zoe are members of the Methodist Episcopal Church Mr Gumpert devotes himself to his business and has achieved a distinctive success He is progressive and up-to-date in his ideas and stands always for the best things in the community life Because of his success and high personal character he enjoys the respect of all who know him

DAN VORHEES STEPHENS was named for Senator Dan Vorhees of Indiana and from this incident one naturally concludes he must have been born a democrat, and in the heyday of Vorhees' career He was born November 4, 1868, among the sycamores on Salt Creek, Indiana, instead of on the Wabash, as was the great statesman for whom he was named

He was reared a Baptist in religion and a democrat in politics He received his early education in the common schools and at Valparaiso College He came to Fremont, Dodge County, Nebraska, in 1887, and taught school for two and a half years and served four years as county superintendent of schools He organized the publishing house of Hammond & Stephens Company in 1894 and began manufacturing and publishing for county and city superintendents of schools He is president of the company and principal owner of the business which now extends over many states

In 1904 he was elected a delegate to the national democratic convention at St Louis In 1908 he was elected delegate at large and chairman of the delegation to the democratic national convention at Denver when Bryan was nominated for president

In 1911 he was elected to Congress from the third congressional district to fill a vacancy caused by the death of Congressman J P Latta He was re-elected in 1912, 1914 and 1916, serving until March, 1919, throughout the dramatic period of the World war He took an active part in the drafting and passage of all the constructive legislation that made the winning of the war possible, such as the federal reserve act, the draft law, the farm loan act, etc He supported the administration of President Wilson from the beginning to the end of the war without exception

In 1920 he was again chosen delegate at large to the national democratic convention which met in San Francisco

Mr Stephens throughout his public service remained essentially a business man, maintaining all his business interests in Nebraska At the conclusion of his term in Congress he organized the Fremont Joint Stock Land Bank under the farm loan act of 1916 with a capital of $300,000 Later he purchased control of the Fremont State Bank and consolidated the management of the Land Bank, State Bank and the Nebraska Building and Loan Association under one head with himself as president of the allied banks Mr. Stephens has been active in promoting the public welfare as well as being a success in attending to his own business

In 1890 Mr Stephens was married to Hannah Boe, daughter of Knute Boe, an old resident of Dodge County Mr and Mrs Stephens had two children, namely: Edith, now deceased, and Estella, who is married to Benjamin Harrison of Omaha

HARLAND L WOLCOTT This family name is practically synonymous with good farming, good citizenship and individual prosperity in Dodge County, where it has been represented since earliest pioneer times For a long period of years the Wolcotts have been farmers in Hooper Township, where H L Wolcott owns one of the best improved places in that locality in section 25

Harland L Wolcott was born in Ohio August 17, 1864, and was about two years of age when he came to Dodge County His father, G W. Wolcott, had first located in Dodge County in the year 1856, when the organization of Nebraska Territory was still being discussed and when there was a mere fringe of settlement along the western bank of the Missouri River G W Wolcott was a native of Ohio and drove to Nebraska with a team He squatted near Fremont, the land subsequently becoming known as Knoell's place He remained there keeping bachelor's quarters for a year in a sod house Leaving Nebraska, he went to the northwest, to Washington, riding horseback all the way

After returning east he married Betsey Jane Baker and in 1866 again came to Nebraska and homesteaded 160 acres near Winslow. Here he went through the grasshopper scourge, many successive droughts, experiencing scarcity of money and low markets for everything the land could raise, but before his death which occurred in 1907 he was rewarded by independent circumstances and was the owner of 480 acres His widow is still living, making her home with her only son and child, Harland L Wolcott

Harland L Wolcott grew up on his father's farm, made good use of such advantages as the district schools afforded, became an able assistant to his father and for many years has carried on the homestead In fact, he has been doing for himself for a quarter of a century and with the resources of 480 acres at his command has been able to carry on general farming and stock raising on a somewhat extensive scale

He has also shared the public spirit of his father in community relationships, particularly in behalf of good schools His father became treasurer of the local School Board when it was first organized, and Harland L succeeded him in that office and has continued to serve for thirteen years In politics his vote is cast as a stanch republican

In 1896 Mr Wolcott married Eunice Bullock Their three children, all at home, are Grace, Harland and George

William Henneman One of the farms longest occupied in Hooper Township of Dodge County is that of William Henneman, who was born there and whose father acquired this tract as a homestead in the very early period of settlement For over half a century the Hennemans have cultivated crops in section 7 of Hooper Township, and in every sense of the word they have been substantial citizens, good neighbors and upholders of the best community spirit

William Henneman was born February 15, 1882 His father, Christie Henneman, was born in Germany and came to this country in 1858. Possessing little capital, he had the courage and resourcefulness to strive to make a home in a new country, and pre-empted land in Dodge County and in spite of many struggles and adversities lived to see his efforts well rewarded He died at the age of eighty years. Of his two sons and five daughters William is the youngest

William Henneman acquired a good education in the local schools and as a youth acquired a thorough training as a farmer, a training that has stood him in good stead In 1907 he rented land from his father and he now owns 200 acres, including the old homestead The father left the farm well improved, and the son has done much to increase its productiveness and general value

In 1911 Mr Henneman married Lulu Panning, who was born in Dodge County, daughter of Fred Panning, one of the early settlers They have one child, Lavier Mr Henneman is an independent voter and is a member of the Lutheran Church.

Ernest Schmidt With a large farm stocked with cattle, sheep and hogs, with all needed equipment, Ernest Schmidt is an adequate picture of a complete and successful Nebraska farmer, and is one of the men relied upon to fill up the quota of agricultural production in Dodge and Washington counties

Mr Schmidt whose fine farm is in section 31 of Elkhorn Township, was born in Dodge County June 24, 1880 Many old friends recall his father, Ernest Schmidt, Sr., one of the pioneers of Nebraska, who for several years as a soldier in the regular army participated in the thrilling campaigns for the redemption of the great west

Ernest Schmidt, Sr., came to the United States from Germany in 1849, being one of those lovers of freedom who were expelled from their native land about that time He landed at New Orleans and in 1853 joined the regular United States army He was in service five years, and was on duty at many points in the great west He was at Salt Lake City at the time of the great Mormon uprising When he left the army he started for Colorado with a pony and cart, and for a time had the experiences of some of the famous mining camps of the state From Colorado he came to Nebraska and for several years was engaged in the overland transportation business, operating ox teams from eastern Nebraska to Denver He made four trips of this kind to Denver and he also freighted goods to Grand Island and Fort Kearney As a pioneer of Dodge County, he bought 160 acres about 1862, and spent the rest of his life in the quiet and industrious pursuit of agriculture He left his farm well improved and had lived in comfort for many years before his death at the age of eighty-five In Dodge County he married Augusta Miller, member of another family of early settlers in this country, who died the same year her husband did at the age of sixty-nine They were members of the Evangelical Lutheran Church

Ernest Schmidt, Jr, was the only son in a family of seven children He grew up on his father's farm of 240 acres, acquired an education in the common schools, and for the past twenty years has been devoting all his time and energies to general farming and the feeding of cattle, hogs and sheep He now has 240 acres, all well improved, and with a complete equipment of barns, while much of the land is tiled

In 1908 Mr Schmidt married Anna Baltz Their three children, all at home, are Erna, Ernest R. and Alberta May Mr Schmidt is an independent voter in politics, and is a member of the Presbyterian faith

GUSTAVUS S STIVER In proportion to its population Dodge County has as great a number of substantial and intelligent agriculturists as any county of its size in Nebraska, and among this number is Gustavus S Stiver, the owner of a farm of finely cultivated land, which, until within a year or two ago, he operated with such judgment as to have made him, financially, a successful and substantial man

Mr Stiver was born in Pennsylvania in 1856, a son of John and Salome Stiver, natives of the Keystone State, who passed their lives there on property of their own, devoting their careers to agricultural work, and being people who were highly esteemed and respected in their community Mrs Stiver was a member of the Lutheran Church, while her husband belonged to the Reformed faith. He was a republican in his political affiliation, and served creditably at various times as member of the Board of School Directors of his township and as overseer of roads Of their children, two are living, Henry, who is carrying on operations on his brother's farm, and Gustavus S.

Gustavus S Stiver resided in Pennsylvania until after he had passed his majority, at which time he turned his face to the West and first started farming in Kansas He remained in that state until 1889, when he came to Nebraska and secured land in section 36, Everett Township, which he developed into a highly productive property, and upon which he made many improvements He continued to be engaged in general farming and stock raising until several years ago, when he retired from active pursuits and rented his land to his brother He still owns the

John W. Haun

land and buildings, as well as valuable farming machinery Mr. Stiver farmed his property with excellent discretion, following methods that were at once practicable and progressive, and this, combined with unfailing industry, won him marked success He is a member of the Reformed Church In politics he is independent, voting invariably for the man in his opinion best qualified for the position While his education was limited to the public schools of his native state, he has been a great reader and close observer of men and things, is well posted on current matters and is excellent company, genial and sociable At one time he served very capably in the office of treasurer of Everett Township

Henry L Gaines came to Dodge and Washington counties nearly forty years ago, but his longest experience as a Nebraska farmer and rancher was in Cheyenne County More recently he has acquired and now lives on a fine farm in section 11 of Arlington Township

Mr Gaines was born near Springfield, Illinois, August 5, 1844 His father, A. C. Gaines, was a native of Kentucky and also came out to Nebraska, where he died at the age of seventy-eight His first wife was Mary Sackert, who was the mother of eight children For his second wife he married Miss Mills Besides Henry L the children of the first marriage were: Thomas R of Kennard, Nebraska, Eliza, a widow, living at Kennard; Robert of Omaha; Mrs Emma Byers of Boyd County, Nebraska; and William, John and Alfred, now deceased William was a pioneer settler of Washington County The two children of the second marriage are L C Gaines of Arlington and Oscar Gaines of Fremont

Henry L Gaines on leaving Illinois in 1881 located near Elk City in Douglas County, Nebraska, renting land there four years In Illinois he married Miss A Archer, and they came out to Nebraska by train. After leaving Douglas County Mr. Gaines went to Cheyenne County and bought a section and a half of land, on which he prosecuted his diversified farming and ranching interests until 1910, when he sold and bought a well improved place of 240 acres in Washington County.

Mr Gaines is the father of eight children Hattie Blanchard of Herman, Nebraska, Harry C of Dodge County; Edwin C of Washington County, Mrs Emma Christensen of Washington County, Newton of Fremont, Henry L, Jr, of Omaha, Carl A, and Lottie, at home

John Haun Dodge County was just within the pale of civilization when the late John Haun cast his fortunes in the locality Death came to him at the end of fifty years of residence, and his name is justly recorded in this history not only for length of residence but for the energy with which he provided for himself and family and the good influence he exercised as a citizen and a successful business man, and is also remembered as one of the former sheriffs of the county

He was born in Germany in 1837, and had gained a common school education in his native land before he came to America He was about fourteen when his parents came to this country and established their home in Michigan From Michigan John Haun went to Wisconsin, was married in that state, and in 1868 reached Dodge County, Nebraska As a youth he had learned the trade of carpenter, was a very skilled workman and at Fremont, his first place of residence, helped put up some of the pioneer houses He also homesteaded, and that homestead, now owned by his son John W, is a highly valuable property, showing the results of half a century of capable management and care from the time John

Haun secured the land from the Government He developed one of the productive farms of the county before retiring, and then for several years lived at the Village of Scribner After the death of his wife he returned to the homestead farm and lived with his son John W until his death, which occurred July 10, 1920

He espoused the cause of the democratic party in politics and his influence added a great deal of strength to the party in the county He was always regarded as one of the most capable sheriffs the county ever had, and whether as a farmer, homemaker or citizen he enjoyed a secure place in popular confidence and esteem Both he and his wife were devout Catholics

John Haun married Theresa Ambruster, who was a native of Wisconsin, and died in 1915 The brief facts concerning their children are as follows Joseph, a resident of the State of California, Frank, living retired at Fremont; Amelia, wife of John Ries of Scotia, Greeley County, Kate, wife of August Stoetzer of Scribner, Mary, wife of Henry Eidam, a Dodge County farmer, Elizabeth, widow of Louis Steil, and now living at the home of her brother John W, who is next in order of birth; and Henry A, concerning whom special mention is made elsewhere in this volume

JOHN W HAUN has always regarded it as an honor to claim Dodge County as his place of birth and the scene of his activities as a successful farmer and stock grower He is a son of the late John Haun, whose career as a pioneer of the county is described above

John W Haun was born in Cotterell Township April 6, 1880 In that township in section 2 and about ten miles from the City of North Bend, he lives today enjoying the ownership of a well improved farm of 280 acres, which includes the old homestead his father took up from the Government half a century ago

Mr Haun was reared on this farm of his father, and is indebted to the public schools of Dodge County for his early educational discipline He has been independently engaged in farm enterprises since the age of twenty-two, and his substantial success has been the direct result of his own industry and well ordered activities He is an independent voter in connection with local political affairs, and some of the interests that identify him with the outside community are as a stockholder in the Farmers' Union at North Bend and at Scribner, and a stockholder in the Douglas Motor Company of Omaha He is also well known as a musician, playing the violin and clarionet, and has been an orchestra leader for over twenty years. He also has many engagements with his clarionet as a band man He is affiliated with the Knights of Columbus and he and his wife are active members of the Catholic Church at Ridgeley

In 1902 he married Miss Addie Feichtinger, daughter of Charles Feichtinger of Dodge County Mrs Haun died six years later in 1908, and since her death Mr Haun's widowed sister Elizabeth has had charge of the domestic economies of his present home. Mr Haun has two children, Elwood and Carroll.

HENRY UEHLING. As one of the native-born sons of Dodge County, Henry Uehling has lived to see many wonderful changes in the development of his home community, both in numbers and class of residents and in importance as an agricultural center He was born November 12, 1862, in Dodge County and is a son of Theodore Uehling, a pioneer who drove through to this region with a team of oxen

During the period of his boyhood, Henry Uehling was better acquainted with the Indians than with white people The redskins were peaceable and friendly and frequently stopped at the Uehling home, where hospitality was extended them by Mrs Uehling, and this familiarity did not tend to increase the youth's awe of the original settlers. Every year tribes of Indians would go west and north in the fall, on hunting expeditions, and in the spring would return to their camps, so that there was almost a constant procession of the tribes coming and going There were very few settlers, the Uehling home eight miles north of Clark's Creek being the first house reached from that point With no fences, when the early settlers desired to go anywhere they merely took the shortest route Omaha was the closest city of any size, and it required three days to make the journey to that place, but of necessity all the grain was hauled there, as the nearest mills were at De Soto and Fort Calhoun After the railroad was built to Fremont, that place became the destination and distributing point of the early farmers

The education of Mr Uehling was acquired in the public schools of Dodge County, and as a youth and young man was associated in farming with his father When he reached the age of twenty-five years he embarked upon operations of his own, first on his father's eighty-acre farm and later on eighty acres of his own From this modest beginning he has extended his activities to cover farming and stock raising on 600 acres of land, all located in Logan Township He is engaged in general farming and devotes a good portion of his time to the raising of thoroughbred live stock, including Jersey hogs and Percheron horses His labors have been attended by satisfactory results and he is regarded as one of the most substantial and prosperous farmers of his county While energetic and progressive, he is nevertheless careful and systematic in his methods of operation, and his farm is one of the most productive and profitable in this section He and Mrs Uehling are members of the Lutheran Church, and as a fraternalist he is affiliated with the Masons While he devotes his attention unreservedly to his farm, he is not indifferent to the duties of citizenship, and a number of years ago served his township in the capacity of treasurer

Mr Uehling was married in 1886 to Miss Marguerite Snyder, daughter of John and Barbara (Krueger) Snyder, settlers of 1874 in Burt County, Nebraska, who are now living in retirement at Scott's Bluff There were seven children in the Snyder family one who died in infancy, Peter, Adam, Marguerite Andrew Conrad and Mary, deceased Four children have been born to Mr and Mrs Uehling Arthur, who is engaged in farming in Dodge County, and Ira, Marie and Ernest, at home

LOUIS F HOLLOWAY The gentleman whose life history is herewith outlined is a man who has lived to good purpose and achieved a gratifying degree of success, solely by his individual efforts By a straightforward and commendable course Mr Holloway has made his way to an influential position in the commercial life of Fremont, winning the hearty admiration of the people of his community and earning a reputation as an enterprising, progressive man of affairs which the public has not been slow to recognize and appreciate Those who know him best will readily acquiesce in the statement that he is eminently deserving of the material success which has crowned his efforts and of the high esteem in which he is held throughout the community

Louis F. Holloway was born in Lawrence, Kansas, December 22, 1862, and is the son of James C and Mary A. (Roy) Holloway The father was a native of the State of Ohio and the mother was born in Troy, New York, their marriage occurring after their removal to Kansas, in which state James C Holloway had been sent by the Government, for whom he was engaged in the forestry service On the outbreak of the Civil war he enlisted in defense of the Union and served faithfully for five years, holding an officer's commission Subsequently he took up railroad construction work and had a part in the building of the Atchison, Topeka & Santa Fe Railroad He and his wife are both deceased, his death occurring at Neodesha and his wife dying in Atchison, Kansas In religious faith, he was a member of the Methodist Episcopal Church and Mrs. Holloway was an Episcopalian In politics he gave his support to the republican party They were the parents of two children, Louis F, of this sketch, and Frederick C, who is engaged in farming at Basalt, Colorado

Louis F Holloway received a good practical education in the public schools and then for four years he was engaged in teaching school in Iowa and Nebraska He came to the latter state in 1884 and his identification with Dodge County dates from 1901, when he bought a small hardware store in Fremont Soon afterwards he had a partner, the firm being known as Holloway & Felt, later Holloway & Fowler, but in March, 1919, Mr Holloway bought his partner's interest in the business, which is now conducted as the L F Holloway Hardware Company The business has enjoyed a steady and healthy growth from the beginning and is now numbered among the leading stores of the kind in Fremont Mr Holloway has applied himself indefatigably to his business and has shown an ability and soundness of judgment that has stamped him as a business man of substantial and permanent qualities He carries a large, well-selected and complete line of all kinds of hardware and his patrons come from a wide radius of surrounding country

In 1888 Mr Holloway was married to Carrie E Lewis, a native of New York, and the daughter of James H Lewis, who came to Nebraska in 1882, settling at Friend, where he engaged in the grain business To Mr and Mrs Holloway have been born two children, Pearl and Ruth The latter became the wife of John Bader of Scribner, Dodge County, but her death occurred on December 17, 1918 She was the mother of two children, Margaret and Gladys, who now make their home with the grandparents

Politically Mr Holloway is independent and he and his wife are members of the Congregational Church Fraternally he is a member of the Independent Order of Odd Fellows, the Ancient Order of United Workmen and the Modern Woodmen of America In the first named order he has passed through all the chairs in both branches He takes a deep interest in all local public and commercial affairs, giving his support to every movement for the upbuilding of the community He has been a director in the Fremont Commercial Club, president for several terms of the Retailers' Association, a director in the Nebraska State Hardware Association, and he has also taken an active and effective part in the interests of the Young Men's Christian Association In every phase of community life he has endeavored to be a booster and as a result of his generous spirit and his excellent personal qualities he enjoys the confidence and good will of all who know him

PETER F. CARY is one of the leading merchants of the thriving little City of North Bend, Dodge County, where he conducts a well equipped furniture store, and his is the distinction of being a representative of a family whose name has been identified with the annals of Nebraska since 1869. He was born at Dunkirk, New York, December 31, 1857, and is a son of Patrick and Bridget (Hayes) Cary, both natives of the Emerald Isle. The devoted mother who would have celebrated in 1920 the eighty-sixth anniversary of her birth, died December 25, 1919, her husband having died in 1912, at the venerable age of eighty-five years.

Patrick Cary was reared and educated in his native land and came from Ireland to America in 1850. He lived for a short period in the City of Boston, Massachusetts, later became a resident of Dunkirk, New York, and from the old Empire State he removed to Ohio, where the family home was maintained until 1869, when he came with his family to Nebraska, which had gained the dignity of statehood only two years previously. After remaining for a time in the City of Omaha Patrick Cary took up a homestead claim in Platte County where he reclaimed and improved a pioneer farm and continued for many years as a respected and influential citizen. After retiring from the farm, in 1900, he established his home at Platte Center, where he passed the remainder of his life and whence his widow later came to the home of their only child, Peter F., of this review, at North Bend, where she received the deepest filial solicitude on the part of her son. She was a devout communicant of the Catholic Church, as was also her husband, and the latter was a democrat in his political proclivities.

Peter F. Cary received a common school education and after the removal of his family to Nebraska he contributed his share to the work and development of his father's old homestead farm, in Platte County. In that county he finally purchased a furniture store at Platte Center, and after conducting the enterprise ten years he removed to Schuyler, Colfax County, where he was similarly engaged for the ensuing two years. He then sold his furniture store at that place and, in 1911, came to North Bend, where he purchased the furniture business of Edward Davis. His store is modern in appointments, range of stock and in service, and he controls a substantial and profitable business. Mr. Cary is independent in politics, and has served as a member of the City Council of North Bend, besides which he held the office of coroner while a resident of Colfax County. He is a communicant of the Catholic Church and is affiliated with the Knights of Columbus.

ROBERT A. LUEHRS, to a brief review of whose life and character the reader's attention is herewith directed, is among the favorably known and representative citizens of Dodge County. Mr. Luehrs has by his indomitable enterprise and progressive methods contributed in a material way to the advancement of his community, and he has ascended through his individual efforts from the bottom of the ladder to a place of importance in business circles in this locality, having ever been known as a man of sound judgment, indefatigable industry and integrity of character.

Robert A. Luehrs was born in Kankakee, Illinois, on September 5, 1882, and is the son of Henry and Margaret (Hess) Luehrs, the former a native of Germany and the latter born in Kentucky. Their marriage occurred in Kankakee, Illinois, and there they have lived continuously since. For a number of years Henry Luehrs was foreman of a brick and tile works, but has long been engaged in the coal business. He and his wife are members of the Baptist Church and in politics he gives his support to the republican party. To these worthy parents were born five children, namely: Harry, who is assistant treasurer of the State of Illinois; Robert A.; Laura, the wife of George Sedorf, a farmer in Kankakee County, Illinois; George, engaged in the banking business in Kankakee; Edna, who is engaged in teaching school at Bisbee, Arizona.

Robert A. Luehrs attended the schools of his native community and at the age of sixteen years he began to learn the carpenter trade, at which he was employed until he came to Fremont in 1907. He here was employed for a few years by his uncle, W. G. Luehrs, and then he entered upon the business of contracting on his own account. He has been eminently successful in this line of endeavor and for a number of years has been numbered among the leading contractors of this locality, having erected some of the finest residences and most substantial business structures in Fremont. Mr. Luehrs has contributed in a very definite way to the welfare and upbuilding of the community in which he lives through his policy of building residences for sale, thus inducing many people to secure homes of their own who otherwise would never do so. In this way he has disposed of about thirty attractive and well arranged homes which he has built in Fremont. He also erected a splendid home for himself at 921 North Clarkson Street, into which he moved in October, 1919.

In 1907 Mr. Luehrs was married to Bessie Faquet, who was born and reared in Saunders County, Nebraska, the daughter of Manassas Faquet, who was one of the earliest pioneer settlers in Saunders County. His death occurred in Fremont, where his widow now survives. To Mr. and Mrs. Luehrs have been born four children, namely: Glen, Wilbur, Arthur and Bessie. Mrs. Luehrs died on December 27, 1919. She was a member of the Baptist Church and a woman of most excellent qualities of character, extremely popular in all the circles in which she moved. Mr. Luehrs also is affiliated with the Baptist Church, while in politics he is a republican. Through his own efforts he has been a success in business and is now the owner of two excellent farms, one located in Dodge County and one in Merrick County, both of which he rents. He carries to successful completion whatever he undertakes and his business methods have ever been in strict conformity with the best business ethics, so that he has ever enjoyed the confidence and esteem of all who know him.

NELS M. JOHNSON. Many of the more enterprising and successful business men of Nebraska are of foreign birth and breeding, and have brought to their adopted country the habits of industry and thrift that have gained them positions of influence, prominent among the number being Nels M. Johnson, of Fremont, head of the prosperous firm of Johnson & Cheney, dealers in coal and lumber. A native of Sweden, he was born March 9, 1873, a son of Carl and Rocina Johnson, who reared a family of six children, four of whom are now living, as follows: Marie, Carl and Anna, living in Sweden, and Nels M., the only member of the family to come to America.

Carl Johnson was born in a little shack on his father's farm and was reared in humble circumstances. Energetic and ambitious, he toiled assiduously during his earlier years at anything he could find to do, and began life on his own account as a hack driver. Prudently saving as much of his earnings as he could, he was subsequently actively identified with various industries, having operated a tannery, a brewery, a creamery, and finally embarking in mercantile pursuits. Possessing

T. L. Matthews

good business ability and judgment, he met with signal success in his undertakings, becoming a fine representative of the self-made men of his country. Both he and his wife united with the Lutheran Church in childhood

Brought up and educated in Sweden, Nels M Johnson determined as a young man to begin life for himself in a newer country, and in 1891 bade his family and friends adieu and came to the United States in search of fortune Locating in Osceola, Nebraska, he clerked in a mercantile establishment long enough to become somewhat familiar with the business methods of this country, and then purchased a store in Madison, Nebraska, where he remained for two years Coming from there to Fremont in 1905, Mr Johnson, in partnership with D W. Hotchkiss, embarked in the lumber business, and soon established a large trade. In 1914 George E Cheney purchased Mr Hotchkiss' interest in the business, which has since been carried on under the name of Johnson & Cheney This firm deals extensively in lumber and coal, handling the different grades of coal and making a specialty of building materials of all kinds

Mr Johnson married, in 1898, Luetta Hotchkiss, a daughter of D W Hotchkiss, who is living in Fremont, retired from active pursuits, as a dealer in coal and lumber having accumulated a competency Mr and Mrs Johnson have four children, namely Martha living at home; Edith and Stanley, attending school; and Raymond, a bright little fellow of two years Fraternally Mr Johnson is a member of the Independent Order of Odd Fellows, the Benevolent and Protective Order of Elks, the Fraternal Order of Eagles, the Modern Woodmen of America and the Turners He also belongs to the Fremont Commercial Club. Religiously Mr and Mrs Johnson are active members of the Methodist Episcopal Church

TREVANYON L. MATHEWS, while not in the pioneer class, has become a prominent and influential personality in connection with the financial, political and other public affairs of Nebraska, and is one of the leading citizens of Fremont

Mr Mathews was born at Florence, Pennsylvania, March 1, 1849, and moved to Illinois in 1865 His early education was acquired in the public schools As a youth he served an apprenticeship in a carriage manufactory, and with this line of industrial enterprise he continued six years, after which he was for one year a clerk in a dry-goods store Illinois was the stage of his early activities where he made an admirable record of achievement prior to coming to Nebraska In 1873 he was appointed deputy sheriff and collector of taxes for Cass County, Illinois, and in 1882 he was elected a member of the Illinois Legislature, his district constituting a part of the territory at one time represented by Abraham Lincoln He was importuned to become a candidate for a second term, but declined this honor on account of having been elected cashier of the Cass County Bank, at Beardstown, Illinois, in 1884 In 1885 he effected a reorganization of this institution, under the corporate title of the First State Bank of Beardstown, and it is worthy of record that this was the first bank organized under the new state banking law of Illinois. Today the bank is one of the strong financial institutions of the central part of that commonwealth. Mr Mathews was elected secretary of the Beardstown Building and Loan Association about the same time he became cashier of the Cass County Bank, and he was a potent force in furthering the success of both institutions In 1884 he was elected city clerk of Beardstown, an office of which he continued the incumbent for eight years, his acceptance of the position having been prompted by his desire to serve the city in the refunding of its bonds, in the building of a municipal bridge, in the installation of a waterworks system and in furthering other important public enterprises which the city was undertaking Mr. Mathews continued his residence at Beardstown, Illinois, until 1892 when he came with his family to Nebraska and established his home at Fremont and the same year organized the Nebraska State Building and Loan Association and was elected secretary and manager, in 1901 he was elected president and manager and continues to be its active head This association with its more than $3,000,000 assets is one of the leading financial institutions of the state Mr Mathews is also first vice president of the State League of Building and Loan Associations In 1899 Mr. Mathews was appointed by President McKinley United States Marshal for the District of Nebraska and was reappointed in 1903 and continued his tenure of office until 1906

In 1908 Mr Mathews was elected cashier of the Fremont Trust and Savings Bank, of which he became president in 1913, as successor to the late R B Schneider In 1914 he reorganized the savings bank as the Fremont State Bank, a commercial bank of which he was elected president For several years he was a director of the First National Bank of Fremont, and for some time served as chairman of the finance committee, and his activities at Fremont have included also his service as a director of the Fidelity Trust Company and a member of the directorate and also the finance committee of the Fremont Hotel Company, which erected the fine Pathfinder Hotel.

For many years Mr Mathews has been active and prominent in the work of the Nebraska Bankers Association and has held several positions of honor and at this time is the treasurer of the Nebraska State Bankers Protective Organization

Always a stalwart in the ranks of the republican party and a forceful advocate of its principles and policies, Mr Mathews has been influential in its councils and campaign activities, both in Illinois and Nebraska He served several years as a charman of the Dodge County Republican Committee and in 1899 he was asked to accept the post of chairman of the State Central Committee of his party in Nebraska, a preferment which he was constrained to decline, by reason of his appointment to the office of United States marshal Mr Mathews has canvassed the state a number of times, as a campaign speaker under the direction of the Republican State Central Committee Concerning another phase of his political activity the following succinct record has been given "In 1898, by unanimous vote of the Republican State Convention of Nebraska, Mr Mathews was nominated for the office of state auditor He accepted this nomination with the understanding that the late Senator Hayward would be nominated for governor Senator Hayward and Mr Mathews together made a vigorous and effective canvass of the state, with the result that the populist majority of the previous year was cut from 19,000 to about 2,500 It developed later that Hayward and Mathews would have been elected had they not be sacrificed by certain interests and influences, to secure the election of a legislature favorable to the election of a certain prominent aspirant to the United States Senate Mr Mathews is now a member of the Republican State Central Committee and treasurer of that organization

Mr Mathews' Masonic affiliations are here briefly noted Fremont Lodge No 15, Ancient Free and Accepted Masons, Signet Chapter No

8, Royal Arch Masons, of which he served one term as high priest, in 1898; Mount Tabor Commandery No 9, Knights Templar, of which he was eminent commander one term in 1898, and of which he served ten terms as excellent prelate, and Arbor Vitae Chapter No 92, Order of the Eastern Star, of which he was a worthy patron in 1897 and 1898

Mr. Mathews holds membership in the Fremont Commercial Club, the Fremont Country Club, the Fremont Men's Club and the local Elks Club He has been a member of the Methodist Episcopal Church since 1872, and both he and his wife have been active and influential in the various departments of church activities He served two terms as president of the Nebraska State Sunday School Association, and in 1894 was a delegate to the general conference of the Methodist Episcopal Church

During the late World war, Mr. Mathews was zealous in all activities through which popular support was given to the Government, and rendered effective service as a speaker in all the Red Cross and loan drives, and was one of the dependable Four Minute men whose service proved of marked value

At Beardstown, Illinois, September 26, 1871, was solemnized the marriage of Mr. Mathews to Miss Louise E Thronsbury, and they became the parents of three children, all of whom were born in Illinois: Earl M, Reece L, and Florence, the last named having died at the age of two years

Mrs Mathews was a charter member of Arbor Vitae Chapter No 92 of the Order of the Eastern Star, and served two terms as its worthy matron, in 1894 and 1895 She served as grand matron of the Grand Chapter of Nebraska in 1900 and 1901, and at the expiration of her second term she declined re-election. During the period of the nation's participation in the World war Mrs Mathews served as chairman of the Woman's Liberty Loan Committee for the Ninth District comprising the counties of Dodge, Washington, Saunders, Thurston, Platte, Colfax and Burt, besides which she was chairman of the knitting committee of the Dodge County Red Cross She is an ex-president of the Fremont Woman's Club and has been especially active in church and club work Mrs. Mathews was a delegate to the Republican State Convention in 1920 and served on the committee on resolutions, and is a member of the County Central Committee of Dodge County

William Schuett. Dodge and Washington counties have been the chosen home and scene of action for William Schuett for more than forty years Coming here practically a stranger, a man of foreign birth, with no capital except his individual energy, he has nevertheless contrived to prosper and make his labor and character win him success Visible evidence of his prosperity is found in the extensive and well-managed farm he owns in section 18 of Hooper Township

Mr. Schuett was born in Germany December 29, 1851, and lived in his native land until he was about thirty-two years of age. In the month of November, 1883, he reached this country and a few days after landing reached Washington County, Nebraska He lived in that county five years and then came to Dodge County where he bought some land and worked steadily in its improvement year after year until his possessions now aggregate 398 acres, with improvements of the very best. For several years past he has done no farming himself, but has a good income from his property which is operated through renters Mr. Schuett is a republican in politics

He married, September 14, 1883, Doris Dierks, who was born in Germany October 23, 1858, where she was reared and married They are the parents of three daughters, Lizzie, Ida and Dorothy Lizzie married Henry L Krohn, of Washington County, Ida married Louis W. Moll, of the same county, Dorothy is at home with her parents Mr and Mrs Schuett are members of the Lutheran Church

CHARLES D. MARR, president of the Fremont Foundry & Machine Company, has secure standing as one of the representative figures in industrial and business circles in Dodge County and as one of the influential citizens of Fremont, the judicial center and metropolis of the county He was born at Sterling, Iowa, February 21, 1856, and is a son of Solomon and Bridget (Haney) Marr, the former a native of Ontario, Canada, and the latter of Ireland The marriage of the parents was solemnized in the Province of Ontario, Canada, whence, in 1853, they immigrated to the West and became pioneer settlers in Iowa, where the father passed the remainder of his life and where for many years he followed the trade of cabinetmaker, his death having occurred, at Sterling, in 1882, and his widow having died about three years later, in 1885, at Fremont, Nebraska David Marr, grandfather of Charles D., was long one of the leading cabinetmakers in Ontario, Canada, where he had a large shop and did an extensive business The maternal grandparents of Mr Marr passed their entire lives in Ireland Solomon Marr was a republican in politics and his wife held membership in the Methodist Episcopal Church. Of their six children only two are now living William, a retired farmer, residing at Sabula, Iowa, and Charles D, of this sketch

In the public schools of the Hawkeye State Charles D Marr continued his studies until he had completed a course in the high school, and there also he learned the sturdy trade of blacksmith, in which he became a skilled workman, his apprenticeship having been partially served while he was still attending school After leaving school he did not turn attention to the work of his trade but became a clerk in a mercantile establishment at Fremont, Nebraska, where he established his home on April 1, 1876 He continued to be thus employed until August 1st of the following year, when he established an independent mercantile enterprise at Schuyler, Colfax County, where he continued in business until he removed to Blair, Washington County In the latter place he conducted a general store until January, 1879, when he returned to Fremont and took charge of the new general store of Z Shedd He continued as active manager of this store until the business was sold, in 1881, and he then purchased the fire-insurance business of L D Richards In connection with this enterprise he served six months as local agent of the American Express Company, and from 1883 he held the post of local editor of the Fremont Tribune His versatility was later shown by his having charge of the coal and lumber office of D Crowell at Fremont, and finally, on September 1, 1886 he found the true initiative point in his successful business career, for he was then elected manager of the Fremont Foundry & Machine Company, to the business of which his able supervision and progressive policies gave distinct impetus, with the result that the corporation has long represented one of the substantial and important industrial enterprises of Dodge County He has been president of the company since 1895, and its operations are based on a capital stock of $50,000 The plant is modern in its equipment and general facilities, with boiler shop and foundry and with facilities for the prompt execution of structural and ornamental steel and iron work of the best type The establishment retains an average corps of fifty men in its various departments, and the business is one of substantial and prosperous order

Mr Marr is now one of the veterans in the business circles of Fremont and has always been liberal and progressive in his civic attitude He has served twenty years as a member of the Fremont Board of Education, and in this connection was a member of the building committee that had control of the erection of the present high-grade public school buildings of the city He is serving at the present time as president of the Fremont Commercial Club and is an enthusiast in the furtherance of its progressive civic and business policies He is also president of the Board of Trustees of the Fremont Public Library, and no citizen is more liberal and public-spirited in connection with community affairs in general Mr Marr is a republican in his political proclivities and is affiliated with the Woodmen of the World and the Fremont Lodge of the Benevolent and Protective Order of Elks, of which he was the second exalted ruler

In 1880 was solemnized the marriage of Mr Marr to Miss Mary E Monroe, who was born in the City of Chicago, and of this union have been born six children Zach, who is superintendent of the foundry of the Fremont Foundry & Machine Company, completed a high-school course at Golden, Colorado, and thereafter took a course in the celebrated Armour Institute of Technology, in the City of Chicago Charles James is one of the principals of the Marr-Hein Candy Company, a prosperous manufacturing concern, and also of the Fremont Bottling Works. He completed a course in the Fremont High School Jennie is the wife of Frank Blum, a farmer near Akron, Iowa. Miss Helen, who remains at the parental home, was afforded the advantages of the Nebraska State Normal School at Fremont and also of those of a Catholic convent in the City of Lincoln She is now a successful and popular teacher in the Fremont High School Miss Madeline likewise attended the normal school at Fremont, as well as the University of Nebraska and she is now an efficient teacher in the public schools of Omaha. Lewis K, who is now on a ranch in Wyoming, completed a course in the Fremont High School, and was one of the gallant young men who represented Dodge County in the nation's military service in the World war He entered service in July, 1916, and was with his command on the Mexican border until he was sent to Camp Cody, where he remained until August, 1918, when he crossed the Atlantic and became a part of the American Expeditionary Forces in France. He there continued in active service until the close of the war and he returned home in May, 1919, having been discharged with the rank of second lieutenant

Henry C. Dahl. An active, prominent, and valued citizen of Fremont Henry C Dahl, a widely known real estate dealer, came to this country from a land beyond the sea when a lad in his teens, and by means of earnest labor, keen foresight, and wise management has accumulated a fair share of this world's goods, and acquired a position of note among the self-made men of today He was born February 13, 1863, in Holstein, Germany, where his parents, Henry and Antje (Suhl) Dahl, were life-long residents, the father having been successfully engaged in business as an architect He is one of a family of four children, three of whom are living in the United States, as follows Henry C, with whom this sketch is chiefly concerned; Mrs George Basler, of Santa Ana, California and Mrs Hettie Mason, of North Bend, Nebraska

Obtaining a practical education in his native land, Henry C Dahl came to the United States as a youth of fourteen summers, locating in 1877 in Dodge County, Nebraska Energetic, enterprising, and not at all afraid of work, he had no trouble in securing a position on a farm, and soon became familiar with the various branches of agriculture Laboring diligently, and prudently saving his wages, he was enabled to buy land from time to time, and is now the owner of 560 acres of finely improved land, a large part of which lies in Dodge County, and yields him a handsome annual income Moving to Fremont in 1910, Mr Dahl lived retired from active pursuits until 1913, when, in partnership with George F Staats, he opened a real estate office, and has since built up an extensive and remunerative business, handling farm property and loans Greatly interested in educational matters, Mr Dahl was instrumental in having the college moved from Atchison to Fremont, and as one of its trustees, and as treasurer of the Ways and Means Committee, devotes much of his time and attention to the affairs of the institution, having himself collected $220,000 of the half million dollar drive that is now in progress

Mr Dahl married, in 1885, Henrietta Schlueter, who was born in Germany, and in 1884 came to Nebraska with her parents, locating on a farm in Dodge County, where both her father and mother spent their remaining years. Mr. and Mrs Dahl have four children, namely: Harry, engaged in farming in Dodge County; Elsie, wife of Carl Carson, a farmer in Sidney, Nebraska; Nora, wife of Henry Wagner, who is engaged in farming at Hooper, Nebraska, and Clarence, employed in the First National Bank of Hooper. True to the religious faith in which they were reared, Mr. and Mrs Dahl are active members of the Lutheran Church Politically Mr Dahl is influential in demorcatic ranks, and is now representing the third ward in the City Council Fraternally he is a member of the Modern Woodmen of America, and of the Fraternal Order of Eagles.

RICHARD T. VAN METRE, M D., has been actively engaged in the practice of his profession in the City of Fremont, judicial center of Dodge County, since 1911, save for an interim of six months, during which, with the rank of captain, he was in service as a member of the medical corps of the United States army, in the late World war, his service having been rendered at Fort Riley, Kansas, and Camp Pike, Arkansas, and his discharge having been received January 2, 1919 He then returned to his home and resumed the interrupted work of his profession Doctor Van Metre is a young man of distinctive professional ambition and spares himself no effort or expense in keeping in touch with the advances made in medical and surgical science, with the result that his technical equipment is always at the highest standard, with resultant success in his well-ordered and representative practice in Dodge County Though his practice is of general order, he specializes in obstetrics and diseases of children He is a loyal and popular member of the Dodge County Medical Society, and is identified also with the Elkhorn Valley Medical Society, the Missouri Valley Medical Society, the Nebraska State Medical Society and the American Medical Association

Doctor Van Metre was born at Cedar Falls, Iowa, July 25, 1879, and is a son of Isaiah and Elizabeth (Thompson) Van Metre, the former a native of Virginia and the latter of Massachusetts, so that there was consummated effective representation of the south, the east and the west when their marriage was solemnized at States Center, Iowa The ability and important activities of Isaiah Van Metre marked him as one of the honored and influential citizens of the Hawkeye State, where, in 1879, he founded the Waterloo Tribune, of which representative newspaper, in one of the most thriving cities of Iowa, he continued the editor and publisher until 1904 He was a leader in the councils of the democratic party in Iowa, and served for several years as state oil inspector Mr. Van Metre continued his residence at Waterloo, that state, until his death, July 5, 1914, at the age of seventy-eight years, and his widow, who was born in 1856, still maintains her home in that city Mr Van Metre was affiliated with the Masonic Fraternity and was a zealous communicant of the Protestant Episcopal Church, as is also his widow Of their eight children six are living Margaret is the wife of Edward L. Carton, city editor of the Waterloo Courier, at Waterloo, Iowa, Doctor Van Metre, of this review, was the next in order of birth, Ricker is vice president of the Joyce-Watkins Company, lumber dealers and dealers in railway ties, in the City of Chicago, Virginia is the wife of John Lund, who is engaged in the jewelry business at Kingsley, Iowa, and Horace and Morris are twins, the former being engaged in the abstract business at Waterloo and the latter being a student in the department of journalism of the University of Iowa.

In the public schools of Waterloo, Iowa, Dr Richard T Van Metre continued his studies until his graduation in the high school, as a member of the class of 1896 Thereafter he was for some time a student in the University of Iowa, in the academic department, and he then entered the medical department of the institution, in which he was graduated as a member of the class of 1905, with the degree of Doctor of Medicine He had early gained varied experience in connection with his father's newspaper business, and from 1896 until 1901, he was actively and successfully identified with newspaper work, in connection with which he indulged itinerant propensities, as shown by his having been an attache of the old Chicago Herald, in the western metropolis, and by his association with newspapers in various other places in the western field.

Soon after his graduation in medicine, Doctor Van Metre engaged in the practice of his profession at Dow City, Iowa, where he remained until May, 1911, when he established his residence at Fremont, Nebraska, where he now controls an excellent practice of representative order He avails himself of the best standard and periodical literature of his profession, and has further fortified himself by recent post-graduate work in the New York Lying-in Hospital and the New York Post-Graduate School of Medicine As previously noted, his active professional work at Fremont has been interrupted only by the period of his professional service in connection with the nation's participation in the World war The doctor maintains an independent attitude in politics, and he and his wife are active communicants of the Protestant Episcopal Church of Fremont He is affiliated with the Masonic Fraternity, in which he is past master of the Lodge of Ancient Free and Accepted Masons at Dow City, Iowa, and holds membership also in the Knights of Pythias and the Benevolent and Protective Order of Elks

On January 17, 1906, was solemnized the marriage of Doctor Van Metre to Miss Marie G Murdock, who was born at Glendive, Wyoming, and the one child of this union is Richard T, Jr. who was born in 1908, and who maintains regal dominion in the pleasant home circle

RAYMOND J MIDDAUGH, whose home is in section 10 of Platte Township, has been one of the leading farmers and stockmen of Dodge County for many years He represents a pioneer family, the Middaughs having come to Nebraska in the early 70s and having gone through all the adversities of grasshoppers, drought, and other hardships that beset the early settlers

His father, the late John C. Middaugh, was born in Luzerne County, Pennsylvania, in February, 1831, son of David and Elsie Middaugh, the former a native of New Jersey and the latter of Pennsylvania. The seven children of David Middaugh and wife were Albert, Margaret, John, Eliza, Ella, Mary and David John C Middaugh lived in Pennsylvania until he was twenty-seven years of age He then moved out to Mercer County, Illinois, and not being possessed of great capital he was a farm renter for eleven years He was only eight years old when his parents died, and he had a limited education and had to mold his circumstances to suit his ambition On June 10, 1862, he married Nancy Braucht, daughter of David and Johanna Braucht, natives of Pennsylvania, whose children were Mary, who died in infancy, Nancy, George, Phoebe, Addie and Henderson

In 1873 John C. Middaugh brought his family to Dodge County and acquired 160 acres of partly improved land in Platte Township Before he died he had the farm highly developed and recognized as one of the most productive tracts in the township The lumber with which he built his first home was hauled all the way from Omaha His widow is now living with her daughter, Mrs Edith Kimmel of North Bend Nebraska John C. Middaugh was a member of the Seventh Day Adventist Church and a republican voter A brief record of his children is as follows George, born April 12, 1864, now deceased, Lyman, born August 19, 1866, Edith, born February 26, 1869, William born July 11, 1872, of whom mention is found on other pages; Raymond J, and Frank, born October 7, 1881

Raymond J Middaugh, who was born in Dodge County May 26 1879 had a common school education and at the age of nineteen assumed entire responsibility for his future Mr Middaugh has had a successful career though for the most part he has been a renter of land owned by others He acquired an increasing equipment of tools and stock, and farmed on rented land until 1918, when he bought 120 acres of the old home estate Since then he has sold this property, and again lives on a rented farm He also owns a large amount of land in Colorado, though he has never occupied it personally Mr Middaugh is an extensive stock breeder, breeding cattle and hogs chiefly, and he keeps a herd of thoroughbred red hogs

February 12, 1901, Mr Middaugh married Miss Bertha Frantz, who was born in Pennsylvania and was four years of age when she came with her parents, Wesley and Amanda Frantz, to Nebraska Her family settled at David City Mr and Mrs Middaugh are the parents of five children Lucile, who died at the age of five years, Edith, Georgia, Julia and Jean Mr Middaugh is a republican voter and has served as road overseer of his district He is a member of the Fremont Gun Club and during the World war was an active and vigilant member of the Council of Defense He is affiliated with the orders of Knights of Pythias, Triumph Lodge No 32, and Elks Mrs Middaugh is a member of the Baptist Church Her parents lived in Dodge County for thirty-one years, and both of them are now deceased

PHILIP S. RINE, president of the Farmers and Merchants National Bank of Fremont, and a heavy landowner of Dodge County, is one of the men who has been instrumental in advancing the interests of this part of the state, and establishing and maintaining the prestige of Fremont He

Philip S Rine

was born in Snyder County, Pennsylvania, on April 7, 1852, a son of John M and Mary Ann (Schnee) Rine, both natives of Pennsylvania, where they died, she in 1865 and he in 1901 Five of their thirteen children are living, namely Kate, who married Adam Winstrel, a farmer and miller of Pennsylvania; Lydia, who is a widow, married Charles Collman, and lives near Dolphin, Nebraska, Philip S, whose name heads this review, Sue, who married Addison Watts, a farmer of Elkhart, Indiana; and George S, who is a farmer of Selinsgrove, Pennsylvania. The parents of this family were devout members of the Evangelical Lutheran Church A democrat in politics, John M Rine was often elected on his party ticket to various township offices, for he was a reliable and trustworthy man, in whom his neighbors placed confidence He operated a tannery and was a man of considerable means, and also owned and conducted a store and a farm Boats owned by him carried lumber and merchandise on the Pennsylvania Canal, and his own outfit freighted these commodities to different points after they were landed from the canal John M Rine was a son of George Rine, also born in Pennsylvania, where his parents had located upon coming to this country from Germany at a very early day The maternal grandfather, Philip Schnee, was born in Pennsylvania, his family being one of the old ones of the Keystone State

Philip S Rine received but a limited education in the public schools of Pennsylvania, which was terminated when he was thirteen years old, at which time he left school to go to work A little later on he took a course of twenty-two weeks at Freeburg College in Pennsylvania His opportunities for obtaining work were those offered by farm labor and in 1873 he went to Michigan and spent a winter in the lumber woods of that state, and then came to Dodge County, Nebraska, arriving at Fremont on April 14, 1874 During his first year he worked in a lumber yard, and then with his savings bought a team and broke up eighty acres of prairie. His father had acquired some land in the vicinity, and with this team Philip S Rine began farming it. Later he bought this land from his father on time, and still owns it Like the majority of the pioneers of the '70s Mr Rine suffered from the grasshoppers and lost his crops for two succeeding seasons However, he was possessed of the sturdy determination which is able to overcome obstacles no matter how unsurmountable they may appear, and so he remained and was amply rewarded for he not only succeeded in placing and keeping his original farm under cultivation, but was able to buy other land until at one time he owned 1,400 acres of land, of which he still owns 560 acres, having sold some of it within recent years He bought it for $10 per acre and sold it in the summer of 1919 for $260 per acre.

For many years Mr Rine was heavily interested in stock, and continued to carry on his stock business and oversee his farm after he moved to Fremont in 1889, at which time he erected a beautiful residence at 1450 North Beard Street, which is one of the real homes of Fremont When the Farmers and Merchants Bank was organized Mr Rine was one of the stockholders and he has been its president for about twelve years

In 1875 Philip S Rine was married to Laura Worminghouse, born in Michigan, a daughter of William Worminghouse, who came to Dodge County about 1868 and died here Mr and Mrs Rine became the parents of three children, namely John, an attorney, is counsel for the Lion Bonding Company of Omaha, Nebraska, and served that city as attorney for eight years, Bertha, who married Dr G G Baird, one of the leading dentists of Dodge County, whose sketch appears elsewhere in this work; and Will, who was on his father's farm, has recently moved to Colorado Mr and Mrs. Rine belong to the Congregational Church He is a democrat, but aside from serving as a director of school district No 69, while on the farm, he has held no office Fraternally Mr Rine belongs to Fremont Lodge No 513, Benevolent and Protective Order of Elks Always a progressive man he has reached an understanding of the public directly and surely and is regarded as one able to give advice it is safe to follow Both he and his wife are convincing in their simplicity and sincerity and give bountifully of their friendships and confidence to those with whom they associate.

BYRON N HEALY There are many ways in which the sound men of the country are giving their encouragement to agricultural effort and expressing their recognition of the principle that it is and must remain our most important industry, but the one adopted by Byron N Healy to render this service is of exceptional merit. For years he has been extensively engaged in calling the attention of the public to different sections of the country, and making such arrangements as will result in the migration to them of denizens of the more congested centers In this way he aids in the development of whole communities, places within the reach of persons of limited means homes of their own, and carries on a business that is congenial and remunerative.

Byron N Healy was born at Milwaukee, Wisconsin, July 7, 1853, a son of James P and Lucinda L (Francisco) Healy, natives of Ireland and Syracuse, New York, respectively, and their marriage occurred in the latter city For some time prior and following his marriage James P Healy controlled practically all of the draying business of Syracuse, but, seeking other fields, he went west to Milwaukee, Wisconsin, at a time when the present metropolis was in its infancy, and the commercial life of the community was carried on in one small log store, which was conducted by a half breed For five years he had dealings only with Indians, during that period acquiring ownership of a tract of land two and one-half miles long and one and one-half miles wide, which was covered with timber As the new settlers came in, he sold land to them, and developed into a man of large means, both he and his wife dying in Wisconsin They had nine children born to them, of whom Byron N Healy is the only survivor All of their mature years they were firm in the faith of the Presbyterian Church, and were instrumental in having their denomination established in their home in the wilderness He had been reared a Catholic, but his wife's persuasions led him to adopt her creed as his own Generous to a fault, he gave lavishly to the support of churches, not only of his own denomination, but others, and schools His political convictions, which were strong ones, led him to give his support to the principles of the democratic party

The educational training of Byron N. Healy was received at Racine, Wisconsin, and he divided his early business life between railroad and farm work Beginning his connection with the railroad as a newsboy, he worked his way up through the various stages until he was a conductor and still later, an engineer, and continued as such for twenty-two years on the Chicago & Northwestern Railroad In the meanwhile he had been gaining a knowledge of men and localities, and, realizing that deep down in the heart of every sound man lies the longing of his nature for possession of a piece of land he can call his own, he decided to go into the land business, and did so, first at Huron, South Dakota, but in

1904 moved his office to Fremont, Nebraska, where he has since maintained his headquarters For some time he was interested in Texas land, but has now disposed of his holdings in that state, and is now operating in Florida, where he owns immense tracts of land On one of his trips he sold $630,000 worth of land, and all of it was disposed of at a very reasonable figure

On October 5, 1874, Mr Healy was married to Mary J. Thomas, born at Yorkville, Racine County, Wisconsin, a daughter of Thomas Thomas, an old settler of Racine County. Mr. and Mrs. Healy became the parents of the following children: Golden Mabel, who married John P Dick, cashier of a bank at Hot Springs, Arkansas, and R Chesley, who married Mayme Johnson, of Fremont This young man is in charge of the Omaha branch of the Healy Land Company, which maintains another branch at Kansas City, Missouri, and the head office at Fremont This company runs its own car to the properties it has for sale, making the trip twice a month Like his father, the son is a splendid land man, and has been eminently successful

Byron N Healy is a thirty-second degree and Shriner Mason, and both he and Mrs Healy belong to the Eastern Star, of which Mrs Healy is past matron They belong to the Congregational Church, and are active in its religious work In politics Mr Healy is a republican, but has never had the time or inclination to come before the public for favors He possesses great mental resourcefulness, and has been able to attain to surprising and big achievements When his eyes were opened to the opportunities of his present business, he responded in wonderful measure, and took up its affairs in a vigorous and efficient manner, convincing those with whom he comes into contract by his flaming sincerity and genuine regard for their welfare

HENRY H. LOOSCHEN Perhaps no class of men render more constructive service to their community than do those who are engaged in the handling of real estate, because without their public-spirited efforts there would be little movement in realty, development work would not be inaugurated or carried out and outside capital interested Of course there are some men in this line of business, as there are in all others, who do not measure up to the highest standards of business probity, but to their credit be it said that the majority of real estate men are reliable and dependable and they form a very important element in the life of the state One of these energetic, alert and thoroughly honorable men who are devoting their talents to the handling of Hooper realty is Henry H Looschen, a former merchant of the place, who is known all over Dodge and Washington counties.

Henry H Looschen was born in Germany in 1854, a son of P O and Johanna (Voght) Looschen, who came to the United States in 1882, locating at Fremont, Nebraska. While living in Germany P O Looschen was a cabinetmaker and furniture dealer, but after coming here he lived in retirement, and both he and his excellent wife died at Fremont, he in 1890, aged eighty-five years, and she in 1898, aged eighty years Their children were as follows George, who died at Fremont in 1917, was in the abstract and insurance business and was registrar of deeds of Dodge County for twelve years, Henry H, who was second in order of birth; John, who was formerly engaged in the banking business at Snyder, Nebraska, now lives in California, Sigmond, who was a clerk in a clothing store, died in 1878; Martha, who married L C Hahn, is deceased, as is her husband, Onoline Schurman, deceased wife of Ernest Schurman, deceased, a former Fremont banker, Justine, who is deceased, married Fred Meyer, a wholesale grocer, and Julia, who married August J Albero, a retired business man of Fremont The family all were Lutherans

Henry H. Looschen came to Fremont in 1872 and attended a commercial college of Omaha, Nebraska, so as to gain a knowledge of American methods of doing business For five years he was employed in a store at Fremont, owned by H Fuhrman, and then came to Hooper and in 1878 founded the store known as Henry H Looschen, general merchandise, and conducted it very profitably until 1892, when he sold it so as to devote all of his attention to handling real estate and making loans In this undertaking he has built up a very valuable connection and is doing a fine business

In 1882 Mr Looschen was united in marriage with Fredericke Heine, a daughter of Vincent Heine, a native of Germany, and his wife Fredericke (Floto) Heine, also a native of Germany They settled in Pennsylvania upon coming to the United States in 1837, and were farmers She died at Hooper in 1892, aged seventy-nine years, but he passed away in Pennsylvania in 1870, when sixty-two years old They were Catholics He was a democrat, and a strong supporter of his party principles Mr and Mrs Heine had the following children born to them: John E, who died at Hooper, was a hardware merchant; August J, who died at Hooper in 1895, was a farmer; George F who was in the cattle business, also died at Hooper, Fred F, who is in the employ of the United States Government, Carrie, who is deceased, and Mrs Looschen, who is the youngest

Mr and Mrs Looschen became the parents of the following children Julia, Delia, Henry and Howard, all of whom are deceased, Paul, who is assistant cashier of the Leshara State Bank of Saunders County, Nebraska, and George H, who is assistant cashier of the Dodge County Bank of Hooper Both Paul and George served in the United States army overseas during the World war Mrs Looschen is a Catholic. In his political belief Mr Looschen is a democrat. He is a Blue Lodge Mason

A J Albers Dodge County, Nebraska, enjoys a high reputation because of the high order of her citizenship, and none of her citizens occupies a more enviable position in the esteem of his fellow citizens than the gentleman whose name appears at the head of this sketch. A residence here of many years has given them a full opportunity to observe him in the various lines of activity in which he has engaged and his present high standing is due solely to the honorable and upright course he has pursued As a leading citizen of his community he is eminently entitled to representation in a work of this character

A J Albers was born in Germany on November 24, 1860, and is the son of O J and Anna (Jansen) Albers, both of whom spent their entire lives in their native land and are now deceased The father was a farmer by vocation, but also had other business interests A J was the only child born of his first marriage By a second union O J Albers also had a son, Albert H, who is now a captain in the Sanitary Corps, a branch of the medical department of the United States army, and is stationed at Camp Grant, Illinois He has been in the military service for several years, having gone to France in June, 1917, and returning in November, 1919, during which period he was in Berlin four months He was promoted to his present rank from private and it is his intention to remain in the army O J Albers and wife were members of the Lutheran Church

A J Albers remained under the parental roof until he was eighteen years of age and received a good practical education in the public schools At the age mentioned he came to the United States and also secured some education in this country In 1882 he came to Fremont and has been identified with this locality ever since For a time he had been employed in a general store at Wahoo, Nebraska, and then was employed in the Farmers and Merchants National Bank at Fremont He later engaged in the general mercantile business at Scribner, Dodge County, for about four years, but at the end of that time he again located in Fremont and entered the insurance business, to which he has ever since devoted his attention In this line he has been very successful and has placed a vast amount of insurance throughout this community He is now district agent for the Northwestern Mutual Life Insurance Company of Milwaukee

In 1884, Mr Albers was married to Julia Looschen, who also is a native of Germany, and they are the parents of one child, Jessie, who is the wife of Albert Van Anda, assistant cashier of the Commercial National Bank of Fremont, and has two daughters, Caroline and Frances

Mr and Mrs Albers are attendants of the Congregational Church Fraternally Mr Albers is a member of the Ancient Free and Accepted Masons, in which he belongs to the Blue Lodge of Master Masons, the Chapter of Royal Arch Masons, the Council of Royal and Select Masters, the Commandery of Knights Templar, the Consistory of the Ancient Accepted Scottish Rite (thirty-second degree) and the Ancient Arabic Order Nobles of the Mystic Shrine, and he has received distinctive recognition by his brethren, having passed through the chairs of the Lodge, Chapter, Council and Commandery, and served one year as grand master of the grand council of the State of Nebraska He is also a member of the Independent Order of Odd Fellows and the Benevolent and Protective Order of Elks Politically he is a republican, though he has not taken an active part in political affairs During the World war Mr Albers took a very active part in the war work in this community, serving as chairman of two Liberty Loan drives, as chairman of the Four-Minute Men and of the last Red Cross drive In many other ways Mr Albers has shown a public spirited attitude toward all movements or enterprises for the advancement of the community's best interests, and because of these things and his business ability he enjoys to a marked degree the respect and esteem of all who know him

Frank W Johnson A man of excellent business ability and intelligence, Frank W. Johnson of Fremont is actively identified with the expansion of the automobile interests of this section of Dodge County, his largely patronized salesroom being one of the busiest places in the city A son of Wallace W Johnson, he was born in 1884 in Fullerton, Nance County, Nebraska, and there grew to man's estate.

Born in Wisconsin, Wallace W Johnson there received his preliminary education, which was completed in the public schools of Kansas Moving from Kansas to Nebraska in the early '80s he took up a claim in Fullerton, where he lived several years Later moving his family to Hitchcock County, Nebraska, he farmed there a number of years He married in Kansas, Mary Perrot, who was born in Canada of French parents, and died in 1892 in Nebraska. Five of their seven children are living: Ida, wife of E H Niles of Marietta, Kansas, Frank W, with whom this sketch is chiefly concerned, John J, who is now an automobile salesman for his brother, Wallace B, who is a resident of Seattle, Washington, and Tryphena, wife of L D Longmiller of Marietta, Kansas

Completing the course of study in the public schools of Fullerton, Frank W. Johnson entered the University of Nebraska, where he took up the course of electrical engineering and incidentally was very active in all athletics, being a member of the Nebraska football team of '07, '08 and '09 Upon graduating he became engaged in the electrical engineering business in Omaha until 1917, when he purchased a half interest in the Zapp Garage in Fremont After its incorporation he became president of this concern In 1918, disposing of his interest in this business, Mr Johnson in April, 1919, opened up his present salesrooms on Sixth Street and has since built up a large and remunerative business in handling the Cadillac, Buick and Oakland automobiles and the G M C truck In fact, his business has outgrown his building and Mr Johnson has recently purchased ground on which he is soon to erect a two-story sales and service station

Mr. Johnson married on June 2, 1910, Nina Chase Hodges, who was born in Almy, Wyoming, a daughter of Frederick and Rose (Chase) Hodges, the former of whom was born in Vermont and the latter in Illinois Mrs Johnson also attended the University of Nebraska

Fraternally Mr Johnson is a member of the Ancient Free and Accepted Masons, in which he has taken the Knight Templar and Shrine degrees, and of Fremont Lodge No 514, Benevolent and Protective Order of Elks and of the Kiwanis Club Both he and his wife belong to the Order of the Eastern Star and Country Club and Mr Johnson is actively connected with the Young Men's Christian Association, being secretary of the special campaign fund committee Mr and Mrs Johnson have no children

Joseph C Cook has made an excellent record in the office of county attorney of Dodge County, a position of which he has been continuously the incumbent since 1916, and in which he has materially advanced his reputation as a resourceful and versatile trial lawyer He has secure vantage place as one of the vital and successful members of the bar of his native state and his private practice has been one of representative order

Mr Cook was born on his father's farm in Washington County, Nebraska, September 1, 1875, and is a son of William S and Jennie A (Unthank) Cook, whose marriage was solemnized in that county, where they had both established residence in the pioneer days—soon after the close of the Civil war The father was born in Vermont, of sterling colonial ancestry in New England, and the mother was born in the State of Indiana In connection with the development of his farm property William S Cook continued in the practice of his profession for a number of years after coming to Nebraska, and became one of the representative members of the bar of Washington County, his political allegiance having been given to the republican party and he having been influential in its local councils in Washington County, where he and his wife still maintain their home Of the six children, Joseph C is the eldest of the four now living; Cortez W is a prosperous farmer near Arlington, Washington County, Roy resides in the City of Los Angeles, California, and is a salesman by occupation, and Hazel is the wife of Otto Ludwig, a successful contractor in the City of Los Angeles

W. M. Cain

Reared to the sturdy discipline of the home farm, Joseph C Cook profited fully by the advantages afforded in the public schools of his native county, and in preparation for his chosen vocation he ambitiously completed the prescribed curriculum of the law department of the University of Nebraska, in which he was graduated as a member of the class of 1895, his reception of the degree of Bachelor of Laws being virtually coincident with his admission to the bar of his native state Since 1897 Mr. Cook has been continuously established in the practice of his profession at Fremont, the judicial center and metropolis of Dodge County, and in addition to building up a substantial and important private practice he has been called upon to serve in various official positions in line with the direct work of his profession Thus it is to be noted that for six years he served on the bench of the Police Court of Fremont, and that his initial election to the office of county attorney occurred in 1908. He held the office for the prescribed term of four years, and after an interval of equal duration he was again elected to this position, in 1916, while the year 1918 recorded his re-election for a term of four years.

His political views mark him as one of the stalwart and effective advocates of the principles and policies of the republican party, he is affiliated with the Knights of Pythias, the Improved Order of Red Men, the Fraternal Order of Eagles, and the Benevolent and Protective Order of Elks, and his wife is an active member of the Methodist Episcopal Church of Fremont

June 15, 1897, recorded the marriage of Mr. Cook to Miss Myrtle Wilson, who was born in the State of Kansas, and of this union were born two children, the one surviving being Jennie, who is the wife of Carl Nelson, of San Francisco, California. Mrs Cook was summoned to the life eternal May 2, 1901, and on August 2, 1905, was solemnized the marriage of Mr Cook to Miss Maude D Clark, who was born near Fullerton, Nance County, this state The one child of this union is a son, Morris, who is attending the public schools.

Hon William M Cain has been engaged in the practice of law in Nebraska for a quarter of a century and is now one of the representative members of the bar of Dodge County, with residence and professional headquarters in the City of Fremont, the judicial center of the county

Judge Cain was born in the Province of Ontario, Canada, November 15, 1868, and is a son of Dr James B and Mary E (Jenkinson) Cain, the former of whom was born in the Province of Quebec and the latter in the vicinity of the City of London, Ontario, where their marriage was solemnized Doctor Cain received his professional education in Rush Medical College and in 1871 he removed with his family to Illinois, where he continued in active general practice until 1880, when he came to Nebraska and established the family home at Leigh, Colfax County, where he continued as one of the leading physicians and surgeons of that section of the state for many years, and moving from there to Omaha in 1905, where he passed the remainder of his life, as did also his wife. Of their three children William M of this review is the elder of the two surviving; Wilmot is a successful contractor at Springfield, Illinois, and John died in childhood Doctor Cain was a stalwart republican in politics, was long affiliated with the Independent Order of Odd Fellows, and both he and his wife were earnest members of the Methodist Episcopal Church

William M Cain gained his rudimentary education in the schools of Illinois and was a lad of eleven years at the time of the family removal to Nebraska He continued his studies in the public schools of Leigh and the State University, and in preparation for his chosen profession he entered the law department of the University of Nebraska, in which he completed the prescribed curriculum and was graduated as a member of the class of 1894, his reception of the degree of Bachelor of Laws soon being followed by his admission to the bar of the state For the ensuing ten years he was established in practice at David City, Butler County, and he then removed to Colfax County and engaged in practice at Schuyler, the county seat, where he became associated with his former law preceptor, George H Thomas, under the firm name of Thomas & Cain Through his effective professional work in two county seat cities of Nebraska, Mr Cain had established a high reputation as a skilled trial lawyer and well fortified counselor, and thus he was fully fortified for further success when, July 15, 1914, he engaged in practice at the judicial center of Dodge County. At Fremont he is senior member of the firm of Cain & Johnson in which his coadjutor is Allen Johnson, and the firm controls a substantial and representative practice of general order While a resident of David City Mr Cain served two terms as prosecuting attorney of Butler County, and he now holds the office of city attorney of Fremont On June 1, 1920, he was appointed by the Supreme Court as one of the judges of the Nebraska Supreme Court Commission, which position he still holds He is a vigorous advocate of the cause of the democratic party but has had no ambition for office other than that in direct connection with the work of his profession He and his wife are active communicants of the Protestant Episcopal Church at Fremont

July 12, 1893, recorded the marriage of Mr. Cain to Miss Grace M De Long, and she passed to the life eternal on June 28, 1900, being survived by two children, John Morley Cain, who is now reading law in the office and under the effective preceptorship of his father, and Marjorie, who is the wife of Albert R Sears, of Fremont Mrs Cain was a member of the Congregational Church

On October 5, 1904, was solemnized the marriage of Mr Cain to Mrs Clara (De Long) Vandermeulen, a sister of his first wife, and she is the popular chatelaine of their pleasant home They have no children

Fred De La Matyr, the pioneer coal merchant of Fremont, is a man who is known all over Dodge and Washington counties as one of the solid and dependable citizens of this region, and one who has taken a constructive interest in its development He was born in Dane County, Wisconsin, in December, 1853, a son of G W. and Catherine (Jacobs) De La Matyr, both of whom were born in New York State, but migrated to Wisconsin in 1852, following their marriage In 1870 they came on further west to Nebraska, and after a stop at Omaha, located at Fremont G W De La Matyr was a Methodist clergyman, and died in California in 1892, but his widow survives him and makes her home at Los Angeles, California They had eight children, four of whom survive, namely Fred, who was the eldest born, Mrs Abbie Cooley, a widow in Los Angeles, California; Thurman E, who is an attorney of Los Angeles, Harry, who is a farmer of British Columbia, Canada, served in France for two years as a member of the Canadian contingent in the World war, and has been given a homestead for this service by the Dominion Government The family all belong to the Methodist Episcopal Church G W De La Matyr was a republican and a Mason The family originally came from France. On his mothers' side Mr. De La Matyr comes of German and Scotch ancestry

Growing up in Wisconsin, Mr De La Matyr attended its public schools and earned his first money working on a farm For a year he was employed in a postoffice in Wisconsin, and when he accompanied the family to Nebraska, he secured a position in the Fremont postoffice, and held it for some years Leaving the Government service Mr De La Matyr went into the Wilson & Hopkins bank and remained with that concern for six years He then moved to Eureka, Nevada, and for six months was connected with its lumber interests, and then for two years he was in the employ of the Union Pacific Railroad at Omaha, Nebraska Returning to Fremont in 1882, he established himself in his present coal business, and has built up a fine trade, handling all kinds of coal

In 1874 Mr De La Matyr was married in Dodge County to Evangaline E Parmele, born at Clinton, New York, and educated at Houghton Seminary For two years prior to her marriage she was engaged in teaching school at Fremont Mrs De La Matyr belongs to the Methodist Episcopal Church, but Mr De La Matyr is not connected with any religious organization He belongs to Fremont Lodge No 513, Benevolent and Protective Order of Elks A strong republican, Mr De La Matyr was elected on his party ticket as city clerk of Fremont, but during late years has devoted all of his attention to his coal business He has found enjoyment and recreation in driving, and takes a pride in always having a fine selection of horses, and is always the first one to be out with his sleigh after the initial snowfall Mr De La Matyr is one of the best examples of the self-made man Dodge County affords Beginning his life career with absolutely nothing but his willingness to work and capacity for saving, he has steadily advanced until he is now one of those who have a competency

Harry Kroeger Among those whose participation in agricultural affairs in Dodge County dates from a comparatively recent period, but who in a short time have substantially established themselves in the farming life of the community, is Harry Kroeger By marked capacity in his vocation, sound methods of management and innate force of character, he has already placed himself well on the road to success

Mr Kroeger was born in Dodge County, May 25, 1889, a son of Chris and Sophie Kroeger His father, a native of Germany, came to the United States at the age of twenty-four years and became one of the early settlers of Dodge County where he homesteaded and proved up on a claim, and where he passed a long and honorable career in the pursuits of the soil When he died, at the age of sixty-four years, his community lost a good and reliable citizen Mrs Kroeger, who is a native of Germany, survives her husband as a resident of Hooper

Harry Kroeger received his education in the public schools of Dodge County and was his father's associate in the work of the home farm until he reached the age of nineteen years At that time he became an operator on his own account, renting land from his father, and since the latter's death has rented land from his mother He carries on general farming, as well as dairying, and maintains a herd of Guernsey cattle The land, located in Hooper Township, is under a high state of cultivation, and its improvements, which were installed by Chris Kroeger, are valuable and attractive in character. Mr Kroeger is a republican in his political views, but has taken only a good citizen's part in public affairs He and his wife are consistent members of the Lutheran Church

Mr. Kroeger married Miss Clara Clark, a native of Virginia, and they are the parents of two children Gretchen and Narelle

HENRY TEIGELER Born and bred in a foreign land, Henry Teigeler of Fremont, a wholesale dealer in eggs, poultry and produce, has brought to his adopted country those habits of industry and thrift that have won him success in the business world, and placed him in a noteworthy position among the self-made men of whom America is so proud A son of the late Henry Teigeler, he was born, July 5, 1864, in Bremen, Germany, where he spent the first eighteen years of his life.

Henry Teigeler, Sr, was a lifelong resident of Germany Living in Bremen City, which is situated on both banks of the "Weser River," he established a saloon in which he served beer, light drinks and coffee, not only to the merchants and laborers but to the sailors, seamen and passengers from the boats, his place being well patronized To him and his wife, whose maiden name was Sophia Hahn, seven children were born, six of whom are living, Henry being the only one in America Two of the boys embarked in seafaring pursuits, and one of they stayed in Spain during the World war, while the other ran a German merchant ship in neutral ports. Both parents were members of the Lutheran Church, and faithfully followed its teachings

Having obtained a practical education when young, Henry Teigeler was employed for three and a half years by H W Stoever & Company, a wholesale leaf tobacco concern, acquiring not much money, but experience of value to him in his future career In 1882, following the tide of emigration, he came to Fremont, Nebraska, arriving here with no other assets than a willing spirit, a courageous heart, and a keen intellect, ready to take advantage of every offered opportunity to advance his financial condition Entering the employ of Osterman & Tremain, produce dealers, he worked for his board, it being a dull season, from the first of November until the middle of the next April, when the firm gave him $25 for his last month's work Mr. Teigeler, with his very limited capital, then went to Scribner, Nebraska, and started in business on his own account, buying poultry, butter and eggs Succeeding fairly well in the venture, he enlarged his operations somewhat by buying produce, too, in the different towns up and down the line from Scribner The first few hundred dollars that he accumulated while thus employed, he had the misfortune to lose all at once, and was forced to again start at the foot of the ladder of attainments.

Coming again to Fremont in 1894, Mr Teigeler became associated with the Fremont Butter and Egg Company Subsequently acquiring an interest in the business, a creamery was established, and George Haskell assumed charge of its management, while Mr. Teigeler looked after the produce end of the business Purchasing his partner's interests, Mr Teigeler now operates the entire business under the name of the Fremont Creamery Company, and has built up an extensive and lucrative trade, shipping produce of all kinds to the eastern markets He is also interested in the Beatrice Creamery Company of Chicago, through which he does considerable business

In 1894 Mr Teigeler was united in marriage with Dora Romberg, a native of Iowa, and they have three children, namely: Henry, Frederick and Paul, a pupil in the Fremont High School Henry, the eldest son, a graduate of the Fremont High School, was attending the Northwestern University in Evanston, Illinois, when the United States entered the World war From there he enlisted in Company A, Three Hundred and Fifty-Fifth Infantry, in which he was made a sergeant, and going with his regiment to France lost his life in the engagement on the Marne The American Legion Post of Fremont is named in his honor the Henry Teigeler, Jr, Post Frederick, the second son, was graduated from the Fremont High School and is now attending the Northwestern University, where he is very active in athletics, belonging to both the football and the basketball teams

Mr Teigeler has been very successful in his business undertakings, and has accumulated considerable property, having large land interests in Dodge County, also being vice president of the First National Bank of Fremont He is a republican in politics, and when but twenty-two years old was elected justice of the peace in Scribner, and served in that capacity for three years He and his family attend the Congregational Church and generously assist in its support.

W E. DURKEE Prominent among the men who have been intimately associated with the development and promotion of the industrial and manufacturing interests of Dodge County is W E Durkee of Fremont, who is carrying on an extensive business as proprietor and manager of the Globe Cornice Works, a long established industry A son of Charles T Durkee, he was born in 1878 in Farmland, Randolph County, Indiana, where his childhood days were spent

Born and reared in New York State, Charles T Durkee migrated to Indiana in early manhood and there started in life for himself as a sheet metal worker Coming with his family to Nebraska in 1884, he worked for Hetty & Son a year In 1885 he established the Globe Cornice Works, at Fremont, where he first located, and subsequently built up a large and lucrative wholesale business, dealing in sheet metal Having achieved both business and financial success, he sold his plant to his son, and, with his wife, moved to California, where he is living retired from business cares He is independent in politics, supportng to some extent the principles of the democratic party Fraternally he belongs to the Independent Order of Odd Fellows, and religiously both he and his wife are members of the Episcopal Church His wife, whose name before marriage was Jennie Bond, was born in New York State, but as a girl moved with her parents to Indiana, where her marriage was solemnized

The only child of his parents, W E Durkee was educated in Fremont, having attended the graded, high and normal schools Completing his studies, he learned the metal worker's trade under his father's tuition, and when familiar with all the details of the business bought from his father the Globe Cornice Works, in the management of which he is meeting with characteristic success, each year increasing its products and extending its trade

Mr. Durkee married, in 1908, Eva Bremer, who was born in Iowa Religiously Mr and Mrs Durkee are worthy members of the Episcopal Church Mr Durkee is a straightforward democrat in politics, and is a member of the Benevolent and Protective Order of Elks, of the Fremont Commercial Club and of the Country Club

HENRY DOERING An enumeration of the enterprising and representative German citizens of Dodge County would be incomplete without special mention of Henry Doering, the successful and well-known hardware merchant of Fremont, for since casting his lot with us he has stamped the impress of his individuality upon the community and benefited alike himself and his neighbors, for while laboring for his own advancement he has not been selfish and neglectful of his duties to the public in general, but he always supports such measures as make for the general good

Henry Doering was born in Germany on August 25, 1874, and is the son of H Carl and Marie (Wehner) Doering His parents spent their entire lives in their native land He was reared under the parental roof and secured his educational training in the public schools In 1904 he came to the United States and located at once in Dodge County, Nebraska, where for a time he engaged in farming However, he was ambitious for a commercial career and, having been employed in the hardware business in his native country, he naturally turned to it here Previous to engaging in business he attended the Fremont Normal School for about six months in order to perfect his knowledge of the English language He then took employment with the Nye, Schneider & Company elevator, and then clerked for Holloway & Fowler for about five years Then he began to carry out his long-cherished plans for an independent business career and opened a small hardware store in Fremont. Success attended his efforts from the beginning and as his business grew he increased his stock until September, 1918, when he occupied his new store, where he has two floors stocked with a complete and well selected stock of shelf and heavy hardware of all descriptions He is well located and now operates one of the best stores in his line in Dodge County

In 1907 Mr Doering was married to Amanda Quesner, who also is a native of Germany, coming to the United States when a child with her parents, who settled in North Bend, Dodge County, where her father clerked in a mercantile business for a time He then conducted a mercantile business in Dodge for several years Mr and Mrs Doering are members of the Lutheran Church and Mr Doering is independent in his political views. Fraternally he is a member of the Knights of Pythias Beginning life practically at the bottom of the ladder, he has climbed to the top with no help but a brave heart, industrious hands and an intelligent brain, and is a living example of what may be accomplished by perseverance and thrift, and now, because of the high ideals and honest motives which have controlled his actions and the success which has attended his efforts, he enjoys the esteem and good will of all who know him

ENDELL N LEAKE, A M, M D A widely known, highly esteemed and eminently successful physician and surgeon of Fremont, Dr Endell N Leake is engaged in the practice of a profession that is particularly exacting in its demands upon the time attention and energies of its devotees, and is meeting with eminent success, his patronage being extensive and remunerative A native of New York, he was born November 9, 1855, in Buffalo, a son of Rev Robert N Leake His paternal grandfather, Rev William Leake, emigrated with his family from England to the United States about 1845, and subsequently had charge of churches of the Methodist Episcopal denomination in different parts of the country, spending his last years in Kansas, where his death occurred at the venerable age of ninety-one years

Robert N Leake was born in London, England, in 1833, and as a lad of twelve years came with his parents to this country, where he completed his early education Entering the ministry as a young man, he served as pastor of various Methodist Episcopal churches of central and western New York, continuing as a minister of the gospel for full

E. N. Leake A.M. M.D.

forty years previous to his death in 1907 Rev Robert N Leake married Margaret Morgan, who was born in Canada in 1836, a daughter of William Morgan, who came from England to the United States at an early day, and settled on a farm near Darien, New York Four children blessed their union, as follows Endell N, Charles W, a dentist in Chicago, Illinois; Mary E, widow of Walter Calkins, resides in Syracuse, New York, and Walter J, one of the leading dentists of Lockport, New York. The father was a republican in politics, and both he and his wife, naturally, were true and faithful members of the Methodist Episcopal Church

Endell N Leake obtained his preliminary education at the Union School, in Lockport, New York, a noted academy which drew its pupils from every part of the state Subsequently entering Syracuse University, he was there graduated with the degree of Master of Arts in 1878, and two years later, in 1880, he received the degree of Doctor of Medicine at the Homeopathic College and Hospital of New York City Locating in Butler, Pennsylvania, Doctor Leake remained there from 1881 until 1894, gaining professional knowledge and skill, and building up a large practice Coming from there to Fremont, Nebraska, the doctor has met with characteristic success, both as a physician and surgeon, winning not only a very satisfactory patronage, but an extended reputation for professional skill and ability

Doctor Leake married, in February, 1881, Mary A Brownell, a native of New York State One child was born of their union, Margaret, who married Elisha B Edwards, and died in Idaho of the Spanish influenza during the nation-wide epidemic in 1918 Doctor Leake is a member of the County, State and American associations of Homeopathy, and while serving as president of the State Medical Association wrote and delivered an address that was very highly spoken of by his professional brethren therein gathered The doctor is independent in politics, and both he and his wife are members of the Congregational Church

WALTER R RECKMEYER While there are some notable exceptions, as a general thing the man who has a thoroughly practical knowledge of his business is the one who has more satisfactory results Walter R Reckmeyer, owner of one of the large planing mills of Fremont, is a carpenter by trade and there is not a single piece of work turned out by his plant that he could not make himself, and so his customers have the advantage of his expert supervision over all of the processes.

Walter R Reckmeyer was born at Fremont on November 25, 1874, a son of Henry and Christine (Kremling) Reckmeyer, both of whom were born in Germany, but were brought to the United States when about twelve years of age, their parents locating in the vicinity of Quincy, Illinois Between 1869 and 1870 they came to Fremont, Nebraska, where the father continued to work as a carpenter all of his life, dying at Fremont in 1900, but the mother survives, and she and all of their children live at Fremont These children are. Julia, who married Dr McGuire Mead, Walter R, whose name heads this review, and Clarence, who is a traveling salesman, lives with his mother There was one other child, but he is now deceased Henry Reckmeyer belonged to the Ancient Order of United Workmen In politics he was a republican His wife early joined the Methodist Episcopal Church, and she still maintains her membership in it

Walter R Reckmeyer attended the public schools of Fremont and also its excellent normal school When he was only thirteen years old he began learning the carpenter trade under his father's supervision, and has always worked in it, although later on he branched out as a contractor Twenty years ago he bought his present planing mill, and turns out all kinds of wooden fixtures for the use of contractors Employment is given to four men in the mill

On August 26, 1908, Mr Reckmeyer was united in marriage with Etta Miller, born at Momence, Illinois, a daughter of Henry Miller, a retired farmer of Yutan, Nebraska Mrs Reckmeyer was the widow of C R Phelps, and had three children by her first marriage, namely Dorothea, who married Al Bencelhemier of Fremont, Vada, who married J O Dolgane of Chappell, Nebraska, and Leona, who lives with Mr and Mrs Reckmeyer The girls are members of the Presbyterian Church, but Mrs Reckmeyer belongs to the Reformed Lutheran Church Fraternally Mr. Reckmeyer belongs to the Elks, the Ancient Order of United Workmen and the Odd Fellows While never seeking for public office he exerts his right of suffrage and votes the republican ticket All that he owns today has come to him through his industry, thrift and good business judgment, and he has not only been successful in a material way, but has also won appreciation as a good citizen and upright man who lives up to his contracts

JAMES H SUTTON An experienced and exceedingly skillful agriculturist, James H Sutton's remarkable success during his active career has been brought about by persistent energy, well directed toil, and exceptional business ability, his highly improved farm in Elkhorn Township bearing visible evidence of his judicious labor and wise management A son of the late James and Ellen Sutton, he was born, in 1864, in New York State, where he lived until 2½ years old when the family moved to Illinois, where they lived until they came to Nebraska in 1870 James Sutton made this long, tedious journey in a prairie schooner, that having been the most expeditious mode of traveling in those days before the western country was spanned by the network of railways that now make journeying so rapid and pleasant Taking up a homestead claim in Saunders County near Wahoo, he erected the necessary buildings, tilled sufficient land to make a good living for his household, and continued a resident of Saunders County until his death at the age of sixty-three years His wife survived him, living to the age of seventy-six years They were both natives of Ireland.

But six years old when his father settled in Saunders County, this state, James H Sutton, began as soon as old enough to assist in the farm labors, and having taken kindly to agricultural pursuits has followed farming as his chief occupation In 1894 he located in Dodge County, and having purchased 480 acres of land that was still in its primeval condition has devoted his time, attention, and means to its management, and his labors have been well rewarded His improvements, all of which he made himself, are of a substantial character, and a large part of his land is highly productive, responding readily to cultivation Mr Sutton carries on general farming and stock raising on a somewhat extensive scale, and in addition to operating his home farm, which is in Elkhorn Township, owns and manages a large ranch of 2,000 acres in Holt County Before locating in Dodge County, Mr Sutton had made a specialty of sheep raising and feeding, and now pays considerable attention to that industry, keeping about one hundred head on his home farm From 1889 to 1896 he made five trips across the country from Oregon and Nevada with large bands of sheep to this county and feed for market Enterprising and progressive, he takes advantage of every opportunity for adding to his agricultural knowledge and efficiency, and is an active and interested member of the Farmers Union He is well acquainted with the western section of our country, in the management of his business interests having made several overland trips to the Pacific Coast.

Mr Sutton married Birdie Pollock, and they have two children, namely James A, born twenty-one years ago; and Rona, nine years younger Politically Mr Sutton is a sound republican, fraternally he is a member of the Ancient Free and Accepted Order of Masons, and of the Independent Order of Odd Fellows Religiously he and his family are affiliated with the Methodist Episcopal Church

George C Campen To a great extent the prosperity of our great country is due to the honest industry, the sturdy perseverance and the wise economy which so prominently characterizes the foreign element that has entered largely into our population By comparison with their old country surroundings, these people have readily recognized the fact that in America lie the greatest opportunities for the man of ambition and energy And because of this many have broken the ties of home and native land and have earnestly entered upon the task of gaining in the new world a name and a competence Among this class may be mentioned George C Campen, of Fremont, who, by indefatigable and honest effort, has not only acquired a well-merited material prosperity, but also richly earned the highest esteem of all with whom he has been associated

George C. Campen was born in Denmark on July 11, 1868, and is the son of Hans and Wilhelmina (Lefeedt) Campen The father was born on October 14, 1837, and died in August, 1870, and the mother, who was born on December 21, 1841, died in Copenhagen in March, 1918 They spent their entire lives in their native land, where the father followed the vocation of a farmer, becoming quite well-to-do On the paternal side, George C Campen traces his ancestry back to Thyge Hansen, of the sixteenth century The paternal grandfather was George C. Campen, who owned a large farm and over one hundred and fifty pure bred cattle, the family occupying a position of prominence and influence in the community To Hans and Wilhelmina Campen were born five children, of whom three are living, namely Caroline became the wife of P B Christenen and they remain in Denmark, Anna became the wife of H Nelson, a railroad engineer at Copenhagen, and George C

George C Campen was reared under the parental roof and secured his education in the schools of his home community. At the age of twenty years he entered the Danish army, with which he served for nine months, and in 1890 he immigrated to the United States He first located in New York, where he followed the painting and decorating trade for a year He then located in Omaha, Nebraska, and in 1892 came to Fremont, where he has remained ever since. Here he established himself in the painting and decorating business and, being a good workman in that line, he met with success from the start, gaining a good reputation because of the high quality of his work In 1905 Mr. Campen established a store on Fifth Street, and has occupied three different locations on that street and is now occupying a fine two-story building erected by him for his business needs He received a large and representative patronage and keeps from seven to twenty-five men constantly busy on his work As a painter and decorator he has perhaps no superiors and few equals in this community and is considered a man of original and artistic ideas When it is remembered that Mr. Campen's sole cash capital when he landed in New York was but $5, it can be appreciated what he has accomplished through his energy, ability and economy.

Mr Campen was married on December 26, 1892, to Sina Jensen, who was born in Denmark, but who, when a child, was brought by her mother to this country, locating in Lancaster County, Nebraska, where she was reared and educated She has borne her husband three children, namely· Agnes, the wife of Harold Eling, a painter and decorator in Fremont, Thorvald, who occupies a homestead at Opton, Wyoming, Edith, deceased

Mr Campen is a republican in his political views and he and his wife are members of the Danish Evangelical Lutheran Church He is a member of the Knights and Ladies of Security Among those who know him best he bears the reputation of a man who uses sound judgment in all his business affairs and who always exercises the duties of citizenship in a conscientious manner Because of his success and his character, he occupies an enviable standing throughout the community.

L H ROGERS In the death of the late L H Rogers, Dodge County, Nebraska, lost one of its representative citizens As the day, with its morning of hope and promise, its noontide of activity, its evening of complete and successful efforts, ending in the grateful rest and quiet of the night, so was the life of this honored man His career was a busy and useful one, and although he devoted his attention primarily to his individual affairs, he never allowed the pursuits of wealth to warp his kindly nature, but preserved his faculties and the warmth of his heart for the broadening and helpful influences of human life, being to the end a kindly, genial friend and gentleman with whom it was a pleasure to meet and converse Through the years of his residence in this locality he was ever true to all trusts reposed in him, whether of a public or private nature, and his reputation in a business way was unassailable He commanded the respect of all by his upright life and engraved his name indelibly on the pages of Dodge County's history

L H Rogers was born in Fayetteville, New York, March 20, 1834, and his death occurred in Fremont in 1903, at the age of sixty-nine years He was educated in the public schools of his native state, having lived in various places owing to the fact that his father was a minister of the Methodist Episcopal Church and was located at several points in the central part of that state. At about the time he attained his majority, L H Rogers left his native state and early in 1857 he arrived in Fremont, being among the earliest settlers in this locality, the town having been established in August of the previous year Here he engaged in farming, which occupied his attention until 1861, when he and his brother established the banking house of E H & L H Rogers This was one of the early banks of this section of the state and became the First National Bank of Fremont, one of the most important and influential financial institutions of the newly settled community Mr. Rogers maintained his active connection with the banking business until 1884, when his health failed and he was compelled to relinquish his active participation in business affairs He and his wife did considerable traveling during the years following, but he maintained his residence here continually up to the time of his death Having become identified with the business interests of this locality in its first stages of development, he was for many years a potent influence in commercial and business circles He was a citizen of high civic ideals and as a citizen he was well worthy of the unqualified confidence and esteem in which he was universally held

In 1864 Mr Rogers was married to Lottie Elizabeth Heaton, who was born September 13, 1844, in the State of Wisconsin, the daughter of Rev Isaac E. Heaton, whose name is linked with the earliest history of this immediate locality. His was the first family to move to Fremont in 1856, he preached the first sermon in Fremont, and organized the first Congregational Church here, the seven charter members of this society having been Reverend and Mrs Heaton, Nathan Heaton (paternal grandfather of Mrs Rogers), E H Barnard, Mrs Seth Marvin, Richard Davis and one other The Reverend Heaton was widely known throughout this section of the state as a Congregational minister of ability and energy, who exerted a powerful influence on the moral standing of the pioneer communities of that day. He was a prohibition republican in his political views To him and his wife were born two children, Mrs Rogers, who is now the oldest living pioneer settler of Fremont, and Mary E, who was the wife of J J Hawthorne, formerly of Fremont, both being now deceased. To Mr and Mrs. Rogers two children have been born, namely C I, who is now retired from business and is living in Fremont, and Belle H, who remains with her mother Mrs Rogers is a member of the Congregational Church and her children are identified with the Methodist Episcopal Church

Mr. Rogers took an active part in advancing the early religious life of Fremont and he was a charter member of the Methodist Episcopal Church here, the others being E H. Rogers and his wife, Mrs Wealthy Beebe and Mrs Mary Flor Politically, L H Rogers gave his support to the republican party and was deeply interested in the public affairs of the community in which he lived Mrs Rogers has lived on the same lot continuously since 1888, though in 1896 her present commodious and attractive home was built It is also worthy of note that Mrs Rogers still owns some of the land that her husband originally purchased here in 1856 There are but few of the pioneer settlers of the '50s still remaining to tell the interesting stories of the development of this locality and to them all honor is due for the part they played in the development of this favored community

FRED F SCOTT has been a resident of Dodge County from the time of his birth, has here proved a successful representative of farm industry, and here his secure place in popular confidence and esteem is indicated by the fact that he is now serving as a member of the county board of supervisors

Mr Scott was born in Union Township, Dodge County, on the 20th of March, 1870, and is a son of David and Isabelle (Johnson) Scott, who were born and reared in Ireland Upon coming to the United States David Scott found employment in a bottling establishment in the City of Philadelphia, though he had learned in his native land the trade of cooper He came with his wife to Dodge County, Nebraska, in the early '60s and purchased land in Union Township, at the rate of one dollar and a quarter an acre. He improved this farm, which he later sold, and thereafter he gave his attention to the management of the fine farm which he owned in section 22, that township, until he finally retired and established his home at North Bend, where his death occurred in 1914 and where his widow still resides

Fred F Scott gained in his boyhood and youth a goodly experience in connection with the work and management of the home farm, and his educational discipline was secured in the public schools of his native county, and by one year of attendance in the Nebraska State Normal School at Fremont. He remained at the parental home until he had attained to his legal majority and then instituted independent operations as a farmer. He utilized for this enterprise a tract of land owned by his father, and finally he purchased also about 120 acres of additional land. He continued as one of the active and successful exponents of agricultural and live stock industry in Union Township until 1914, when he retired and established his home at North Bend, though he still retains ownership of his well improved farm property, which comprises 360 acres. Mr Scott is a vigorous advocate and supporter of the cause of the republican party and is serving his first term as a member of the county board of supervisors He is a stockholder in and stanch supporter of the Farmers' Union in his native county, and is affiliated with the Masonic fraternity and the Modern Woodmen of America

The year 1895 recorded the marriage of Mr Scott to Miss Mina Hatcher, who was born in West Virginia and who was a child at the time of the family removal to Nebraska Mr. and Mrs Scott have two children: Irma A, a skilled stenographer who now holds a position in an insurance office in the City of Omaha, and Marvin F, who is still a student in the public schools of North Bend

JACOB R BADER, president of the J R. Bader Furniture Company, of Fremont, has one of the most beautiful stores in Nebraska, and during the years he has been connected with this city he has always proven himself a man of probity, excellent business endowments and a factor in the moral uplift of his community Mr Bader was born in Hugsweier, Baden, Germany, on July 24, 1864, a son of Carl and Caroline (Lieb) Bader. Carl Bader was district treasurer for forty-five years, and both he and his wife were very pious, their main concern in life being the spiritual welfare of their children Their efforts in this direction met with very gratifying results for three of their sons are successful preachers, one of them now being at the head of the house publishing all of the religious literature of his denomination Another son served as a missionary to India, and a daughter married a missionary to India.

After attending the public schools of Germany, Jacob R Bader came to the United States, and took a commercial course in the business college at Nebraska City, Nebraska He has no degrees After two years' work on a Nebraska farm, Mr Bader secured employment as a bookkeeper in a brewery of Nebraska City, and later went into a furniture store of that same place as a clerk, holding that position from 1886 until 1890, and learning the business in all of its details

In 1890 Mr Bader came to Fremont and, after working for M H Hinman, bought the business in October, 1890, taking Ernest Elsner as a partner Later the firm saw several changes, becoming in turn Bader & Anderson, Bader & Rogers Furniture Co, Bader Bros Company, and finally the J R Bader Furniture Company, of which Mr Bader is president and owner of sixty per cent of the stock He is a member of the Fred Bader & Company, undertakers His furniture business has increased its annual sales from $11,000 to $160,000

On May 25, 1886, Mr Bader was married on the farm of his father-in-law, E Elsner, at Arlington, Nebraska, to Emma E Elsner,

whose father is one of the successful farmers of Nebraska The following children have been born to Mr and Mrs. Bader Carl G, who is a minister of the gospel, married Edna McAfee of Worcester, Massachusetts, Ernest F, who is advertising manager of the United Phonograph Corporation, married Nellie Baldwin, Eleanore O, who married Clarence King, a lumberman of Sterling, Colorado, Alma E, who is a music teacher, resides at home, Clara B, who is a student of the Art Institute, of Chicago, Illinois, and Jean R., who is attending the Fremont High School

Mr Bader is an active republican and has never failed to vote He is a Methodist, and has been licensed to preach since 1886 While he has been very successful in his enterprises there is no doubt but that Mr Bader takes more satisfaction in the work he has been able to accomplish in raising the standard of morality, and bringing additional souls into the fold A man of unblemished private life, he sets an example for others to follow, and certainly in every act practices the religion he so fervently preaches

CHARLES C POLLARD is a leading representative of the real estate and insurance business in the City of Fremont, and his operations in the handling of real estate extend far beyond the immediate confines of Dodge County, though his attention is given principally to the handling of city property and to his substantial general insurance business

Mr Pollard is a scion of the stanchest of colonial New England stock and claims the old Green Mountain State as the place of his nativity. He was born at Wilmington, Vermont, July 4, 1854, and it may consistently be said that his patriotism and civic loyalty have ever been in consonance with the spirit of the great national holiday which figured as the day of his nativity. He is a son of Jonas S. and Louisa D (Cunningham) Pollard, both natives of the State of Massachusetts, where the former was born November 10, 1810, and the latter March 20, 1818, their marriage having been solemnized May 16, 1844 The parents were residents of their native state at the time of their death, though they had lived for several years in Vermont Mrs Pollard passed away in 1873, and her husband survived her by nearly a score of years, his death having occurred in 1890 Of the five children Charles C is the elder of the two now living, and Joshua H is a machinist at Worcester, Massachusetts Jonas S Pollard was a man of energy and industry, but in the cultivation of his small and none too prolific farm in Massachusetts he was able to gain only modest prosperity, his original dwelling on his farm having been constructed of logs which were hewed by him He was a stanch republican and he and his wife were zealous members of the Congregational Church His father, Jonas Pollard, was born at Bolton, Massachusetts, July 12, 1778, and was a son of William Pollard, born at Billerica, Massachusetts, August 3, 1698 Thomas, father of the last mentioned, William Pollard, was born in Coventry, England, as was also his father, William Pollard, who came with his family to America and settled at Billerica, Massachusetts, in 1692 John Cunningham, maternal grandfather of Charles C. Pollard, was born at Phillipston, Massachusetts, and he likewise was a representative of one of the sterling colonial families of the old Bay State

Charles C. Pollard acquired his early education in the public schools at Clinton, Massachusetts, and supplemented this by continuing his studies two winters under the direction of a private tutor. His initial business experience was gained as an employe in a carpet factory, and thereafter he was employed for a time in a shoe shop and grocery store at Spencer, Massachusetts In 1882, when twenty-eight years of age, he came to the West, and in September of that year he established his residence at Cherokee, Iowa, where he was employed as clerk in a store until the spring of the following year, when he removed to what is now the State of South Dakota For four years he was engaged in the lumber business at Howard, that state, which was then still a part of Dakota Territory, and on the 1st of April, 1887, he arrived at Fremont, Nebraska For the ensuing eight years he had the management of a lumber business at his place, and he then turned his attention to independent enterprise in the real estate and insurance business, with which he has since continued his effective alliance and with marked success He is now one of the veteran exponents of these lines of business in Dodge County, and his reputation, won through years of honest and effective service, is one of the most valuable assets of his business Mr Pollard has had no ambition for political activity or official preferment, but is a stanch advocate of the principles of the republican party He is actively affiliated with the local Blue Lodge, Chapter, and Commandery of Knights Templar of the Masonic fraternity, and has served as high priest of his chapter, besides having held official chairs in the lodge He has been actively identified with the Independent Order of Odd Fellows for thirty-five years, and he and his wife are earnest members of the Congregational Church in their home city

October 19, 1886, recorded the marriage of Mr Pollard to Miss Sarah J Harrison, who was born in the City of London, England.

John H Hoebener An intelligent and enterprising agriculturist of Dodge County, John H Hoebener has a well appointed farm in Platte Township, on which he has erected a conveniently arranged residence, modern in every respect, a substantial barn, and all other necessary buildings for carrying on farming, cattle and sheep raising after the most approved methods, everything about the premises indicating the thrift, industry and keen judgment of the proprietor He was born, July 22, 1853, in Lucerne County, Pennsylvania, a son of J. H and Elizabeth Hoebener, life long residents of the Keystone State

Brought up and educated in his native county, John H Hoebener spent the earlier years of his life in that vicinity Migrating to Nebraska in 1881, he located in Dodge County, and having opened a meat shop in Fremont continued in business nine years Changing his occupation, Mr Hoebener began dealing in sheep, driving flocks of them from Oregon, and feeding them in Fremont, where later, for a period of nine years, he was engaged in the hide and wool business Giving that up, Mr Hoebener lived retired for a while, and then bought his present farm of 248 acres in Platte Township, two miles from town, an advantageous location In addition to carrying on mixed husbandry successfully he makes a specialty of feeding cattle, hogs and sheep In 1916 Mr. Hoebener erected his fine residence, one of the most attractive in the township and is constantly adding to the improvements already inaugurated

Mr Hoebener married, in Illinois, Anna H Hoefer, a native of that state, and into their household six children have made their advent, namely: Dorothy, Bertha, Frieda, Iona, Henrietta, and John In his political affiliations Mr. Hoebener is independent, voting for the best men and measures He has never aspired to public office, and belongs to no fraternal or social organizations Religiously he and his family worship at the Presbyterian Church

PETER PARKERT, JR. Possessing superior business ability, enterprise and judgment, Peter Parkert, Jr. of Everett Township, has gained a position of prominence and influence in the financial, industrial and agricultural interests of Dodge County, and well merits representation in a work of this character. A son of Peter Parkert, Sr., he was born, August 30, 1887, in Dodge County, Nebraska, which he has always proudly claimed as home.

Born in Germany seventy-one years ago, Peter Parkert, Sr., came to this country in early life, locating first in Michigan. Being assured that better opportunities for advancing his interests awaited him in the then far West, he came to Nebraska in 1869, and for a short time worked in Fremont. Subsequently taking up a homestead claim in Dodge County, he was prosperously engaged in farming and stock raising until 1904, when he retired from agricultural pursuits, and took up his residence in Hooper. He is now serving as vice president of the First National Bank of Hooper, and is a stockholder in the Hooper Land & Investment Company, and in the Hooper mills. He is a democrat in politics, and for about twenty years served as county supervisor of Dodge County. In religion he is a Catholic.

Peter Parkert, Sr., married Mary Tillman, a daughter of Frank M. and Anna (Enderley) Tillman, natives, respectively, of Germany and Switzerland. After coming to this country to live, Mr. Tillman lived first in Detroit, Michigan, where his marriage was solemnized, and later was hotelkeeper in Holton, Michigan, for a number of years. In 1868 he settled in Dodge County, this state, and carried on farming in Ridgeley Township until 1881, when he removed to Hooper, where his death occurred at the age of ninety-one years, in 1915, seven years after that of his wife, who died in 1908, aged eighty-two years. Their children were as follows: Joseph, deceased; Mary, now Mrs. Parkert; Margaret, wife of Charles S. Basler, of Hooper; Lizzie, wife of W. F. Basler, of Hooper, Frank A., of Hooper, Catherine, wife of Edward Wickhorst, of Santa Ana, California; and A. M., a prominent business man of Hooper.

Of the union of Peter Parkert, Sr., and Mary Tillman, six children were born, as follows: George, a farmer in Dodge County, Peter, Jr., of this sketch, Anna, wife of Harry Heine, a farmer, living near Madison, Nebraska; Ella, wife of William Schuler, a Dodge County farmer, Isabelle, wife of H. R. Katz, who is engaged in farming in Dodge County, and Julia.

After leaving the Fremont Normal School, where he completed his early studies, Peter Parkert, Jr., was bookkeeper for a year for the Farmers Grain & Stock Company, at Hooper. Beginning to farm on his own account in 1906, he made a specialty of dealing in Shorthorn cattle for a period of six years, holding annual sales, and is still interested to some extent in that industry, keeping a good grade of stock, and feeding for the markets. He is prominent in business circles, having served as secretary of the Farmers Grain & Stock Company until it was sold to the Farmers Union, in which he is a stockholder, and having been secretary of the Hooper Mill & Grain Company since its organization. Mr. Parkert is also a stockholder in the First National Bank of Hooper; a stockholder and director of the Stock Show Company of Hooper; and one of the stockholders of the Hooper Land & Investment Company. He is a democrat in politics, but is not active in public affairs. Religiously he is a member of the Catholic Church; and fraternally belongs to the Knights of Columbus.

Mr Parkert married, in 1909, Miss Edith S Drayer, a native of Iowa

W A. GUIDINGER, M D Engaged in the practice of one of the most exacting of all of the higher lines of occupation, W A Guidinger, M D, is devoting his time and energies to his professional duties, and is meeting with gratifying success, having won an extensive patronage, not only in Dodge, but throughout the surrounding country A son of John G Guidinger, Sr, he was born, June 11, 1882, in Colfax County, Nebraska, on the parental homestead.

Born in Wisconsin, John G Guidinger, Sr, selected farming as his occupation, and in 1855 made his way to the newer country of Nebraska, where there were large tracts of Government land for sale at a minimum price Settling in Colfax County, he cleared and improved a valuable farm, on which he lived and labored many years Having accumulated a competency, he is now retired from active business, his home being at Hollister, California To him and his wife, Annie G Guidinger, eight children were born, two of whom, a son and a daughter, have passed to the life beyond, while W A, of this sketch, and his brother John, of Fremont, are the only two sons now living in Nebraska The mother died when but sixty-five years old

After leaving the rural schools, W A Guidinger attended the Fremont Normal School four years, and subsequently entered the Chicago College of Medicine and Surgery, from which he was graduated with the degree of Doctor of Medicine Locating in Dodge in 1907, Doctor Guidinger has labored earnestly and successfully, and has made rapid strides in his professional career, being numbered among the leading physicians and surgeons of Dodge County He has won the confidence of the general public to a marked degree, and through his recognized skill and ability has built up a large and lucrative practice

Doctor Guidinger married, in 1906, Minnie Johnson, who was born in Appleton, Wisconsin, a daughter of James and Anna (Hansen) Johnson, her father having been a millwright. The doctor is independent in politics, casting his vote for the best men and measures regardless of party prejudices Fraternally he belongs to the Ancient Free and Accepted Order of Masons, and religiously he is a Congregationalist

GRANT S REEDER, M D The record made by the physicians and surgeons of Nebraska stands to the credit of the profession, and the men, who, sacrificing personal interests, proffered their services to the Government, and whole-heartedly gave their time and skill to the needs of their country in time of war, deserve special consideration on the part of the public, although they are the last ones to even admit this obligation. One of these patriotic young men of the profession who went out from Dodge County, is Dr Grant S Reeder, of Fremont, who has achieved more than local distinction because of his specialization on children's diseases.

Doctor Reeder was born at Tipton, Iowa, on March 25, 1885, a son of John W and Sarah E (Lee) Reeder, both natives of Ohio. John W Reeder came West to Iowa on October 10, 1852, and he is still living, although eighty-four years old His wife came to Cedar County, Iowa, in 1849, and at the age of seventy-six years, is one of the oldest surviving settlers of that county They were married in Cedar County, Iowa Until his retirement, John W. Reeder was active as a stockman, and is

C. H. Rogers

still interested in affairs in spite of his years After the organization of the republican party, he espoused its principles and still adheres to them He was one of the organizers of the first free school west of the Mississippi River For many years he has maintained membership with the Knights of Pythias The paternal grandfather, George Reeder, was born in Pennsylvania, and came to Iowa many years ago, and died in that state He was a circuit rider of the Methodist Church, and one of the best-known men in early days in Cedar and other counties His farm, which he homesteaded, is now owned by Mrs Reeder John W. Reeder was brought up in the faith of his father, and, while not entering the ministry, has always been exceedingly active in church work and is very religious The maternal grandfather, William Lee, was born in Virginia, from whence he moved to Ohio and later to Iowa, where he died

Doctor Reeder attended the public schools of Tipton, and was graduated from the high school of that place in 1903 He then took a collegiate course at Cornell, Iowa, in which he was graduated in 1907, following which he matriculated at Rush Medical College, Chicago, Illinois, from which he was graduated in 1911, with the degree of Doctor of Medicine

Immediately following his graduation Doctor Reeder engaged in a general practice at Kirkland, Illinois, but at the expiration of four years came to Fremont, Nebraska, arriving here in the spring of 1916, and has been engaged in the practice of his profession in this city ever since with the exception of the time he was in the army. He enlisted in July, 1918, and was discharged in July, 1919, having, during that period spent six weeks at New Haven, Connecticut, in the United States General Hospital No 16, when he was assigned to examine the soldiers for diseases of the lungs at Camp Funston, and in the Carolinas Still later he was placed in charge of convalescents, especially those suffering from lung and heart trouble, and rendered a magnificent service to the Government and soldiers

Doctor Reeder was married on October 4, 1911, to Wilda Chace, born at Stanton, Nebraska They have one son, Robert Chace Reeder, who was born on August 9, 1912, and one daughter, Jane Chace Reeder, who was born on February 13, 1920 Both Doctor Reeder and his wife belong to the Methodist Episcopal Church He is a member of the Masonic fraternity, the Knights of Pythias and the Modern Woodmen of America. While he votes the republican ticket, he is not in any sense a politician, devoting himself to his profession In connection with it he maintains membership with the Dodge County Medical Society, the Nebraska State Medical Society and the American Medical Association, and is secretary and treasurer of the county organization

Possessing as he does the personality which wins the confidence and affection of children, Doctor Reeder is making considerable strides forward in his special line, and patients are brought to him from a wide territory. Conscientious as well as skilled, he gives to each little one careful thought and attention, and his success has been really remarkable, not only in the curing of maladies, but the prevention of disease and the stamping out of conditions which might, if left, terminate in serious results

ELIPHUS HIBBARD ROGERS Born in humble circumstances, and reared in a school of stern experience, the late Eliphus Hibbard Rogers, an early pioneer of Fremont, was a man of strong personality and remarkable force of character, and through persistent effort overcame the almost seemingly insurmountable obstacles constantly appearing in his pathway, obtaining positions of influence in business, political and religious circles, and becoming prominent in the public affairs of our country A native of New York State, he was born, January 12, 1830, in Litchfield, Herkimer County, a son of Rev Lucius Carey and Fannie (Locke) Rogers, his father, a minister in the Methodist Episcopal denomination, having belonged to the Oneida, New York, Conference

Manifesting a decided thirst for knowledge very early in his life, Eliphus Hibbard Rogers was sent to a school resembling in some respects the kindergarten schools of today, where he was regarded as an infant prodigy, having been especially brilliant in declamation He continued his education in the different places in which his father was located, taking a special course in a select school at Springfield, Otsego County In the summer of 1842, he entered the employ of Spencer Field, a tavern keeper, who owned a large farm, and in addition to raising considerable stock, fed all of the cattle passing through the place to the Eastern markets, and although it was a hard position for a boy of his age he stuck to it for quite a while

Going to Lowville, New York, in the spring of 1844, he became a clerk in the general store of W L Easton, but was forced ere long to give up the position on account of ill health At the age of sixteen years he began teaching school and later was again employed for a time as a clerk Desirous of further advancing his education this courageous lad subsequently journeyed by stage over the muddy spring roads to Cazenovia, New York, and there pursued his studies at the Cazenovia Seminary, in the meanwhile supporting himself and paying his college expenses, working at any honorable employment that he could find

Going then to Columbus, Pennsylvania, Mr Rogers accepted a position as bookkeeper in the store of his cousin, Enfield Leach, but the long hours and his close application to the work proved too much for his physical health and he resumed his professional labors as a teacher, teaching winters and farming summers Marrying soon after attaining his majority, Mr Rogers bought a small farm, partly on credit, and there he and his brave young wife spent two long years, making barely enough money to live on and pay the interest on the mortgage Stricken with the Western fever in the spring of 1854, he sold his farm, receiving $1,500 in cash after the mortgage was paid, and journeyed to Jo Daviess County, Illinois, where he worked as a farm hand for his uncle, J H Rogers, while his wife assisted her aunt in the house

Subsequently moving to Wisconsin, Mr Rogers purchased eighty acres of land in Jefferson County, and in trying to improve it used the oxen with which he and his wife had made the trip from Illinois At that time his particular friend, E H Barnard, was employed in a real estate office at Des Moines, Iowa, and through a lively correspondence the two men were planning great things for their future In the summer of 1856 Mr Barnard located in Omaha, Nebraska, and in October of that year he was joined by Mr Rogers. They had intended to there establish themselves in the real estate business, but Mr Barnard, who was then recovering from an attack of typhoid fever, had laid out a new town on the Platte River, about fifty miles northwest of Omaha, and was going to settle there Mr Rogers decided to remain in Omaha during the winter, and in order to eke out his income, and not encroach on the $1,500 that he had received for his farm, he was engaged in hauling wood until February, 1857

Going in that month to the newly laid out Town of Fremont, Mr Rogers secured a room in one of the three log houses already erected, and in that room he and his wife lived until their house, which he built with his own hands, was completed, some three months later Having previously studied law to good purpose, Mr Rogers was admitted to the bar in 1858, and that same year was elected as a representative to the State Legislature Going to Pike's Peak during the gold excitement, he located at Russell's Gulch, and having built a cabin for himself and family began the practice of his chosen profession in earnest Taking charge of law cases for both the miners and the mine owners, he built up a fair practice, and in February, 1861, was elected judge of the Miner's Court Returning to Fremont in June, 1861, Mr Rogers was kept busy for a few months attending to the farm which he had purchased before going to Colorado Accompanied by his family, he then went East on a visit, and remained there during the winter of 1865 and 66 In the fall of 1866, Mr Rogers was made a member of the Territorial Council, and took an active part in its proceedings

In the summer of 1866 the Union Pacific Railroad was extended through Fremont, and Mr Rogers, in partnership with his brother, L H Rogers, embarked in the real estate business, and opened a private bank, which has since developed into the First National Bank of Fremont In 1870 Mr Rogers was a candidate for the United States Senate, but after the first ballot withdrew his name, and Mr Hitchock was elected as senator On account of ill health, Mr Rogers, accompanied by his wife, went to Florida for the winter of 1877, and in 1879 spent the winter in New Mexico Although his health was not very much improved when he returned to Fremont, he continued at his desk throughout the summer, but in the fall of 1880 resigned his position in the bank. Taking his wife and daughter to Florida, he rented a house, and camped out, hoping in that balmy climate to recover some of his former physical vigor In May, 1881, Mr Rogers was appointed United States Consul at Vera Cruz, Mexico, and having accepted the position resided there until his death, on August 1, 1881, when his body was laid to rest on Mexican soil

Mr Rogers was a devout Christian, very active in the Methodist Episcopal Church, and a faithful friend of the circuit riders and the Methodist preachers, whom he gladly welcomed to his hospitable home. He was a prominent member of the republican party, in his younger days being what was then termed a black abolitionist He was a man of sterling worth and integrity, and through good management acquired considerable wealth

In New York State, on September 17, 1851, Mr. Rogers was united in marriage with Lucy J. Goff, and of the children that blessed their union, but two are now living, namely Mrs Ida J Moe, of Fremont, Nebraska, and Mrs Joseph Yager, also of Fremont Mrs Moe was born at Augusta, Oneida County, New York, May 7, 1852. She was only six years old when she came to Fremont with her parents in 1857 and was reared here. With exceptions of time spent in school her life has been spent in Fremont She was educated in Houghton Seminary, Clinton, New York She married, October 11, 1874, Lewis S Moe, who was a native of Tioga County, New York, where he was reared and educated He was in the militia and was clerk in the Treasury Department in Washington, D C After the war he came West to Fremont and was in the show business for a time with a brother. He later clerked and also worked for Doctor Smith He died February

27, 1909 Mr and Mrs Moe have three sons Rex R Moe was educated in Fremont High School and at Cornell, Iowa, and filled the pulpit while in college; in the fall of 1890 he went to the Philippine Islands as missionary, was in Tarlac for five years, then came home for a year, was then in Pangasinan Province two years and in Cagayon three years, then in November, 1919, he came home on a year's furlough to visit his mother He married Miss Belle Noyes and they have two daughters, Corrall Eugenie and Margaret Rogers, both born in the Philippines

Locke Barton Moe is in the laundry business at Le Grande, Oregon He married Ella Douglass and has one son, Lewis Douglass Grant S Moe is a farmer near Central City, Nebraska In 1911 Mrs Moe joined her son in the Philippine Islands She has always been active in the Woman's Foreign Missionary Society here for a great many years

FRED C LAIRD, who was engaged in the practice of his profession at Fremont, judicial center of Dodge County, until December 3, 1919, when he entered the Government service, is a native of Fremont County, Iowa, and has gained a place as one of the representative younger members of the bar of Dodge County, Nebraska He is now internal revenue inspector under civil service, assigned to the Nebraska district He was born on his father's fine old homestead farm in Fremont County, Iowa, May 22, 1880, and is a son of Francis M. and Phoebe (Reeves) Laird, both likewise natives of that county of the Hawkeye State, where the respective families were founded in the pioneer period of the history of that favored commonwealth The father is now the owner of two valuable farm properties in his native county, and his entire active career was one of close association with the basic industries of agriculture and stock growing Since 1893 he and his wife have maintained their residence at Tabor, Iowa, where he is living virtually retired, Fred C of this review being the elder of their two children, and Belva being the wife of Dr. B B Miller, a representative physician and surgeon at Tabor. Francis M Laird is a stalwart democrat in politics and has been active in local politics, besides which he has served in various offices of public trust, including two terms of effective service as a member of the State Legislature of Iowa He and his wife are earnest members of the Congregational Church His father, John Laird, was born and reared in Pennsylvania, and became an early settler in Fremont County, Iowa, where he secured Government land and developed a productive farm, the remainder of his life having been passed in that county. Asa Reeves, maternal grandfather of Fred C Laird was a native of Ohio and he likewise was a pioneer of Fremont County, Iowa, where he reclaimed a valuable farm and where he continued to reside until his death, he having served during practically the entire period of the Civil war and having been wounded in battle

Fred C Laird gained his preliminary education in the public schools of his native county and in 1903 he was graduated in Tabor College, at Tabor, Iowa In preparing himself for the profession of his choice he entered the law department of the University of Nebraska, and in this institution he was graduated in 1906, with the well-earned degree of Bachelor of Laws, and with concurrent admission to the bar of the state. His initial work in his profession was in the capital city, Lincoln, and in the nearby Village of Havelock, but after this novitiate of a few months, he came to Fremont in December, 1906, and established himself in independent practice He developed a successful law business and in 1913 he formed a professional alliance with George L. Loomis, with whom he associated under the firm name of Loomis & Laird This firm has a substantial and well ordered law business and a clientele of representative order Mr Laird is unfaltering in his allegiance to the cause of the democratic party, and he served two years as police judge of Fremont Both he and his wife are members of the Congregational Church in their home city A scion of stanch colonial ancestry, Mr. Laird is eligible for and is affiliated with the Society of the Sons of the American Revolution, in which he is secretary of the local organization at Fremont In the Masonic fraternity he has received the chivalric degrees and is a popular member of the Fremont Commandery of Knights Templar, and Sesostris Temple Mystic Shrine, at Lincoln, Nebraska, while both he and his wife are active members of the local chapter of the Order of the Eastern Star, of which he is past patron Mr. Laird is serving, in 1920, as secretary of Fremont Lodge, Benevolent and Protective Order of Elks, and maintains affiliation also with the Knights of Pythias, besides which he is a member of the Alpha Tau Omega college fraternity

The year 1911 was marked by the marriage of Mr Laird to Miss Leo Loomis, daughter of his law partner, George L Loomis, and they are popular factors in the representative social life of their home city

JOSEPH C SINK An active, earnest and honest tiller of the soil, Joseph C Sink, of Platte Township, is numbered among the enterprising and self-reliant men who are so ably conducting the farming interests of this part of Dodge County, everything about his premises bearing evidence of his wise care and supervision A son of Abram Sink, he was born, October 30, 1857, in Virginia, where he lived and labored for upwards of forty years

Abram Sink was born in Virginia ninety-nine years ago and has there spent his unusually long life, during his active career having been engaged in agricultural pursuits To him and his wife, whose name before marriage was Elizabeth Fisher, nine children were born, Joseph C being the fifth child of the parental household and the only one living in Nebraska

Bred and educated in Virginia, Joseph C. Sink obtained a thorough knowledge of agriculture while young and continued to farm there until 1900 Being seized with the wanderlust and wishing to take advantage of more favorable conditions for enlarging his operations, he came to Nebraska in that year, locating in Colfax County, where he was engaged in his chosen calling seven years Coming to Dodge County in 1907, Mr Sink purchased 120 acres of land in Platte Township, near Ames, and in its improvement has shown good judgment, the buildings being in excellent repair and his farm under a good state of cultivation Having toiled assiduously many years, Mr Sink is now living retired from active labor, having resigned the management of his estate to his son

In 1879, while still a resident of Virginia, Mr Sink married Mary Kingry, and of their union eight children have been born, namely Susie McKinery, Henry, Mattie, Carl, Isaac, Rosie, Burrell, and Scyrel Mr Sink is independent in politics, voting without regard to party restrictions. Religiously, he is a Dunkard

HENRY KUSS Many of the more thriving and enterprising citizens of our great republic have been born and bred in far-off countries and from their native lands have brought the habits of industry and perseverance that have steadily overcome all obstacles that beset their pathway and won them places of note in business and industrial circles. Prominent among this number is Henry Kuss, a well known grain operator and farmer of Winslow A son of Frederick Kuss, he was born, November 14, 1868, in Hanover, Germany, where he acquired a good education

A native of Germany, Frederick Kuss began life for himself as a farmer and remained in the fatherland for a number of years after his marriage. Coming with his family to the United States in 1884, he spent six months in Illinois, from there coming to Washington County, Nebraska, where he resumed his agricultural labors Meeting with excellent results as a farmer, he accumulated a fair share of this world's goods, and is now living in Winslow, retired from active cares His wife, Lena Kuss, died on the home farm, aged seventy-two years

Bidding his parents a loving farewell in 1883, Henry Kuss immigrated to the United States in 1883, hoping in the land of bright prospects to find remunerative employment Locating first in Illinois, he was engaged in general farming in the vicinity of Chicago for two years becoming accustomed to the agricultural methods used in his adopted land Coming to Nebraska in 1885, he worked on Kupp's Ranch in Washington County, for six years, and was afterwards on his father's farm two years. Giving up farming in 1907, Mr. Kuss entered the employ of the Nebraska-Iowa Grain Company, and still operates the elevator in Winslow, although for the past few years he has been also engaged in agricultural pursuits, living on the farm which he bought in 1913. He casts his vote independent of party restrictions and has served as road overseer for several terms In religion he is a member of the Lutheran Church and faithful to its teachings

Mr Kuss married Lizzie Panning, and into their attractive home five children have been born, namely Lottie, Arthur, Fred, Howard and Paul Mrs Kuss is a daughter of Henry Panning, Jr, and granddaughter of Henry Panning, Sr, both natives of Germany Henry Panning, Sr, came with his family to the United States in 1852, and having bought land in Dodge County, Wisconsin, improved his little farm of forty acres, on which he lived twelve years Migrating to Nebraska in 1864, he located in Dodge County, very near Winslow, on the fourth of July, and bought 320 acres of land and there improved the farm on which he and his wife Margaret spent their remaining days, her death occurring at the age of three score years, and his at a ripe old age. They reared three children, as follows Mrs Kate Wager, deceased, Frederick, living on the home farm, and Henry, Jr

Born in Hanover, Germany, April 15, 1844, Henry Panning, Jr, was a lad of eight years when he accompanied his parents to Wisconsin, where he was reared and educated When the family came to Nebraska he drove across the country with an ox team, traveling with a caravan of thirteen families and being five weeks en route Nebraska was then very sparsely settled, Indians were plentiful, but usually friendly There were no railroads in this part of the country and the new settlers bravely endured all the hardships and privations of frontier life Mr Panning has seen wonderful changes in the face of the country, and in the grand transformation has contributed his full share

Henry Panning, Jr, married Mado Mayer, who was born in Germany, their marriage having been solemnized in Dodge County, Nebraska. Eleven children were born of their union, five of whom are living, as follows: Mary Bergt, of Altona, Wayne County, Nebraska; Fred G., living on the home farm in Dodge County, Lizzie, wife of Henry Kuss, of this sketch; Gustaf, a resident of Dodge County, and Anna Schmidt, of Thayer, York County, this state Mr. Panning is a democrat in politics and a member of the Lutheran Church

THOMAS H. WRIGHT Sterling integrity, keen insight and a willingness to work are leading characteristics of Thomas H Wright, one of the successful produce merchants of Blair, and a sterling citizen of Washington County He was born at Abingdon, Virginia, September 30, 1871, a son of Thomas M and Margaret J (Neeley) Wright, both of whom were born in Virginia. At the outbreak of the war between the North and the South, Thomas M Wright enlisted in the Confederate Army and was engaged in some of the leading battles of that great conflict until he had the misfortune to be so severely wounded as to lose a portion of one of his hands Following the war he found conditions unfavorable in his native state, and so, like a number of the Confederate veterans, came West, locating in Washington County March 4, 1872, and here he bought land and was engaged in operating it until 1894, when he moved to Kennard, where both he and his wife died. They were consistent members of the Methodist Church. In politics he was a democrat, and served as town assessor He and his wife had eight children, of whom four are living, namely: Sarah, who married J. A. Chamberlain, a retired farmer of Norfolk, Nebraska, Thomas H, who was second, John B, who is a confectioner of Kennard, Nebraska, and Walter E, who is with the Cudahy Packing Company of Chicago, Illinois

Thomas H Wright attended the rural and Kennard schools, where he gained a sound knowledge of the fundamentals of an education His early experience at making himself useful was gained on his father's farm, but his actual contact with the business world was acquired as a clerk in a general store at Kennard, and he worked as such for ten years, and then for four years was with the Anchor Grain Company at Wayne and Hartington, Nebraska In 1907 he came to Blair, and in 1913, after being connected with several lines, embarked in a poultry, eggs and produce business, and has built up a very desirable connection, handling all kinds of produce and shipping in carload lots to Omaha and eastern markets

In March, 1901, Mr Wright was married to Dora Sherwood, who was born in Virginia, and they have two children, namely Margaret and Helen, both of whom are attending the Blair public schools. Mr Wright has been very active in establishing the Odd Fellows, belonging to both branches and the Modern Woodmen of America, serving the former as secretary and the latter as clerk Both he and his wife belong to the Daughters of Rebekah, and they are very zealous members of the Methodist Episcopal Church of Blair While he votes the republican ticket, Mr Wright has never sought public honors, as his time is fully occupied with his business In every respect he is a fine type of the energetic business man of which Nebraska is so justly proud, and he holds the esteem of his fellow citizens in a marked degree

JOHN HAVEKOST. Enterprising and progressive and possessing good business talent and tact, John Havekost, of Hooper Township, holds a noteworthy position among the more successful farmers and stock growers of this part of Dodge County, his large and well-kept farm bearing visible evidence to the most casual observer of the owner's thrift and industry A native of Dodge County, he was born, July 30 1872, in Logan Township, of German lineage

Herman Havekost, his father, was born, bred and married in Germany In 1866, with his wife, Margaretta, he came to the United States, the land of promise, and for two years lived in Newton, Iowa, where he followed the carpenter's trade Then, with himself, family and household goods packed into two covered wagons, he drove, in typical pioneer style, to Dodge County, Nebraska, camping and cooking by the wayside Taking up a homestead claim in Logan Township, he first used as a dwelling place one of the wagons in which he had journeyed, and with the small means he had at his command began the improving of his land. By means of sturdy labor, he met with desired results in his undertakings, and by future investments became owner of 401 acres of land at the time of his death, which occurred at the age of seventy-eight years and eleven months He was very well-to-do, his entire property having been acquired through his own efforts His widow, now well advanced in years, still occupies the old homestead

The fifth child in a family of eleven children, John Havekost began doing the chores incidental to farm life in a new country as a boy, obtaining a practical knowledge of the rudiments of farming when young In 1895, soon after attaining his majority, he bought land in Cedar County, and was there engaged in tilling the soil for fourteen years. Returning to Dodge County in 1909, he purchased his present place of 360 acres of land in Hooper Township, and in its improvement has spared neither time nor expense ,Using excellent judgment in his work, he has placed his land in good condition, and each year adds to its value and attractiveness, his improvements and equipments being up-to-date in all respects In addition to carrying on general farming successfully, Mr Havekost raises Duroc Jersey hogs and feeds cattle on a somewhat extensive scale

Mr Havekost married, in 1895, Gesina Suhr, a daughter of Herman Suhr Mr Suhr immigrated to the United States with his family in 1884, locating in Dodge County, Nebraska, where he was engaged in agricultural pursuits until his death, at the age of fifty-nine years Eight children have been born of the marriage of Mr and Mrs Havekost, namely. Mrs Bertha Olteman, of Dodge County, Mrs Olga Wurdeman, of Dodge County; Mrs. Alma Moeller, also a resident of Dodge County, Alvin, Harland, Bernard, Gerald and Woodrow. Politically, Mr Havekost casts his vote without regard to party lines, and though not an office seeker has served as a member of the local school board a number of terms Religiously, he and his wife are active members of the Lutheran Church Hs is a member and the president of the Farmers Elevator Company of Hooper, and a member and director of the state organization of the Farmers' Union

Adolph F Diels has been a resident of Dodge County from infancy, as his parents established their home at Fremont in 1866, when he was but a few months old and prior to the admission of Nebraska to statehood Here he is now living retired from active business, after having been for many years engaged in the milling, grain and lumber business at Scribner, this county.

Mr Diels was born in the city of Brooklyn, New York, December 4, 1865, and is a son of John M and Anna M (Kuehn) Diels, both natives of Holland, whence they came to America when young, their marriage having been solemnized in Brooklyn In 1866 they came to the Territory of Nebraska and established their home at Fremont, where the father opened a meat market and became one of the pioneer business men of

the vital little town He here continued his residence until 1873, when he removed with his family to Scribner and established himself in the lumber and grain business, in connection with which he erected and operated a large flour mill He developed a prosperous business, and was long numbered among the representative business men and influential citizens of Dodge County He lived retired during the latter period of his life and both he and his wife died in the City of Los Angeles, California Of their eight children, five are living: Gustave A is living retired at Redlands, California, in which vicinity he is the owner of two valuable orange groves, John A is living retired at Los Angeles, that state; Adolph F, of this review, is the next younger son, Mrs. Joseph P. Hahn, the only daughter, resides at Glendale, California; and Henry M. owns and operates a transfer line in Kansas City, Missouri John M Diels was a communicant of the Catholic Church, but his wife was of the Protestant faith He was a staunch democrat and while a resident of Scribner he served as member of the village council and the board of education

Adolph F Diels acquired his early education in the public schools of Fremont and Scribner, and as a youth he became associated with his father's business He finally purchased this business, and he continued to operate the mill, which was kept up to the best modern standard, and to deal in grain and lumber at Scribner for sixteen years, the business having been greatly expanded and having yielded large returns under his effective management He finally sold the property and business and, on March 17, returned to Fremont, his boyhood home, where he has since lived retired

Mr Diels is a democrat in politics, and his constructive interest in community affairs was shown by thirteen years of service as a member of the village council and the board of education at Scribner He is affiliated with the Ancient Order of United Workmen, the Modern Woodmen of America, the Fraternal Order of Eagles and the Sons of Hermann, his wife being an active communicant of the Catholic Church

December 7, 1892, recorded the marriage of Mr Diels to Miss Anna Josephine Verba, who was born at Schuyler, Colfax County, this state, a daughter of Matthew and Anna (Karel) Verba, the former a native of Iowa and the latter of Bohemia, Mrs Diels being the elder of their two surviving children, and Emma being the wife of James Moore, a merchant at Schuyler Mr Verba came to Nebraska in the early days and was for many years a leading merchant at Schuyler Mr. and Mrs Diels have four children Arthur J is attending a business college in the City of Omaha, Victor A and Mildred A are students in the Fremont High School, and Gladys is a grade pupil in the city schools

Abram Castetter is one of the ablest of the pioneer citizens of Washington County and is particularly well known for his extensive interests as a banker and as founder of the A. Castetter banking house of Blair

He was born in Ohio, February 13, 1831, and grew up and received his education in his native state A young man seeking broader opportunities in the opening of a new western country, he came to Nebraska Territory in 1856, when the interest of the nation was being turned in this direction as a result of the discussion over the Kansas-Nebraska Bill in Congress. His first settlement was in De Soto In 1868 he moved to Blair, and the following year established a bank which has been in existence for over half a century as the banking house of A Castetter

He was an active republican, served as county clerk of Washington County, and has many business and civic interests to lend importance to his name He was affiliated with the Independent Order of Odd Fellows.

Mr Castetter, whose honored career came to a close on April 23, 1900, married in 1854 Helen M Phelps of Williston, Vermont. She followed her husband to Nebraska in 1857 and was his personal assistant while he was in the office of county clerk She was one of the woman pioneers of Washington County, and was long prominent socially Her death occurred May 29, 1909

FREDERICK H CLARIDGE Occupying a place of prominence and influence in the business and financial life of Washington County, Frederick H Claridge, of Blair, is widely known as the president of the banking house of A Castetter, which is one of the oldest institutions of the kind in the state, it having been established in 1869 A native of Massachusetts, he was born in 1861 in Boston, of honored New England ancestry.

James R Claridge, his father, was born and educated in Maine, and as a young man went to Boston in search of congenial employment. After his marriage he removed to Baltimore, Maryland, where he was engaged in commercial pursuits until his death, having been employed in foreign trade, shipping goods on ocean bound vessels He married Fannie R Whipple, a native of Boston, and of the six children born of their union, four are living, Frederick H. being the eldest child Both he and his wife were members of the Presbyterian Church He was a true blue republican in politics, and a member of the Independent Order of Odd Fellows.

Growing to manhood in Baltimore, Frederick H Claridge was educated in its schools Coming to Blair, Nebraska, in 1883 he entered the banking house established by A. Castetter, the pioneer banker of this section of the state, and has since been actively identified with the institution, which he has served in various capacities, and of which he is now president, a position of responsibility for which his knowledge, experience and ability amply fit him

Mr Claridge married in 1886 Miss Helen M Castetter, who was born at De Soto, Nebraska, in 1862 daughter of the late Abram Castetter. Mr and Mrs Claridge have no children and both are members of the Episcopal Church Politically, Mr Claridge is a republican, but has never been an aspirant for public office, his banking affairs demanding all his attention and time

N T. LUND. A man of mark and unusual achievement in Washington County, Nebraska, is found in N T Lund, county superintendent of schools, and for a number of years engaged in educational work in this and other sections Since the age of fourteen years he has been the arbiter of his own fortunes

N T Lund was born in Denmark, December 13, 1874, the youngest in a family of seven children born to Thomas J and Dorothy (Dahn) Lund, the others being as follows H. T, who is a prominent citizen of Amery, Wisconsin, a hotel proprietor and stockman, Mrs Marie Fisher, a widow, who lives at Eugene, Oregon, J. T, who is a Lutheran minister at Hutchinson, Minnesota, Marian, who is the wife of P J Ostergard, a retired minister living at Los Angeles, California; P D, who is a farmer near Vermilion, South Dakota, and A W, who is in charge of a Lutheran church at Minneapolis

The parents of Mr Lund came to the United States about 1882 and lived one year at Minneapolis, Minnesota In Denmark the father had been a blacksmith, but after moving to Clay County, South Dakota, he bought a farm near Vermilion and spent the rest of his life there The mother died in Wisconsin They were members of the Lutheran Church and in politics the father was a republican

N T Lund left home at the age of fourteen years and after attending school in Minneapolis, came to Blair, Nebraska, in 1892, intent on procuring a college education. After two years at Blair he spent two terms in the Normal school at Fremont, then took charge of the Larsen School, situated seven miles north of Fremont, which position he held for seven years In order to complete his college course he attended summer school during this period at Fremont College, and later an entire year, receiving his A B degree in 1903.

Mr Lund then accepted a position on the faculty of Luther College, Racine, Wisconsin, where he remained a year and a half. During the next year he was out of the educational field, being associated with a partner in a book and stationery store at Des Moines, Iowa, at the end of which time he returned to Blair and accepted a place on the faculty of Dana College, where he continued for the next ten years, becoming so favorably known that in 1914 he was elected county superintendent of Washington County He was twice re-elected, then declined to serve further, having made plans to retire from the educational field in favor of an agricultural life He owns a fine farm of 120 acres, situated south of Blair, and he promises himself a vast amount of enjoyment in making improvements on this land and making it a model modern farm

In 1903 Mr Lund was united in marriage to Miss Marie Hansen, who was born at Hampden, Nebraska, and they have children as follows: Ray, Una, Lona, Ruth, Norma, Russell and Dorothy Louise, the last named being an infant, the older children being in school, the eldest being in the high school Mr Lund and his family belong to the Lutheran Church.

During the great war Mr Lund was one of the active and loyal supporters of the Government and worked unceasingly and freely in many official positions of responsibility He was chairman of the Council of Defense of Washington County, and was Government Appeal Agent on the draft and also was chairman of the Junior Red Cross Commission in Washington County He is zealous in his support of the republican party and in full sympathy with its claim of true Americanism, for he loves his adopted country with most loyal devotion

EDWIN DIFFEY has been a resident of Nebraska since boyhood and his parents here established their home about three years after the admission of the state to the Union, so that pioneer distinction may justly be applied in connection with the family name He whose name introduces this paragraph has won for himself success and prestige as one of the progressive agriculturists and stockgrowers of Dodge County, and his well-improved farm, comprising 160 acres, is situated in Cotterell and Union townships

Mr Diffey was born in England, in the year 1863, and is a son of Charles and Sarah (Holland) Diffey, who came from their native land to America when their son was a child, and they arrived in Omaha, Nebraska, in 1870 In that city the father was for a time employed as teamster, and finally he came with his family to Dodge County and rented a farm near the village of Webster Here he continued operations eighteen years, at the expiration of which he took a homestead in Holt County, where he developed and improved a good farm and where he passed the remainder of his life, his death having occurred in 1901, and his wife likewise having passed away Of the five children Edwin, of this review, is the eldest, Martha is the wife of William Hull, a farmer in Dodge County, Rose is deceased, Elizabeth is the wife of William Butterfield and they reside in Holt County, Fannie is the wife of George Gans, a farmer in Howard County The father was a republican in politics and during the residence of the family in Dodge County the mother was a zealous member of the Presbyterian Church at North Bend

Edwin Diffey gained his early education principally in the public schools of Dodge County and here he continued his association with the work of his father's farm until he had attained the age of twenty-six years, when he initiated his independent career as an agriculturist and stockraiser. His present farm of 160 acres is one of the well improved places of this vicinity and in connection with diversified agriculture he gives special attention to the raising of pure-blood Shorthorn cattle and Poland-China hogs His political support is given to the republican party, he is affiliated with the Modern Woodmen of America, and he and his wife hold membership in the Presbyterian Church at North Bend

In 1891 Mr Diffey was united in marriage to Miss Matilda Catherwood, daughter of Johnson Catherwood, who was a pioneer settler in Dodge County Mr and Mrs Diffey have two children: Edna is the wife of Arthur Mapes, a prosperous young farmer of Dodge County, and Harold is associated with the activities of the home farm, where he remains at the parental domicile

HENRY BENNER No small amount of the development represented in Ridgeley Township in the way of good farms, productive homesteads, roads, schools and other facilities must be credited to members of the Benner family, who have lived here for nearly forty years

The family was established by John Benner, who was born in Germany in 1851 and married in his native land Helene Roemer. When he was thirty-three years of age he brought his wife to the United States and at once settled in Dodge County Being without capital and without influential friends, he chose a road to prosperity by renting, and was a farm renter seven years before he bought his first land Before renting, he worked three years as a farm laborer at $15 per month He experienced nearly all the hardships to which the farmers of Nebraska were subjected twenty-five or thirty years ago, and sold his corn crop for as low as eleven cents a bushel His persistent industry has brought its sure reward, and he acquired 275 acres of Dodge County lands, made excellent improvements, and is now able to take life in comfort and leisure, his only regular employment being tending his own garden He is a member of the Lutheran Church and an independent voter John Benner had six children Charles, who died at the age of twenty-one, Louis, who passed away at the age of thirty-three; Henry, Laura, Louise, who died at the age of fifteen; and Mrs Carrie Joens, who lives in South Dakota

Of this family, Henry Benner is one of the high-class modern farmers of Dodge County, a young man college trained and well fitted for the responsibilities imposed upon the young men of this generation

He was born in Dodge County September 17, 1888 He grew up on his father's farm and after the common schools attended the Grand

Joseph Roberts.

Island Business College, Highland Park College, at Des Moines, Iowa, and spent three years in the University of Nebraska He began farming on his own account in 1914 and now has 140 acres devoted to crops and livestock He feeds some stock for market every year and runs a small band of sheep His farm is modern in every respect.

In 1915 he married Dora Ditson of Lincoln, and they have one son, Robert Edwin Mr. Benner and family are Lutherans, while in politics he chooses an independent course He is now a director of his local schools

JOSEPH ROBERTS was a young man of twenty years when he first made his appearance at Fremont, the judicial center of Dodge County, and that the impression which he has here made has been most excellent needs no further evidence than the fact that he is now serving as treasurer of the county.

Of sturdy English lineage, tracing back to the time when the memory of man runneth not to the contrary, Mr Roberts was born in the rugged old county of Cornwall, England, on the 4th of August, 1854, and is a son of John and Catherine (Dungey) Roberts, who passed their entire lives on the "right little isle" of England, where the father was a farmer by vocation Of a family of four children Joseph Roberts, of this review, is the youngest of the three surviving, Mary is the widow of Louis Jennings and resides in the state of Iowa, and the elder sister, Elizabeth, is the wife of Charles Long, a prosperous farmer of Dodge County, Nebraska The father achieved success in connection with his agricultural activities and continued to reside in Cornwall until his death, both he and his wife having been earnest communicants of the Church of England

Joseph Roberts attended the schools of his native land until he was thirteen years of age, when he was brought to the United States by William H Hicks, who became a farmer in the state of Illinois and with whom he remained until he had attained to adult age There Mr. Roberts continued his association with agricultural pursuits until 1884, when he came to Nebraska and purchased a farm near Fremont, Dodge County To the work and improvement of this farm he continued to give his attention four years, and during the following six years he traveled extensively through the state as a representative of the business of Mark M Code, an extensive importer of horses In the meanwhile he sold his original farm, but after leaving the employ of Mr Code he purchased the well improved farm on which he still resides, a short distance east of Fremont, the place receiving his general supervision and affording him relaxation from his official duties as county treasurer

Upon becoming a naturalized citizen of the United States and thereby gaining the franchise, Mr Roberts allied himself with the republican party, of whose principles and policies he has since continued a loyal advocate He has been influential in the councils of his party in Dodge County, and has represented the county as a member of the State Legislature, 1903-1905, in which connection he made a record of effective service in behalf of his constituent district and the state at large In 1905 he was elected to the Nebraska State Board of Agriculture and re-elected to same and has served as president of the board for two terms For eight years he was a valued member of the board of county commissioners and in 1918 further evidence of his secure place in popular confidence was given by his election to the office of county treasurer As a citizen Mr. Roberts has been emphatically progressive and liberal, and in this connection it should be noted that he has been specially influential in connection with the promotion of effective drainage systems through the county. He has served fourteen years as a director of the board of drainage commissioners of the county and has been president of the board since 1915, having been re-elected president in 1920 Within his incumbency the county has expended more than $200,000 and thereby effected the drainage of fully 40,000 acres of land which has been brought to a high state of cultivation. The service of the drainage board involved the straightening of the course of the Elkhorn River, and by this means valuable land was redeemed to cultivation

Mr Roberts is the owner of a fine farm of 168 acres, improved with modern buildings of the best type and yielding large returns annually He has made his farm enterprise specially successful, and he has availed himself of the best of modern facilities as well as scientific methods, and he has reason to feel gratified in the substantial prosperity which he has won through his well ordered efforts during the period of his residence in Nebraska, a state to which his loyalty is marked by deep appreciation of its attractions and advantages

Within the period of his residence in America Mr Roberts has made two trips to his native land, and on the last occasion, in 1911, he was accompanied by his wife. They witnessed the coronation of the present king of England, and prior to returning home they visited Switzerland, Belgium and Germany While in England they met numerous kinsfolk and other friends of earlier days

Mr Roberts is affiliated with the local organizations of the Independent Order of Odd Fellows and Fraternal Order of Eagles, and both he and his wife hold membership in the Presbyterian Church of Fremont

In 1892 was solemnized the marriage of Mr Roberts to Miss Emma M Hicks who was born in Illinois and who is a daughter of William H Hicks, with whom Mr Roberts came to America when a boy, as previously noted Mr and Mrs Roberts have no children of their own, but their adopted son, Albert Roberts, is now married and has the active management of the farm of his foster father

John H Bader The premier honors of breeding more championship hogs in the year 1919 than any other man in America rests with John H Bader of Dodge County His stock farm, known and appreciated for its products in many states, is located in section 2 of Ridgeley township

Mr Bader is a young and enthusiastic stockman, and was born at Toledo, Illinois, in 1883 His parents were Asa and Clara Bader His father was born and reared in Ohio and his mother in Illinois, where they married. Asa Bader was a good farmer, and in 1893 came to Wahoo, Nebraska, where he farmed until his death in 1903 He and his wife had seven children Elmer, a farmer at Webster, Nebraska, Rono, of Fremont, Cora Bishop, of Hooper, Della Linquist, of Scribner, Lizzie Van Horn, of Fremont, Fannie Van Horn, of Dodge, and John H

John H Bader received most of his early training and education in Nebraska and began for himself in 1908 He was farming as a partner with his mother near Hooper until after his marriage and then rented and in 1910 bought his first land, 240 acres Six months later he sold that, and his present farm comprises 120 acres. On this farm he has built the finest modern home in this section of the county Some years ago he purchased his first thoroughbred big type Duroc-Jersey and has had wonderful success with this breed, and it is now the chief feature of his business Mr Bader is an independent voter, a member of the Masonic order and the Congregational Church

Mr Bader married Miss Cora Hallett, a native of Toledo, Illinois She died in 1911, the mother of two children, Howard and Mable, who live with their father

JOHN MATTSON Numbered among the prosperous agriculturists and respected citizens of Dodge County, John Mattson is the owner of a fine and well appointed farm, pleasantly located on section 22, in Logan Township, where he is laboring with excellent and highly satisfactory results as a general farmer, the land, under his gentle persuasion, yielding profitable harvests each season. A son of the late Matts Mattson, he was born, August 18, 1865, in Omaha, Nebraska, where the first five years of his life were spent

Born, bred and married in Sweden, Matts Mattson immigrated to the United States early in 1865, and for five years thereafter followed his trade of a stone mason in the City of Omaha Coming with his family to Dodge County about 1870, he secured eighty acres of land in Logan Township, and with true pioneer courage and faith began the improvement of his land His first dwelling was a rude, one-room shack, in which he and his family lived, and in addition took for a boarder the first school teacher employed in that district Laboring earnestly and faithfully, he was quite successful as a farmer, and in course of time added materially to his landed possessions, at the time of his death, at the advanced age of four score and four years, owning 280 acres of rich and fertile land, the greater part of which was under culture and with improvements of an excellent character. His wife survived him, passing away at the venerable age of ninety years Of the eight children that were born of their marriage, but two are now living, as follows John, the subject of this brief sketch, who was the seventh child of the parental household in order of birth; and Matts, of Uehling, Nebraska

Brought up in Logan Township and educated in the public schools, John Mattson was initiated into the mysteries of agriculture as early as possible, beginning as a boy to assist his father on the home farm The free and independent occupation appealing to his tastes and temperament, he began life as a farmer on his own account at the age of twenty-one years, renting a piece of land from his father Full of push and energy, Mr. Mattson labored diligently and each year has materially added to the value and productiveness of his farm, which is one of the best in the community in regard to its improvements and appointments, its neat and attractive appearance bearing evidence of his good management

Mr. Mattson married, in 1889, Carrie Peterson, a daughter of Lars Peterson, of Uehling, Nebraska, and they are the parents of five children, namely Mrs Ruby Larson, of Uehling, Josie, Marvin, Franklin and Geneve, at home Mr Mattson is a strict prohibitionist in politics and in addition to having served four years as township clerk was school treasurer nine years A member of the American Sunday School Union, he served as Sunday school superintendent for ten years, in that capacity doing efficient and appreciated work

JOHN McQUARRIE The interesting activities of John McQuarrie, a retired coal and lumber merchant of Blair, first touched this community nearly fifty years ago when for a time he had his headquarters at Blair and engaged in the real pioneer business of buying up from local hunters quantities of prairie chicken and shipping them to market. It was some four or five years later that Mr. McQuarrie became a permanent resident of Blair and continued for forty years the leading coal and lumber dealer of that community.

Mr. McQuarrie was born on Prince Edward Island December 24, 1847, son of Charles and Mary (Matheson) McQuarrie Both his grandfathers were natives of Scotland and his parents were born and lived all their lives in Prince Edward Island. Charles McQuarrie was a boat builder, was captain of sailing craft a number of years, also cultivated a small farm and reared his family in a rural district He and his wife were stanch Scotch Presbyterians Of their eleven children five are now living, all residents of Prince Edward Island except John The others are Isabelle, wife of Joe Clemens; Ann, a widow, Robert, Jane, a widow

John McQuarrie received his early education in his native province, and in 1868, at the age of twenty-one, left home and removed to Rhode Island The following year he came West to Omaha, but during that summer found work as a farm hand near Sioux City, Iowa He remained there five months, being paid twenty-two dollars a month He had come West with about $200 and it was through the exertion of his physical energies and taking advantage of opportunities presented by experience that he eventually laid the foundation of a business he prosecuted to success and which enabled him to enjoy life at ease After leaving the farm Mr McQuarrie was for two and a half years in the Government service as a carpenter During that time he was sent to an Indian agency in Nebraska, working there from September, 1873, until February, 1874 Then he returned to Sioux City, Iowa, worked as a carpenter there and at Yankton, South Dakota, for a brief time, and in the fall of 1874 paid his first visit to Blair in the novel business previously referred to In 1875 he worked as a carpenter in Omaha and in 1876 went West to Cheyenne, Wyoming, again in the Government service During the summer of 1877 he was employed in helping build Fort Custer Montana, a memorial to the gallant General Custer who fell in the massacre the preceding year He worked in Montana from July to October and then started down the Yellowstone River from Fort Custer and on a steamer down the Missouri River, a journey of 348 miles

Having returned to Blair, Mr McQuarrie in 1878 entered the lumber business, conducted a yard for handling lumber supplies, and also sold coal and was in the business consecutively until 1919, when he sold out to the Christiansen Lumber Company

In 1880 Mr McQuarrie married Margaret Higgins, who was born in Prince Edward Island, a daughter of Theophilus Higgins Mr and Mrs McQuarrie have had their home in Blair for a number of years They are parents of four children Miss May, at home; George, in the automobile business at Blair, Jeannette, a teacher at Kenesaw, Nebraska; and Marian, a student in the State University at Lincoln

The family are members of the Presbyterian Church and Mr McQuarrie has filled various chairs in the Lodge of Odd Fellows In politics he has been aligned with the republican party ever since he acquired American citizenship While in the midst of his business career at Blair he was elected and served two terms as a member of the city council and for two terms was mayor of the municipality

HENRY L. BEEBE, whose home is in section 4 of Platte Township, is one of the oldest native sons of Dodge County, and his father was one of the very first white pioneers in this region of old Nebraska Territory. H. L. Beebe has interesting memories of many things he saw and took part in as a boy and young man. The prairies were still covered with buffalo and wild Indians while he was growing up and practically the entire history of Dodge County has been enrolled as a panorama before his eyes.

Mr. Beebe was born in Dodge County March 4, 1860, just one year before Abraham Lincoln was inaugurated president of the United States. He is a son of Henry P. Beebe, whose record appears again and again in connection with the early annals of Dodge County. Born in New York State, he arrived in Nebraska Territory September 27, 1856. He started for the country west of the Missouri from Green Bay, Wisconsin, and traveled overland with a team of horses and two teams of oxen. Locating on a land grant of 160 acres, he built a log house, the building in which Henry L. Beebe was born. At that time the nearest trading point was Council Bluffs, Iowa. H. P. Beebe married Lavina J. Hager, who was born near Montpelier, Vermont. Of the ten children born to this pioneer couple, six are still living: Stedman P., Curtis E., Henry L., Mrs. Welthie S. French, Mrs. Sarah J. Howe and Mrs. Rosie A. Bower. H. P. Beebe died at the age of seventy-two and his wife aged fifty-nine.

During the sixties and seventies, while Henry L. Beebe was passing through the period of youth, school facilities were very poor in his section of Dodge County. But he had abundant opportunity to exercise his strength and practical skill in assisting the family to make a living in those poverty-stricken days. His present farm is a portion of the old homestead, comprising 152 acres, and during his active life he has done much to improve and develop its resources. For many years it was a difficult struggle to make a living, however cheap and plentiful land was. Mr. Beebe many times ground corn and wheat in a coffee mill and after shelling corn by hand hauled it to market at Fort Kearney, a distance of 150 miles, being a week on the trip and getting hardly enough money for his crop to supply the household with groceries. There were a number of winters when the Beebe household was snowed in for weeks at a time and this family also passed through the discouraging periods of great drought and devastation by grasshoppers. Mr. Beebe personally witnessed the tremendous prairie fire of 1881, when thousands of tons of hay went up in smoke. Those adversities are now largely a matter of memory and Mr. Beebe and others who went through the trials of that period now find themselves blessed with abundant prosperity. He is still active, farming ninety-five acres, and does some stock raising.

Mr. Beebe is a member of the Masonic Lodge and in politics is a republican in national affairs and an independent in county elections. He served six years as justice of the peace of his township and for nineteen years was a member of his local school board.

March 25, 1902, he married Jennie Thompson. She was born in Canada and when six months old was brought to the United States by her parents, John and Martha (Kirk) Thompson. Her mother is still living. Her father, who died in 1888 when about fifty years of age, settled near Morse Bluff in Saunders County, Nebraska. Mrs. Beebe has two brothers, Joseph and Robert Thompson. The only child of Mr. and Mrs. Beebe is Henry A., born May 20, 1905.

CLAUS G TANK has become one of the successful representatives of farm industry in the county that has been his home from the time he was about two years old, and as an agriculturist and stockgrower in Dodge County he is the owner of a well-improved farm of 120 acres in section 11, Cotterell Township Energy and good management have brought to him substantial success and he is a citizen who has secured place in popular esteem He is a stockholder in the corporation owning and operating the well equipped grain elevator at North Bend, and his progressiveness is further shown in his being likewise a stockholder and loyal supporter of the stock show held annually at Scribner. A democrat in politics, he takes lively interest in all things touching the welfare and advancement of his home county, and though he has had no desire for public office he gave most effective service during his incumbency of the position of treasurer of School District No 30 Mr. Tank is indebted to the public schools of Dodge County for his early education, has been continuously associated with farm enterprise since boyhood and began his independent activities as an agriculturist and stockgrower when he was twenty-four years of age, his success having been continuous and cumulative since that time

Mr. Tank was born in Germany November 3, 1874, and thus was about two years old when his parents immigrated to the United States in 1876 and established their home in Dodge County, Nebraska. Here the father was employed for seven years in the grain elevator at Fremont and he then purchased land and engaged actively in general farm enterprise, in which he here continued until his death, which occurred in 1904 at the age of 56 years, his widow still continuing to maintain her home in Dodge County and being a devout communicant of the Lutheran Church at Fremont, as was also Mr Tank, whose political allegiance was given to the democratic party Of the nine children, Claus G is the eldest, Celia is a resident of North Bend, Henry resides in Morrill County, Mary and Edward remain in Dodge County, Niel, Amelia and Emil are residents of Cheyenne County, and John is a farmer in Dodge County

In 1902 was solemnized the marriage of Claus G. Tank to Miss Iowa Miller, who was born in the State of Kansas, and they have four children, all of whom remain at the parental home. Glenn J Alta C, Edwin A and Melvin M

ALBERT E BUCHANAN, M D Admirably fortified in personality and technical ability are the physicians and surgeons who are upholding the honors of their profession in Dodge County, and among the number whose success and popularity are adequate indices of professional ability and effective service is he whose name introduces this paragraph Doctor Buchanan has the distinction of being a native son of the historic Old Dominion commonwealth, with whose civic and material affairs the name which he bears has been identified for numerous generations The doctor was born in Smyth County Virginia, August 21, 1872, and is a son of Hickman S and Laura (Sexton) Buchanan, both natives of that state, where the father died in 1889, at the age of fifty-two years, and where the widowed mother still maintains her home, at the age of sixty-seven years (1920). Arthur E is the eldest in a family of ten children, all of whom are living except one Hickman Buchanan was a successful planter in his native state and was a man of ability and fine personal character and standing His political allegiance was given to the democratic party and he held membership in the Presbyterian Church,

as does also his widow. His father, Patrick C Buchanan, was born in 1799, of Scotch-Irish ancestry, and three representatives of the name came to America in early days, one having settled in Pensylvania, one in Tennessee and one in Virginia

Afforded the best of educational advantages in his youth, Doctor Buchanan finally entered Emory & Henry College, one of the historic and well ordered institutions of Virginia, and in the same he was graduated in 1896, with the degree of Bachelor of Arts. Thus fortified in the academic education that has been all too frequently neglected by aspirants for professional service, Doctor Buchanan was matriculated in the Virginia Medical College, in the City of Richmond In this institution he was graduated as a member of the class of 1900, and after thus receiving his degree of Doctor of Medicine, he was for three years engaged in practice in his home state He then, in May, 1903, came to Nebraska and established his residence at Cedar Bluffs, Saunders County, where he developed an excellent practice and where he continued his activities until 1910, when he found a broader field of service, he engaging in practice at Fremont. Here his success has been unequivocal and he is distinctly one of the representative physicians and surgeons of Dodge County, with a substantial practice that shows a constantly cumulative tendency He is actively affiliated with the Dodge County Medical Society, of which he is president in 1920; the Elkhorn Valley Medical Society, the Nebraska State Medical Society, the Missouri Valley Medical Society, and the American Medical Association The doctor inherited his full quota of ancestral patriotism, and this was distinctly shown when the nation became involved in the great World war, for in 1918 he subordinated all else to tender his professional services to the Government. On August 1st of that year he was assigned to service at the base hospital of Camp Mead, Maryland, and he continued in active base hospital work with marked fidelity and efficiency, until he received his discharge, December 6, 1919 He is an appreciative and valued member of the local post of the American Legion, is affiliated with the Masonic fraternity, in which he has received the thirty-second degree of the Ancient Accepted Scottish Rite and in which his maximum York Rite affiliation is with Mount Tabor Commandery of Knights Templar, at Fremont, besides which he is identified with the adjunct organization, the Ancient Arabic Order Nobles of the Mystic Shrine, as well as the Fremont lodges of the Knights of Pythias and the Benevolent and Protective Order of Elks. The doctor is a member of the Fremont Rotary Club, and through this and other mediums shows his civic loyalty and progressiveness He attends and supports the Congregational Church, of which Mrs Buchanan is an active member

In 1901 was solemnized the marriage of Doctor Buchanan to Miss Grace Pratt, who likewise was born and reared in Virginia, and they have three children. George Warren is a member of the class of 1920 in the Fremont High School, Edna Virginia is likewise a student in the high school, as is also Laura Marie.

GUSTAVE C PANNING Leading an active and useful life on the farm which he owns and occupies, and which he is so skillfully managing, Gustave C Panning, of Hooper Township, is a fine representative of the American yeomen, and is eminently worthy of the respect and confidence so generously accorded him by his neighbors and friends. A son of Henry Panning, he was born, August 11, 1877, in Dodge County, of German lineage

A native of Germany, Henry Panning was born, reared and educated in Hanover He immigrated to the United States, and after living for a time in Watertown, Wisconsin, made his way to Nebraska, locating in Dodge County, where, in 1856, he settled on Government land and after the Homestead Act was passed he homesteaded in 1863 Improving his land, he carried on general farming and stock raising with the best of results, and became prominently identified with several important enterprises, having been one of the original stockholders of the Winslow State Bank, and also of the Hooper Telephone Company He married Meta Meyer, a native of Oldenburg, Germany, and to them five children were born, as follows: Mary wife of J C. Berght, who is engaged in farming in Wayne County; Eloise, wife of Henry Kuss, manager of the Nebraska and Iowa Grain Elevator at Winslow, Anna, wife of Paul Schmidt, of Thayer, manager of an elevator, Frederick G, a well known agriculturist of Dodge County, and Gustave C, with whom this brief sketch is principally concerned.

The youngest child of the parental household, Gustave C Panning had ample opportunities when young for obtaining a practical education and having finished his studies he was well drilled in the different branches of agriculture on the home farm Beginning farming on his own account at the age of thirty years, he bought land on section 18, Hooper Township, and has since devoted his time and energetic efforts to its management A thorough-going farmer, he has been constantly adding to the improvements previously inaugurated, and his labors have always proved satisfactory and remunerative, his land being in an excellent state of culture, and the buildings in good condition, everything about the premises bearing visible evidence of the owner's enterprise, intelligence and managerial ability Mr Panning is a good general farmer and as a successful stock raiser handles pure-blood Shorthorn cattle almost entirely He is greatly interested in the advancement of agriculture as a science, and is a stockholder in the Farmers' Union at Winslow

Mr. Panning married, in 1907, Anna Langewish, a daughter of William Langewish, of Dodge County, and they have three children, namely: Floma, Elert and Florence Politically, Mr Panning is a stanch republican, and religiously he and his wife are faithful members of the Lutheran Church.

C A SCHMIDT. A man of tried and trusted integrity, C A Schmidt, of Blair, president of the State Bank, has been an important factor in promoting the financial prosperity of this section of Washington County, and occupies a position of prominence in the business activities of the city He is a native-born citizen, his birth having occurred in Blair on September 15, 1880

His father, the late Christ Schmidt, was born in Benningen, Germany, and as a young man, immigrated to the United States He married, in Memphis, Tennessee, Wilhelmina Ufrecht, a native of Germany, and in 1870 came with his bride to Nebraska Locating in Blair, he was associated for nineteen years with the Crowell Lumber & Grain Company Investing his money in land at the end of that time, he turned his attention to agriculture, and was subsequently actively engaged in farming until his death, in 1912, at the age of seventy-one years He was identified with the democratic party until Bryan appeared in the political arena, after which he voted the republican ticket Ever interested in local affairs, he served as councilman one or more terms Beginning life with but scant capital, he was fairly successful in his undertakings, accumulating considerable property His wife survived him and is now a resident of Blair Four children were born of their union, as follows: Otto D, an architect, lives in St. Louis, Emil F, of Denver, Colorado, is manager of a large foundry, C A, of this brief sketch; and Carl J., employed in the State Bank

Completing his early studies in the city schools, C A Schmidt assisted his father on the home farm for three years, and then accepted a position in the State Bank, with which he has been actively identified for twenty-two years. Beginning in a minor position, he proved himself faithful, trustworthy, and eminently capable, performing the duties devolving upon him in whatever capacity he served with such promptness and ability that he was frequently promoted On January 1, 1906, Mr Schmidt was made cashier of the institution, and ten years later, on January 1, 1916, he had the distinction of being made president of the bank, being the youngest man in the state to hold such a responsible position. The State Bank, which has a capital of $50,000, with surplus and undivided profits of $50,000, receives annually, on an average, upwards of $900,000 in deposits, it being one of the most substantial and prosperous institutions of the kind in Washington County.

Mr. Schmidt is a steadfast republican in politics, and for twelve years has rendered acceptable service as city treasurer He belongs to the Ancient Free and Accepted Masons, being a Knight Templar, and is also a member of the Ancient Arabic Order Nobles of the Mystic Shrine. He has never married, but lives with his widowed mother

Henry W Schoettger No one element has more to do with the permanent prosperity of a community or section than sound banking institutions The history of nations is involved in financial transactions, and no large commercial enterprises anywhere can survive without adequate bank securities In this matter the progressive little city of Arlington, Nebraska, is amply provided for, its leading financial institution being the Arlington State Bank, of which Henry W Schoettger is cashier, and is a prominent citizen in other directions

Henry W. Schoettger was born at Quincy, Illinois, in November, 1864 His parents were William and Margaret (Toebban) Schoettger, the former of whom was born in Germany in 1812, and the latter in Germany in 1846 The father came to the United States in 1849, escaping from his native land after the Revolution of 1848 His first marriage took place in Germany and three children were born to that union He settled at Quincy, Illinois, and remained in that city and vicinity until 1868, when he came to Nebraska and purchased a partly improved farm in Washington County, for which he paid $15 per acre This land he made very valuable through cultivation and further improvement and to his original farm kept adding other tracts until, at the time of death, in 1894, he was a heavy landowner and a man of ample fortune

While living in Quincy, Illinois, William Schoettger married Margaret Toebban for his second wife, and five children were born to this marriage, as follows: Fred, who is engaged in farming near Enterprise, Nebraska, Henry W, who is a representative citizen of Arlington, Nebraska, Frank, who still lives on the old homestead; H D, who also resides on the old home farm, and Mrs A E Woodman, who resides at Omaha, Nebraska In political matters, the father of Mr Schoettger was a staunch democrat Both he and wife were members of the Lutheran Church The mother did not reach the father's advanced age, her death occurring in 1898.

Henry W Schoettger enjoyed school privileges at Quincy and afterward took a special commercial course in the Gem City Business College After returning to Nebraska he gave his father assistance, but in 1886 became bookkeeper in the Bell Creek Valley Bank at Arlington, and ever since has been identified with bank interests He was one of the founders of the Arlington State Bank, of which he is cashier. This is a flourishing institution, operating with ample capital and affording financial accommodation over a wide section As cashier, Mr Schoettger is held in high regard, his strict and careful methods being recognized by patrons as wise and judicious

In 1892 Mr Schoettger was united in marriage to Miss Emma Ehninger, who was born at Niles, Michigan Her parents, John and Katherine Ehninger, were farmers near Niles, where the father died In 1868 the mother came to Washington County, Nebraska, and bought land She now resides with Mr. and Mrs Schoettger They have two children, namely George E, who is pursuing his studies in the Nebraska State University, and Clara K, who is a student in the high school at Arlington The family belongs to the Methodist Episcopal Church

Mr Schoettger is a prominent factor in democratic politics in Washington County and frequently takes part in councils and conventions with other influential democrats He has served at times in public office, with complete efficiency, has been township collector and both village and city treasurer, and because of his deep interest in educational matters has accepted membership on the school board

Jacob Kavich Many of the more enterprising and prosperous business men of Dodge County are of foreign birth and breeding, prominent among the number being Jacob Kavich a well and widely known furniture dealer of Fremont, who has achieved success through his own efforts A son of the late Phillip Kavich, he was born, January 20, 1875, in Poland, the home of his ancestors for many generations.

Born, reared and educated in Poland, Phillip Kavich was there engaged in the milling business during the greater part of his life In 1888, when well advanced in years he came with his family to the United States, locating in Fremont, Nebraska, where he spent the remainder of his life, passing away in 1904 His wife, whose maiden name was Esther Robnowich, was born in Poland, and is now living in Fremont She is a very pleasant and religious woman, and a devoted member of the Jewish Synagogue, to which her husband also belonged Of the six children born of their union, five are living, as follows Henry, engaged in the furniture business at Fremont, Louis, of Omaha, proprietor of the Bee Hive Grocery Company, Samuel, engaged in the furniture business at Columbus, Nebraska, Belle, wife of Max Rosenbloom, of Omaha, a traveling salesman, and Jacob, of this sketch

Having acquired an excellent knowledge of books in his native land, Jacob Kavich attended school but six weeks after coming to Fremont As a lad of fourteen summers he began his business career and for three years thereafter traveled through the country, selling goods from a pack, and during the three years he was so employed gained business knowledge and experience that has been of inestimable value to him since Giving up the pack, Mr Kavich embarked in the furniture business, beginning in a modest way and as his means increased, gradually enlarging his operations until now he has one of the largest and best patronized stores of the kind in the city, his stock being large and varied enough to suit the tastes of all customers Beginning life for himself without a dollar to his name, Mr Kavich has met with genuine success in business affairs and gained a noteworthy position among the self-made men of our country

On December 25, 1903, Mr Kavich was united in marriage with Elizabeth Pearlman, a native of Poland, and they have a fine family of seven children, namely: Ruby, born in 1904, Dorothy, born in 1907, Minnie, born in 1909, Libbie, born in 1911, Anna, born in 1913, Phillip, born in 1915; and David, born in 1918. Mr and Mrs Kavich are both members of the Jewish Synagogue Politically, Mr Kavich is an adherent of no special party, voting for the best men and measures. Fraternally he is a member of the Ancient Order of United Workmen, of the Woodmen of the World, of the Knights and Ladies of Security, of the Fraternal Order of Eagles and of the Independent Order of B'nai B'rith

Gus H Weber A newspaper man of wide experience and marked ability, Gus H. Weber, editor and proprietor of the Uehling Post, has been associated with various Nebraska journals, and has ever devoted his thought and energy to making the papers with which he was connected bright, readable and, above all, clean. A native of Switzerland, he was born December 24, 1878, a son of Albert and Anna Weber, life-long residents of that country His father, a railroad engineer, was accidentally killed while yet in the prime of life They were the parents of seven children, of whom but two, Gus H, and his sister Emma, were the only ones to come to America

When but fourteen years of age Gus H Weber, who was of an adventurous spirit, came to the United States, and for seven months after his arrival made his home with an uncle at Westpoint, Nebraska. He had acquired a high school education in Switzerland and had there attended a Conservatory of Music Leaving his uncle's home, he joined Ringling Brothers' Circus, and as a member of its band toured the country for two years Deciding to locate in Nebraska, Mr Weber purchased the Banner, a paper published in Snyder, and managed it successfully for four years. The following three years he was in service as a member of the Twenty-Second United States Infantry Band, the greater part of the time in the Philippine Islands, and on receiving his discharge returned to Snyder and again assumed management of the Banner

Going to Petersburg, Nebraska, the ensuing year, Mr Weber was there engaged in journalistic work eight years and later was foreman on two of the Albion, Nebraska, papers, the News and the Argos He subsequently worked on the Omaha Bee and the Fremont Tribune, well known papers. From Fremont Mr Weber came to Uehling and having bought the Uehling Post has since edited it most successfully, the paper under his management being one of the brightest and most newsy and popular papers published in Dodge County

Mr. Weber married, in 1911, at Albion, Nebraska, Mabel Cooper, a daughter of Henry Cooper, who is living retired in Petersburg, this state, and they are the parents of four bright, interesting children: Albert Conrad, Francis Henry, John Pershing and Virginia Elizabeth Mr Weber supports the principles of the republican party by voice and vote. Mrs Weber is held in high esteem by her many friends and acquaintances and is a consistent member of the Congregational Church

JAMES F HANSON, coming to Fremont from Kansas with his parents in 1864, became one of the early settlers of the city and has, barring absence at college, made Fremont and Dodge County his home ever since He was born at Wathena, Kansas, just across the river from St. Joe, Missouri, in the stormy John Brown and anti-slavery days of 1857, and his first childhood memories are those of marching soldiers of the Civil war times, and of his father and older brother taking their turns in the citizens guards watching the Missouri River nights against Missouri "bushwhackers" and a possible repetition of Quantrell's Lawrence massacre

His parents were James C and Ellen Christina Hanson, people of comfortable circumstances and good education, devout members originally of the Lutheran Church, who came to America and settled in Kansas in 1854 from a suburb of the fine capital city of Copenhagen, Denmark The senior Hansons lived for many years in Copenhagen The father was a soldier in the Danish war of 1848 with Prussia, and with the strong French sympathies of the family, his great-uncle was a soldier in the armies of the great Napoleon

The Hansons were not well pleased with their first rough pioneering and war-torn experiences in America, and in 1864 set out to find something better than Kansas and Missouri seemed to afford, and found it to their entire satisfaction, at first for a number of months in the then small city of Omaha, and then permanently at Fremont The family landed first at Fremont in their "prairie schooner" drawn by four yoke of oxen, there being no railroad, but as a Sioux Indian war was on, they spent the fall, winter and spring of 1864-65 in Omaha, returning to Fremont in the spring of 1865 James F Hanson, the subject of this sketch, then seven years old, remembers as distinctly as if it were yesterday, the rejoicing and the public decorating of Omaha with flags and bunting in celebration of the fall of Richmond in the spring of 1865, and the mourning and crepe of a few days later upon the assassination of President Lincoln He attended the notable civic and military funeral services for Lincoln at the Territorial Capitol building then at Omaha

At Fremont the Hansons witnessed the great overland traffic carried on in prairie schooners and stages to Denver Salt Lake and beyond; and the building soon thereafter of the Union Pacific Railroad up the Platte Valley, the first Nebraska railroad After five years the family located on a "homestead" farm ten miles out from Fremont where the senior Hanson, being a blacksmith by trade, conducted a shop and was the local rural postmaster, while James F, thirteen years old, but big for his age, did the farming The neighborhood and postoffice were named Jamestown, in honor of the senior Hanson, the first postmaster, and James Beeman, an old resident of the neighborhood

At Jamestown the Hanson family all became members of the Methodist Episcopal Church and were active in surrounding rural church and Sunday school work James F became a Sunday school superintendent at seventeen and a member of the first board of trustees of Bethel Church at nineteen, a church still existing and prospering A much-beloved sister of young Hanson, Marie E., died at Jamestown His parents died a number of years afterward at Fremont, the father at sixty-eight years of age, the mother at eighty-one

Mr Hanson's education was had at the Fremont public schools and at Jamestown, and at seventeen years he began a five-years' course at Doane College, Crete, Nebraska, which he pursued with increasing regularity until 1880, graduating from an elective course and receiving a

James F. Hanson

diploma from that excellent school that year Among Mr Hanson's educational accomplishments at Doane College was a thorough reading, speaking and writing mastery of the German language, which he completed by an after-stay of one year with the educated and noted German families of Grosshans and Bonekemper at Sutton, Nebraska, Rev Mr Bonekemper having been pastor of the German Reform Church of that town and having been a graduate of Goettingen University of Germany

Having completed his schooling, Mr Hanson in 1881 became a member of the working force of L. D. Richards, later Richards, Keene & Co, then and since an investment concern of great strength, and of which Mr Hanson became a member in 1885 Richards, Keene & Co. represented at that time millions of dollars of eastern money for farm loan investment, great widely extended areas of farm lands in Nebraska and Iowa, including the northeast Nebraska land grants of the old Fremont, Elkhorn & Missouri Valley and Sioux City & Pacific railroads Mr Hanson became the main expert for the company on real estate values and titles, and industrial and corporate organizer in the large and public spirited activities of the company in the building up of industrial Fremont Mr. Hanson traveled much in this connection and his subsequent extensive investment activities over the East and in the South and on the Pacific Coast and Canada

Mr Hanson, in 1897, sold out his interest to Richards, Keene & Co and developed his present business of J F. Hanson & Co, comprising himself and his four sons, Donald E, James R, Alfred L and Willard B Hanson, doing business on a very considerable scale in Nebraska, Kansas, Missouri, Colorado and South Dakota as conservators of estates, financial and confidential brokers, corporate auditors and title men

Mr Hanson was married in 1884 to Miss Lelia Stanton Wightman Mrs Hanson was of an educational family of high standing and from a long line of New York State and Connecticut ancestors, the Wightman family having an unbroken American genealogy from Groton, Connecticut, from 1632 down Her father was a graduate of Union College, Schenectady, New York, and bore the degrees of A M and Ph. D. Her mother was a New York State college graduate with the degree of A M Her father was for a number of years dean of Nebraska Wesleyan University Mrs Hanson was educated in the schools of her native New York State and of Nebraska, and took a special course of music at Buffalo, New York

Mr and Mrs Hanson's family consists of six children, all living, namely, Grace M Hanson, their only daughter, and Howard W, successfully engaged in farming at Davenport, Nebraska, and James R, Donald E, Alfred L, and Willard B, all associated with their father in the business of J F Hanson & Co, of which they are members James R and Donald E became sergeant-majors at Camp Funston in great war, and Donald E was private secretary to General Wood at the camp Willard B. was in the radio service in the Navy

Mrs Hanson died, sixty years of age, on May 14, 1920, possessed of a strong constitution that would ordinarily have guaranteed her twenty more years of useful, happy life, but dying of a malignant incurable disease Besides raising her considerable family, which her friends say she did well, she was for twenty years a power in Fremont and in the State in defense and reclamation of helpless children and of unfortunate girls and women, and in support of prohibition and of salutary public morals She was for years a member of the executive committee of the Nebraska Woman's Christian Temperance Union.

Mr. Hanson has always taken an active interest in public affairs As a member of Richards, Keene & Co, Secretary of Fremont Stock Yards & Land Co, and an executive officer for many years of the Fremont Commercial Club, he became a recognized local authority on manufacturing industry and has done a great deal in the course of the years in the industrial and general community development of Fremont, securing the Nebraska enactment of helpful drainage, road making and park laws, and playing a leading part in the organization of surrounding drainage districts, building of dikes and levees to keep the river out of Fremont, building good roads

Mr Hanson was an active adherent for a number of years of Theodore Roosevelt and his progressive party, sitting in the associated Republican Progressive National Convention of 1916 at Chicago and being progressive candidate that year for governor of Nebraska in that closing period of the party's history These progressive associations gave him a personal acquaintance with Mr Roosevelt and correspondence and conferences with him

ALBERT A NEHRBAS The career of Albert A Nehrbas, president of the Fremont Milling Company, affords an excellent example and incontrovertible proof of the fact that nothing is impossible to the industrious, thrifty and upright man in this country Starting out in life with absolutely nothing, having had no special training, not even the ordinary educational advantages, backed by no capital or influence, he has steadily advanced until today he is at the head of a large industrial plant, and is recognized as a man of moment in his home city

Albert A Nehrbas was born at Pittsburgh, Pennsylvania, on January 21, 1868, a son of George and Rachael (Miller) Nehrbas, natives of Germany and Pennsylvania, respectively, who were married in Pennsylvania In 1886 George Nehrbas brought his family to Fremont, Nebraska, and here he worked as a carpenter, until his retirement, but while living in Pennsylvania, he was an iron worker Seven children were born to him and his wife, of whom five are now living Albert A, who is the eldest, Laura, who is unmarried, lives with her parents, George, who has worked for the Fremont Tribune for thirty years; Letitia, who married T L. Watson, a traveling man of Kansas City, Missouri, and Charlotte, who married David Fowler, bookkeeper for Wiley & Moorehouse The family all belong to the Lutheran Church They are strong in their support of the doctrines of the republican party After attending school in Pennsylvania for a brief period, Albert A Nehrbas began to be self-supporting as a clerk in a grocery store, and later entered one of the rolling mills of Pittsburgh, Pennsylvania, with which industry he was connected until the time of the family migration to Fremont in 1886 Upon his arrival in this city he secured employment with May Brothers, and then engaged with the Chicago & Northwestern Railroad, remaining with it for ten years, alternating the selling of tickets with work in the freight office All of this time he was saving his money with a definite end in view, and in 1902 was able to realize his ambition to own a milling business of his own, at that time buying a substantial interest in the Fremont Milling Company of which he is now the president Quite recently this company has acquired by purchase the property of the Brown Mill, and consolidated the interests of the two organizations Mr. Nehrbas is also a heavy stockholder in the Fremont Building & Loan Association, but takes no active part in the latter, all of his energies being expended in the conduct of his mill

Like the other members of his family Mr Nehrbas is a republican, but has never aspired to public honors Fraternally he belongs to the Elks and Odd Fellows Mr Nehrbas is unmarried From boyhood he has striven to develop those qualities which now enable him to multiply his productiveness and his value to his community, in his case they being grit, vision and a really marvelous ability to overcome obstacles.

HENRY TANK There is no other occupation which yields such gratifying results as does that of farming, and especially is this true in Nebraska, the fertile lands of that commonwealth responding splendidly to the care and attention lavished on them by the more progressive of the agriculturalists Dodge and Washington counties form a portion of the state that has been specially favored by natural conditions and these in turn have been developed in a commendable manner until this region now stands as a monument to the foresight and industry of its pioneers One of the men who is making a great success of his farming and stockraising, and yet is finding time to attend to his duties as a public-spirited citizen is Henry Tank of Maple Township

Henry Tank was born in Dodge County, February 23, 1875, a son of Hans and Katherine Tank, natives of Germany Hans Tank participated in the war between Germany and Denmark, and came to the United States in 1869, and making his way West to Nebraska, was first in the employ of Mr Sievers, one of the first settlers of the county Carefully saving his money, Hans Tank was soon able to begin farming for himself, and if it had not been for the forces of nature, would doubtless have soon become independent for he was very industrious and economical, but unfortunately for him he began farming at a period when this region was liable to be afflicted with the scourge of grasshoppers, and more than one crop was lost in this manner Then a devastating prairie fire wiped out all of his improvements and destroyed his crop However, he belonged to that type of self-reliant human beings who will not allow himself to be discouraged no matter what the conditions may be, and he went to work repairing the damages and in time prospered He was spared to see the neighborhood he had selected acquire a substantial standing in this state and his farm become one of the valuable ones of Dodge County, for he attained to the age of eighty-two years, his wife passing away, however, when seventy-four They had twelve children, two sons and six daughters still living

Growing up on his father's farm Henry Tank attended the local schools and remained at home until he had attained to his majority, at which time he began farming in partnership with his brother, the two renting land from D W Dorsey for ten years and working the 160-acre farm together, but at his death Henry Tank bought his share of the 160 acres Later he added to his farm until he now owns 400 acres of splendidly developed and improved land, and here he is engaged in general farming and stockraising, specializing on Red Polled cattle and Jersey Red hogs In addition to his farming activities, Mr Tank is a director of the Farmers Elevator of Nickerson, and of the First National Bank of Ames

Mr. Tank was united in marriage with Rose Knoell, born and reared in Dodge County Mr. and Mrs Tank have seven children, as follows: Ernest, Louie, Harold, Marie, Alice, Dorothy and Donald For fifteen years Mr Tank served on the school board of his district, and he has also been road supervisor Interested in the progress of his community, Mr Tank has sought to secure for it the various improvements necessary to bring it up to standard ideas of development, and among other things was active in promoting the organization of the Dodge County Telephone Company of which he has been a director for twelve years His personal affairs and public duties have been too arduous for him to form any fraternal affiliations, but he maintains many warm personal attachments among the leading men of this and other counties, and is recognized as one of the representative citizens of Nebraska

M. R. LIPPINCOTT, a former county clerk of Washington County and for many years engaged in the lumber and grain business at Blair, represents the third generation of the Lippincott family in Washington County. The Lippincotts were among the first pioneer settlers and the family name has always enjoyed dignified associations with the best interests of the community

The pioneer was J C Lippincott, who came to Nebraska about 1858 and took up a homestead in the vicinity of Blair. He was a very poor man when he settled in Nebraska and he experienced many of the trials and vicissitudes of pioneering and lived out his life in the county.

His son, Thomas P Lippincott, was born in Washington County, Indiana, and was a child when brought to Nebraska He was reared on a farm but for a number of years was engaged in the implement business at Blair Successful in business affairs, he was also a leader in the life of the community, and was elected on the republican ticket and served one term as county clerk of Washington County In later years he became a socialist in politics He was a member of the Episcopal Church Thomas P Lippincott died at Blair in 1916, and his widow is still living in that town He married Hettie Camp, who was born near Buffalo, New York They were married in Blair, and she had come to Nebraska about 1874 Of their five children three are still living M R Lippincott, who was born at Blair in 1877, Lydia R., living with her mother, and Paul Thomas, a locomotive fireman living at Chadron, Nebraska

M R Lippincott grew up in his native town, attended the grammar and high schools, and soon after completing his education went to work in the lumber and grain business Almost continuously through all the years of his manhood he has been associated with the coal, lumber and grain company, and for a number of years past has been manager of the Blair Elevator and Yards of that corporation He has given his time and energies to business affairs with marked success, and is known as an able executive and man who accomplishes all that he undertakes

In 1902 Mr Lippincott married Augusta Mayle, a native of Blair. Her father, John Mayle, was an early settler at Blair, coming from Pennsylvania, and for many years was in the confectionery business Mr and Mrs Lippincott have two daughters, Marjorie and Pauline, both attending the Blair schools The family are members of the Episcopal Church. Mr and Mrs Lippincott are members of the Eastern Star chapter and he is affiliated with other branches of Masonry The cause of good government and politics has always interested Mr Lippincott, and he gave a very efficient administration during his term as county clerk He is a republican

JOHN G OSTERLOH One of the first pale faces to invade that domain of the Indian in Dodge County, the part since christened Logan Township, was the late Gerhard Osterloh, a cabin-dweller who took up Government land and converted the same into a valuable and paying property, and who established a precedent of life and labor since maintained by the members of his family One of the representatives of this worthy and honorable name is John G Osterloh, a son of the pioneer, who is carrying on extensive operations in Logan Township

Mr. Osterloh was born in Germany, in 1866, and was two years of age when his parents, Gerhard and Gisine Osterloh, brought him to the United States The family came at once to Dodge County, where the father homesteaded a tract of eighty acres of Government land, near what is now the Town of Hooper, not then in existence At the time of his arrival he possessed $200, and his first home was a cottonwood-board dwelling, through the yard of which the old Indian trail passed The Indians were still numerous, although they never made serious trouble Gerhard Osterloh continued to be engaged in farming during the remainder of his life, and at his death, in 1895, was the possessor of about three hundred acres of good land His widow, now well advanced in years, survives him

John G Osterloh grew up on the home farm in section 20, Logan Township, and secured his education in the public schools As a youth he adopted farming as his life work, and at the age of twenty-four years began farming on his own account Later he purchased 160 acres of land from his father, and to this he has added from time to time until he is now the owner of 750 acres. He has modern improvements on his property installed by himself, and in every respect his property is up-to-date He has always carried on general farming, in addition to which he has been a cattle and hog raiser of some prominence He has numerous business interests, and is identified financially with the First National Bank, of Hooper, and the Logan Valley Bank, of Uehling He and Mrs Osterloh are consistent members of the Lutheran Church where Mr. Osterloh has served as chairman of the board of trustees for a long time and also has served as Sunday school superintendent for a number of years As a citizen he has discharged his duties faithfully and conscientiously, and has served as a member of the local board of school directors for a long period and as clerk of Logan Township four years

In 1891 Mr Osterloh was united in marriage with Meta G Behrens, who was born in Germany, a daughter of Gerhart Behrens, who never came to the United States Four children have been born to Mr and Mrs Osterloh Bertha, the wife of Adolph Moeller, a farmer of Dodge County, Alma, the wife of John A Schroeder, also engaged in farming in Dodge County; Henry, who is carrying on agricultural operations in Nickerson Township, this county, and Emil, residing at home, who is assisting his father

A J Miller Well known in financial circles as a man of keen foresight and much ability, A J. Miller, of Dodge County, has achieved success in the business world through industry and meritorious work, at the present time being president of the First National Bank, a responsible position which he is filling with credit to himself, and to the satisfaction of the officers of the institution, and of its numerous patrons A son of the late Vaclav Miller, he was born, in December, 1881, in Dodge County, which he has always claimed as home.

Born in Bohemia, Vaclav Miller immigrated to the United States, the land of hope and promise, in early life, coming to Dodge County, Nebraska, in 1861, soon after his arrival in New York Taking up a homestead claim, he improved a good farm, which he managed successfully for many years, subsequently living retired until his death, at the age of seventy-two years To him and his wife, Margaret, whose death occurred in Dodge County, twelve children were born, a goodly number of sons and daughters

Acquiring a practical education in the Dodge schools, A J Miller began the battle of life on his own account at the age of eighteen years and for four years was employed as a clerk in a general mercantile establishment In 1903 he began his banking career, accepting a minor position in a local bank, receiving for his work the munificent salary of $25 dollars a month Faithful to the duties devolving upon him in that capacity, he won promotion from time to time, and at the present time is not only president of the First National Bank of Dodge County, but has an interest in several other banks, and is an extensive and successful dealer in real estate The bank with which he is officially connected was first capitalized at $10,000, which has been increased to $50,000, and its annual deposits, which were $35,000 the first year of its existence, now amount to $706,000, an increase that bears visible evidence of the safety and popularity of the institution The building in which it is housed was erected in 1910, and is of modern construction, conveniently arranged for carrying on business

Mr Miller married, June 30, 1901, in Omaha, Clara Schulte, who was born and reared in Cuming County, Nebraska, and of their union four children have been born, namely Nitha, Roma, Gladys, and Imogene Active in local affairs, Mr Miller is a member of the parochial school board, and is serving as mayor Fraternally he belongs to the Catholic Workmen, the Knights of Columbus, and to the Catholic Order of Foresters

William C Wiley Conspicuous among the active, wide-awake business men who are contributing so largely toward the advancement of the mercantile prosperity of Dodge County is William C Wiley, of Fremont, an official member, and general manager, of the Stacey-Wiley Company, wholesale dealers in fruit A son of John Wiley, he was born, September 23, 1862, at Camptown, Bradford County, Pennsylvania, of Irish ancestry

Born in County Monaghan, Ireland, John Wiley lived there until after his marriage with Jane Dougherty, a native of the same county Soon after that event he immigrated, in 1848, to America, locating in Pennsylvania, where both he and his wife spent their remaining years Subsequently buying a small tract of land, he improved a cozy little farm, on which he lived and labored hard in order to support his large family He was a republican in politics, and both he and his wife were faithful members of the Presbyterian Church Of the sixteen children, seven sons and nine daughters, eight girls and one boy are living, all being residents of Pennsylvania with the exception of the son, William C

Having completed his early education in the Camptown High School, William C Wiley, impelled by the restless spirit characteristic of the Americans, left Pennsylvania in 1881, and coming directly to Nebraska, located in Fremont Securing a position in the wholesale house of the May Brothers, he continued with that firm three years, after which he was for ten years employed in the freight depot of the Northwestern Railroad Company, and for another ten years owned and operated a dray line Wise in his savings, and prudent in his expenditures, Mr Wiley accumulated money, and in 1907 established himself in business as a wholesale dealer in fruits, and met with good success in his venture

Wm. R. Wiley

Admitting Carlos Morehouse as a partner in 1911, he continued the business as head of the firm of Wiley & Morehouse until January, 1920 This firm was then merged into a stock company, and incorporated, with a paid up capital of $100,000, as the Stacey-Wiley Company, of which Mr Wiley is second vice president and general manager Under his superintendence an extensive business is being carried on, amounting to $500,000 per annum In addition to the other employes, four commercial salesman are kept constantly on the road, the payroll of this enterprising firm being $2,000 each month of the year, an amount bearing evidence of its volume of business and financial prosperity

Mr Wiley married, in 1887, May A Reynolds, whose birthplace was Devils Lake, Michigan, and of their union five children have been born, namely Imo, wife of Harry Prater, who is traveling for Mr Wiley, Nellie, wife of Fred O'Dell, a cigar manufacturer, of Fremont; Hazel, wife of John B Freeman, of Fremont, a traveling salesman, Warren C, of Fremont, a traveling salesman, enlisted during the World war in Company B, One Hundred and Ninth Iowa Engineers, and served for two years, one year having been spent in France, and Harold, who is in school Mr and Mrs Wiley are members of the Methodist Episcopal Church Politically Mr Wiley is a straightforward democrat, and takes an active part in local affairs, having served as a member of the city council six years, and in 1917 was elected mayor of the city, a position for which he was amply qualified, and which he filled most ably and satisfactorily Fraternally he is a member of the Independent Order of Odd Fellows, in which he has passed all the chairs of the local lodge, and belongs to the grand lodge, and is likewise a member of Fremont Lodge No 513, Benevolent and Protective Order of Elks Having had but one dollar to his name when he arrived in Fremont in 1881 Mr Wiley has been in truth the architect of his own fortunes, and the above brief review of his life may well furnish to the rising generation a forcible example of the success to be achieved by persevering industry, thrift and good management

C E CUYKENDALL Active, enterprising and progressive, C. E Cuykendall occupies a place of prominence and influence in the industrial and business circles of Dodge County, in the management of his large canning factory at Fremont showing excellent judgment and marked ability A son of E C. Cuykendall, he was born December 2, 1879, in Milford, Delaware, where his early life was passed

A native of New York State, E C Cuykendall was born in Owasco, Cayuga County, in 1832, and was there reared, educated and married Moving to Delaware, he was engaged in the drying of fruit for many years, an industry that proved highly remunerative He is still residing in that state, a venerable and highly respected citizen, now retired from business cares He married Carolina Roosa, who was born in Owasco, New York, in 1834, and is now a bright and active woman of fourscore and six years Four children were born of their union, as follows John W, born sixty-four years ago, is prosperously engaged in the canning business at Atlantic, Iowa, J R, of Hoopeston, Illinois, is likewise engaged in the canning business. Katherine is the wife of James Kurtz of Dannemora, New York, who has charge of the food supplies for the penitentiary and asylums of the county in which he lives, and C E, of whom we write The father is a democrat in politics and during his active life served in various public offices He is a member of the Dutch Reformed Church, to which his wife also belongs

C E Cuykendall received his elementary and academical education in Delaware, and afterwards attended a noted institute in New York, and completed the course of study at the Northwestern University in Chicago In 1895, in partnership with his brother John he embarked in the canning business at Atlantic, Iowa, and during the six years he remained there became proficient in all the details connected with the business Coming from there to Dodge County, Nebraska, in 1901, Mr Cuykendall and brother John W bought the canning factory in Fremont, and in its management has met with unquestioned success In 1914 the business was incorporated, with a paid-up capital of $50,000, and Mr Cuykendall was made vice president and manager of the company The factory, which has been recently modernized as to its equipments, is devoted exclusively to the canning of corn, and its annual output of 2,000,000 cans finds a ready market, it being extensively and favorably known throughout the great Middle West

Mr Cuykendall married in 1908 at Atlantic, Iowa, Bernadette O'Donnell, a native of Pennsylvania, and they have one daughter, Jean, born in 1913 Mr Cuykendall is a straightforward democrat in his political affiliations and has rendered his fellow-citizens excellent service as a member of the Fremont City Council Fraternally he belongs to Lodge No 445, Benevolent and Protective Order of Elks, at Atlantic, Iowa He is a member of the Fremont Commercial Club and of the Rotary Club Religiously he is a Presbyterian and Mrs Cuykendall is Catholic.

Ezra Phillips Long years of industry, well-directed management of his affairs, close application to the details of his work, and a thorough and comprehensive knowledge thereof, combined to place Ezra Phillips among the foremost and substantial promoters of agriculture in his part of Dodge County From the prairies his unaided industry brought forth ample means, permitting his retirement to Fremont in 1908 and his consigning to younger hands the tasks that made up the sum of his existence for thirty-one years He has a modern and well-furnished home on Broad Street and is regarded as one of the financially strong and morally high retired farmers

Mr Phillips was born in Pickaway County, Ohio, August 6, 1852, a son of John M and Sarah (Reed) Phillips, both of whom are deceased His father, who was reared in Ohio, passed his active career in agricultural pursuits in that state, and was a highly esteemed citizen of his community, where he served twenty-seven years as a member of the Board of Supervisors of Woodford County He died at the advanced age of eighty-eight years There were seven sons and seven daughters in the family, but Ezra is the only one now living in Dodge County

Ezra Phillips was reared on the home farm and acquired his educational training in the public schools, after leaving which he worked for a time with his father, and later for other agriculturists in his home community Eventually he decided that better opportunities awaited him in the West, and in 1877 made his way to Dodge County and bought 160 acres of land, a part of which has been improved, paying $9 35 per acre Mr Phillips went to farming seven miles north and seven miles west of Fremont and his industry gained him success from almost the start Since his original purchase he has added 120 acres to his holdings, the greater part of this land having been secured at a purchase price of $40 per acre During the period of his active career he made numerous improvements on his land, adding to its value and attractiveness, and became known throughout his part of the county as a man dependable and upright, one who regarded his word as he would his bond, and who ever maintained the highest methods of farming and the noblest ideals of home and community life. In 1908 he retired from active pursuits and moved to Fremont, where he took up his residence at 1137 North Broad Street, where he is surrounded by the comforts that reward the man of industry.

In 1877, in Illinois, Mr. Phillips was united in marriage with Miss Louise Cooper, who was born in the Prairie State, and to this union there have been born seven children: Clifford, who is looking after some of his father's agricultural interests in Dodge County; Mrs. Effie Bradbury, a resident of Fremont; Earl, who is also a farmer of Platte County; Mrs. Elsie Olson, living on a farm in this county; Mrs. Nina Richardson; Mrs. Allie Wagner of Fremont; and Mrs. Frieda Wallick. Mr. and Mrs. Phillips are faithful members of the Christian Church. Fraternally he is affiliated with the Benevolent and Protective Order of Elks and local republican politics has found a staunch supporter in him for many years. At various times his fellow citizens have made manifest their confidence in him by electing him to office, and he has faithfully and efficiently discharged the duties of assessor, township clerk and school director, having held the latter position for fifteen years.

D. Z. Mummert. A man of versatile talents, possessing a thorough knowledge of law as well as of modern business methods, D. Z. Mummert of Blair occupies a place of prominence in the legal and financial circles of Washington County, and in all respects is considered a valuable member of his community. A son of the late S. L. Mummert, he was born in 1867 in Pennsylvania, where his childhood days were passed.

S. L. Mummert, a son of George Mummert, a farmer, was born, reared and married in Pennsylvania, the maiden name of his wife having been Nancy Unger. Continuing in the free and independent occupation to which he was reared, he moved with his family to Illinois, locating in Carroll County, where both he and his wife spent their remaining days. He was a stanch republican in politics, and an active member of the Lutheran Church. His family consisted of three children, of whom two are living, D. Z. of whom we write, and William D., a well-known merchant tailor of South Dakota.

Completing his early education in the Lanark, Illinois, High School, D. Z. Mummert remained on the home farm for awhile, but agriculture seemingly had no charms for him. Coming to Blair, Nebraska, in 1888, he read law under the tuition of Judge W. C. Walton to such good purpose that he was admitted to the bar, and in 1890 entered upon the practice of his profession, for which he was well prepared, continuing in it for three years. Opening the Citizens State Bank in 1904, Mr. Mummert became its cashier, and successfully managed its affairs for ten years. In 1915 he disposed of his interests in the institution, which he had placed upon a substantial basis, and has since devoted his time and abilities to the management of his financial affairs, being very successful in either loaning or investing money. Mr. Mummert's prosperity in life is entirely due to his efforts, as he came to Blair with a very limited capital, and has since accumulated a handsome property. At one time he was quite an extensive landholder, but he disposed of the last of it in 1918. Although he is practically retired from law, Mr. Mummert has charge of the legal business not only of his personal friends but of the Citizens State Bank, and of several corporations. He is identified in politics with the republican party and he and his family attend the Methodist Episcopal Church.

Mr. Mummert married, in 1890, Mary A. Pound, who was born near Tipton, Iowa. Her father, the late Albert O. Pound, settled in Iowa as a young man and after teaching school a number of terms bought land, and subsequently carried on general farming until his death. Two children have been born of the marriage of Mr. and Mrs. Mummert, namely: David, a high school pupil; and Gretchen, attending the grammar school.

James Tilton Young. One of the foremost osteopaths of Dodge County, James Tilton Young of Fremont has achieved distinction in his especial method of treating the various diseases to which human kind is heir, oftentimes relieving the sufferings of his patients, and effecting a permanent cure when medical aid has been of no avail. He was born March 7, 1874, in Kansas City, Missouri, coming on the paternal side of English ancestry.

His father, the late John Young, was born in 1850 in England, and as a young man immigrated to the United States, settling in Missouri, where he was engaged principally in general farming until his death in 1902. His wife, whose maiden name was Kesiah C. Allen, was born in Virginia, but came to Dallas County, Missouri, where they were married in 1872. She is still living, making her home in Fremont, Nebraska, with her son James. She is a consistent member of the Christian Church. John Young was usually a democrat in politics. Five children were born of their union, as follows: James Tilton, of whom we write; Nathan M., of Paris, Missouri, a farmer; Mary E., a graduate nurse, living in Fremont; George J., engaged in farming in Cass County, Missouri; and Harvey A., a newspaper man in Los Angeles, California.

Having acquired his elementary education in the common schools, James Tilton Young attended the normal school at Stanberry, Missouri, and the State Normal School at Warrensburg, that state. Thus equipped, he taught school six years, having served as principal of the first consolidated high school established in Missouri. Resigning the position, Mr. Young studied osteopathy in Des Moines, Iowa, and having acquired a thorough knowledge of the art and science thereof located in Superior, Nebraska, where he practiced successfully for five years. Coming from there to Fremont in 1910, Doctor Young has built up a large and lucrative practice in this city. He is active and prominent in professional organizations, having served as president of the State Association of Osteopathy for two terms, and was a member of the State Board of Osteopathy, of which he was secretary two years.

Doctor Young married, in 1911, Jeannette Dysart, who was born in Ohio, a daughter of William Dysart, who in 1881, bought land in Superior, Nuckolls County, Nebraska, for $7 an acre, and recently sold the same for $116 an acre. He still resides in Superior, being retired from active pursuits. Dr. and Mrs. Young have two children, Jean, born in 1912, and John D., born in December, 1913. Both Dr. and Mrs. Young are members of the Congregational Church. The doctor is usually independent in politics, voting according to the dictates of his conscience. Fraternally he belongs to the Knights of Pythias and is an active and prominent member of the Rotary Club.

John H. Knowles. Possessing in a large measure the energy, ability and sound judgment that invariably commands success, John H. Knowles was widely known as the longest established shoe dealer in

Dr. Andrew Harvey

Fremont He is held in high esteem in business, political and social circles A son of the late James Knowles, he was born in 1865 in Upper Sandusky, Ohio, coming on the paternal side of Irish ancestry

Born in Ireland, James Knowles was brought up in the northern part of the Emerald Isle, and as a young man immigrated to the United States He lived first in Ohio, from there moving to Wisconsin, where he was engaged in farming a number of years, and eventually going to Iowa, where he spent the later days of his life He served for two or three years as a soldier in the Civil war and was at one time taken prisoner, but was fortunate enough to escape from his place of confinement He was a republican in politics a member of the Presbyterian Church and belonged to the Grand Army of the Republic He married, in Ohio, Eliza Lowery, a native of this country, and of their eight children five are living, as follows· John H, of whom we write, William, a Kansas farmer, J. D, engaged in farming in Clarinda, Iowa; Mary, wife of L B Turner of Kansas, a farmer, and Elizabeth, wife of John M Dodge, who is engaged in mercantile pursuits in the State of Washington

Having completed the course of study in Carroll College, Waukesha, Wisconsin, John H Knowles first turned his attention to agriculture, and later clerked for awhile in a retail store Changing his occupation, he subsequently traveled fourteen years for a wholesale shoe house, acquiring while thus employed a pretty good knowledge of the shoe business. In the meantime, in 1898, Mr Knowles and his brother Robert opened a shoe store in Fremont, the brother assuming charge of the store, while Mr Knowles continued traveling Robert Knowles died in 1911, and John Knowles had entire charge of the establishment until September, 1920, when he sold the store and is now a traveling salesman Mr Knowles began business for himself with very limited means, and by strict attention to the details of his business met with unquestioned success in his undertakings

Mr. Knowles married, in 1896, Margaret Turner, who was born in Waukesha, Wisconsin, a daughter of Robert Turner, a lifelong farmer of Wisconsin Of the marriage of Mr and Mrs. Knowles two children have been born, namely Isabel, who attended the University of Wooster, in Wooster, Ohio, and now teaching in the high school in Fremont and Elizabeth, a student in the Fremont High School Independent in politics, supporting the best men and measures, Mr Knowles has served in the City Council, and in 1907 and 1908 represented his district in the State Legislature Fraternally he is a member of Fremont Lodge No 514, Benevolent and Protective Order of Elks, of the Knights of Pythias, and of the Modern Woodmen of America Religiously Mr and Mrs Knowles are members of the Presbyterian Church.

ANDREW HARVEY, M D As far back as there is any definite record of the human race there have been men who devoted their lives to the healing of disease, but it is only within practically recent times that the physician has exerted himself with equally beneficent results in the prevention of disease by the introduction of practical sanitary regulations and the application of discoveries relative to the cause of maladies once believed incurable With the expansion in the field of usefulness has come to the members of the medical profession added esteem and honor, and those belonging to it are easily ranked among the best citizens of the community in which their work is performed Dodge County, as one of the most progressive sections of Nebraska has some of the eminently representative physicians and surgeons of the state, and one of them is Dr Andrew Harvey of Fremont

Doctor Harvey was born in Dodge County, Nebraska, on October 26, 1884, a son of Andrew and Margaret (Ritchie) Harvey The father was born in Ayr, Scotland, and the mother in Dundee, Scotland About 1871 he came to the United States and located in Nebraska, and the mother came to the state some time later, and they were here married Both survive and are making their home in North Bend, Nebraska, where for a number of years the father was a farmer and engaged in raising fruit He and his wife belong to the Presbyterian Church In politics he is a democrat and he served as mayor of North Bend for three terms Fraternally he belongs to the Woodmen of the World He and his wife became the parents of the following children Mrs W A McPherson, whose husband is a retired farmer of Fremont, Mrs Elizabeth Bailey, who is a widow living at Mitchell, Nebraska, Mrs Mary H Robinson, a widow residing at Ponca, Nebraska, Mrs J A Ross, whose husband is a farmer of North Bend, Nebraska Mrs O. J Walker, whose husband is a lumberman of Gibbon, Nebraska; Doctor Andrew, who was the sixth in order of birth Mrs James Ferguson, whose husband is a Dodge County farmer, and David, who lives at Lyons, Nebraska The paternal grandfather, Andrew Harvey, came to Dodge County, Nebraska, in the '70s and lived on a farm in this county for many years He reached the advanced age of ninety-six years before he was claimed by death The maternal grandfather, James Ritchie, came to Dodge County, Nebraska, at an early day He, too, is deceased, passing away at North Bend, Nebraska, after useful life spent as a farmer and preacher

Doctor Harvey attended the local schools of Dodge County and North Bend, and was graduated from the high school of the latter place in 1903, following which he took a four-years' course in Bellevue College, from which he was graduated in 1907 with the degree of Bachelor of Science, and then taught for the subsequent two years He matriculated at the University of Nebraska, in the medical department, and was graduated therefrom in 1913 with the degree of Doctor of Medicine Immediately following his graduation Doctor Harvey began the practice of his profession at Craig, Nebraska, where he remained for two and one-half years, and then came to Fremont, locating permanently in this city in November, 1915, and has built up some very excellent connections, and his practice shows a steady and normal increase

On October 22, 1913, Doctor Harvey was married to Mabel Thom, born at North Bend, Nebraska, a daughter of Alexander Thom, mayor of North Bend, president of the First State Bank of that city, and a man of more than ordinary prestige Dr and Mrs Harvey have two children, namely: Dorothy Jean and Alexander They belong to the Presbyterian Church Fraternally Doctor Harvey is a Mason Although he exercises his right of suffrage by voting the democratic ticket, Doctor Harvey does not take a very active part in politics, being absorbed in his practice Professionally he maintains membership with the Dodge County Medical Society the Nebraska State Medical Society, the Elkhorn Valley Medical Society and the American Medical Association While living at Craig he was president of the Burt County Medical Society for a year A close student and conscientious practitioner, Doctor Harvey has been very successful and has honorably won and holds the confidence and respect of his neighborhood both as a physician and as a man

HERMAN G SASSE Among the younger men who have assumed the active burdens of agricultural management in Dodge County, one is Herman G Sasse who has always believed that the best and fullest life is to be found in the country He has remained on the homestead farm, where he grew up, and has laid a sure foundation of success in the work for which he was trained

The Sasse farm is in section 26 of Maple Township Mr Sasse was born there April 12, 1891, grew up with an education in the common schools, at the age of twenty-three married and began farming for himself He has since operated his father's place of 280 acres, and does both general farming and stock raising In 1920 he purchased an improved farm of eighty acres in Nickerson Township, Dodge County, which he took charge of in March, 1921.

Mr Sasse is independent in political affiliations In 1914 he married Sarah Knoell who was born in Dodge County

WILLIAM J MAHER One of the best known of the younger attorneys of Washington County is William J Maher, of Blair, an honored native son who has always tried to measure up to the standard of correct manhood and this locality is proud to number him among its progressive and representative men, having always maintained his home here In all the relations of life he has proved true to every trust reposed in him and no one is worthier of the high esteem in which he is held

William J Maher was born in Blair, Washington County, Nebraska, on October 25, 1894, and is the son of James E and Grace A (Hayes) Maher, both of whom also are natives of Washington County and are now living in Blair James E Maher was born in October 27, 1858, and is the son of William and Catherine (Walsh) Maher, both of whom were natives of Ireland The father was born in 1824 and died on May 7, 1888, and the mother who was born in 1824, died in 1891 William and Catherine Maher were married at Davenport, Iowa, where they first settled after coming to this country, and in that city he ran a hotel for two years In 1858 he came to Washington County, Nebraska, and homesteaded a farm, on which he lived for about six years at the end of that time moving into Blair, where they spent the remainder of their lives They were members of the Roman Catholic Church and in politics he was a democrat He served as a member of the City Council and also on the School Board for several years in Blair Of the six children born to them, four are living, namely. Mrs R A Heaton of Wahoo, Nebraska, James E., father of William J, of this sketch; Mary, the widow of J. T Powers, living at Muskogee, Oklahoma; Lizzie, the wife of Fred Cunningham of Muskogee.

James E Maher was educated in the public schools of Blair and on attaining mature years he engaged in the mercantile business, which occupied his efforts for a number of years He was successful in business and in 1897 retired from the mercantile business and now gives his attention to his farms, several of which he owns in this locality In 1890 he was married to Grace Hayes, who was born and reared in Blair, the daughter of Patrick Hayes, who was born in Ireland and came to Blair in 1869, when the town was first started He ran a lumber yard here for a number of years and was successful in his business affairs To James E and Grace Maher were born seven children, namely. Ruth, the wife of Reed O'Hanlon of Blair, William J, of this sketch; Roland, who is a student in the law department of Georgetown University at Washington, D. C Robert, who graduated from the Blair High School in the spring of 1920, Charlotte, who is attending St Mary's Academy, Notre Dame, Indiana; James and Margaret The family are identified with the Catholic Church and in politics James E Maher is a democrat

He has taken an active part in public affairs and served for eleven years as a member of the Board of County Commissioners and twenty-four years as a member of the School Board.

William J Maher attended the public schools of Blair, followed by a year's attendance at the University of Nebraska, and then was a student in Creighton College, where he was graduated in 1916, with the degree of Bachelor of Laws Immediately thereafter he formed a law partnership with Clark O'Hanlon and has been actively engaged in the practice of his profession continuously since As a lawyer he has won the reputation of a safe and sound practitioner, and by a straightforward, honorable course he has built up a good legal business, being considered one of the leaders of the Washington County bar

In 1915 Mr Maher was married to Winifred Donahue, who was born in Omaha, Nebraska, and they have one child, John Joseph. They are members of the Catholic Church and Mr Maher is a member of the Knights of Columbus He is also a member of the Gamma Eta Gamma, a college law fraternity In every respect he merits the high esteem in which he is universally held, for he is a man of public spirit, professional ability and exemplary character

JAMES J McFARLAND A man of talent and enterprise, James J McFarland, who has recently turned over to his son the management of the Dodge Criterion, was for many years proprietor of that paper, and successfully devoted all his thought and energy to making it a bright, reliable, and above all, a clean sheet, nothing of worth being too small to claim his attention, and no topic so large that he could not handle it intelligently A son of the late A M McFarland, he was born March 9, 1857, in Clinton County, Indiana, where his childhood days were spent

A pioneer of Nebraska, A. M McFarland trekked across the country with a colony of thirteen families from Indiana to Nebraska, camping and cooking by the way in true pioneer style Locating in Stanton, then a little settlement of six families only, he took up land in what is still called Hoosier Hollow, on Pleasant Run Creek, becoming a homesteader in 1868, and on the farm which he reclaimed spent the remainder of his seventy-five years of earthly life He was a Baptist minister, and in addition to preaching was known far and wide as the best auctioneer in the Elkhorn Valley His wife, whose maiden name was Elizabeth Couger, attained the advanced age of seventy-nine years Their children, eight in number, were reared on the homestead and educated in the district school

Well trained in agricultural pursuits under his father's instructions, James J McFarland spent all of his earlier life on the home farm, as a boy doing all the chores incidental to farm life. Having a decided taste and talent for journalism, he became familiar with its rudiments in Stanton, and subsequently edited and published the Stanton Democrat for five years, and later managed the Stanton Register for twelve years, making it one of the best papers of the kind in Stanton County

Coming to Dodge in 1901 Mr McFarland assumed charge of the Dodge Criterion, and in its management met with assured success from the start It has a large and constantly increasing circulation, its many readers getting all of the latest reliable news in a condensed form, whether foreign or domestic, and keeping well informed on local affairs Mr McFarland recently installed his son as manager of the paper, but still assists in the office if necessary, although he is practically retired from active work

Mr. McFarland married, in 1878, Hannah E Lovett of Stanton and into the household thus established six children have been born, namely Lillie Daniels, living on a farm in Stanton County, Elmer M, in charge of the Criterion, Chester died in infancy; Orvil, who lived but eleven years, Reginald, engaged in farming in Stanton County, and Maurice, also a farmer in Stanton County Mrs McFarland passed to the life beyond on February 15, 1919 She was a member of the Congregational Church, to which Mr McFarland belongs Politically Mr McFarland is a republican, and although he has never held public office, he has ever heartily endorsed all projects conducive to the advancement and prosperity of his home town

Elmer M McFarland, the eldest son of his parents, began working for himself at the age of eighteen years, being engaged in farming for two years Subsequently serving an apprenticeship at the printer's trade, he followed it until 1906, when he removed to Ashland, Nebraska, where he was in the employ of the Chicago, Burlington & Quincy Railroad Company until 1919, doing clerical work at first, but afterward having been employed as a mechanic in the roundhouse Resigning the position, he bought a half interest in his father's paper, the Dodge Criterion, of which he has now full control, in its management meeting with acknowledged success. He is a republican in politics, and a member of the Highlanders

Elmer M McFarland married, October 23, 1909, Jennie R Bricker, whose parents reside in Ashland, Nebraska, and they have one child, Wynona, born in 1911

John B. Janssen The steady tides of immigration which have flowed into the fertile states of the northwest have had their part in the marvelous growth of this region, but they take away none of the credit from the men who dared the hardships and endured the privations of life in the early days, although many of them now sleep in death One of these men of Nebraska, now gone from this life, was John Janssen of Dodge County, who in dying left behind him a keen appreciation of his sterling characteristics which are not easily forgotten, any more than they were overlooked while he was living He was a good man, a kind neighbor and worthy citizen, and no higher praise can be accorded anyone

John Janssen was born in Hanover, Germany, January 15, 1841, a son of John Henry and Katherine Janssen, natives of Germany, both of whom died in their native land In 1871 John Janssen came to the United States and first stopped at Toledo, Ohio, where he secured employment chopping wood Later he spent a short time in Illinois, where he was married to Katherine Brandt, a native of Illinois, and a daughter of Henry and Mary Brandt, natives of Germany, who came to the United States and became farmers of Illinois After his marriage Mr. Janssen came on west to Nebraska, and for a time lived at Fremont, where he worked at whatever he could find to do As soon as possible he rented land, then bought a farm, and on it did general farming for thirty years. Feeling that he had by this time earned a rest, he retired and moved to Hooper, where he died November 2, 1904 He was an independent voter Zion Lutheran Church held his membership, and he lived up to its creed in his every-day life

Mr and Mrs Janssen became the parents of the following children Anna, who married Willis Marshall, a farmer of Belgrave, Nebraska, and she died March 9, 1920, John, who is a farmer of Dodge County,

Herman, who is also a farmer of Dodge County; Emma, who is the wife of Peter Miller, a farmer of Dodge County, Mary, who died March 1, 1906, was the wife of Gust Agers, Amelia, who is the wife of Henry Johanning, a farmer of Dodge County, Lucy, who married George Bower, a farmer in the vicinity of Scribner, and he died April 6, 1920, Carrie, who died in infancy, Charles, who is an attorney; Fred, who is also an attorney, and two who died in infancy Fred Janssen is a veteran of the World war, and served in Company L, Three Hundred and Fifty-Fifth Regiment, Eighty-Ninth Division of Infantry, for six months abroad after a training of thirteen and one-half months at Fort Funston For ninety-three days he was under fire and was a brave soldier He received his honorable discharge on June 13, 1919, and is now a member of Hooper Post No 18, American Legion. Charles Janssen was also in the service as a member of the balloon corps, receiving his first training at Omaha, Nebraska, from whence he was sent to Camp Dodge, Virginia, where he was honorably discharged, after being in the army for eighteen months He, too, is a member of the American Legion.

NATHANIEL W SMAILS Seventy-one years have dissolved in the mists of the irrevocable past since Nathaniel W Smails, one of the best known citizens of Dodge County, first saw the light of day He has lived through one of the most remarkable, and in many respects the most wonderful, epoch in the world's history There will never be another like it, for it embraced the period when the strong-armed homeseekers from the eastern states invaded the great west (he being among the number) and redeemed it from the wilds, bringing it up through various stages to its present high state of civilization. To all this he has been a most interested, and by no means a passive, spectator, having sought to do his full share in the work of progress in the locality which he selected as his place of abode He talks most interestingly of the early days when customs and manners were different in many respects, but when real manhood and womanhood were valued at their true worth

Nathaniel W. Smails was born in Monroe, Michigan, on August 6, 1849, and is the son of James and Margaret (Levington) Smails Both parents were born and reared in England, immigrated to the United States and were married in Philadelphia, Pennsylvania, the officiating clergymen being Rev Nathaniel West, who afterwards was the first chaplain appointed by President Lincoln. James Smails was a tailor by trade and for a number of years followed that trade in New York In the early '40s he went to Michigan, living in Monroe and Coldwater, where he was engaged as a merchant tailor until 1882, when he retired from active business and came to Fremont, Nebraska, where he spent his remaining years, both he and his wife being now deceased He was a republican in his political faith and a member of the Presbyterian Church To him and his wife were born nine children, of which number three are living, namely Nathaniel W , Robert L , and Abraham L., all of whom live in Fremont and are partners in business

Nathaniel W. Smails received a good public school education, completing his studies in the high school He then apprenticed himself to learn the printing trade in Coldwater, Michigan, receiving $50 for a year's work In 1869 he came to Fremont, Nebraska, secured the ownership of the Nebraska Statesman and ran it until 1875 Then for a short time he was employed on another paper here, afterwards buying the Herald and conducting it for a short time. During this period he also issued a daily edition for a short time About 1904 Mr Smails and his

F. W. Fuhlrodt.

two brothers, Robert L and Abraham L, engaged in the job printing business here and are still so engaged. They operate under the name of the Electric Print Shop and have built up a large and representative business in their line

Politically Mr. Smails has been a lifelong supporter of the democratic party and has for years taken an active part in political affairs, having served for ten years as secretary of the Democratic State Central Committee In 1914 he was appointed postmaster of Fremont and served for four years, then resigning He proved himself a competent, painstaking and courteous public official and was popular with the patrons of the office

In 1895 Mr Smails was married to Cora B Kemp, a native of Minnesota, whose family came to Fremont many years ago Her father, who was a lawyer by profession, was a railroad right-of-way man and first came through here when the railroad was being built from Dubuque to Minneapolis. Mr. and Mrs Smails have one child, Judith Margaret, who is now attending Midland College Mrs Smails is a member of the Episcopal Church A public-spirited citizen, Mr Smails has stood at all times for those things which make for the best phase of community life The qualities of keen discrimination, sound judgment and executive ability have entered very largely into his makeup and have been contributing elements to the success which has come to him

FRANK W. FUHLRODT Widely and favorably known as the efficient postmaster of Fremont, Frank W Fuhlrodt is thoroughly acquainted with the duties of his responsible position, his remarkable aptitude having been developed by years of consecutive service in the postoffice, during which time he familiarized himself with the work of each of its various departments A son of the late Conrad Fuhlrodt, he was born April 10, 1878, in Chicago, Illinois, coming from French and German ancestry.

Born in France, Conrad Fuhlrodt came to the United States when very young, and for a long time lived in Illinois During the '70s he moved to Chicago, from there coming, in 1878, to Fremont, Nebraska, where he was engaged in mercantile pursuits a number of years. Moving to Washington County, this state, he opened a store in Telebasta, and in addition to running a general store also served as postmaster there until his death He married, in Illinois, Elizabeth Hausfeldt, a native of Germany, and they became the parents of eight children, as follows Ida, wife of Henry Schafersman, a retired farmer, living near Norfolk, Nebraska, Albert, engaged in farming at Wisner, Amelia, wife of Arthur Lamb, a retired farmer of Albion, Nebraska Emma, wife of Frank Felder, a shoe manufacturer of Seattle, Washington; Frank W, of this sketch, William L of Fremont, with the Bader Furniture Company, August C, a metal worker in Seattle, Washington, and Conrad A of Omaha, a traveling salesman. The father was a republican in politics, and both he and his wife were members of the Methodist Episcopal Church

Educated in Fremont, where his parents brought him when he was an infant, Frank W Fuhlrodt attended the public and normal schools, and at the age of seventeen years began life as a wage earner, working on the railroad. In September, 1903, Mr. Fuhlrodt entered the postoffice at Fremont in a minor capacity, and through deserved promotions has been an active worker in all of its departments, in 1915 having been made assistant postmaster, and on May 11, 1920, having received his appointment as postmaster, a position he is filling with credit to himself and to the satisfaction of all concerned, having been acting postmaster since March, 1919

Mr. Fuhlrodt married June 15, 1904, Lucinda Mallette, who was born in Burt County, Nebraska, a daughter of Thomas Mallette, a prosperous farmer. Mr and Mrs Fuhlrodt have no children Both attend the Methodist Episcopal Church and contribute liberally towards its support Politically Mr. Fuhlrodt is a republican and fraternally he is a member of the Ancient Free and Accepted Masons and the Benevolent and Protective Order of Elks

ANDREW JENSEN Self-acquired prosperity, liberal ideas, ambitions expressed in promoting agriculture, education, religion and simplicity of living, as well as unquestioned public and private integrity, constitute the fundamentals upon which rest the enviable standing of Andrew Jensen a pioneer of Platte Township, Dodge County, of 1866, and at present a retired resident of the suburbs of Fremont

Mr Jensen was born in the Kingdom of Denmark, July 26 1840 and there received his education in the public schools He was reared to agricultural pursuits, and when he immigrated to the United States, in 1865, it was with the intention of settling in a community where he could work his way to the ownership of a farming property Upon his arrival, he was possessed of but six dollars, but his ambition and willingness to work were assets that discounted his lack of financial resources, and he made his way to Wisconsin where he began his career in this country In 1866 he came on to Nebraska where he purchased the homestead of his brother, in Platte Township, Dodge County, and here the entire period of his active career was passed Through industry and good management he became the owner of 148 acres of valuable farming land, which he brought to a high state of cultivation and upon which he made modern improvements In 1906 he retired from active farming and moved to a home in the suburbs of Fremont, where he now has ten acres of land, having disposed of his other property His position in the community is that of a man who has lived according to the best that he knew, whose abilities have been trained upon the things that are worth while, and whose general character is such as to win him those most splendid and satisfying of rewards, the consciousness of welldoing and the esteem of his fellow-townsmen Mr Jensen is a member of the Lutheran Church, to which his family likewise belongs Since his location in the county he has exerted a controlling interest upon many phases of its growth Few happenings of moment but have profited directly or indirectly by his judgment or pecuniary assistance Various township offices, including those of road overseer for seven years, constable for one year and member of the School Board for a long period, have been invested with dignity and non-partisan largeness through his occupancy He is an independent voter.

Mr Jensen was first married in 1868 to Miss Dorothy Peterson, and they became the parents of four children: Mrs Katie Davis, a resident of Missoula, Montana Mrs Bertha Patterson, who died at the age of thirty-two years, Mrs Sennie Scutter of Lincoln County, Nebraska, and Hans, who died at the age of two years The mother of these children died in 1878, and in 1880 Mr Jensen married Miss Anna Jeppisen, six children being born to this union Dorothy and Mary, who died as small children; Andrea, who died in infancy, Hans, Minnie and Andrew, Jr, who reside with their parents

CARL KROEGER One of the substantial and best known citizens of the flourishing Town of Hooper Nebraska, is Carl Kroeger, who, while having large interests in several other sections of the state, has maintained his home here for forty years. He has also been one of the vigorous citizens, active in business affairs and practical in furthering the interests of the town Although now retired from active life, he is still influential in the town's general affairs, concerning which his sound judgment is frequently consulted, the fruits of his ripened experience being recognized as most beneficial

Carl Kroeger was born in Holstein, Germany, in 1850 His grandfather was a lieutenant in the Danish army His parents, Gustaf and Amelia (Hansen) Kroeger, were born in Germany, and the mother died there. The father, who was a tanner by trade, came to the United States in 1881, joined his son Carl in Dodge County, Nebraska, and died here in 1897 Of his eight children, Carl was the eldest, the others being as follows Amelia, who lives in Idaho, Johanna, who is the wife of Peter Eggers; Theodore, who is a dentist, lives in Idaho, Hermoine, who is the widow of Hans Harlow; Herman, who is deceased, Helen, who is the wife of William Moshage, a rancher near Wood Lake, Nebraska, and Gustaf, who is an attorney in active practice at Boise, in Ada County, Idaho He and wife were members of the German Lutheran Church and were people held in high regard in Germany

Carl Kroeger had school privileges in his native land and then learned the trade of a tanner He was twenty-three years old when he came to the United States and for one year afterward worked in a tannery at Fremont, Ohio In 1874 he came to Omaha, Nebraska, and for the next six years engaged in farming near that city In 1880 he located at what was then the Village of Hooper, but he had the foresight to recognize that it offered business opportunity, and he started a meat market, in partnership with his brother Theodore, which they continued as the Hooper Market for thirteen years When he retired from the market business he still kept his home at Hooper, although for the next nine years he was connected with the Heine Brothers in a cattle ranch in Cherry County and in buying and selling as well as raising livestock

After disposing of his ranch interests in this connection, he entered into another ranch enterprise, in partnership with William G J. Dau, in Brown and Cherry counties, Mr Kroeger subsequently buying his partner's interest and operating alone until he saw a favorable opportunity to sell Once more he bought a ranch in Cherry County and carried on a large and successful business until 1918, when he sold out and retired from active business

In 1880 Mr. Kroeger was united in marriage to Miss Emma Winkleman, then of Hooper but a native of Holstein, Germany, like himself, and the following children were born to them Minnie, who is the wife of William R. Hoabak, who is a banker at Dodge, Nebraska, Gustaf and Theodore, both of whom died in infancy, Anna, who died at the age of four years, and Mary, who is the wife of W H Rogers, manager of the Hooper Electric Light and Power Company

Mr Kroeger is prominent in local politics, a strong republican, and has served faithfully and efficiently in many offices of trust and responsibility For nine years he was precinct assessor, was treasurer for twenty years of the School Board of Hooper, has served several terms on the Town Board and in other ways and offices has proved his excellent citizenship He belongs to the Masonic fraternity at Hooper He was reared in the German Lutheran Church but has been liberal in his support to other religious bodies and to worthy enterprises of all kinds

FREDERICK E. BRAUCHT, M D, D D S As a specialist in the treatment of diseases of the eye, ear, nose and throat, Dr Frederick E. Braucht has developed a large and representative practice in the City of Fremont, Dodge County, and is essentially one of the representative physicians and surgeons of the state, besides which he was graduated also from the Northwestern Dental College at Chicago

Doctor Braucht was born in Mercer County, Illinois, February 2, 1868, and is the only child of George W and Frances (Douglass) Braucht, the former of whom was born in Ohio and the latter in Mercer County, Illinois, where their marriage was solemnized, and where the latter died in 1869, within a few months after the birth of her only child In 1872 George W. Braucht came to Nebraska, and with headquarters at Fremont, engaged in the buying and shipping of horses Later he was for a few years engaged in farming west of Fremont, and within this period he contracted a second marriage, Miss Kate Burner becoming his wife. They thereafter resided at Fremont about twelve years, and then Mr Braucht removed to Idaho From that state he finally removed to the State of Washington, where he resided until July, 1919, when he returned to Fremont, where he passed the closing days of his life in the home of his son, Doctor Braucht, of this review, his death having occurred October 14, 1919. Of the four children of the second marriage, three are living Jesse, in the employ of a wholesale millinery house in the City of Minneapolis, Minnesota; Myrtle is the wife of Arthur Callan of Portland, Oregon, and Roy L is manager of a large ranch near Artois, California

Doctor Braucht received excellent educational advantages in his youth, including those of Battle Creek College, at Battle Creek, Michigan, and also those of the great University of Michigan, at Ann Arbor In preparation for the profession in which he has achieved unequivocal success, he entered the celebrated Rush Medical College, in the City of Chicago, and from this great institution he received his degree of Doctor of Medicine in 1894, the following year having marked his graduation in the college of dentistry A very exceptional experience marked the practical novitiate of Doctor Braucht in the work of his profession, for he went to the Samoan or Navigators Islands, in the Southern Pacific Ocean, where he engaged in the practice of medicine and where he remained somewhat more than eight years He there built up a substantial and profitable practice, but in 1903 he returned to the United States and engaged in practice in the City of Omaha. One year later, however, he went to Honduras, Central America, where he remained nine months, and after his return he was engaged in practice at Licking Valley, Pennsylvania, for six months In 1906 he became superintendent of the Kansas Sanitarium, at Wichita, and in this position he continued the incumbent until 1909, when he became interested in gold mining in the Nome district of Alaska, where he passed two seasons He thereafter passed one year at Wichita, Kansas, and he then engaged in active general practice in Cedar County, Nebraska, where he remained until, in January, 1918, he further diversified his somewhat remarkable experience, by entering the medical corps of the United States army He was assigned to service with the signal corps of the aviation section, and in this capacity remained at Omaha six months He was then sent to the Government Aeronautic

School at Arcadia, California, and three months later he was transferred to the surgical division and ordered to Letterman Hospital, at San Francisco After there continuing in service two months he was ordered to Camp Crain, Allentown, Pennsylvania, and he was the commanding medical officer of the One Hundred and Twenty-Seventh Base Hospital when the war closed. He arrived at his home January 7, 1919, and on the first of the following May he established his residence at Fremont, where he has since continued in active practice, as a specialist in treatment of diseases of the eye, ear, nose and throat He had previously taken special post-graduate courses in these special lines, at the Chicago Post-Graduate School of Medicine and Surgery, his first work of this order having been in 1895, and a further post-graduate course in that institution having been completed in 1904, a four months' course Doctor Braucht is a close student of the best standard and periodical literature of his profession, is at all times in touch with advances made in medical and surgical science and practice, and is admirably equipped for the special line of service to which he is devoting his attention He is associated in practice with Dr D G Golding, is a member of the Nebraska State Medical Society, and also holds membership in the American Medical Association The doctor is independent in politics and while a resident of Samoan Islands he served as a member of the Municipal Council of the city in which he maintained his home He was a member of the Board of Health while engaged in practice in Cedar County, Nebraska In the Masonic fraternity he is affiliated with both the York and the Scottish Rite bodies, in which latter he has received the thirty-second degree, and also with the Mystic Shrine At Fremont he and his wife attend and support the Methodist Episcopal Church, and they are popular in the representative social life of the community

The year 1893 recorded the marriage of Doctor Braucht to Miss Mina A Owen, who was born at Hastings, Michigan, and they have two children: Frederick A. is now associated with the Taylor-Jenkins Optical Company in the City of Omaha, and Dorothy Frances is attending the public schools of Fremont

ERNEST DAU One of the chief industries of the thriving little City of Scribner is that pertaining to the handling of lumber, grain, coal and live stock, and it is in this field of endeavor that Ernest Dau, manager of the Crowell Lumber and Grain Company, has won recognition of his business ability He has been identified with this concern for fifteen years, during which time he has materially developed its interests, while at the same time advancing himself in the estimation of his associates

Mr Dau is a Nebraskan by nativity, born January 27, 1880, and a history of his parents will be found in the review of his brother, William G J. Dau, elsewhere in this work His education was acquired in the public schools of Dodge County, and as a young man he began his career as a farmer, a vocation to which he applied himself until twenty-three years old. In 1903 Mr Dau disposed of his agricultural interests and located at Scribner, where he entered the employ of the Crowell Lumber and Grain Company, an old established and responsible concern which had been founded as early as 1869 A demonstration of ability and fidelity won him promotion from the start, and eventually he was placed in the position of manager of the business, an office of which he is the incumbent at this time In 1908 he resigned and engaged in farming in this county for five years, when on account of his wife's health he again disposed of his farming interests and again took his old position with the Crowell Lumber and Grain Company This company does a large business in the handling of all kinds of lumber, grain, coal and live stock, and Mr Dau allows no other interests to distract his attention from the management of the concern's affairs In political affairs he acts independently, giving his vote to the candidate whom he deems best fitted for the office, irrespective of party lines He is a Blue Lodge Mason and has numerous friends in that order, as he has also in business circles

On November 6, 1907, Mr Dau was united in marriage with Miss Mary Soll of Blair, Nebraska, and to this union there were born three children Mildred, born in 1906, Catherine, in 1911, and Lucille, in 1915

P G Johnson Of the residents of Dodge County who have retired from active pursuits after spending long years in agricultural operations is P G Johnson Like many of those who have won success and position in this locality, Mr Johnson is a native of Sweden, and, also like others, has been the architect in the rearing of his own fortune's structure At present he is the owner of a pleasant home in Fremont, where he is surrounded by the comforts that form the awards for a life of industry directed by a policy of integrity

Mr Johnson was born in Sweden, April 11, 1852, a son of Johannus Johnson His father joined the Swedish army in his younger years, but later turned from a military career and took up farming, being engaged in the pursuits of the soil until his death at the age of eighty-five years Of his children, Helen is deceased, Johanna accompanied her brother to the United States and is now a resident of Ainsworth, Nebraska and P G is a resident of Fremont P G Johnson was educated in the public schools of his native land, and was twenty-nine years of age when he immigrated to the United States in 1881 At that time he came to Fremont, where he resided for three years, then going to Burt County, where he spent eight years in farming While there, he was married in 1884, to Augusta Christina Carlson, who was born in 1860, in Sweden, and who came to the United States in 1881, her parents having passed their entire lives in their native land, where they died Nine children were born to Mr and Mrs Johnson Mrs Phoebe Sweet of Dodge County, Mrs Helma Sight of Dodge County, Gilbert, a farmer of this county, Mrs Grace Johnson and Mrs Ruby Harris, also residents of Dodge County, Carl, who is engaged in agricultural operations here, Mrs Helen Kenyon, a resident of Saunders County, Emil, who farms in Dodge County; and a child who died in infancy

After spending eight years in Burt County, Mr Johnson returned to Dodge County, where, eleven years after his arrival in the United States, he purchased a farming property He accumulated a valuable tract of land, upon which he made numerous improvements, and for many years carried on farming and stock raising and became known as one of the practical, substantial and successful agriculturists of his community With advancing years came the feeling that he had earned a rest from his labors, and he accordingly turned his responsibilities over to younger shoulders and removed to his present pleasant home at 1120 East First Street, Fremont While Mr Johnson is retired from agricultural pursuits, he still maintains an interest therein and is the owner of forty acres of good Dodge County land

Mr and Mrs Johnson are consistent members of the Swedish Lutheran Church and are contributors to worthy religious and educational movements Politically he gives his support to the candidates of

Fred Bader

the republican party He is a great lover of his home, and that is perhaps the reason that he is not affiliated with any fraternal or secret order

FREDERICK BADER The Bader family is one of the best-known ones of Dodge County, and has as its representatives some of the sound and dependable men of this region, one of them being Frederick Bader of Fremont, who, with his brother, Jacob R Bader, is engaged in the undertaking business under the name of Fred Bader & Company, and he is also engaged in the jobbing of caskets under the name of the Fremont Casket Company.

Frederick Bader was born in Hugsweier, Baden, Germany, on November 13, 1870, a son of Carl and Caroline (Lieb) Bader, most estimable parents who brought up their children in an atmosphere of piety, and so turned their attention to spiritual matters that all of them have been upright Christians, two have gone into the ministry, and two have gone to India, one as a missionary and the other as the wife of a missionary

Up to the time he was eighteen years of age Fred Bader remained at home and attended the public schools of his native place, but then came to the United States, and coming west, settled in Nebraska, his arrival at Nebraska City being in 1888 For two seasons he was employed during the winter months as shipping clerk in the sausage department of the Chicago Packing Company, and for one summer he was on a farm in Washington County Mr Bader then came to Fremont and for three months worked in the tub factory An opening occurring for him in the furniture business, he went into it and remained in it through the various changes in name and partners until he and his brother, Jacob R Bader, became the owners of the undertaking part of the business, in 1900, and operated it under the name of the Bader Brothers Company Later Fred Bader bought an interest in the furniture business and subsequently he and his brother purchased the stock of Mr Rogers conducting both the furniture and undertaking branches under their firm name of Bader Brothers Company The volume of business increased to such an extent that in 1916 the brothers decided to divide it, and Fred Bader took over the undertaking branch, leaving his brother in charge of the furniture, since then operating as Fred Bader & Company As an adjunct to his business, Mr. Bader is engaged in the jobbing of caskets under the name of the Fremont Casket Company, and does a jobbing trade in them in Nebraska, South Dakota and Colorado Two men represent the latter company on the road Mr Bader is a highly trained undertaker, whose license bears the date of June 20, 1900 He is noted for his reliability in sympathetic service and moderation in charges incurred in the hour of bereavement.

On November 26, 1895, Mr Bader was united in marriage with Laura Cochran, born in Ottumwa, Iowa and they have had two children born to them, namely Ruth, who is connected with M A. Disbrow & Company of Omaha, Nebraska, was graduated from the Fremont High School, the Northwestern University of Evanston, Illinois, and the Van Sant Business College of Omaha, Nebraska, and Marian, who was graduated from the Fremont High School, is now taking a post-graduate course at the Midland College Mr. Bader is a member of the Methodist Episcopal Church Well known in Masonry, he is a Knight Templar, thirty-second degree and Shriner Mason, and he also belongs to the Odd Fellows in both of its branches, the Knights of Pythias and the Modern

Woodmen For a number of years he has been a director of the Commercial Club, and is serving the church as treasurer In politics he is a republican, but has not cared to compete for public honors In addition to the business enterprises already mentioned, Mr Bader is a director of the First National Bank of Fremont His time and attention have been fully occupied with his business affairs, but he and his family have pleasant recollections of a recreation period, when for three months they visited Europe in 1907, long before the terrible devastating war had plunged the world into conflict and destroyed so many of the former pleasure grounds Both Mr. Bader and his brother are men of the highest standing in the community in which they have worked for so long and faithfully, and none are held in greater esteem because of personal characteristics than these two

EUGENE L MAHLIN is another of the native sons of Nebraska who is here making an excellent record in the practice of law, and he is one of the representative younger members of his profession in Dodge County, with residence at Fremont, the county seat Mr Mahlin was born in Butler County, this state, August 14, 1890, and is a son of George S and Sadie E. (Garman) Mahlin, who were born in Pennsylvania and whose marriage was solemnized in the State of Illinois Two years later they came to Nebraska and established their residence in Butler County, in 1884, the father having become one of the prosperous farmers of that county, where he continued to reside until his death, in October, 1916, his widow being now a resident of Fremont Of the four children, the eldest is Harvey, who is a farmer near Rising City, Butler County, Edgar F, likewise is a progressive agriculturist in that locality, Jay C. is engaged in the banking business at Smithfield, Gosper County, and Eugene L., of this review, is the youngest of the four sons George S. Mahlin was a man of strong mentality and well fortified opinions, his political allegiance having been given to the democratic party, he having been affiliated with the Ancient Order of United Workmen, and his religious faith having been that of the Christian Church, of which his widow likewise is a devoted member He was influential in community affairs in Butler County, where he served in various township offices, and through his well ordered farm enterprise he achieves substantial prosperity after coming to Nebraska

The public schools of his native county afforded to Eugene L Mahlin his early educational discipline, which was supplemented by the completion of the scientific course in the Fremont College at Fremont, in which he was graduated in 1910 In consonance with his ambition and well matured plans, he then went to the City of Omaha and completed the curriculum of the Creighton College of Law, in which he was graduated as a member of the class of 1915, his reception of the degree of Bachelor of Laws having been attended also by his admission to the bar of his native state He forthwith engaged in the practice of his profession at Fremont, and here his ability and close application have enabled him to develop a substantial and representative law business His valiant spirit was shown by his attending the night classes of the law school and defraying his incidental expenses by working during the daytime It is needless to say that the same dauntless spirit attended his initial efforts in establishing himself in practice, and he has made a record of success worthily achieved In 1916 he was elected police judge of Fremont, and of this office he continued in tenure until he subordinated all personal interests to tender his services to the Government when the nation became involved in the great World war In 1917 he entered the Atlantic transport service, at Norfolk, Virginia, and with this important arm of the service he continued to be identified until the close of the war, his honorable discharge having been received December 31, 1918 He then returned to Fremont, where he has since continued in the independent practice of his profession He is a popular and appreciative member of the American Legion, composed of those who served in the late war, and in November, 1919, he had the distinction of being elected commander of the Fremont Post of this fine patriotic order He is affiliated also with the Benevolent and Protective Order of Elks, is a democrat in politics and his wife is an active member of the Methodist Episcopal Church

In September, 1919, Mr Mahlin wedded Miss Lula M Walker, who was born near the City of Peoria, Illinois, a daughter of Frederick J and Anna Walker, who now reside at Fremont, Dodge County, where the father is a prosperous retired farmer

CHRIST H CHRISTENSEN is one of the sturdy sons of the far Norseland who has proved his constructive powers most effectively since establishing his residence in Nebraska, where he has maintained his home in Dodge County for fully thirty-five years He now owns and conducts a prosperous general insurance business in the City of Fremont, and in connection with this enterprise he has given no little attention to the real estate business As an insurance underwriter he represents a number of the best and most popular fire, life, accident and tornado insurance companies, and his agency is one that controls a large and representative supporting patronage

Mr Christensen was born in the Province of Vandsyssel, Denmark, on June 18, 1862, and is a son of Christ and Mary (Petersen) Nelson, his own surname being derived from the personal or Christian name of his father, in accord with the ancient Danish custom His parents passed their entire lives in Denmark, where the father, a man of superior education, was long a successful teacher, as well as a citizen of prominence and influence in community affairs, both he and his wife having been earnest communicants of the Lutheran Church Of the ten children five are now living, and two of the number reside in the United States—Christ H. of this review, and Louis, who is engaged in the hotel business in the City of San Francisco, California To the excellent schools of the Town of Sterup, in his native province, Christ H Christensen is indebted for his early education, besides which he had the advantages of a home of distinctive culture and refinement As a youth he served an apprenticeship to the blacksmith's trade, and he continued work at his trade in his native land until 1884, when he came to the United States, his arrival at Fremont, Nebraska, having occurred on April 17th, of that year For the first few months he was employed at farm work in Dodge County, and for four years thereafter he was employed at his trade, in the shops of the Fremont Foundry and Machine Company He then, in 1887, initiated an independent business as owner of a cafe and as a dealer in cigars, which enterprise he successfully conducted at Fremont for several years Through this business he won substantial success, and it may well be understood that this fact gave him special satisfaction when he reverted to his having arrived in Fremont with an available capital of less than $2, besides which he still owed the price of his transportation from Denmark to America Mr Christensen has been engaged in the insurance business since 1902, and his careful and progressive policies have enabled him to build up a most prosperous business, to the management of which he gives the greater part of his time, Loyal and public spirited, he is aligned in the ranks of the democratic party, but has had no ambition for public office He and his wife are devoted and influential communicants of the Danish Lutheran Church of Fremont, of which he is not only a trustee but also the treasurer He is affiliated with the Independent Order of Odd Fellows, the Fraternal Order of Eagles, in which he is secretary of the aerie at Fremont; and the Danish Brotherhood, in which he is secretary of the local lodge. He is well known in Dodge County and his circle of friends is limited only by that of his acquaintances.

In 1888 Mr Christensen was united in marriage to Miss Anna Jensen, who likewise is a native of Denmark, and who is a daughter of Jens Jensen, whose death occurred in Denmark when a young man, and whose widow later married Hans Wolf and still resides in this city Mr Wolf died in Fremont in 1917. Mr and Mrs Christensen have three children: Lillie is the wife of Arthur W Lucas, train dispatcher at Fremont for the Chicago & Northwestern Railroad; Alfred is assistant cashier of the Fremont National Bank, and Henry a registered pharmacist for the firm of Kerlin & Christensen, one of the leading drug stores of Fremont He had the distinction of serving eleven months in Field Hospital No 12 in France during America's participation in the late World war, and thereafter he was with the allied forced in occupying German territory along the Rhine until June, 1919, when he departed for home, his honorable discharge having been given on July 5th of that year

Louis M Warner was born and reared in Dodge County and has never wavered in his allegiance to and appreciation of his native county and state, within the borders of which he has found ample opportunity for the achieving of worthy success through association with farm enterprise He is now one of the representative farmers of the younger generation in Cotterell Township, where his operations are carried on in section 18, his farm comprising the eighty acres that he owns and 460 acres also in this part of Dodge County He is a son of John H Warner, of whom specific mention is made on other pages of this volume, so that in the present connection further review of the family history is not demanded

Louis M Warner was born on the old homestead farm of his father in Everett Township, this county, and the date of his nativity was August 11, 1881 He early gained practical experience in connection with the operations of the home farm and his youthful education was acquired in the excellent schools of Dodge County. He began his independent career as a farmer when he was twenty-two years of age, and he has since improved his land in many ways including the erection of buildings and the providing of the various equipments that mark the up-to-date farm He gives his attention to diversified agriculture and the raising of excellent grades of live stock, is loyal and liberal in community affairs, is a stockholder in the Farmers' Union at North Bend, is independent in politics and is now serving as treasurer of the School Board of his district

The year 1905 recorded the marriage of Mr Warner to Miss Mabel Snover, who was born in Dodge County and who is a daughter of Sylvester Snover, now a resident of Fremont, the county seat Mr and Mrs Warner have five children, Hazel B, Howard L, Grace L, Bernice E and Irene M

JAMES CASSELL endured his full share of the hardships and trials marking the pioneer period in the history of Nebraska, his parents having come to Dodge County when he was a lad of six years—and within a short time after the admission of the state to the Union His memory compasses the time when grasshoppers laid waste all growing crops of the pioneer farmers and entailed privation and distress, he recalls seasons of drought, with attendant failure of crops, but he was reared under the conditions that begat courage and self-reliance and in the later years has shared in the prosperity that has attended those who remained in Nebraska and had faith in the now great and progressive commonwealth He still has active supervision of his well improved farm of 120 acres, in section 30, Elkhorn Township, as well as of the adjoining farm of eighty acres owned by his venerable mother.

Mr Cassell was born in Whiteside County, Illinois, July 28, 1862, and is a son of John and Fannie (Green) Cassell, the latter of whom still remains on the old homestead, with her son James, as one of the most venerable and loved pioneer women of Dodge County John Cassell was born and reared in Scotland and was about twenty-five years of age when he came to the United States and established his residence in Illinois, where his marriage was solemnized In 1868, with team and covered wagon, he brought his family overland from Illinois to the new State of Nebraska, and he established the family home on the farm now owned by his son James, of this sketch He hauled lumber from Omaha to erect the primitive dwelling on the pioneer farm and earnestly applied himself to reclaiming the wild prairie and making his land productive He bravely met the trials incidental to pioneer life, but did not live to realize the prosperity of the later years, as he died about six years after coming to Nebraska, his wife and children being left to face the heavy burdens entailed by his death Indians were still much in evidence through this section of the state and the prospect that faced the widowed mother was not an alluring one It has been her good fortune to witness the splendid development and progress of Nebraska and to enjoy the gracious rewards that compensate for earlier trials and privations. She is a devoted member of the Methodist Church, as was also her husband

James Cassell acquired his early education in the pioneer schools of Dodge County, and he reverts with satisfaction to the fact that as a boy and youth he attended the Sunday school that was held in the old-time railroad station at Arlington He was but twelve years old at the time of his father's death and yet his youthful courage and determination did not fail in the face of the heavy responsibilities and arduous labors that came to him. He and his mother did not leave the home farm, but he assumed the practical management of its operation and as the years passed by he achieved worthy and enduring success through his zealous labors as an agriculturist and stock-grower His appreciation of present conditions is enhanced by his memory of those of the pioneer days, and he is one of the loyal and public-spirited men of the county to whose civic and industrial development he has contributed his full quota His farm is equipped with good buildings and he has made profitable both the agricultural and live-stock departments of the industry to which he has here devoted himself during his entire active career Mr Cassell is not constrained by strict partisanship in politics, but supports men and measures meeting the approval of his judgment He has served as a member of the Township Board and has been moderator of the School Board of his district for thirty-six years He and his wife, and also his venerable mother, hold membership in the Methodist Episcopal Church at Arlington and he is affiliated with the Modern Woodmen of America.

March 23, 1896, Mr Cassell wedded Miss Nora Clark, who was born and reared in Kansas, and they have three children Edward, George and Fannie, the daughter now being the wife of Robert Hansby of Arlington, Nebraska

HERMAN MONNICH Occupying a noteworthy position among the esteemed and valued citizens of Everett Township, Herman Monnich was for many years conspicuously identified with the agricultural interests of this section of Dodge County, and having through wise management secured a comfortable annual income is now living retired from active pursuits, enjoying a well-earned leisure A son of Gerhard and Anna (Osterloh) Monnich, he was born November 3, 1855, in Iowa County, Iowa, where his parents lived for three years

Born reared and married in Germany, Gerhard Monnich immigrated to the United States in 1854, and having taken up Government land in Iowa was there engaged in carpentering and farming until 1857. Coming with his family in that year to Dodge County, he journeyed across the intervening country with ox teams, the trip being long and tedious Taking up a homestead claim in what is now Everett Township, he improved his land, and was actively employed in farming and stock raising until his death in 1878 at the age of sixty-three years His wife survived him, passing away in 1907, at the advanced age of eighty-two years He was a democrat in politics, and both were members of the Lutheran Church. Of the thirteen children born of their union, four are living, as follows· Mary, wife of Menke Von Zeggen of California; Herman, of this brief personal review, Bernard, residing in Hooper, and Dora, wife of Caspar Heller of Hooper

Having acquired a practical education in the common schools of Dodge County, Herman Monnich, who was of an active and enterprising disposition, turned his attention to agriculture, and having become thoroughly familiar with its many branches, began farming on his own account. When ready to settle permanently, he bought his present property in section 1, Everett Township, and in its improvement met with unquestioned success, his place being one of the most attractive in the vicinity, reflecting credit on his good judgment and ability Mr Monnich was actively engaged in general farming and stock raising until 1917, when he gave up hard labor, and has since lived retired from active business cares An active and influential member of the republican party, he has served a number of terms as county supervisor Fraternally he is a thirty-second degree Mason He is not affiliated with any religious organization, but his wife is a devout member of the Catholic Church

Mr Monnich married, in 1881, Margaret Parkert, and into the household thus established seven children have been born, namely· George W, managing the home farm, John, a garage owner of Fremont, Bernard, engaged in farming in Dodge County, Nettie wife of Norman Schaffer of Hooper, cashier of the First National Bank; Edward served in the signal corps during the World war, being trained at Lincoln, Nebraska, Fort Leavenworth, Kansas, and at Baltimore, Maryland, and now a resident of Oakland, California; Celia, a nurse, resides in Ohio, and Clarence, now at home, enlisted May 21, 1918, in the field artillery, and after being trained at Camp Jackson went with his command overseas, took part in the Argonne Forest engagements, and was discharged from the service May 10, 1919

Fred W. Vaughan

FRED W VAUGHAN, an influential citizen of the City of Fremont and a representative member of the Dodge County bar, has been engaged in the practice of his profession in Nebraska for fully forty years, and his qualities of leadership have been manifested not only in connection with the activities of his profession but also in the field of politics and general civic affairs, where his influence has been marked by high ideals and utmost loyalty

It is most gratifying to find in this vital western commonwealth of the Union a man who can claim the stanchest of American lineage for generations, for representatives of Colonial ancestry are all too few in this day of rampant commercialism and heterogeneous social standards It is to be recorded that Mr Vaughan is a scion of fine Colonial ancestry in both the paternal and maternal lines, and that ancestors on both sides were found aligned as patriot soldiers in the War of the Revolution Richard Vaughan, great-grandfather of Fred W, was in service in the Revolution, as a member of Capt Peter Grant's company in the regiment commanded by Colonel Grayson, in the Continental foot forces commanded by Col William Gearson He enlisted as a private September 1, 1777, and made a record of loyal and efficient service in the ranks May 1, 1789, Governor Thomas Mifflin of Pennsylvania appointed him a lieutenant of the Fifth Company in the Second Battalion of Militia in Luzerne County His commission, attested by Charles Biddle, secretary to the governor, is now in the possession of him whose name introduces this sketch Elias Vaughan, son of Lieut Richard Vaughan, was one of the very early settlers in the vicinity of Wyalusing, Bradford County, Pennsylvania, where he reclaimed a farm from the virgin forest, his land holdings being such that he was able to give to each of his sons a farm of good area, as gauged by the standards of the locality and period On June 8, 1812, Elias Vaughan was commissioned deputy postmaster at Asylum, Luzerne County, and his commission is still retained as an interesting family heirloom He likewise received appointment as lieutenant of the Fifth Company One Hundred and Forty-Fourth Regiment, Pennsylvania Militia, which was a part of the Second Brigade of the Ninth Division This commission, for four years' duration, was signed by Governor Thomas McKean and Secretary T M Thompson

Evander R Vaughan, son of Elias and father of Fred W Vaughan, to whom this sketch is dedicated, was born and reared in the old Keystone State, and became the founder of the family in Nebraska, where he passed the remainder of his life, his death having occurred at Fremont November 12, 1900 While still in his native commonwealth he was commissioned first lieutenant of the Wyalusing and Asylum Invincibles, attached to the Fourth Battalion of the uniformed militia of the state, besides which, at the time of the Civil war, he enlisted for service as a private in the military body formed to repel invasion of Pennsylvania by Confederate troops, Governor Curtin having called for volunteers for this temporary service

In 1882 Evander R Vaughan came with his family to Nebraska and established himself in the furniture business at Fremont He continued this enterprise until about 1890, when he sold the business and retired, by reason of advanced age, and he was one of the revered citizens of Dodge County at the time of his death

On the maternal side Fred W Vaughan is a scion of the seventh generation in descent from James York, who was a member of the royal house of Orleans and who came to America in 1635 He became seized of a large landed estate in Connecticut One of his descendants, Amos

York, great-grandfather of Fred W Vaughan, was taken prisoner by the Indians and Tories in 1778 and all his live stock was confiscated, besides which he suffered the indignity of being compelled personally to drive this stock to the British lines. After being held a prisoner several months his exchange was effected in New York, whence he made his way on foot to Connecticut, where his death occurred a few days prior to that of his wife, who had escaped from the fort at the time of the historic Wyoming massacre in Pennsylvania, she having eluded the Indians and escaped by making her way in a canoe down the Susquehanna River and thence to her home in Connecticut

Evander R Vaughan, as a young man, was united in marriage to Miss Jessie E Hinman, a native of Bradford County, Pennsylvania, and she preceded her husband to eternal rest, her death having occurred, at Fremont, October 13, 1901 Her father, Curtis Hinman, of Wysox, Pennsylvania was the first abolitionist in that part of the state, and his home was a station on the famous "underground railroad," by means of which many slaves were assisted to freedom, in Canada, prior to the inception of the Civil war

Fred W Vaughan, the only child of his parents, was born in Wyalusing, Pennsylvania, on December 9, 1858, and he acquired his early education in the public schools of Pennsylvania and the Susquehanna Collegiate Institute, at Towanda, that state Thereafter he was graduated in the Wyoming Commercial College, at Kingston, Pennsylvania, and in August, 1879, shortly before his twenty-first birthday anniversary, he came to Nebraska and found hospice in the home of his uncle, Beach I Hinman, at North Platte There he studied law in the office of Hinman & Neville, of which firm his uncle was the senior member, and he was admitted to the bar of Nebraska September 28, 1881 On February 22d of the following year he established his home at Fremont, and here he has since continued in the active practice of his profession, as one of the leading members of the bar of this section of the state An effective resume of his political career is gained by quoting from records appearing in a recent publication "Mr Vaughan had always been a democrat, but upon the division of the party in 1892, on the silver question, he became identified with the gold-standard wing of the party, of which he was a representative as a member of the state central committee of Nebraska until 1897 In the preceding year he was a delegate to the Democratic National Convention, in Chicago, and with others of the Nebraska delegation, he was unseated by the convention On the 23d of the following July he was a member of a conference of forty-five gold democrats, from the states of Illinois, Indiana Michigan, Ohio, Wisconsin, Kentucky and Nebraska, who assembled to protest against the Chicago platform of the democratic party. As a result of this conference was held the National Gold Democratic Convention, at Indianapolis, in which were nominated the standard bearers of the gold or single standard branch of the democratic party, with General John M Palmer as presidential nominee Mr Vaughan was a delegate to this convention, and he was secretary of the Sound Money Democratic League of Nebraska in 1895 In 1897 believing that the sound-money democrats must choose either the free silver democratic party or the republican party, he transferred his allegiance to the latter, with which he has since continued his active and loyal affiliation He wielded influence in political councils, but the only office to which he was elected was mayor of Fremont in April, 1899."

Mr Vaughan was one of the organizers and incorporators of the Fremont Club, and has served as president of the same He is prominently identified with the Masonic fraternity, in which he has served as grand commander of the Nebraska Grand Commandery of Knights Templar He takes deep interest in the affairs of the Society of the Sons of the American Revolution, and was president of the Nebraska state organization of this great patriotic order one term He and his wife are active members of the Presbyterian Church in their home city He has been for a number of years a member of the Board of Trustees of the Fremont public library

In 1904 was solemnized the marriage of Mr Vaughan to Miss Ora Reynolds, daughter of M C Reynolds of Culbertson, Nebraska, and the three children of this union still remain at the parental home—Maude, Jessie and Reynolds

OSCAR WIDMAN was reared and educated in Sweden and was a youth of seventeen years when he established his residence in Nebraska Here he has gained independence and prosperity through his own efforts and he is now one of the successful merchants of the City of Fremont, Dodge County, where he owns and conducts a grocery store of the best standard of equipment and service

Mr Widman was born in Sweden on January 6, 1868, and is a son of Carl and Eva (Danielson) Widman, the former of whom passed his entire life in that fair country of the far Norseland, where his widow still resides, he having followed the carpenter's trade during his entire active career. Of the four children three are living' Sophia is the wife of David Saunders, a farmer in Saunders County, Nebraska, Oscar, of this review, was next in order of birth, and Emily remains in Sweden The religious faith of the family has long been that of the Lutheran Church

After having profited by the advantages afforded in the schools of his native land, Oscar Widman, at the age of nineteen years, manifested his youthful ambition and self-reliance by severing the home ties and coming to America For three years thereafter he was identified with farm enterprise near West Point, Cuming County, Nebraska, and in 1890 he came to Fremont and began work as a railroad section hand While thus engaged he sent home honey to repay the amount which he had borrowed to pay his passage to America He continued to follow railroad work three years and then, in 1902, became a clerk in a grocery store at Fremont With characteristic ambition, he applied himself to learning all details of this line of enterprise, and in 1911 he established his independent grocery business, in which he has since continued with marked success, his finely appointed establishment receiving a liberal and representative patronage

Mr Widman is a democrat in politics and his high standing in the community is shown by his having been twice elected a member of the Board of Supervisors of Dodge County, a position of which he is still the incumbent, through election in the autumn of 1918 He is affiliated with the local lodge of the Knights of Pythias and he and his family are earnest communicants of the Lutheran Church

In 1890 Mr Widman was united in marriage to Miss Selma Swanson, who was born on a farm in Burt County, this state, and of the eight children of this union six are living Luther is employed in the office of the Fremont Tribune; Gladys is the wife of Otto Sticker of Fremont; Violet is a popular assistant in her father's store, Allison died in January, 1920, at the age of twenty-three years· Daphne died in 1913, aged fourteen years, Phyllis remains at the parental home, as do also Oscar, Jr, and Gwendolyn, who are attending school

WILLIAM H BRADBURY Among other interests those connected with the handling of grain are exceptionally heavy at Hooper, owing to its location with reference to fertile farming regions and the railroads, and some of the most enterprising of Dodge County men are engaged in this important line, one of them being William H Bradbury, manager of the Latta Grain Company

William H Bradbury was born in Dodge County in 1874, a son of James Bradbury, and grandson of William Bradbury, the latter being a native of England, who came to the United States and became superintendent of a coal mine in Pennsylvania He and his wife, who bore the maiden name of Anna Markland, had fourteen children

James Bradbury was born in 1850 in the State of Pennsylvania, where he resided until 1874, working in the coal mines In that year he came to Dodge County, Nebraska, where he obtained employment in the harvest fields during that summer, and then worked for Peter Neabose, a contractor at Fremont Still later he bought a farm on Maple Creek, adding to his original purchase until he had over 400 acres and he farmed this until 1908 when he came to Hooper where he is still living He married Mary Swemhat, born in Pennsylvania, and they became the parents of the following children William H, who is the eldest; Esther is the wife of E M Havens, Alice, the wife of Walter Spinner, Mary is deceased, Florence, the wife of William Meyer; Mary, the wife of Earl Phillips, James, a Dodge County farmer; Fred, with his brother James on the farm; Charles, also a Dodge County farmer, Josephine, the wife of George Parker; and Sarah, who is deceased

William H Bradbury remained with his parents on their farm until 1895 when he commenced farming on his own account, and was engaged in general farming and stock raising until 1903, when he moved to Washington, where he continued to be interested in agricultural matters and handled agricultural implements for three years Going to Spokane, Washington, he was in the employ of Mitchell, Lewis & Staver, but in 1914 returned to Dodge County, and entered the elevator business at Hooper for two years, being manager for the elevator owned by Henry Roberts, and then went with his present company This company handles all kinds of grain and coal, and does a big business

In 1898 Mr Bradbury was married to Effie Phillips, born in Nebraska, a daughter of Ezra Phillips of Fremont Mr and Mrs Bradbury have one child, Merle, who is the wife of Jesse B Jarvia of Fremont, in the employ of the electric light plant of that city. Both Mr Bradbury and his wife are active and valued members of the Methodist Episcopal Church Mr Bradbury is a republican, but aside from voting does not participate much in politics He maintains membership with the Knights of Pythias Having attended both the public schools of Dodge County and Fremont College Mr. Bradbruy had better educational opportunities than some, and is a well informed man on many subjects, and is interested in seeing this part of the state develop

O A PETERSON A man of artistic tastes and talents, handy with chisel and tools of all kinds, O A Peterson of Fremont has won an extended reputation as a skillful worker in marble and granite, and as a manufacturer of monuments and headstones has built up a substantial business Like many other of Nebraska's valued citizens, he was born on foreign soil, his birth having occurred September 14, 1874, in Sweden

His father, Andrew Peterson, was born, reared and educated in Sweden and is there successfully employed in agricultural pursuits, being an extensive farmer and stock buyer He married Christina Benson, and to them four children have been born, as follows: Nels, engaged in farming in Sweden, O A, of this brief personal record, K A, living retired from active pursuits in Blair, Nebraska and Anna, residing in Sweden Both parents are members of the Lutheran Church

Immigrating to the United States in 1897, O A Peterson located in Blair, Nebraska, where he served an apprenticeship at the marble worker's trade, acquiring proficiency in the monumental arts Removing to Fremont in 1908, Mr Peterson established himself in business as a manufacturer of monuments, and met with success from the start, it having grown to such proportions that, in 1914, he erected, on Main Street, his present fine two-story, marble front business building, which is well adapted for his work In addition to the skilled workmen he employs in his factory, Mr Peterson keeps several salesmen on the road, and sells goods throughout Nebraska, South Dakota and Iowa

On October 8, 1918, Mr Peterson was united in marriage with Emma Carlson, a native of Oregon, and their pleasant home is ever open to their many friends and acquaintances, all of whom there find a warm welcome from the hospitable host and hostess Both Mr and Mrs Peterson are faithful members of the Lutheran Church. Politically Mr. Peterson casts his vote with the republican party Fraternally he is a member of the Benevolent and Protective Order of Elks, the Knights of Pythias, Woodmen of the World and the Royal Highlanders

JOHN PETROW Occupying a place of note among the more active and prosperous business men of Fremont, John Petrow has been a conspicuous factor in advancing the manufacturing and mercantile interests of Dodge County, as a candy and confectionery maker and seller having built up an exceedingly extensive and substantial trade, the toothsome products of his factory appealing to the tastes of the old and the young, and to the rich and the poor alike He was born March 3, 1881, in Greece, where his parents, Christ N and Helen (Constantine) Petrow, were lifelong residents His father was a very successful business man, in addition to having engaged in mercantile pursuits, was a farmer and stock dealer, and at the time of his death was very well-to-do His family of three girls and five boys are all living, four of the boys being in America, as follows Nicholas of Omaha, Nebraska, John, of this sketch, James, of Fremont, and George, engaged in the candy business at Fort Dodge, Iowa All of these boys are candymakers and dealers, and all have become wealthy since coming to this country

Educated in Greece, John Petrow immigrated to the United States in 1899, going directly to Minneapolis, Minnesota, where he and his three brothers were all at one time engaged in manufacturing candy and confectionery of all kinds Coming to Fremont, Nebraska, in 1903 Mr Petrow embarked in his present business, starting in on a very modest scale, and has since increased his operations a hundred fold He needed but little assistance at first, but now employs eighteen people, and has started twelve boys, former employes of his, in the same business, and all of them are succeeding well in their undertakings. Mr Petrow, in partnership with his brother James, is the owner of valuable property in the City of Fremont, Nebraska, and in Dodge County, Nebraska

Mr Petrow married, in Tamaqua, Pennsylvania, Vasiliky Petropoulou, who was born in Athens, Greece, and they are the parents of three children, namely Christ, born in 1916, Helen, born in 1917, and George, born in 1920 True to the religious faith in which they were reared, Mr. and Mrs Petrow are devout members of the Greek Orthodox Church Fraternally Mr Petrow is a member of the Ancient Free and Accepted Masons, in which he has taken the thirty-second degree, of the Ancient Arabic Order Nobles of the Mystic Shrine, of the Knights of Pythias and of Fremont Lodge No 514, Benevolent and Protective Order of Elks.

JOHN H MELICK A wide-awake and successful representative of the lumber and coal interests of Dodge County, John H Melick, of Fremont, head of the Melick Coal & Lumber Company, is thoroughly conversant with the business, both as to its conduct and safe advancement, and as general manager is keen and alert to take advantage of offered opportunities, and broad and bright enough to handle the extensive trade he has so ably established A son of J J Melick, he was born, January 13, 1881, in Neligh, Nebraska, where he obtained his first knowledge of books, and of business

J. J. Melick was born, reared and educated in New Jersey Industrious, thrifty, and anxious to succeed, he labored while young at any honorable employment, and in course of time accumulated some money Desirous to better his condition he came to Nebraska in 1876, locating in Neligh, where, as he had no money, he began work as clerk in a grocery, and was later made postmaster When ready to establish himself in business, he purchased a grain warehouse and later a lumber and coal yard, and met with such almost unprecedented success from the start that he was enabled to buy land at different times, and in a few years found that his limited capital with which he began life had reached comparatively large proportions, and he had acquired title to much valuable property Moving to Omaha in 1910, he has since carried on an extensive business as a dealer in real estate, and has gained a prominent position in the industrial and financial life of the city

J J. Melick married Mary Trowbridge, who was born in Wisconsin, and of their union five children have been born, as follows John H, with whom this sketch is chiefly concerned, Charles, engaged in the coal and lumber industry at Neligh, Nebraska; Amy, wife of K A. Whitmer, who is managing a coal yard at Elgin, Nebraska, for Mr Melick, Dema, wife of J C Schwichtenberg, a clothing merchant at Norfolk, Nebraska, and Edward, of Neligh, Nebraska, a dealer in coal and lumber Both parents united with the Congregational Church when young

Becoming familiar with the details of the lumber business in early manhood, John H Melick worked with his father for a while, and then embarked in the furniture, lumber and coal business in Carroll, Wayne County, this state, remaining there until 1914 Wishing to broaden and enlarge his scope of action, he then bought a lumber and coal business in Fremont, and as head of the Melick Lumber & Coal Company, and general manager of the concern, has since built up an extensive and lucrative trade, and gained an excellent reputation for business ability and integrity

Mr Melick married, in 1904, Mary Alice Cratty, a native of Elgin, Nebraska Mrs Melick is a very pleasant and accomplished woman, and an esteemed member of the Methodist Episcopal Church Mr Melick

WILLIAM H. CLEMMONS

is a stanch republican in politics, and fraternally is a member of the Benevolent and Protective Order of Elks Mr and Mrs Melick have no children

PRESIDENT WILLIAM H CLEMMONS In the educational annals of Dodge County, a full chapter belongs to the personality, achievements, and influence of William H Clemmons, late president of Fremont College, and State Superintendent of Instruction President Clemmons was a native of Madison County, Ohio, and was born, April 6, 1857, the son of William M and Mrs Ellen O (Bethards) Clemmons The death of his mother, when he was a child, and the consequent breaking up of his home life, resulted in his removal to Van Wert County, in the same state, and in his being bound out to a farmer By the strange contract he was to remain in the service of this employer until his majority, and at that age to receive one suit of clothes, a horse, saddle and bridle Being a lad of resolution, and independent mind, he emancipated himself from this thralldom at the age of sixteen, purchasing his freedom by clearing forty acres of timber-land, and fencing the same into ten acre lots This task he accomplished in a period shorter, by six months, than the time that had been allowed him Up to the age of twenty-one he had been in school but two months in the year But being free, he took a course of study at Valparaiso College, and received supplementary training at the Indiana State University After graduation, he served effectively as superintendent of schools in Tipton, Indiana, for a period of six years, and then, interested in the West, came to Nebraska, arriving here in 1886 After a period of preliminary teaching in smaller places he accepted the principalship of the Fremont Normal School, out of which he developed Fremont College, of which he was the able and efficient president for thirty years In the three decades involved, his school steadily grew, multiplied its departments and faculty, and became an institution increasingly influential, attracting a multitude of students from all surrounding and many distant localities Classical, commercial and normal courses were offered, music and art departments were added, and in several years the student body numbered above a thousand

The normal department met the need of a large element of youth, whose early educational privileges had been meagre, but who were of an age to be serious-minded, and vigorous in application And in consequence there were graduated through the years hundreds of teachers, who rose to prominence in their profession, and many to distinction Over all these, President Clemmons exerted a powerful influence, and extènded the potency of his personality throughout a wide domain When in 1916 he was elected State Superintendent of Instruction, he further extended his usefulness, and, in two years of incumbency, advanced greatly the systematization of public school work in the state President Clemmons was a man of great firmness of character, and of the highest ideals His industry was marvelous, and his labors boundless Few men in the whole West have achieved so much in a generation And his influence upon young manhood and womanhood for the highest ends of character, service and American citizenship cannot be overestimated A thorough patriot, a faithful disciplinarian, a man of highest ethical and spiritual conceptions, a lover of educational work, and all culture, he attained a potency of influence, and won a love and reverence, scarcely paralleled among educators. The Alumni banquets given at each Commencement season were most memorable as testimonials to the gratitude and admiration, cherished by thousands of graduates for the president of their Alma Mater.

Mr. Clemmons was married at Tipton, Indiana, October 8, 1885, to Miss Dell U Harding of that city, and his life-partner proved through all his educational career a helpmeet and comforter indeed Closely associated in all the administration of the college, with her husband, Mrs. Clemmons shares with him, in the honor of achievement attained, and in the love and helpful influence, that remain forever their wealth and distinction President Clemmons was for years identified with the First Congregational Church of Fremont, and when suddenly, in January, 1920, he was called to a higher world, his pastor, Rev Wm. H Buss, preached his funeral sermon, in the church auditorium in which he had worshipped for over thirty years The memorial service was remarkable for the vastness and personnel of the congregation In addition to the populace of the city, there were present a small army of students and alumni, several representatives of the faculty of the State University, and of the State House at the Capital The tributes were many and varied, and the whole occasion was an object lesson, upon the possibilities of youth in America, who battling against poverty and all imaginable difficulties, may attain eminence in scholarship and wide influence, and wear the crown of usefulness, and public gratitude, never to be tarnished by the flight of years

R H CHAPPEL is one of the progressive young men of the capital city of Dodge County, where his attractively equipped book and stationery store is one of the popular and prosperous retail establishments of Fremont Here he is also secretary of the Chappel-Stuart Printing Company, of which more specific mention will be made in a later paragraph

Mr Chappel was born at Carroll, Iowa, in 1887, and is a son of William and Ida (Mark) Chappel, the former a native of England and the latter of Pennsylvania, in which state their marriage was solemnized, their removal to Iowa taking place in 1883 The father was for a number of years employed as a railroad man, and he is now living virtually retired and resides in the home of his son, Ray M, of Fremont, his wife having passed to eternal rest in 1917 and being survived by her twin sons, Ray M and R H The father is a republican in political allegiance, is affiliated with the Masonic fraternity and is a member of the Methodist Episcopal Church, as was also his wife

In the public schools of the Buckeye State R H Chappel continued his studies until his graduation in the high school at Tama, as a member of the class of 1905 For four years thereafter he was employed in the postoffice at Tama, and then he came to Fremont, Nebraska, where for the ensuing ten years he was in the employ of the Hammond Printing Company. During the last six years he was manager of the company's stationery department, and the knowledge thus gained proved of distinct value to him when, November 2, 1915, he opened his book and stationery store at Fremont He initiated this enterprise with a capital of $2,000, and the marked success that has attended the business is now indicated by his carrying a stock valued at more than $8,000 The establishment caters to a large and appreciative patronage of representative order and is metropolitan in its appointments and general equipment

In the spring of 1920 Mr Chappel became associated with his brother, Ray M, and with E M Anderson and A L Stuart in the organization of the Chappel-Stuart Printing Company, which is incorporated with a capital of $50,000 and which has fitted out a thoroughly modern plant for the execution of the best class of commercial printing, with facilities also for book printing. An inviting field is offered the new company and under its vigorous and progressive executive control its success is assured. The officers of the company are as here noted: Ray M Chappel, president; A L Stuart, vice president, R H Chappel, secretary, and E M. Anderson, treasurer

Mr Chappel gives his allegiance to the republican party and in his civic attitude is liberal and public-spirited. He is an influential and popular member of the Fremont Lodge of the Benevolent and Protective Order of Elks, of which he became exalted ruler on the 1st of April, 1920 He belongs to Fremont Lodge No 15, Ancient Free and Accepted Masons, Mount Tabor Commandery No 9, and Scottish Rite and with Lodge of Perfection No 5 He is a member of the Rotary Club During the great war he saw service in camp five months His name is still enrolled on the list of eligible young bachelors in Dodge County

HAMILTON M MORROW, M D, has been engaged in the practice of his profession in the City of Fremont since 1905, has gained secure vantage-ground as one of the representative physicians of Dodge County and has done some special work in diseases of children His substantial practice indicates the high estimate placed upon him and his ability

Doctor Morrow was born at Ballibay, Bradford County, Pennsylvania, April 6, 1875, and is a son of Newton and Adelaide (Nesbit) Morrow, both of whom were born and reared in that same locality, where the father still maintains his residence, the mother having passed to eternal rest in March, 1916 She was a daughter of John Nesbit, who was born at Ballibay, Ireland, and who was young at the time when he established his residence in the vicinity of Ballibay, Pennsylvania, where he became a successful farmer and where he passed the remainder of his life Newton Morrow has been associated with farm industry in his native county during the entire period of his active career, and he still owns the valuable farm that in the early days was cleared and reclaimed by his father, Hamilton Morrow, who was born at Ballibay Ireland, and who was twenty-one years of age when he established his home in Pennsylvania, the old homestead farm having continued as the stage of his activities during the residue of his life The lineage of the Morrow family is traced back to stanch Scotch origin, but representatives of the family left Scotland and became early settlers in the north of Ireland Newton Morrow has long been one of the influential men of his community, has served in various township offices in his native county, is a republican in politics and holds membership in the Presbyterian Church, as did also his wife. Of their children the eldest is Mary, who is the wife of Frank R Mitten, chief clerk in the office of the county commissioners at Towanda, Pennsylvania, Doctor Morrow of this review was the next in order of birth, Andrew resides at Towanda, Pennsylvania, and is serving as assistant county superintendent of schools, and Helen is a successful teacher in the schools of Camptown, Pennsylvania

Passing the period of his childhood and early youth on the old home farm, Dr Hamilton M. Morrow continued his studies in the public schools of his native state until he had completed a course in the high school at Camptown, and thereafter, in 1905, he was graduated in the Susquehanna Collegiate Institute, at Towanda, Pennsylvania For the ensuing year he was engaged in teaching in the schools of the old Keystone State, and he then came to Tekamah, Nebraska, where for a year he held a clerical position in the general store conducted by the firm of which his maternal uncles, John and William Nesbit, were members This occupation he held but a means to an end, for he had determined to prepare himself for the medical profession In the pursuance of this ambition he availed himself of the advantages of Rush Medical College, Chicago, one of the greatest and most celebrated medical institutions of the country He was there graduated as a member of the Class of 1901 and shortly after thus receiving his degree of Doctor of Medicine he engaged in the active practice of his profession at Tekamah, Nebraska, where he became associated in practice with his maternal uncle, Dr Andrew Nesbit There he continued his successful work in his profession for four years, at the expiration of which, in December, 1905, he initiated practice in the broader field afforded at Fremont and in its tributary territory in Dodge County Here his success has been distinctive—a due reward for his earnest service and a voucher for his marked professional ability The doctor served two years as health officer of Fremont, is an active member of the Dodge County Medical Society, of which he has served as secretary and counselor, and while engaged in practice at Tekamah he served as president of the Burt County Medical Society He is president of the Elkhorn Valley Medical Society, a member of the Nebraska State Medical Society and the American Medical Association, as is he of the Missouri Valley Medical Society

Doctor Morrow is a stanch supporter of the cause of the republican party, and is affiliated with the Masonic fraternity and the Independent Order of Odd Fellows, both he and his wife being active members of the Presbyterian Church. The attractive family home is at 406 East Sixth Street, where the doctor also maintains his office

The year 1904 was marked by the marriage of Doctor Morrow to Miss Edythe Trowbridge, who was born at Halstead, Pennsylvania, and whose early education included the discipline of the high school, besides which she completed a course of two years in the Moody Bible Institute She gave special attention to the study of both vocal and instrumental music, and is one of the talented musicians of Fremont, even as she is a popular factor in the representative social life of her home city Doctor and Mrs Morrow have three children, all of whom are still attending the public schools of Fremont, their names being here entered in order of their birth Adelaide, Hamilton, and Paul

HARVEY W SHAFFER Farm management at its best is well exemplified by Harvey W Shaffer, whose home is in section 28 of Hooper Township Mr Shaffer is young, progressive, an expert not only in handling his fields and crops, but in raising and handling livestock

He enjoys practically a lifelong acquaintance with the agricultural community of Dodge County His father is the well known early settler, Jacob Shaffer, mentioned on other pages Harvey W. Shaffer was born in Dodge County, April 15, 1882, and had a thorough apprenticeship at farming on his father's place Besides the advantages of the country schools, he graduated in the commercial course of the Fremont Normal School in 1905 Then starting for himself he has made a specialty of stock raising, and has fed many carloads for the market His progressiveness is not alone in evidence on his farm, but through his active affiliation with many organizations that have the welfare and prosperity of the farmer as their object

Mr Shaffer is a director in the Farmers' Co-operative Association at Nickerson, a stockholder in the Farmers' Union at Hooper, stockholder in the Farmers State Bank and Co-operative Store at Nickerson, in the Farmers Creamery at Fremont, and in the Farmers Union State Exchange of Omaha The management of the 350-acre farm owned by his father makes his voice entitled to be heard in the organizations as a real factor in agricultural affairs

In 1912 he married Miss May Tookey She was born in Illinois, but grew up in Nebraska, being a daughter of Fred Tookey of Fremont To their marriage was born one daughter, Wilmetta Elizabeth Mr and Mrs Shaffer are members of the Methodist Church at Hooper and in politics he is independent

J C. NELSON Noteworthy among the active and prosperous agriculturists of Dodge County is J C Nelson, a well-known resident of Elkhorn Township, where his fine and well improved farm gives substantial evidence of the excellent care and skill with which it is managed, presenting to the passer-by a glimpse of country life as it now exists Like many another of our more successful and esteemed citizens, he was born across the seas, his birth having occurred, in 1872, in Denmark, where his parents spent their entire lives

J. C Nelson, it is needless to say, received a good education in his native land, and there acquired some knowledge of agriculture In 1890, having determined to seek his fortune in America, he secured passage on an ocean bound vessel, and immediately after landing in the United States made his way to Nebraska, locating in Holstein, Adams County, where he was employed as a farm laborer three years Going then to Omaha he was variously employed for a number of years, making and saving money In 1904 Mr Nelson located in Dodge County, and having purchased 240 acres of land has since been busily employed in general farming and dairying, in the latter industry keeping a fine line of Holstein cattle He has made many and varied improvements on his home farm, and is cultivating his land with good results, the rich and fertile soil yielding abundant crops, well repaying him for his labors

Mr Nelson married, in Omaha, Matilda Kruger, who has ably assisted him in his undertakings. He is a republican in politics, and a Lutheran in religion.

SETH F STILES. Distinguished not only for his active services in many of the more important battles of the Civil war, but as a man of sterling integrity and worth, Seth F Stiles, late of Fremont, was held in high respect as a man and a citizen, and it is eminently fitting that a brief review of his life should be given in a work of this character He was born, January 23, 1842, in Zanesville, Ohio, and being left fatherless when a boy fourteen years old, was taken by his mother to Iowa, where she settled on a farm in Dallas County, and where he completed his early education

In 1862, inspired by patriotic enthusiasm, he enlisted in Company B, Fourth Iowa Volunteer Infantry, and with his brave comrades participated in fourteen regular battles, and several skirmishes, doing his duty willingly and faithfully Discharged from the service after the surrender at Appomattox, Mr Stiles began work as a carpenter and builder, and was busily employed in Iowa for upwards of twenty years Coming to Nebraska with his family in 1887, he continued at his trade a few years, was contractor, pension agent, chief of police, deputy sheriff

A stanch republican in politics, Mr Stiles had been serving as city clerk for eight years at the time of his death, on September 20, 1911. Fraternally he was a member of the Ancient Free and Accepted Order of Masons, in which he had taken several degrees, and was a member, and past commander of Fremont Post, Grand Army of the Republic, of which he was adjutant when the final summons came

.Mr. Stiles married, in September, 1865, three weeks after receiving his discharge from the army, Frances E Peters, who was born in Lafayette, Indiana, a daughter of James and Mary (Simpson) Peters, both of whom were natives of Ohio, having been born in the vicinity of Cincinnati Her father migrated from Ohio to Indiana, from there going to Illinois, and later to Perry, Iowa, where both he and his wife spent their later years Mr. Peters was for many years engaged in mercantile pursuits, and as a general merchant acquired considerable wealth, including among other properties valuable farming lands

Eleven children blessed the marriage of Mr and Mrs Stiles, namely Mary, wife of J R Gay, of Fremont, Mrs Lois Koyen, living on a farm lying east of Fremont, J E, a traveling man, with headquarters in Sacramento, California, William W, of San Francisco, California, who has charge of the carpet department of the Sloan establishment, Orville D, employed in the Fremont Canning Factory, lives with his mother, Mrs Ethel Zachan, of San Francisco, whose husband is city salesman for the Union Lithographing Company, and five children that have passed to the life beyond

Moses Theodore Zellers, M D Some of the most capable and dependable physicians and surgeons have found that they could increase their usefulness by specializing on some branch of their profession, and one of them of Dodge County, who is making his name known in this region as an eye, ear, nose and throat specialist, is Dr Moses Theodore Zellers, of Hooper.

Doctor Zellers was born at Oriental, Juniata County, Pennsylvania, on May 15, 1861, a son of George and Rebecca (Miller) Zellers, both natives of Pennsylvania, now deceased, the mother passing away in 1901, aged seventy-seven years, and the father in 1907, aged seventy-three years. By trade George Zellers was a shoemaker and he was also engaged in farming, all of his life being spent in the Keystone State He and his wife had the following children Jonas, who is a farmer of Pennsylvania; John, who is a farmer of Ohio; Moses T, whose name heads this review, and George, who is also a farmer of Pennsylvania The family were Dunkards, and the men republicans

Doctor Zellers attended the common and high schools of his native state, and took his medical course in the Western Reserve College at Cleveland, Ohio, from which he was graduated on March 6, 1889, with the degree of Doctor of Medicine In November of that same year he came to Hooper, Nebraska, and until 1908 was in a general practice, but since then has confined himself to diseases of the eye, ear, nose and throat, having built up a wide connection He has taken post-graduate work and in 1907 studied at the Chicago Eye, Ear, Nose and Throat College, and in 1908 went abroad to pursue his studies at Vienna, Austria, and is now recognized as an authority on these special subjects, being often called into consultation by others of his profession

In 1880 Doctor Zellers was married to Alice Troutman, a native of Pennsylvania, and they became the parents of the following children William M, who is manager of the Farmers' Co-operative Association,

Dr M. V. Zellers

at Hooper, served during the Spanish-American war in the Third Nebraska Volunteers under Capt J M Vickers, J Sherman, who was graduated from the Kansas Dental College, is a dental surgeon of Hooper, Nebraska, Henry C, who is a dental surgeon of Lincoln, Nebraska, was graduated from the Kansas City Dental College, and was for eleven months in France during the World war as a member of the Dental Reserve Corps, Monroe T, who was graduated from the Hooper High School, is now a resident of Hooper, George G, who was graduated from the Hooper High School, was a navy cadet during the World war, was discharged and is now a student at Lincoln Business College, Lincoln, Nebraska, and Margaret R, who married Carl von Seggeon, owner of an elevator at Gregory, South Dakota

Doctor Zellers is a Blue Lodge Mason. He belongs to the Dodge County Medical Association which he served at one time as president, the Nebraska State Medical Society and the American Medical Association Mrs Zellers is a member of the Lutheran Church He is a republican and during 1899 was the successful candidate of his party to the State Assembly It would be difficult to find a more representative citizen or successful professional man than he and he deserves his present prestige for he has honorably earned it through his ability and personality

GEORGE W SHEPHARD A man of scholarly attainments, energetic and far-sighted, the late George W Shephard, for many years an esteemed and highly respected resident of Fremont, was distinguished not only as a pioneer school teacher of Saunders County, Nebraska, but as an able assistant in developing the agricultural prosperity of that part of the state A native of Illinois, he was born, February 1, 1845, in Menard County, where he acquired his preliminary education

After his graduation from the high school, Mr Shephard attended the University of Illinois for a year, and subsequently taught school in his native state for a number of terms Coming as a young man to Nebraska, he bought land in Saunders County, and in addition to improving a good farm continued his professional labors as a teacher for several years, teaching in all about a quarter of a century He met with unquestioned success in all of his undertakings, and at his death, which occurred in Fremont, where he had lived for nearly twenty years, in 1907, he was considered quite wealthy He was influential in public affairs, being a prominent member of the republican party, and for two terms represented his district in the State Legislature

Mr Shephard married, in 1889, Miss Grace Snyder, who was born in New York State, and in 1870, at the age of five years, came with her parents, F G and Mary (Smith) Snyder, to Saunders County, Nebraska, where her father, who died in 1903, was for many years prosperously engaged in tilling the soil Mr. and Mrs Snyder reared five children, as follows Mrs Shephard, E G Snyder, an extensive farmer at Cedar Rapids, Nebraska, Victor, Rudolph and James, all of whom are single, and living with their widowed mother in Canada Mr and Mrs Snyder both united with the Methodist Episcopal Church when young

The union of Mr and Mrs Shephard was blessed by the birth of two children, namely James, now assistant city engineer, attended the State Agricultural School in Lincoln, and Grace, a student in the University of Nebraska, is a member of the Phi Phi Sorority Mrs Shephard, who owns valuable property both in Fremont and

Saunders county, recently bought a lot, and erected a beautiful residence at 746 East Fifth Street, Fremont, where she welcomes her friends with a gracious hospitality

JOHN EDELMAIER There are many practical, sensible men who are prospering in a business way at Hooper, Nebraska, where they are quietly carrying on enterprises and producing standard commodities for which at all times there is demand and ready sale An instance is the manufacture of brick, successfully carried on here by John Edelmaier, an experienced man in the business While the manufacturing of brick is a very old employment, it being remembered that in Biblical days the requirement to "make bricks without straw" was one of the grievances of the chosen people, it has come on down to the present time as one of the basic industries and promises to continue so Wood, marble, stone, cement and steel, all enter more or less into modern building, but brick still holds its own in all durable construction work.

John Edelmaier, who owns an extensive brick manufacturing plant at Hooper, where he is a substantial citizen in every way, was born at Miltonburg, Monroe County, Ohio, November 25, 1865 His parents were David and Caroline (Knaus) Edelmaier, both of whom were born in Germany After coming to the United States they located on a farm in Monroe County, Ohio, and their eldest son, John, was born there in the same year They had other children as follows Carrie, who is the wife of J W Sharp, a machinist, and they live in California, Henry, who is cashier of the Farmers State Bank at Scribner Nebraska Albert, who is a Farmer and bricklayer near Dale, in Spencer County, Indiana, Anna, who lives at Evansville, Indiana and Edward, who is pastor of a Methodist Episcopal Church at Mount Vernon Indiana The parents were members of the above church after moving to Indiana in 1870 The mother died in July, 1914 The father lives retired

John Edelmaier was five years old when his people moved to Indiana He attended the public schools and also took a commercial course in the Gem City Business College at Quincy, Illinois, so that when he came to Washington County, Nebraska, in 1885, he was well prepared for any business opportunity that presented itself He worked on a farm near Fontanelle, for a time, but later went to work in the Waterman brickyard at Fontanelle, subsequently buying a half interest in the business In 1889 the partners moved their plant to Scribner, Nebraska, Mr Edelmaier continuing with Mr Waterman in the business for five years, at Scribner Both partners proved keen, far-sighted business men and when, in 1894, they had the opportunity to buy the brickyard of John Heimrick, at Hooper, they took advantage of it and have been established at this point ever since Mr Edelmaier is a man of progressive ideas and soon found it advisable to greatly enlarge the plant at Hooper, where, during the operating season, he employs from 35 to 40 first class men It has become one of the important industries at Hooper

Mr. Edelmaier was married in Indiana to Miss Louise F Kreie, who was born at Mount Vernon, in that state, and they have one daughter, Susanna Ruth, who resides with her parents Mr and Mrs Edelmaier attend the Methodist Episcopal Church In politics he is a republican as is his father, and on many occasions has been urged to accept public office but has declined, his own business affairs sufficiently engaging his attention He is a stockholder in the Hooper Light & Power Company and has some valuable land interests in Texas He is a member of the United Workmen and Knights of Pythias at Hooper Mr Edelmaier is numbered with the reliable business men and worthy citizens of Dodge County

CARL N RALPH, D D S It is stated that one of the first things noticed about the American troops when they landed on foreign shores was their well-cared for teeth, and a leader of the English forces is reported as having declared that there was no doubt but that the "Yanks" would outfight the "Tommies" because of the superiority of their teeth which would enable them to properly digest army rations Back of these magnificent young men of ours were the efficient and conscientious members of the dental profession, who, through their care and ability, preserved the teeth in a manner not to be equalled in any other country in the world Although the majority realized the debt owned this profession, the truth was brought home through contact with those of other nations where this same care is not given to the teeth with disastrous results There probably is not a community in the whole United States of any appreciable size which has not its competent, regularly qualified dental surgeon, and one of this profession at Hooper who has fully gained the confidence of the people of Dodge County is Dr Carl N Ralph

Doctor Ralph was born in Germany in 1893, a son of Nicholas and Dorothea (Tiegens) Ralph, natives of Germany, who came to the United States in the early '90s and located in the vicinity of West Point, Nebraska, where they were engaged in farming until 1905, when they left their farm, moved to West Point and are now living there in retirement They became the parents of the following children Henry, who is engaged in conducting the old homestead; Katie, who is the wife of Gus E Grunke, a farmer of West Point, Nebraska, Marie, who is the wife of Joseph Zich, a street car conductor of Omaha, Nebraska; Doctor Ralph, who was the fourth in order of birth, Ellen, who is in the nurses training school connected with the Nicholas Senn Hospital of Omaha, Nebraska The parents are consistent members of the Lutheran Church In politics the father is a republican.

Doctor Ralph remained with his parents until he was twenty years of age, and attended the schools of Cuming County In 1909 he was graduated from Creighton University, Omaha, Nebraska, and located at Hooper, where he has built up a large practice to which he devotes all of his time, being now recognized as one of the best dentists in Dodge County

On December 24, 1912, Doctor Ralph was united in marriage with Byrdee E Zuhlke, born in Dodge County Doctor and Mrs Ralph have one child, Sheridan, who is a bright little one Like his father, Doctor Ralph is a republican, but he has never been willing to enter public life. He and his wife belong to the Lutheran Church

P HARRY LARSON Possessing excellent business ability and judgment, P Harry Larson holds a place of importance in the public affairs of Fremont, as acting commissioner of the local Water, Light and Power Company, having full charge of the plant, and in that capacity rendering the city very satisfactory service A son of John Larson, he was born, December 6, 1882, in Fremont, which has always been his home

Born in Sweden, John Larson immigrated to this country when very young, and a short time after his arrival in the United States located in Dodge County He was engaged in the grocery business in Fremont for a while, and later, in company with his brother, L P Larson, was employed in the wholesale liquor business until 1892 Retiring from active pursuits in that year, he continued his residence in Fremont until his death, in 1894 Beginning life even with the world, he met with good success in his undertakings, accumulating a good property He married, in Fremont, Louisa Larson, who is still living in this city, and of their five children, P Harry, is the only survivor The father was independent in politics, and both he and his wife united with the Swedish Lutheran Church when young

Brought up in Fremont, P Harry Larson was educated in the graded and normal schools, and began life as a wage earner in the office of the brewery with which his father and uncle were connected He was afterwards in the employ of the Nye, Schneider & Fowler Company until 1916, when he was made acting commissioner of the Fremont Water Light & Power Company, a position that he is filling ably and acceptably

Mr Larson married, in 1906, Hedwig Holmberg, who was born in Wahoo, Saunders County, Nebraska, where her parents were early settlers Mr and Mrs Larson have no children They are both members of the Swedish Lutheran Church, having remained faithful to the religious beliefs of their parents A sound democrat in politics, Mr Larson represented the Fourth Ward in the city countil for six years Fraternally he is a member of the Knights of Pythias, of the independent Order of Odd Fellows; and of the Benevolent and Protective Order of Elks

George W Moyer, Sr, who was born in 1843, went to Illinois with his mother when young He was a resourceful pioneer citizen, who was well fortified in energy and ambition when he came to Dodge County and began the work of reclaiming and improving a farm having purchased 160 acres in section 12, Cotterell Township, and among his first activities was the building of a modest house to serve as habitation for his family With the passing years, his energy and good management brought to him abundant success in his farm enterprise and he continued as one of the substantial farmers and highly esteemed citizens of Dodge County until his death January 23, 1904, at the venerable age of sixty-one years He was a democrat in politics and was earnest in his Christian faith, as is also his widow, a member of the Christian Church She stills remains on the old homestead Mrs Moyer, whose maiden name was Sabra Mark, was born in Kentucky April 1, 1862, and reared in Indiana They were married September 25, 1889, and became the parents of seven children John, who is now a resident of Lodgepole, Cheyenne County, Mrs Margaret Matthews resides in the City of Fremont, judicial center of Dodge County; Mrs Iva Johnson and her husband reside on one of the excellent farms of Dodge County, Mrs Myrtle Bishop is a resident of Beatrice, Gage County, Theodore, George W Jr, and Harry, remain on the old homestead with their mother and have active management of the farm, which is devoted to diversified agriculture and to the raising and feeding of a due complement of live stock, including Duroc-Jersey hogs George W. Moyer, Jr, is well upholding the prestige of the family name and is one of the vigorous and popular exponents of farm industry in Dodge County, where he was born in the year 1898 and where his educational advantages were those offered in the excellent public schools

G. H. Rathbun

GROVE H RATHBUN, M D Among the prominent and esteemed citizens whom Fremont has been called upon to mourn within the past few years none are more genuinely missed than Grove H Rathbun, M D, an able and skilful physician and surgeon, whose professional services are entitled to honorable recognition and praise A native of Iowa, he was born, December 3, 1881, in Bedford, Taylor County, and died in Clarkson Hospital, Omaha, Nebraska, September 5, 1919, while yet in manhood's prime, his death being a loss not only to his immediate family and friends, but to the entire community and the medical profession

Brought up in Iowa, Grove H. Rathbun was graduated from the Exira High School, and at the age of fifteen years was ambitious to enter a medical college. Being altogether too young to do so, he began the study of medicine under private tutorship, and in 1902 was graduated from the Omaha Medical College with the degree of Doctor of Medicine Doctor Rathbun began the practice of his profession in South Dakota, connected with a hospital at Lead and had charge of the hospital at Roubiax, and also being physician for the mining companies of those places He subsequently located at Bellefourche, South Dakota, where associated with Dr L J. Townsend, of Sioux City, Iowa, where he remained seven years, having a large private practice, and doing much surgical work in the local hospital

Coming to Fremont in 1912, the doctor confined his practice exclusively to surgery and consultation, in both of which he had a fine reputation, his skill as a surgeon being widely known, and his diagnosis of the different diseases to which human flesh is heir being unexcelled Some time prior to his death, Doctor Rathbun purchased a large and conveniently arranged building on Nye Avenue, and after having it equipped with all the modern appliances used in surgery, performed there all of his operations, which were many, and ofttimes very serious A man of brilliant intellect, he was considered an authority on medical and surgical matters, and at the time of his death was enjoying a large and lucrative practice. In August, 1918, he entered the service, and as the armistice was signed just after he had received orders to go across the sea he was discharged in December, 1918

In February, 1903, he married, in Lead, South Dakota, Mollie McArthur, who was born in that city, and completed her early education in the State Normal School, at Spearfish, South Dakota Her father, John McArthur, was born in Nova Scotia, and as a young man came to the United States He located in Lead, South Dakota, where he was engaged as a mining engineer and in later life, mining contractor in South Africa His wife, whose maiden name was Margaret Johnston, was born and reared in Scotland, and is now living with Mrs Rathbun Three children blessed the union of Doctor and Mrs Rathbun, namely. Grove A, born February 13, 1904; Jeanne, born April 13, 1906, and Sanford, born February 24, 1911 Mrs Rathbun is a member of the Episcopal Church The doctor, who had taken several post-graduate courses, belonged to all of the medical societies and associations, and was a member of Fremont Lodge No 514, Benevolent and Protective Order of Elks

SAMUEL I BLOCK The commercial enterprise of Fremont owes a great deal to the progressive spirit and energy of Samuel I Block, who came to this Nebraska city twelve years ago and began on a modest scale the merchandising career which has steadily expanded until it is one of the best stores in Dodge County He specializes in women's ready-to-wear garments and his success has been due to his correct estimate of the tastes and demands of the people of Dodge County who have given him a splendid patronage

Mr. Block was born in Poland in 1886, coming to America at the age of twenty, and has shown great ability in adapting himself and assimilating himself with American life and customs His parents were C H. and Bertha (Yorckshire) Block who spent all their lives in Poland and were of the Jewish faith Three of their eight children came to the United States Harry I, a prominent merchant of North Platte, Nebraska; Samuel I, and Edith, wife of a merchant at St Joseph, Missouri On account of the World war the children in America did not receive news of the death of their parents during the influenza epidemic in 1917 until nearly two years later

Samuel I Block was educated in the schools of his native country, and came to America with neither capital nor any knowledge of American ways and customs His first location was at Gouverneur, New York, and he sold goods from a pack until he had accumulated the capital necessary to bring him to the West In August, 1908, he arrived at Fremont and on the third of that month opened his first store with a modest stock of merchandise valued at $1,500 He worked, studied the local situation, and proved his ability to adapt himself to changing circumstances Consequently he saw his business steadily grow and expand, and his store now meets the exclusive demands of a large part of the population for ready-to-wear garments and furnishings

In 1912 Mr. Block married Libbie Brown who was born at Nebraska City and was educated in Omaha Her parents were Henry and Mollie Brown Her father was a furniture man and died at St Louis, while her mother is still living at Omaha Mr and Mrs Block have two children, Milton, a schoolboy, and Florence, who was born in 1918 The family are members of the Jewish Church Mr Block is affiliated with the Independent Order of Odd Fellows, with the Elks, is a member of the Fremont Commercial Club and the Young Men's Christian Association Since coming to Dodge County his prosperity has been represented not only by a steady growth of his mercantile enterprise, but he has been enabled to purchase, and still owns, two farms and one of the comfortable residences of the Town of Fremont

Charles J Robinson. Among the essentials which contribute to the enjoyment of mankind, not the least is that which caters to our entertainment In this connection the motion picture industry, comparatively a new enterprise, has come to occupy an important place As one of the pioneers in this field at Blair, Charles J Robinson has won his way to success and position, and his Home Theater is one of the most popular and best patronized family amusement places of the city Mr. Robinson's career has been one in which poverty and affluence have both had a part and in which success has come only after much discouragement and the overcoming of numerous obstacles.

Born January 7, 1861, in York County, Pennsylvania, Mr Robinson is a son of James W and Catherine (Overlander) Robinson, natives of Pennsylvania His father entered the Union army at the outbreak of the Civil war, and fought with bravery and fidelity until stricken by typhoid fever, subsequently passing away in a Southern hospital, in 1865 Mrs Robinson, a member of the Presbyterian Church, survived her husband until 1870. They were the parents of four children:

Catherine, who married Elijah Heffner of York County, Pennsylvania, Charles J, George W, a farmer of Moorfield, Nebraska, and A M, a railroad man of Arlington, this state

Charles J Robinson was but four years of age at the time of his father's death and as his mother possessed no resources he was placed in an institution at Mount Joy, near Lancaster, Pennsylvania, where he received his education and remained until he was sixteen years of age At that time he left the Soldiers' Orphans Home and walked a distance of twenty-seven miles to the farm of his uncle He had been promised the sum of $100 for a year's work, but after he had faithfully fulfilled his part of the contract, his relative refused to pay him for his work Chafing under a spirit of injustice, the youth left his uncle's farm and accepted employment with a Mr Gamble, for whom he worked three years and seven months at a wage varying from $4 to $8 per month At this time many ambitious young men were turning their faces toward the West, and in 1882 Mr Robinson gave up his Pennsylvania farm work for the uncertainties of a new country His first settlement was in Henderson County, Illinois, where he secured employment on a farm, but after working for three months was stricken with fever and ague, and at one time his case was so serious that all hope was given up for his recovery However, he managed to pull through, and in September, 1882, again took up his journey, eventually arriving in Seward County, Nebraska, with the sum of $4, borrowed capital Here he found employment putting up windmills in the country districts, working three weeks at a wage of $9 per week, and during the next period of his training had various experiences, in which were included work in a restaurant and a clerkship in a dry goods store for one year He was also employed by George W. Gibbs, a wholesale boot and shoe dealer, after leaving whom he went to Holt County, Nebraska, with the intention of taking up a homestead Upon his arrival, however, the proposition did not look attractive, and after he had spent all of the money he had made he went to Albion, Nebraska, and worked on a farm for one month, securing in this manner the sum of $19 Later he went to Grand Island and then to Ord, Nebraska, where he worked in the general store of Perry & Cover for one year, being later with R. Harris & Company. He first came to Blair in 1886, but subsequently removed to Herman, where he was engaged in farming for a year He also worked for five years in a general store at Spiker, Nebraska, and a peddling outfit was his next means of income, he traveling through the country districts around Arizona, Burt County, Nebraska, and also conducted a store in Burt County

Selling out his Arizona interests, Mr Robinson came to Washington County, where he was married August 13, 1894, to Miss Marrilla J. Newkirk, a daughter of Clifton and Mary Katherine (Ray) Newkirk, the former a native of Lawrence County, Indiana, and the latter of Jackson County, that state The parents of Mrs. Robinson were married in Indiana and came to Washington County, Nebraska, in 1869, homesteading a farm on which they spent the balance of their lives Of the eight Newkirk children, six are living A B, who lives on his farm in Washington County, Mrs Robinson Edward, a farmer of Washington County, Henry C., a farmer of Revinna, South Dakota, Vernon, of Montrose, Minnesota and Elizabeth, the wife of Dr W H Pruner, a surgeon of Omaha Mr Newkirk was a soldier in the Union army during the Civil war from October, 1861, until February, 1862, when he was wounded and secured his honorable discharge because of disability He carried the bullet in his body until his death

Three sons have been born to Mr and Mrs Robinson: Raymond Harold, born May 9, 1895, who was in the Sandstorm Division of the United States Expeditionary Forces during the World war for twenty-two months and went to France, although he did not reach the front lines before the signing of the armistice; Edward James, born August 27, 1897, who was an aerial gunner during the World war and had training at the Great Lakes Naval Training Station and at Pensacola, Florida, and Clifton N, born November 25, 1902, who enlisted for four years in the United States Navy as an aerial photographer, and is now attending the United States Government School at Washington, D C

Following his marriage, Mr. Robinson located at Arlington, Nebraska, where he was engaged in the hotel business for one year, after which he purchased a farm and engaged in agricultural pursuits for eight years Returning to Blair at that time he established himself in business as the proprietor of a grocery, but after one and one-half years disposed of his interest therein to take advantage of the larger opportunities offered by the motion picture industry. Buying the Home Theater in 1907, he has since built up a large and profitable patronage which appreciates his efforts to give it wholesome, clean and enjoyable entertainment at popular prices Mr Robinson has made himself a recognized fixture in business circles of Blair, not alone through his theater, but through his transactions in real estate Some years ago he began to engineer transactions in the realty field and each year has seen the further increase and development of his operations in this line He occupies a place high in the esteem of his associates and in the confidence of his fellow citizens

F W Arndt. A prosperous hardware merchant of Blair, and one of its substantial and prominent business men, F W Arndt has built up a large and lucrative trade, his upright and honorable transactions, and his ready willingness to oblige all patrons, having won him an extensive business A son of the late Bernard Arndt, he was born, May 4, 1862, in Cincinnati, Ohio, of German parentage

Born and bred in Germany, Bernard Arndt immigrated to this country soon after his marriage, and with his bride settled in Cincinnati, Ohio, where he remained as a cigar manufacturer until 1871 Coming in that year with his family to Blair, Nebraska, he continued the manufacture of cigars during the remainder of his active life, and subsequently continued a resident of the city until his death, at the advanced age of ninety-four years He was a republican in politics, and a member of the Lutheran Church, which, at his death in December, 1919, lost one of its most respected and valued members His wife, whose maiden name was Dorothea Albrecht, was born in Germany, and died in 1910, in Blair, Nebraska Eight children were born of their marriage, three of whom are living, as follows. F. W., the special subject of this sketch, Mrs. Londelius, living in Spokane, Washington, where her husband owns a fruit ranch, and Mrs Fred Michael, Tekamah, Nebraska

Attending first the public schools of Cincinnati, F. W. Arndt completed his early education in the public schools of Blair His first salaried occupation was that of a clerk in a mercantile establishment Giving up that position, he learned the sheet metal trade, which he followed for nine years Embarking then in the hardware business, he was in partnership with G G Lundt for fifteen years, when, in 1903, he bought his partner's interest in the firm, and has since conducted the business alone. Enterprising and progressive, he has enlarged his operations, having added an auto salesroom and shop, in which he handles the Dodge and Nash cars, having a large salesroom and a wareroom. He has three floors in the hardware department, and carries an extensive and varied line of hardware and electric supplies, endeavoring to keep in stock everything required in his line in an up-to-date establishment. Mr. Arndt is a member of the Blair Commercial Club, and of the State Hardware Association, in each of which he takes much interest.

In 1886 Mr. Arndt was united in marriage with Sophie E. Riddler, who was born in Fort Calhoun, Nebraska. Her father, the late James S. Riddler, served in the Regular Army during his earlier life, being stationed at Fort Calhoun at an early day. He served in the cavalry, a military branch in which he was ever interested. After leaving the army, Mr. Riddler engaged in contracting and building, and in addition to erecting many of the church edifices in Blair put up many of the Government buildings in the Indian Agency near Sioux City, Iowa. Mr. and Mrs. Arndt are the parents of three children, namely: Wilfred B., in business with his father; Mrs. Josephine Bunting, whose husband is a jeweler in Akron, Iowa; and Dorrette, wife of H. H. Struve, a bookkeeper in Omaha. Mr. Arndt is a sound republican in politics, and has rendered acceptable service as councilman. Serving as director on the board of the Columbia Life Insurance Company of Fremont, Nebraska, also Nebraska Retail Hardware Mutual Insurance Company. Aggressive pusher in any enterprise tending to upbuilding of his home city.

JOHN H. WARNER. The retired farmer of ample means is very often the most useful citizen of a community in which he takes up his residence. Very often he will be found to be a stockholder in the town's soundest business concerns, and these are apt to prosper, for the farmer, in transferring his interests from rural to urban life, does not lose his personality. If he has been able to make his undertakings along agricultural lines profitable, the same good judgment will make him careful, observing and prudent in relation to the town's affairs and enterprises. One of the well-known retired farmers and useful, highly respected citizens of Hooper, Nebraska, is John H. Warner, who has been a resident of Dodge County since he was eleven years of age.

John H. Warner was born at Henderson, in Knox County, Illinois, May 13, 1855, the eldest of six children born to Lewis and Mahala (McCoy) Warner, natives of Indiana. Lewis Warner was a farmer in Indiana, Illinois, Iowa and Missouri. During the Civil war he served in the Missouri State Militia, and afterward moved with his family to Dakota, and from there, in 1866, came with their household goods in a covered wagon to Dodge County. Here he secured land which, in the course of time, and after many family hardships, became of some value, and he carried on general farming and raised stock as did his neighbors. He was a man of sterling character, was a member of the Christian Church, was a justice of the peace for many years and as a republican was elected several terms as a county commissioner. On account of failing health he finally sold his farm and moved to Brownsville, Oregon, where he died March 28, 1900, aged sixty-eight years. In Illinois he married Mahala McCoy, who survived him, her death occurring February 28, 1911, at the age of seventy-six years. Besides John H. they had the following children: William, who is deceased; Mary Jane, who is the wife of Frank Watson, a farmer near Brownsville, Oregon; Robert E., who is a rancher and lumberman in Oregon; and Myra and Sarah, both of whom died in infancy.

John H Warner was eleven years old when the family came to Dodge County and he has a very vivid recollection of early days here He assisted his father after his period of school attendance was over, then bought land for himself and for many years was one of the busy and prosperous farmers and stock raisers of the county. In 1910 he decided to give up the hard duties that had engaged him so long and take life a little easier, a resolution that met with the approval of his family

Mr Warner was married in 1879 to Miss Clara Mitchell, who was born in Pennsylvania, a daughter of Jeremiah and Amelia (Boyer) Mitchell, who came to Dodge County in 1877. Both are deceased The following children were born to Mr and Mrs Warner Maude, who is the wife of Charles Hansen, a farmer near Dickson, Nebraska, Lewis, who is a farmer near North Bend Harvey E who is a farmer in Dodge County, Mabel, who is the wife of William Van Horn, a farmer near Haxtum, Colorado, Ray, who is a farmer near North Bend, Myrtle, who is the wife of John Schmela, a veterinary surgeon at Spencer, Nebraska; and Merle, who is a student in the Hooper High School

Mr Warner has always voted the republican ticket He has never desired political honors and has never accepted any office except that of school director of District No 75, in which he served many years before coming to Hooper He is a stockholder in the Farmers Union Elevator at Hooper This is one of the fine, typical families of Dodge County

DAVID BROWN As the woodman in clearing his land leaves here and there some stalwart maple or cedar, which long years after stands alone in the midst of some green and fertile field, a solitary remembrance of the past, so the relentless Reaper, in his grim harvest of men has spared here and there a pioneer who forms a connecting link between the past and the present David Brown, now retired from active affairs, is one of the surviving pioners of Dodge County, where he came in 1871 and where for many years he was engaged in successful farming operations

Mr Brown was born in Ontario, Canada, in 1839, a son of John and Ellen Brown, the former a native of Ireland, who emigrated to Canada and died there at the age of seventy-two years David Brown was given a common school education in Canada, where for nine years he was engaged in teaching school Coming to the United States in 1866, he first located in Benton County, Iowa, where he was engaged in farming for one year. Following this, he was unsettled for a time, moving from place to place in search of a location that would satisfy him, and in 1871 decided upon Dodge County. For a short time he lived at Fremont, but eventually moved to a farm fifteen miles northwest of that city, which he at first rented Later he became the owner thereof through purchase, and as the years passed not only improved his own land and kept pace with the ever-changing developments of his county's history, but also played his own part well in assisting the advancement of the forces of education and religion and serving for a number of years as a member of the School Board He is a Presbyterian in his religious affiliation, his wife having passed away in that faith in 1917, at the age of seventy-two years In the evening of life, Mr Brown stepped aside from the path of active labor to allow younger men to assume the burdens and exercise their ambitions Although he has passed the Psalmist's threescore and ten by a large margin, he still maintains an interest in the work of the property, as well as in other matters of importance occurring about him

Mr. Brown was married in Ontario, Canada, to Catherine Raycraft, and to this union there were born six sons and three daughters: Alfred D., William J., Emma V., Agnes S., who is deceased, Helen M., George S., Earl R., Owen D. and Ernest H. These children have all been given excellent educational advantages and have been reared to habits of industry, integrity and sobriety, their father having always been a stanch adherent of prohibition, not only personally but as a national measure.

Owen D. Brown, son of David Brown, was born on his father's farm in Dodge County, Nebraska, in 1885, and received his education in the public schools. Reared as an agriculturist, he adopted that vocation upon attaining years of maturity, and for the past six years has been operating successfully a highly productive farm in section 4, Maple Township. Mr. Brown is accounted one of the progressive agriculturists of the younger generation in his community, where he has been a representative of the highest type of agricultural citizenship. He is fraternally affiliated with the Masons, holds membership in the Presbyterian Church, and as a voter maintains an independent attitude.

In 1914 Mr. Brown was united in marriage with Miss Arvida Maryott, who was born in Dodge County, and to this union there have been born two children: Oravetta and Dorathea.

EDWARD N. MORSE came to Nebraska almost immediately after the close of his loyal service as a soldier of the Union in the Civil war, and nearly two years before Nebraska was admitted to the Union. He was one of the pioneer merchants of Fremont, and for over half a century until his death one of the city and county's ablest business men and most public spirited citizens, fully earning the high esteem paid him during his lifetime and the many tributes of honor given after his death.

He was born in 1846 in Knox County, Illinois, where he was reared and educated. His parents were Nelson D. and Amanda (Glass) Morse, the former a native of New York State and the latter of Ohio. They were married in Illinois. Nelson D. Morse was a stonemason by trade, and was a very prominent member of the Masonic fraternity, serving as grand master of the Grand Lodge of Illinois as well as lecturer of the Grand Lodge. In 1848 he went out to California and while on the Pacific Coast organized a number of pioneer Masonic lodges. He died when his son Edward was a boy. The only other child is Mrs. Emma J. Brown, a widow living in Iowa. The mother died in Iowa, and was a devout member of the Christian Church.

Edward N. Morse was about fifteen years old when the Civil war began. As soon as he became eligible in 1863 he enlisted in Battery H of the Second Illinois Light Artillery. He served two years until the close of the war, and was in a number of campaigns including the great battle of Franklin, Tennessee. After his honorable discharge he returned to Illinois, but two weeks later came to Nebraska Territory in 1865. The work that brought him to the territory was employment during the construction of the Union Pacific Railroad. He was practically without financial resources when he came here, and his individual earning power, his prestige as a loyal citizen, and his great capacity for friendship gave him the advantages that made him successful when he established one of the pioneer mercantile enterprises at Fremont. For several years he continued his business as a merchant at the little village, but in 1868 began supplying in a modest way the local demands for ice. Probably no other business man of the state had a longer continuous connection with the ice business than Mr. Morse, who founded and until his death was nominally head of the Fremont Ice and Sand Company He was its principal owner, as well as president and general manager The business is a corporation with capital of $18,000 He was also a director in the First National Bank of Fremont, a stockholder in the Pathfinder Hotel, and was owner of a large amount of valuable real estate in his home city.

By many years of hard work Mr Morse thoroughly satisfied his modest and honorable ambition for material accumulations, and all the time he gave something of himself and his influence to the welfare of friends and community He was an unfaltering democrat in politics, served several terms on the Municipal Council of Fremont, but his greatest hobby was education and for about thirty years he was a member of the Board of Education and its president at the time of his death He was a valued member of the Fremont Commercial Club, serving at one time as president In Masonry he was secretary of the local lodge several years, was active in various Masonic bodies, and a thirty-second degree Scottish Rite Mason and Shriner. He was also a member of the Independent Order of Odd Fellows, and for fifteen years commander of the local post of the Grand Army of the Republic and for an equal time a member of the Soldiers' Relief Committee of Dodge County

His prominence as a business man and a citizen can be well understood even from this brief outline of his activities He was at once one of the oldest and best known men of Fremont, and the community felt a large sense of loss when the news came of his death at San Diego, California, June 30, 1920

In October, 1870, he married Miss Emma J Goodman, who died in 1886 She was the mother of five children, but only one is now living, Edna, wife of William S Balduff of Fremont In 1887 Mr Morse married Miss Lillian L Green, who keeps her home at 320 West Military Avenue in Fremont She became the mother of six children, five of whom are living, as follows Harry S, who was the active associate of his father in business, and for several years executive manager of the Fremont Ice and Sand Company, Jennie C, formerly a popular teacher in the Fremont schools, is the wife of Alfred Carstens of Fremont, May, who gave much of her time to her father's business until his death; Edith M, who is secretary for the Fremont superintendent of schools, and Robert S Robert S enlisted in July, 1917, for service in the World war and was with the colors twenty-three months, though an attack of influenza prevented him from accompanying his regiment overseas. He has a soldier's land claim near Baggs, Wyoming He is now married and living in Fremont and connected with the Fremont Ice and Sand Company

Dan Swanson. One of the most prominent men of Dodge County is Dan Swanson, member of the Lower House of the State Assembly, and commissioner of public lands and buildings, with headquarters at Fremont He is one of the best-known men in this part of the state, and has not only acquired distinction as a public official of unquestioned probity, but also as a business man of recognized acumen, much of his efforts as such being directed along the line of extensive realty operations

Mr Swanson was born in Sweden on May 1, 1857, a son of Swan Pierson and Maria (Anderson) Swanson, both of whom were born and reared in Sweden, where they rounded out their useful lives, he being an extensive landowner and farmer and a man of prominence locally He and his wife had eight children, of whom three are now living,

Dan Swanson

namely. Matilda, who is unmarried, lives in Sweden; Amelia, who is also unmarried and a resident of Sweden, and Dan, whose name heads this review The parents belonged to the Lutheran Church At one time the father was very wealthy, but lost some of his means as he grew older.

Growing up in his native land Dan Swanson acquired an excellent educational training in the public schools and Lund University at Lund, Sweden, and after completing his studies became a clerk in a general store In 1877 he came to the United States, and for a time after landing worked in a tobacco store in Connecticut However, one of his sisters had located in Nebraska, and Mr Swanson joined her and lived at Wahoo, although he had the misfortune to lose his sister within two weeks after they were reunited During the time he was at that point he was engaged in clerking, but in 1892 came to Dodge County and obtained employment in the store owned by Mr Bloomenthal at Fremont, where he remained for six or seven years, and was promoted to be manager of this large department store His attention was then turned toward real estate, and he gained a working knowledge of the business with Richard Keen & Company, and he maintained his connections with this concern until he was elected to the Legislature in 1900 and served in it for one term He was then appointed postmaster of Fremont in January, 1903, and served in that office for eight years and three months Mr. Swanson then went into the real estate business and carried it on very profitably as secretary and treasurer of the Fremont Real Estate Company, and was discharging the duties of these positions when, in 1918, he was elected commissioner of public lands and buildings In 1920 he ran for re-election as commissioner of public lands and buildings without opposition with reference to his nomination on the republican ticket In this election he received the largest vote for re-election of any candidate in the state, his majority being 110,744 votes.

In March, 1884, Mr Swanson was united in marriage with Matilda Streed, born in Sweden, who came to the United States with her parents when she was only six years old They settled at Wahoo Mrs. Swanson is a daughter of John Streed, who was a merchant tailor of Wahoo for many years. Following the death of his wife, Mr Streed returned to Sweden and died there. Mr and Mrs Swanson became the parents of three sons, namely Fred W., who is bookkeeper and assistant manager of the Fremont Beverage Company of Fremont; Carl, who is employed in the state engineering department at Lincoln, Nebraska, and Ray, who was employed in the Ashland Bank for a number of years, is now engaged in conducting large realty operations The family are Lutherans Mr Swanson has always been active in state and local politics in the republican party, and has served as chairman of the County Central Committee of this party Since his election as commissioner he has devoted his care and attention to the duties appertaining to it and is rendering a very satisfactory service One of the acts of Mr Swanson was to raise the school tax assessments from $624,312 to $2,380,522, making an annual increase for the state of nearly $105,374 He is a man of broad vision and one who cannot be swerved from a position when he is convinced that his stand is the right one, and he believes that the responsibility rests upon him to see to it that the interests of the general public be protected and he is utterly fearless in living up to his own conception of his duty Such men as he are very valuable adjuncts to the state, and Mr Swanson's record proves that he is worthy of all the confidence reposed in him by his fellow citizens

PERRY SELDEN The record of pioneer activities and personalities in Washington County must always give an important place to the late Perry Selden He was an early freighter over the great plains, located in Washington County soon after the close of the Civil war, and his name is especially associated with the community of Blair where Mrs Selden is still living and Blair is also the home of his daughter, Mrs L A. Williams

Perry Selden was born at Hornellsville, New York, May 2, 1842 When he was twelve years of age his parents came West and settled at Omaha, then a river town and an outfitting post for the caravans of commerce and travel that started for the West and Northwest Perry Selden received his early education in Michigan, but could not long be kept out of the current of western life which surged through Omaha At the age of eighteen he began driving freighting wagons to the Far West, and he also carried mail over the plains. He was engaged in this adventurous occupation until 1867, when he returned to Omaha He completed his education with one year in Grinnell College

In 1869 Perry Selden came to Washington County and homesteaded and in a few years had achieved a place of leadership in county affairs Besides farming he engaged in the newspaper business and was editor and proprietor of the Blair Pilot for a number of years. A stanch republican, he was elected to the Legislature in 1876 and he also held the office of county judge of Washington County Judge Selden is remembered as a man absolutely fearless, honest, straightforward, possessing sound judgment in business and his record is one that can be recalled with distinct pride He was superintendent of the Yankton Indian Agency Government School at Yankton, South Dakota, and Mrs Selden was matron from 1884 to 1888 Judge Selden's death occurred September 16, 1896 He was affiliated with the Knights of Pythias and the Independent Order of Odd Fellows

On April 9, 1869, Judge Selden married Eliza Newell, member of an even earlier family of settlers in Washington County She was born at Amherst, Massachusetts, October 12 1843, a daughter of Samuel and Rebecca (Hall) Newell Her parents settled in Washington County, Nebraska, in 1865, when she was twenty-two years of age, and her father homesteaded and became one of the very substantial farmers in the Blair community where he lived out his life

Mr and Mrs Selden became the parents of four children, only two of whom are now living, Mrs L A Williams of Blair and J. W Selden, a lawyer at Tacoma, Washington

Minnie A Selden was born April 28 1870, on the homestead of her Grandfather Selden, who settled there in 1854 and which has since been incorporated in the City of Omaha Miss Selden was reared and educated at Blair and on August 16, 1893, became the wife of Lyman A Williams

Mr Williams was born at Middleton, Wisconsin, November 24, 1869, and came to Blair in 1891 He was well educated and for several years was a successful teacher in the schools of Scribner and Blair, and Mrs Williams also did work as a teacher in the schools of these communities Mr Williams had completed his education in the Plattville State Normal of Wisconsin After the death of Judge Selden he was editor of the Blair Pilot for a number of years, also served as mayor of the town, and for a number of years has enjoyed a distinctive success in the insurance field He was formerly general superintendent of agencies for the Guarantee Fund Life Insurance Company and for the past seven or eight years has maintained his business headquarters at Omaha, and directs the agency work of his company in the states of Iowa and Nebraska Mr Williams also owns two farms in Western Nebraska and another farm in California

The two children of Mr and Mrs Williams are Bert Selden Williams, born June 17, 1900, and Letha A, born March 8, 1911. The daughter is still in school The son Bert, now attending the State University of Nebraska at Lincoln, is also working with his father in the insurance business Bert Williams was in training for a time at Fort Sheridan and also as a member of the Student Army Training Corps at Lincoln On August 31, 1918, he married and has a son, George Bert

Mr Williams is a thirty-second degree Scottish Rite Mason and Shriner and has been deeply interested in the success of the republican party and has participated in several local campaigns Mrs Williams is a member of the Methodist Episcopal Church She and her mother have long been prominent in fraternal and social and educational affairs at Blair. Mrs Williams is a member of the Eastern Star and a past matron of the Chapter, present secretary, also served as Grand Martha for one year She and her mother are members of the Daughters of the American Revolution and both are active in the work of the Woman's Relief Corps, one of the strong organizations in Blair Mrs Williams has been president of the local corps about seven years Both are members of the Rebekahs and have filled the various chairs in that order Mrs Williams took a prominent part in the organization of the Woman's Auxiliary to the American Legion and served as county chairman of the Red Cross after the close of the great war

REV A M. ANDERSEN, of Blair, is one of the oldest and most prominent ministers of the Danish Lutheran Church in the West More than forty years ago he did his first missionary work among the scattered communities of western Nebraska He first came to Blair in the early '80s, and while his duties have called him away from Washington County at different times, his chief interests and work have centered at Blair Rev Mr Andersen was the founder of Dana College at Blair, and for a number of years has been editor of the Danskeren, published at Blair by the Danish Lutheran Publishing House, a journal of wide circulation throughout the West

Rev Mr Andersen was born in Denmark March 8 1847, son of Anders Jorgensen and Maren (Andersen) Andersen His parents, who spent all their lives on a farm in Denmark, were devout Lutherans, and had seven children, five sons and two daughters Three are still living Therkel was for many years a teacher in a private school in Denmark and is now retired The second is Rev A M Andersen, and the third is Jens a retired wheelwright still living in Denmark

A M Andersen acquired a public school education in Denmark, attending a high school at Ryslinge Fuen He was a young man of twenty-five when he came to the United States in 1872 His first destination was Madison, Wisconsin, but during the summer he worked on a farm in Orfordville in Rock County, and in the fall of 1872 he removed to Minneapolis and there took up active study in preparation for the ministry of the Danish Lutheran Church He spent two terms in a seminary, and in 1874 took examination and was ordained to the ministry October 11, 1874 While preaching during the summer he taught a term of school at Elmdale, Minnesota, and when ordained the church gave him a missionary assignment in Nebraska For a year and a half he was located at Dannebrog in Howard County, Nebraska, having charge of the local church and being missionary pastor for five other churches at a distance of from 10 to 120 miles from Dannebrog It was a new country and Mr Andersen's duties involved strenuous labor and all the difficulties of pioneer travel He frequently rode great distances on horseback, and also had a buggy to which he hitched a mule. On leaving Nebraska he was pastor of a church at Racine, Wisconsin, two and a half years, but in the fall of 1879 returned to Nebraska and located in Burk County. In 1882 he began his work at Blair, and the following year moved his family to that city, built a home, and also erected the first church of his denomination Soon afterward he entered the work of organizing an institution of higher learning He secured a donation from local citizens to the amount of $3,000, while the church board furnished about $4,000 This was the fund with which Trinity Seminary and Preparatory School was established, though the first real work of instruction was done in Mr. Andersen's own home in 1884 He continued as president of the college from its beginning until 1889 On retiring from that post he took charge of a church at Hampton, in Hamilton County, Nebraska, where he remained five years On returning to Blair he became a member of the theological faculty of the college, and continued in that work until the school was taken over by another branch of the church and given its present name of Dana College For a time Mr Andersen was pastor of a church at Viborg, South Dakota, and on his return to Blair he became editor of the Danskeren

The Danskeren was established in 1892 and is one of the oldest publications of the Danish Lutheran Church in the western states It was for a time published twice a week and has a circulation between 3,000 and 4,000 copies Mr Andersen for a number of years has devoted his time and energies to this publication, though he has also performed incidental work of importance in connection with other departments of his church In politics he is a republican

March 5, 1875, Mr Andersen married Laurina Marie Larsen, a native of Denmark They are the parents of seven children Agnes Christina, wife of George W Larsen, a farmer at Beresford, South Dakota, Andrew M, a farmer at Wakonda, South Dakota, Silas C, studying medicine at the University of Minnesota, Miss Emma A, at home, Anton M., proprietor of a men's furnishings store at Ringsted, Iowa, Ruthven C, a teacher in the schools of Washington County, and Allen Emil, a student in the Nebraska State University at Lincoln

HARRY HIGLEY was one of the very successful business men and leading citizens of Blair for a number of years Besides the importance attaching to his individual career, his name is interesting since it recalls one of the very first pioneer families of Washington County The Higleys have been well known in this section of the state for sixty years

Harry Higley was born at Waukesha, Wisconsin September 12, 1861, son of Thomas and Sarah E (Welch) Higley His parents were natives of Wisconsin, and about 1862 they came west and settled in Washington County, Nebraska Thomas Higley was postmaster of a town in Washington County during the Civil war For many years he was a successful merchant, and he died at Kearney while his wife passed away at Blair She was an active member of the Congregational Church They were the parents of four sons, the only one now living being Vernon, a resident of Davenport, Iowa, who for twenty-four years has been employed in the United States Arsenal at Rock Island

Harry Higley grew up in Washington County when it was a pioneer region, acquired a common school education in the schools of that time and his mature years were a progressive record of sound business achievement For a number of years before his death he was proprietor of a high-class confectionery and wholesale ice cream business at Blair

Mr Higley's death on March 3, 1919, was a severe blow to the community in which he had lived for many years He was one of the prominent Masons in Washington County, had filled all the chairs in the Blue Lodge, was an eminent commander of Knights Templar Commandery, also a Shriner, and was affiliated with the Independent Order of Odd Fellows and Knights of Pythias Mrs Higley is an active member of the Eastern Star and is one of the officials of her Chapter Both Mr and Mrs Higley were identified with the Episcopal Church

Some years before his death Mr. Higley built a large home on South Street and Mrs. Higley still occupies that residence in Blair

Mr Higley was twice married, his wives being sisters His first wife was Mary E Cain, and after her death he married Miss Sadie Cain, on June 8, 1904 By the first union he had five children, and the two now living are Mrs Eva Cook, a clerk in the Blair postoffice, and Myron E, a salesman living at Ogden, Utah Mrs Sadie Higley was born at O'Neill, Nebraska, and has the distinction of having been the first girl born in that town. She is a daughter of Thomas and Elizabeth (Miller) Cain, who still live at O'Neill Her father is a retired farmer and has been identified with agricultural affairs in Nebraska for a long period of years He was born in Ireland and his wife in England. Mrs Higley is the second of three living children Her older sister is Mrs John Ratterman, of Columbus, Nebraska, and her younger sister, Elizabeth, is a stenographer at Los Angeles, California Mrs Higley's parents are active members of the Catholic Church, and her father is a republican

MRS MARY M SIEKKOTTER, a resident of Blair, is a daughter of the late Soren Jensen, long prominently identified with the agricultural community of Washington County Mrs Siekkotter's first husband was John Reeh, whose citizenship in Washington County also deserves some reference on these pages.

John Reeh was born in Germany in 1870, and the following year his parents brought him to the United States The family were early settlers in Washington County, and his father was an honored resident of Blair at the time of his death John Reeh took up the vocation of farming and acquired and managed some important interests in Washington County. He was a man of good judgment, successful and a highly esteemed friend and neighbor He died in 1903 He was a member of the German Lutheran Church and the Modern Woodmen of America

Mrs Siekkotter by her marriage to John Reeh had three children Lyle, employed in the State Bank of Blair, Blanche, a successful teacher in the schools of Tekamah, Nebraska, and Odella, who graduated from the Blair High School in 1920

In 1905 Mrs John Reeh was married to Mr Charles Siekkotter of Blair Mr Siekkotter was the owner of some extensive and valuable farming lands in Sarpey County, Nebraska, and managed that property until his death, which occurred in 1908 Mr and Mrs Siekkotter had one daughter, Gladys, now attending school Mr Siekkotter was a member of the Lutheran Church, and his widow and children are members of the Baptist faith In politics he was a republican

The parents of Mrs Siekkotter, Soren and Anna Sina (Jensen) Jensen, were both natives of Denmark They came to the United States when young people, settled at Omaha, and when most of eastern Nebraska was still a wilderness they located on a homestead in Washington County Her father became one of the well-to-do farmers of the region and spent his last years in comfort and the enjoyment of the fruits of his early trials and labors He died in 1917, and his widow is still living at Blair They had thirteen children, all of whom are still living, and including them and their children and grandchildren there are now a hundred descendants of this worthy couple of Danish pioneers in Washington County Soren Jensen was a member of the Danish Lutheran Church and a democrat in politics.

FRANK JAHNEL Formerly engaged in agricultural pursuits in Washington County for many years, and now well known in insurance circles of Blair and the surrounding country Frank Jahnel is accounted as one of the successful retired farmers and leading representatives of fire risk companies in his locality His career has been one in which hard work, enlightened views and sound integrity have all played a prominent part, and the not inconsiderable success that has come to him has been well and fairly earned

Mr Jahnel was born in Barlt, Holstein, Germany, December 8, 1851, a son of Frank and Margaret (Kruetzfield) Jahnel, both of whom passed their entire lives in Germany and died in the faith of the Lutheran Church The father, a man of excellent education, was a school teacher throughout his life Mr Jahnel has one brother, August, who when last heard from was still a resident of Germany Frank Jahnel, of this review, secured his education in the public schools of Germany, and had passed his majority, in 1873, when he came to the United States At first he made settlement in Missouri, where he remained about two months, then came to Nebraska and located at Grand Island, working there two years, when he went to Omaha and clerked a couple of years He then located on tax title land in Washington County, from which he secured two crops while breaking it Later Mr Jahnel secured other land, adding to his holdings from time to time as his resources increased, and at present is the owner of 600 acres of well-cultivated property lying in Washington County In 1907, after his long and successful career as an agriculturist, he retired from operations as a tiller of the soil and took up his home at Blair, where he occupies a modern and comfortable residence At the time of his arrival he began selling fire insurance, and at the present time is the accredited representative of the Columbia Underwriters Farm Insurance Company of Omaha and the German Mutual Fire Insurance Company He has built up an excellent farm insurance business, which not only adds to his income, but occupies his energetic mind All that Mr. Jahnel owns in the world he has made himself, for he has never relied upon others, preferring to depend upon his own ability, the strength of his mind and the skill of his hands He is a faithful member of the Lutheran Church In politics a republican, he has been a prominent and leading factor in his party in the community for many years, and for twenty-five years was school treasurer For six years he was a member of the Board of County Commissioners, during which time the new courthouse was erected, and in 1903 and 1905 he was sent as the representative of his district to the Nebraska General Assembly, in which body his work was constructive and beneficial He is a member of the Masons

Rainsford C. Brownell

Mr Jahnel was married in 1876, at Omaha to Miss Bertha M Munster, who was born in Holstein, Germany, and to this union there were born eight children Fritz, who is carrying on operations on his father's farm, Frank, who owns a farm in Washington County, Willie, who is farming on his father's property, Lena, who married O E Anderson, a farmer of Wisconsin; Dora, who married Charles Cravens, a farmer of Pierce County, Nebraska; Rosie, who married Ed Mathiesen, in the clothing business at Blair, Elsie, the wife of Elmer Miller, a farmer of Washington County, and Christ, farming on his father's property. The mother of these children died July 16, 1907, and October 8, 1908, Mr. Jahnel married Mrs Sophia (Benck) Alberts, a widow, at Sterling, Illinois Mrs Alberts was born in Marne, Holstein, Germany, November 1, 1851, and came to the United States in 1873, first settled at Sterling, Illinois, but later, in 1908, came to Nebraska By her former marriage she has two sons John, auditor for a wholesale house at Chicago, and Albertus, a fruit rancher of Santa Ana, California

RAINSFORD C BROWNELL was a lad of twelve years at the time his parents came to Nebraska and established the family home in Saunders County, where he was reared to adult age, was afforded the advantages of the public schools of the period and where he eventually became a successful exponent of farm industry, besides which he became a leader in the breeding and raising of fine standard-bred horses in Nebraska After retiring from his farm he established his residence at North Bend, Dodge County, where he has since remained and where he is a popular and influential citizen

Mr Brownell was born in the Province of New Brunswick, Canada, on January 12, 1860, and is a son of John H and Mary (Taylor) Brownell, who were born and reared in the province and who were honored pioneer citizens of Saunders County, Nebraska, at the time of their deaths, the father having passed away in 1886, at the age of seventy-four years, and the mother having been eighty-six years of age at the time of her death, in 1904 In New Brunswick John H Brownell had not only followed farm enterprise but had also operated a sawmill and was a successful representative of the lumber business in his community In 1872 he came with his family to Nebraska and purchased a tract of land in Saunders County, where he devoted the remainder ot his active life to agricultural pursuits and the raising of live stock He was a republican in his political allegiance, was affiliated with the Masonic fraternity and both he and his wife held membership in the Methodist Episcopal Church While a resident of his native province he served for some time as justice of the peace His son, William J Brownell, was a sea captain for many years and was a resident of New Brunswick at the time of his death He was the father of ten sons and one daughter, and of the number four are living, Rainsford C, whose name introduces this sketch; H C, engaged in the real estate business in the City of Denver, Colorado, A R, living retired at Aurora, Hamilton County, Nebraska, and T C, a resident of Hay Springs, Sheridan County, where he is living retired

Rainsford C Brownell early began to contribute his quota to the work of his father's farm in Saunders County, where also he initiated in due time his independent career as an agriculturist and stock grower There he eventually became the owner of a well improved landed estate of 640 acres, and substantial success attended his progressive activities as a representative of farm enterprise He achieved special reputation in the raising of standard-bred horses, and from his farm went forth some of the finest horses that have maintained the reputation of Nebraska in turf events Thus it may be noted that Mr Brownell raised and owned the famous gelding, "Spill," which made a splendid record and won more cash prizes on the turf than any other horse in Nebraska On his farm property Mr Brownell made the best of modern improvements, and in all ways he exemplified the most scientific and advanced methods and policies applied to farm industry He remained on the farm until 1912, when he removed to North Bend, Dodge County, where he has since lived retired, though he still owns his valuable farm property in Saunders County He has taken loyal and vital interest in the welfare and progress of his attractive home city of North Bend, where he served three terms as mayor and gave a most progressive and satisfactory administration. He is unwavering in his allegiance to the republican party and has been influential in its local councils, as shown by the fact that in 1895 he was elected to represent Saunders County in the State Legislature, in which he served one term In that county he served as a member of the School Board of his district, and within the period of his residence at North Bend he has given effective service as a member of its Board of Education He is affiliated with the Masonic fraternity, including the Mystic Shrine, and is identified also with the Modern Woodmen of America He and his family are members of the Methodist Episcopal Church

The year 1904 recorded the marriage of Mr Brownell to Mrs Cedelia (Easom) Collins, who was born and reared in Nebraska and who is a daughter of the late William H Easom Mr. and Mrs Brownell have one son, Donald L, who is attending the public schools of North Bend Mrs Brownell by her former marriage has a daughter, Miss Agnes Collins, who is a teacher of French in the schools of Lafayette, Indiana

William Douglas Gross Among the best-known families of Blair, Nebraska, is that bearing the name of Gross, which was founded in this state by William Douglas Gross, one of the early settlers of the state and long a resident of Blair, where he was well known as a public official He was born at Hillsboro, County Albert, New Brunswick, Canada, on April 13, 1837, a son of Richard and Mary (Steeves) Gross The Gross family was long associated with the history of the American colonies, and Richard Gross, grandparent, was born at Hingham, Massachusetts, and was reared there, but in young manhood he moved to New Brunswick, Canada, and there rounded out his useful life Mrs Gross was a descendant of Henrick Steeves, who with his seven sons founded the Village of Hillsboro

Growing up in his native village William D Gross attended its schools and learned the carpenter trade, which he followed at Hillsboro, New Brunswick; Boston, Massachusetts, and Omaha, Nebraska, coming west to the latter city in 1868 In 1869 he moved on a homestead in Grant Precinct, Washington County, proving it up in 1872 In the meanwhile he was engaged during the winter months in working for the Union Pacific Railroad in the extension of its tracks and the erection of necessary sheds

In 1873 Mr Gross moved to Blair, where he embarked in the hotel business and carried it on for many years, and at the same time he became interested in different enterprises, which, together with his agricultural holdings gained him a wide acquaintance throughout Washington and adjoining counties

During the war between the states Mr Gross served as sergeant of Company E, Third Massachusetts Cavalry, from April 1, 1864, until October 8, 1865, and was honorably discharged at Fort Leavenworth, Kansas During his period of service he was with General Sheridan in the Shenandoah Valley, Virginia

A republican, stanch in his support of the principles of that party, he became a leading figure in it, and was acting mayor of Blair during one year, and was a member of its city council for a number of years In 1881 he was elected sheriff of Washington County, and held that office for four years, proving himself a fearless and competent official, and also during his second term in the same office During 1896-1897 and 1897-1898 he was supervisor of Blair, representing it on the county board He was a Mason, belonging to Howard Lodge No 15, Hillsboro, New Brunswick, and he was also a member of the post at Blair of the Grand Army of the Republic

On November 15, 1865, Mr. Gross was married at Hillsboro, New Brunswick, to Maria Theresa Martin, a daughter of George Martin, of Saint John, New Brunswick. Mr and Mrs Martin died when Mrs Gross was a child They were of Irish descent and were very early settlers of New Brunswick

Mrs Gross was a brave woman, and used to remain alone with her little children when Mr Gross was away from home working on the railroad, at a time when the surrounding country was practically unsettled Mr Gross died November 4, 1904, after an illness extending over ten years, but his widow survives him and is very well known in this region, particularly because of her hospitality and her thoughtfulness to those who are deprived of active participation in the life of the community by reason of disability She is a member of the Eastern Star and the Woman's Relief Corps

Anna Gross, daughter of William D Gross and his wife, was one year old when brought by her parents to Omaha, Nebraska On September 25, 1884, she was married to James H Stewart, a son of James S Stewart, one of the pioneers of Washington County She was graduated from the Blair city schools, and for many years has taken a constructive part in their development Her two daughters are Abbie and Marguerite, both of whom were graduated from the Blair High School and the University of Nebraska, and both are well known among the alumni of the latter institution. Abbie Stewart was married to Lyle D Milliken, a son of James Milliken, of Fremont, Nebraska, where the family is well known both socially and in a business way. Mr and Mrs Milliken have one son, James Stewart Milliken, named for his two grandfathers, James Stewart and James Milliken Marguerite has also studied at Columbia Univeristy, New York City, and the University of Colorado, and is now a very successful teacher of home economics in the Smith-Hughs schools of Wyoming and Nebraska. The second daughter of William D Gross and his wife is Miss Frances Gross, an educator of Omaha, Nebraska, and one of the principals of its city schools. She has been connected with the schools of Blair and Lincoln, Nebraska. She belongs to the Eastern Star at Blair Both she and her sister are members of the Daughters of the Revolution, she maintaining membership with Isaac Saddler, and Mrs Stewart with Nikumi Chapter, Daughters of the American Revolution.

These ladies are entitled to membership in this organization through members of the Gross family. Two brothers, Isaac and Edmund Gross, came from England to Massachusetts in the seventeenth century, receiving grants of land, and their descendants served in the American Revolution This land, received by Isaac in 1636, and by Edmund in 1639, was around Hingham and Andover, Massachusetts Their line of the family descends direct from Isaac Gross, and another Isaac Gross was one of Major Thaxter's company in the Crown Point Expedition of 1756

W W WILKINSON Of the men who have lent dignity of character, excellence of labor and largeness of general co-operation to affairs in Washington County for a considerable period, few are more widely known or generally respected in their neighborhood than W. W Wilkinson, now living at Blair It has been the privilege of this man to have lived close to the heart of nature, to have partaken generously of her awards and to have responded with enthusiasm and clear judgment to her opportunities for advancement

Mr. Wilkinson comes of sturdy and honorable lineage and one which has furthered the universal gospel of industry He was born at Elk City, Nebraska, in 1876, a son of Thomas and Lucy (Jackson) Wilkinson, natives of England, who upon their arrival in the United States, about 1865, settled near Elk City In that community Thomas Wilkinson purchased land at from $2 50 to $5 per acre and continued to be engaged in agricultural pursuits until moving to Blair about 1886, in which year he retired He continued to make Blair his home during the remainder of his life and died in July, 1912, since which time his worthy widow, who survives him, has made her home with her daughter at Omaha They were the parents of four children Ida, who married J F Smith, engaged in the manufacture of brick at Omaha, Emma, who married Herman Shields, also engaged in the brick business in that city; Nettie, who died in 1913, as the wife of George B Dyball, of Omaha; and W W The parents were faithful members of the Episcopal Church Thomas Wilkinson joined the Masonic fraternity at an early day and was a member thereof throughout his life A democrat in politics, he took an active interest in civic affairs and served as postmaster at Blair under the administration of President Cleveland, in addition to which he was a member of the board of county commissioners for a number of years and of the board of school directors He was a well-to-do, self-made man and one who had the respect and esteem of the people of his community A more complete sketch of Mr and Mrs Thomas Wilkinson appears elsewhere in this publication.

W W Wilkinson attended the public schools of Blair and Wesleyan University, Lincoln, but after two years in the latter institution, returned to his home town, where he assisted his father and also worked in the postoffice At the end of his father's term as postmaster the young man began to give his undivided attention to agricultural pursuits, in which he engaged until 1920, at that time retiring and renting his farm in Washington County. When he gave up active pursuits he moved to Blair, where he now occupies the attractive and comfortable home in which his parents formerly lived He is a Royal Arch Mason and takes a keen interest in fraternal work, and in political matters maintains an independent attitude

In 1901 Mr Wilkinson was united in marriage with Miss Mae Pierce, who was born at Blair, daughter of E C Pierce, one of the earliest undertakers of the state who is now living in retirement at Blair Three children have been born to this union Marjorie, born in 1902, Alice, born in 1906; and Thomas, born in 1909, the latter two now attending school Mrs Wilkinson, a woman of numerous graces and accomplishments, is an active member of the Episcopal Church and belongs to the Daughters of the American Revolution

MAURICE MEHERNS In nearly every community are individuals who, by innate ability and sheer force of character, win for themselves conspicuous places in public esteem. Such a one is the well-known gentleman whose name appears above, who has been identified with the history of Washington County for about forty years, practically his entire life having been spent here His mature years have been closely interwoven with the material growth and development of the county, while his career as a progressive man of affairs and an able public official has been synonymous with all that is upright and honorable in citizenship

Maurice Meherns was born in Harrison County, Iowa, on November 29, 1875, and is the son of Gayhart and Lucy (Pipher) Meherns, the former a native of Germany and the latter of Tennessee The father came to Washington County, Nebraska, in young boyhood and received the major part of his educational training in the public schools here He was married in Blair and for a time devoted his energies to farming He then engaged in the flour and feed business in Blair, which he successfully conducted up to 1910, when he retired from active business pursuits, and he and his wife are making their home at Long Beach, California They are members of the Church of Christ and in politics he is a republican. They became the parents of five children, as follows: Maurice is the immediate subject of this sketch, Zena became the wife of J H Warrick, a farmer at Lorenzo, Nebraska, W H and Alex, both of Minneapolis, Minnesota, and Tressa, who is the wife of Ross VanLiew, a farmer near Blair.

Maurice Meherns was reared under the parental roof and secured his education in the public schools His boyhood years were spent on a farm, and to that vocation he devoted his energies until 1905, when he engaged in the flour and feed business with his father. Five or six years later he entered the employ of an oil company, and while thus employed, in 1916, he was elected to the office of Sheriff of Washington County, entering the office in January, 1917 So satisfactory was his discharge of his official duties that two years later he was elected to succeed himself, and is thus the present incumbent of the office His official career has been characterized by the faithful performance of his duties, and he has won the confidence and respect of the people of Washington County thereby

In March, 1898, Mr Meherns was married to Ella Reed, who came to Washington County a number of years prior thereto with her parents, both of whom are now deceased To Mr and Mrs Meherns have been born four children, Sterling, Maude, Milford and Helen Politically Mr. Meherns gives his support to the democratic party and fraternally is a member of the Independent Order of Odd Fellows and the Woodmen of the World He is a member of the Baptist Church, but his wife is affiliated with the Church of Christ Such, in brief, has been the record of Mr. Meherns, than whom a more whole-souled or popular man it would be difficult to find within the borders of Washington County, where he has labored not only for his own individual advancement, but also for the improvement of the entire community, whose interests he has ever had at heart.

E. B. CARRIGAN It is a well-attested maxim that the greatness of a state or nation lies not in the machinery of government, nor even in its institutions, but rather in the sterling qualities of the individual citizen, in his capacity for high and unselfish effort and his devotion to the public welfare In these particulars he whose name appears at the head of this review has conferred honor and dignity on his county and community, and as an elemental part of history it is consonant that there should be recorded a resume of his career, with the object in view of noting his connection with the progress of one of the most flourishing and progressive sections of the commonwealth, as well as his official relations with the administration of the legal affairs of his county

E B Carrigan was born in De Soto, Washington County, Nebraska, on the 5th day of November, 1869, and is the son of John and Carrie L (Palmer) Carrigan, the former a native of Maryland and the latter of Pennsylvania They were married in Illinois and in about 1867 came to Washington County While living in Bureau County, Illinois, Mr. Carrigan had studied law and been admitted to the bar, and he first entered upon the practice of his profession in De Soto, Nebraska Subsequently he moved to Blair and took a prominent part in the early history of that city He built one of the first houses in that city and remained closely identified with the interests of that community up to the time of his death In the practice of the law John Carrigan early gained a leading position at the bar of his own county, and eventually he became celebrated throughout the state because of his special success in the practice of criminal law For many years he was connected with many of the most important and celebrated cases in the courts of this and other counties, and at the time of his death he was engaged in the celebrated Ketcham murder case In politics he gave his support to the democratic party His death occurred on April 21, 1880, and he is survived by his widow, who still resides at Blair They were the parents of two children, the subject of this sketch and Nora, the wife of Robert Smock, a merchant in Spokane, Washington

E B. Carrigan received his education in the public schools at Blair graduating from the high school, and he then entered Northwestern College in Iowa, where he was graduated He then gave his attention to the study of law, and in 1892 was admitted to the bar, since which time he has continuously been identified with the active professional life of this county He soon gained an enviable reputation as a successful practitioner and enjoyed a large clientele For twelve years he served as county attorney, and in 1918 was elected county judge, entering upon his official term in 1919 Since occupying the bench, Judge Carrigan has won the commendation of all classes by his fair and impartial rulings and his rendered decisions have been models of clearness and learning

On August 3, 1892, Judge Carrigan was married to Frances Lawson, a native of Pennsylvania, and they have become the parents of three children, namely: Phyllis, the wife of H C Morttock, an oil geologist at Chelsey, Oklahoma; Lila, the wife of G L Dixon, who is engaged in the insurance business at Blair, and Jack, who is a student in the law department of Michigan University, at Ann Arbor, Michigan

Judge Carrigan is a republican in his political views and he holds fraternal relations with the Independent Order of Odd Fellows and the Knights of Pythias Mrs Carrigan is a member of the Methodist Episcopal Church Judge Carrigan possesses in a high degree the elements that make men succesful, pre-eminent among his qualities

James Bradbury

Mary C Bradbury

being that sound judgment which is ordinarily called common sense He has the ability to grasp facts and infer their practical significance with almost unerring certainty, his good judgment extending to men as well as to related facts, for he possesses a keen insight into human nature. In all the relations of life he has displayed that public spirit and unswerving integrity that has commended him to the confidence and respect of all who know him

P T MITTERLING came to Fremont, Dodge County, about the time of attaining to his legal majority, and after here being identified with business enterprises for many years he was finally recognized as a specially eligible candidate for the office of clerk of the district court, to which position he was elected in 1916 and the duties of which he assumed at the beginning of the following year His facility in handling the work of this office has fully justified the popular choice which composed his installation therein, and he is one of the well known and distinctively popular officials of the county.

Mr. Mitterling was born at Richfield, Pennsylvania, December 21, 1867, and is a son of George S and Margaret (Wise) Mitterling, who likewise were born and reared in the old Keystone State, whence they came to Nebraska in 1888 and established their home at Fremont, where they still reside, in an attractive home at 105 East Twelfth Street, the father having passed the four-score milepost on the journey of life and being now retired from active business George S Mitterling followed the carriagemaker's trade in Pennsylvania for some time, and there also he operated and owned a flour mill prior to coming to Nebraska, besides which he served for a short time as a member of a Pennsylvania regiment in the Civil war During his active career at Fremont, Nebraska, he followed the carpenter's trade and became a successful contractor and builder He is a republican of the stanchest loyalty, is affiliated with the Grand Army of the Republic, and both he and his wife are earnest members of the Methodist Episcopal Church For several years Mr Mitterling gave efficient service as street commissioner of Fremont, and within his regime was effected noteworthy improvement of the thoroughfares of the city Of the six children only two are living and the subject of this review is the elder, the younger son being Dr E S Mitterling, an osteopathic physician, who is engaged in the practice of his profession at Webster City, Iowa

The public schools of his native state afforded P T Mitterling his early educational discipline, and after coming to Nebraska with his parents in 1888, he attended Fremont College for a time His initial business experience was gained as clerk in a shoe store in the City of Elkhart, Indiana, and in Fremont, Nebraska, he became a popular salesman in the shoe store of J Knowles, his service in this capacity continuing until he was elected to his present office, that of clerk of the district court, in 1916 He is a candidate for re-election without opposition His political faith is that of the republican party, and he is affiliated with the Independent Order of Odd Fellows, the Benevolent and Protective Order of Elks and the Fraternal Order of Eagles He still clings to the independence of bachelorhood and resides with his venerable parents in their pleasant home at Fremont

JAMES BRADBURY. After years of sincere and earnest endeavor, James Bradbury is now enjoying his ease and comfort at Hooper where he is regarded as one of the representative men of the place and a constructive element among its citizens He was born in Schuylkill County, Pennsylvania, March 5, 1850, a son of William and Anna (Marland) Bradbury, natives of Great Britain William Bradbury became a superintendent of a coal mine in Pennsylvania after his arrival in the United States He came to this country after his marriage, which occurred over 100 years ago. His wife was an orphan girl when he married her, and they became the parents of fourteen children, three of whom survive, namely Mary Ann, who is the wife of James Bracey, of Pennsylvania, William, who is a mechanic, and James, whose name heads this review.

James Bradbury was reared in his native state, where he attended the public schools and Mount Pleasant Seminary, and he worked around the coal mines, first as a mule driver and later as stationary engineer, and he also learned the carpenter trade In 1874 he left Pennsylvania for Dodge County, Nebraska, and during the season worked in the harvest fields He then came to Fremont and was employed by Peter Neabose, a contractor, and while with him assisted in the erection of the old Kittle Opera House and the Anderson store

Mr Bradbury, however, had come West with the idea of securing land, and after he had secured a little money from his carpenter work he came to Maple Creek and rented for a few years when he bought eighty acres of land, paying $10 an acre, and began farming He kept on adding to his farm until he had over 400 acres, and carried on general farming and stockraising until 1908, when he retired, moved to Hooper, and has maintained his residence there ever since

On June 29, 1874, Mr Bradbury was united in marriage with Mary Sweinhart, a native of Pennsylvania, born February 16, 1849, a daughter of Fred and Esther (Steirley) Sweinhart, both natives of Pennsylvania, where they died, and where he worked as a carriage maker Mr and Mrs Sweinhart had the following children Mrs Bradbury, and Elmyra and Howard, both of whom are deceased The children born to Mr and Mrs Bradbury are as follows· William, who is manager of the Latta Grain Company of Hooper; Esther, who is the wife of E M Havens of Hooper, Alice, who is the wife of Walter Skinner, a Dodge County farmer, May, who is deceased, Luruqua, the wife of William Meyer, vice president of the Dodge County State Bank; Mary, the wife of Earl Phillips, a farmer of St Edwards, Nebraska, James, who is a Dodge County farmer, Fred, who is with his brother James on the farm; Charles, who is a Dodge County farmer, Josephine, the wife of George Parker, a Dodge County farmer, and Sarah, deceased

Mr. Bradbury cast his first vote for General Grant for the presidency, and has continued to support the principles of the republican party ever since For twenty-five years he has been a director of District No 38 In religious belief Mrs Bradbury supports the creed of the German Reformed Church, while he is a Methodist They are fine people in every respect and have brought up a family of children who do them credit and are a valuable addition to the several communities in which they have settled

Frederick E Calkins, M D The technical ability and loyal stewardship that insure success and prestige in the exacting profession of medicine have been significantly exemplified in the career of Doctor Calkins, who is one of the representative physicians and surgeons of Dodge County, where he has been established in practice at Fremont, the county seat, since 1902, and where he has developed a substantial and profitable professional business

Doctor Calkins was born at Wyoming, Jones County, Iowa, October 7, 1866, and is a son of Kirkland James Calkins and Lorilla (Williams) Calkins, who were born in the State of New York and whose marriage was solemnized at Wyoming, Iowa, prior to the Civil war—a fact that indicates that they were pioneer settlers of the Hawkeye State When the Civil war was precipitated on the nation, Kirkland J Calkins enlisted in Company K, Twenty-Fourth Iowa Volunteer Infantry, with which regiment he served during the entire period of the conflict between the states of the North and the South, principally as a member of the gallant forces commanded by General Grant After the war he continued his residence in Iowa until 1873, when he came with his family to Nebraska and took a homestead claim in Polk County There he reclaimed and developed a good farm and continued his residence a number of years, when he retired, and he died February 14, 1920 His wife resides at York, the judicial center of the Nebraska county of that name. Of the five children, Doctor Calkins of this review, is the eldest, Lucy is the wife of Mark Ravenscroft of York, who is an extensive land owner, Dr Albert E is a dentist by profession and is engaged in practice at York; Dr Charles A is a dentist at York, and Dr Royal W is a physician and surgeon of Cortez, Colorado The father is a republican in politics, is affiliated with the Grand Army of the Republic, and he achieved substantial success through his active association with farm industry He is a son of Samuel Calkins, who was an early settler in Illinois, where he passed the major part of his life Royal S Williams, maternal grandfather of Doctor Calkins, was a pioneer in Iowa, where he continued to reside until his death

Doctor Calkins obtained his early education in the public schools of Wyoming, Iowa, and those of York County, Nebraska, he having been about seven years old when the family came to this state He finally returned to Iowa and completed a course in the high school at Wyoming, and in pursuance of his ambitious purpose he entered the medical department of the University of Iowa, in which he was graduated as a member of the Class of 1899 and with the well won degree of Doctor of Medicine. His professional novitiate was served at York, Nebraska, and later he engaged in practice at Hill City, South Dakota There he remained until 1902, when he came to Fremont, Nebraska, where he has since been engaged in general practice and where his noteworthy success represents the result of his ability, close application and effective ministrations He has served fully fifteen years as county physician, of which office he is now the incumbent, and for a number of years he was local surgeon for the Union Pacific Railroad He is state medical director of the Modern Woodmen of America, and is an active member of the Dodge County Medical Society and the Nebraska State Medical Society He is affiliated with the local Blue Lodge and Chapter of the Masonic fraternity and is a very active member and a past chancellor commander of Triumph Lodge No 32 of the Knights of Pythias, Fremont, Nebraska, which he represented in the Grand Lodge of the state for eight years He was a member of the medical board during the World war, devoting the greater part of his time to its work for several months, neglecting his private practice His political allegiance is given to the republican party

The year 1900 was marked by the marriage of Doctor Calkins to Miss Elizabeth T Dickerson, who was born and reared in Dodge County, where her father settled in the pioneer days She is a daughter of Edward Dickerson, who came to Nebraska in the Territorial period and who in the later '50s was engaged in overland freighting from Fremont to Denver, Colorado Doctor and Mrs Calkins have no children.

EDWIN W MARTIN, M D, is consistently to be designated as the dean of the medical profession in Dodge County, where he is still engaged in active general practice and where he has maintained his residence at Fremont, the county seat, since 1886 Here he has achieved the success that has not only been his due as an able and faithful physician and surgeon, but has also gained inviolable place in the confidence and high regard of his fellow citizens

Doctor Martin, in both the paternal and maternal lines, is a scion of fine old Kentucky ancestry, and is himself a native son of the Bluegrass State, within whose borders were born his grandfathers, William Martin and David Sellara who there passed their entire lives Doctor Martin was born near Cynthiana, Kentucky, March 11, 1845, and is a son of M D Martin and Zarilda Ann (Sellars) Martin, who continued their residence in that state during their entire lives the father having passed away in 1915 and the mother in 1918, both having been of venerable age at the time of death. Of their ten children Doctor Martin is the eldest of the four survivors; Emma is the wife of Rev. E W. Elliott, who is a clergyman of the Christian Church, and they reside at Glasgow, Kentucky, Belle is the wife of James G Van Daren, a retired farmer residing at Cynthiana, Kentucky, and George P is a farmer near Frankfort, that state The parents were earnest members of the Christian Church, and the father was affiliated with the Masonic fraternity and was a stalwart democrat in politics He served three terms in the Kentucky Legislature, and was one of the honored and influential citizens of his county, where he gave his active life to agricultural industry

Doctor Martin acquired his early education in the schools of his native city, and prior to preparing himself for his profession he had had a number of years' experience in retail mercantile business. Finally he entered one of the leading medical colleges in the City of Cincinnati, Ohio, and after his graduation in 1881, he was for five years engaged in practice in his native place, Cynthiana, Kentucky He then, in 1886, came to Nebraska and established his permanent home at Fremont, which has been the central stage of his earnest and successful professional activities during the intervening years The doctor was burdened with an indebtedness of about $4,000 when he arrived at Fremont, and for a time he was compelled to travel on foot in ministering to his patients He frequently traversed many miles in this way, but he did not need the muscular exercise to heighten his efficiency in his professional work, so that he did not deem it inconsistent when he was able to provide a horse and vehicle as a means of transportation in his visitations He has long controlled a good practice of a representative type, and has the affectionate regard of the community in which his able ministrations have been given He is essentially one of the representative physicians of Dodge County, has served as president of the Dodge County Medical Society, in the affairs of which he continues to take deep interest, and he is affiliated also with the Nebraska State Medical Society and the American Medical Association The doctor is the owner of a fine farm of 160 acres near Fremont, and in this city, in addition to his attractive home property he is the owner of six houses, all in the same block He is a democrat by conviction and ancestral predilection, is loyal and liberal as a citizen but has never desired public office, as he considers his profession worthy of his undivided time and attention, the while he trusts that he may be able to continue his humane ministrations until the close of his life

The year 1866 recorded the marriage of Doctor Martin to Miss Julia Doyle, who was born at Concord, Kentucky, and they have two children Kate is the wife of Albert O Morse, of Omaha, who has been for twenty years associated with the Nebraska Telephone Company, and M. Dell, who resides at Fremont, is the widow of Edward C. Blakesley Mr and Mrs Morse have an adopted daughter, Kate, who is six years old in 1920 Mrs Blakesley has one son, Edwin W, who is now a student in the Iowa State Agricultural College at Ames Doctor and Mrs Martin are members of the Christian Church

JOHN W GOFF A representative citizen of Dodge County, J W Goff has gained distinction not only for his activity and prominence in the business life and public affairs of Fremont, his home city, but for his service as a brave and courageous soldier in the Civil war He was born March 4, 1843, in Oneida County, New York, coming on the paternal side of New England ancestry

His father, Henry Goff, was born and bred in Connecticut Moving to New York, he bought land in Oneida County, and was there prosperously engaged in agricultural pursuits during his remaining years. He was identified with the Whigs until the formation of the republican party, when he became one of its ardent supporters. He was a strong abolitionist and prior to the Civil war was associated with the "Underground Railway" He married Elizabeth Sturdevant, a native of the Empire State, and of their eight children, two are living, as follows: James, a retired farmer of Waterloo, Iowa, and John W, the subject of this sketch Both parents were faithful members of the Methodist Episcopal Church

Brought up in New York State, John W. Goff was educated in the public schools and at different academies, and afterwards taught school three years, during vacations assisting in the labors of the home farm Enlisting in 1862 in Company G, one Hundred and Forty-Sixth New York Volunteer Infantry, he served three years in the Civil war, during the last ten months of the time having been confined in Andersonville Prison He took part in many of the important battles of the war, including among others, the engagements at Fredericksburg, Chancellorsville and the battle of the Wilderness While in prison Mr Goff suffered untold privations, and when at the end of the war he was released, was unconscious Recovering consciousness, he found himself in the Naval Academy at Annapolis, Maryland, from whence he was sent home, arriving there in a very weak and debilitated condition

Subsequently Mr Goff attempted to resume his studies for a college course, but his health would not permit Having partially recovered his former physical vigor, he took a commercial course of study, and later taught bookkeeping and mathematics in both Utica, New York, and the neighboring city, Syracuse Coming to Fremont, Nebraska, on March 1, 1869, to visit E. H Rogers, a pioneer banker of the city, he was induced to accept a position in his friend's banking institution, and has remained here since Resigning his position as bookkeeper with E H Rogers & Company in 1872, Mr Goff was for three years associated with Nye, Colson & Company, dealers in grain and lumber, but left that firm to enter the employ of L D Richards Proving himself eminently capable and trustworthy, he was later admitted to partnership with his employer, becoming a member of the firm of Richards, Keene & Company, and on the incorporation of this firm was made its vice president, which position he now holds

Mr Goff was at one time vice president of the Western Trust & Security Company, which was organized to make real estate loans, and which was later taken over by Richards, Keene & Company, and he was also vice president of the Security Savings Bank, which was formed in connection with the Western Trust & Security Company and was located in the rooms occupied by Richards, Keene & Company On the removal of the Security Savings Bank to the rooms of the Fremont National Bank Mr Goff became its president, which position he held for several years

Mr Goff married Miss Myra Gilley, a native of Maine, and they have two children, Daisy L, wife of Frank H Brown, a member of the Omaha and Chicago Grain exchanges, and Erma, wife of Fayette Leard, financial manager of the jobbing house of the Milligan Grocery Company, of Springfield, Missouri A prominent member of the republican party, Mr Goff has served two terms as city clerk, and as city assessor for the same length of time Fraternally he is a member of the Benevolent and Protective Order of Elks, and belongs to the Grand Army of the Republic. He is a member of the Country Club, which he has served as president two years, and is very fond of golf, being, as he says, "an enthusiastic, if not a good, player."

Mr. Goff is a very pleasing speaker, and had the distinction of being selected to deliver the address at the centennial anniversary of Lincoln, an address spoken of in very complimentary terms by the newspapers, and he was urged to repeat the address at other places He has also lectured to large audiences on his experiences at Andersonville, his talks being always interesting and entertaining

At seventy-seven years he is still actively engaged in business, and attributes his good health largely to his life-long habit of alternating work with play

John Sonin The history of every community reveals the fact that its real progress is the result of the vision and faith of a few men who in spite of obstacles and discouragements were willing to go ahead and invest heavily in its realty, and to develop enterprises which could not help but advance it in every way This determination and enthusiasm on the part of a few have always resulted in prosperity for the many, and Fremont is no exception to this long ago proven fact In the past each step forward has been taken through the efforts of the men who had the real good of the community at heart, the same is true of conditions today, and viewing the future in the light shed by events of the time gone by the responsibility will still rest on the shoulders of similar good citizens One of these men of moment of the recent past, the active present and likely future is John Sonin, one of the leading merchants of Fremont, who through his purchase in January, 1920, of the Gumpert Building adjoining his present store building secures a site for what he intends will be the finest department store building in this portion of the state In commenting upon his purchase, one of the largest realty deals ever consummated in the business district of Fremont, Mr Sonin said

"I have great faith in the future of Fremont, and for that reason made the purchase," in these pregnant words thus placing himself in the foremost ranks of the worth-while citizens and constructive business men of Dodge County

John Sonin is of European birth, and was born in April, 1881, a son of B and Rose (Ginsberg) Sonin, also natives of Europe, who came to the United States in 1896, seeking a refuge from oppressive conditions in their native land, and a country in which their children would be given opportunities to develop They located in Grand Island, Nebraska, where the father was engaged in the clothing business for two years, and in 1898 came to Fremont and opened a clothing store that he conducted until his death Of his six children, John Sonin is the only one living in Fremont

John Sonin attended the public schools of Grand Island and Fremont, and at the same time made himself useful in his father's store, in this way learning the business thoroughly In 1904 he went into business for himself, and now has one of the best clothing stores in this part of the state, his establishment occupying two stories and basement His trade is a very large one and comes from a wide territory surrounding Fremont as well as from the city itself He is also a stockholder in several of the banks of Fremont, is prominent in commercial club work and owns improved farms in Nebraska and Colorado which he rents.

In August, 1910, Mr Sonin was united in marriage with Hazel Sampter, born at Fremont, a daughter of Nathan Sampter, one of the early clothing merchants of Fremont Mr and Mrs Sonin have no children Mr Sonin belongs to Temple Israel of Omaha, Nebraska Well known in Masonry, he is a thirty-second degree and Shriner Mason He also belongs to Fremont Lodge No 514, Benevolent and Protective Order of Elks, and the Knights of Pythias, and Woodmen of America, and is very popular in all of these organizations Having been brought up in a republican household, he learned his political sentiments as a child, and his experiences of mature years have but strengthened his love for the republican party

Mr Sonin is an earnest, purposeful man, deeply interested in the progress of Fremont and willing to do everything in his power to prove that his faith in its future is justified

George Turner Although he no longer is in the ranks of the living, the influence of George Turner is felt in the actions of those with whom he formerly associated, and his name is connected with much of the constructive work of Fremont, where so many years were spent by him He was born in England on September 5, 1829, and he died at Fremont, Nebraska, on June 10, 1870 On April 13, 1856, he was united in marriage with Nancy S Gilley, who was born in Maine on January 12, 1834, and still survives, although now eighty-six years old

But a baby when he was brought to the United States by his parents, George Turner was reared at Needham, Massachusetts, and there he received his educational training His father established the first knitting factory at Needham, and in it he gave employment to about forty men, manufacturing underwear He was much interested in the discovery of gold in California, and had he been younger, doubtless would have made the trip, but instead, encouraged his son, George, to do so He was a most excellent man and very religious, belonging to the Baptist Church

George Turner went to California by the long route around Cape Horn, and was meeting with considerable success when his claim was washed away in a flood, and left him bankrupt In about 1853 or 1854, he returned to Massachusetts, and, following his marriage, decided to come West He and his wife first located at Dubuque, Iowa, but after a year, came to Nebraska, and after a brief period went on to Omaha, which continued to be their home until 1858, when they returned to Fremont and filed on a claim, the site of their farm being now included in the city limits Mr Turner gave the right-of-way to the Union Pacific Railroad through his property, but before the building of the road he was engaged in freighting to Pike's Peak from Fremont for a number of years Mrs Turner still resides in the large brick house at 78 South C Street that was built on the homestead, and she still owns the greater portion of the lots platted from the farm, also about seventy acres unplatted Later in life Mr Turner embarked in a wholesale and retail grocery business with W R Wilson. They were very prosperous and Mr Turner maintained these connections until his death A strong democrat, he was the nominee of his party for State Senator, but was defeated, although his personal popularity caused him to run far ahead of his ticket He was very active in civic affairs, gave liberally to charitable movements, and it is said of him that no one in need ever appealed to him in vain Although many years have passed since his death, his memory is still cherished by those who had the privilege of meeting and associating with him

Mr and Mrs Turner became the parents of the following children George Alfred Turner, who is a pioneer of Hot Springs, South Dakota, having located there in 1880, and owns a large ranch in the vicinity of that city; Edward Gilley Turner, who is living in the vicinity of Waldo Oregon, was extensively engaged in copper mining in that vicinity for a number of years; Nannie E, who married Frank L Joy, has three children, and now lives with her mother, Mrs Turner The children of Mrs Joy are as follows Mrs Ruth Hopkins, who lives at Pasco, Wyoming, where her husband is employed by the Middle-West Oil Company, Marvin A Joy, who is with the Baush Manufacturing Company of New York City, and Marion, who is attending school at Fremont For many years Mrs. Turner has been a consistent worker in the Episcopal Church, is very generous in her donations to it, and is interested in its good work Not only is the Turner family one of the pioneer ones in this neighborhood, but it is also one of the most prominent, and its representatives are living up to the name in every respect

CHARLES LESTER WALLINGFORD A prominent, prosperous and progressive agriculturist of Elkhorn Township, Charles Lester Wallingford is a typical representative of those citizens of Dodge County that came here poor in pocket but rich in energy, ambition and ability, and who, by persevering labor and efficient management, have steadily climbed the ladder of attainments, reaching one of its higher rungs through their own efforts A son of the late James G Wallingford, he was born August 10, 1864, in Muscatine County, Iowa

A native of England, James G Wallingford studied when young for the ministry, but never filled a regular charge His father was a native of England and was a Baptist minister He came to the United States and was engaged in ministerial work in Nebraska in an early day. After coming to the United States, James G Wallingford lived first in Ohio, from there going to Illinois, and thence to Iowa, where he was engaged

CHARLES L. WALLINGFORD

in agricultural pursuits until his death, when but fifty-three years old His wife, whose maiden name was Elizabeth Painter, came to Iowa in 1885, where her death occurred at the venerable age of four score years

Acquiring a practical education in the common schools, Charles L Wallingford remained in his native state until 1882 Coming to Nebraska in that year, with just $2 50 to his name, he secured employment in Fremont, and was afterwards variously employed in that vicinity for several years, nine months of the time working on a farm Gaining a good knowledge of many of the branches of agriculture, Mr Wallingford began farming on his own account in 1891, buying in Knox County 160 acres of land Disposing of that he returned to Dodge County and rented land for two years He subsequently bought land in Boone County, but never lived on it In 1900 Mr Wallingford purchased 160 acres of unimproved land in section 30, Elkhorn Township, and in its improvement has spared neither time, labor, nor expense Laboring wisely and unceasingly, he has now one of the choice farms of the County, it being highly cultivated and yielding abundantly of the crops common to this part of the state

Mr Wallingford married, in 1895, Nettie Harkins, who was born in Dodge County, Nebraska, where her parents, William and Rosie Harkins, improved a homestead from its original condition, and on the farm which they cleared spent the remainder of their lives Mr and Mrs Wallingford have six children: Lyda, James, Jessie, Pearl, Louis, and Hazel Mr Wallingford is a steadfast republican in politics, and has rendered good service as road overseer and as township clerk. Fraternally he is a member of the Ancient Free and Accepted Masons A loyal citizen of Dodge County, and one of its most persistent boosters, he has so thoroughly identified himself with its interests that he never visited the scenes of his childhood for a period of thirty-six years, being then recalled, in 1919, by the death of his brother, who was killed by lightning

FREDERICK MOLLER, SR In touching upon the life history of the gentleman whose name forms the caption to this sketch and who is one of the best known and most highly esteemed citizens of Fremont, the writer aims to avoid extravagant praise, yet he desires to hold up for consideration those facts which have shown the distinction of a true, useful and honorable life—a life characterized by perseverance, energy, broad charity and well defined purpose To do this will be but to reiterate the dictum pronounced upon the man by the people who have known him long and well

Frederick Moller, Sr, was born in Hamilton, Canada, on October 25, 1857, and is the son of John and Lizzie (Senges) Moller Both of these parents were born and reared in Germany, but immigrated to the United States and were married in New York State Subsequently they moved to Canada, but came back to New York City, and thence went to Philadelphia, where they remained until they came to Fremont, Nebraska Here Mr Moller homesteaded and pre-empted tracts of land, to the improvement and cultivation of which he devoted himself for several years Then selling his rights in this land, he moved into Fremont and engaged in the mercantile business on Broad Street for some time By trade he was a pocketbook maker and dyer, but never followed that line of work after coming to this locality He and his wife were members of the Lutheran Church and in politics he was a democrat Fraternally he was affiliated with the Independent Order of

Odd Fellows and the Improved Order of Red Men To him and his wife were born five children, three of whom are living, namely: John, of Fremont, who followed the barber's trade, but is now well-to-do and retired; Frederick, the subject of this review, and Leopold, who accumulated considerable property through his gardening operations and is now retired

Frederick Moller received his educational training in the public schools of Fremont to the age of twelve years, when he entered the office of the Fremont Herald to learn the printing trade, and it is worthy of note that he was the first boy to sell newspapers on the streets of Fremont He worked at the printing trade until twenty-one years of age, when he learned the trade of a barber, at which he worked for fourteen years Since then, for almost twenty years, he has been carrying mail in this city and is numbered among the oldest employes of the Fremont postoffice During these years, in storm and sunshine, he has faithfully served the public and his courtesy and careful attention to duty has not been unappreciated by those whom he has served

On June 15, 1884, Mr Moller was married to Mary Dierks, who was born in Monee, Illinois, the daughter of John and Gesche Catherine (Behrens) Dierks Both of her parents were born in Germany and came to Nebraska in 1871 Here Mr Dierks engaged in the elevator business for a number of years at Fremont, but both he and his wife are now deceased To Mr. and Mrs Moller have been born three children, namely Leonard, who was a traveling salesman, died on March 1, 1919, Gesche became the wife of Fred Lueders, a carpenter and harnessmaker in Fremont, and they have two children, Wade Frederick and Mary Anna, Gerald, who for two years has been a letter carrier in the postoffice

Mr and Mrs Moller are members of the Congregational Church, and in his political views Mr Moller supports the republican party He is a member of the Independent Order of Odd Fellows In his early life he was a successful hunter and has killed practically all kinds of game to be found here including such as deer and antelope In athletic sports he was greatly interested in playing semi-professional base ball, foot racing, trap shooting, and while in training was very successful, winning many first and second prizes Always quiet and unostentatious in manner, he nevertheless has left the impression of his strong individuality upon all who came in contact with him, and he enjoys a deservedly high standing among his fellow citizens

William A Shaffer A resident of Dodge County for forty-two years, and during a large part of this time personally identified with the agricultural activities of the thriving community of Everett Township, William A Shaffer holds a position second to none as a thorough farmer and breeder of high grade live stock His career has been one in which success has come as a direct result of well-directed enterprise and unfaltering industry, and the integrity that has guided his actions in the winning of material prosperity has served also to gain him a position in the unqualified esteem of his fellow-citizens

Mr Shaffer was born in Pennsylvania, January 11 1872, a son of Abel and Mary Ann (Hellwick) Shaffer, who were also born in that state Abel Shaffer learned the shoemaker's trade in his youth, and followed that occupation in the Keystone State until 1878, when he came to Nebraska and rented a farm in Dodge County A man of industry, he eventually accumulated means sufficient to buy a farm, and during the rest of his life he applied himself to the vocations of farming and stock raising, becoming known as a capable farmer and a good judge of live stock. As a citizen he stood high, and his integrity was inviolate. Politically, while not a seeker for honors, he was a stanch republican, and he and Mrs. Shaffer, a most estimable woman, were faithful members of the Lutheran Church. They were the parents of six children, James M., who is successfully engaged in farming in Maple Township, Dodge County, William A., Emma, the widow of Joe Barner, of Kearney, Nebraska; Luzetta, the wife of Henry Stiver, who is engaged in farming in Dodge County, Jacob, a resident of Kearney, and Abel, who is deceased.

William A. Shaffer was about six years of age when he accompanied his parents and brothers and sisters in their long and arduous journey across the country from Pennsylvania to Nebraska, and in the new community of Dodge County acquired his education in the district schools. He was only twenty years old when he began an independent career as the owner of land, and from that time to the present he has extended the scope of his activities until now he is known for his accomplishments as a general farmer and a breeder of a good grade of live stock. He has splendid improvements on his property, which is modern in every respect, and is a stockholder in the Farmers Union of Hooper and a member of the Omaha Stock Exchange. Mr. Shaffer has given all of his attention to the farm, taking little part in public affairs, although he feels a loyal pride in the prosperity and welfare of the community he has helped to build. The respect which is accorded him by his neighbors and fellow-citizens in general is proof of his worth. He votes independently.

Mr. Shaffer was married January 31, 1897, to Wilmina K. Schafer, who was born in Dodge County, January 15, 1876, and they are the parents of two children: Alois Raymond, who is connected with the Goodyear Tire Company, and Dorothy Fern, who resides with her parents. Mrs. Shaffer belongs to the Christian Science Church.

H. Charles Hansen. In the life history of H. Charles Hansen, one of the substantial agriculturists of Maple Township, Dodge County, the young can see what industry and temperance can accomplish, the farmer, the mechanic, the professional man, all can learn the results of energy and the possibility of the combination of a substantial success with unsullied citizenship. Mr. Hansen is one of the worthy sons of Denmark now numbered among the valued citizens of Dodge County, and was born January 11, 1866, his father, now deceased, having been Rasmus H. Hansen, a farmer who never left his native land. Of the children, one, N. Lena, still resides in Denmark, and four came to the United States: H. Charles; Fred, a resident of Omaha; Peter, of Tennessee, and Chris, of Oklahoma.

H. Charles Hansen was educated in the public schools of his native land, and was still a young man when he immigrated to the United States in 1887. At the time of his arrival he was possessed of $4.50, of which amount he spent $4 for a pair of boots. Thus he began his career in this country with the sum of 50 cents, but he was likewise the possessor of ambition and willingness to work, and these proved sufficient to get him started on the road to independence. Making his way to Nebraska, Mr. Hansen settled in Dodge County, where for the next three years he worked in the field as a farm hand. He then started independent operations as a renter, which continued to be his status for seven years, and he then purchased his first property, a tract of 100 acres This he subsequently sold, then purchasing the 160-acre tract which comprises his present farm in Maple Township, section 12 For the greater part he applies himself to general farming, in which he has won much success, although he has also been prosperous in his experiments in raising live stock He has splendid improvements on his land, including large and substantial buildings and the most modern equipment and up-to-date accessories Mr Hansen is a republican, and belongs to the Danish Brotherhood and the Modern Woodmen of America He is a great friend of education and for four years served as a member of the board of school directors

In 1893 at Fremont, Nebraska, Mr. Hansen was united in marriage with Katie Hansen, who was born in Denmark, and to this union there have been born two children Roy and Edel, both residing with their parents.

Fred Osterloh Of the agriculturists who have assisted in sustaining the integrity of the farming and stockraising interests of Dodge County during an extended period of years mention is due Fred Osterloh, the owner of a well-cultivated and valuable farming property lying in section 26, Cuming Township Mr Osterloh has passed his entire career in this county, where he is well known, and his manner of conducting his affairs has so met with the approval of his associates that he is held in general esteem as a man, citizen and farmer

Fred Osterloh was born on a farm in Dodge County October 22, 1873, a son of Henry and Anna (Egbers) Osterloh The parents, natives of Oldenburg, Germany emigrated to the United States during the '60s, at which time they made their way across country to Omaha, and then drove overland to Dodge County, where the father took up a homestead During the early years, when the crops were small and money not easily secured, he added to his income by freighting with an ox-team, but in later years his well-developed farm paid him well for his labors and he was able to furnish himself with many of the comforts of life, the farming advantages being added each year and the improvements progressing in modernity Henry Osterloh passed away on this farm in 1903, at the age of sixty-eight years, while his widow survived him until 1917 and was seventy-seven years of age at the time of her death They were faithful members of the Lutheran Church, and Mr Osterloh was independent in his political views There were six children in the family Fred, Catherine, who is the wife of Henry Peters, a farmer in Washington County, this state, and four deceased

Fred Osterloh was given his educational training in the public schools of the rural districts of Dodge County, and passed his boyhood in much the same manner as other farmer's sons of his day and community He continued to reside under the parental roof, and it was not until he was twenty-seven years of age that he began farming operations on his own account In 1901 he was united in marriage with Miss Marie Romberg, who was also born in Dodge County, and to this union there have been born eight children Christina, William, Martin, Anna, Herbert, Elmer, Marguerite, and Glenville

Mr Osterloh devotes his activities to carrying on general farming and also raises a good grade of stock for which he finds a ready and satisfying market He has a number of business interests and is a stockholder in the Douglas Motor Company of Omaha His record in business affairs has given him a good reputation among his associates,

IRVING J. POLLOCK

and this statement holds good also as to his status as a citizen, for he has always discharged his duties in a conscientious manner. He is an independent voter and is rather a farmer than a politician, but at this time is the incumbent of the office of Clerk of Cuming Township

VICTOR E KOYEN An industrious and well-to-do farmer of Elkhorn Township, Victor E. Koyen, who succeeded to the ownership of the parental estate, is interested in mercantile pursuits as well as agricultural, having a well patronized store on his farm A son of the late Frederick and Christina Koyen, he was born March 31, 1881, on Washington Island, in Lake Michigan, of thrifty Danish ancestry

Born in Denmark, November 28, 1848, Frederick Koyen remained in his native land until attaining his majority Coming then to this country, he located in Wisconsin, where he worked as a lumberman and farmer for eleven years He then came to Dodge County, Nebraska, and bought 160 acres of prairie land in Elkhorn Township, which he improved He there carried on general farming until ready to give up active pursuits, when he removed to town, and spent his later years of life enjoying the fruits of his early labors His wife, whom he married in the Empire State, died on the home farm at the age of sixty-nine years. Their children were five in number, and three of them, William, Albert and Victor E, are living. The father was independent in politics, and a member of the Danish Lutheran Church, to which his wife also belonged

Choosing the independent occupation with which he became familiar in early life, and having been but a child when he came with his parents to Dodge County, Victor E Koyen was educated in the district schools and began farming on his own account about 1906 Since assuming possession of the parental homestead he has added to the improvements previously inaugurated, and now has a conveniently arranged dwelling house, modern in every respect

The land is well improved and most of it tiled, everything about the premises giving evidence of the owner's prosperity and wise management

On the first day of January, 1906, Mr Koyen was united in marriage with Anna Benson, who was born in St Louis, Missouri, came with her parents to Dodge County, Nebraska, in pioneer days, and was then living in Fremont, where their marriage was solemnized Two children have blessed their union, Bernice J. and Rodney Victor Mr. Koyen is a stanch republican in politics, and both he and his wife are valued members of the Baptist Church

IRVING J POLLOCK has been a resident of Dodge County from the time of his birth and is a representative of a well known pioneer family of Nebraska He is also one of the substantial and prominent exponents of agricultural and live stock industry in his native county, where he owns and resides upon a well improved farm estate of 220 acres, and is one of the influential citizens of Elkhorn Township, where his homestead place is situated in section 25

Mr Pollock was born in Elkhorn Township, Dodge County, October 19, 1872, and is a son of Joseph and Elizabeth Pollock, whose marriage was solemnized in this county Joseph Pollock was born and reared in Scotland, a scion of the staunchest of Scottish ancestry, and he was eighteen years of age when he came to America and settled in Whiteside County, Illinois, where he became actively identified with farm industry and whence he went forth as a gallant young soldier of the

Union in the Civil war, a service in which he proved most effectively his loyalty to the land of his adoption He was twenty-one years of age when he came to Nebraska and settled on a pioneer farm three miles west of the present Village of Arlington, but in Dodge County, that village being in Washington County In the early period of his residence in Nebraska he followed the line of construction on the Union Pacific Railroad as far westward as Cheyenne, this state, and had charge of the eating house maintained for the construction men He developed and improved his farm in Dodge County and was still the owner of a good farm of 160 acres at the time of his death in 1899, when sixty-four years of age, his wife passing away at the age of fifty years and both having been active members of the Methodist Episcopal Church Of their eight children the subject of this review was the second in order of birth and of the number, seven, one having died at the age of twenty-eight, are now living (1920). The father held a secure place in popular confidence and esteem and was one of the honored citizens and pioneers of Dodge County, where he served for some time in the office of justice of the peace

Irving J Pollock received his early education in the public schools of Dodge County and as a youth gained full fellowship with the work of the home farm, a preliminary experience that well fortified him for his later and independent activities as an agriculturist and stock-grower His fine farm estate of 220 acres bears every evidence of thrift and good management, and is devoted to diversified agriculture and the raising and feeding of a due complement of live stock for the market. In politics Mr Pollock is a democrat, and he has given effective and loyal service as township clerk, as road overseer and as a member of the school board of his district He and his wife hold membership in the Methodist Episcopal Church, and he is affiliated with the Modern Woodmen of America

In 1896 was solemnized the marriage of Mr Pollock to Miss Esther DeLong, and they have eight children Joseph, Nellie, Mildred, Gladys, James, Ivan, Dorothy, and Esther Nellie, the eldest daughter, is the wife of Fred Brown, and they maintain their home in the City of Fremont, Dodge County

E C Diers The experiences of those men who are numbered among the pioneers of Nebraska form an interesting part of the history of each division of the state Through the efforts of these sturdy men present conditions have been developed, and it is only fair to render to them the credit which is their due. Among these residents of Dodge County who belong to the pioneer class is E C Diers of section 32, Nickerson Township, whose finely developed farm of 880 acres demonstrates the value of careful farming and intelligent use of the facilities at hand He is a native son of Nebraska, having been born at West Point, Cuming County, November 13, 1868 His father, Charles Diers, and his mother, Ernestine Diers, were natives of Germany, who came to the United States in 1868 and settled in Cuming County, Nebraska, where they homesteaded The father was a farmer and stockman, but had retired, and he died in Pasadena, California His widow survives him

Remaining on his father's farm until he was twenty-one years old, and during his youth attending the district schools and acquiring a practical working knowledge of farming, Mr Diers then began to work on his own account, and came to Dodge County during its pioneer period At the time he came here the Indians were still hostile and there were no facilities other than natural ones offered the men brave enough to take up homesteads, but those who did so and persisted until they proved up and developed their claims have been amply rewarded and are now men of means and high standing in their community. The original homestead of Mr. Diers has been increased until it now contains 880 acres. While all of his stock is of a good grade, he does not handle thoroughbred strains. Nearly all of his stock is bred on his farm, and he raises all of his feed. He averages about three carloads of sheep annually.

Mr. Diers was married to Erma Levy, born and reared in Saunders County. They have two children, Walter C. and Eugene Donald, both of whom are at home. In his political faith Mr. Diers is an independent democrat, but aside from exercising his right of suffrage he does not participate in politics. In the Congregational Church he finds a medium for the expression of his religious faith, and he is a liberal contributor to the local church. Fraternally he is an Odd Fellow. His accounts of really thrilling experiences with the Indians are well worth preservation. He was born in a dugout, and if his children had to go through the hardships he and his wife took as a part of their everyday life, they would feel that fate was according them an unfair portion, and yet both Mr. and Mrs. Diers realize that these very hardships played an important part in the development of their characters, and that without them they might not today be what they most certainly are, self-reliant and dependable citizens of a mighty commonwealth.

HENRY KNOELL. In connection with his progressive farm enterprise Mr. Knoell is proving himself fully equipped with success-winning qualifications and is to be classed among the substantial and popular representatives of the basic industries of agriculture and stock-growing in his native county, where he is a scion of a sterling pioneer family. His farm of 160 acres consists of rich valley land in section 2, Platte Township, Dodge County, and he is making it one of the model places of the township. The farm has good buildings, and its general appearance gives full evidence of thrift and prosperity.

Mr. Knoell was born in Nickerson Township, this County, August 29, 1871, and is a son of Christopher and Dora (Strom) Knoell, whose marriage was solemnized at Fremont, the judicial center of the county. Christopher Knoell was born in Germany and was fourteen years of age when the family came to America and established a home in the State of Wisconsin, where he was reared to adult age and where he continued to be employed, principally at farm work, until he became one of the pioneer settlers of Dodge County, Nebraska. Here he rented land for some time, and eventually he purchased land until he was the owner of seven quarter-sections. He was one of the prosperous farmers of the county for many years prior to his death, when well advanced in age. His wife died in 1901. The subject of this review was the eldest of their seven children, all of whom are living.

Henry Knoell was reared to the sturdy discipline of the farm and gained his early education in the public schools of his native county. In 1900 he rented land and engaged in farming in an independent way, and with increasing resources he finally purchased his present farm, which he has since operated with unequivocal success, the place being devoted to diversified agriculture and the raising of live stock of good grades. Mr. Knoell maintains an independent attitude in politics, and the only office in which he has consented to serve was that of school director of his district, a position of which he continued the incumbent from 1917 until 1920 He is affiliated with the Fraternal Order of Eagles

March 7, 1900, recorded the marriage of Mr. Knoell to Miss Mary Hoffman, who likewise was born and reared in Dodge County, and their pleasant home is still brightened by the presence of their seven children, namely: Theodore, Lora, Henry R, Raymond, Mabel, Herbert and Marian Clara, the eldest in order of birth, died at the age of seventeen years.

Eric Olson Among the many successful agriculturists who are quietly pursuing the even tenor of their way in the counties wherein they were born is Eric Olson, of Logan Township, who during his active career has been a tiller of the soil, and in his chosen occupation has found both pleasure and profit A son of the late Matts Olson, he was born December 13, 1873, in Dodge County, coming from pioneer stock.

Born and bred in Sweden, where his birth occurred in 1841, Matts Olson, who was not at all satisfied with his future prospects in his native land, immigrated to the United States in 1868 and having secured employment on the Union Pacific Railroad, which was then in process of construction, worked on it as far westward as Salt Lake City He subsequently worked for a time in Omaha, but about 1870, finding himself $50 in debt, he decided to turn his attention to agriculture Coming, therefore, to Dodge County, he homesteaded eighty acres of land in Logan Township and built the sod house in which he and his family first lived Industrious and thrifty, he not only improved his homestead property, but through his agricultural operations was enabled from time to time to purchase other tracts, and at the time of his death, at the age of seventy-three years, owned 718 acres of good land He married in 1871, and reared a family of six children and a step-son, as follows Eric, the special subject of this sketch, Willie, of Pleasant Valley, Mrs Mary A Anderson, of Iowa; Alfred, of Burt County, Nebraska, Mrs. Christie Erickson, of Dodge County, Mrs Glen Carson, of Burt County; and A B Jacobs, of Thurston County, Nebraska In politics the father was independent, voting for the best men and measures regardless of party restrictions The mother died in Dodge County at a good old age.

Acquiring his education in the rural schools of Dodge County, Eric Olson began working as a boy on the parental homestead, and finding that occupation congenial to his tastes has since continued in it Starting for himself at the time of his marriage he rented land of his father and in its management was quite successful When he had accumulated a sufficient sum to warrant him in so doing he bought land, and has now a well improved and well equipped farm of 118 acres, and being a skillful and practical farmer, systematic and thorough in his methods, he is being amply rewarded for his labors, his land yielding abundant crops each year

Mr. Olson married, in 1903, Hilda Lundberg, who was born in Sweden and as a child was brought by her parents to Fremont, Nebraska, where she grew to womanhood Mr and Mrs Olson have three children Geraldine, Evelyn and Howard As a prosperous farmer and stock raiser Mr Olson, who is a man of strict integrity and a trustworthy citizen, has the esteem and respect of the community in which he resides and in the advancement of which he takes a genuine interest. He is independent in politics, and for several years served acceptably as a member of the local school board

Florence Adda Winkelman

HENRY BOHLING, late of Logan Township, was for many years well known throughout this part of Dodge County as an industrious and prosperous farmer, a highly respected citizen, a kind neighbor and a loving husband and father, and his death, which occurred September 30, 1918, at the homestead where he had so long resided, was a cause of general regret, being mourned not only as a loss to his family but to the entire community He was born May 5, 1862, in Germany, where he was reared and educated

Immigrating to this country at the age of nineteen years, Mr Bohling came directly to Dodge County, Nebraska, and after working three years for Mrs. Panning went to Washington County, where he was busily employed for two years Starting in life on his own account then, he rented the farm in Logan Township now occupied by his widow and children, and meeting with success in its supervision subsequently bought the place. He added to the improvements previously inaugurated, erected substantial farm buildings and a good residence, and continued his operations as a farmer and stock raiser, in the prosecution of his calling meeting with highly satisfactory results, his valuable farm of 215 acres being at the time of his death one of the most desirable pieces of property in the neighborhood His first house was a mere shack, and the one he erected was a modernly built structure, furnished with all the comforts, necessities and conveniences commonly found in the homes of the more progressive and successful agriculturists of today

Mr Bohling married, April 10, 1888, Caroline Seabuhr, who was born in Washington County, Nebraska, where her parents, Christopher and Mary Seabuhr, natives of Germany, located on coming to Nebraska from Wisconsin, their first home in America. Twelve children were born of their union, namely: Mrs M Katt, Mrs Lizzie Prigge, and Mrs Minnie Katt, of Washington County, and Dorothy, Henry, Louis, Adolph, Willie, Lena, Emil, Otto, and Alma, living at home Mr Bohling was independent in politics, voting for men and measures he deemed best, and was a faithful member of St Paul's Lutheran Church, to which Mrs Bohling also belongs

MRS FLORENCE ADDIE WINKELMAN is one of the successful business women of Dodge County, and is proving that her sex is no bar to her entering into competition with men and setting a pace for them that many find difficult to keep up She is a worthy daughter of her father, the late Gideon West, who will long be remembered as a man of sterling character and fine business ability At the time of his demise he was serving Fremont as city marshal, and was the owner of a large amount of realty in the city and Dodge County

Gideon West was born in Canada while his mother was there on a visit but was taken to Vermont in infancy, where he spent his childhood days From there he came West to Wisconsin, and thence to Nebraska, where he arrived in 1867. During the war between the North and the South he served in the Union army and held the rank of sergeant His enlistment took place from Wisconsin and he was disabled and honorably discharged at the end of nine months This military service resulted in subsequent ill health, and doubtless terminated his life, for he passed away in the latter '70s

After coming to Nebraska he met and was married to Martha Jensen, born near Copenhagen, Denmark Her parents brought her to the United States when she was six years of age, and they lived at Fremont, Nebraska, for a number of years, but later moved to Iowa and there died Mr and Mrs West became the parents of two children, Florence A, whose name heads this review, and Lila, who married Ray Pankow, of Sioux Falls, South Dakota Both Mr and Mrs West were consistent members of the Methodist Episcopal Church from an early age, and brought up their daughters in the same faith Mr West was a Mason and one of the most prominent men in the fraternity in Dodge County. His was the first Masonic funeral ever held in the county, and one of the first held in the Methodist Episcopal Church When he died Mr West owned a half a square of property in Fremont and farm land in Dodge County, and acquired that property during the last few years of his life

When Mr and Mrs. West were young married people Mr West had a long period of illness, and his devoted wife threw herself into the breach and did washing in order to supply the necessities of life, not only doing it cheerfully and willingly, but so acceptably that she built up a large connection and made money After her husband's death she so managed her property that she has become very wealthy and now owns five farms Later she was married to Charles A. Devine, and they live at North Bend, Nebraska.

Florence A West was married to Frank Winkelman, of Fremont, a railroad conductor, who later became a merchant He died on January 14, 1918 They became the parents of the following children: Gideon W, who is a farmer of Saunders, Nebraska, Jennie Edith, who married J. R Carroll, of North Platte, Nebraska, Tyrone, who married George Devine, lives on a farm near North Bend, Nebraska; and Richard A, who is attending high school

Mrs Winkelman is a very shrewd business woman and knows how to make her effort pay her a good return She owns and operates a high-class, modern rooming house at 140 East Second Street, and has other city and farm realty Being an excellent judge of real estate, she does considerable in this line, and during the summer of 1919 handled two and one-half sections of farm land in Kimball County, Nebraska, in such a way as to treble her money and awaken the admiration of some of the most astute realty operators of the state

She and her family belong to the Episcopal Church For a number of years she has been very active in the local chapter of the Eastern Star, and holds the degree of honor in the Ancient Order of United Workmen and is a past grand of this order for the State of Nebraska

It is such capable women as Mrs Winkelman who are proving to their communities that they are fully competent to handle any problems While she has been so successful in business life, Mrs Winkelman has not neglected any of her home responsibilities but has reared a family of fine children

LARS PETERSON Having accomplished a satisfactory work in his free and independent occupation and acquired a competency to live on in his declining years, Lars Peterson, a retired farmer of Uehling, is now enjoying a well-earned leisure Born in Sweden in 1841, he remained there twenty-two years

After a long and tedious ocean voyage he landed in New York on July 14, 1863 Proceeding westward, he arrived in Chicago with $5 00 in gold in his pocket, which he soon changed into scrip, receiving $7 50 in that currency Here he worked at his trade as a carpenter until 1864 In that year he was one of three Swedes selected to find a favorable location for a colony of their countrymen Going to Omaha, he was there told that the only land available for that purpose lay west of Columbus, but as the Indians in that locality were very hostile the committee decided to form a settlement in Logan Valley instead The venture proved successful, and Mr Peterson is now the only survivor of the founders of that settlement

His father, who followed him to this country in 1864, came to Nebraska, where he took up a homestead claim and carried on general farming with good results, residing on his ranch until his death, at the age of seventy-eight years His wife, Justine Peterson, survived him, living to be eighty-two years old

Taking up a homestead claim in Dodge County, Lars Peterson went from Chicago by rail to St Joseph, Missouri, and thence by boat to Omaha, Nebraska, and before leaving for the farm homestead at Logan Valley, Nebraska, he spent his last $10 00 for flour, purchasing 200 pounds, an amount that by strict economy lasted him and his bride, whom he married in Omaha, a long time He cleared and improved his homestead of 160 acres, and lived upon it until he had accumulated a sufficient sum to warrant him in giving up active labor, and since 1898 has lived retired, having a most desirable home in Uehling, Nebraska

Mr Peterson married October 10, 1864, in Omaha, Hanna Anderson, and to them several children have been born, namely Peter, who died at the age of fourteen years, having accidentally shot himself, Carrie Mattson, wife of a Dodge County farmer, Anna Bennett, living in California; Mary Peterson, of Los Angeles, California; Clara Taylor, also living in Los Angeles, Turah, who died at the age of twenty years; Elmer, living on the parental homestead, Lillie, wife of Dr Chris Johnson, a veterinary surgeon living near Uehling, and Roy, a resident of California Mr Peterson has traveled in the west, after retiring from the farm, having spent five years in Denver before settling permanently in Uehling He is a never changing republican in politics and a member of the Lutheran Church

Frank B Knapp, president of the Fidelity Trust Company of Fremont, was born at Sloan, Iowa He was engaged in the banking business at Cedar Bluffs, Nebraska for several years He came to Fremont in 1910 as cashier of the First National Bank, later became president of the Fidelity Trust Company, and is an officer or director in a number of Nebraska banks and financial institutions Mr Knapp was married to Lula A. Meeker, of Wahoo, Nebraska Of this union one child, a daughter, Marjorie, was born and is living with her parents.

James C Badger, the popular and efficient postmaster at Arlington, Washington County, was about ten years of age at the time of the family removal from Michigan to this progressive Nebraska county, his birth having occurred near Niles, the Metropolis of Berrien County, Michigan, on January 12, 1870 His father, William D Badger, was likewise a native of that county, where he was reared and educated and where was solemnized his marriage to Miss Margaret Mead She was born in the State of New York and was young at the time of her parents' removal to Michigan In his native county William D Badger continued his active association with farm enterprise until 1880, when he came with his family to Nebraska and established a home in Washington County, he having been a resident of Arlington since the autumn of that year Here he was for ten years successfully engaged in the buying and shipping of grain and live stock as junior member of the firm of Shepard &

Badger, and he then became one of the organizers of the Belle Creek Valley Bank at Arlington He continued as one of the executive officials of the institution until it was reorganized as the First National Bank. His political allegiance is given to the democratic party, and he is affiliated with the Masonic fraternity Of their two children the subject of this review is the elder, and the younger is O D Badger, who is employed in a general merchandise establishment at Arnold, Custer County. In his youth the father received not only the advantages of the public schools of Michigan, but also those of the great University of Michigan, of the Eastman Business College in the City of Poughkeepsie, New York He has been influential in politics in Washington County and has been known for his civic loyalty and public spirit

James C Badger acquired his rudimentary education in the public schools of Michigan, and after the family removed to Nebraska he continued his studies in the schools at Arlington, his higher academic training having been received in the celebrated Notre Dame University at South Bend, Indiana As a youth he became associated with his father's banking business, and thereafter he was for one year employed in the Government military postoffice service in the State of Utah After his return to Arlington he held a position in what is now the First National Bank for a period of about ten years, and for one year thereafter he was in the Pullman car service of the Union Pacific and Chicago & Northwestern Railroad. In 1915 he was appointed postmaster at Arlington, of which position he has since continued the incumbent and in which he has given a most effective and popular administration

Mr Badger has been active and influential in the councils and campaign activities of the democratic party in Washington County, and he is actively affiliated with the Masonic fraternity

In 1892 was recorded the marriage of Mr Badger to Miss Honora Fink, daughter of John Fink, a well-known citizen of Washington County Mr and Mrs Badger have two children, Ralph and Loren, both of whom are still attending school at the time of this writing in 1920

Laurence M Peterson While the art of preserving and repairing the teeth was known in a crude form by the very ancient peoples, it has been only within recent years that dental surgery has received the consideration it has always merited on account of its importance, and consequently men of much greater intellectual attainments have been attracted to the profession, which now includes some of the ablest men of the country One of the skilled and dependable operating dentists of Dodge and Washington counties, who draws his patients from both localities, is Dr Laurence M Peterson of Arlington

Doctor Peterson was born at Arlington in 1894, a son of J A and Emma J (Gustafson) Peterson, natives of Sweden and Iowa, respectively J A Peterson came to the United States in 1868, locating in Iowa, where he remained for four years, and then came west to Nebraska and settled permanently at Arlington, which still continues to be his home He is now in the employ of a hardware and general store at Arlington The children born to him and his wife were as follows. Bernita, who is now engaged in teaching at Scottsbluff, Nebraska, L M, who was the second in order of birth; Erma M, who is in her brother's office; and Theodore R and J Rodney, both of whom are attending the Arlington schools The parents of these children are members of the Congregational Church, and the father is a republican in politics and a member of the Modern Woodmen in his fraternal affiliations.

After completing his high school course at Arlington, Doctor Peterson entered the dental department of the Nebraska State University and was graduated therefrom in 1917, with the degree of Doctor of Dental Surgery and as a member of the Greek letter fraternity, Beta Theta Pi. Immediately following his graduation Doctor Peterson located at Arlington, where he has built up a valuable practice and has firmly established himself in the confidence of the public He is a Blue Lodge Mason Like his father he is a republican, and also like the elder man he has not aspired to public honors, all of his energy being conserved for the practice of his profession However, like all intelligent men, he realizes the need for a constructive interest in civic affairs by the best element of any locality, and so stands ready to do his part in keeping Arlington in the front rank among similar municipalities along all lines

WILLIAM SCHAFERSMAN The claim of William Schafersman upon the good will and consideration of his fellow townsmen at Blair is based upon many years of effective work as an agriculturist, upon his meritorious record as a citizen and upon his activity in promoting education and kindred accompaniments of advanced education While he is now employed in the produce business, Mr Schafersman is still the owner of a splendid farm in the vicinity of Herman, and the business with which he is identified keeps alive his interest in things agricultural

Born at Quincy, Illinois, June 23, 1868, Mr Schafersman is a son of Gottlieb and Hannah (Westerbech) Schafersman, natives of Germany His father left his native land at the age of twenty-one years, in order to escape the hated compulsory military service, and on arriving in the United States became employed as a laboring man, accepting such honorable work as fell to his hands He was living in Illinois when the Civil war came on, and while he had left the home of his birth because he did not want to be forced into the army, in the land where his inclinations were given consideration he voluntarily offered his services to the country of his adoption and was accepted as a member of Company H, Sixteenth Regiment, Illinois Volunteer Infantry, a regiment with which he served four years He took part in many of the hardest-fought engagements of the great struggle, and was slightly wounded at Gettysburg and Bull Run. After receiving his honorable discharge he returned to his home in Illinois, but in 1868 turned his face to the West and settled at Blair, in which community he bought 200 acres of school land at $7 00 an acre Mr Schafersman lived to see this land increase many times in value, and under his good management and industry it flourished and became splendidly productive He was a man of integrity and fidelity to trust and had the esteem and respect of all with whom he came in contact His religious faith was that of the German Lutheran Church, and his political belief that of the democratic party He and his worthy wife were the parents of six children, William being the second in order of birth, and two others live in Washington County, Edward, proprietor of a general store at Telbasta, Nebraska, and Minnie, the wife of August Carlston, a farmer near the Village of Dale

William Schafersman received his education in the country school of his locality, to reach which he was compelled to walk three miles, and as a youth adopted farming as his life work He was engaged in farming successfully until his fortieth year, and is still the owner of a large and highly productive property near Herman, for which he paid at the rate of $35 an acre, while this land is now worth $300 an acre. When he gave up active participation in farming work he identified himself with the produce business at Herman, and continued therein for eleven years, coming to Blair in July, 1918, and associating himself as clerk with the produce business of Mr. Wright In 1920 he took the management of the Valley Poultry Company of Blair, Nebraska He is regarded as one of the substantial men of his community and as a citizen who backs worthy measures with his means, abilities and time. Mr. Schafersman is a member of the Lutheran Church, as is his wife, who belongs to the Rebekahs and the Knights and Ladies of Security, of which her husband is also a member He is also an Odd Fellow In civic life he has taken an active and prominent part As a democrat he was elected to the office of road overseer for nine years, subsequently serving four years as mayor of Herman He has been successful in his affairs and has varied interests, among them a directorship in the Farmers State Bank

In the spring of 1896 Mr Schafersman was united in marriage with Miss Reka Richter, who was born in Washington County, Nebraska, a daughter of Herman Richter, one of the early farmers of the county To this union there has come one daughter, Opal, who is attending the public school

E S Beaty It is nearly forty years since E S Beaty came to the Blair community, arriving here with practically no assets except his skill and experience in his trade He has been building bridges and doing other contracting and construction work ever since, is active head of the Beaty Contracting Company, and is widely known as a most substantial business man and one whose success is the product of his own energies and initiative.

Mr Beaty was born in Massachusetts December 10, 1855, a son of J. J and Mary F (Snowden) Beaty His mother was a native of Boston and his father of Nova Scotia, and they were married in Medford, Massachusetts. After a number of years in Massachusetts the family emigrated to the Northwest in 1857, settling in Minnesota Territory J J Beaty developed a pioneer homestead in that territory, though in the east he had been a carpenter and contractor When the Civil war came on he enlisted in Company E of the Eleventh Minnesota Infantry, and served as second lieutenant during the last ten months of the war He was also a county surveyor in Minnesota and held other minor offices, was a stanch republican in politics, a Mason and a member of the Episcopal Church Of a family of twelve children eight are still living, E S being the sixth in age

E S Beaty was an infant when the family moved to Minnesota, and his first recollections were of that pioneer country He acquired a district school education, grew up on a farm, but also learned the carpenter's trade, and early in life began taking independent contracts

On moving to Blair in 1883 Mr Beaty was for eleven years foreman of railroad bridge construction He then set up in business as an independent contractor, building bridges for railroads and the county, and finally incorporated the Beaty Contracting Company, with a capital of $25,000 This is a family corporation and Mr. Beaty is now to a large extent retired, having turned the active management of the business over to his son

He married in 1884, in Iowa, Miss Lucretia Maun She is a native of Nebraska and her father, John Maun, was a Nebraskan of prominence, a thoroughly well educated man who was in the newspaper business, an Indian agent, a druggist, and spent his last years on a farm He had been educated for the Catholic priesthood Mr and Mrs. Beaty have

Eugene W Burdy

two children The son Mark, now in business with his father, is a graduate of the high school and of the Armour Institute of Technology at Chicago The daughter, Enid, is a graduate of the Blair High School and of the Rockford Woman's College in Illinois, and is the wife of Fred Rankin of Sioux City, Iowa Mr Rankin served as a lieutenant in the World war, having been trained at Camp Grant and also at the School of Fire at Fort Sill, Oklahoma Mrs Beaty and her children are Catholics Mr Beaty is a prominent Mason, having filled all the chairs in the lodge, past high priest of the Royal Arch Chapter, past eminent commander of the Knights Templar, and is also a Mystic Shriner. He is a member of the Modern Woodmen of America and a republican in politics In 1900 Mr Beaty built the beautiful home in Blair where he and his family reside, and he also owns some valuable farm lands in Washington County

EUGENE W BURDIC The value in business of concentrating one's forces upon a given line of activity, of correctly gauging its importance among the needs of the world, and keeping pace with the ever-changing conditions surrounding it, is confirmed anew in the success of E W Burdic, vice president of the Plateau State Bank of Herman A resident of Washington County since 1877, in his earlier years he was interested in farming, merchandise and stock shipping, but for many years has centered his attention in financial matters

Mr Burdic was born November 16, 1861, in Steuben County, Indiana, and was a lad of fifteen years when brought to Nebraska in 1877 by his parents, Fred and Ann Burdic, natives of Indiana, who settled in Washington County, near Herman There the father rounded out a long and honorable career in the pursuits of agriculture, and died at the age of seventy-four years, highly esteemed and respected The widow still survives There were four children in the family R L, a resident of Ashland, Oregon; E. W , Mrs Maude Hasbrook of Hood River, Oregon, and Alva, who is deceased

E W Burdic received his education in the public school at Herman, and when about twenty-three years of age began farming on his own account After two years spent in agricultural activities, he turned his attention to merchandising and the shipping of stock, pursuits which he followed for eighteen years at Herman At the end of that time he purchased an interest in the Plateau State Bank, of which institution he has been vice president ever since and to the success of which he has contributed materially by his good judgment, foresight and natural business ability Mr Burdic is a Knight Templar Mason and Shriner and a member of the Benevolent and Protective Order of Elks In political matters he considers the character of the aspirants for office and is not bound by party lines He has rendered efficient and conscientious service to his community in public positions for many years, having been for fourteen years a member of the Board of County Commissioners, a member of the Board of School Directors for upwards of twenty years, and a member of the town board for a long period

Mr Burdic was united in marriage March 12, 1885, with Miss Cora Rose, who was born at Omaha, Nebraska, but reared in Washington County, a daughter of S C and Mattie Rose, the latter of whom makes her home with Mr and Mrs Burdic, Mr. Rose being deceased In the Rose family there were five children George, Edward, Eugene, Cora and Jessie Four children have been born to Mr and Mrs Burdic Earl, Lloyd, Neil and Gretchen

C. HENRY PETERSEN. A well-known and prosperous business man of Washington County, C Henry Petersen has achieved success in the various lines of industry with which he has been associated, his keen foresight and earnestness of purpose having proved his chief assets during his career as a farmer, stockraiser and merchant He was born in 1873 in Clinton County, Iowa, a son of Nichols D and Margaret Petersen, natives of Germany

Born in 1842, Nichols Petersen remained in Germany until attaining his majority In 1865, following the footsteps of many of his companions, he immigrated to the United States, settling first in Iowa, where he was employed in general farming and stock raising, and was also engaged in business at Bennington, Nebraska, where he owned and operated a meat market Coming from Clinton County, Iowa, to Washington County in 1876, he was here a resident until his death, on January 1, 1916 He was a democrat in politics, and both he and his wife united with the Lutheran Church at Bennington, this state They were the parents of six children, as follows Peter C, of Bennington, Nebraska, a butcher, C Henry; Catherine, widow of John Missfeldt; John of Bennington, a well-known garage man, William, engaged in farming in Washington County, Nebraska, and Emma, wife of Richard Johnson, who is engaged in farming in Douglas County, this state

Obtaining a practical education in the rural schools of Washington County, C Henry Petersen acquired valuable knowledge and experience in the art of agriculture on the home farm Finding the work profitable as well as agreeable, he carried on general farming for several years, making a specialty of raising a good grade of stock Locating in Washington in 1916, Mr Petersen opened a store, and having put in a complete stock of general merchandise has since been actively and prosperously engaged in mercantile pursuits, his trade being large and constantly increasing He has acquired considerable property, owning land in Cheyenne County, Nebraska, and being a stockholder in the Omaha Wholesale Grocery

Mr Petersen married, in 1893, Mary Voss, a native of Ohio and into their home circle ten children have made their advent, namely Alvina, wife of Charles Wrick, a farmer in Washington County, Clara, postmistress in Washington, Dora and Celia, in Omaha, Carl, engaged in agricultural pursuits in Washington County, Catherine, working in her father's store, Herbert, Otto, Louise and Lorraine Mr Petersen is independent in politics, voting according to his convictions, regardless of party affiliations

W. L. JAPP The man who today owns Washington County farm land is to be accounted one of the most fortunate men of Nebraska This is one of the great agricultural states of the Union and its present state of fertility has been brought about through the efforts of the men who have devoted their time and energy to the development of its natural resources One of the men who has borne his part in the establishment and maintenance of this supremacy is W L Japp, of Richland Township, owner of 200 acres of valuable farm land in section 3

W L Japp was born in Dodge County, Nebraska, in 1876 a son of John and Christine Japp, natives of Germany John Japp came to the United States when a young man and homesteaded in Dodge County, Nebraska At the time of his death he owned 1,200 acres of land, and was a man of prominence in Dodge and Washington counties His death took place in 1879, but his widow survives him and lives in Dodge County, being now seventy-five years old

Until he was twenty-one years old W L Japp remained at home and secured his education in the district schools of Dodge County When he reached his majority he began farming for himself, first on land he rented from his father, but later he bought his present farm, and on it he is carrying on a general farming and stockraising business, and has been very successful He has made improvements upon his place and it is now in good condition and reflects credit upon his skill as a farmer

Mr Japp was married to Dora Harder, a daughter of Joseph Harder of Dodge County, now deceased Mr and Mrs Japp have twelve children, as follows John, August, Emil, George, Edward, Ernest, W. L, Kate, Minnie, Emma, Lora and Lizzie In politics Mr. Japp is an independent thinker and voter His elder sons are engaged in farming in the same neighborhood as he, while the younger ones are on the farm with him, and all of them are doing well They are held in high respect in their community as hard-working and thrifty men and good citizens.

HARVEY C KENDALL, advertising manager and director of the Fremont Evening Tribune, is one of the leading business men and public-spirited citizens of Fremont, who has done much for the advancement along industrial civic lines of this locality He was born in Iowa County, Wisconsin, in 1885, a son of William H and Minnie (Hoskins) Kendall They were born in Iowa County, Wisconsin, where they lived for many years engaged in farming, but in 1905 he sold his farm and retired to Dodgeville, Wisconsin, where he and his wife are still living They had four children born to them Alma, who married John Campbell, mayor of Dodgeville, died in 1918; Harvey C, who was second in order of birth, James H, who is treasurer of Iowa County Wisconsin, is the youngest man ever elected to such an office in Wisconsin; and Dr Charles H, who is practicing dentistry at Milwaukee, Wisconsin, was graduated from the Northwestern University at Evanston, Illinois, and was president of his class during his senior year Mr. and Mrs Kendall are consistent and earnest members of the Congregational Church He is a republican in politics He has been fairly successful in his undertakings, and has won the confidence of his fellow citizens The paternal great-grandfather, Henry Kendall, founded the family in this country when he came from England to the United States and located in Iowa County, Wisconsin, about seventy years ago When he settled there he was one of the very earliest pioneers in the county, and became one of its prominent men, always holding some of the township offices Possessed of sterling traits of character, principal among which was strict integrity, he stated in his will that all of his debts must be paid first of all The maternal grandfather, William Hoskins, was also an Englishman, born in Cornwall, England, and he, too, was an early settler of Iowa County, Wisconsin

Mr. Kendall's first occupation was in newspaper work, at which time he was in the employ of his uncle in North Dakota Six years later he returned to Wisconsin and became the manager of the Dodgeville Chronicle, which has the largest circulation of any weekly newspaper in Wisconsin

While in North Dakota Harvey C Kendall met Alice McKay, to whom he was married September 11, 1912, and in January, 1913, he moved to Fremont to become manager of the Fremont Herald Later he went with the Hammond Printing Company and held the position of advertising manager for three years He resigned his position with the Tribune at that time and organized the Golden Rod Ice Cream Company, incorporating it at $50,000, and F. E Pratt is its president; Carl Thomsen is vice president, and Mr Kendall was secretary and general manager The company ships its product all over Nebraska, Iowa and South Dakota, and is represented on the road by two traveling salesmen. In January, 1920, Mr Kendall sold his interests in the Golden Rod Ice Cream Company and purchased a substantial interest in the Hammond Printing Company He was elected a director of the firm and advertising manager for its publication, the Fremont Evening Tribune, which position he now holds Mr Kendall has other interests, owning stock in several concerns, and his nice modern residence

Fraternally Mr. Kendall is a Knight Templar Mason He also belongs to the Modern Woodmen of America, Ancient Order of United Workmen and other similar organizations Always interested in the work of the Young Men's Christian Association, he is now serving as one of the directors of the association at Fremont, is president of the Fremont Boy Scout Council, is secretary of the Fremont Aerial Club, and is a member and official of the Fremont Rotary Club and an active member of the Commercial Club He is one of the officials of the Congregational Church During the late war he served as county merchant representative, and took a very active part in all of the war drives A strong republican, he served as chairman of the county central committee and as chairman of the congressional committee of the Third District of Nebraska of his party. Mr. Kendall is a man of more than ordinary strength of will and is oftentimes called into counsel with other representative men of his community Having devoted much thought to current events, he is recognized as an authority on public questions and local politics Among other qualities without doubt he is possessed of grit, vision and a really marvelous ability to overcome obstacles, and he has contributed of them freely to civic undertakings as well as to the advancement of his own interests

E P Hanson Strict attention to business and undaunted faith in his ability to succeed have been influential factors in the rise of E P Hanson, president of the Herman State Bank His original business equipment consisted of a good name, a fair endowment of intellect and a practical education, and with these he has worked his way to business and financial prominence among the people of his community

Mr Hanson was born on a farm in Washington County, Nebraska, May 4, 1870, a son of H. V. and Anna Hanson His father, a native of Sweden, came to the United States a poor young man in 1865, and after four years in Utah settled in Washington County and purchased a relinquishment of eighty acres For his first board home he hauled lumber all the way from Omaha, but in later years this residence was replaced by a more commodious and pretentious one, for Mr. Hanson rose rapidly in fortune through his industry and good management, and at the time of his death in 1902, when he was sixty-four years of age, was the owner of 720 acres of land and considered one of the successful men of his locality. His wife, Anna, died when forty-two years of age, leaving six children Mrs R B Wilson, a resident of Omaha, E P; Mrs Dr J F. Peddleford of South Dakota, Mrs Swan Johnson, living on the old homestead in Washington County, E A, a former banker of Decatur, this state, now deceased, and Francis, a member of the First Nebraska Volunteer Infantry, who met his death in the Philippines April 27, 1899

After attending the local schools E. P Hanson pursued a course at the normal school at Fremont, from which he was duly graduated, and at the age of nineteen years entered upon a career of his own He farmed until he reached the age of twenty-eight years, at which time he became a salesman on the road for the Cudahy Packing Company, with which concern he remained three years, then entering the employ of the Standard Oil Company, with which he remained five years Mr. Hanson then spent one year at the Exposition grounds, Omaha, following which he came to Herman, and in 1907 founded the Herman State Bank, of which he is president This institution has an excellent standing among the financial concerns of the county, and is capitalized at $50,000 A large part of the confidence placed in it by the people of this community is by reason of their faith in Mr. Hanson's motives, which have always been found above board and free from double dealing He has various farming interests in Washington and Thurston counties, and is a member of the board of directors of the First National Bank of Decatur As a fraternalist he is a thirty-second degree Mason and a Shriner, and a member of the Knights of the Maccabees, in both of which orders he has numerous friends

In 1901 Mr. Hanson was united in marriage with Lucy D Cooper, who was born and reared at Cameron, Missouri, and to this union there has been born one son, Howard, who is still attending school

HIRAM JEFFERSON ROSENBAUM For thirty years Hiram Jefferson Rosenbaum was numbered among the industrious farmers, good citizens, trusted friends and neighbors of Washington County. His life record is one to be remembered in his community Besides Mrs Rosenbaum and his children he left material evidences of his activity in a substantial farm property and country home, now occupied by Mrs Rosenbaum.

This farm home is in Arlington Township, section 1, a half mile north and five miles east of Arlington

Mr Rosenbaum was born in Washington County, Virginia, a son of Joel and Nancy (Ramsey) Rosenbaum His father was a Virginia farmer and at one time held the office of constable The family were Presbyterians in religion

Hiram Jefferson Rosenbaum in 1874 married Sarah Garrett, who was born in the same county as himself The following year, in 1875, they came out to Washington County, Nebraska They first bought land near Fort Calhoun, where they remained eight years, after which they removed to the community west of Kennard where Mr Rosenbaum spent the rest of his years A carpenter by trade, which he had learned in Virginia, he used that trade during many seasons in Nebraska, also cultivated his farm, and built up a considerable business in fire insurance He identified himself from the first with the progressive element of the community, and was a very popular and highly esteemed citizen He died in 1916 at the age of sixty-one Fraternally he was affiliated with the Woodmen of the World, Modern Woodmen of America and the Knights of Pythias. Mrs. Rosenbaum is a member of the Baptist Church

To their marriage were born ten children· Carrie, wife of Reese French, a Washington County farmer, Joe who farms the old homestead. Edward, in the real estate business at Omaha; Mattie, widow of Jens Hoteling of Oklahoma, Nancy, wife of Charles Robinson, a farmer at Denver, Colorado, Buck, a farmer near Kennard, May, wife of Charles Peterson of Kennard, Jesse, a railroad man living at Spokane, Washington, Hiram B, a prospector near Spokane, and John, a salesman for the Goodyear Tire Company of California

THOMAS T. OSTERMAN, proprietor of the Tribune, of Blair, has been enrolled in the printing and newspaper service since boyhood With all his devotion to this profession, he has likewise been a leader in politics and in the civic affairs of his home community.

He was born at Fremont, Nebraska, June 9, 1876, fourth among the ten children of Charles Osterman and Catharine Kerl His father was born in Germany in 1840, came to America at the age of sixteen, and was identified with the pioneers at Fontanelle, Nebraska Mr Osterman's mother was born near Jefferson City, Missouri Her half-brother, Simon Kerl, was a noted author and grammarian, and was private secretary to the secretary of the treasury in Abraham Lincoln's cabinet

At the age of thirteen, when in the seventh grade of the old Fremont Central School, Tom Osterman went to work in the office of the Flail, to learn the printer's trade When three years later he left home he was competent as a compositor and in other branches of printing, and as a journeyman he worked in a number of eastern Nebraska towns In 1895 he leased a weekly paper at Arlington, and at that time was regarded as the youngest editor in Nebraska. The lease terminated in 1896 and in September of that year he began his long and permanent connection with Blair, where he became foreman of the Courier He was in charge of the business while its editor was in the South during the Spanish-American war in 1898

In 1903 Mr Osterman was appointed deputy county clerk He resigned that office March 1, 1904, to assume the ownership of the Blair Republican, changing its name to the Blair Democrat In 1907 he purchased the Courier, consolidating the two papers In 1912 a building and lot was purchased in the central business part of the city, to which the Democrat was moved It was published under that title until 1917 when Mr. Osterman participated in the purchase of the Tribune and has since used the latter name for his publication

Always active in politics as a stanch democrat, in recognition of the services he had rendered the party in Washington County Mr Osterman was appointed postmaster at Blair on the recommendation of Congressman C O Lobeck and took charge of the office July 1, 1914 While this necessitated turning over the active management of his newspaper to others, he has found time to keep in touch with its conduct and policies and has never for a moment lost sight of its welfare nor allowed it to lag in a single particular. A second commission as postmaster was given Mr Osterman under date of October 3, 1918, Congressman Lobeck informing him of his reappointment with the announcement that "The department had not a single mark against his record"

Something should also be said of Mr Osterman's influential activities in civic affairs. With the aid of his newspaper he has worked steadily for the betterment of the community. In a great measure his persistent efforts were responsible for the organization of Blair's present Chamber of Commerce, and it is a source of personal satisfaction to him that the local Commercial Club has brought about an extensive program of paving and sewer construction at Blair, to say nothing of the many other aids the chamber has rendered the city since its organization a few years ago

Mr Osterman has been interested in lodge work, being a Mason, Odd Fellow and Knight of Pythias, and for the last two years has been chancellor commander of Garfield Lodge No 6, Knights of Pythias, at Blair, during which time the lodge has enjoyed an unprecedented growth in membership

THOMAS T. OSTERMAN

November 23, 1898, Mr Osterman married Miss Minnie A Parish, a daughter of Joel D Parish Their only child was born in 1901 and died during a scarlet fever epidemic in 1905 Mr Osterman's brother, Theo M, of Central City, is serving his fourth term as a member of the Nebraska House of Representatives and is minority floor leader Merrick is his home county and he is prominently mentioned as a candidate for democratic gubernatorial honors in 1922

F J HOVENDICK was born in Washington County about the time Nebraska was suffering its worst era of vicissitudes through grasshoppers, drought and other adversities His people were early settlers here, and since youth his own efforts have been put forth as a practical farmer, and largely on the land where he was born and reared He has shared in the great prosperity of modern times and is owner of one of the highly improved places in Richland Township, in section 24

He was born October 24, 1875, son of Herman Henry Hovendick His father, a native of Germany, came to the United States in 1858 and for several years lived in Quincy, Illinois, a community from which came many of the early colonists of Dodge and Washington counties He was employed as a teamster there and when the Civil war broke out he enlisted in an Illinois regiment and gave valiant service to the Union cause Several years after the war, in 1869, he came to Nebraska and settled on land now included in the farm of his son, F J Hovendick His first purchase was a relinquishment of eighty acres, and later he added another eighty acres and gave to this farm the best efforts of his life He lived there honored and respected until his death on May 11, 1917, at the age of seventy-eight He was married in Quincy and his wife died in 1903 In the family were five sons and four daughters

F J Hovendick grew up on the home farm, acquired a common school education At the age of twenty-one he entered the employment of his father, and nine years later took entire charge of the place and has lived there ever since He now owns 120 acres and has been a very successful stock raiser, that being the most profitable branch of his enterprise.

Mr Hovendick had a place on his local school board for seventeen years He is a member of the non-partisan league, which expresses most of his views on politics and economic subjects He and his family are members of the Lutheran Church.

May 6, 1908, Mr Hovendick married Miss Frieda Tranton, daughter of the late August Tranton She was four years old when her father died, and her mother is now Mrs Emma Hawk The children of Mr and Mrs Hovendick, all at home, are Francis, Opal and Herman

CHRISTOPHER C CROWELL Of all the names associated with the commercial and civic history of Blair from pioneer times to the present that of Crowell has been perhaps most distinctive of widespread commercial enterprise, affairs and movements of first magnitude in the community and this section of the state In earlier generations the Crowells were a wealthy and prominent family of Massachusetts and later they supplied capital and personal initiative to the great task of railroad building in the Missouri Valley, both in Iowa and Nebraska. A member of the same group of capitalists and railroad builders was the Colonel Blair for whom the county seat of Washington County was named

While his life for the most part was spent in Massachusetts, Prince S Crowell, father of C C Crowell, was the first of the family whose name deserves recognition in the history of Washington County. He was of old Puritan stock and a lineal descendant of Elder Brewster, the first churchman in the New World C C Crowell's grandfather, Capt David Crowell, was in the War of 1812, and his father, Christopher, was in the War of the Revolution. Thus the Crowell family story goes back well to the beginning of American history Prince S Crowell was a man of remarkable business ability and unusual energy, and those qualities were transmitted to the succeeding generation In younger years he commanded one of the first merchant vessels sailing from American ports to China He retired from the sea quite young to become a shipbuilder, and he constructed a great many vessels in his home town of East Dennis, Massachusetts, that contributed to the prestige of the American merchant marine in the early half of the nineteenth century

Some years later Prince Crowell became interested with John F Blair and others in a construction company which built many of the railroads developing the western country Some of these pioneer railroad lines were the Chicago, Iowa & Nebraska, from Clinton to Cedar Rapids, the Cedar Rapids & Missouri River, from Cedar Rapids to Council Bluffs; The Sioux City & Pacific in Iowa, from Missouri Valley to Sioux City; all of which are now integral parts of the Chicago & Northwestern system In Nebraska this company built the Fremont, Elkhorn & Missouri Valley Railroad Prince Crowell was president of two banks, and in Massachusetts conducted a large marine insurance He was a devoted friend of the public school system, was a radical abolitionist, and his home was the meeting place of such historic personages as William Lloyd Garrison, Wendell Phillips, the Burleighs, Lucy Stone, Anna Shaw and others who molded the thought and action of that generation. Though of a retiring disposition, his power was nevertheless a strong factor in public affairs He amassed a large fortune through his personal efforts and was ever a liberal supporter of all charitable movements

A son of this New England capitalist was the late Christopher C Crowell, Sr, many of whose life activities were identified with Blair and vicinity He was born at East Dennis, Massachusetts, May 19, 1844, and was educated in the common schools and in Eastman's Business College at Poughkeepsie, New York After leaving school he was clerk in a ship chandlery store at Boston, and at the age of twenty-four entered the fish oil manufacturing business at Portland Harbor, Maine

It was in 1869 that Christopher C Crowell removed to Nebraska He lived a short time in Omaha, and then rented and operated for a year a flouring mill near De Soto in Washington County Locating at Blair, he engaged in the grain business and during his lifetime developed the extensive business now represented by the Crowell Lumber and Grain Company and Crowell Elevator Company, which during his lifetime operated lumber yards and elevators at fifteen different points in Nebraska along the Fremont, Elkhorn & Missouri Valley Railroad

He maintained a home in Los Angeles California, a number of years before his death, which occurred in California in April, 1910 Even at that distance he maintained a deep personal interest in the welfare of the towns in Nebraska where his business intersts lay He was one of the first men to undertake to utilize the salt springs at Lincoln for making commercial salt Thinking he would have to pay royalties for the benefit of some of the state officials who had the leasing of the lands under control, he abandoned this enterprise. In the contemplated salt manufacturing venture he was associated with Thomas F. Hall of Omaha, and both were important witnesses later in the impeachment trial of Governor David Butler. His political record shows a noteworthy independence. He was first a republican, later a labor party advocate, for a single campaign was a democrat and after 1884 was a stanch prohibitionist. In 1900 he was the candidate of his party for treasurer of Nebraska, and served as the first full term mayor of Blair in 1870. He was a pioneer in the prohibitionist movement and he left a fund of $10,000 in trust to be used for the purpose of promoting the interests of the prohibition party. The trustee of this fund was his son, C. C. Crowell, Jr., who used the money to the best advantage and has had the satisfaction of seeing the results which his father so ardently desired in his lifetime.

December 5, 1867, Christopher C. Crowell, Sr., married Polly D. Foster. She likewise was of Mayflower ancestry, and her grandfather at one time was a slave owner in the Town of Brewster. The old house of the Fosters in Brewster was later owned and occupied by a descendant of one of these slaves, and was one of the oldest residences in the state. Christopher C. Crowell and wife had eight children, two of whom died in infancy. Those to reach mature years were Grace E., Edwin F., C. C., Jr., Lydia S., Nathan and Harland. Of these Lydia is the wife of L. M. Weaver, a wealthy rancher and sheep man of Spokane, Washington, and whose father was a Nebraska pioneer, serving as a member of the first Constitutional Convention. Harland Crowell is a fruit farmer at Olympia, Washington. Nathan is a former banker and lives at Stuart, Nebraska.

Since the death of his father Christopher C. Crowell, Jr., has been at the helm of the business affairs of the Crowell Lumber and Grain Company and the Crowell Elevator Company. The Crowell estate is still intact and as manager of the business he has greatly enlarged it. There are now twenty-three stations where they operate lumber yards or elevators in Nebraska controlled by these companies.

Mr. Crowell was born in Blair July 6, 1874, was well educated and practically grew up in the atmosphere of his father's business and was thoroughly qualified for the responsibilities that have devolved upon him during the last ten years. He began business personally with the company in 1894.

He married Augusta Saare, of Newman Grove, Nebraska. They have four children: Herman and C. C. III, both students in the Nebraska Wesleyan University at University Place, and Mildred and Pauline, attending the public schools of Omaha, where the family have their city home.

JOHN ROSENBAUM, who is now living practically retired in the Village of Kennard, Washington County, is one of the pioneers who did effective service in connection with the civic and industrial development of this county, where he remained and improved an excellent farm and became one of the representative agriculturists and stock growers of the county. His loyalty as a citizen has been unstinted and marked by liberality and public spirit, while he has so ordered his course in all the relations of life as to retain secure place in the confidence and good will of the community in which he has long maintained his home.

Mr Rosenbaum claims the historic old Dominion State as the place of his nativity, and was there reared and educated, he having been a child at the time of his mother's death and his father having there remained until he, too, passed away Mr Rosenbaum is a son of Joel and Nancy (Ramsey) Rosenbaum, and his father's active career was marked by close association with farm enterprise in Virginia, where he died when about sixty-seven years of age. He was a republican in politics and he and his wife held membership in the Baptist Church They became the parents of five children Hiram J who came to Washington County, Nebraska, in 1871, and is one of the well-known pioneer citizens of the county, John, immediate subject of this sketch, the next in order of birth, Aaron, who still resides in the State of Virginia; Caroline, who died in that state, and Emanuel, who came to Nebraska in 1882 and here passed the remainder of his life

John Rosenbaum was born in Washington County, Virginia, on August 30, 1850, and there received his early education in the common schools of the period, he having been about eleven years old at the inception of the Civil war and having been deeply impressed with the struggle that brought so much of disaster and devastation to his native state In 1872, shortly after attaining to his legal majority, he came to Washington County, Nebraska, where he purchased a tract of wild land and stanchly girded himself for the arduous work of reclaiming a productive farm With the passing years generous success attended his efforts as an agriculturist and stock grower, with the result that he is now one of the substantial men of the county, where he still retains a valuable and well-improved landed estate of 180 acres, though he removed from his farm to Kennard in 1912 and has since lived virtually retired His political allegiance is given to the democratic party, he is affiliated with the Modern Woodmen of America, and his wife is an active member of the Methodist Episcopal Church at Kennard

On March 22, 1887, was solemnized the marriage of Mr Rosenbaum to Miss Ruth McCann, who likewise was born in Washington County, Virginia, and whose parents, Isaac and Margaret (Wright) McCann, became early settlers of Washington County, Nebraska, where he was a successful farmer at the time of his death at the age of seventy-two years, and his wife was seventy-six years of age at the time of her death Mr and Mrs Rosenbaum have seven children Jasper H, Clyde, Ethel, Blanche, Hazel, Glenn and Roscoe All of the sons are actively identified with farm enterprise in their native county, and in this connection, as well as in loyal citizenship, they are well upholding the honors of the family name Ethel is the wife of Dudley P. Rosenbaum, a carpenter and contractor, residing at Arlington, Washington County Blanche is the wife of Frank Naeve, who resides at Kennard, and Hazel is the wife of Samuel Wright, who is prominently associated with the grain and elevator business at Kennard.

EDWARD PILCHER The late Edward Pilcher was for many years one of the leading citizens of Washington County, and after he had retired from the agricultural labors with which he had occupied himself he moved to Blair, although he did not enter its business life He was not born in this country, but became one of its most devoted adherents, and exemplified in his life and associations the principles upon which the government is founded

Edward Pilcher was born in England, October 22, 1833 a son of George and Mary Pilcher, who were born, lived and died in England

When only a lad Edward Pilcher came to the United States all by himself, and until he enlisted for service during the war between the two sections of the country, lived in New York After a military service of one year he was honorably discharged, and then began looking about him for a good opening This he found in Washington County, although his resources were nearly exhausted by the time he reached his destination Here he homesteaded and for many years continued to conduct the farm he proved up In 1903 he left the farm, moved to Blair, and there he died, August 17, 1904 Both he and his wife were members of the Baptist Church In politics he was a republican, and he served on the school board for fifteen years

In 1865 Mr Pilcher was married to Mary Teeter, who was born in Pennsylvania, a daughter of David and Teressa (Raidey) Teeter, both of whom were born in Pennsylvania, where he died, his widow then coming to Nebraska, where she passed away On both sides of the family the ancestry is of German origin Mr Teeter had four children, and his widow, when she married again, had four more children Mr and Mrs Pilcher became the parents of twelve children, six of whom survive, namely Jane, who married Del Ballard, a Dakota farmer; Dora, who married Mike Wilson, a Nebraska farmer, Grace, who married Burdett Hancock, a farmer, resides at Cuming, Edward C, who lives on the old homestead, Charles, who is engaged in farming in the vicinity of the old homestead, and Lloyd L, who is living on a portion of the homestead

When Mr and Mrs Pilcher began their married life they were poor, and for years they had to work very hard, but in time they prospered and became the owners of a large amount of land, some of which has been sold, but Edward C owns the homestead Mrs Pilcher maintains her residence at Blair, where she is very highly regarded She is proud of her children, all of whom are doing very well, and looks back with pride on the days when she was able to render so much assistance to her husband in his uphill climb to prosperity.

Norman Wilkins Born and reared on a Nebraska farm, herding cattle in Washington County when most of the land was unfenced, and after experiences in other vocations and seeing a good deal of the world Norman Wilkins made the happy choice of farming as his steady vocation, and has seen his affairs prosper until he is now one of the substantial land owners and good citizens of Blair Township, his home being in section 17, three miles west and one mile south of Blair

He was born in Washington County November 11, 1873, and after getting his early education left home and for about three years traveled over the country, most of the time as a railroader. About sixteen years ago he started for himself and is now living on one of his father's farms, comprising 200 acres Besides the general farm management he is specializing in thoroughbred livestock, Hereford cattle and Poland China hogs

Mr Wilkins married Sophie Rathman Her father, George Rathman, was an early settler in Washington County and died during the Spanish-American war Mr and Mrs Wilkins have two children Norman, Jr, born July 4, 1918, and Marietta, born May 28, 1920 Mr Wilkins and family are members of the Christian Church He is a thirty-second degree Scottish Rite Mason, and for several years has interested himself in the cause of public education as a member of the school board

MANNASSES FAUQUET The success of men in business or any vocation depends upon character as well as upon knowledge, it being a self-evident proposition that integrity of motive and action is the best policy Business demands confidence, and where that is lacking business ends In every community some men are known for their upright lives, strong common sense and moral worth rather than for their wealth or political standing Their neighbors and acquaintances respect them, the young generations heed their example, and when they "wrap the drapery of their couches about them and lie down to pleasant dreams," posterity listens with reverence to the story of their quiet and useful lives Among such men of a past generation in Nebraska was the Mannasses Fauquet who was not only a progressive man of affairs, successful in material pursuits, but a man of modest and unassuming demeanor, of a high type of mental calibre, a reliable, self-made man, a friend to the poor, charitable to the faults of his neighbors and always ready to unite with them in every good work, and active in the support of laudable public enterprises He was a man who in every respect merited the high esteem in which he was universally held, for he was a man of public spirit, exemplary character and business ability

Mannasses Fauquet was born in the Province of Picardy, France, on January 8, 1840, and his death occurred at his home in Fremont, Nebraska, on October 5, 1916 He was reared and educated in his native land until 1858, when, at the age of eighteen years, he came to the United States, locating first in Ohio, where he learned the trade of a cooper Subsequently he entered the oil business, drilling wells for different companies, and at length became manager of one of the most successful of the oil concerns He was successful not only as a workman and a manager of men, but he also possessed a business acumen and shrewdness that enabled him to make use of opportunities for business advancement He lived in Ohio and West Virginia until 1872, when he moved to Saunders County, Nebraska, where he bought eighty acres of land, comprising the present site of Cedar Bluffs Some time later this land was sold to a railroad company and Mr Fauquet bought a larger place, on which they lived for fourteen years and to the improvement and cultivation of which he devoted himself with energy and splendid financial results Then, selling that place he bought another farm near Wahoo, Saunders County, and lived there until 1910, when he and his wife moved to Wahoo, where they resided three years Then, in 1913, they came to Fremont, where Mrs Fauquet still lives For several years prior to Mr Fauquet's death he and his wife had spent their winters in the South, spending one winter in Florida and three in Texas When they came to Nebraska their total cash capital was $1,700, and with this nucleus Mr Fauquet by persistent and well-directed industry succeeded in accumulating a handsome property and was able to spend his last years free from any necessity for active participation in business affairs, enjoying that rest which he had so richly earned

In 1865 Mr. Fauquet was married to Mary J. Prince, who was born and reared in West Virginia, the daughter of Hubbard and Elizabeth (Kincheloe) Prince, both of whom were natives of eastern Virginia, though they spent practically all of their lives in West Virginia Mr Prince was a minister of the Methodist Episcopal Church, though he afterward transferred his labors to the Baptist Church In connection with his religious work he also carried on agricultural pursuits To Mr and Mrs Fauquet were born seven children, of which number six are living, namely Cleophine, who is the wife of Alfred Softley, of

Ma Fauquet

Dodge County; Emile, who is a graduate of the Nebraska State University, is now living on his mother's farm in Saunders County, Arsene W, who is a graduate of the Nebraska State University, is now a college professor at Sioux Falls, South Dakota, Bertha is the wife of William Luehrs, a farmer in Dodge County, Ernest has moved to a large farm which he owns near Mason City, Nebraska; and Ephriam J is a farmer in Dodge County

Mr Fauquet was a supporter of the republican party and formerly took an active interest in political affairs In an early day he served as postmaster of Cedar Bluffs Religiously he and his wife were earnest and faithful members of the Baptist Church, to which they gave generously During the Civil war Mr Fauquet rendered good service as a teamster, and was always a loyal and stanch supporter of the government of his adopted country One special phase of his makeup was recognized by all who became acquainted with him, namely, the keen quality of his mind Though he possessed but an ordinary education, he wrote many articles for the newspapers, and wrote in an attractive and graceful style that always rendered his articles interesting Had he possessed a more complete education he undoubtedly would have occupied a definite position in the literary field, for he was a keen and analytical thinker and possesses naturally strong powers of expression. By a straightforward and commendable course Mr Fauquet made his way from a modest beginning to a respectable position in the business world, winning the hearty admiration of his fellow citizens and earning a reputation as an enterprising, progressive man of affairs and as a broad-minded, charitable and upright citizen, which the public was not slow to recognize and appreciate He was a man whom to know was to respect and admire, and his loss was keenly felt by a large circle of friends and acquaintances.

LOUIS CHRISTENSEN At the age of fourscore Louis Christensen has a retrospect of half a century spent in Washington County, and that half century has been well employed and involves many years of fruitful labor, well ordered industry, and a giving of service both to further his own ambitions and benefit his community

Now retired from the heavy responsibilities of farming, Louis Christensen was born in Denmark April 2, 1840 He and his brother came to the United States by the way of Canada in 1862, and located at Monmouth, Illinois Louis Christensen almost immediately signalized his loyalty to his adopted country, enlisting and serving in the Union army with Company I of the Sixty-First Illinois Regiment. After the war he continued to live and work at Monmouth until 1870, when with a team of mules and a covered wagon he made the interesting and lengthy overland journey to Washington County, Nebraska He took up his homestead near the Town of Washington, acquiring at first only forty acres, but eventually extended his land holdings until he is now the prosperous owner of 480 acres of well-improved land

Two years before coming to Nebraska, in 1868, he married Miss Anna Paulsen, at Omaha, Nebraska She died in 1891, the mother of three children · F W Christensen, whose career is briefly noted on other pages, Mary, who died at the age of twenty-six, and George, who lives on the home farm in Washington County

For a number of years past Mr Christensen has lived in the Town of Washington, and his sons have taken over the management and work of the farm He was always a hard worker, and deserves all the credit for his prosperity The first home he owned in Washington County was a little one-story frame board shack, but many years ago that was replaced by a modern farm home surrounded with a group of other buildings Mr. Christensen has performed his duties as a citizen through his record as a Union soldier and through the quiet and effective management of his private affairs He has always cast his vote as a republican and is a member of the Lutheran Church

JOHN FINEGAN The career of John Finegan since coming to Dodge and Washington counties represents real achievement An Irish youth recently arrived, he recommended himself by his willingness to do hard work and was satisfied with the slow but sure progress of laying a foundation and accumulating capital The rewards have come in later years in the possession of valuable farming land and an extensive business as a stock raiser

Mr Finegan, whose home is in section 32 of Nickerson Township, Dodge County, was born in County Galway, Ireland, September 23, 1864 He grew up and received his education in his native country and at the age of twenty years came to the United States, going directly to Washington County, Nebraska For a number of years he was employed as a farm hand, using his limited savings to purchase lands and gradually getting the equipment to start farming on his own account in Dodge County The years have brought a steady increase of prosperity until he now owns 257 acres in Dodge and Washington counties and recently he completed a modern home, one of the best in this section The first year he came to the land he set out an orchard and for many years has had abundance of fruit He is one of the successful sheep growers of Dodge County and he also feeds hogs and cattle

Mr Finegan married Miss Julia Delaney, a native of Dodge County, member of the well-known Delaney family of Dodge County (to whom reference will be found on other pages of this edition) They have six children: Gertrude, Julia, Agnes, John, James and Edward, all of whom live with their parents and have a part in the management of the household and the farm. Mr Finegan is a democratic voter, a member of the Catholic Church, and for a number of years has given much of his thought and time to the affairs of the local school district He is affiliated with the Modern Woodmen of America and the Knights of Columbus

HARRY L SWAN In journalistic circles of Washington County a name that has become well and favorably known is that of Harry L Swan, publisher and proprietor of the Herman Record In something over three years Mr Swan has so managed the affairs of this weekly that he has made it an important factor in the molding of public opinion, and at the same time has established himself firmly in the confidence of the community as a man of breadth of view and sound judgment

He was born in New York state in 1859, a son of Samuel P and Calista (Crandall) Swan, natives of New York, the former of whom died when sixty-five years of age and the latter at the age of seventy-three years On both sides of the family the ancestry is traced back to pre-Revolutionary days Taken to Missouri in boyhood, Harry L Swan received his education in the public schools of that state, and at the age of nineteen years entered upon his career in southwestern Missouri, where he taught in the rural district for two years He also conducted small country nwspapers from 1880 to 1890, and in the latter year went to Denver, where he was associated with several city papers In 1885 he accepted a position with the Associated Press, and continued with that organization until coming to Herman in May, 1918 At that time he purchased the Record, a weekly publication of which he has been the owner and publisher ever since He is furnishing his readers with a well-edited, well-printed and entirely reliable paper, and has the support of a large subscription list and of advertisers who have found his publication a valuable and business-bringing medium While Mr Swan is a democratic voter, his paper maintains an independent stand as to party matters He is a member of the Masonic Lodge, the Sons of the American Revolution, the Woodmen of the World and the Brotherhood of American Yeomen, while Mrs Swan belongs to the Order of the Eastern Star and the Neighbors of Woodcraft

In 1886, at Schell City, Missouri, Mr Swan was united in marriage with Sarah A Herrick, and to this union there have been born seven children. Herrick, a resident of Billings, Montana, Robert, Ernest and Harry L., Jr., all of whom reside with their parents, Helen and Maude, who died in infancy, and Eula, deceased, who was the wife of Harold Gorham

HENRY MENCKE. Only those who come into personal contact with Henry Mencke, of Blair, scion of one of the worthy old families of Washington County, and one of the popular and successful attorneys of this locality, can understand how thoroughly nature and training, habits of thought and action have enabled him to succeed in his life work and made him a fit representative of the enterprising class of professional men to which he belongs He is a fine type of the sturdy, progressive American of today, doing thoroughly and well the work that he has to do, and because of his ability and character he enjoys an enviable reputation among his fellowmen

Henry Mencke was born in Washington County on June 28, 1876, and is the son of Claus and Tina (Rathmann) Mencke, both of whom were born in Germany, and who now live in Blair Claus Mencke came to Washington County in 1869, bought land and devoted himself to its improvement and cultivation for a number of years He was elected sheriff of Washington County, and so satisfactory was his service that he was retained in the office for the unusual period of twenty-two years He is now a bonded abstracter and is numbered among the leading citizens of Blair He is a democrat in politics and a member of the Modern Woodmen of America To him and his wife were born seven children, five of whom are living, as follows Henry, the subject of this sketch, Bessie, who is engaged in the millinery business at Tekamah, Nebraska, George, who is engaged in the lumber business at Seattle, Washington; Emma, the wife of E J Lazure, who is engaged in the grocery business at Florence; and John, a bookkeeper at Brush, Colorado

Henry Mencke was reared at home and attended the public schools, graduating from the Blair High School, in addition to which he took a commercial course in a business college He then read law and in 1900 was admitted to the bar During the following years he was variously engaged, being in the lumber business for a year or two, then spending six years in the banking business in Buffalo County, was deputy sheriff under his father for about a year, and four years was deputy county treasurer In 1912 Mr. Mencke entered upon the active practice of law at Blair, and during the subsequent years he has enjoyed a large and lucrative business Well versed in the principles of law, a constant student of the latest court decisions and keen and sagacious in his comprehension of a case, he is considered one of the leaders among the attorneys of the Washington County bar

In 1900 Mr Mencke was married to Eliza McCoy, who was born in Missouri, and they have a son, Ralph W, born on August 27, 1901 Mr and Mrs Mencke are active members of the Methodist Episcopal Church Mr Mencke is a democrat in his political views and fraternally he is a member of the Independent Order of Odd Fellows and the Modern Woodmen of America He has served as city attorney of Blair four years and in other ways his popularity among his fellow citizens has been recognized He is a public-spirited, unassuming, conservative, genteel gentleman whom to know is to respect and admire

GABRIEL RICHARD STEWART, who is familiarly known as "Dick" Stewart in his home community in Washington County, came with his parents to Nebraska prior to the admission of the state to the Union, and in his youth he gained a plethora of experience in connection with life on the frontier. In 1883 he engaged in farm enterprise in Washington County, where he continued his successful activities as an agriculturist and stock-grower until 1913, since which year he has lived retired in the attractive Village of Kennard, this county.

Mr Stewart was born in Champaign County, Illinois, on December 29, 1854, and is a son of David M. and Nancy (Barnes) Stewart, both of whom were born in the State of Ohio In the pioneer days the father became actively identified with the great western cattle industry, in connection with which he drove cattle from Indian Territory and Kansas into Nebraska, as well as from Texas to Nebraska In 1861 David M Stewart came with his family to Nebraska and established a home at Omaha Thereafter he was for some time engaged in overland freighting from Omaha to Denver and Salt Lake City, and he was one of the first to make a cattle trail from Texas to Omaha He died at the early age of thirty-five, and his widow passed the closing period of her life in Washington County, where she died at the age of sixty-two years Of the children the subject of this review is the eldest, Alma H is the widow of Rufus Clair and resides at Blair, Washington County, Charles F. is deceased, Jacob A operates a grain elevator in York County After the death of her first husband Mrs Stewart became the wife of Jonathan Alloway, and two sons of this marriage survive her—Oliver S, engaged in the oil business at Enid, Oklahoma, and Simon B, a telegraph operator residing at Dayton, Iowa The father of Mr. Stewart was a democrat in politics and the mother was a zealous member of the Free Methodist Church

Gabriel Richard Stewart was a lad of seven years at the time when the family home was established in Omaha, and he gained his early education in the public schools of Nebraska Territory When eleven years old he made one trip with his father to Kansas, to procure 250 steers that were to be broken and used for freighting After the death of his father Mr Stewart was given charge of the live stock of Sheely Brothers, who then conducted the largest butchering business in the City of Omaha. Thereafter he was engaged in running cattle to the Omaha and Winnebago Reservation in the employ of Edwin Loveland, and in 1873 he came to Washington County and became associated with his stepfather, Jonathan Alloway in farm enterprise. At this time he purchased land in the county, but in 1876 he began as a cowboy on the range in western Nebraska for the firm of Keith & Barton, of North Platte In 1883 he returned to Washington County, where he married Miss Lucy Magee, a native of Pennsylvania, and they established their home on the farm, to which he later added until he had a total of 160 acres He developed one of the well-improved and valuable farm properties of this county and still owns the same Here he continued his active operations as an agriculturist and a grower of good grades of live stock for fully thirty years, and his energy and good management brought him a generous measure of prosperity with the advancing years Upon retiring from his farm he established his residence in the Village of Kennard, as previously stated in this article, and here he and his wife have an attractive home in which they delight to extend welcome to their many friends Mr Stewart is a stanch democrat in politics, is affiliated with the Masonic Fraternity and the Modern Woodmen of America, and his wife holds membership in the Methodist Episcopal Church To them have been born five children Belle is the wife of Claar LeCrone, who is engaged in the sawmill business at Kennard, Edna is the wife of William Nelson, and they reside on her father's old home farm, Jennie became the wife of David Pritchard and is now deceased; Winnie is the wife of Soren C Cook, engaged in the real-estate business at Kennard, and Donivan C, who is now identified with farm enterprise in Washington County, was for fourteen months in service in the United States navy at the time of the late World War He went to Manilla, Philippine Islands, China Sea and Siberia, and returning home received his honorable discharge at Denver before he was eighteen years old, he having enlisted before he was seventeen years of age

EDMUND R. GURNEY, who is now president of the Lion Bonding & Surety Company in the City of Omaha, has been a resident of Nebraska since boyhood, and here he has found ample opportunity for his effective activities in connection with business enterprises of important order He has been specially influential in connection with banking enterprise and is known as one of the representative and influential figures in the financial circles of the state, with a record of splendid achievement in the development and managing of strong banking institutions Though his activities are now centered in the City of Omaha, he rendered so valuable a service in connection with the affairs of the First National Bank of Fremont, Dodge County of which institution he is still vice president, that it is but consonant that in this publication be entered a brief review of his career

Mr Gurney was born at Monticello Iowa, on May 22, 1870, and is a son of Mark and Emma (Goodrich) Gurney, who were born in Massachusetts but whose marriage was solemnized in Iowa, prior to the Civil war. Mark Gurney developed a prosperous enterprise as a manufacturer of furniture at Monticello, Iowa, and after his retirement from active business he came to Nebraska in 1883, and settled in Cedar County, where he made investment in real estate Later he removd with his wife to Kansas, where they passed the remainder of their lives and where he was serving as county judge of Graham County at the time of his death Mr Gurney was a man of fine mentality and sterling character, was prominently affiliated with the Masonic fraternity, in which he passed various official chairs, including those of the Knights Templar order, and in politics he was a stanch advocate of the cause of the republican party Of the four children Edmund R, of this review, was the third in order of birth, and of the number one other likewise is a resident of Nebraska, Clara, who is the wife of B H Williamson, of Arlington, Washington County.

Edmund R Gurney gained his preliminary educational discipline in the public schools of his native state and was a lad of thirteen years at the time of the family removal to Nebraska, where he continued his studies in the schools of Cedar County, besides having been for one year a student in Fremont College, of which William H Clements was then the executive head His first remunerative occupation was that of teaching in the schools of Nebraska, and after having served two years as principal of the high school at Ponca, Dixon County, he initiated his banking career by taking a position as assistant cashier of a bank in the little Village of Dixon, that county, where he thus continued his services three years His initiative energy, his ambition and his resourcefulness were then shown by his effecting the organization of the Laurel State Bank at Laurel, Cedar County, and under his five years' regime as cashier of this institution it developed a prosperous business. Upon leaving Laurel Mr Gurney purchased control of the Merchants State Bank of Winside, Wayne County, and he continued as president of this bank for three years In January, 1904, he came to Fremont and as vice president assumed forceful executive functions in connection with the First National Bank, the affairs of which were greatly advanced under his vigorous and progressive administration He still holds the office of vice president of this institution, which continued to receive the major part of his time and attention until January 1, 1919, when he was elected president of the Lion Bonding & Surety Company of Omaha, to which representative financial institution he has since given characteristically effective promotive service, his connection with the corporation marking still further advance in his peculiarly successful career as a constructive force in financial affairs This company bases its operations on a capital stock of $600,000, its surplus fund aggregating $400,000, and its business being disseminated over fifteen states of the middle west and southwest Mr Gurney is actively interested also in the First Bank of Nickerson, Dodge County, the Scribner State Bank of Scribner, this county; the First State Bank of North Bend, this county, the Farmers State Bank of Ames, likewise in Dodge County, and the Arlington State Bank at Arlington, Washington County The success that has attended the earnest and prolific activities of Mr Gurney is the more gratifying to contemplate by reason of the fact that his advancement has been entirely due to his own ability and efforts He has manifested a fine sense of personal stewardship in connection with his various banking enterprises, and has also been conspicuous for his civic liberality and progressiveness —especially in connection with the furtherance of the general advancement of the City of Fremont, where he still maintains active executive connection with the First National Bank, though he now resides in the City of Omaha

Well fortified in his opinions concerning governmental and general economic policies, Mr Gurney has always given unwavering allegiance to the republican party and has been active in its service In 1916 he was a delegate at large from Nebraska to the Republican National Convention in the City of Chicago, where he served as chairman of the Nebraska delegation He has been for a number of years treasurer of the State Central Committee of his party in Nebraska In a fraternal way he is actively affiliated with the Masonic fraternity and with the Knights of Pythias

In the year 1893 was solemnized the marriage of Mr Gurney to Miss Minnie Reynolds, who was born in the State of Pennsylvania, and they have five children Norris is superintendent of the Baker White Pine

Lumber Company of Baker, Oregon; Clair, who served nearly two years in the Marine Corps during the nation's participation in the World war, is now assistant cashier of the First National Bank of Fremont; Marion is a member of the class of 1921 in the University of Nebraska, and Theodore and Louise continue to impart youthful buoyancy in the parental home Mr and Mrs Gurney hold membership in the Presbyterian Church

R G WIESE Just half a century ago the Wiese family put in its first crop in the soil of Washington County, and through all successive years they have been here, have contended with the difficulties of soil and climate and economic conditions, and have contrived to prosper and achieve something creditable to their name

One of the prominent representatives of the family is R G Wiese, owner of a large and valuable farm in Richland Township, in section 15 He was born in Germany March 23, 1865, and just a year later his parents, Asmus and Dorothy Wiese, set out for the United States The first three years they lived in Iowa In Germany they were like many others, poor, living from day to day and when they came to America they did not possess money enough to pay their passage across This passage money was furnished by a brother of Asmus, Hans Wiese, who had come to America some years before and lived at Davenport, Iowa He was the only other member of the Wiese family to come to this country Asmus Wiese in 1869 came to Nebraska He rented some land and in 1870 put in his first crop For about eight years he provided for his family by renting and then bought eighty acres, and from that time forward his affairs were moderately prosperous and at one time he owned 400 acres Altogether he has been a very successful citizen, and is still living, making his home with his son R G, and was ninety-two years of age on November 2, 1920 His wife died at the age of forty-nine They had four children, two of the sons, Henry and George, being deceased, while the only living daughter is Mrs Katrine Japp

R. G Wiese grew up in Washington County from the age of five years and shared with the family in some of their early hardships He has done well in his mature career, and at the present time owns a farm of 320 acres, devoted to crops and live stock He is also a director and treasurer of his local school board and has filled that office for a number of years He is a republican voter, he and his family are Lutherans and his is affiliated with the Modern Woodmen of America

In 1888, at Blair, Nebraska, Mr. Wiese married Lena Schlapkohl, who died August 3, 1900, the mother of five children: Claus, Rudolph, Bertha, Amanda and Mata, all living except Mata For his present wife Mr Wiese married Lena Harder, a daughter of Joseph and Christina Harder, of Blair To this union were born eight children, all at home, named Herman, August, Arthur, Clarence, Christina, Asmus, Dorothy and Henry

JOHN H. GRIMM. Washington County has profited by the stable citizenship and faithful industry of the Grimm family since the '60s Practically all bearing the name have been interested in agriculture, but their services have been extended also to politics, education, religion and society John H Grimm, a resident of Blair, and for many years known as a prominent farmer and stockman, represents the second generation of his family in the county He was born at Blair in 1872, and is a son of Hans and Elizabeth (Harders) Grimm.

To the man who took up his abode in the prairies of the central west more than a half a century ago was vouchsafed a wealth and diversity of experience beside which that of those active in the twentieth century pales in insignificance If the men of the frontier suffered, they also lived, and their existence was turned to far higher purpose than the mere getting and parading of wealth and its luxuries In those days a code of honor prevailed which made it possible for a man to borrow money without putting up gilt-edged securities, and instances were rare in which the debt was not paid as agreed upon. These and other advantages of a non-commercial age are recalled in the life of the late Hans Grimm, whose earthly pilgrimage passed by sixty-eight milestones, and who became one of the substantial and highly respected agriculturists of Washington County

Hans Grimm was born May 6, 1841, in Germany, and was about twenty-four years of age when he came to the United States and located at Blair At the time of his arrival he had but small means, but his judgment was good and his foresight accurate, and he began buying land at the city limits During the early years he experienced all the hardships of the frontier, but as time went on his resources increased, as did his comforts, and he continued to add to his holdings while employing himself in cultivating the soil and feeding cattle and other stock. Through wise investment and marked industry be became one of the large land-holders of his community, as well as a citizen who was held in the highest esteem, his declining years being crowned with the love and respect of all who knew him. At his death he left his eight children an inheritance of money, as well as a heritage of ability and an honorable name, and each of the children has put his inheritance to good use and has upheld the name of what is known as one of Washington County's most highly esteemed families

Hans Grimm passed to his final rest in 1909. He was married at Blair in 1869 to Elizabeth Harders, who was born in Germany March 29, 1842, and died in 1903, and they became the parents of eight children, of whom seven are living C H, who occupies the old home place near Blair; Dr P. G, a physician and surgeon of Spirit Lake, Iowa, John H, Louis, who occupies a farm north of Blair, Dr Arthur, a dental practitioner of New York City, Edward, who occupies a farm in Washington County, and Mrs K A Petersen, of Blair.

John H Grimm was educated in the public schools of Blair, and when entering upon his independent career chose the vocation of farming as his life work He has been engaged therein throughout his career, and at this time is the owner of three large farms in Washington County, all of which are highly improved and in an excellent state of development Mr Grimm has made a specialty of raising live stock, and in 1920 shipped twenty-seven carloads of cattle to the market He is a man of the highest integrity and enjoys the confidence of his associates in business life and in several social and civic bodies to which he belongs He is unmarried and makes his home at Blair in a comfortable and modernly-furnished residence

James B Anderson, M D, has been since 1912 engaged in the practice of his profession at Kennard and is one of the able and representative physicians and surgeons of Washington County He was born at Buffalo, Dallas County, Missouri, on October 17, 1887, and is a son of Rev Moses Anderson and Maria (Burns) Anderson, the former a native of Missouri and the latter of Illinois The father went to Iowa in the pioneer days, and at Red Oak, that state, he received his higher educational training. He became a clergyman of the Methodist Episcopal Church, and held pastoral charges both in Colorado and Nebraska, to which latter state he came as a pioneer. His political allegiance is given to the republican party, and he holds membership in the Independent Order of Odd Fellows Of the children James B is the only son, Nellie P is the wife of Roy Beman, who is engaged in the drug business at Ceresco, Saunders County, Nebraska; and Faye, Elsie and Carroll remain at the parental home at Ceresco, the father having had pastoral charge of a number of churches in different counties in Nebraska

In the public schools of this state Doctor Anderson continued his studies until he had completed the curriculum of the high school at York, where also he attended York College one year In preparation for his chosen profession he entered the medical department of Creighton University in the City of Omaha, and in this institution he was graduated as a member of the class of 1910 After thus receiving his well earned degree of Doctor of Medicine he was engaged in practice at Arcadia, Valley County, about one year, and on January 15, 1912, established his residence at Kennard, where he was associated in practice with Dr William H. Pruner, Sr, until the death of the latter in 1915. Since that time he has continued in the control of a large and representative general practice, with high reputation in his exacting profession, and active as a member of the Washington County Medical Society, besides which he is a member also of the Elkhorn Valley Medical Society, the Nebraska State Medical Society and the American Medical Association The doctor is a stalwart advocate and supporter of the principles of the democratic party is affiliated with the Independent Order of Odd Fellows and the Masonic Fraternity, in which latter he has received the Knights Templar degree, and he and his wife hold membership in the Methodist Episcopal Church in their home village

In October, 1910, was solemnized the marriage of Doctor Anderson to Miss Cleo Pruner, daughter of his former and honored professional associate, Dr William H Pruner, Sr, and the three children of this union are Ella Sue, James B, Jr, and Robert P, the two older being students in the public schools of Kennard at the time of this writing, in 1920

CHRIS SCHUMACHER Some of the best farms and some of the best farmers in Dodge and Washington counties are to be found in Richland Township of the latter county. One of the country places that immediately attract attention in that locality is the farm of Chris Schumacher in section 16 He has lived in this locality all his life and has always exemplified the qualities of the sound agriculturist and public-spirited citizen

He was born in this county July 17, 1880 His father, Henry Schumacher, was a native of Germany and was an early settler around Fort Calhoun, where he started as a worker, until he was able to homestead and acquire property of his own

Chris Schumacher, as a boy, acquired a common school education and established a home of his own in 1904 by his marriage with Miss Louise Stender, of Washington County, daughter of Chris and Charlotte Stender Mr. and Mrs. Schumacher have three children, all at home, Henry, Doretta and Freddie

The farm which Mr Schumacher so industriously and intelligently manages comprises 290 acres, with good improvements and highly pro ductive He has been interested in the affairs of the community, serving on the school board for twelve years, is a member of the Farmers Union of Washington, casts his vote independently and affiliates with the Lutheran Church.

WILLIAM JAHNEL, one of the prosperous farmers and business men of Washington County, is a son of Frank Jahnel, who came to this section of Nebraska more than forty years ago and is a retired citizen of Blair

William Jahnel was born in Washington County in 1880 The story of his family appears on other pages While he had only the advantages of the common schools, he has always shown that progressiveness which has made him an interested student of local conditions and has kept him in touch with the leading issues of the time He grew up at home, worked with and for his father, and since 1908 has been established for himself on the old homestead of his father, where he has 240 acres, exemplifying some of the best equipment and some of the best live stock and crops in Richland Township His farm is in section 11 and is two miles east and a mile and a half south of Kennard The chief feature of his live-stock farming is a herd of Polled Shorthorn cattle

Besides his farm he has co-operated with other citizens to secure better marketing and other economic advantages, and is president of the Farmers Grain and Lumber Company of Kennard and also one of the organizers and president of the Home State Bank of Kennard Just recently he was elected and began his service as a director of the home school Mr Jahnel is a republican and is affiliated with the Independent Order of Odd Fellows

In 1906 he married Margaret Kahlke, who was born in Holstein, Germany, the same section from which the Jahnel family came The Kahlkes came to the United States, where the mother died at the age of seventy-three, and her father then went back to Germany Mr. and Mrs Jahnel have five children, all at home, named Bertha, Frank, Helen and Margaret and Marian, twins

NICKELS PETERSEN While the life record of Nickels Petersen has been closed his family are still prominently represented in Washington County, and the farm where he spent so many industrious years is still a substantial evidence of his character and enterprise This fine old country home is one mile north and two and a half miles east of Washington in Richland Township, section 27

Mr Petersen was born in Germany in 1842, and was reared and educated in his native land, where he acquired the habits of thrift associated with the German people In 1866 he came to America and for the first ten years lived in Clinton County, Iowa. He saw his efforts prosper in a moderate degree in Iowa and when he came to Nebraska in 1876 he was able to buy a quarter section of land at $10 an acre It was a tract of prairie but had no improvements He broke the virgin sod, erected a house and other buildings, cultivated and harvested many successive crops, and was esteemed as a prosperous farmer and good citizen of that locality for forty years About five years after coming to Nebraska Mr Petersen bought eighty acres adjoining the 160 acres in section 34 He died January 1, 1916 He was a democrat in voting and a member of the Lutheran Church

While living in Iowa he married Margaret Rathgens, who is still living on the home farm Twelve children were born to their marriage,

five of whom died in infancy, while the daughter, Mrs Kopke, is also deceased The six children living are Peter C, a marketman at Bennington, Nebraska; C H, a merchant at Washington, Mrs John Misfeldt, a widow living at Bennington, John F, in the garage business at Bennington; William, who is a practical farmer at home with his mother, and Mrs Richard Jansen, wife of a farmer in Douglas County, Nebraska

Oliver C. Roberts. Scarcely any feature of the landscape seems to more forcibly impress a traveler from other lands with the wealth and abundance of the vast western section of the United States than the number of great elevators that line the railroads and often seem to dominate every other business in some communities The name of Roberts has been identified with grain and elevator interests in Washington County, Nebraska, for many years, and to this line of commercial life Oliver C Roberts, formerly mayor of Arlington, devotes much attention

Oliver C. Roberts was born on a farm one mile east of Arlington, Nebraska, February 14, 1870, and is a son of Robert Ellis and Nancy Jane (Sage) Roberts, the former of whom was born in Wales and the latter in the State of Indiana. The father came to Washington County in the early '50s and homesteaded here, for some years afterward freighting between Council Bluffs and Denver He was a man of foresight and great business enterprise Not satisfied with his original homestead, he kept on acquiring land, and at the time of his death owned 1,560 acres in Washington County Later he went into the grain business, purchasing a mill and 160 acres of land, but later sold the land for $2,000 and moved the mill in 1880 to Arlington, where it subsequently was destroyed by fire, entailing a loss of $20,000 He owned three elevators, situated at Kennard, Washington and Arlington He was considered one of the county's most substantial citizens at the time of death, which occurred December 25, 1910, when aged eighty-two years. After disposing of a large amount of his property and retiring from active business life he made a visit to his old home in Wales He was influential in democratic politics and was one of the early members of the Odd Fellows at Arlington

Robert Ellis Roberts married Nancy Jane Sage, who died July 5, 1915. Of their ten children, Oliver C is the third in order of birth, the others being as follows: Mrs F P. Van Wickle, whose husband is in the grain business at York, Nebraska, Mrs N P Borick, whose husband is in the real-estate business at Arlington; Will E, who is in Montana engaged in the harness and saddlery business, Mrs G I Pfeiffer, whose husband is cashier of the First National Bank of Arlington; Mrs J A Dixon, whose husband is at the head of the telephone company at Arlington; Ray F, who is a traveling man, and three who are deceased The mother of the above family was a member of the Congregationalist Church.

Oliver C Roberts completed the public school course at Arlington, then took a commercial course in the Lincoln Business College, and subsequently spent ten weeks in 1887 in the Fremont Normal College He was associated with his father in the grain business until the latter's death, when he took over the elevator interests of the estate and continues their management He has other interests and owns 480 acres of fine land in Brown County, South Dakota

In 1892 Mr Roberts was united in marriage to Miss Laura Louise Fitch, who was born in Iowa and is a daughter of Ambrose T Fitch

They have three children The eldest daughter is the wife of C I. White, who is connected in business with the Burroughs Stock Food Company; Dorothea is a student in Midland College at Fremont, and Lawrence Gilbert is attending the Nebraska State University The family attends the Congregational Church Mr. Roberts belongs to the Odd Fellows and has passed through the chairs of the local lodge. In political life he has always been active in the democratic party, and at one time his political friends elected him mayor of Arlington He consented to serve but one year, during which time he gave the city a first-class business administration

W J McCANN Nearly fifty years a resident of Washington County, where he was reared from early childhood, William J McCann has spent a busy life, most of the time as an agriculturist, and is still giving his time and labors to the operation of a valuable and systematically handled farm in Richland Township, section 11 His home is three miles east and a half mile south of Kennard.

Mr McCann was born in Washington County, Virginia, January 29, 1868, a son of Isaac and Margaret McCann, natives of the same state. His father was a planter, served in the Civil war and early in 1872 came to Nebraska and acquired land near Arlington, from which he retired in 1900, moving to Kennard There the mother died in 1916 They were the parents of eight children, William J being the oldest

William J McCann was four years of age when he came west, grew up in Washington County, and after getting an education in the common schools worked for his father and others, but since the age of twenty-two has been going it alone He lived for thirty-five years in Arlington Township, but his home is now in Richland Township He left the farm in December, 1909, and for a time was employed by the telephone company and in other occupations In 1916 he returned to the land, and has continued farming during this modern period of high prices and a shortage of farm labor He has 120 acres, well improved and modern in every respect Mr McCann was elected a member of his local school board in 1920 He votes independently and is affiliated with the Independent Order of Odd Fellows and Modern Woodmen of America Mrs McCann is a member of the Baptist Church

In 1892 he married Miss Mamie Blazier, who died in August, 1910, the mother of four children, two of whom are living, Gladys, now a music teacher at Omaha, and Gertrude, at home. The mother of Mamie Blazier is still living In 1912 Mr McCann married Hettie Rodman and they have two young children, Florence and Ione

AUGUST KAHNK While he is a native of Illinois, August Kahnk has spent practically all his life in Washington County, and the farm where he grew to manhood is the scene of his present industrious efforts The buildings and other improvements on that land are to be credited jointly to the enterprise of Mr Kahnk and his father The substantial farm home is in section 16 of Richland Township, a mile east and two and a half miles north of Washington.

Mr. Kahnk was born in Illinois in 1867. His father, John C Kahnk, was born and married in Germany, and in 1865 brought his family to the United States, living in Illinois, where his first employment was in a paper mill In 1869 he came to Washington County, traveling to Omaha by railroad, and then freighted his goods overland to his destination twenty miles away He did not choose to locate on public lands and homestead, but bought a piece of school land at a dollar an acre. His first home was only a board shack, and while his early life was not greatly in contrast with that of the other pioneers, he had to make shift with practically no capital and very few facilities for farming and living. It is said that for a number of days the sole diet of the Kahnk family was turnips But better days came with the passing years, larger comforts, and John C Kahnk enjoyed much prosperity before his death, which occurred at the age of sixty-seven. He acquired the ownership of 120 acres His wife died in 1916 at the age of eighty-eight They had five children: John and Dolf, both deceased, August; Peter, who was drowned at the age of three years; and Mrs Anna Cornelius, a resident of Douglas County

August Kahnk, only surviving son, grew up on the home farm, attended the local schools and worked for his father to the age of twenty-three, after which he took over the management of the farm and has conducted it successfully ever since. Mr. Kahnk is an independent voter and a member of the Lutheran faith.

He married for his first wife Anna Matthesen, who died the mother of four children John, Mata and Margaret, all at home, and Gustaf, deceased Mr Kahnk married for his second wife, Lena Matthesen, and to their union were born nine children, all of who remain in the home circle Their names are Gustaf, Anna, Louis, Harry, Marie, Albert, Lillian, Arthur and Clara

CHRIS PAULSEN. Agriculture is now generally recognized as the most important of all of the basic industries, for upon the production of the farmer depends practically all business operations Therefore much credit must be accorded the man who tills the soil and handles the difficult problems of securing labor and marketing his produce Nebraska has some of the most industrious and successful of these agriculturalists, and among them one deserving of mention in a work of this high character is Chris Paulsen of Blair Township

Chris Paulsen was born in Germany in 1864, a son of John and Catrina Paulsen, both of whom were born in Germany, where they died, he when seventy-two years of age and she when sixty-three They were farming people, hard-working and honest, and brought up their four children to habits of thrift and industry Of these children Chris Paulsen is the only one who came to the United States

The arrival of Chris Paulsen in this country was in 1892, and he came here with the purpose of acquiring land of his own, something he could not do in his own country with his lack of capital Going west to Nebraska, he rented land in the vicinity of Calhoun for two years, and then was able to buy his present 120-acre farm in Blair Township, and at once began to improve the property The present substantial house and barns have been built by him, and he has put up fences and bought machinery, and is now carrying on his farm operations in a thoroughly modern manner

In February, 1892, Mr Paulsen was united in marriage with Margarita Schrader, also born in Germany, and they became the parents of the following children Charles and May, who are at home, and one that died in infancy While Mr. Paulsen had had experience in farming in Germany, conditions were so different when he reached this country that he deserves a great deal of credit for what he has been able to accomplish since coming here He is now accounted one of the best farmers in his part of the county, and his neighbors are adopting many of his methods, for they see that they are excellent A man of strong personality, Mr Paulsen likes to choose his own candidates and so has remained an independent voter

OTTO F OLSEN, editor and publisher of the Kennard Weekly News, in connection with which he conducts a well equipped job-printing department, is one of the progressive and influential young business men of the Village of Kennard, Washington County, where he holds in 1920 the office of water commissioner of the municipality and where he is a stalwart and effective advocate and supporter of all measures and enterprises tending to advance the civic and material welfare of the village and the county

Mr Olsen was born at Fremont, judicial center of Dodge County, Nebraska, May 3, 1894, and is a son of Zacharia and Mary Anna (Christiansen) Olsen, who now reside at Kennard, where the father, a shoemaker by trade, conducts a repair shop in which he has developed a prosperous business Of the eight children in the family four are living: Anna, the wife of Henry Hansen, a farmer in Washington County, Jennie, the wife of Harry R Redfield, manager of the Western Union Telegraph Company's office at Fremont, Otto F, of this sketch, the next in order of birth; and Ruby, an assistant in her brother's printing office. The father is independent in politics, and both he and his wife are members of the Seventh Day Adventist Church

Otto F Olsen acquired his early education in the public schools of Fremont, and in 1907 he entered upon an apprenticeship to the printer's trade in the office of the Kennard Enterprise, then published by E L Tiffany Within the ensuing seven months he gained no little proficiency as a compositor, and in 1908 took a position in the Danish Lutheran Publishing House at Blair, the judicial center of Washington County He continued his connection with this representative concern until 1914, when he assumed charge of the office of the Superior Daily Express, at Superior, Nuckolls County. In the following year, however, he came to Kennard and founded the Kennard Weekly News, the first edition of which appeared on the 14th of June of that year He has made this paper an effective exponent of the interests of the community and has gained for it a representative circulation throughout the territory normally tributary to Kennard His office is modern in equipment and service and its job department receives a substantial supporting patronage

In politics Mr Olsen is not constrained by strict partisan lines, and his paper likewise is independent in the domain of politics He is serving as water commissioner of Kennard, as previously stated, and he is a vigorous advocate of progressive policies in connection with all municipal affairs Both he and his wife are communicants of the Danish Lutheran Church.

October 21, 1914, recorded the marriage of Mr Olsen to Miss Minnie Rohwer, daughter of Carl Rohwer, of Washington County, and the two children of this union are Lucille Marian and Vera Louise

E V. HEATH One of the oldest farms under continuous cultivation in Washington County is two miles west of Blair in section 8 of Blair Township. Its present owner and occupant is E V Heath and family.

Mr Heath was born in Illinois in 1861, and three years later his parents, Marvin and Lucy Heath came to Nebraska His father was a native of Pennsylvania Coming to Nebraska, they settled in Burt County, where he homesteaded and where he lived until his death at the age of sixty-five. His wife passed away at the age of seventy-four

E V Heath was one of a family of ten children The Heaths were among the pioneers of the country west of the Missouri River, lived here in buffalo and Indian days and when there were no railroads and the scarcely recognized trails were traveled either by wagons or riders on horseback

In 1881 Mr Heath married Mary Raver, who was born in Washington County, a daughter of H J Raver and wife, who came to this region in 1858 Mr and Mrs Heath had eight children Burt, now manager of the Nebraska Power Company garage at Omaha; Elmer, chef in a cafe on Broadway, New York City, Charles, who served as an engineer in the late war and lives in Wyoming; Vera, wife of Thomas Griffin, of Wood Lake, Nebraska; Harry, a garage owner at Brownlee, Nebraska, Oria, Earl and Vernie, both at home

Mr. Raver was born August 24, 1836, at Johnstown, Pennsylvania At the age of twenty, he went with his parents to Des Moines, Iowa, and there married Sarah Mann To this union seven children were born Mrs. Raver died January 2, 1918, at the age of seventy-eight Mr Raver died April 21, 1918, at the age of eighty-one He came to Washington County in 1858 from St Louis by way of Omaha, up the river on a steamboat, and from Omaha traveled to his destination by ox team Mr Raver witnessed the first legal execution in Omaha during the summer of 1863. Their first home was a dugout containing one room and situated about five miles west and north of Blair Later he lived for five years in the Missouri River bottom and later returned to the homestead Just fifty years have passed since Mr Raver moved to the place where Mr and Mrs Heath now live At that time the landscape showed no trees, and there were no other evidences of cultivation and civilization such as mark this farm today. Mr Raver set out the orchard which is still bearing Much of the land in the Heath farm was broken out by Mr Heath himself.

Mr and Mrs Heath are proud of the fact that two of their sons were enrolled in the cause of democracy during the World war. Corp Charles W Heath entered the service July 17, 1917, at Fort Logan, and was assigned as a truck driver He went overseas as corporal of Company F of the Tenth Engineers, and was assigned the task of sawing lumber near the front lines He was in the service twenty-one months and was honorably discharged at Camp Funston on February 22, 1919

The other son, Corp Elmer H Heath, entered the army March 4, 1918, was trained at Fort Riley and went overseas June 13, 1918, landing in Italy, and being with the first American troops sent to that quarter of the allied front. He was with the Thirtieth ambulance section, with the First Army Corps, and was on duty until the armistice of November 11th His unit carried 1936 wounded men off the field in seven days He received the Italian war cross for bravery, and was discharged June 10, 1919 He then re-enlisted at Camp Dix, New Jersey, and is now in the Medical Corps

William Murley. An honored veteran of the Union army during the Civil war still living in Washington County, William Murley has been a Nebraskan for over thirty years, and his earnestness and industry have brought him many of the substantial rewards of good citizenship

He was born in England in 1842, and at the age of eight years was brought to the United States by his father, John Murley, who settled in Wisconsin John Murley was a miner and was employed in the mines of Wisconsin until he was killed at the age of fifty-five William Murley and five brothers entered the Union army, and while they participated in some of the hardest fought campaigns of the war not one was wounded William Murley was in Company I of the Sixteenth Wisconsin Infantry, and was all through from the beginning to the end, being under the commands of Grant and Sherman After the war he took a homestead near Schuyler, Wisconsin, in 1871, and at that time married Miss Louise John To their marriage were born three children, James, Hattie and Annie Mrs Murley died in 1882

Mr Murley moved to Washington County in 1888, bought land in the county, and now enjoys the comforts of a good home in section 23 of Arlington Township, his being the first house north of Dale Store.

In 1917 he married Mary Googen, whose family were pioneers of Washington County Her parents came here about 1866, were homesteaders, and went through all the experiences of pioneering Her father died at the age of seventy-five and her mother is now living at Elk City in Douglas County.

FRED HEUERMANN The enterprise that manifests itself in good farms, good livestock and good homes, and the co-operative movements that advance and improve the general welfare is typical of the career of Fred Heuermann, one of the very well known citizens of Washington County. Mr Heuermann for many years has been a livestock breeder and farmer, interested in other lines of business, and has a complete and adequate country home and farm in section 10 of Arlington Township, located three miles east of the Village of Arlington

Mr Heuermann was born in Ohio in 1868, son of D B and Louise (Strobmann) Heuermann. His parents were both natives of Germany, settled in Ohio when they came to America, and were early settlers in Nebraska Fred Heuermann was reared and educated in Washington County, attending country schools, and has been in business for himself since the age of twenty-three For several years he specialized in the raising of Shorthorn cattle on his farm, and his chief business has been the breeding and feeding of hogs and cattle Among other features of his farm is a fine orchard, which was set out by his father Mr Heuermann is vice president and a director of the Farmers Lumber & Grain Company, and for ten years served as director of School District No. 4 In 1909 he was elected a member of the Board of County Commissioners, and gave much of his time to the duties of that office for nine years He owns a modern country home, built in 1915

In 1893 he married Kate Hartung, a native of Washington County and a daughter of Fred Hartung, of an old and well known family of the county To their marriage were born eleven children, nine of whom are still living Florence, who was a graduate of Nicholson Hospital at Omaha and died in November, 1919, Edna, wife of Alfred Smith, a farmer in Washington County, Emma, who is taking the nurse's training course at Nicholson Hospital in Omaha, Chester, Lotta, Arthur, Fred, Jr, Mattie, Lucile and Elva, all at home with their parents, and Dorothy, who died in infancy The family are members of St Paul's Lutheran Church. Mr Heuermann is active in the republican party, serving as township committeeman

HANS HANSEN. Many years of earnest and well directed labor have brought Hans Hansen the merited reward of substantial property interests and the substantial esteem of the community in which he lives Just outside the city limits of Arlington is the Hansen farm, which was cleared from the condition of timber and brush by his labors and made productive

Mr Hansen was born in Denmark in 1861 and was twenty-one years of age when he arrived in the United States in 1882 For about a year he lived around Chester, Pennsylvania, and then came out and joined the people of Dodge County, which was still a comparatively new district Without capital, he was unable to buy land and satisfied himself with the slow but sure route to independence as a farm worker, and continued his employment with others until 1904 Most of that time, especially after his marriage, he rented land.

Mr. Hansen married Christina Madsen, a native of Denmark, and the only member of her family to come to this country. Her father was Johan Madsen She came over on the same boat with her husband, and they were married at Fremont March 19, 1885 Six children have been born to their union Marie, of Fremont; Mrs Nellie Phillips, of Wahoo, Nebraska; Mrs L W Weigand, of Central City, Nebraska, Fern, of Fremont, Julius, at home, and Agnes, of Fremont

The eighty-acre farm adjoining Arlington Mr Hansen has improved with good buildings, and for many years has been a successful general farmer and dairyman He began life with only a common school education, but has made the best possible use of all his opportunities He is affiliated with the Modern Woodmen of America and the Danish Brotherhood, is a member of the Congregational Church at Arlington, and is a republican voter

CORTEZ U COOK By no means all the young men in Washington and Dodge counties are being recruited into the trades and professions and other activties of urban life The business of farming offers substantial rewards sufficient to hold and draw young men to this oldest of all professions and vocations.

One of the younger men actively identified with the agricultural affairs of Washington County is Cortez U Cook, owner of a valuable farm in section 20, Arlington Township, a mile east and a mile south of the Village of Arlington

Mr. Cook, who was born in Washington County in 1881, is a son of W. S. and Jennie (Unthank) Cook. His father, who was born in Iowa, studied law under Judge Walton and for many years practiced as an attorney in Washington County with offices at Arlington After he retired from his profession he gave general oversight to his landed interests until his death, November 17, 1920 The Unthank family is one of the oldest in this section of Nebraska Jennie Unthank was seven years of age when in 1855, her parents, Mr and Mrs John A Unthank, migrated from Indiana, her native state, to Washington County, Nebraska Territory Her father homesteaded, and besides farming conducted one of the pioneer elevators of the county at Old Bell Creek W S. Cook and wife had four children Joseph C, of Fremont, Cortez U; Roy R, a lawyer and real estate man at Los Angeles, California, and Hazel, wife of Otto Ludwig, a carpenter and mason at Los Angeles

Cortez U Cook acquired his early education in the public schools of Arlington and has given his best energies and efforts to farming since 1900 In 1917 he began the development of a herd of Duroc Jersey hogs, and has made that one of the important features of his farm enterprise His interests have extended to other affairs, and he is a stockholder in the Farmers Lumber & Grain Company's elevator at Arlington, the Nebraska Foundry & Manufacturing Company at Fremont, and the Waterloo Creamery of Omaha The scene of Mr Cook's well ordered industry as a farmer and stockman is known as the Golden Gate Farm In politics he is a republican, as was his father.

Mr Cook married Amy Krajick, of a family whose history is given on other pages To their marriage were born four children, three still at home, named William, Lawrence, Mabel and Raymond Raymond Cook passed away on the 25th of October, 1920

JOHN BLACO is another of the representative men who have gained substantial prosperity through association with agricultural and live-stock enterprise in Washington County, where he has maintained his residence since the spring of 1883 and where he is now living virtually retired in the Village of Kennard

Mr Blaco was born in Lancashire, England, on the 28th of January, 1869, and is a son of John and Jane (Burkett) Blaco, who there passed their entire lives, the father having been a farmer by vocation, and both of whom were devoted communicants of the Church of England Two of their sons came to America, and both are residents of Washington, County, Nebraska, Richard being one of the representative farmers in the vicinity of Kennard

John Blaco was reared and educated in his native land and was about twenty-three years of age when he severed the home ties and came to America On the 21st of April, 1883, he arrived at Blair, the judicial center of Washington County, Nebraska, and for the ensuing four years was employed at farm work in this county. He then initiated his independent activities as a farmer, and with the passing years he accumulated and improved a valuable farm property of 240 acres, which he still owns and to the active management of which he gave his effective attention until 1914, when he removed to the Village of Kennard, where he has since maintained his home and where he has one of the modern and attractive residences of the community In his farm enterprise Mr Blaco made a specialty of feeding cattle for the market, and at all times he kept a good grade of livestock He was one of the organizers of and is a substantial stockholder in the Home State Bank at Kennard, is also a stockholder in the Farmers Grain & Lumber Company of this place and has been from the time of its organization a stockholder of the Blair Telephone Company at the county seat, of which corporation he is a director

A staunch supporter of the cause of the republican party, Mr Blaco has been somewhat active in political affairs of local order and served four years as a member of the Board of County Commissioners of Washington County He has always given effective co-operation in the support of enterprises and measures advanced for the general good of the community, and is deeply appreciative of the advantages that have enabled him to win independence and prosperity within the period of his residence in Nebraska, to which state he came as a young man of most limited financial resources but with a full endowment of energy, ambition and integrity of purpose He is serving his third term as master of the Masonic Lodge at Kennard, and is affiliated also with the local camp of the Modern Woodmen of America Reared in the

John Blaco.

Mattie Blaco

faith of the established Church of England, he has retained the faith in America as a communicant of the Protestant Episcopal Church, his wife being a member of the Christian Church.

On January 13, 1887, was solemnized the marriage of Mr Blaco to Miss Mattie Robertson, at that time a resident of Blair, Washington County, though she claims Kentucky as the state of her birth She came with her parents to Nebraska when she was six years old Mr and Mrs Blaco have but one child, Blanche, who is the wife of Leonard E Peterson, of Sidney, Cheyenne County, Nebraska, where he is associated with a leading mercantile establishment

Buck Rosenbaum is a native son of Washington County, Nebraska, and has here proved his ability and enterprise in connection with successful farm industry Mr Rosenbaum and his wife are the owners of a well improved farm estate of eighty acres, as well as of a modern and attractive residence and twelve acres in the Village of Kennard, where he established his home on removing from his farm in 1917 He is one of the popular and progressive young men of his native county

Mr. Rosenbaum was born on his father's farm in Washington County, August 9, 1881, and is a son of H J. and Sarah (Garrett) Rosenbaum, both of whom were born in Washington County, Virginia, where they were reared and educated and where their marriage was solemnized In 1871 the parents came to Washington County, Nebraska, where the father bought land near Fort Calhoun and developed one of the excellent pioneer farms of the county He was one of the well known and highly respected pioneer citizens of this county at the time of his death, which occurred February 8, 1915, the date of his birth having been September 10, 1848 His widow still remains on the old homestead farm Mr Rosenbaum was a democrat in political adherency and was affiliated with the Knights of Pythias, the Modern Woodmen of America and the Woodmen of the World Of the children the eldest is John, who is now a resident of the City of Spokane, Washington, Carrie is the wife of G R French, a farmer in Washington County, Martha is the widow of James Hotele and resides in this county, Minnie is the wife of Charles Robinson, and they reside in the State of Colorado, J. D Lives at Spokane, Washington; Joseph R is a successful farmer in Washington County; Edward maintains his home in the City of Omaha; Buck, of this review, was the next in order of birth, May is the wife of Chris Peterson, of Kennard, and Binkley resides at Spokane, Washington.

Buck Rosenbaum is indebted to the district schools of Washington County for his early education, and on the home farm he gained in his youth the experience that well equipped him for independent farm enterprise when he initiated his activities as an agriculturist and stockgrower when twenty-four years of age He made a genuine success in this important field of industrial enterprise, and made his farm a center of vigorous and progressive activities with a due combination of agriculture and the raising of good grades of live stock He is a stockholder of the Farmers Grain & Elevator Co-operative Company at Kennard, is an independent voter in politics and is affiliated with the Modern Woodmen of America

In 1905 Mr. Rosenbaum wedded Miss Emma Japp, who likewise was born and reared in Washington County and who is a daughter of John and Catherine (Weise) Japp, sterling pioneers of this county. Mr and Mrs Rosenbaum have two children Ida and Harry

MARTIN T CEDERLIND, cashier of the Home State Bank at Kennard, one of the substantial financial institutions of Washington County, is a native of Nebraska and a member of a family whose name has been identified with the history of this state for more than forty years He was born on his father's old homestead farm near Newman Grove, Madison County, Nebraska, on the 18th of February, 1892, and is a son of Alfred and Louise (Lyon) Cederlind, who were born and reared in Sweden They established their residence at Omaha, Nebraska, in 1875, in which city they were married Within a short time thereafter they removed to Madison County, where the father purchased land near Newman Grove and developed a fine farm, a property which he still owns, though he has lived virtually retired since 1911 His political support is given to the republican party and he and his wife are members of the Free Mission Church Of their seven children the subject of this sketch was the fifth in order of birth

Martin T Cederlind passed his boyhood days on the old home farm and acquired his preliminary education in the district schools Later he attended the Nebraska State Normal School at Wayne, as well as the one at Fremont, in which latter he took a course in the commercial department For one year he was a teacher in a district school near Newman Grove, and he then took a clerical position in the general offices of the Union Pacific Railroad in the City of Omaha. Later he assumed a similar position in the general offices of the Great Northern Railroad at St Paul, Minnesota, where he continued his services three years For the ensuing year he was employed as bookkeeper in a leading department store in the same city, and in 1917 he accepted the position of which he has since continued the efficient and popular incumbent, that of cashier of the Home State Bank at Kennard, with the upbuilding of the substantial business of which institution he has been closely and effectively identified This bank, organized and incorporated in 1915, bases its operations upon a capital stock of $15,000, has a surplus of $4,000, and its deposits in 1920 are somewhat in excess of $100,000.

Mr Cederlind takes loyal interest in all things pertaining to the welfare and advancement of his home village and county, is a republican in politics, is affiliated with the Independent Order of Odd Fellows, and Masons, and both he and his wife hold membership in the Methodist Episcopal Church at Kennard

The year 1915 recorded the marriage of Mr Cederlind to Miss Donna Cunningham, who was born and reared in Washington County, where her father, Charles C. Cunningham, is a substantial and prosperous citizen, his attention being given largely to the growing and feeding of cattle, in which he conducts business upon a somewhat extensive scale Mr and Mrs Cederlind have three children Eldon C, Willis J and Irvin M

LEWIS E WARD, who came to Nebraska in the year 1879 and for a time was in the employ of one of the leading attorneys at Blair, judicial center of Washington County, eventually became one of the leading merchants at Kennard, this county, where he built up a large and prosperous hardware business, with which he continued his active association until the spring of 1920, when he sold the stock and business and removed to Firth, Lancaster County, where he is now associated with his son, Homer E, in the drug business A man who achieved success and influence during the many years of his residence in Washington County, where his circle of friends is limited only by that of his acquaintances, it is but due that Mr Ward be accorded recognition in this publication

Lewis E Ward was born in Branch County, Michigan, on the 29th of May, 1860, a son of Robert and Sarah (Freeman) Ward, who were sterling pioneers of that beautiful county in the southern part of the Wolverine State, both having been natives of the State of New York In the old Empire State the father learned the trade of shoemaker, and this he followed successfully in the early period of his residence in Michigan He also owned and developed a good farm in Branch County, where he and his wife continued to reside until their death, when venerable in years. Both were consistent members of the Presbyterian Church The father was a stanch republican in politics and served many years as a justice of the peace Of the five children the subject of this review is now the only one living

The public schools of his native county afforded Lewis E Ward his early education, which was supplemented by a course in what is now Valparaiso University at Valparaiso, Indiana He came to Nebraska in 1879, as previously noted, and in 1888 he engaged in independent farm enterprise in Washington County After having been for eight years one of the vigorous and successful exponents of agricultural and live-stock industry in this county Mr. Ward removed to the Village of Kennard, where in 1896 he purchased the hardware stock and business of Martin Hansen He developed a substantial and prosperous enterprise in the handling of heavy shelf hardware, and he continued as one of the leading representatives of this line of enterprise in Washington County until 1920, when he sold his business to E O Fairchild, his removal from the community having been greatly regretted by his many friends in both business and social circles Mr Ward was known as one of the liberal and progressive citizens of the county and assisted in the organization of the Grange, in the affairs of which he was active and influential In politics he votes for men and measures meeting the approval of his judgment, rather than being constrained by strict partisanship He has passed the official chairs in the Modern Woodmen of America and his wife is an active member of the Methodist Episcopal Church.

In 1881 occurred the marriage of Mr Ward to Miss Emily Renshaw, a resident of Michigan, though she was born in England, and of this gracious union have been born six children Merton C and Carl H are associated with business activities at Kennard, Homer E is engaged in the drug business at Firth, Lancaster County, Mildred is the wife of Ferdinand Ziegler, a farmer near St Paul, Howard County, Leland E. holds a position in a hardware store at Kennard, and Nina A is at the time of this writing, in 1920, a successful and popular teacher in the public schools of Fort Calhoun, Washington County

CHARLES C CUNNINGHAM A life long resident of Eastern Nebraska, son of a Nebraska pioneer and old soldier, Charles C. Cunningham has had a varied experience but chiefly as a farmer and stockman He is owner of one of the fine country homes in Washington County, located in section 12 of Arlington Township, five and a half miles east of Arlington Village

He was born in Douglas County Nebraska, in 1868, son of William G and Eliza (Wetz) Cunningham, the former a native of Virginia and the latter of Iowa William G Cunningham though a native of Virginia came West early in life, and when the Civil war came on enlisted with a regiment of Nebraska cavalry and saw much frontier and other army duty He was once wounded As a pioneer of the country west of the Missouri he was engaged in freighting from Omaha out to Salt Lake City He conveyed a number of herds of cattle across the plains, and also freighted with ox teams. On returning to Omaha he frequently walked the entire distance. Later he homesteaded in Douglas County, and in 1870 traded his homestead there for a homestead in Washington County, where for many years he was an esteemed and useful citizen, engaged in farming and stock raising He died in May, 1920, at the age of ninety-four, being at that time one of the oldest surviving western pioneers He was a Baptist in religion and a democrat in politics. In his family were six children Mamie, wife of Jake Stewart, an elevator man at Charleston, Nebraska, Minnie, deceased, Charles C, Frank, a retired resident of Blair; O A, a Washington County farmer, and Emma, wife of Elmer Bates, a Washington County farmer.

Charles C Cunningham grew up in Washington County, attended the common schools, and for three years of his early life was associated with his brother, Frank, in operating a store at Washington When he sold out his mercantile interests he turned to general farming, and for the past thirty years has devoted his time and energies to his business as a farmer and the general improvement of his locality

In 1889 Mr Cunningham married Ethel Robertson, a native of Kentucky and a daughter of William Robertson, who took his family out to Perkins County, Nebraska Four children have been born to Mr. and Mrs. Cunningham· Ellis, a farmer in Washington County; Donna, wife of M T Cederlind, the Kennard banker, and William and Marie, the former an employe of the Home State Bank at Kennard and the latter a teacher living at home The family are members of the Methodist Church at Kennard Mr Cunningham is independent in politics, and is a member of the Masonic Lodge and the Modern Woodmen of America

EDWARD F. CUSHMAN, the efficient and popular station agent for the Chicago & Northwestern Railroad at Kennard, Washington County, has been a resident of Nebraska since he was a lad of fifteen years, save for one year passed in Wyoming and Utah, and for twenty-seven years (1920) he has been in active railway service He was born at Ironton, Wisconsin, June 19, 1873, and is a son of Charles and Almira (Warner) Cushman, the former of whom was born in Ohio, where he was reared and educated, and the latter was born in the State of New York From Ohio the father removed to Wisconsin, where he engaged in the work of his trade, that of carpenter, and became a successful contractor and builder He founded the town of Lime Ridge, Wisconsin, gave to the village its name and served as its first postmaster His political allegiance was that of the republican party, and his wife was a member of the Methodist Episcopal Church for many years, though she was a birthright member of the Society of Friends. The parents were residents of Wisconsin at the time of their death In addition to Edward F, parents are survived by six other children Charles, railroad agent at Hooper, Nebraska, Blanche, who is the wife of Edward Trucks, engaged in the real estate business at Meadow Grove, Nebraska, Julia, widow of Roscoe J Sanders, of Hastings, Nebraska, who now resides in Colorado, Belle, wife of R L Bohn, retired business man, who resides in the Town of Lime Ridge, Wisconsin, Nelson Ackley, owner of the Cushman Poultry Ranch of Reedsburg, Wisconsin, and Wellington B, ticket agent for the Missouri Pacific at Independence, Kansas

Edward F Cushman gained his preliminary education in the public schools of Wisconsin and after coming to Nebraska in 1888, he continued his studies in the high school at Hastings and later in that at Wisner, besides having attended the Western Normal College in the City of Lincoln For a time he was employed at farm work near Hastings, and he then learned the trade of telegraph operator at Wisner, Cuming County He has continued for twenty-seven years in the service of the Chicago & Northwestern Railroad as operator and station agent and was for one year employed as a relief telegraph operator for the Union Pacific Railroad in Utah and Wyoming For three years he was operator in the Northwestern Railroad station at Scribner, Dodge County, and he was then assigned to duty as station agent at Snyder, that county, where he remained until he was transferred to a similar position at Anoka, Boyd County, where he remained three years. For six months thereafter he was station agent at Pierce, judicial center of the Nebraska county of the same name, and for a similar period he served as station agent at Cornlea, Platte County, when in August, 1911, he came to Kennard and assumed his present position

Mr Cushman is a stanch republican, and while a resident of Anoka he served as a member of the village board of trustees At the time of this writing he is a valued member of the Board of Education of Kennard He is a past master of the Blue Lodge body of the Masonic fraternity, past senior warden of the Chapter of Royal Arch Masons, and actively affiliated also with Blair Commandery of Knights Templar at Blair, Nebraska, besides which he holds membership in the adjunct organization, the Ancient Arabic Order Nobles of the Mystic Shrine and is also a member of the Woodmen of the World Both he and his wife hold membership in the Methodist Episcopal Church in their home village and Mr Cushman is a member of the Order of Railway Telegraphers

In 1899 was recorded the marriage of Mr. Cushman to Miss Lulu Osborn, who was born and reared in Nebraska, and their home is brightened by the presence of their two children: Loraine and Gail

Harry C. Blaco The year 1920 finds Mr Blaco giving efficient and progressive administration as mayor of Kennard, Washington County, and he is one of the substantial and influential citizens of his native county, where he still owns and gives a general supervision to his fine farm property, besides which he controls a prosperous business at Kennard, where he is engaged in the handling of farm implements and machinery

Mr Blaco was born on his father's old homestead farm in Washington County, and the date of his nativity was August 28, 1872 He is a son of Richard and Eliza A (McFadden) Blaco, the former a native of England and the latter of the State of Iowa Richard Blaco came to Washington County, Nebraska, in 1870, and here purchased a relinquishment to a claim of land, to the development and improvement of which he directed his attention with marked energy and discrimination. He eventually became the owner of one of the large and valuable landed estates of the county and was a citizen of prominence and influence in the county, as shown by his having been chosen to serve not only as county commissioner but also as a member of the State Legislature, his political alignment having been with the republican party He achieved abundant success through his well ordered activities as an agriculturist and stock-raiser, and was one of the honored pioneer citizens of Washington County at the time of his death, in September, 1906, his wife having passed away in 1899 and having been a devoted member of the Presbyterian Church Of the children Harry C, of this review, is the eldest, Nellie is the wife of Harry Wardell, a farmer near Creighton, Knox County; Myrtle is the wife of Herman O Wulff, who is engaged in the mercantile business at Benson, Douglas County, Bessie E is the wife of Albert L. Cook, a teacher in the public schools at Benson and former superintendent of schools of Washington County, and Gertrude is the widow of Joseph C Neal, of Kennard.

Harry C Blaco is indebted to the public schools of Washington County for his early educational discipline, and from his boyhood he has been closely associated with farm industry, his entire career in this connection having been marked by connection with the operations of the fine old home farm on which he was born and reared and of which he is now the owner, he having been the only son and having acquired his sisters' interest in the property after the death of his honored father This well improved and admirably managed farm property comprises 240 acres and constitutes one of the model farms of Washington County, the same being devoted to diversified agriculture and to the raising and feeding of excellent types of live stock. Mr. Blaco continued his residence on the farm until February, 1917, when he removed to the Village of Kennard, where he has since been established in the farm implement and machinery business, in which he handles both heavy and light implements and machinery demanded in connection with modern farm operations He is also a director of the Farmers Grain & Lumber Company at Kennard and of the Farmers Grange & Mutual Insurance Company of Washington, Burt County, besides which he is a director and influential member of the county Grange of the Patrons of Husbandry His political allegiance is given to the republican party, and his popularity in his home community needs no further voucher than his incumbency of the office of mayor of Kennard, and his being also a member of the Board of County Commissioners, in which latter office he is serving his first term at the time of this writing, in the spring of 1920 He is also a member of the republican committee of Richland Township Mr Blaco is affiliated with both the Lodge and Encampment bodies of the Independent Order of Odd Fellows and also with the local camp of the Modern Woodmen of America, in which he has passed the various official chairs, as has he also in the Odd Fellows Lodge His wife holds membership in the Presbyterian Church

April 26 1899, recorded the marriage of Mr Blaco to Miss Meric Johnson, who was born and reared in Douglas County, and who is a leader in the social activities of her home community They have no children

HERMAN JUNGBLUTH A disciple of modern farming, who does his farming with his brain as well as his brawn, Herman Jungbluth has lived his life in Washington County, and while others of the family have gone into business and acquired substantial positions he has been well satisfied in the exercise of his business capabilities as a farmer and stockman His well improved and handsome home is in section 22 of Arlington Township, half a mile west of Dale

He was born in Washington County March 14, 1881, a son of Bernard H J. and Ida (Fisher) Jungbluth, the former a native of Germany and the latter of Toledo, Ohio Bernard Jungbluth located in Chicago in 1871 and was employed in the McCormick Harvester Company's plant when the historic fire swept over that city in 1871 Some years later, in 1878, he came out to Washington County, Nebraska, bought land and for many years was engaged in general farming and stock raising For eight years he also operated at Arlington what was known as the Arlington Steam Brickyard, and made great quantities of brick, part of which was used in building the residence on his home farm He was a democrat, and he and his wife were members of the Catholic Church at Fremont They were the parents of five children: Bertha, wife of S R Batson, a traveling salesman living at Lincoln; Herman, Julian, a farmer in Washington County; Zella, wife of F. J Emerson, who is vice president of the Union Stock Yards Bank at South Omaha, and Wilma, wife of Robert Kimball, manager of a wholesale tire company at Lincoln

Herman Jungbluth acquired a public school education in Washington County, attended the Lincoln Business College, and at the age of twenty-eight became an independent farmer While he has grown many successive crops, his big interest as a farmer is the breeding and raising of livestock Since 1917 he has taken great pains and expended a large amount of capital in developing a fine herd of choice hogs First he bred the Duroc Jersey, but now has laid the nucleus of a herd of Poland Chinas He is also an extensive feeder for the market, and during the last year fed five hundred cattle and fifteen hundred sheep He has given all the extensive equipment and facilities to his farm He is a member of the Farmers Union and is a stockholder in the Mid-West Creamery at Omaha

In 1909 Mr Jungbluth married Mata Oft, of Bennington, Nebraska They have four children. Kermit, born in 1910; Sylvia R., Vernon, born in 1913, and Bernard, born in 1916 Mr Jungbluth is a Catholic, while Mrs Jungbluth is a Lutheran Politically he is independent in voting.

George B Riker is one of Blair's most substantial business men, and his business career has been accompanied by an equally praiseworthy record in every matter affecting the general welfare and the progress of his community Mr Riker has lived in Washington County many years and first came to Blair as a railroad man After giving up his duties with the railroad company he took up the real estate business, and his many years of experience make him one of the best judges of realty values in this section of Nebraska

Mr. Riker was born in New York State in 1865, son of George W and Angeline E. (Benedict) Riker The Riker family is of remote German ancestry, but was established in this country in the early part of the eighteenth century Mr Riker's paternal grandfather, Henry Riker, was a native of New York State, and his maternal grandfather, Smith Benedict, was also a New Yorker Both parents were born in New York State, were married there, and in 1871, moved west to Iowa and settled on a farm They lived out their lives as agriculturists The father was devoted to the republican party in politics, and his wife was a member of the Presbyterian Church. They had three children. The oldest, Smith H is in New York City with the American Telephone & Telegraph Company, the second is George B, and the third is Adeline S, wife of R. T Huston, a farmer and livery man at Russell, Iowa

George B Riker was six years of age when the family settled on the Iowa farm He had considerable experience in the tasks of the field and at the same time acquired an education in country schools As a youth he learned telegraphy and at the age of sixteen was first regularly employed on a railroad He was in the railroad service eleven years, enjoying well deserved promotions, and the last four years was joint ticket agent at Blair, Nebraska

Leaving the railway company he entered the real estate business with Charles McMenemy in 1892 Mr McMenemy was a veteran citizen and business man of Blair, having established his home there in 1868, a year before the town was laid out. Mr Riker was associated with Mr McMenemy for sixteen years, until the latter's death In 1901 S W Chambers came into the firm, and since then the business has been conducted as Riker & Chambers Mr Riker is still doing business in the same room where he started nearly thirty years ago He handles general real estate, and in former years has done a great deal of immigration and colonizing work, selling large tracts of Colorado and South Dakota lands He still handles some large bodies of land in Eastern Colorado and also does a large business in farm loans

In 1886 Mr. Riker married Dora Marquis, a native of Iowa, daughter of Samuel N and Rachel Marquis Her parents died in Iowa, where her father was a farmer. Mr and Mrs Riker have one son, Atlee C Riker, now assistant cashier of the Wyoming National Bank at Casper, Wyoming.

Mr. Riker is fraternally affiliated with the Masonic Order and the Modern Woodmen of America He and his wife belong to the Eastern Star and he is worthy patron of the Chapter He is also a member of the Order of Railway Telegraphers and in politics casts his vote as a republican For one term he rendered some creditable service to Blair as a member of the City Council, and it was during his term that the municipal plant was erected

Israel C Eller The most elaborate history is necessarily an abridgement, the historian being compelled to select his facts and materials from a multitude of details So in every life of honor and usefulness the biographer finds no dearth of incident, and yet in summing up the career of any man the writer needs touch only the most salient points, giving only the keynote of his character, eliminating much that is superfluous Consequently in calling the reader's attention to the life record of I C Eller, the well known and able lawyer of Blair, no attempt shall be made to recount all the important acts in his useful life, for it is deemed that only a few of them will suffice to show him to be eminently worthy of a place in a work of this character

Mr Eller has been a resident of Washington County forty years, and his residence is an important fact in the county history because of his enviable position as a lawyer, his efficient services in several county offices and as a member of the 1907 Legislature He was born in Jefferson County, Iowa, on December 17, 1853, and is the son of Harvey and Mary Caroline (Vannoy) Eller Both of these parents were born and reared in Wilkes County, North Carolina, the father's

I. C. Eller

birth having occurred on March 24, 1819, and the mother's on February 18, 1823. They are both deceased, the father dying on November 4, 1906, at Hedrick, Iowa, and the mother on January 18, 1904, at the same place They were married in North Carolina, and in 1852 moved to Jefferson County, Iowa, where the father applied himself to farming The family was a large one and the trip was made in a "prairie schooner," the typical conveyance used by the pioneer emigrants of those days Harvey Eller was a poor man at the time he located in Iowa, but he was energetic, industrious and ambitious For a time after settling in Jefferson County he rented a farm, which he operated so successfully that at length he was enabled to buy land, which he improved and sold at a profit, eventually buying a farm of a 160 acres, which he improved and to the cultivation of which he devoted himself with gratifying success until he was able to retire from active business affairs sometime prior to his death. This last farm is the 160 acres on which the town of Farson, Iowa, is now located. He and his wife were members of the Missionary Baptist Church; in politics he gave his support to the republican party, and during the Civil war he was a strong supporter of the Union

To Harvey and Mary C Eller were born fifteen children, ten sons and five daughters, all of whom grew to years of maturity, and of this number eight sons and two daughters are now living Only three of the children have ever been identified with Washington County, Israel C, now being the only one The survivors are as follows· William H, who was first a minister of the Baptist Church and later a successful lawyer, was an early settler of Washington County, coming here in 1876, but in 1893 he returned to North Carolina and now lives at Greenboro, that state, Cleveland is a general merchant at David City, Nebraska; James Anderson is a successful market gardener at Glenwood, Iowa, Jesse F is engaged in the real estate business at Red Bluff, California, I C. is the immediate subject of this sketch, Mrs Mattie C Dickins is a widow and lives at Farson, Iowa, Thomas A is a retired farmer living at Stratton, Nebraska, Jacob H is a successful merchant at Clay Center, Nebraska, Margaret is the wife of Edward Delos Davis, a farmer at Hedrick, Iowa; Otis R is United States postal clerk at Lincoln, Nebraska

I C Eller received his elementary education in the public schools of Iowa, and then for three years was a student in Central University at Pella, Iowa After teaching one term of school he came to Blair, Nebraska, and applied himself to the reading of law under the direction of his brother William, who at that time had relinquished the work of the ministry and was practicing the legal profession at Blair In February, 1883, he was admitted to the bar at Tekamah and immediately thereafter entered upon the practice of law at Blair He was soon afterward elected clerk of the District Court, which office he held for eight years, and after the expiration of his official term he resumed practice, which commended his attention until 1908, when again he was appointed clerk of the District Court, serving as such three years He then was appointed to the office of county judge, of which he was the incumbent by election thereafter for eight years, and since then he has devoted himself to office practice chiefly Judge Eller in addition to high qualifications as a case lawyer enjoys a wide reputation as an accurate and reliable examiner of abstracts of titles, one of the most important departments of law office work As a lawyer, Judge Eller won a reputation as a sound and safe practitioner. Years of conscientious work have brought with them not only increase of practice and reputation, but also that growth in legal knowledge and that wide and accurate judgment the possession of which constitutes marked excellence in the profession In discussions of the principles of law he is noted for clearness of statement and candor His zeal for a client never leads him to urge an argument which in his judgment is not in harmony with the law, and in all the important litigations with which he has been connected no one has ever charged him with anything calculated to bring discredit upon his profession

When Washington and Bent counties chose Mr. Eller as their representative in the Legislature for the session beginning in 1907 they bestowed that responsibility upon a well trained lawyer with a broad knowledge of public affairs and public men in Nebraska. He entered the Legislature therefore with a prestige that enabled him to exercise an influence throughout the memorable session, and his record therein is one that reflects credit on his home community It has been generally conceded that this session was prolific of more progressive laws than any previous or subsequent sessions It is not inappropriate to name some of the laws passed by that Legislature They included the Railway Commission Bill, the Primary Election Bill, the legislation providing a fifteen per cent cut on express rates, a two-cent fare for railroads—bills which in themselves comprise a program that only occasionally can be credited to the legislative output of any state

On November 3, 1886, Mr Eller was married to Ella E Kemp, who was born near East Troy, Wisconsin, and to their union four children were born, two of whom are living Mary Louise is the wife of Harry L Morris, who was manager of the city electric light plant of Blair from the time it was established to April, 1920, when he resigned and has since been manager of the Blair Canning Factory, Francis Pauline is the wife of Ralph J. Roush, who was manager of a tire and automobile accessory store at Fort Dodge, Iowa, for two years, but now resides in Des Moines

Judge Eller is a member of the Baptist Church, while his wife was a member of the Congregational Church up to the time of her death, which occurred June 14, 1914, the daughters also being affiliated with the latter denomination The judge is a member of the Ancient Free and Accepted Masons and the Independent Order of Odd Fellows In the local lodge of the later order he has been honored by being passed through the chairs several times, and has been a trustee of the lodge for thirty successive years

Politically he is an earnest supporter of the republican party, and has been active in public affairs, having served on the county and state central committees of his party Locally he has served as member of the school board and as city clerk Strong and forceful in his relations with his fellowmen, he has not only made his presence felt, but has also gained the good will and commendation of his associates and the general public, ever retaining his reputation among men for integrity and high character

BERNHARD ABELS has been one of the substantial business men and popular and influential citizens of Kennard, Washington County, since the year 1891, and is a son of John B and Anna (Behrens) Abels, who passed their entire lives in Germany, and four of whose sons are residents of Nebraska Bernhard, of this review George, a retired farmer residing at Papillion, Sarpy County; Henry, a market gardener at

DeBolt Place, Douglas County; and Anton, employed in a meat market in the City of Omaha

Bernhard Abels was born in Minsen, Germany, on the 19th of February, 1855, and was there reared and educated In 1881 he immigrated to America, and in the same year came to Nebraska, where for two years he was employed as a laborer in the City of Omaha Thereafter he was engaged in business as a market gardener at Happy Hollow, near that city, for seven years, and in 1891 he came to Kennard, Washington County, where he purchased the hardware stock and business of George Jessen For the ensuing thirteen years he continued as a dealer in hardware and furniture, and he then sold his stock and business and engaged in the confectionery business, in which he has since successfully continued, with a well stocked and appointed establishment that caters to a representative patronage and with special attention given to the manufacturing and sale of high-grade ice cream during the summer months

An independent voter in politics, Mr Abels has always been loyal and public-spirited in his civic attitude, and in addition to having served three years as township clerk he was for twelve years a member of the board of trustees of the Village of Kennard He has passed the official chairs in the local camp of the Modern Woodmen of America, in which he holds the position of manager in 1920, and he and his wife are communicants of the German Lutheran Church at Blair, the county seat

In 1882 was solemnized the marriage of Mr Abels to Miss Johanna Dannanmann, who likewise was born and reared in Germany, and they have three children Ella, the wife of James Edwards, of Cleveland, Ohio; Bertha, the wife of William P Seybold, assistant superintendent of the Ford automobile assembling plant of the City of Omaha, and Tillie, the wife of Robert L Patrick, superintendent of one of the leading dairy concerns in Omaha

M H Mueller Born and reared and having lived in Washington County forty years, M H Mueller has labored faithfully at the vocation of agriculture since early youth, has experienced some of its unpleasant features, but on the whole his career has been marked by growing success and the enjoyment of the many advantages now characteristic of the country life of Washington County

Mr. Mueller, whose home is in section 22 of Richland Township, two miles north and a mile and a half east of Washington, was born in Washington County July 24, 1879 His father, Michael Mueller, a native of Germany, came to the United States in 1864, at the age of twenty-two He possessed a fair education, and at that time was a young man of ambition and industry, although all the capital he possessed when he reached Council Bluffs, Iowa, was 50 cents Out of necessity he immediately went to work, and most of the time he lived in Iowa, his work was in a brick yard In 1867 he came to Washington County, Nebraska, and took up a homestead of eighty acres His equipment to begin farming consisted of an old team, a wagon and plow, and he had to improvise a harrow to tying together quantities of plum brush with which he dragged his fields In those early days Omaha was the principal market, and it was a two days' trip to that city There followed many years of very slow advancement, due to grasshoppers, drought and other plagues, but eventually he possessed a farm of 300 acres and had all those things which moderate ambition craves He died in Washington County in 1913, at the age of seventy-two His widow, still living, bore the maiden name of Anna M Kahnk, and they were married in Washington County The father was a member of the Masonic Order There were just two children, M H and Mrs. Anna M Wesemann, wife of a Washington County farmer

M H Mueller grew up on his father's homestead and became well acquainted with its duties even when a boy. He attended the common schools and at the age of twenty-six started for himself, but his work has always been on the homestead His father had given the land a great deal of improvement, including buildings, and had also set out many trees. Mr Mueller is a republican in politics, he and his wife are Lutherans in religion, and since 1917 he has served as a director of his home school district

In 1906 he married Caroline D Logemann, who was born in Douglas County, Nebraska, daughter of William and Sophia Logemann, early settlers of that county. Mrs Mueller was the second of three children, the others being Marie and August Mr. and Mrs Mueller were married January 10, 1906, and they have two sons, still at home, Ervin and Arthur

George T Hedelund Prominent among the younger generation of active and progressive men who are contributing largely toward the advancement of the financial interests of Washington County is George T Hedelund, who is widely known as cashier of the State Bank at Washington A native of Nebraska, he was born January 1, 1895, in Blair, coming on both sides of the house from honored Danish ancestry

J S and Dorothy Hedelund, his parents, were born, brought up and married in Denmark Hoping to better his fortunes, J S Hedelund came with his family to the United States in the latter part of the '80s, taking a step that he never regretted, although it had taken him quite a while to make up his mind to forsake his native land Locating in Washington County, Nebraska, he was for thirty years janitor of the schools in Blair He became identified with the democratic party in politics, and both he and his wife belonged to the Danish Lutheran Church Eleven children blessed their marriage, as follows Soren, of Fergus Falls, Minnesota, pastor of the Episcopal Church; John S, engaged in the grain business at Omaha; Mary, wife of J B Dickson, a linotype operator in Omaha, Albert, associated with the United Grain Company in Omaha, Electa, wife of Frank Nelson, who is with the Lyman Sand Company, Anna, wife of H W Lang, foreman of the Union Pacific Shops at Omaha, Martin J, of Omaha, with the Bankers Mortgage & Loan Company, George T, of whom we write; Gertrude, in the employ of the Omaha Taxi Company at Omaha, Carrie, connected with the Pacific Storage Company of Omaha, and Dorothy, with the Nebraska & Iowa Steel Tank Company

Acquiring his early education in Blair, George T Hedelund was graduated from the high school with the class of 1912, and later continued his studies in Dana College Beginning life for himself as a teacher, he taught in the Blair High School two years Abandoning his profession, he was in the employ of the Crowell Grain & Lumber Company for a year, and later served as assistant cashier of the Citizens Bank of Blair for four years, gaining in the meantime knowledge and experience of value Coming from there to Washington County Mr Hedelund assumed his present responsible position as cashier of the

Washington State Bank on May 1, 1919, and has since performed the duties devolving upon him in that capacity ably and faithfully This bank, of which Mr Hedelund is a director and a stockholder, has a paid up capital of $15,000, a surplus fund of $3,000, and individual deposits of $190,000

Mr Hedelund married in September, 1917, Vera McCracken, a daughter of John McCracken, of Blair Mr Hedelund is a republican in politics, but has never been an aspirant for official honors, his time and energies being devoted to the interests of the bank with which he is officially connected He has had some experience in naval affairs, having served five months in the United States Navy Mrs Hedelund is a consistent member of the Danish Lutheran Church

J F McCANN Those who own and cultivate the land are very properly entrusted with other responsibilities in the business and social life of the community J F McCann had made a reputation as a successful farmer before he became identified with several community enterprises in Arlington Township, where he has lived and become well known for many years His home is in section 12, five miles east of Arlington, on the Blair highway

Mr McCann was born in Virginia February 4, 1871, but has spent most of his life in Nebraska His parents, Isaac and Margaret McCann, were also natives of Virginia His father was a Virginia farmer, served in the Civil war, and in March, 1872, came out to Nebraska, traveling by train as far as Omaha, where he was met by some friends He never homesteaded, but bought land near what was known as Bell Creek, now Arlington In that community he lived forty years, until his death in 1913, and had brought his affairs to a high degree of prosperity. His wife died in 1916 His accumulations at one time aggregated 460 acres, most of which he divided among his children before his death The children number eight William, of Washington County; Mrs Ruth Rosenbaum, of Washington County, J F; Henry, a farmer and stockman in Canadian County, Oklahoma, Mrs. Lydda Demaree, wife of a Scottsbluff farmer, Mrs Salley Weidner, the deceased wife of a farmer of Washington County, Mrs Dell Whorlow, of Washington County; and Delmar, deceased

J F McCann was about a year old when brought to Nebraska, and he grew up on his father's farm and acquired a common school education At the age of twenty-one he began on his own responsibility and after working for a time for his father, rented some of the homestead When he married he bought forty acres, and now has a well improved and ably managed farm of eighty acres, devoted to general farming and some stock raising Mr. McCann helped organize the Blair Telephone Company in 1902 He also became a charter member of the Home State Bank of Kennard, which was chartered and began business in 1915 He served as its vice president three years He also helped organize the Farmers Grain & Lumber Company of Kennard Other interests to which he has directed his time have been particularly the cause of education He served as a member of the school board for several years. Politically he is independent and is affiliated with the Masons and Modern Woodmen of America.

In 1895 Mr McCann married Miss Mertie LeCrone, whose father, John LeCrone, was a native of Illinois, spent many years in Washington County but is now living in Alfalfa County, Oklahoma Mr and Mrs McCann have six children, all at home, named Addie, Lyle, Lloyd, Alice, Leroy and Lester

DERVIE HALL is, with but one exception, entitled to the distinction of being the oldest business man at Kennard, Washington County, in point of continuous identification with representative business activities in this thriving village He was born in Denmark in 1874, and was there reared and educated, besides which he there learned the painter's trade He is a son of Jens and Margaret (Jensen) Hall, the former of whom is a carpenter by trade, though he is now engaged in farm enterprise in Denmark, where he served in the national army and took part in the war with Germany when the latter empire encroached upon the rights of sturdy little Denmark His wife died at the age of thirty-five years, a devout member of the Lutheran Church, as is he also. Of the children, the subject of this sketch and two of his brothers, Fred and Martin, came to the United States, where all have won independence and prosperity, Fred being now engaged in farming near Irvington, Douglas County, Nebraska, where he also continued to work at his trade, that of painter, and Martin being a carpenter and builder at Elkhorn, Iowa

Dervie Hall was about eighteen years of age when he came to America and established his residence at Hampton, Iowa, in 1892. He there followed his trade until the following year, when he came to Nebraska and worked at his trade in the City of Omaha. Before the close of that year, however, he came to Washington County and engaged in business as a painter and decorator in the new Village of Kennard, besides which he was here associated with his brother Fred in the general merchandise business, of which they disposed at the expiration of five years Dervie Hall thereafter opened another store, which he still conducts and in which he handles groceries, paints and wall paper. He also owns and operates a well equipped greenhouse in the village, besides which he is serving as justice of the peace He is a republican in politics, is affiliated with the Modern Woodmen of America and he and his wife are active members of the Methodist Episcopal Church in their home village, where they hold an inviolable place in popular esteem

In 1894 was solemnized the marriage of Mr Hall to Miss Sarah J McCracken, who was born in the State of Virginia, a daughter of Frank McCracken, who settled in Washington County, Nebraska, in 1883 A great-uncle of Mrs Hall married a daughter of the famous Indian chief, Blackhawk Mr. and Mrs Hall have three children Angie, who remains at the parental home and has active charge of her father's store, Wilbur, a painter by trade and vocation and now at home in Washington County, was in the aviation service of the Government during the World war and was stationed in Texas the greater part of the time, he having made a trip across the continent on a motorcycle, and Elsie, in 1920, a student in the Kennard High School

GEORGE MENKING owns and conducts a modern garage which gives to the Village of Kennard, Washington County, the most approved facilities in connection with the automobile business, and in addition to carrying a full line of supplies and accessories and maintaining a well-equipped repair department Mr Menking is also local agent for the celebrated Buick and Chevrolet automobiles

Mr Menking was born in the immediate vicinity of the City of Cincinnati, Ohio, on September 1, 1871, and is a son of Frederick and Dora Menking, who came to Nebraska and established their residence in Washington County in 1872, the father here taking up a homestead and developing one of the excellent farms of the county, where both he and his wife passed the remainder of their lives, his death occurring in 1908 and his widow having passed away in 1912 They were honored pioneer citizens of the county, were earnest communicants of the Lutheran Church, and Mr Menking was affiliated with the lodge of the Independent Order of Odd Fellows at Arlington, his political support having been given to the republican party Of the six children the first born, Sophia is deceased; Frederick C. conducts a garage at Arlington, this county, William is engaged in the same line of enterprise at Geneva, Fillmore County, Lena is deceased; George, of this review, was the next in order of birth, Edward is engaged in farming near Fort Morgan, Colorado

George Menking was not yet one year old at the time of the family removal to Washington County, where he was reared on his father's farm and where he gained his early education in the rural school of District No. 10. His initial activities of independent order were in connection with farm enterprise, with which he here continued his active association until 1909, when he engaged in the agricultural implement business at Kennard Later he turned his attention to the automobile business, and his garage is now one of the representative business establishments in this thriving village, he having sold his implement business.

Mr Menking is a loyal supporter of the cause of the republican party, is serving as a member of the Kennard Board of Education and is affiliated with the local organizations of the Independent Order of Odd Fellows and Modern Woodmen of America

In the year 1892 Mr Menking was united in marriage to Miss Elizabeth French, who was born and reared in Washington County, and they have four children Bertha is the wife of Harry Edward, a farmer near Herman, this county; Ethel is the wife of Arthur Andressen, who is engaged in farming near Lyons, Bert County, Lola is the wife of Frank Vibrial, assistant cashier of the Farmers and Merchants Bank at Kennard; and Keith is attending the public schools of Kennard

Homer A Wright, who is now engaged in business at Kennard, Washington County, has been a resident of this place since 1896 and has been here identified with varied lines of business enterprise He was born in New York in 1862, a son of Thomas and Phoebe (Rogers) Wright, both of whom passed their entire lives in the old Empire State, where the father was engaged in farm enterprise during the greater part of his active career His political allegiance was given to the democratic party, and both he and his wife were members of the Presbyterian Church.

The public schools of his native state afforded Homer A. Wright his youthful education, and upon coming to Nebraska in 1896 he became associated with his brother, Charles L, in the general merchandise business at Kennard, his brother having later returned to the State of New York, where he is still giving his attention to this line of business. The store at Kennard was conducted under the firm name of Wright Brothers for eight years, and after his retirement from this business Mr Wright served one year as mail carrier on a rural route For five years thereafter he was in the employ of the Chicago & Northwestern Railroad, and he then established himself in the draying business at Kennard, in which line of enterprise he developed a prosperous business and continued the same for five years He is now one of the well known business men and popular citizens of Kennard He is independent in politics, is a member of the Christian Church, and his wife holds membership in the Church of God. His marriage to Miss Mary Jane Jones occurred in 1908, but no children were born of this union

EMIL GOTTSCH. A resident of Washington County for thirty years, Emil Gottsch discovered some real opportunities in this Nebraska country, though almost entirely through the avenue of hard work and his own initiative, and has attained a position as one of the prominent farmers and citizens of Richland Township His farm is in section 35 and his home a half mile north and three miles east of the Town of Washington

Mr Gottsch was born in Germany in 1870 and acquired most of his education in that country He had only the advantages of the common schools At the age of fifteen he came to America and for four years lived in and around Davenport, Iowa, and from there came to Washington County His parents, Frederick and Anna Gottsch, followed their son to America seven years later, and the mother died in 1916 Frederick Gottsch now lives with his daughter Emil Gottsch, after coming to Washington County made his work available to others as a farm hand for many years With a modest equipment and capital he rented farms for seven years, and since then has been on the way to independence as a land owner and agriculturist He has 160 acres in his farm, practically all well improved and highly cultivated The cyclone of 1913 destroyed all the buildings on the farm, but these have been replaced with structures of a most substantial character. He raises a good deal of stock and carries on diversified operations

For nine years Mr Gottsch served as a member of his local school board He is a republican, is affiliated with the Modern Woodmen of America and is a member of the Christian Church of Bennington.

He married Hattie Dornacker, a native of Washington County and daughter of the late Nick Dornacker, who was born in Germany and was an early settler in Washington County Mr and Mrs Gottsch had eleven children, one of whom died in infancy The others, all at home, are Theresa, Louis, Lillie, Fredie, Helen, Irene, Francis, Herbert, Earline and Henrietta

A J. CAMERON, M D Twenty years of effort to maintain the health of a large part of the population of Herman and community have drawn the career of Dr A J Cameron within the fold of a large and emphatic need, giving him an increasing outlet for a wealth of professional and general usefulness

He was born at Watford, Ontario, Canada, May 17, 1875, a son of Donald and Mary (Kline) Cameron. His father, a native of Scotland, went to Canada in young manhood and there passed the rest of his life in agricultural pursuits, dying at the age of seventy-five years Mrs Cameron still survives Doctor Cameron is the third youngest in a family of four sons and six daughters One daughter died at the age of thirty, seven of the children live in Canada, and Doctor Cameron and his sister, Mrs Spears of Detroit, are the only ones in the United States.

A. J. Cameron attended the public schools of his native place and began teaching school at the age of seventeen years After three years as an educator he again attended high school for one year, and then entered the University of Toronto, where he pursued a four-year course and graduated in 1900, with the degree of M D, C. M On September 25th of the same year he embarked upon the practice of his profession

Allan J. Cameron

at Herman The doctor has a well-equipped office and appliances for the most delicate and exacting demands of his profession He has been deservedly successful, is thorough, and energy and enthusiasm enable him to carry a heavy burden of indispensable service to the community. During the period of the World war Doctor Cameron was a member of the Medical Advisory Board of Washington County, and later volunteered and was commissioned a captain in the Medical Corps, United States Army, and had a regular assignment of duty for six months He was in New York on his way overseas when the armistice was signed. Doctor Cameron is a member of the County, State and American Medical Associations, and the Elkhorn and Missouri Valley Medical Association He is a past master of Landmark Lodge, Ancient Free and Accepted Masons, a Knight Templar and a Shriner, and also a member of Omaha Lodge, Benevolent and Protective Order of Elks

September 18, 1901, Doctor Cameron married Miss Mamie B Eccles of Watford, Ontario, where she was reared and educated They have one daughter, M Evelyn, now in high school Mrs Cameron is a member of the Order of Eastern Star

Doctor Cameron has filled various public offices with efficiency and conscientiousness and has been a member of the village board for six years and of the Board of School Directors for a like period As a voter, he maintains an independent stand Personally he is a man of rare discretion, tact and helpfulness, an earnest and painstaking exponent of the best tenets of medical science, and an indefatigable seeker after those things which produce health and therefore happiness to the human race

LESLIE T. BERRY now owns the controlling interest in the Kennard Co-operative Store, a well-equipped general merchandise establishment in his native Village of Kennard, and is one of the popular and progressive young business men of Washington County He was born at Kennard on October 8, 1898, and is a son of Charles and Elizabeth (Leasburg) Berry, the former a native of the State of Virginia and the latter of Denmark, their marriage having been solemnized in Washington County The father was reared and educated in the historic Old Dominion State and was a young man when he came to Nebraska and settled in Washington County He was one of the early business men of Kennard, where he developed a substantial and prosperous enterprise as a dealer in agricultural implements and machinery and where he became a stockholder in the Farmers and Merchants Bank He was one of the honored and representative citizens of Kennard at the time of his death, in 1900, and his widow still resides in this village, she being a communicant of the Lutheran Church and he having held membership in the Methodist Episcopal Church. Mr Berry was a stanch democrat, was affiliated with the Modern Woodmen of America and was a loyal and public-spirited citizen who commanded unqualified popular esteem Of the four children, the eldest is Charlotte, who is now serving as postmistress at Kennard, Ellen is a clerk in the Kennard Co-operative Store, as is also Charles; and Leslie T, of this review, is the youngest of the number.

The public schools of Kennard afforded Leslie T Berry his earlier education, which was supplemented by his completing a business course in the Nebraska State Normal School at Fremont For a time thereafter he was in the employ of A Kroigard, a merchant at Kennard, and he then took a clerical position in the Farmers and Merchants Bank of this village, in which institution he continued his effective service until February, 1919, when he purchased the controlling interest in the Kennard Co-operative Store, to the management of which he has since devoted his attention with characteristic energy and good judgment. His political allegiance is given to the republican party, and he is affiliated with the Independent Order of Odd Fellows and the Modern Woodmen of America.

GUSTAVE E KRONBERG is distinctively one of the representative business men of the younger generation in his native county and is the efficient and popular cashier of the Farmers and Merchants Bank of Kennard, Washington County, where he is also a stockholder in the Farmers Co-operative Company's general merchandise store.

Mr. Kronberg was born on his father's farm near Blair, judicial center of Washington County, on January 31, 1882, and is a son of Olaf and Matilda Kronberg, both natives of Sweden Upon coming to Nebraska the father first located in the vicinity of Florence, Douglas County, and within a comparatively short time thereafter he came to Washington County and purchased land near Blair, where he reclaimed a productive farm and achieved substantial and well merited prosperity He is now living retired at Blair, is independent in politics and is a zealous communicant of the Lutheran Church, as was also his wife, who died in 1911, at the age of sixty-two years

Gustave E Kronberg was reared to the sturdy discipline of the home farm and gained his early education in the public schools of Washington County He remained on the home farm until 1906, when he took a position in the employ of R E Roberts, operator of the grain elevator at Kennard He was thus engaged about one year, and in 1907 he assumed the position of bookkeeper in the Farmers and Merchants Bank of Kennard, of which institution he was made assistant cashier in 1909 and of which he has been the cashier since 1915 This substantial bank bases its operation upon a capital stock of $30,000, its surplus fund is $7,000, and its deposits at the time of this writing, in 1920, are somewhat in excess of $290,000 Mr Kronberg is a member of the American Bankers Association, is affiliated with the Independent Order of Odd Fellows, is independent in his political attitude, and is one of the wide-awake and progressive young men of Washington County He and his wife hold membership in the Lutheran Church.

In 1910 Mr Kronberg was united in marriage to Miss Elizabeth Kempcke, who was born in Douglas County, this state, where her father is a representative farmer, and the two children of this union are Lester and Twila

FRED E JUNGBLUTH For twenty years Fred E Jungbluth has carried some of the heavy burdens of farm enterprise in his particular section of Washington County. Nearly all his undertakings have prospered and his net experience constitutes a fine farm home and a position among the capable men of affairs of Washington County His farm is a mile and a half south of Dale in section 35 of Arlington Township

Mr Jungbluth was born in Washington County in 1881, a son of Joseph and Nellie (Renard) Jungbluth While his father was born in Germany his mother was born in Wisconsin Joseph Jungbluth came to Washington County in May, 1871, was an early settler and went through all the trials and hardships of pioneering. He was a farmer and stock raiser, and was actively affiliated with the Catholic Church In his family were five children Della, wife of Clayton Beck, a stockman at Harold, South Dakota, Fred E, Minnie, wife of Otto Siesch, a farmer of Washington County, Alfonso, and Gus, deceased. Alfonso for two years was with the colors during the late war He was trained at Camp Cody, and was honorably discharged at Camp Dodge. He was both in the machine gun and cavalry branches of the service, being a member of Company H of the One Hundred and Twenty-Seventh Machine Gun Battalion While he went overseas he was never in action on the front line He is now completing his education in Midland College at Fremont

Fred E Jungbluth was educated in Washington County and took a thorough business course in the Nebraska Business College at Omaha for two years In 1901 he began farming, and has kept steadily at this occupation through subsequent years He has his land well improved and handles much livestock, but for several years has featured mules He is a members of the Farmers' Union and of Washington Hall

In 1903 Mr Jungbluth married Mellie Johnson, who was born in Denmark, a daughter of J P Johnson To their marriage were born seven children Chester, Frances and Lloyd, still at home, Erma, who died at the age of ten years, Mildred, who died aged twenty-one months, Allen, who died at the age of ten months, and Marjorie, the youngest of the children, is at home The family are members of the Kountz Memorial Church of Omaha Mr Jungbluth is affiliated with the Woodmen of the World, votes independently, and is treasurer of his school district, No 41

Austin W Beales One of the first points to attract settlement in Washington County was historic old Fort Calhoun, a frontier post that prior to and during the Civil war period guarded this portion of the Missouri River Valley from Indian incursions The site of that old Indian post is on the land now known as the Austin W Beales farm, which adjoins the Village of Fort Calhoun on the east At one time Fort Calhoun Village was a place of considerable population and trade

This interesting and historic farm is now owned and occupied by Mrs Hannah Beales, widow of the late Austin W Beales The latter was an old soldier and Nebraska pioneer He was born in England in 1836 and at the age of ten years came to the United States As early as 1856 he was in Nebraska, at Fort Calhoun, and later he went into the army and served as a Union soldier during the Civil war During 1865-66 he was engaged in freighting across the plains to Denver, but after his marriage he settled down on his land and continued the occupation of farming until his death in January, 1912 He was a highly esteemed citizen, a successful man in managing his affairs, left a well-improved property and had also given much of his time to public affairs. He was a school director for a number of years, also served as city clerk, and was a member of the Masonic Order He had homesteaded 158 acres in 1864 and proved up on it in 1869, and continued to own it until 1885, when he traded it to the Newton Clark heirs as part payment on his farm he owned at the time of his death

In April, 1868, Austin W Beales married Miss Hannah Hall, who is also a pioneer of Washington County She was born at Springfield, Ohio, in 1849, and came to Nebraska June 7, 1857 Her father, John A Hall, was born at Zanesville, Ohio, in 1816, was a saddler by trade, and on coming to Nebraska first settled at Florence and his later years were spent at farming near Herman He died in February, 1874 John A Hall married Catherine C Mitchell, and they were the parents of two sons and four daughters The oldest daughter is Mrs Catherine Bailey of New York City

Mrs Beales for more than half a century has lived in the environment of Fort Calhoun, and here she reared her children To her marriage with Mr Beales six children were born: Elizabeth, born in 1869 and died in 1870, Catherine C, born November 10, 1871, still at home, Sarah C, born October 29, 1874, wife of Fred H Frahm, of Fort Calhoun, Isabel C, born March 6, 1880, died in October, 1884, Park G, born April 23, 1883, at home with his mother on the farm, and J Howard, born June 18, 1886, living near Fort Calhoun

ELMER M MILLER Just a mile west of Kennard in Richland Township appears the prosperous home and farm of Elmer M Miller, one of the stanch and progressive citizens of Washington County Mr. Miller has spent practically all the days of his life in one community, and has found here ample opportunity to busy him usefully and with a degree of credit to himself and to the community

He was born near Kennard, son of Nels and Christena (Christensen) Miller His parents were both natives of Denmark, though his father was born in the old German Province of Schleswig Nels Miller came to this country from Denmark in 1872 and was an early arrival in Washington County, where he married and where he bought and improved a tract of railway land He proved an industrious and capable citizen, and was frequently honored in his community, serving on the school board, as township assessor and as director of the local cemetery He was a member of the Methodist Church at Kennard, and as a republican attended several state conventions as a delegate His widow is still living at Kennard at the age of sixty-three There was one other son, Leonard N, who graduated in medicine from Creighton University of Omaha in 1908 and enjoyed an extensive and growing practice as a physician at Carthage, South Dakota, until his death

Elmer M Miller acquired his early education in the Kennard schools and since the age of twenty-one has been doing for himself and has been developing more and more extensive interests as a farmer He is a dairyman, stock raiser and feeder and has a highly improved farm in section 6 Politically he gives his allegiance to the republican party, is a member of the Royal Arch Chapter of Masons, the Modern Woodmen of America, the Independent Order of Odd Fellows, and he and his family attend the Methodist Episcopal Church.

In 1898 Mr. Miller married Elise Jahnel Their three children are Leonard, Marvin and Bernice, all at home

WILLIAM E SWIHART, who is now living retired in the Village of Kennard, is one of the venerable and sturdy pioneer citizens of Washington County, and was a lad of eleven years when his parents came to this county and became pioneers of Nebraska Territory, nearly a decade prior to the admission of the state to the Union He has had broad and varied experience in connection with pioneer life in the west, and as a skilled artisan at the blacksmith's trade he for many years conducted a shop and worked mightily at his forge in the village in which he now maintains his home

Mr Swihart was born in Stark County, Ohio, March 24, 1847, and is a son of Israel and Mary (Brewster) Swihart, the latter a descendant of Nathaniel Brewster one of the Pilgrim Fathers who came to America on the first voyage of this historic ship Mayflower Israel Swihart was born in Pennsylvania, a representative of a sterling family, of German lineage, that was early found in the old Keystone State, and his wife was a native of Ohio, where their marriage was solemnized and whence they removed to Indiana when their son William E of this review was a boy. In 1854 they numbered themselves among the pioneers of Dubuque County, Iowa, where the father followed the blacksmith trade and also operated a sawmill In 1858 he came with his family to Nebraska and settled in the old Town of De Soto, Washington County, where he arrived on the 5th of May. He became a prominent and influential citizen of the pioneer community, where his versatility was shown in his following the blacksmith trade, in his serving several terms as sheriff of the county, and in his serving also as a minister of the Christian Church, of which both he and his wife were devout members At the time of the discovery of gold in the Black Hills he joined in the stampede to the new field, where he erected the fourth house at Lead City, a place now known as Lead He there engaged in mining with marked success, and also served as notary public After selling his interests in that locality he went to Hot Springs, South Dakota, where he was engaged in the raising and feeding of cattle until "rustlers" stole so much of his stock as to make his operations unprofitable He then returned to Lead City, and there his death occurred in 1896, when he was about eighty-seven years of age, his remains being brought back to Kennard, Nebraska, where they were laid to rest beside those of his wife, in the cemetery which he himself had laid out a number of years previously, his wife having died when about forty-eight years of age They were numbered among the organizers and charter members of the Christian Church at De Soto, and in politics he was a stalwart republican Of the three children William E of this review is the eldest, Nancy E is the wife of Ezra Spink of Council Bluffs, Iowa, and John H is now a farmer at La Junta

William E Swihart received the advantages of a good home, but, reared under pioneer conditions, his entire attendance in school in his youth did not exceed a year in duration, his broader education having been gained through self-discipline and in the stern school of experience He learned the blacksmith trade under the direction of his father at De Soto, and as a young man he entered a claim to a homestead in Washington County two and one-half miles northeast of Kennard After going to the Black Hills with his father he lost this property He was but fourteen years old at the inception of the Civil war, but before its close he entered service in defense of the Union by enlisting in the First Nebraska Black Horse Battalion, which later became a part of the First Nebraska Volunteer Infantry He participated in several skirmishes and continued in service, principally in Nebraska, until the close of the war From what is now the State of South Dakota, after a varied experience in the Black Hills district, Mr Swihart returned to Washington County, Nebraska, and opened a blacksmith shop at Kennard, where he continued to work vigorously at his trade until 1902, when he retired He has served as township assessor, as census enumerator and as justice of the peace, with secure place in the confidence and good will of the community that has represented his home during the major part of his life His political allegiance is given to the republican party, he holds membership in the Christian Church, and he is affiliated with the Grand Army of the Republic and the Independent Order of Odd Fellows

In 1867 Mr Swihart married Miss Sarah E Allen, who was born in the State of Illinois and whose death occurred in 1901. Of their eight children six are living Charles H is a prosperous farmer in Knox

County, Pearl is the wife of Elmer Wild of Fremont, Dodge County, Jessie E is the wife of Charles A Olson of Los Angeles, California, John A is his father's successor as the village blacksmith at Kennard; Mark I is engaged in farming in Wayne County, and Grace is the wife of George A Rathman, who conducts an automobile garage at Blair, Nebraska

In 1904 Mr Swihart was united in marriage to Mrs Sarah E French, widow of James R French She was born in Kentucky, a daughter of Taylor B Meadows, who was killed in battle in the Union army in 1863 Four children by her first marriage are living G R is a successful farmer in Washington County, Elizabeth is the wife of George Menken of Kennard, Thomas E conducts a meat market in this village; and Taylor is a farmer near Herman, Washington County.

MAGNUS JOHNSON is the son of one of the early pioneers of Washington County, has lived in the county himself for over half a century, has been successfully identified with farming, banking and public affairs, and is undoubtedly one of the best known and most highly esteemed residents of Blair

He was born in Sweden February 25, 1856, only child of Mous and Anna Johnson His parents immigrated to the United States in 1865, when he was nine years of age, and for two or three years lived in Omaha It was in 1868 that the Johnson family homesteaded in Washington County, and the parents spent the rest of their lives on their homestead, seeing their efforts rewarded with a comfortable home before their deaths They were active members of the Lutheran Church, and the father after acquiring American citizenship voted as a republican

Magnus Johnson from the age of twelve lived on a Nebraska farm and supplemented his education acquired at Omaha in country schools He began his career as a practical farmer, and his enterprise was chiefly directed to agricultural lines and he lived on the farm until 1913, when he moved to Blair. A man of substantial property interests, well known for his integrity of character and good business judgment Magnus Johnson has had many interests in his home community He helped organize the Farmers and Merchants Bank of Kennard, and has been its president since its organization twenty-one years ago At Blair he served a term as mayor, and for four years was a member of the County Board of Washington County and was on the school board about twenty-four years when on the farm

In 1882 Mr Johnson married Miss Anna Anderson, a native of Sweden They have five children Nellie C, who married Al Payne of Chelsea, Oklahoma; Ida, at home, Emma, who has been employed in railroad service for fourteen years and while the Government had charge of the railroads she was employed as one of the officers of the railroad administration at Washington, District of Columbia, and still has that position, Alma, wife of Robert Foley, a Washington County farmer, and Lawrence William, the only son, who was the soldier representative of the family during the World war He was in the field artillery with the One Hundred and Twenty-Seventh Regiment, was in training and in service two years, went overseas but was not put on the front line of action prior to the signing of the armistice

Mrs Johnson is a member of the Lutheran Church while Mr. Johnson attends the Episcopal Church In politics he is a stanch republican

WILLIAM H. BUSS

F W. CHRISTENSEN. One of the live and enterprising farmers and stockmen of Washington County is F W Christensen, whose thoroughly improved and systematized farm is in section 26 of Arlington Township, his home being just a half mile south of Dale Store

Mr Christensen was born in Washington County August 16, 1870, son of Lewis Christensen Mr Christensen grew up and acquired a public school education in Washington County and for a number of years was associated with his father on the farm In 1900 he began doing for himself, purchasing 157 acres, all of which he has now devoted to the purposes of general farming He is also a stockholder in the Farmers Livestock Exchange at Omaha He is a member of the Methodist Church at Elk City and is affiliated with the Modern Woodmen of America For a number of years he served as school director and has been deeply interested in all matters of community progress

November 7, 1900, Mr Christensen married Emma Gaines, daughter of H L Gaines of Washington County, whose career has been described elsewhere Mr and Mrs Christensen have three children, all at home Mary Irene, Glen Leroy and Loren William

REV WILLIAM HENRY BUSS The publishers welcome this opportunity to tell briefly something concerning the life and service of the supervising editor of this history, Rev William Henry Buss, who has been a part of the community at Fremont for more than a quarter of a century

He was born in Lamberhurst, Sussex County, England, February 6, 1852, and in the following year his parents, Rev. Henry and Charlotte (Miles) Buss, came to the United States His father, a Congregational minister, gave a pioneer service to his church in Wisconsin and Illinois, his pastorates covering a period of forty years Both parents died in Aurora, Illinois, at a ripe old age

William H Buss acquired his early education in Wisconsin and Illinois, and his higher education in Wheaton College in Illinois and Oberlin College in Ohio He took the four-year classical course at Oberlin, graduated with the degree of Bachelor of Arts in 1879, and ranking fifty in his class of fifty members In his junior year he was elected class poet, and his commencement composition was an "Ode to Oberlin" Mr Buss was not supplied with liberal funds to attend college, and practically paid his way, serving as clerk, accountant and school teacher Immediately on leaving Oberlin he entered the Chicago Theological Seminary, taking the three years' divinity course including Hebrew The expenses of his senior year at the Theological Seminary were defrayed from his returns from missionary preaching in Chicago He was graduated in 1882 with the degree Bachelor of Divinity

Rev Mr Buss was ordained a minister of the Congregational Church at Burlington, Iowa, June 6, 1882, and for two years was the assistant pastor of the First Congregational Church of that city in association with Rev. Dr. William Salter. He then organized a new church and built a new house of worship at West Burlington, where he served until February, 1887, when he was called to the pastorate of the Deadwood Congregational Church, in which he continued until October, 1890

It was in that month, just thirty years ago, that he accepted a call to the First Congregational Church of Fremont, Nebraska, where he served eleven consecutive years. In 1901 he was summoned to the pastorate of a church at Aurora, Illinois, but was recalled to Fremont January 1, 1906 Rev Mr Buss has served as a delegate to national and international councils of his denomination at Syracuse and Boston, also as a delegate to an international convention of Christian Endeavor at Baltimore, and has twice delivered the annual baccalaureate sermon at the University of Nebraska He managed the fortieth and the fiftieth anniversaries of the Fremont church, which were elaborately celebrated and has been closely identified with the religious, civic and educational affairs of the city for twenty-six years

During his pastoral work he has composed and published many poetical writings, not a few of which have attracted wide attention In 1917 he contested with 400 competitors for the price of $100 offered by Hon John D Haskell, president of the Farmers' National Bank of Wakefield, Nebraska, for the best state hymn that should be written by a Nebraska author in honor of the semi-centennial of the commonwealth Mr Buss won the prize, which naturally brought him congratulations from all over the West The "Hymn to Nebraska" was set to music by John Prindle Scott of New York City and has been sung not only during the anniversary celebration but also by great numbers of school children in various parts of the state ever since His gifts as a poet were additionally inspired during the World war, when he composed many poems on various phases of the war situation and upon prominent American persons and events Many of these were published in the local press and by outside journals Mr Buss has a collected volume of poems now ready for publication

October 29, 1885, at Burlington, Iowa, he married Miss Annie Rachel Woepking, who has been from the beginning a true helpmeet, comfort and inspiration in all his labors Their family consists of one daughter and two sons Edith Emily is a business accountant and a church choir soloist Ralph Harold is master of the department of discounts and collateral in the Federal Reserve Bank of Chicago William Kenneth, the other son, was with the United States Marines during the World war, is now local adjutant of the American Legion Post at Fremont, and a salesman and accountant in his native city

In the spring of 1917 Rev Mr Buss, suffering with an affliction of his eyes and having served in the gospel ministry for thirty-six years, decided to resign from his pastorate and undergo special treatment The First Congregational Church accepting the resignation expressed great love and appreciation of the extended pastorate and unanimously elected him pastor emeritus for life He is now living in comparative retirement, much improved in health, and his memories of the past and the love of his people fill his heart with gratitude and joy, intangible assets that he regards as the truest wealth But he is not allowed to be idle, is constantly called upon for special sermons and all varieties of pastoral work, and the early evening of a useful life he still finds richly fraught with the gladness of the service of mankind

Mrs. Dora Luse, whose home is in section 9 of Blair Township, two miles west of the Town of Blair, is the widow of the late George Luse, and was herself born in Dodge County and represents one of the earliest families to settle in this section of Nebraska

Her father, H. J Raner, was a native of Ohio, and on going west first settled in Lynn County, Iowa For a time he lived in St Louis and in 1859, with his wife, whom he married in Iowa, came in a covered wagon to Washington County, Nebraska He homesteaded eighty acres, and began life there practically without capital He and his wife made their first home in a dugout Experiencing low markets drought, grasshoppers and other plagues that beset the early settlers, he went steadily ahead and achieved notable success He early began to acquire more land, trading a threshing machine for some and paying $8 an acre for other tracts and at the time of his death had 400 acres Despite the hard work he did and the hardships he passed through he lived to a good old age and passed away April 27, 1917, at the age of eighty-two H. J. Raner married Sarah Mann, who died January 2, 1917, at the age of seventy-seven They were the parents of seven children Stephen, a farmer in Brown County, Nebraska, Mrs Mary Heath, wife of a Washington County farmer, Delbert, a broom-maker by trade, living at Herman; Mrs Dora Luse, Charles, deceased; Mrs Lora Steed, of Blair; and Theodore, deceased

At Blair in 1894 Miss Dora Raner became the wife of George Luse Mr Luse grew up in Pennsylvania, and at the age of fifteen went out to northwestern Nebraska, locating in Cherry County He came to Washington County about twenty-five years ago, and during his married life successfully and profitably managed the farm where Mrs Luse and her family now reside. They had four children: Gladys Peterson, of Washington County, Harry, of Washington County, Adelbert, deceased, and Georgia, at home with her mother.

William R Goll Prominent among the reliable business citizens who have maintained the prestige and business integrity of Fort Calhoun during a long period of years is William R Goll, the proprietor of a modern pharmacy. Mr. Goll has not alone been prominent in business affairs, but in public life as well, having been formerly postmaster here for nearly a quarter of a century and at present acting efficiently in the capacity of city treasurer.

Mr Goll was born on a farm in Washington County, Nebraska, in 1864, a son of Jacob J and Margaret (Frees) Goll, natives of Holstein, Germany His father on first coming to the United States in 1827 settled in Pennsylvania, but later moved to Cal Junction, Iowa, and in 1847 or 1848 came to Washington County, Nebraska. He located or preempted a claim near Blair, when Nebraska was still a territory He being one of the first to locate in this section and continued to live on the same farm and received title from the Government He was married in 1862 Later in life they were numbered among the substantial agricultural people of their region, owning 100 acres of land and carrying on farming and stock raising on a large scale It happened that father Goll had located his claim before this region had been surveyed by the Government, and had erected his log house on a site which proved to be immediately upon the corners of four sections, making it necessary for the surveyors to plant their stake in the middle of his home In later years this historic old log house was replaced by a more modern one, and finally Mr and Mrs Goll retired entirely from active pursuits and moved to Blair, where the father passed away at the age of eighty years and the mother when she was seventy-two years of age They were faithful members of the Lutheran Church, and in politics Mr Goll was a republican He held office on several occasions, having been school moderator and director of Goll School, District No 12 in Washington County, the school having been erected in his honor. There were seven children in the family, of whom four are living at this time: Amelia and Mary, who are unmarried and reside at Blair; Matilda, the wife of Mr. Linstrom, of that place, and William R.

William R Goll attended the country schools and resided on the home farm until he was seventeen years of age, at which time he decided to make his own way in the world. For seven and one-half years he was employed by Dr. S. B Taylor, of Blair, in his drug store, and during this time took a business and pharmacy course at Elliott's Business College, Burlington, Iowa, graduating in the latter study in 1887 Later he went to Pueblo, Colorado, where he worked in a wholesale drug house, and then went to Pilger, where he was employed for one year by C W Howe Coming to Fort Calhoun in 1891, he became postmaster here and held that position for twenty-four years In March, 1891, he brought in a drug stock which he had purchased and established himself in the drug business He now conducts a general pharmacy, compiling prescriptions and handling A D S drugs, and has built up an excellent patronage through his thorough knowledge of his calling, his business perspicacity and a courteous and obliging personality that readily makes friends Mr Goll has long been a prominent figure in the ranks of the republican party in this section, and after serving fifteen years in the capacity of city treasurer resigned in January, 1921 He belongs to the Masons and the Modern Woodmen of America, and Mrs Goll is an Adventist

On December 31, 1890, Mr Goll was united in marriage with Miss Sadie M Conger, a native of Illinois, and three children have been born to them: Harold, in the United States postoffice at Omaha; Walter Creighton, attending the Omaha Medical College; and Willard, at home

Frank C Adams Like the majority of his contemporaries in the field of journalism in the smaller cities of Nebraska Frank C Adams began his connection with newspaper work at the case. Throughout a somewhat extended career he has been identified with the printing business, largely in association with newspapers, and the varied experience which he gained in numerous communities has been of no little value to him in his work of producing the Fort Calhoun Chronicle, of which he has been the editor and publisher since his arrival in this city in 1915

Mr Adams was born on a farm in Sherman Township, Washington County, Nebraska, in 1876, a son of J. K and Elizabeth (Love) Adams; the former born in Pennsylvania and the latter in Scotland From Pennsylvania, where they were married, the parents removed first to Wisconsin and then to Iowa, where the father engaged in farming and stock raising until 1869, when he took up a homestead in Sherman Township, Washington County, Nebraska He continued his farming operations there for fourteen years, but his wife died in 1881, at the age of forty years, and two years later he went to Tekamah and embarked in the drug business, being associated therein with his brother, Robert L After eight years of this association it was mutually terminated and Mr Adams removed to Lyons, this state, where he is still engaged in business as the proprietor of a pharmacy known as Adams Drug Store He is eighty-three years of age, but still active in attending to the daily routine of his duties He is a member of the Independent Order of Odd Fellows and of the Presbyterian Church, and in politics is a republican Four children were born to Mr and Mrs Adams· A. C., engaged in the drug business at Omaha, R W, an insurance man of Boise, Idaho; Maria, the widow of William Scott, of Tekamah, and Frank C

Frank C. Adams received his education in the public schools of Lyons, Nebraska, and at Bellevue College, which he attended two years, and then began to learn the printing business of M W. Warner, of Lyons. After he had been employed by Mr Warner for two years he went to

Bentley, Iowa, where he conducted The Argus, and later went to Atlanta and was the proprietor of the Atlanta Record Subsequently he worked on the Fremont Tribune and following this the Tekamah Herald and the Pender Times, and then spent four years in job shops of Omaha Next he went to Bloomfield, where he was proprietor of the Journal for one year, and in 1915 came to Fort Calhoun and founded the Chronicle, which he has conducted to the present time This is a well-printed, well-edited weekly publication, which by reason of its reliability, cleanness and interesting character has attained a large circulation at Fort Calhoun and in the country surrounding, while as an advertising medium it is accounted to be valuable In connection with his newspaper Mr Adams operates an up-to-date and well-equipped job printing department, where high-class work of all kinds is done. He is likewise interested in handling local real estate, being associated in this business with W. P. Cook.

Mr. Adams was married in 1899 to Miss Tessie Cleveland, who was born in Burt County, Nebraska, and to this union there have been born five children DeLena, residing at Lyons; Robert and Julia, residing with their parents, Ruth, who lives at Omaha; and Giles, at home The family holds membership in the Presbyterian Church at Fort Calhoun Fraternally Mr. Adams is identified with the Modern Woodmen of America, while his political adherence is given to the republican party Since coming to Fort Calhoun he has served efficiently as postmaster two years

J F JAPP Since earliest pioneer times in Washington County one of the very prominent families has been that of Japp. A prominent representative of that name today in the argicultural enterprise of Richland township is J F Japp, whose home is in section 22, a mile and a half east and two and a half miles north of the Town of Washington.

Mr. Japp, whose life of earnest effort and successful enterprise has been entirely spent in Washington County, was born on the site of his present home September 24, 1869, oldest of the twelve children of John and Catherine Japp. His mother is still living John Japp, a native of Germany, came to the United States with all his capital comprising only $70. As a pioneer in Nebraska he homesteaded eighty acres of prairie land, and a very modest frame structure furnished the first habitation for him and his family The nearest town to his place of settlement was old Fort Calhoun, and he took his grain to be ground at the grist mill in that village While he always remained a farmer his life's industry was well rewarded and at one time he owned 960 acres He and his family were active members of the Lutheran Church John Japp died at the age of seventy-nine years.

J F Japp has always lived close to the home environment, and after being educated in the local schools he assisted in the work of the farm and at the age of twenty-six established a home of his own, buying land from his father He has 160 well-cultivated acres and handles a considerable amount of live stock every year Mr Japp is an independent in politics

In December, 1898, he married Bertha Schroeder, who was born in Germany and at the age of two years was brought to the United States by her parents Her father, Peter Schroeder, is a retired farmer at Brunswick, Antelope County, Nebraska Eight children have been born to Mr. and Mrs Japp, and they are all in the home circle Their names are Dorothy, Minnetta, Meta, John, Pauline, Olga, Sylvia and Leonard

CHRIS WRICH In section 16 of Richland Township, a mile east and two and a half miles north of Washington, is a farm and home which shows the evidence of the thrifty labors of two generations of the Wrich family The present owner and occupant is Chris Wrich, who has lived there practically all his life and whose years have borne every token of industry and good citizenship

Mr Wrich was born in Washington County in 1874, son of Carsten and Marie Wrich. His father came from Germany to the United States in 1869, and made his first settlement at old Fort Calhoun He possessed less than $50 when he reached Nebraska, and for the first five years he lived at Calhoun Village and found varied employment in the life and affairs of this district. He then bought eighty acres of state school land, and with that as a foundation he developed his land holdings until at the time of his death his estate comprised 800 acres, including several very high-grade farms He died at the age of eighty-three and his wife is also deceased They were the parents of four sons and one daughter Carsten Wrich put up on his first farm a rude board barn and house, but eventually erected a very substantial home, with all the comforts of good living

Chris Wrich had all the experiences of the average farm boy, attended district school, and helped his father in the fields, and since the age of twenty-seven has been doing for himself as a successful general farmer and stock raiser. He has also served on the school board as clerk for a number of years, is a democratic voter, and he and his wife are affiliated with the Lutheran Church

In 1899 Mr. Wrich married Miss Emma Kuhr. The four children born into their home are Mary, Margaret, Dora and Alma

HANS WRICH has spent nearly all his life in the community where he still lives and since early infancy has been associated with the rural environment of Dodge and Washington counties His life has been one of strenuous effort, particularly in the years when he had to combat those vicissitudes so well known to the Nebraska farmer, but in more recent times has seen his affairs grow and prosper and is now the contented owner of a fine farm property in Richland Township of Washington County, located in section 22.

Mr Wrich was born in Germany February 27, 1869, son of Carsten and Marie Wrich A few months after his birth his parents started for America. They completed their journey at Fort Calhoun, Nebraska, and the father had only $75 when he reached there. For three years he worked out by day and month wages, then rented land two years, after which he secured eighty acres of school land in township 17, and put up for the accommodation of his family an old country style house of plain boards As he improved his land he bought more and at one time owned 840 acres. He was always busy as a farmer and stockman, never held any public offices, and was one of the prosperous citizens of the county when he died in 1914 at the age of eighty-three. His wife died at the age of eighty-four

Hans Wrich grew up on his father's homestead, learned the lessons taught in the common schools, and assisted his father in proportion to his growing strength on the farm. At the age of twenty-six he started for himself, buying a tract of 170 acres of improved land and gradually increasing his holdings until he now has 410 acres, all in Washington County and devoted to general farming and stock raising Mr Wrich, like his father, has never dabbled in politics, and gives his vote to the

J. T. Smith

man or principle which he deems most worthy He is affiliated with the Modern Woodmen of America.

In 1895 Mr. Wrich married Bertha E Kuhr, member of one of the older families of Dodge and Washington counties Mr. and Mrs. Wrich are the parents of six children: Chris, a farmer near Oram, Nebraska, George, at home; William, who died at the age of eighteen years, Otto and Marie, both at home, and Herman, who died at the age of ten years

JOSEPH TOWNER SMITH While it was a real distinction that he arrived at Fremont in 1856 among the very first settlers, it was the character and capabilities of Joseph Towner Smith that made his career impressive as one of the real pioneers At the time of his death he was the largest taxpayer in Dodge County, and for upwards of half a century the name of Towner Smith possessed a significance due as much to his character as to his extensive possessions He was a shrewd and far-sighted business man, very plain and unassuming, and his life illustrated the possibilities of substantial achievement without superficial show

He was born November 28, 1831, in Wyoming County, Pennsylvania, and died at Fremont, Nebraska, November 12, 1902 His father, Tilton Smith, was a native of Orange County, New York, while his mother, Catherine Draper, was born in Otsego County, New York They were married in Luzerne, now Wyoming, County, Pennsylvania, and of their family three sons became identified with the pioneer life of eastern Nebraska

Towner Smith grew up and acquired his early education in Pennsylvania On October 28, 1856, he crossed the Missouri River into Nebraska at Omaha His companion in travel was his brother, Charles A They proceeded up the Nebraska side of the river to Fremont, where their older brother, Judge James G Smith, had preceded them several months, in time to help lay out the Town of Fremont in August of that year Towner Smith saw the village when it contained only a few log houses and dugouts It was a real frontier community, surrounded by a greater Indian population than whites. It was only in that year that any of the permanent settlements were established in this part of Nebraska Territory. Preparatory to approaching winter the three brothers constructed a dugout 8x12 feet, and here they had their home and headquarters during the winter of 1856-57 During the spring and summer of the following year the brothers erected a hewed log house, 16x24 feet This by virtue of its service was one of the real historic landmarks of early Fremont, serving as residence, boarding house, postoffice, store and trading house for both whites and Indians In 1858 Towner Smith and his brother, James G, opened the first store in Fremont, and James was appointed the first postmaster. This store was on the corner of Military and Broad streets, but later they erected a store building at Sixth and Broad in block 125, opposite the present postoffice building and on the site now occupied by Hammond & Stephens' large publishing house For many years Towner Smith and his brother, Judge James G, were together in the merchandise business. James G Smith removed from Fremont to Chattanooga, Tennessee, in 1906, and later lived in Los Angeles, where he died July 5, 1915 The other Smith brother, Charles A, died in Fremont October 2, 1916

After Towner Smith and his brother James dissolved partnership, the former devoted his time to his extensive landed interests and for many years did a large business buying and selling lands His investments were varied and his acute judgment made him almost invariably successful in his investments He owned much Chicago property, coal lands in Missouri, and other interests besides those in his home county

An early settler who had known Towner Smith from the time he came west paid this significant tribute to him "He was a great saver but was generous to people whom he knew to be in need Whenever he performed an act of kindness it was done without ostentation and many deeds of this nature never came to the public notice He was scrupulously honest and whatever he said could be depended on" He was never actively affiliated with lodge or church, but contributed to causes represented by such organizations, was a republican in politics, and for several years represented the third ward in the City Council He was one of the founders and was the first chief of the Fremont fire department Undoubtedly the substantial character of Towner Smith entered into the very foundation of the modern City of Fremont, and it was his good fortune to see that community grow from an outpost of the wilderness into one of the real cities of the state

The first wife of Towner Smith was Charlotte Adelia Miller. On November 25, 1882, he married Augusta Wilhelmina Knopp, a native of Nebraska, who died July 8, 1889 To this marriage were born three children. Charlotte, wife of Carlos Morehouse of Fremont, Franklin Perry, who was born in 1888 and died March 10, 1919, and Joseph T, Jr

Joseph T Smith. A successful young business man who has always counted it a part of his good fortune that his destiny has been allied with the City of Fremont, Joseph T Smith is a son of the late Towner Smith, and was born at Fremont November 22, 1886

He acquired his early education in the Fremont High School, spent three years in the Culver Military Academy at Culver, Indiana, and nine months in the Fremont Normal School His education finished he was connected with the Fremont State Bank until reaching his majority and for the past thirteen years has had full charge of the J T Smith Estate, Incorporated, which owns and controls the widely scattered and valuable properties accumulated chiefly during the lifetime of the late Towner Smith Included in the estate are some valuable coal properties in Missouri conducted as Smith, Marriott & Company of Moberly, Missouri, of which Mr Smith is president Mr Smith has shown executive and financial ability of a high order in the management of this estate, but as a business man has not neglected the claims and duties of good citizenship

September 6, 1917, he joined the colors and trained as a soldier for the World war at Camp Funston, Kansas He was in the army eleven months, being corporal of his company, and received an honorable discharge on account of ill health July 26, 1918 Following his military service he spent five months recuperating in California, and after partly recovering his physical vigor returned to his home in Fremont In 1910 he built at 1452 North Park Avenue a very attractive home, planning it after some of the beautiful modern houses of Southern California This home was in readiness for the reception of his bride, Leonora K Pierce, whom he married June 21, 1911 Mrs Smith was born in West Virginia, daughter of Frederick G and Bertha E Pierce Their only daughter, Marjorie Elizabeth Smith, was born in 1912. Mr and Mrs Smith are active members of the Presbyterian Church and he is a trustee of the church and secretary of the Sunday school Well known in social and fraternal life, he is a member of the Fremont Commercial Club, the Country Club, is affiliated with the Masonic order, the Benevolent and Protective Order of Elks, and since the war has been active in

American Legion work He is a republican, and during the primary campaigns of 1920 was secretary of the "Leonard-Wood-for-President-Club."

CHRISTOF BERGMANN is a Washington County pioneer. His home has been here for over forty years. His activities for the most part have been identified with the land, and in earlier years he experienced all the hardships and ups and downs of the Nebraska farmer He was persistent, hard working and eventually saw the sun of prosperity shine upon his efforts and is now well satisfied to enjoy the comforts won by earlier years and allows the responsibilities of farming to rest upon the sturdy shoulders of his son.

Mr Bergmann was born in Hanover, Germany, in 1845, and was reared and educated in his native country. At the age of twenty-three he came to America, and from 1870 for nine years lived in Chicago He was in that city at the time of the great fire of 1871 His chief employment while there was with an express company.

In 1879 Mr. Bergmann came to Nebraska, bringing his family He did not homestead, but soon after coming bought eighty acres of unimproved land He gave that farm its substantial improvements, and still lives there His home adjoins the Town of Washington on the east, and is located in section 32 of Richland Township. Mr Bergmann out of his personal experiences is able to appreciate the wonderful contrast in conditions affecting the farmer In the early days he was hardly able to sell corn even at 10 cents a bushel, and he sold his hogs for $3 80 a hundred He and some of the other early settlers in the locality usually did their trading at Omaha, many miles away

In Chicago in 1873 Mr Bergmann married Mary Seedorf, who was also a native of Hanover Five children were born to their marriage Mrs Emma Rathmann, living near Bloomfield, Nebraska; Mrs Mary Cunningham, whose home is near Kennard in Washington County, Chris, at home, looking after his father's farm, Margaretha, also at home, and Mrs. Adela Goedeker, of Washington County Mr. Bergmann is a democratic voter For two years he served as a member of his local school board

CARL F. PULS Through all the years of his mature life Carl F Puls has been identified with one prosperous agricultural community of Washington County, Richland Township, where he owns a well-improved farm in section 26

The esteem paid him as a good citizen has been acquired in the same county where he was born and reared Mr Puls was born in Washington County February 9, 1875, son of Carl and Margaretha Puls His father, a native of Germany, came to the United States in 1866, a poor man, and for two years worked out for day and month wages in Scott County, Iowa By dint of much saving he accumulated the modest fund that enabled him to come to Nebraska and homestead eighty acres of raw land in Washington County On this land he built a humble board shack, but eventually saw his efforts meet their proper rewards, although he suffered many hardships Before his death he owned 200 acres in Washington County He died January 19, 1912, at the age of seventy-eight, and his wife passed away November 1, 1895, at the age of fifty-four. They had nine children, three of whom died in infancy, and the six still living are: August Adolph, a Wisconsin farmer, Mrs Herman Klindt, of Washington County, Carl F., Martha Hiese, of Cuming

County, Nebraska, F. J, who lives on the old homestead farm, and Mrs Emma Echtemkamp, of Boone County

Carl F Puls was reared on the farm, acquired a common school education, and worked with his father for a number of years, helping improve and operate the land At the age of twenty-nine he bought some land from his father and in that one locality has continued his enterprise as a general farmer and stockman, and at the same time has manifested a commendable interest and public spirit in connection with all progressive affairs in his locality

April 20, 1904, Mr Puls married Miss Dorthea M Wiese They have four children, all at home, named Rheinhardt, Margarthea, Louie and Anita Mr Puls is affiliated with the Modern Woodmen of America, in which he has held the various chairs and is now past consul, and is a member of the Royal Neighbors of America His interest in good schools led him to retain his position as director of his local district for a number of years For two years he served as township assessor and for a long time was road overseer He is a republican voter

GEORGE M ANTILL is one of the highly respected business men of Blair, where he has lived a number of years and where his efforts have brought him commendable success and a place of confidence in his community.

Mr Antill has been the architect of his own fortunes. He was a small boy when his father died, and he had to make the best of his own opportunities from early youth He was born in Monroe County, Ohio, March 15, 1875, son of Samuel Hudson and Mary J (Torchey) Antill In 1880, when he was five years of age, his parents left Ohio and moved to Iowa, where his father died a year later The Antills were farming people Of ten children five are still living, George being the eighth in order of birth His father was a Mason, a democrat in politics and a member of the Christian Church

George M Antill was about six years of age when his father died He had a very limited education in the country schools of Iowa, and had to practice self-reliance and contrive means to support himself at a very early age He learned the cabinet-maker's trade in Iowa, and followed it for four years Following that he was a shipping clerk in a wholesale fruit house at Omaha, and then came to Blair, where he has become extensively interested in the sale of real estate He also operates a garage, though real estate is his chief business Mr Antill has sold great quantities of Colorado lands to individual settlers and is still heavily interested in that state

HENRY WESTPHALEN is able to record a residence in Dodge County of forty years, and those have been the most productive and successful years of his life He is one of the leading farmers of Ridgeley Township, his home being in section 26

He was born in Wisconsin in 1860 His father, John Westphalen, was a native of Germany and an early settler of Wisconsin, where he lived a number of years About 1880 he came to Dodge County, Nebraska, and bought eighty acres near Scribner At the time of his death he owned 200 acres

Henry Westphalen was twenty years of age when he came to Nebraska, had a common school education and some knowledge of farming, and has turned those advantages to good account in his work as an agriculturist and his varied relations with the community He owns a farm of 200 acres, and has put its improvements among the very best He is a republican voter and a member of the Lutheran Church

His first wife was a Miss Roemer, who at her death left two children For his second wife he married Alice Roemer, and they have five children

THOMAS T. WILKINSON The Civil war was still in progress when Mr and Mrs Thomas Wilkinson came West to seek a home in the sparsely settled country of Nebraska They shared in practically all the experiences of the frontier. They came to Nebraska poor, had to depend upon their thrift and exertions to provide a living for themselves and their children, and it is a tribute to their substantial virtues that they subsequently achieved a gratifying degree of prosperity and independence Mr Wilkinson enjoyed the comforts and fruits of his early toil for a number of years before his death, and Mrs Thomas Wilkinson, whose home is at Blair, is one of the interesting pioneer women who can recount some of the hardships and struggles the early settlers went through

Thomas Wilkinson was born in England July 1, 1838, son of James and Sarah Wilkinson, life-long residents of England His father was a worker in a clothing factory in England Thomas Wilkinson came to America when a young man of about seventeen, and for several years followed the trade of painter and paperhanger He lived in northern Illinois, not far from Chicago, and in 1859 married at Barrington, Illinois, Miss Lucy S Jackson She was born in England September 3, 1840, daughter of John and Sarah Ann Jackson. The Jackson family left Lincolnshire and came to the United States about 1842, locating in Illinois John Jackson was a veterinary surgeon Of his nine children Mrs Thomas Wilkinson is the only one now living. Her parents both spent their last years in Elk City, Nebraska

After their marriage Mr and Mrs Wilkinson spent two years at Lake Providence, Louisiana, where he followed his trade With the breaking out of the Civil war he returned north, resumed his residence in Illinois, but in 1864 started west to Elk City, Nebraska They reached their destination July 27, 1864 They brought with them the two children born in Illinois, Ida and Emma The wagon and team that carried the family from Illinois to Nebraska represented a large part of the fortune of Thomas Wilkinson, and consequently when one of his horses died soon after coming here it was a calamity such as can hardly be understood at this late date Later he bought another horse from the Government and named it Sam At that time land was cheap, selling from $2 50 to $5 an acre, the same land that fifty years later commands a price of between $250 and $300 an acre Mr and Mrs Wilkinson acquired a tract of railroad land, and at the price of great self-denial and close economy they eventually paid for their property Mrs Wilkinson tells many anecdotes showing that the high cost of living was a problem even more troublesome in those days than at present Mr Wilkinson at one time traded a good watch for a bushel of potatoes There was also a scarcity of labor. Mr. Wilkinson sometimes employed Indian squaws to husk his corn Indians frequently came to the Wilkinson home, begging Mrs Wilkinson for beef and corn, but would never accept pork This original home of Mr and Mrs Wilkinson in Nebraska was twenty-five miles from Omaha, then a small town Mrs Wilkinson was a champion butter-maker in her neighborhood, and the surplus of this product she sold in Omaha Gradually their affairs prospered and in 1887 they were able to retire from their farm and move to Blair, where they enjoyed the comforts of a good town home At Blair Mr Wilkinson passed away July 18, 1912, nearly forty years after he had come to Nebraska

After Mr and Mrs Wilkinson settled in Nebraska two other children were born to them at Elk City, Nettie and William Of their four children the oldest is Ida, wife of J F. Smith, who is in the brick business at Omaha Mr and Mrs Smith have four children, named Harry, William, Ralph and Marvel The second daughter, Emma, is the wife of Herman Shields, also a brick man at Omaha Mr and Mrs Shields had two children, their daughter Mildred being a high school girl Their other daughter, Lucy Louella, married Clarence Simpson, of Blair, and she died November 3, 1918, her only child, Lu Ella Ruth, surviving and living in Blair Mrs Wilkinson's daughter Nettie is now deceased Her only son is William W Wilkinson, a sketch of whom appears elsewhere in this publication.

The late Thomas Wilkinson was an active member of the Episcopal Church, a democrat in politics, and throughout his life was deeply interested in local affairs He served a term of the County Board of Supervisors and was also a member of the school board at Blair He was postmaster under Cleveland's administration from 1893 to 1896 Mr Wilkinson became a Master Mason at Algonquin, Illinois, in September, 1860, and was loyally affiliated with that order the rest of his life While living near Fremont he became a charter member of the lodge there, subsequently a charter member of the lodge at Waterloo, Nebraska, and finally a member of Blair lodge and the Royal Arch Chapter Though he went through some difficult struggles during his early years in Nebraska Mr Wilkinson always had a great faith in the future of the country, and invested wisely in land and left a large estate

WILLIAM VOSS Through a long period of years the Voss family has been substantially identified with the farming interests of Richland Township, Washington County, and representing this name is William Voss, Jr, whose effective management is given to a fine farm in section 14, two miles east and two and a half miles south of Kennard

He was born in Washington County in 1884, son of William Voss, Sr After completing his education in the local schools the son remained at home until 1914, when he took charge of one of his father's farms and now has 120 acres devoted to crops and live stock Most of the substantial improvements on the land were placed there by his father

March 23, 1910, William Voss, Jr, married Bertha Koepke, daughter of William Koepke, one of the early settlers of Washington County They have five children, Katherine, Dorothy, John, Wilma and Aveline Mr Voss is an independent voter in politics and a member of the Lutheran Church

MRS ROSE MCGIVFRIN, whose beautiful home is situated on East Sixth Street in the City of Fremont, judicial center of Dodge County, has been a resident of Nebraska for more than forty years, and few have manifested deeper interest in the civic and material development and progress of this commonwealth Mrs McGivern has been specially prominent and influential in various fraternal and general civic organizations, as well as a leader in social activities A woman of fine intellectuality and gracious personality, she finds ample demand upon her time and attention in connection with the various social and benevolent organizations with which she is identified, and her beautiful home is a center of generous hospitality

Mrs. Rose Saxton McGiveran

Mrs McGiverin was born in Green Lake County, Wisconsin, December 19, 1857, and is a daughter of Ray and Phoebe (Clark) Saxton, both natives of the State of New York and both representatives of families founded in America in the early colonial period of our national history The marriage of the parents was solemnized in the State of Ohio, but later they numbered themselves among the pioneers of Green Lake County, Wisconsin, where Mr Saxton developed and improved a farm, as did he later one of the valuable farms of Minnesota, where both he and his wife passed the closing years of their lives In his youth Mr Saxton learned the mason's trade, but the greater part of his active life was devoted to farm enterprise On the paternal side Mrs McGiverin is a great-granddaughter of Ezekiel Pearce, who was a resident of Rhode Island when he enlisted in the Continental line and entered service in the War of the Revolution He served with utmost patriotism and loyalty and was severely wounded in one of the battles marking the progress of the great struggle for national independence Though he lived several years after the close of the war, his death was the distinct sequel of the wounds he had received in battle. Representatives of the Pearce family likewise were patriotic soldiers in the Revolutionary war, and thus strongly fortify Mrs McGiverin's credentials as a member of the Society of the Daughters of the American Revolution

Mrs McGiverin received her early education in the schools of Wisconsin and by the self-discipline gained through comprehensive reading and study she has become a woman of distinctive culture and fine mental poise In 1876 was solemnized her marriage to Francis McGiverin, and three years later they came to Nebraska From Wisner, Cuming County, they proceeded by stage to Stanton, the judicial center of Stanton County, where they established their home There they remained twelve years, and they then came to Fremont, where Mrs McGiverin has since maintained her home Of this union were born two children Ethel is the wife of Paul Colson of Fremont, and Daisy, who became the wife of Charles Derick, was a resident of this city at the time of her death

Mrs McGiverin was a member of the first Chautauqua class formed at Stanton, this state, and she is one of the two original members of the American Historical Association from Fremont, the other being George L Loomis She has taken specially lively interest in the affairs of that noble patriotic organization, the Society of the Daughters of the American Revolution, and has served as regent of the Lewis & Clark Chapter of this organization at Fremont She is one of the influential members of this chapter, and has been active and prominent also in the Order of the Eastern Star, in which she served two years as treasurer of the Grand Chapter of Nebraska In the Daughters of Rebekah, an adjunct of the Independent Order of Odd Fellows, she served one year as vice president and one year as president of the state organization of the order in Nebraska She is actively identified with the Ladies' Charity Club of Fremont, as well as with the Woman's Club, of which she was the organizer and of which she has served as president She has been very active in the home-service section of the Civilian Relief Department of the American Red Cross and to its work gave the major part of her time and attention during the period of America's participation in the great World war and is continuing in the care of the discharged soldiers at the present time (1920) Her influence was potent also in the local activities of the Red Cross and other war-time organizations and services Having traveled extensively through the Orient and Europe in 1900 on a Mediterranean cruise and in 1910 having spent five months in Germany and the British Isles, Mrs McGivern has a great deal of data, especially on Belgium and France, and when the war came on she was familiar with those countries, which was a great help to her in her war and Red Cross work. She has been one of the leading members of the Physical Research Club of Fremont, and has taken loyal interest in all things pertaining to the social and material welfare of the community While a resident of Stanton she was a member of the Congregational Church of that place, but she is not actively identified with any church at the present time A woman of high ideals, her life has been one of gracious service, and to her is accorded the affectionate regard of the community in which she has so long maintained her home

WILLIAM OSTERMAN, a retired farmer of Arlington, and formerly quite prominent in the agricultural life of Washington County, was born in Germany on May 9, 1852, a son of Karl and Rachel (Sprick) Osterman, both of whom were born in Westphalia, Germany Coming to Washington County, Nebraska, in 1857, he pre-empted land and continued to live on his homestead until his death He and his wife had six children, of whom two survive, namely. Mary, who married Samuel S. Dugan of Shawnee, Oklahoma, and William. Karl Osterman was a democrat in politics He and his wife were consistent members of the Lutheran Church Although he began his struggle with the world without any capital, he died a man of some means

William Osterman attended the schools of Washington County and took a course at the first college established in Nebraska, which was located at Fontanelle When the time arrived for his selection of a life occupation he selected that of farming, and was engaged in that line of endeavor throughout the remainder of his active career, always operating on his own property, and he still owns the old family homestead In 1915 he left the farm and came to Arlington, where he has since been numbered among the worth-while men of this locality

In March, 1880, Mr Osterman was united in marriage with Louise Ruwe, a daughter of William Ruwe, a prominent farmer and pioneer of Washington County The children born of this marriage are as follows: William, who is on his father's farm, was educated at Arlington and in the Fremont Normal School, Harry Roscoe, who was also educated at Arlington and in the Fremont Normal School, was formerly a farmer, but has left that occupation and is now employed at Arlington, and Alice, who was educated at Arlington, is unmarried and living at home

Although he was born and reared a Lutheran, Mr Osterman is now attending the services of the Congregational Church He is a democrat in his political convictions, and has served on the federal jury and on the School Board, occupying the latter office for over fifteen years Through persistence and hard work Mr Osterman has made a success in life, and now owns many acres of well-improved land, a beautiful residence at Arlington and the Terry Hotel building at Fremont Mr Osterman's success has not come to him through any spectacular operations, but is simply the result of whole-hearted endeavor along legitimate and congenial lines What he accomplished anyone can do if he is only willing to work hard, apply himself and save his money.

MRS MARY VAN ANDA Daughter of a Nebraska pioneer, Mrs Van Anda since her marriage has been identified with the farm and rural life of Dodge County, has seen some capable children grow up in this community and is widely known for the effective part she has played as a home maker

She was born in Camden County, Missouri, in 1861 Her father, George W Mitchell, was born and reared in Jackson County, Kentucky He was an expert cabinet-maker by trade, also a farmer and a Methodist minister He was honored five years by service in the Missouri State Legislature For five years he was in the army as a Union soldier, and while protecting the frontier paid his firse visit to Dodge County in 1865 He was also a Mason He married Louise Jane Wilson, of Nashville, Tennessee, and Mrs Van Anda was one of ten children

Mrs Van Anda was married at Fremont February 22, 1883. She became the mother of nine children · George E, of Arlington, Nebraska, James C., of Fontanelle, Carmi Huston, of Centerville, South Dakota, John L, Catherine, at home; Ralph W, of the Moody Bible Institute, Francis W, Fletcher W and Merrill C, at home with their mother

When they married Mr and Mrs Van Anda moved on a farm, and Mr Van Anda was one of the hard working and prosperous citizens of the community until his death October 25, 1909 Since then Mrs Van Anda has kept her home on the old homestead of sixty-five acres She is a member of the Methodist Church and her husband was a republican voter

Asa Dixon, Jr. A live, wide-awake man, energetic and progressive, Asa Dixon, Jr, of Blair, a well-known operator in real estate, began life for himself when young, and in the course of his active career has steadily followed the pathway leading onward and upward to success A son of Asa Dixon, Sr, he was born, March 21, 1877, in Washington County, Nebraska, of pioneer stock

Born and educated in Peoria, Illinois, Asa Dixon, Sr, served as a soldier in the Civil war, enlisting in Company C, Twenty-second Iowa Volunteer Infantry, and was with Sheridan in the Shenandoah Valley campaign. Being seriously wounded at the seige of Vicksburg, he was confined in a hospital four months Recovering his health, he again entered the service and fought bravely until the close of the conflict, having the distinction of being the youngest soldier in his regiment He came to Nebraska in 1865, took up a homestead claim in Washington County, and in addition to carrying on general farming successfully was engaged in the real estate business at Blair for about thirty years Retired from active business, he is now a resident of California He belongs to the Grand Army of the Republic, and is a consistent member of the Methodist Episcopal Church, though in his earlier life he was a preacher in the United Brethren Church

Asa Dixon, Sr, married, in 1866, in Nebraska, Alice Manigal, who was born in Cincinnati, Ohio, and came with her parents to Washington County, Nebraska, in 1864 She passed to the life beyond on October 28, 1918. Of the fifteen children born of their marriage, twelve are living, as follows Mrs T E King of Los Angeles, California; James M, engaged in the real estate business in Blair; Frank, formerly a farmer in Tekamah, Nebraska, is now living retired in Los Angeles, Mrs L. E Robinson, also a resident of Los Angeles, Emil of Blair, a dealer in real estate, Asa, Jr, of this sketch, Oscar, operating a laundry in Blair, Wallace P, a well-known real estate dealer at Tekamah; Charles, who has served as a mail clerk in Los Angeles for fifteen years, Mrs William Nichols, also of Los Angeles, Mrs Russell Thapp, whose husband is pastor of the First Christian Church at Seattle, Washington, and Fred, who has a studio at Carnegie Hall, New York City, was the third man in the United States to make records for self-playing pianos

After his graduation from the Blair High School, Asa Dixon, Jr, embarked in agricultural pursuits, and for twelve years carried on general farming and stock raising and dealing Establishing himself in Blair in 1910, he has since been busily and prosperously engaged in business as a real estate dealer, his operations extending throughout Nebraska, and even to the Pacific Coast, as he has sold some land in California He is interested in lands on his own account, and by wise investments has acquired a goodly property

Mr Dixon married, in 1895, in Blair, Jessie Sheets, who was born in 1877 in Washington County, Nebraska, on the farm of her father, Henry Sheets Five children have been born into their household, namely. Gifford of Blair, now an insurance agent, was for three years state manager for the National Auto Insurance Company, Arthur, engaged in the insurance business at Blair, Mrs D. D Kinyoun, whose husband is engaged in farming at Formoso, Kansas, and Mildred and Jennie, attending school. Politically Mr Dixon is a steadfast democrat, and fraternally he belongs to the Knights of the Maccabees Religiously he is a member of the Methodist Episcopal Church, and has ever been active and prominent in church and Sunday school work Mrs Dixon is a member of the Roman Catholic Church, and faithful to its teachings

Mrs Mary Barry All of the farm land is not owned by men, for some of the most successful farmers of the country are women, and one who has achieved a gratifying success in agriculture is Mrs Mary Barry of section 26, Blair Township, Washington County, Nebraska She is the widow of Michael Barry, and a daughter of James Manny, a native of Ireland. who came to the United States at an early day and settled first in New Jersey, from whence he came to Nebraska, making the trip early in 1865 As far as St Joseph, he made the trip by water, but on account of the shallows at that point was forced to conclude the journey with wagons, to Calhoun The first winter the family lived in a log cabin, near Calhoun fort, where the overland travelers stopped on their way to the Black Hills and further West. In the spring the family moved on a farm and at that time had an ox team and one cow They underwent hardships, including trouble from unfriendly Indians, but in time prospered, and when the father died he owned 400 acres of land in Washington County and 320 acres in Kimball and Antelope counties He passed away when he was fifty-five years old, his widow surviving him until she was sixty-eight years old. Mrs Barry is the only one of their children living, as her brother, James, was shot while on duty as a watchman at Benson, and her sister, Johanna, died in 1907.

Michael Barry was born in Canada, and came to the United States in 1856, first living for a time at Omaha, Nebraska, and then going on a farm near Calhoun, his father, Thomas Barry accompanying him when he located on this farm In 1880 he and Mrs. Barry were married and they became the parents of the following children Thomas, Mrs James Thompson, Mrs Edgar Rose, Joseph, Mrs Jim Sip, James and John, who are at home, Paul, who lives in Dodge County, Bryan, who is at home, Grace, who is a trained nurse of Chicago, Illinois, and Charles, who is also at home Mr Barry was a Catholic For some years he was a member of the School Board of his district, and for many years was road overseer He was an independent voter Fraternally he maintained membership with the Woodmen of the World His death occurred January 17, 1913, and in his passing his community lost a good citizen, and his family a kind and loving husband and father Since his death his widow and several of her sons are conducting a 160-acre farm, where they live, and another farm of 120 acres in the neighborhood, and are doing very well with their work They are fine people in every respect and stand pre-eminently well with all who know them.

ALBERT F GERICKE. A prominent and prosperous citizen of Elkhorn Township, Albert F Gericke is closely identified with the agricultural and industrial interests of this part of Dodge County, being profitably engaged in general farming on the parental homestead, which he is managing with ability and success A son of Charles L and Frederica Gericke, he was born August 28, 1884, in Dodge County, which has always been his home

Born March 15, 1845, and brought up in Germany, Charles L Gericke was early impressed with the superior advantages America offered the laboring man, and in 1868 immigrated to the United States After spending a while in Illinois, in 1870 he made his way to Fremont, Nebraska, where he worked a time, then rented and spent about a year in the employ of the Government, freighting on the plains Returning to Nebraska in 1884, he bought 120 acres of prairie land in Dodge County and immediately began the improvement of a ranch He succeeded well in his undertakings, and as his wealth increased he invested in other tracts of land At his death, which occurred May 28, 1913, he had title to 240 acres of rich and arable land, much of which was under cultivation His wife, Frederica Weierhausen, was born in Germany January 13, 1860, and came to the United States in 1876, settling in Fremont, Nebraska, where she married Charles L Gericke in 1880 To them were born six children, as follows: Will, a professor in the University of California, Ernest, of Nickerson, Nebraska, Emma, living at home; Frieda, also at home; Louise Katherine, who died at thirteen years; and Albert F., unmarried, is the subject of this brief sketch. Charles L Gericke was an active member of the Evangelical Church

Acquiring a substantial education in the district schools, Albert F Gericke became thoroughly familiar with agricultural labor while young, and having decided that farming was not only an agreeable but a profitable occupation he selected it as his own, and since the death of his father has carried on mixed husbandry on the home place, in its management displaying rare discrimination and judgment Mr Gericke makes a specialty of raising Poland China hogs and Shorthorn cattle, a branch of industry in which he is meeting with characteristic success Taking a keen interest in everything pertaining to the advancement of agriculture Mr Gericke is one of the wide-awake members of Dodge County Farm Bureau and of the Farmers' Union A stanch republican in politics, he has held various township offices, performing the duties devolving upon him ably and promptly. Religiously he belongs to the German Evangelical Church

JOHN A. VAN ANDA came to Nebraska in the year following that which marked the admission of the state to the Union and he was one of the honored pioneer citizens of Fremont, Dodge County, at the time of his death, July 10, 1903 He had given valiant service as a soldier in the Civil war and was a young man of sterling character and ambitious purpose when he numbered himself among the pioneer settlers in Dodge County, Nebraska, where he did well his part in connection with social and industrial development and progress and where he ever commanded inviolable place in popular confidence and esteem

Mr Van Anda was born at Mount Vernon, Ohio, March 15, 1840, and thus was sixty-three years of age when he died He acquired his early education in the schools of the old Buckeye State and his youthful ambition had been to prepare himself for the medical profession, but enlisting in the service of his country prevented the realization of this laudable purpose He was twenty-two years of age when, in September, 1861, he tendered his aid in defense of the Union He had in the meantime become a resident of Iowa, and there he enlisted in Company H, Twelfth Iowa Volunteer Infantry He proceeded with his regiment to the front and took part in the historic battle of Shiloh, in connection with which he was captured by the enemy, April 6, 1862 He was held as a prisoner of war for seven months, within which he endured the hardships and horrors of infamous old Libby Prison at Richmond, Virginia, where his physical powers ebbed to the lowest point, with the result that when he was paroled and taken to Annapolis, Maryland, it was supposed that his death was imminent He recuperated, however, sufficiently to be transferred to a government hospital at St Louis, Missouri, where, during his period of convalescence, he assisted in the care of other patients in the institution After receiving his honorable discharge Mr Van Anda returned to Iowa, where he remained until March, 1868, when he came to the new state of Nebraska, and filed entry on a homestead of eighty acres, fifteen miles northwest of Fremont. He remained on this pioneer farm until he had perfected his title to the property, after which he purchased another farm, upon which likewise he made good improvements He continued his active association with farm enterprise in Dodge County until 1880, and in the meanwhile had gained financial independence, though he had no monetary resources when he came to the state In the year mentioned he removed with his wife to Fremont, and in this city he passed the remainder of his life in well earned retirement

Mr Van Anda was a stalwart republican, and was actively affiliated with the local post of the Grand Army of the Republic, as well as the Independent Order of Odd Fellows He was for several years engaged in the retail grocery business at Fremont, but he lived retired from active business during the closing period of his life He was fully forty years a member of the official board of the Methodist Episcopal Church and was influential in all departments of the work of the church of this denomination at Fremont Mrs Van Anda, who still retains her home in this city, has likewise been zealous in church work and is one of the revered members of the local Methodist Church

The year 1870 recorded the marriage of Mr Van Anda to Miss Elvina Taggart, who was born February 6, 1845, in the City of Cleveland, Ohio, a daughter of Henry and Mary (Walker) Taggart. The parents were born near Concord, New Hampshire, and were representatives of fine old colonial families of New England Their marriage was solemnized in their native state, and after removing to Ohio Mr Taggart became a successful contractor, he having learned both the carpenter's and the cooper's trades and his father having been a shipbuilder in New Hampshire Mr. Taggart became a pioneer settler in Iowa, where he purchased and improved a farm, in Dubuque County, and there he and his wife passed the remainder of their active lives, though the death of both occurred at Colorado Springs, Colorado. Their religious faith was that of the Methodist Episcopal Church Mrs Van Anda is the eldest of a family of five children, of whom three are living She was educated in the public schools and at Epworth Seminary, in Dubuque

County, Iowa, and in that county she had been a successful and popular teacher for six years prior to her marriage John A., the only child of Mr. and Mrs. Van Anda, is assistant cashier of the Commercial National Bank of Fremont, the maiden name of his wife having been Jessie Albers and they have two children, Caroline M. and Francis E.

Mrs. Van Anda had her full share of pioneer experiences in Dodge County and takes pleasure in having a witness of the splendid development of the county and its attractive judicial center, the while she has a wide circle of friends in the community that has long represented her home.

CPSIA information can be obtained
at www.ICGtesting.com
Printed in the USA
BVHW041208020619
549919BV00009B/17/P

9 781345 298178